Isaiah: Prophet, Seer, and Poet

Isaiah: Prophet, Seer, and Poet

Victor L. Ludlow

Deseret Book Company
Salt Lake City, Utah

Library of Congress Cataloging in Publication Data

Ludlow, Victor, L.
    Isaiah—prophet, seer, and poet.

    Bibliography: p.
    Includes index.
    1. Bible. O.T. Isaiah—Criticism, interpretation,
etc. 2. Isaiah (Biblical prophet) I. Title.
BS1515.2.L78   224'.107   82-1444
ISBN 0-87747-884-8
AACR2

CONTENTS

PREFACE

I would like to give special thanks to the Commissioner's Office of the Church Educational System of The Church of Jesus Christ of Latter-day Saints for its help and support with this book. Commissioner Jeffrey R. Holland appointed me as a special research fellow and scholar for 1980 and 1981. This fellowship gave me time, research funds and help, and other aids that greatly assisted my Isaiah studies. In September 1981 I submitted a manuscript of almost nine hundred pages to the Church Commissioner's Office. This manuscript became the foundation for this book.

For help rendered during the research project, I would like to thank Barney Madsen, Duncan Barber, and Susan Wallace, my research assistants; Charlotte Webb, my secretary; Carin Greene, manuscript typist; Su Jones, BYU Bookstore buyer; and the many students who have encouraged and inspired me as we studied Isaiah together.

I also appreciate the fine work of Jack Lyon, associate editor at Deseret Book, as he and I carefully reduced the manuscript to two-thirds its original size. Readers requiring information about the unedited manuscript may contact me at Brigham Young University.

I must also give special thanks to my wife V-Ann and our six children for their support of this project and book.

Preparing this book has greatly strengthened my understanding and appreciation about how and why our Heavenly Father works through prophets to deliver divine truths and profound prophecies to God's children. Likewise, I hope the reader will not only gain insights into Isaiah's writings, but will also enhance his ability to communicate with God the Father.

INTRODUCTION

Students and scholars of the scriptures all acknowledge the importance of Isaiah's words, but many of them have difficulty understanding them. His insights are prophetic and fascinating, but since he uses poetry and symbols, readers often become discouraged and confused.

The main purpose of *Isaiah : Prophet, Seer, and Poet* is to help readers of Isaiah to understand his writings. Readers sometimes come across ambiguous passages in Isaiah, and they wonder, "What is he saying?" The ambiguity often results from confusing or unfamiliar vocabulary, phraseology, or sentence structure. In order to clarify Isaiah's words, this book explains Isaiah's obscure terminology, poetic style, symbolism, and teachings. Charts, maps, outlines, illustrations, and alternate English translations are included to further elucidate his writings.

Helpful background chapters are given in the first section of this book to provide information about Isaiah and his prophetic role and to give suggestions on why and how one should study Isaiah. They also help answer a more challenging question: "What does Isaiah mean?" In order to answer this question, Isaiah's writings are discussed in terms of historical context, literary style, scriptural context, and doctrinal application. This "four-dimensional" approach is used in this book to build up progressive layers of knowledge about Isaiah's message. Through the historical dimension, the reader learns about the cultural setting and history of the ancient Middle East. The literary dimension enables the reader to analyze the poetic and prophetic style in which Isaiah wrote. The third dimension reveals Isaiah through the eyes of other prophets, some contemporary, others his successors. Each borrows from Isaiah according to his needs and prophetic perspective. The insights of these prophets help the reader appreciate key words, symbolism, and figurative and spiritual meaning in Isaiah. The last and most important dimension is doctrinal; it highlights Isaiah's prophecies and allows the reader to apply his teachings.

My approach in this book has been to provide information and ideas from which readers can make their own value judgments. Probably the most important question any reader should ask about Isaiah's writings is, "What is the value of his words to me today?" Although I will give some suggestions as to how Isaiah's message can be applied to contemporary situations, the readers should not feel restricted to these applications. Because Isaiah's prophecies are powerful and prophetic, any limited or single interpretation may restrict their meaning and application. Instead of following one line of thought, I prefer to share a variety of insights I have gained through years of study of Isaiah, the Old Testament, the Hebrew language, and the Near East. My perceptions and suggestions should simplify Isaiah's writings and help readers to study and ponder the prophet's message. However, readers should consider my ideas only as possible suggestions and then build upon them, going beyond them to seek an individual relationship with Isaiah's work. In other words, follow the admonition of Nephi and "liken" Isaiah unto yourself! (1 Ne. 19:23-24.)

I hope that the ideas and materials in *Isaiah—Prophet, Seer, and Poet* will motivate Latter-day Saints toward a greater appreciation and comprehension of the great words of a great prophet. I also hope that a better understanding of Isaiah's writings will strengthen the readers' testimonies and that his messages will motivate them toward becoming true sons and daughters of our Heavenly Father.

KEY TO ABBREVIATIONS

AB   Amplified Bible
ABC   *Abingdon Bible Commentary*
AGQ   *Answers to Gospel Questions,* Joseph Fielding Smith
AOJ   *Antiquities of the Jews,* Josephus
ASV   American Standard Version of the Bible
BD   Bible Dictionary, Latter-day Saint edition of the King James Version of
        the Bible
BMC   *Book of Mormon Compendium,* Sidney B. Sperry
BOI   *The Book of Isaiah,* George Adam Smith
BOJ   The Book of Jasher
CHMR   *Church History and Modern Revelation,* Joseph Fielding Smith
COR   *Crusader of Righteousness,* Melvin J. Ballard
CR   *Conference Report*
CSBM   *A Companion to Your Study of the Book of Mormon,* Daniel H. Ludlow
CSOT   *A Companion to Your Study of the Old Testament,* Daniel H. Ludlow
DS   *Doctrines of Salvation,* Joseph Fielding Smith
DNTC   *Doctrinal New Testament Commentary,* Bruce R. McConkie
DWW   *Discourses of Wilford Woodruff,* edited by G. Homer Durham
GNB   Good News Bible
HC   *History of The Church of Jesus Christ of Latter-day Saints,* Joseph Smith
IB   *Interpreter's Bible*
IDB   *Interpreter's Dictionary of the Bible*
IDYK   *Israel! Do You Know?* LeGrand Richards
JB   Jerusalem Bible
JD   *Journal of Discourses*
JPS   Jewish Publication Society translation of the Old Testament (The Holy
        Scriptures according to the Masoretic Text)
JST   Joseph Smith Translation of the Bible (Holy Scriptures)
JTC   *Jesus the Christ,* James E. Talmage
KJV   King James Version of the Bible
LB   Living Bible
LOF   *Lectures on Faith,* Joseph Smith

MA	*Messenger and Advocate*
MD	*Mormon Doctrine,* Bruce R. McConkie
MFP	*Messages of the First Presidency,* compiled by James R. Clark
MLB	Modern Language Bible
MM	*The Mortal Messiah,* Bruce R. McConkie
MS	*Millennial Star*
MWW	*A Marvelous Work and a Wonder,* LeGrand Richards
NAS	New American Standard Bible
NEB	New English Bible
NIV	New International Version of the Bible
NJV	New Jewish Version of the Book of Isaiah
PM	*The Promised Messiah,* Bruce R. McConkie
RSV	Revised Standard Version of the Bible
SOT	*Signs of the Times,* Joseph Fielding Smith
SWK	*Spencer W. Kimball,* Edward C. Kimball
TEV	Today's English Version of the Bible
TG	Topical Guide, Latter-day Saint edition of the King James Version of the Bible
TPJS	*Teachings of the Prophet Joseph Smith,* compiled by Joseph Fielding Smith
VIP	*The Voice of Israel's Prophets,* Sidney B. Sperry
VLL	Translation by Victor L. Ludlow
WJS	*The Words of Joseph Smith*
WTP	*The Way to Perfection,* Joseph Fielding Smith
WW	*Wilford Woodruff,* Cowley

(Note: References in this book to the Topical Guide, Bible Dictionary, Maps, Gazetteer, Appendix, footnotes, and chapter headings pertain to the Latter-day Saint edition of the King James Version of the Bible, published in 1980 in Salt Lake City by The Church of Jesus Christ of Latter-day Saints.)

WHO WAS ISAIAH?

Solomon's magnificent temple in Jerusalem was approaching its bicentennial anniversary in 760 B.C. when a young lad named Isaiah first walked through its courtyards. The venerated structure with its long porches, spacious courts, and numerous auxiliary buildings must have strongly impressed the boy. Around the temple, large crowds dressed in fine robes and jewelry displayed the prosperity of a resurgent Judah, and Isaiah was undoubtedly proud to be a citizen of such a strong, noble nation. His own name, which meant "Jehovah's salvation," reflected the Lord's protection and blessings which seemed to flow unceasingly upon the people.

Isaiah's associations with the temple continued, culminating twenty years later in a vision of the Lord seated upon a high throne within the celestial temple. (Isa. 6.) After receiving his prophetic call, Isaiah visited the temple courtyards often to deliver the Lord's messages to the people. His visions penetrated the apparent prosperity of the people and condemned their prevailing unrighteousness. He declared how and why the Lord's long-suffering was coming to an end, and he prophesied of impending destruction, declaring that Jehovah's salvation would have to wait until his people were chastened and humbled.

Isaiah's warnings of judgment and promises of hope were transmitted to later generations in both oral and written form. The collection of his writings became one of the most important books of the Old Testament. Indeed, his words are so significant that he is quoted more in the New Testament, Book of Mormon, Doctrine and Covenants, and Dead Sea Scrolls than any other prophet. His prophecies became the Lord's word for later generations of Israelites as they studied his writings and anticipated their fulfillment.

In spite of the comparatively large collection of Isaiah's writings, very little information was recorded about the man and his family life. Isaiah was born about 770 B.C., and it is known that his father's name was Amoz (not the Old Testament prophet Amos; see Isa. 1:1), that he lived in Jerusalem, was married, and had at least two sons. (Isa. 7:3; 8:3.) Ancient Jewish tradition says Isaiah was related to the royal family of Judah, and the scriptures record that his ministry spanned the reigns of four Judean kings—Uzziah, Jotham, Ahaz, and Hezekiah. (Isa. 1:1.) He received his prophetic call near the end of Uzziah's reign (about 740 B.C.) and served for almost half a century until Hezekiah's death (about 692 B.C.). Jewish tradition states that Hezekiah was Isaiah's son-in-law, and some works record that Hezekiah's son, King Manasseh, had Isaiah encased within a tree trunk and sawn asunder with a wooden saw. (See Josephus, *Antiquities of the Jews* 10:3; L. Ginsberg, *Legends of the Jews* 4:279; and the Talmud, Yebamoth 49b.) Christian tradition also supports the idea that Isaiah was sawn asunder and that he was among those martyred prophets mentioned by Jesus in Matthew 23:37 and by Paul in Hebrews 11:37.

Although little is recorded about the personal history of this great man, through his writings his noble character, sensitive compassion, political astuteness, and prophetic insight become apparent. The key to knowing the man Isaiah is the careful study of his words.

Isaiah as a Prophet

One valuable step in understanding Isaiah is to evaluate his unique prophetic role and teachings. He was the last major prophet to teach all the Israelite tribes before they began to scatter from the Holy Land. His words went with them to the four corners of the earth to instruct, inspire, and comfort them throughout following generations. However, as their descendants and other readers study his messages today, they experience difficulty in comprehending them because of the varied and complex nature of the prophecies. Most readers also lack an understanding of Isaiah's terminology, symbolism, imagery, phraseology, and style.

As people become more familiar with Isaiah's writings, they gradually begin to recognize and understand Isaiah's dominant themes, key words, and ideas. They see how Israelites throughout the ages can receive inspiration from his messages. They also see how his prophecies can be expanded from an ancient Israelite setting to a latter-day universal context. This universality is especially evident in the last half of Isaiah's book, although many of his early pronouncements also have at least a double fulfillment, with application to his own time and also to a later age. Nephi recognized that many of Isaiah's teachings could be applied to his own people, so he "likened" or compared Isaiah's messages to his generation for their "profit and learning." (1 Ne. 19:23.) Modern readers continue to learn from Isaiah as they study his gospel insights and witness the fulfillment of many of his prophecies.

According to his own writings, Isaiah did not perform many great miracles, although he did promise a miraculous deliverance to Jerusalem (ch. 37), and after prophesying health to Hezekiah, he gave a sign or miracle by having the sun's shadow recede (ch. 38). His greatest power came not as a law-giver (like Moses) or a miracle worker (like Elijah) but as a prophet and seer who foretold many future events in the history of the world.

Isaiah's warnings and prophecies cover almost three thousand years of Israelite history. They also foretell the first and second coming of the Messiah, the restoration of the gospel, the gathering of the house of Israel, the events and leaders before the Millennium, and some characteristics of the Millennium. As Christ said about Isaiah, "surely he spake as touching all things concerning my people which are of the house of Israel." (3 Ne. 23:2.)

Isaiah as a Poet

Few English readers realize that over ninety percent of Isaiah's writings are in poetic form. Isaiah was an eloquent master of the Hebrew tongue, and his vocabulary exceeds that found in any other Old Testament book. Some of the extensive vocabulary is due, no doubt, to the length of the book and the variety of subject matter, but much of it results from Isaiah's development as a poet. He delivered his prophetic messages in such sophisticated and exalted poetry that his writings attain heights of spiritual, intellectual, and artistic expression almost unparalleled in world literature.

Scholars are undecided as to whether his book is a collection of carefully prepared compositions by the prophet himself, or whether his inspiration was simply so intense that his poetry is an expression of the mind of God. After comparing his works with the writings of numerous other prophets, most students of the scriptures would agree that Isaiah's style is unsurpassed. Other inspired writers may reach similar heights of expression, but they can rarely sustain such a constantly high level or mastery of form and poetry as does Isaiah. It is granted that his prophetic insights and much of his power of speech were divinely inspired, but these talents must have been polished and refined by his personality, intelligence, and communication skills.

The Writings of Isaiah

Considering the length of Isaiah's ministry, it is probable that he gave many more messages than those recorded in his book. Old Testament prophets usually delivered their messages orally at the city gates or in a public assembly place, such as the temple courtyards in Jerusalem. Their important warnings and prophecies were written down by the prophet, his scribe, or one of his disciples. These written prophecies had only a limited circulation, however, and most ancient Israelites did not have any prophetic writings or scrolls in their own homes. They learned of the prophetic messages as they were repeated and discussed orally. Because of this oral transmission, prophets, poets, and psalmists organized their material into forms that could be easily remembered and transmitted. The written copies of their literature were primarily used to verify the correct oral transmission and, especially in the case of the prophetic works, to serve as a witness or record of the Lord's counsel and promises to the people.

It is assumed that Isaiah personally recorded his prophecies or at least supervised their recording. At least twice, he was commanded to preserve his messages as a testimony for later ages. (Isa. 8:16; 30:8.) His works were not only passed on to later generations, but they also became a prophetic foundation used constantly by later prophets and apostles. Without a doubt, the writings of Isaiah constitute the most important prophetic discourses of the Old Testament. As mentioned earlier, Isaiah is quoted more in the New Testament, Book of Mormon, Doctrine and Covenants, and Dead Sea Scrolls than any other Old Testament prophet. Jesus quoted Isaiah throughout his ministry. (For example, compare Isa. 61:1-3 with Luke 4:16-21.) Jesus also promised that all of Isaiah's prophecies would be fulfilled, and he commanded his followers to search Isaiah's words. (3 Ne. 20:11-12, 23:1-3.) It is also significant that Christ chose the words of Isaiah to open our dispensation (compare Isa. 29:13 with JS-H 1:19) and to instruct the boy Joseph Smith (compare Isa. 11 with JS-H 1:40).

Outline of Isaiah

The book of Isaiah easily divides into two main collections of prophecies, which are joined by a few historical chapters: collection one (ch. 1-35), historical segment (36-39), collection two (40-66).

A more detailed description of the segments within the two halves of Isaiah and the historical chapters between them is presented below:

Prophecies of Judgment (ch. 1-35)

Warnings to Israel. Prophecies to ancient Israelites and their leaders. Includes Isaiah's call to repentance, a description of his first vision, his Immanuel and other messianic prophecies, and his promise of millennial peace when the lamb, lion, and other animals will lie down together (1-12).

Pronouncements to the foreign nations. Prophecies or "burdens" to the Gentile kingdoms. Contains warnings to Babylon, Moab, Syria, Africa, America, Egypt, Phoenicia, and other places. Countries of the last days, especially Babylon, or the "wicked world," are symbolically represented (13-23).

Revelations of the Lord's judgments and blessings. Prophecies, psalms, prayers, and promises of God's punishments and rewards. Includes Isaiah's "apocalypse" (24-27) and warnings to Israel of her suffering and to the wicked world (or Edom) of its destruction before the Millennium, with promises to the righteous of hidden treasures of knowledge, scriptures coming from the dust, justice, peace, noble leaders, and the earth blossoming as a rose (24-35).

Historical Narrative (36-39)

Record of the Assyrian invasion and King Hezekiah's sickness. Written mostly in prose rather than in poetry. Describes political events between Judah, Assyria, and Babylon and portrays Isaiah's relationship with the royal line of Judah (36-39).

Promises of Redemption (40-66)

Affirmation of God's power and salvation. Prophecies to Israel and the whole world (including "Babylon," 47) concerning the Lord's strength, glory, deliverance, and other attributes. Contains the first of Isaiah's "servant songs," which describe God's servants (messianic, religious, and secular) who will deliver the righteous from death, wickedness, and oppression (40-47).

Redemption of Israel by the Messiah. Invitation to scattered Israel to enjoy the blessings of salvation provided by God's atoning servant. Includes a call to those who call themselves Israelites (either by lineage or covenant) to join with those who live in the land of Israel and to enjoy the blessings of righteousness in Zion (48-52), the great servant song of the Messiah and his glory (53), and a universal invitation to join in the Lord's work, to trust in his ways, to keep his commandments (such as the Sabbath, morality, fasting, and charity), and to always turn away from sin (54-58).

Glorious prophecies of the last days. Warnings of the great and dreadful day of the Lord immediately preceding the Millennium. Contains promises of the gathering of Israel, the Restoration, temple work, temporal and spiritual blessings, the return of Christ, and the creation of a new heaven and a new earth (59-66).

5

Isaiah's works are extensive, and it is assumed that he himself arranged his writings into their present order, although a scribe or disciple may have done so. Other records of Isaiah may also have been the source for some of the historical information about this period and his involvement in it. (See 2 Kgs. 14-21; 2 Chr. 26-33.) One other major work of his was known anciently but has since been lost—his history of Uzziah. (See 2 Chr. 26:22.) Some of Isaiah's records may have been edited or deleted as the Jewish scribes returned from Babylon and collected various sacred writings before they prepared standardized copies of the biblical texts. The accepted Old Testament version of the canonized Hebrew translation (the Masoretic Text) of Isaiah's writings is a result of this scribal editing tradition. The contents of a parallel Greek translation (the Septuagint) and the portions translated from the brass plates of Laban (quoted in the Book of Mormon) differ slightly from the Masoretic text, although the Isaiah material remains basically the same in all three versions.

In spite of the passage of time and the ravages and pressures without and within Judaism, most of Isaiah's writings have remained intact. They provide powerful warnings and prophecies to the world from an Old Testament prophet who was great like unto Moses (Deut. 18:15) and who truly communed with God (2 Ne. 11:2).

WHY AND HOW TO STUDY ISAIAH

Numerous prophets and leaders have served the Lord. Of all the prophets who prepare us for the future through messianic and millennial prophecies, Isaiah is by far the most significant. Although Christ has endorsed the words of all his servants, the prophets (D&C 1:38; 68:3-4), he singled out Isaiah's words in particular and commanded his followers to study Isaiah's message:

> Yea, a commandment I give unto you that ye search these things diligently; for great are the words of Isaiah. For surely he spake . . . concerning my people which are of the house of Israel; therefore . . . he must speak also to the Gentiles. And all things that he spake have been and shall be, even according to the words which he spake. (3 Ne. 23:1-3.)

Why? *All Isaiah's words will be fulfilled.* Isaiah spoke to Israel and the whole world, delivering many prophecies concerning the Lord's work. In speaking to the Nephites, Jesus promised that all Isaiah's prophecies will be fulfilled, just as Isaiah gave them.

How? *Read Isaiah.* Isaiah's words help only those who read them. And because of the complexity of his message and style, it is usually not until the second or third reading that his ideas become clear and his wisdom appears bright.

It is also very helpful to read more than one translation of Isaiah. Obviously, reading his book in the original Hebrew would be of greatest value, but any foreign language version or alternate English translation helps the reader view Isaiah from a different perspective. An additional English translation is also helpful because it often provides alternate meanings for troublesome words, idiomatic expressions, and language patterns. The main value of a second translation is that it stimulates a closer evaluation of the text itself. As one reads the material in a different language, new meanings appear. This is important, since all scripture must be read, pondered, and prayed about before it can be fully understood. (See Moro. 10:3-5.) A second or third reading of Isaiah, especially if one reads an alternate translation, stimulates meditation and enhances understanding.

Since a great number and variety of new English translations have appeared recently, this book includes a second English translation for each Isaiah chapter to complement the standard King James Version. The second version will appear within the text of the commentary on each chapter.

As you set aside time for daily scripture study and read and reread Isaiah, you will come to understand and feel more comfortable with his writings.

> And it came to pass that I, Nephi, did teach my brethren . . . And I read many things unto them . . . : but that I might more fully persuade them to believe in the Lord their Redeemer I did read unto them that which was written by the prophet Isaiah; . . . that it might be for our profit and learning. (1 Ne. 19:22-23.)

Why? *Isaiah inspires and teaches.* Many of the great prophets and teachers took material for their messages from Isaiah: when Nephi tried to persuade his brothers to believe in Christ, he read from Isaiah; as Abinadi taught about the Messiah, Resurrection, and Atonement, he preached from Isaiah (Mosiah 14-15); while the resurrected Lord ministered to the Nephites, he incorporated and elucidated much of Isaiah within his teachings (3 Ne. 16, 20-23); and as Moroni concluded his records, he exhorted his readers to search the prophecies of Isaiah (Mor. 8:23). The Lord and these Book of Mormon prophets recognized the universal application of the inspired teachings and prophecies of Isaiah. Just as they used his words to teach their audiences, we too can reap insights from Isaiah to inspire ourselves and others.

How? *Search and study Isaiah's gospel teachings.* It is not enough simply to *read* the scriptures, or to *read* Isaiah; Christ said that one must *search* the scriptures (John 5:39) and *search* Isaiah (3 Ne. 20:11; 23:1). It is only after careful and deep examination, comparison, and synthesis that the words of Isaiah burn brightly and his images reveal themselves.

As most of us read Isaiah, trying to ponder his words and understand their meaning, we are like the Ethiopian who was reading an Isaiah scroll while riding home in his chariot from Jerusalem. Philip met him and asked, "Do you understand what you are reading?" The man replied, "How can I, unless some man guides me?" (Acts 8:30-

31.) Since Isaiah's inspired writings reflect both his time and culture and also reveal the Lord's work throughout later generations, the question, "What does Isaiah say?" is not as important as the more insistent query, "What does Isaiah *mean*?" This second question should motivate everyone's search into the words of Isaiah.

One aid to understanding is to study Isaiah within the context of the gospel dispensation of Moses. Many Israelites of Isaiah's time knew the elements of the plan of salvation (premortal existence, purpose of earth life, resurrection, etc.), the basic principles and ordinances of the gospel, and the prophetic promises about the Messiah, who would free them from spiritual and physical bondage. Isaiah builds upon this gospel foundation and teaches it in greater depth. For example, his ideas in chapter 14 elaborate on the account of Lucifer and his hosts being cast down to spirit prison. And in chapter 1, he teaches in his unique vocabulary the basic gospel principles of knowing one's master (faith), changing scarlet sins to white (repentance), washing oneself (baptism), and hearing the word of the Lord (the gift of the Holy Ghost). His servant songs and insights about a prophet's burdens culminate in chapter 53 with his great discourse on the atoning servant, Jesus Christ.

Before we can understand Isaiah's teachings and share the inspiration he received, we must study his words, ponder how they fit within the gospel, and pray about them. A careful study requires us to look at Isaiah theme by theme, chapter by chapter, concept by concept, verse by verse. As we come to share his insights, we will come to a greater understanding of the gospel.

> I, Nephi, did . . . read unto them that which was written by the prophet Isaiah, for I did liken all scripture unto us, that it might be for our profit and learning. Wherefore I spake unto them, saying: Hear ye the words of the prophet . . . and liken them unto yourselves, that ye may have hope. And now I, Nephi, write more of the words of Isaiah, . . . For I will liken his words unto my people, . . . for he verily saw my Redeemer. (1 Ne. 19:23-24; 2 Ne. 11:2.)

Why? *We can learn from Isaiah today*. Nephi includes many historical passages in his Isaiah extracts and gives them not as history lessons so much as lessons from history, showing the past types and patterns that can influence later generations. The fate of ancient unrighteous nations (and individuals) was all too familiar to Nephi. Having seen the destruction of Jerusalem and the future destruction of his own people in vision, and knowing the awful destiny of most latter-day Gentiles, he strove to motivate those who would repent, both among his own people and later readers. (Compare 1 Ne. 12 with 2 Ne. 28:32.) He recognized that scripture will help only those readers who can personally relate to its message. A modern prophet, Bruce R. McConkie, has expressed similar feelings:

> Scriptural understanding and great insight relative to the doctrines of salvation are valuable only insofar as they change and perfect the lives of men, only insofar as they live in the hearts of those who know them. (*Ensign*, Oct. 1973, p. 83.)

How? *Liken Isaiah to yourself.* You might take the words of Isaiah and place them in a modern context by:

1. Rewriting a chapter to express the same ideas, only using your own vocabulary and imagery.
2. Preparing a talk or home evening lesson based upon one of Isaiah's themes.
3. Writing a poem that conveys the same feelings as one of Isaiah's.
4. Drafting a sermon as a general authority might address one of the doctrines stressed by Isaiah.

But whatever method you choose, take the ideas, feelings and teachings of Isaiah and see how they apply in your own life and how you can use them in teaching and inspiring others.

> Isaiah spake many things which were hard for many . . . to understand; for they know not concerning the manner of prophesying among the Jews. . . . And my soul delighteth in the words of Isaiah, . . . and I know that the Jews do understand . . . the prophets, and there is none other people that understand . . . save it be that they are taught after the manner of the things of the Jews. (2 Ne. 25:1, 5.)

Why? *Isaiah is profoundly prophetic.* Just as many Nephites did not understand Isaiah because they did not know "the manner of prophesying among the Jews," most people today continue to lack understanding for the same reason. While Nephi's writings are simple and plain, Isaiah's compositions are complicated and eloquent. Isaiah's messages contain many levels of meaning and are thus comparable to the Savior's parables, which were addressed to different audiences of varied spiritual backgrounds. Isaiah's audience included the people of his own time and place, Israelites in exile, Jews returning from Babylon, Jews at the time of Jesus, early Christians, and the Nephites. Now it includes modern Christians, Jews, Moslems, and Latter-day Saints. He has something to say to all of us, and in order to teach and inspire us, his poetry is superb, his prophecy sublime, and his style of teaching unique.

Isaiah's mechanical techniques (his "manner of prophesying") were probably understood by the Nephites. That is, they understood Isaiah's types, figures, symbols, and poetic structure. Their ignorance was not so much in the mechanics of prophecy as in spiritual comprehension, as suggested by Nephi's brother Jacob:

> The Jews were a stiffnecked people; and they despised the words of plainness . . . and sought for things that they could not understand. Wherefore, because of their blindness, which blindness came by looking beyond the mark . . . God hath taken away his plainness from them, and delivered unto them many things which they cannot understand, because they desired it. And because they desired it God hath done it. (Jacob 4:14.)

Nephi and Jacob are saying, in other words, "Isaiah is hard for many people to understand because they do not know the way the Lord commanded Isaiah to prophesy. Since they have desired complicated messages, God has given them prophetic utterances which they do not comprehend."

Isaiah's prophesying is usually cryptic, for he often veils his message from his audience. (See the commentary on Isaiah 6 in this book.) Elder McConkie illustrates this technique as follows:

> The virgin birth prophecy is dropped into the midst of a recitation of local historical occurrences so that to the spiritually untutored it could be interpreted as some ancient and unknown happening that had no relationship to the birth of the Lord Jehovah into mortality some 700 years later. Similarly, many chapters dealing with latter-day apostasy and the second coming of Christ are written relative to ancient nations whose destruction was but a symbol, a type, and a shadow, of that which would fall upon all nations when the great and dreadful day of the Lord finally came. . . . Once we learn this system and use the interpretive keys found in the Book of Mormon and through latter-day revelation, we soon find the Isaiah passages unfolding themselves to our view. (*Ensign*, Oct. 1973, pp. 82–83.)

How? *Study Isaiah's manner of prophesying.* Four major stylistic elements must be understood before Isaiah's "manner of prophesying" can be unraveled. First, his mode of communication should be studied, since most of his writings are poetry. A careful look at his poetic style, called "parallelism," is necessary to understand the form of his writing.

The second element in Isaiah's "manner of prophesying" is his use of symbolism. Symbolic names (such as Immanuel, and those of Isaiah's two sons—Shear-jashub and Maher-shalal-hash-baz, Shiloh, etc.), titles (servant, the blind, Holy One, etc.), places (altar, temple, mountain of the Lord, Edom, Babylon, etc.), and acts (washing, sacrifice, shedding blood, etc.) are scattered throughout Isaiah. By

11

studying the history and context of Isaiah's ministry, one can see how he uses contemporary symbols both to teach his immediate audience and to provide images and lessons for later generations.

The third element in understanding Isaiah's prophesying is more difficult since it requires a careful look at his prophetic role and philosophy of teaching. Because of the spiritual limitations of his audience, he could not always be exact and straightforward in his teaching. His insights are often well hidden within a poetic discourse. He thereby not only challenges our understanding through his writing expertise, but also deliberately obscures his ideas in imagery and symbolism.

The last element necessary to understand Isaiah's prophesying is the use of inspired interpretation. Revealed insights and interpretive keys are found in the New Testament, the Book of Mormon, and latter-day revelation, though much remains to be revealed as the prophecies of Isaiah continue to unfold. (See Article of Faith 9.)

In summary, Isaiah's "manner of prophesying" follows certain patterns that require sensitive interpretive skills before one can understand his teachings. The four major elements of his prophesying must be studied on two levels: (1) the mechanics or technique of his writings, and (2) the meaning or interpretation of his teachings. The basic keys are diagrammed in the following chart:

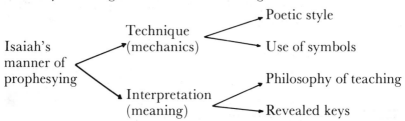

Ancient Israelites (such as Nephi's brothers) understood the prophetic technique but, since they were often not spiritually sensitive, looked "beyond the mark" and missed the correct interpretation. Today we should be able to interpret Isaiah because of the many scriptures and inspired interpretations available to us. However, we often hesitate to study Isaiah because we do not or cannot appreciate the mechanics of his prophesying, and therefore we stumble over his style and symbols. As we both study his technique and learn how to interpret his writings, we will master his "manner of prophesying" and come to understand his message.

I [Christ] say unto you, that when they [the words of Isaiah] shall be fulfilled then is the fulfilling of the covenant which the Father hath made unto his people, O house of Israel. (3 Ne. 20:12; see also 23:2.)

I [Nephi] speak unto all the house of Israel, . . . he [the Lord] surely did show unto the prophets of old all things concerning them; . . . that they might know concerning the doings of the Lord. . . . Hear ye the words of the prophet [Isaiah], which were written unto all the house of Israel. (1 Ne. 19:19, 21, 22, 24.)

I [Jacob] have read these things [from Isaiah] that ye might know concerning the covenants of the Lord that he has covenanted with all the house of Israel. (2 Ne. 9:1.)

Why? *Isaiah taught Israel concerning her covenants with the Lord.* Isaiah was the last great prophet who spoke to all of Israel while they were still one people in the Holy Land. He taught the Israelites how the Lord had worked with their ancestors and why they were his covenant people. He reminded them of how they were breaking their covenants and why the Lord's punishment would come upon them. In short, he was the greatest teacher of Israel since Moses, and the last prophetic witness before the scattering.

How? *Review the Lord's covenants in the ancient scriptures.* Read and reread the Old Testament to appreciate how God dealt with his children anciently. In particular, study chapters 12-50 of Genesis to review how the Lord established covenants with Abraham, Isaac, and Jacob (Israel). Then review the book of Deuteronomy to see what Moses taught assembled Israel concerning their laws and covenants. Finally, read the book of Psalms to capture some of the love and emotion expressed by many authors (poets, kings, priests, and prophets) as they told about God's relationship with his chosen people.

The Book of Mormon is also a key to understanding ancient covenants. Review especially 1 Nephi 10 (Lehi's teachings on Israel), 2 Nephi 25-33 (Nephi's teachings), and Jacob 5 (Zenos's allegory) to see how the Lord's covenants developed within that branch of Israel. Also note how the law of Moses was fulfilled as recorded in 3 Nephi 1:24-25 and 9:16-22.

The fulfillment of the Mosaic dispensation, the preparation of the Jews for Christ's dispensation, and many other Isaianic prophecies are also recorded in the New Testament. All these ancient scriptures show how the Lord worked through the prophets (particularly Isaiah) and other servants (psalmists, poets, etc.) to teach Israel her proper relationship with God.

> And I [Nephi] did rehearse unto them the words of Isaiah, who spake concerning the restoration of the Jews, or of the house of Israel; and after they were restored they should no more be confounded, neither should they be scattered again. (1 Ne. 15:20.)

Why? *Isaiah promises the return of Israel.* Isaiah not only taught Israel about her ancient history and covenants, but he also prophesied that the Jews and other remnants of Israel will return to the Lord and their promised lands in the last days. His ideas stimulated the Book of Mormon prophets to seek for further insights into these future events. Isaiah also gives signs and promises concerning the other remnants of Israel, the Ten Tribes and Lamanites; some of these prophecies were used by Christ as he taught the Lamanites about their latter-day destiny. When the Ten Tribes return and their scriptural record is revealed, Isaiah's words will probably be frequently quoted in them as a major teaching source and witness. (See 2 Ne. 29:13.) In short, Isaiah's words have inspired all the dispersed groups of Israel, and his promises concerning their return will certainly be fulfilled.

How? *Study Jewish and Lamanite history.* A study of Jewish and Lamanite history over the past hundred and fifty years will demonstrate the fulfillment of many Isaianic prophecies pertaining to the return of Israel in the last days. Many Jewish history books evaluate modern Jewish history (since 1800), the development of Zionism, and the modern state of Israel. Not as many sources are available for American Indian or Lamanite history, but articles in the *Church News*, *Ensign,* and other Latter-day Saint publications often highlight the current social and religious development of the Lamanites as they join the Church in large numbers in Central and South America. Of course, many prophecies of these two remnants of Israel remain to be fulfilled, but a review of their movements and growth indicates the tremendous progress they have made from their ancient apostate traditions since the keys for the gathering of Israel were restored by Moses to Joseph Smith in 1836.

> But behold, I [Nephi] proceed with mine own prophecy. . . . In the days that the prophecies of Isaiah shall be fulfilled men shall know of a surety, at the times when they shall come to pass. Wherefore, they are of worth unto the children of men, . . . for I know that they shall be of great worth unto them in the last days; for in that day shall they understand them; wherefore, for their good have I written them. (2 Ne. 25:7-8.)

Why? *People in the last days will witness the fulfillment of Isaiah's prophecies.* Although some of us may wish that we had lived in the days

14

of Isaiah, when his visions and revelations might have been explained to us personally, most of us would still be confused, since we could not then have comprehended the scientific achievements and religious developments to come in the last days. From an ancient perspective, our modern age would have appeared astonishing with its labor-saving machines, communication systems, transportation devices, and other advances; yet it would also have baffled us that so much poverty, inequality, and wickedness could still be a part of the "advanced" society of the last days. We would also have a difficult time appreciating how the plain, simple, restored truths of the gospel could come forth and grow in such a sophisticated and wicked world. Since Isaiah used imagery and symbols to describe the latter days and did not completely and literally describe all that he saw, his audience would have been even more confused about modern events and how they would fulfill Isaiah's prophecies.

In the Book of Mormon reference quoted above, Nephi promises that those who live in the last days will witness the fulfillment of Isaiah's prophecies and understand them! We can build upon our hindsight of history with knowledge of contemporary events and Isaiah's visions of our day to see how his words are being fulfilled.

How? *Review the restored gospel and the signs of the times.* In modern revelation, the Lord has interpreted, clarified, and expanded the meaning of many of Isaiah's words. Many quotations from Isaiah are found in the latter-day scriptures, and explanations of his meaning are contained in the teachings of the prophets and apostles of this dispensation.

Moroni quoted Isaiah to Joseph Smith at the opening of this dispensation (JS-H 1:40), and the Doctrine and Covenants is especially rich in phraseology from Isaiah. For example, section 113 interprets parts of Isaiah 11 and 52; section 133 repeats many phrases and ideas from Isaiah 35, 51, 63, and 64; and section 101 presents some keys to understanding Isaiah 65. Also, numerous Isaianic terms and phrases are found in sections 1, 45, 88, 109, 124, and 128.

Later prophets and apostles of this dispensation also have taught from Isaiah and explained difficult points of his message. Elder Bruce R. McConkie points out the value of these modern, inspired commentaries:

> There are also, of course, numerous allusions to and explanations of the great seer's words in the sermons of Joseph Smith and the other inspired teachers of righteousness of this dispensation. So often it takes only a propheti-

cally uttered statement, revealing the age or place or subject involved in a particular passage in the writings of any prophet, to cause the whole passage and all related ones to shine forth with their true meaning and import.

It truly takes revelation to understand revelation, and what is more natural than to find the Lord Jehovah, who revealed his truths anciently, revealing the same eternal verities today and so tying his ancient and modern words together, that we may be blessed by our knowledge of what he has said in all ages. (*Ensign*, Oct. 1973, p. 81.)

In seeking to understand more of Isaiah by reviewing the restored gospel and studying the signs of these last days, we should study the Doctrine and Covenants carefully, especially the sections noted above. We should know the important events and movements of Latter-day Saint and world history. We should study the general conference addresses and review the scriptures that prophesy of the last days. All these things will not only help us to understand how Isaiah's prophecies are being fulfilled, but also prepare us to become better servants in fulfilling the prophesied events of this dispensation.

Wherefore, hearken, . . . and give ear unto my words; for because the words of Isaiah are not plain unto you, nevertheless they are plain unto all those that are filled with the spirit of prophecy. (2 Ne. 25:4.)

Why? *Isaiah's words are plain to those with the spirit of prophecy.* An angel told John the Revelator that "the testimony of Jesus is the spirit of prophecy." (Rev. 19:10.) Peter likewise recorded that no man can know the things of God without enlightenment by the Spirit. (2 Pet. 1:20-21.) Since the spirit of prophecy makes plain the words of Isaiah, a living knowledge and testimony of the gospel truths, especially the divine mission of the Lord Jesus Christ, is imperative for understanding Isaiah's writings.

With this spiritual gift, we can understand Isaiah through the same spirit of prophecy that inspired Isaiah. Isaiah's inspired writings and all other scriptures come from God through the power of the Holy Ghost. As any man studies scripture, that same Holy Ghost enlightens him as to the meaning and value of revealed truths. (See Hel. 9:20; 1 Cor. 2:11; 1 Ne. 10:17-19; D&C 75:10.)

How? *Gain the spirit of prophecy.* The value of all spiritual gifts depends upon our worthiness to receive them and our diligence in developing them. God's Spirit does not come to the unworthy and, as demonstrated in the parable of the talents, gifts from God profit neither him nor us if they are not used and magnified. (See Hel. 4:12-14; Matt. 25:15-30; Ether 12:35.) Thus, in order to receive the spirit of prophecy, we must strive to keep all the commandments and retain the Holy Spirit at all times. The development of this spiritual gift through constant study, pondering, and prayer can eventually lead us to receive the same spirit of instruction that inspired Isaiah originally.

> And now I, Nephi, write more of the words of Isaiah, for my soul delight-eth in his words . . . for he verily saw my Redeemer, even as I have seen him. (2 Ne. 11:2.)

Why? *Isaiah has seen the Lord.* Nephi loved to quote Isaiah because he shared Isaiah's spiritual manifestations and insights. Both Nephi and Isaiah had seen the Lord, and they foresaw how his work would unfold among the children of men.

Of all the prophetic writings on the brass plates, Nephi specifically chose the writings of Isaiah to use in persuading his brothers and the whole house of Israel to believe in the Lord their Redeemer, Jesus Christ. (1 Ne. 19:18-23.) Isaiah received and recorded messianic insights that continue to inspire God's children. As Elder McConkie writes,

> Isaiah is everywhere known as the messianic prophet because of the abundance, beauty, and perfection of his prophetic utterances foretelling the first coming of our Lord. And truly such he is. No old world prophet, whose inspired sayings have come down to us, can compare with him in this respect. Moreover, the first coming of the Messiah is past, and so even those among us who are not overly endowed with spiritual insight can look back and see in the birth, ministry, and death of our Lord the fulfillment of Isaiah's forecasts. (*Ensign*, Oct. 1973, p. 81.)

How? *Develop yourself spiritually.* During our mortality, most of us may not be privileged to see Christ in vision as did Isaiah and Nephi, or in the flesh as did others, but all of us can draw nearer to the Lord through following his teachings and example. As we attain greater spiritual heights and develop an intimate relationship with him through mighty prayer, we will naturally come to a greater love and appreciation of him. And as we give Christian service and increase our love toward others, we will become more like him. Then we will understand more of the words and feelings of Isaiah and the other prophets who loved the Lord and served him with all their power. As our spiritual life becomes more like Isaiah's, his writings will communicate to us on a higher spiritual level and teach us great truths about ourselves, others, the Lord, and the divine plan for this earth and its inhabitants.

17

We can derive many values from studying Isaiah's book, for as we follow the necessary steps in understanding his writings, they will help us come closer to the Lord's goal for the children of men— immortality and eternal life. (Moses 1:39.)

HISTORICAL BACKGROUND

Almost one-fifth of Isaiah's chapters and prophecies are directed specifically to foreign nations. (Isa. 13-23, 46-47.) Major sections of other chapters are also set in the historical and sociopolitical context of his age. (Isa. 1-10, 28-39.) In order to understand Isaiah's message to the foreign nations and to Israel and Judah, one must have a basic knowledge of historical events in the eighth century B.C.

During Isaiah's ministry, Assyria dominated the Middle East, although Egypt still harbored hopes of regaining previously lost territories and prestige.

Assyria

During much of its early history, Assyria was controlled by various powers that periodically invaded Mesopotamia, conquered Babylon, and extended their rule over the Assyrian inhabitants. During the years 1300 to 800 B.C., the Assyrian kings engaged in continual struggle to keep their boundaries intact, with the primary military objective of freeing Assyria from foreign domination. This Assyrian preoccupation, coupled with the weakness of Egypt and Babylon, left David and Solomon free to extend their own boundaries and maintain their kingdoms independent of foreign domination. However, with the ascension of Adad-Nirari II (909-899 B.C.) to the Assyrian throne, the Assyrians began to expand their territories and annex newly-conquered areas to the Assyrian state. Succeeding kings improved upon this policy, increasing the army's power and reputation and building a vast empire that ruled many peoples with a harshness and terror previously unsurpassed in history. It was the rise of this Assyrian Empire that figures so heavily in the prophecies of Isaiah and the political policies of Israel's neighbors.

As the Assyrians, under the new imperialist dynasty, began to take more vigorous military action against the tribes that resisted them, they were able to build up a ring of vassal countries surrounding the Assyrian homeland. Often, princes would free themselves and join in anti-Assyrian ventures. Assyria would then be forced to undertake new campaigns. This brought about the need for a strong standing army, which in turn required civilian and military officials accountable only to the king. The king's powerful army, with its cruel professional soldiers, soon became the dread of the conquered peoples in the Assyrian Empire.

In the middle of the ninth century B.C., Shalmaneser III extended Assyria's rule from Urartu (Turkey) to the Persian gulf, and from Media (Iran) to the Syrian coast. (See the dark lines on Map 10.) When, in 857 B.C., Shalmaneser III captured the city of Carchemish in Syria, the cities to the southwest were alerted to action; the feuding states surrounding Israel and Judah quickly made peace and formed a coalition against the oncoming Assyrians.

The armies of Assyria met the armies of this coalition in 853 B.C. at Qarqar, and while this battle is not mentioned in the Bible, Assyrian inscriptions state that King Ahab of Israel was a major participant. The outcome of this battle being indecisive, it led to other unsuccessful Assyrian attacks. These indecisive battles became a thorn in the side of the Assyrians and served as a catalyst for the explosive situation between Assyria and the West during Isaiah's day.

Shalmaneser III died in 810 B.C., and the Assyrian Empire entered a dormant period during which the various kingdoms of the western Fertile Crescent gained more and more power and independence. In fact, Jeroboam II (792-747 B.C.) of Israel was able for a short time to expand his rule to encompass both Syrian and Judean territories.

Although Assyria lost control of some territories and the taxes from most vassal states, no one directly tried to challenge her power because of her fearsome reputation. The dormant period and years of ineffectual rule ended with a palace revolution just a few years before Isaiah was called as a prophet.

Tiglath-pileser III (745-727 B.C.; called Pul in the Bible) took immediate action to strengthen the empire. Under his able leadership, the Assyrian Empire reached the pinnacle of its power. He developed a new type of imperialistic foreign policy and strengthened royal authority and administration by changing the great Assyrian provinces to small administration districts owing direct allegiance to the king himself. Also, instead of forming a loose vassal relationship with surrounding states, he destroyed, step by step, the political independence of those petty states and incorporated them into the provincial structure of the empire. The process of his conquest is outlined below.

First stage: Pul brought the states to a vassal relationship by demonstrating his military might through harassment and threats. Each vassal state was required to pay an annual tribute and furnish auxiliary troops. This policy was no different from those of Pul's predecessors.

Second stage: When the vassal states revolted or were suspected of plotting against the crown, the Assyrians removed the unfaithful ruler and replaced him, if possible, with someone more loyal from the ruling family. In most instances, Pul reduced the size of the vassal's kingdom and gave it to a more loyal vassal. If necessary, he deported segments of the upper class and other societal leaders to distant parts of the empire. In any case, Pul increased the annual tribute and watched the vassalage more closely.

Third stage: At the slightest sign of further anti-Assyrian activities, the military directly intervened, removing the vassal king, liquidating the political resistance in the nation, and establishing the area as an Assyrian province under the jurisdiction of Assyrian officials. Again, they deported the native upper class and placed a foreign one in its stead.

As Assyrian territory expanded toward Israel and Judah during Isaiah's lifetime, Israel underwent all three stages of conquest while Judah suffered only the first stage, barely escaping the other stages. Since both Israel and Judah had enjoyed great independence during the period of Assyrian dormancy, this encroachment was particularly frustrating and frightening.

Egypt

Egypt was the second major ancient power in the Middle East. Indeed, when Moses led the Israelites through the Red Sea, Egypt was the strongest imperial power in the area. Within a couple of centuries, however, the dynasties of the Egyptian New Kingdom period weakened and then finally crumbled. Although the pharaohs of the post-imperial period (1100-700 B.C.) often took forays into Palestine and Syria, Egypt was unable to reassert full control over her former vassals. Egypt's weakness in foreign affairs was due largely to domestic weakness and internal dissension; the Egyptian rulers were unable to control the various provinces that composed the country. Often the provinces remained petty independent states or banded into two larger states, upper and lower Egypt.

During Isaiah's youth, while the twenty-second dynasty continued to rule at Tanis-Zoan in the delta area of lower Egypt, a twenty-third dynasty was already establishing a power base in the south, near Thebes. Neither dynasty was able to gain substantial control because of weak leaders, resulting in a civil war centered at Thebes. Hoshea, the last king of Israel, foolishly relied upon one of these weak pharaohs as a source of military aid in his rebellion against powerful Assyrian masters. It is no wonder that help never came to save Samaria from its fall.

The short-lived twenty-fourth dynasty (715-709 B.C.) was confined to a single pharaoh, Bocchoris, whose only mark of significance was his codifying of many Egyptian laws. However, during the reign of Bocchoris, a new power entered into Egyptian history, the Ethiopian or Cushite pharaohs. By the middle of the eighth century, these Ethiopian rulers consolidated their rule in their African homelands around the fourth cataract of the Nile and were ready to move north against a weakened Egypt.

Although from south of Egyptian Nubia, these Ethiopian pharaohs were thoroughly Egyptian in culture. By 720 B.C., one of these rulers, Piankhy, had already laid claim to Thebes and had taken upper or southern Egypt as a protectorate. He then went north and temporarily subdued lower Egypt to keep Thebes safe from an Egyptian counterattack. As the Assyrian influence expanded into Palestine-Syria and then toward Egypt, the pharaohs only occasionally committed major military forces to resist the Assyrian campaign. They preferred diplomatic intrigue through inciting the weak rulers of Palestine-Syria.

As the Assyrians grew in power during Isaiah's ministry, they extended their control over Palestine-Syria to consolidate that area before attacking the real prize, Egypt. In the 730s, Pul of Assyria penetrated as far south as Gaza, and a decade later, Sargon II defeated the Egyptians at Raphia, having already taken Samaria in 721. Egypt, under the weak rulers of the twenty-fifth dynasty, finally took up an aggressive military campaign against the Assyrians. When Sennacherib attacked Judah and laid siege to Jerusalem in 705 B.C., the Ethiopian Pharaoh Shebiku sent his brother Terhakah to oppose Assyria. (See 2 Kgs. 19:9; Isa. 37:9.) It appears that the promise of Egyptian support prompted King Hezekiah of Judah to rebel against the Assyrians. It also appears that the Egyptians were interested only in keeping the Assyrians busy with revolts throughout their empire, thus making it impossible for them to mount a campaign against Egypt. A statement made by one of Sennacherib's generals to the soldiers of Jerusalem sums up both Egypt's perpetual weakness and Hezekiah's folly in relying upon Egyptian strength: he assured the Jews that their reliance upon pharaoh was like trusting a "broken reed" that could only injure him who leaned upon it. (Isa. 36:6.) After Sennacherib's setback at Jerusalem (Isa. 36), he eventually defeated the Egyptian forces at Eltekeh in southern Palestine in 700 B.C. (See Map 10 for political boundaries.)

In summary, the Egyptians figured very prominently in Israel's and Judah's history during the ministry of Isaiah. The Egyptian intrigues helped to bring about the downfall of Israel in 721 and greatly threatened Judah's security in 705 B.C. Egypt's greatest weakness always was her own internal disunity. No wonder the Lord counseled Judah not to trust in Egyptian chariots but in the God of Israel, Jehovah. (Isa. 31.)

Historical and Religious Setting

Isaiah was born about 770 B.C. during the reigns of two strong Israelite kings, Jeroboam II and Uzziah. In the northern kingdom of Israel, Jeroboam II was beautifying Samaria and expanding his country's borders and influence to their greatest extent since Solomon's time. Likewise, in the southern kingdom of Judah, Uzziah was serving as Jerusalem's most powerful king since Solomon. This was a time of peace for both kingdoms, since neither Assyria (to the northeast) nor Egypt (to the southwest) had strong rulers who threatened that part of the Middle East. Both Israelite countries were becoming more cosmopolitan as increased trade and prosperity improved the wealth of the urban upper classes. Meanwhile, the lower classes and rural dwellers experienced increased taxes, land expropriations, and social inequities. Idolatry and wickedness permeated all social levels. Thus, wealth, social injustices, immorality, and growing pagan worship came to characterize both societies, with the greatest decadence being in Samaria.

Israel and Judah

During Isaiah's youth and early manhood, the southern Israelite kingdom of Judah was ruled by the strong King Uzziah (also known as Azariah). Uzziah expanded Judah's borders southward and eastward, thus controlling areas of Edom and territories reaching to Elath and the Red Sea. After Uzziah attempted to usurp some priestly functions and was stricken with leprosy (c. 750 B.C.), his son Jotham ruled with him as co-regent. (2 Kgs. 15:5; 2 Chr. 26:21.) In 740 B.C., the year of Uzziah's death, Isaiah received his calling as the Lord's prophet. (Isa. 6.) As can be seen from Uzziah's long reign of over fifty years, Judah experienced strong, stable rule during Isaiah's early life.

In the north, political conditions were much more chaotic during this period. At the time of Isaiah's birth, Jeroboam II ruled the northern kingdom of Israel as the fourth king of Jehu's dynasty and one of Israel's most illustrious rulers. (2 Kgs. 14:23-29.) Because Assyria was preoccupied with other nations, Jeroboam II was able to advance aggressive expansionist policies, thus restoring Israel's boundaries almost to their extent under Solomon. (See Maps 7 and 9.) Jeroboam ruled for over forty years (787-746 B.C.), including the last ten years of his life, when he ruled as coregent with his son Zechariah. Six months after Zechariah ascended the Israelite throne in 746, he was murdered by Shallum, who by this act overthrew the Jehu dynasty and fulfilled an earlier prophecy. (2 Kgs. 10:30.) However, Shallum ruled only one month before he was cut down by another usurper, Menahem. Menahem (745-736 B.C.) suppressed several serious revolts against his rule and became a vassal of Pul (Tiglath-Pileser) to strengthen his position. (2 Kgs. 15:19-20.) Menahem's tribute payment to Pul brought Israel into the first stage of vassalage to the Assyrians. This alliance became disastrous for Israel and eventually ended in the complete annexation of Israel to the Assyrian Empire. With Menahem's death in 736 B.C., his son Pekahiah ruled and probably continued his father's unpopular policy of submission to Assyria. (2 Kgs. 15:23-26.) In the second year of his reign, Pekahiah was murdered by Pekah, a zealous nationalist. After the ascension of Pekah to the Israelite throne, the Assyrians became much more involved in Israelite politics.

Israel's prosperity was threatened by the necessity of increased defense expenditures and tribute payments to Assyria. In order to recover assessments required by the king, the wealthy oppressed the poor even more. For example, consider the dilemma of a struggling rural farmer who found his taxes increased anywhere from one-third to one-half of his produce. This increase, along with additional assessments, was required regardless of good years or bad, rains or drought. Many farmers were forced to sell their lands and to become indentured servants or slaves to the wealthy, who became even more powerful. Religious conditions also deteriorated as pagan worship increased through Assyrian influence and as people became more insensitive to the needy and oppressed among them. Similar economic and religious problems developed in Judah to the south, although they were not as extensive or serious as in Israel.

As opposition to Assyria grew in Israel and the surrounding states, Pul of Assyria moved his armies into the area in 734 B.C., plundered the seaports of Phoenicia, and imposed heavy tribute upon some Philistine cities. At this time, Judah was ruled by a young, new king, Ahaz, the son of Jotham. The events in Philistia were very near Judah's border, and Ahaz undoubtedly observed the harsh way in which the Assyrians dealt with opposition. Thus, when Rezin of Damascus and Pekah of Israel attempted to draw Ahaz into an anti-Assyrian coalition, he refused.

In 734 B.C., both Rezin of Damascus and Pekah of Israel were under the first stage of Assyrian vassalage. However, for reasons unknown, they felt the time was right to unite in an anti-Assyrian coalition. They strengthened themselves politically and militarily and then attempted by diplomatic means to persuade Ahaz to participate in their coalition. When Ahaz refused, they prepared their troops to march against Jerusalem to place a loyal Aramaean upon the throne. Ahaz knew that Jerusalem could not withstand the combined Syrian-Israelite army, since Judah's forces were scattered throughout the country defending the nation against other ambitious neighboring states. (2 Kgs. 16:1, 5-6; 2 Chr. 28.) (See map, p. 26.)

Against Isaiah's advice, Ahaz sent a contribution to Tiglath-Pileser III and requested Assyrian aid against the Syrian-Israelite coalition. In doing so, Ahaz deliberately moved his nation into the first stage of Assyrian vassalage.

Tiglath-Pileser III immediately moved against the anti-Assyrian coalition. Rezin and Pekah were forced to move their troops away from Jerusalem and to fight against Assyria long before they had planned to. As was to be expected, the Assyrian army proved much stronger than their resistance, and it quickly defeated the combined Syrian-Israelite forces; Damascus was taken and its inhabitants deported, and Rezin's officers were impaled on stakes and his gardens were destroyed (a severe punishment for any people living near the desert). In dealing with Syria, Tiglath-Pileser skipped the second stage of vassalage and simply made all of the country into an Assyrian province.

Israel, the weaker of the two nations in the coalition, received a

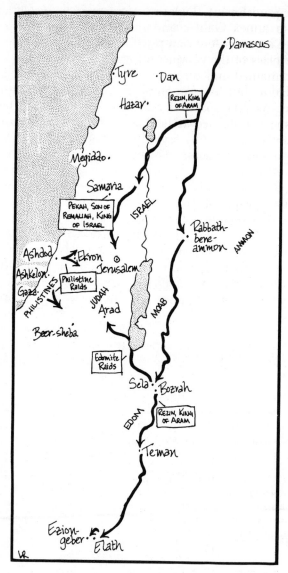

Syrian-Israelite March against Jerusalem

much lighter punishment. Tiglath-Pileser appeared in Israel as early as 733 B.C. to annex Galilee and the area east of the Jordan and establish both areas as Assyrian provinces. Here too, he deported the urban upper class of the conquered territories to Assyria. The rural population remained and received a new foreign upper class. Pekah was not replaced, but he soon fell victim to a conspiracy among the ranks of a pro-Assyrian party in Samaria. The leader of this conspiracy was Hoshea, confirmed as Israel's king by his Assyrian overlord. He began his rule in 732 B.C. Assyrian control over Hoshea's ascension constituted the second stage of vassalage for the northern kingdom. (See map, p. 28.)

As can be seen by this short historical review, within the early years of Isaiah's prophetic ministry, he witnessed Israel's transformation into a weak, dependent vassal state of Assyria. At the same time, Judah had entered the first stage of vassalage and was vulnerable to further Assyrian encroachment. In this troublesome period, therefore, Isaiah received prophecies for Israel, Judah, Assyria, Egypt, and the other nations in the area. The following chronological chart provides a historical overview and a framework for the history of Isaiah's discourses.

HISTORY OF THE PALESTINE AREA, 760-690 B.C.

Judah	Israel	Assyria (and Syria)
760: *Uzziah* (or Azariah, 791-740) has served as co-regent (791-771) and king of Judah since he was sixteen years old. (2 Kgs. 15:1-4; 2 Chr. 26:1-15.)	760: *Jeroboam II* (787-746) has served as co-regent (787-782) and then expands Israel's borders and influence to their greatest extent since Solomon's time. (2 Kgs. 14:23-29.)	760: Ashur-dan III (772-755) and Ashur-Nirari V (754-745) continue a period of Assyrian decline and weakness; one of these kings probably ruled greater Nineveh during *Jonah*'s visit and then called upon his people to repent. (Jonah 3:4; 2 Kgs. 14:25; Matt. 12:40-41.)
c. 760-740: *Amos* and *Hosea* serve as prophets and warn Israel of her wickedness and pending destruction.	751: *Pekah* (751-732) sets himself up as a rebel king in the Transjordan (area east of Jordan River).	
750: Uzziah tries to burn incense in the temple and becomes leprous; his son *Jotham* (750-735) acts as co-regent or king. (2 Chr. 26:16-23; 2 Kgs. 15:5, 32-38.)	746: Jeroboam's son, Zechariah (746-745), rules for six months before he is murdered by Shallum, who rules for one month	745: *Tiglath-Pileser III* (745-727; called Pul in the Bible) becomes king, subjects Babylon, and begins empire expansion to Egypt

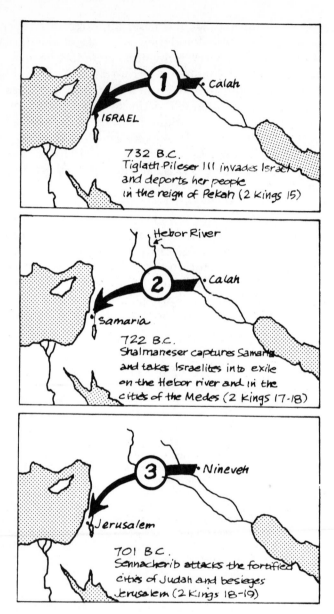

Assyrian Invasions

743: Ahaz begins to serve as "crown-prince" or co-regent with his father Jotham, while his grandfather, Uzziah, is a leper.

740: King Uzziah dies, and *Isaiah* has great vision. (Isa. 6.)

735: Jotham finishes his strong reign (2 Chr. 27) and his son *Ahaz* (735-720) begins wicked rule and then is invaded from the north; he seeks Assyrian aid against Isaiah's advice. (2 Chr. 28; 2 Kgs. 16; Isa. 7.)

Micah and Isaiah denounce Ahaz.

728: Hezekiah begins to serve as a co-regent with his father, Ahaz. (2 Kgs. 18:1.)

727: Hezekiah, as acting ruler, initiates strong religious reforms. (2 Chr. 29; 2 Kgs. 18:3-8; Num. 21:4-9.)

720: Ahaz dies and Isaiah urges on *Hezekiah* (720-692) in his radical religious reforms. (2 Chr. 30-31.)

before he is slain by Menahem (745-736), who rules Samaria for ten years. (2 Kgs. 15:8-18.)

c. 740: Israel pays tribute to Assyria. (2 Kgs. 15:19-22.)

736: Menahem's son, Pekahiah(736-735) rules for two years before being murdered by Pekah, who then rules all of Israel (Samaria and Transjordan) for four years. (2 Kgs. 15:23-28.)

732: *Hoshea* (732-722) slays Pekah and establishes pro-Assyrian policy. (2 Kgs. 15:30; 17:1-3.)

c. 726: Hoshea refuses to pay Assyrian tribute and seeks Egyptian alliance.

722: Wicked Israel falls to the Assyrians. Over 27,000 Israelites exiled to northeast Assyria. Other settlers in Samaria intermarry with remaining Israelites

on the west and the Indus River (India) on the east.

740: *Rezin* (740-732) becomes king of Syria.

735: Rezin and Pekah form a Syro-Israelite alliance and attempt to get other neighboring countries to join them in fighting against Assyria. They invade Judah to force her support, but Ahaz decides to favor Assyria.

732: Tiglath-Pileser III (Pul) destroys Syria, slays Rezin, and invades Israel, taking many captives. (2 Kgs. 15:29; 16:9.)

730-727: Pul conquers and annexes Transjordan, deporting a large part of the population (including portions of Israelite tribes of Manasseh, Gad, and Reuben.)

726: *Shalmaneser V* (726-722) begins reign and invades Israel, besieges Samaria for three years and takes ten tribes captive. (2 Kgs. 17:4-6; 18:9-12.)

721: *Sargon II* (721-705) completes conquest of Samaria and destroys the kingdom of Israel.

and become the semi-pagan Samaritans. (2 Kgs. 17:7-41.)

c. 707: Hezekiah's sickness and gifts from Babylon. (Isa. 38-39; 2 Kgs. 20.)

701: Sennacherib's generals besiege Jerusalem and employ psychological warfare; Hezekiah's tunnel, Isaiah's counsel, and a plague from the Lord preserve Judah. (2 Chr. 32; 2 Kgs. 18:17-36; 19:1-37; Isa. 36-37.)

696: Perhaps because of Hezekiah's ill health (he died about 692) *Manasseh* (696-642) begins co-regency at the tender age of twelve. He quickly establishes a strong pagan and perverse policy (2 Chr. 33:1-9; 2 Kgs. 21:1-18), although he may have repented somewhat in his later years (2 Chr. 33:10-20). However, according to Jewish traditions, he slew many of the prophets and had Isaiah encased in a tree trunk and sawn asunder with a wooden saw. Some Jewish traditions also state that Hezekiah's wife was Isaiah's daughter—if true then Isaiah would have been killed by his own grandson.

712: Sargon II travels down the seacoast west of Judah, besieges Ashdod, and forces the Egyptian twenty-fifth (or Ethiopian) Dynasty to open trade relations with Assyria.

705: Sargon II slain in battle, his son, Sennacherib (704-681), begins powerful reign; he receives temple tribute from Hezekiah. (2 Kgs. 18:13-16.)

PARALLELISM IN OLD TESTAMENT POETRY AND PROPHECY

Hebrew poetry comprises about one-third of the Old Testament. It extends beyond the so-called poetic books (Job, Psalms, Proverbs, etc.) throughout the scriptures, and it is especially prominent in the prophetic books (Isaiah, Jeremiah, Hosea, Amos, etc.). For example, approximately ninety percent of Isaiah is written in poetry.

The ancient poets and prophets recognized that their works were usually received and transmitted orally. Although written copies of their works (usually in the form of parchment scrolls) would have been available from generation to generation, most Israelites would not have had copies in their own homes because of the expense and effort required to make the scrolls. Temple or synagogue scrolls were usually not readily available, and in times of war or religious persecution they would have been easily suppressed or destroyed. Rather than relying upon written records, the ancient Semites were trained to remember long passages. The development of their oral retention allowed them to pass on religious records, poetry, psalms, family histories, and other important information.

The ancient poets, prophets, writers, and scribes would assist their followers by organizing their material into an easily remembered form. Old Testament authors often used key phrases or words as verbal flags to alert the listener to important passages that would be coming up shortly in their presentation. They also used memory devices or patterns that made the poems easy to remember and still allowed the composer spontaneity of expression.

The most common pattern in Hebrew poetry was parallelism. Two thousand years after Hebrew had ceased to be a common spoken language, Bishop Robert Lowth of the Anglican Church rediscovered this memory aid and poetic style in 1753. Later studies have expanded his ideas and have made major strides in understanding Old Testament poetry and why words and ideas are repeated in many verses.

Parallelism is the most distinctive quality of Hebrew poetry, and it is found in most of the famous biblical passages. In parallelism, a thought, idea, grammar pattern, or key word of the first line is repeated or continued in the second line. There are two basic types of parallelism, grammatical and semantic. Grammatical or "form" parallelism is often difficult to identify, especially in non-Hebrew translations, because the rhyme schemes, grammar forms, conjugation patterns, prefix or suffix parallelisms, and so on may not carry over into the new translation. However, semantic parallelism is more easily recognized in English and other non-Semitic language translations since it is a "theme rhyme" or "idea pattern" in which the thought or meaning in one line is related to an idea of another line in a variety of parallel patterns. Among the types of semantic parallelism are the following:

1. Synonymous parallelism: a theme of the first line *repeats* itself in the second line, but in slightly different words:

   (a) A fool's mouth is his ruin, and
   (b) His lips are the snare of his soul. (Prov. 18:7.)

   (a) An ox knows his owner, and
   (b) An ass his master's crib. (Isa. 1:3.)

This most common form of parallelism might be compared to the two rails of a railroad track, because although close together, the parallel rails seem to join into a single point on the horizon. The repeated ideas of synonymous parallelism reinforce each other and provide a more complete perspective of a single, major concept.

Many ideas are repeated throughout the scriptures. Repetition is a necessary educational process, whether in learning a new vocabulary word or in understanding complex religious doctrines. But using synonymous parallelism, the ancient authors could repeat their messages and reinforce the learning of their listeners.

2. Antithetic parallelism: a thought of the second part of a couplet *contrasts* with an opposite theme in the first:

   (a) When pride comes, then comes disgrace.
   (b) But with the humble is wisdom. (Prov. 11:2.)

   (a) If you are willing and obedient, you will eat the good things of the earth:
   (b) But if you refuse and disobey, you will be devoured by the sword. (Isa. 1:19-20.)

This form is very common in Proverbs, and the use of *opposites* clarifies both extremes. It might be compared to a black silhouette, which brings the exact outline of a figure into sharp focus as it is placed on a white background.

Through antithetic parallelism, the poet mirrors the opposition of all things. (See Eccl. 3:1-8.) As in life, where sensitivity to ugliness and suffering can lead one to better appreciate beauty and goodness, so also in poetry the sharp contrast of opposites brings the desired message into sharper focus.

3. Emblematic parallelism: the ideas of two lines are *compared* by means of a simile or metaphor:

(a) Like clouds and wind without rain
(b) Is the man who boasts of a gift he does not give. (Prov. 25:14.)

(a) Though your sins be [red] as scarlet,
(b) They shall be white as snow
(a') Though they be red as dyed wool,
(b') They shall be [white] as fleece. (Isa. 1:18.)

These comparisons can usually be recognized by the prepositions "like" or "as." Often, symbolic, emblematic parallelism is like a shadow, which can be distinct or hazy.

Symbolic representations allow the listener's past experiences to enrich his understanding. Like parables, they allow the listener to comprehend the parallelism according to his own background and insights. Thus, every listener can immediately relate to the material and yet still be challenged to discover additional meanings.

These first three types of parallelism are all used in the second example above:

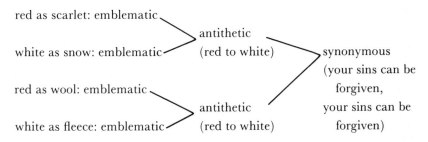

4. Synthetic parallelism: the second line *completes* or *complements* the thought of the first in a variety of possible combinations (question-answer, proposition-conclusion, situation-consequence, protasis-

apodosis, etc.). An idea is introduced in the first line, which is incomplete or generates questions about that idea. The second line then completes the idea, or answers a question raised by the first line. Note how the first line in the two following examples leaves you searching for more information and how the second line satisfies that desire:

(a) Yea, though I walk through the valley of the shadow of death, I will fear no evil:
(b) For thou art with me; thy rod and thy staff they comfort me. (Ps. 23:4.)

(a) I [the Lord] have nourished and brought up children,
(b) And they have rebelled against me. (Isa. 1:2.)

The two lines of the synthetic couplet are often loosely connected as the second line continues or completes the thought of the first. Like a belt and buckle, this parallelism joins or blends two ideas in any of several possible relations.

Sometimes difficult to identify, synthetic parallelism encompasses good educational psychology as it generates and then answers questions, completes statements, and amplifies ideas. If the first line of a verse seems incomplete or if it causes you to want to know how or why that statement is true (for example, Why should I not be afraid in the shadow of death? or, What happened to the children?), then this line probably begins a synthetic parallelism.

5. Composite parallelism: three or more phrases *develop* a theme by amplifying a concept or defining a term:

Blessed is the man
(a) Who walks not in the counsel of the ungodly,
(b) Nor stands in the way of sinners,
(c) Nor sits in the seat of the scornful. (Ps. 1:1.)

(a) Ah nation of sin!
(b) A people laden with iniquity!
(c) A brood of evildoers!
(d) Children that are corrupters:
They have forsaken the Lord. (Isa. 1:4.)

By presenting a variety of ideas that radiate about a central theme, this parallelism is often an advanced combination of synonymous and synthetic parallelisms and is like the spokes of a wheel, combining ideas to provide a complete message. Sometimes the central idea (or hub) of these ideas is expressly stated, as in the first example above (qualities of a blessed man). Other times no central theme is mentioned; or a general theme or summary (hub) might be stated, as with the second example, and the listener must still organize the component parts within a general framework (or rim) and complete the model (the wickedness of the society).

Notice in both examples above how the poets provided additional memory aids. In the first, the verb sequence is natural and easy to picture and remember: "walks," "stands," "sits." In the second, the size of the group decreases in each line: "nation," "people," "brood (extended family)," "children (immediate family)."

Through composite parallelism, the poet extends an idea beyond its simple meaning into its varied component parts. Complex issues are presented in as many facets as the poet wants to develop. He provides the definitions and interpretations that give the listeners a more complete understanding of the whole theme.

6. Climactic parallelism: part of one line (a word or phrase) is repeated in the second and other lines until a theme is developed which then *culminates* in a main idea or statement:

(a) Ascribe to the Lord heavenly beings
(b) Ascribe to the Lord glory and strength
(c) Ascribe to the Lord the glory of his name
Worship the Lord in holy array. (Ps. 29:1-2.)

(a) Your country is desolate
(b) Your cities are burnt down
(c) Your land is devoured by strangers before your eyes
It is desolate; as overthrown by strangers. (Isa. 1:7.)

Sometimes the theme statement is given first and then followed by the repeated term (a phrase or word) with its attached phrases:

The daughter of Zion is left
(a) Like a booth in a vineyard
(b) Like a hut in a cucumber field
(c) Like a city beleaguered. (Isa. 1:8.)

The main point and the ideas (or steps) leading toward it can be joined in various combinations. In the first example above, the climax presents a new idea in contrast to the introductory lines. The first three lines stress the majesty of God to the listener, and in the fourth he is exhorted to worship God. In this psalm, David develops the idea of respect for the Lord by stressing varied manifestations of divine glory. However, he wants the listeners to do more than just fear the

ISAIAH: PROPHET, SEER, AND POET

Lord, so he shifts emphasis in the last line and challenges the listeners to worship God in reverence. This poetic style is much more effective than simply saying, "Worship God because he is almighty."

In the second example, the major ideas and key words ("desolate," "strangers") are contained within both the steps and the climax. Thus, the climax is not a surprise but a summary.

The third example is also an elaborate model of emblematic parallelism, in which the climactic idea, the "daughter of Zion," is defined through the three following examples, each of which is an emblematic parallelism.

This progressive model of parallelism is like a set of steps that lead to or descend from a main point. To help distinguish this from composite parallelism, look for a word or phrase repeated in each line leading to (or from) the climax.

This complicated form of parallelism is often made by combining a composite form of semantic parallelism with a more obvious example of grammatical parallelism. Grammatical parallelism deals with the structure or form of the original Hebrew, while semantic parallelism consists of the message or idea of the poetry. For example, the syntactical patterns (the way in which words are joined to form phrases and sentences) or metrical similarities (the measured rhythm or patterns of accented and unaccented syllables) would be types of grammatical parallelism, while repeated patterns using similar symbols and comparable vocabulary words would be types of semantic parallelism. Grammatical parallelism is usually present in most semantic parallelisms, but it is often disguised by the English translation.

In climactic parallelism, watch for a word, phrase, grammar unit, or other form to repeat itself in each line. By using a number of close, successive steps, the poet channels the listener's attention toward a culminating point. This climax could be a summary of the earlier-mentioned ideas, or it could be a new idea derived from the context of the earlier ones. In any case, the poet uses climactic parallelism to lead the listener toward a major theme or idea.

7. Introverted parallelism: a pattern of words or ideas is stated and then repeated, but in a *reverse* order. This parallelism is also called chiasmus:

    (a) *We have escaped* as a bird
    (b) From *the snare* of the fowlers
    (b') *The snare* is broken,
    (a') And *we have escaped*! (Ps. 124:7.)

36

(a) Ephraim shall not envy
(b) Judah
(b') And Judah
(a') shall not harass Ephraim. (Isa. 11:13.)

The poet can develop and then introvert as many ideas as he desires:

(a) Make the *heart* of this people fat,
(b) And make their *ears* heavy,
(c) And shut their *eyes*,
(c') Lest they see with their *eyes*,
(b') And hear with their *ears*,
(a') And understand with their *heart*,
And convert [return], and be healed [heal themselves]. (Isa. 6:10.)

(abc) Come to the *house* of the *God of Jacob*, . . . and *we will walk* in his paths
(d) And he shall judge among the *nations*, . . .
(ef) And they shall beat their *swords* into *plowshares*,
(e'f') And their *spears* into *pruninghooks*:
(d') *Nation* shall not lift up sword against *nation*, . . .
(a'b'c') O *house of Jacob*, . . . *let us walk* in the light of the *Lord* (Isa. 2:3-5.)

Chiastic patterns can be expanded to include many verses, whole chapters, and even (according to some authorities) groups of chapters. With the more elaborate patterns, a main theme or message is usually stressed in the center of the chiasmus; thus it might be compared to an hourglass, with the focal point being in the middle. The separate halves of the chiasmus can also be in parallel patterns to each other (synonymous, antithetic, synthetic, etc.), so this becomes a very sophisticated style of Hebrew poetry.

Chiastic parallelism is a common literary and public communications style used by Israelite poets and prophets. Just as contemporary students in public speaking classes are taught to organize their talks with an introduction, major ideas or illustrations, and a conclusion, ancient Israelite poets would use chiasmus along with other forms of parallelism to present their messages.

Introverted parallelism is found in much of the inspired prophetic literature,[1] suggesting the possibility that revelation was received by

---

[1]For two clear Book of Mormon examples, see Mosiah 3:18-19 (humble—children—atoning blood of Christ—natural man—God—has been * will be—Holy Spirit—natural man—atonement of Christ—child—humble); and Mosiah 5:10-12 (name—called—left hand of God—remember—blotted out—transgression * do not transgress—blotted out—remember—

the prophets in this structured form. Chiasmus transmits sublime, divine teachings, and as the Bible reader understands this style, he can better appreciate God's messages for today.

Why Parallelisms Are Sometimes Difficult to Recognize

Hebrew poetic parallelisms, as they are found in the English translations of the Bible, are often hard to identify and understand. There are several reasons for this difficulty:

1. English readers are often unfamiliar with the forms of speech and symbolism used by the biblical authors.
2. The cultural settings differ so much between ancient and modern times that the context and original application of the messages are sometimes unclear to contemporary readers.
3. Poets and prophets do *not* usually explain everything in clear, black-and-white terms, and they often use imagery and symbols to convey complex ideas. They purposefully leave the clarification and applications of their messages up to us, the readers, as they apparently want us to study and ponder their words before we can say that we understand them.
4. Whenever a message is delivered in highly structured patterns, (such as in chiastic parallelism) it may lose its clarity and power as concepts and words are stretched and forced by the author to fit the pattern. Thus, the message may be stilted or awkward even though it is presented in an organized and polished poetic form.
5. Sometimes a reader misinterprets some words or reads more into the passage than the author originally intended. The reader then becomes confused and frustrated at what, to him, appears to be a difficult part of the work.
6. Any new field of learning is difficult at first. For example, American teenagers are usually confused in their high school English classes as they are initially introduced to the sonnet, with its characteristic fourteen lines which are, on the one hand, "made up of an octave and a sestet embodying the statement and the resolution of a single theme" (*American Heritage Dictionary*, p. 1232), but

---

left hand of God—called—name). For further examples, see John W. Welch, "Chiasmus in the Book of Mormon," *New Era*, Feb. 1972; Noel Reynolds, "Nephi's Outline," *BYU Studies* 20:131-49 (Winter 1980); and Wayne A. Larsen and others, "Who Wrote the Book of Mormon? An Analysis of Wordprints," *BYU Studies* 20:225-51 (Spring 1980).

* = pivot point of these patterns.

on the other hand contain "typically five-foot iambics rhyming according to a prescribed scheme" (*Webster's Third New International Dictionary*, p. 2173). However, with patience, through careful explanations, and after studying many examples, the students can understand the sonnet as a form of poetry. Soon many of them begin to appreciate how the sonnet is used, and some may even try their hand at writing one. Likewise, these patterns of parallelism described earlier are difficult to recognize and understand—especially at first. Be patient, for as you study this poetic form and see examples of it scattered throughout the scriptures, you will appreciate the beauty and power it gives to the inspired words of the prophets and poets.

In summary, for the people of Old Testament times, parallelism served not only as an oral memory device, but it also enriched the messages of the prophets. Today, an awareness of parallelism aids the reader in his comprehension of vague and repetitive biblical passages. Although one should not attempt to rigidly identify each Bible verse as an example of parallelism, an understanding of this poetic style can increase one's appreciation of the literary qualities and religious messages to be found in the scriptures.

PROPHETS CONTEMPORARY
WITH ISAIAH

The Old Testament is primarily the inspired journal of ancient Hebrew prophets. Starting with the record of Moses and ending a thousand years later with the prophecies of Malachi, this work of scripture contains the names, activities, and teachings of dozens of prophets. During long periods within that millennium, however, no prophetic activities were recorded, such as during the period of the judges, before the time of Elijah, and after the ministry of Elisha. At other times, two or more prophets were contemporary with each other. At no other Old Testament time period were as many prophetic works and significant writings recorded as during the lifetime of Isaiah. The exact time spans of these contemporary prophetic ministries is not known, but the following chart lists the prophets of Isaiah's time and provides an overview of how their ministries may have overlapped.

Prophetic Ministries During the Eighth Century B.C.

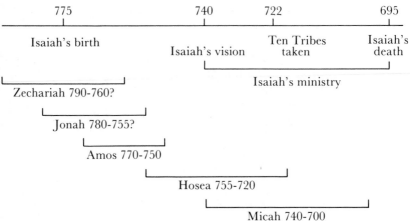

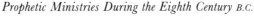

Zechariah

Prior to Isaiah's counseling of the Judean kings, Ahaz and Hezekiah, an earlier prophet, Zechariah, served as an advisor to King Uzziah. His prophetic ministry is recorded in a single Bible verse which states that he "had understanding in the visions of God." (2 Chr. 26:5.) Over two centuries later, a prophet with the same name encouraged the Jews to rebuild the temple after their return from Babylon, and he left many important prophecies which are found in the Old Testament book, Zechariah.

Jonah

Jonah lived during the reign of King Jeroboam II, who ruled Israel from 787 to 746 B.C. (2 Kgs. 14:23-25.) The story of Jonah as now found in the Bible, however, was written some centuries later. Since Isaiah grew up during Jeroboam's reign over Israel, it is probable that he heard of Jonah and his calling to the Assyrians at Ninevah. Indeed, Isaiah later gave his own prophecies concerning the Assyrians, although it is doubtful that he ever traveled there personally to deliver his warnings. (See BD "Jonah.")

Amos

Amos was probably acquainted with both Zechariah and Jonah, since he lived in Judah when Zechariah advised King Uzziah (Amos 1:1) and he traveled to Israel, where he had a confrontation with King Jeroboam's chief priest (Amos 7:10-13).

Although Amos died before Isaiah received his prophetic calling, scrolls containing Amos's warnings and prophecies were probably available for Isaiah to read and study. Indeed, so many similarities exist between the writings of Amos and Isaiah that Isaiah was undoubtedly inspired by Amos. Both prophets recorded a vision of the Lord near his altar and both shared similar teachings and style. For example, they both received visions of the Lord (Amos 9:1; Isa. 6:1-6); delivered prophecies to the same foreign nations (Amos 1-2; Isa. 14-23); denounced the lack of Israelite charity (Amos 2:6-8; Isa. 1:17; 58:7); rebuked the people's rejection of the prophets (Amos 2:12; Isa. 30:9-10); used biting wit to belittle secular leaders (Amos 4:1, 11; Isa. 1:10); prophesied that only a tenth of the Israelites would be left in the land after its destruction (Amos 5:3; Isa. 6:13); criticized the religious festivals and sacrifices of hypocritical Israelites (Amos 5:21-23; Isa.

1:11-14); warned of heavenly manifestations of judgment (Amos 8:9; Isa. 13:10); told of baldness as a sign for mourning or destruction (Amos 8:10; Isa. 3:24); foretold an apostasy or period of spiritual darkness (Amos 8:11-12; Isa. 60:2); and concluded their writings with promises of peace, productivity, and righteousness in the last days (Amos 9:11-15; Isa. 65-66). In addition, similar words and phrases demonstrate an affinity between Amos and Isaiah. In order to appreciate the life and teachings of Amos and to understand how they may have influenced Isaiah, a careful study of Amos is important.

In spite of many similarities between their writings, these two prophets came from very different backgrounds. Isaiah led a highly educated and social life in Jerusalem; Amos raised flocks and tended orchards in the small village of Tekoa, about ten miles south of Jerusalem. As a shepherd and wool producer, Amos traveled throughout Judah and Israel. Before he was called as a prophet, he had probably made several trips into the northern towns of Israel, where he had seen the religious and social corruptions he would later denounce. Amos did not receive any formal training for his calling; instead, he listened to the Lord's promptings while tending his flocks. Although he lived in Judah, his call was to go and preach to the inhabitants of Israel. (Amos 7:14-15.)

Because of their lineage through Abraham and "the covenant," the Israelites considered themselves above reproach and protected by adherence to the Mosaic law. Amos tried to instruct the people as to what the covenant and law really required in terms of obedience. First, he warned that lineage and nationality give no impunity from punishment, but that greater punishment follows in the wake of greater knowledge. Second, he tried to lift the people above the empty rituals of the law which, by themselves, lack power to save. Rejecting the sacrifice and ritual of the Israelites, Amos preached justice and righteousness.

As revealed through this straightforward, unsophisticated message, Amos was a common man, untrained in all the technicalities of religious law and unacquainted with the intellectual and theological "prophetic" schools of his day. His message was, therefore, not written as a polished, eloquent masterpiece like Isaiah's, but developed out of his experience as a rural dweller, shepherd, and dresser of fig trees. (Amos 7:14.) The imagery in his visions came naturally from the scenes around him and present a harsh and unrelenting picture of the desert in which he dwelt.

Most scholars divide the writings of Amos into three sections:

1. Chapters 1-2: *Prophecies* of the destruction of Israel and surrounding nations through a cataloging of their sins and the modes of their judgments.
2. Chapters 3-6: *Teachings* that the sins of Israel will bring destruction, and why such harshness is due to Israel's unique position as the chosen people.
3. Chapters 7-9: *Visions* of judgment followed by a final promise of eventual restoration.

Through repetition of parallel syntactical structures in chapters one and two, Amos lists judgments to come upon the neighboring nations, building to a climactic pronouncement upon Judah and Israel. These two countries, ruled as they are by the descendants of Jacob, are in a particularly precarious position, since they alone know the law of Jehovah. Two specific and major sins are associated with the country of Israel, Amos's distinct charge, and his complaint against her centers around them—social injustice and idolatry.

Indeed, although Amos's background and style were in sharp contrast to Isaiah's, both prophets delivered similar messages and held great hope for the future. The two men may not have had direct contact with each other, but Amos's simple feelings, concerns, prophecies, and promises later inspired Isaiah and were repeated and amplified by him in his characteristic majestic style.

Hosea

Fewer similarities exist between Hosea and Isaiah than between Amos and Isaiah, in that while Isaiah and Amos lived in the southern kingdom, Hosea lived and preached many miles north of Jerusalem in the kingdom of Israel. Like Amos, his vocational and social background differed greatly from Isaiah's. Though Hosea recorded very little about his lifestyle and background, the agricultural images that he uses leads some readers to believe that he was a farmer (see Hosea 2:5, 8, 22; 4:16; 6:4; 10:12 for some examples), while others derive from the references in chapter seven that he was a baker. Infrequently, if ever, would this rural prophet from the north have associated with Jerusalem's urban prophet, Isaiah.

As the only northern prophet whose writings have survived, Hosea's love for his nation, Israel, is apparent. Unlike Amos and Isaiah, who prophesied concerning surrounding countries, he focused strictly upon Israel's relationship with the Lord and rarely referred to foreign nations except in terms of how the Lord uses them in relation to Israel. Also unlike Amos, Isaiah, and Micah, his prophetic warnings encompass little beyond the immediate future (the impending Assyrian captivity) and the continued love of God for his people. Therefore, of Isaiah's contemporaries, Hosea's writings are at once the most immediate and personal. Because of his sensitivity, he has been described as "the prophet of love," the prophet with a "broken" or "tender" heart, and, along with Jeremiah, "the weeping prophet."

The biographical sketch at the beginning of his work provides insights into his soul through his feelings toward his wayward wife. His experiences with her helped him to identify with the Lord's love toward an apostate, immoral Israel. Therefore, it is not surprising that woven throughout his teachings is a most personal and familiar metaphor—marriage.

Previous to Hosea, sexual symbolism had been avoided as a way of expressing the relationship between Yahweh and his people, because sex was central to the mythology of the fertility cults of the nations that surrounded Israel. But since Israel's increased participation in the rituals and religion of the idolatrous Canaanites had become the nation's greatest sin, Hosea's symbol of the adulterous wife was perfectly fitting. He was able to grasp the peoples' attention by incorporating Canaanite images and themes into the context of the Israelite covenant. The cultic marriage of Baal and nature needed to be replaced with a remarriage between Yahweh and his estranged people.

The book of Hosea, then, develops the metaphor of marriage and the unfaithful wife on two levels, personal and national. The first three chapters deal primarily with Hosea's personal marital problems, while chapters four through fourteen expand the metaphor to place Yahweh and Israel in a marital or covenant relationship.

In short, four major phases in Hosea's relationship with his wife are presented in the first three chapters:

1. Hosea's covenant relationship with his wife is broken. (Hosea 1.)
2. They separate. (Hosea 2:1-13.)
3. They prepare for reunion. (Hosea 2:14-23.)
4. They renew their covenant. (Hosea 3:1-5.)

These same four phases are then developed in national terms by Hosea in chapters 4-14 as he teaches the Iraelites concerning their relationship with God:

1. Israel breaks her covenants with God. (Hosea 4-6.)
2. Israel is scattered and separated from God. (Hosea 7-10.)
3. God reviews how he had earlier brought Israel out of the wilderness and how the people must prepare to return again to him. (Hosea 11-13.)
4. The renewed, prosperous relationship between Israel and the Lord is promised. (Hosea 14.)

By comparing these eleven later chapters with the earlier biographical chapters, the reader can appreciate Hosea's personal experiences, which gave him great insight into the Lord's feelings and actions toward Israel.

Isaiah undoubtedly shared these feelings and borrowed from Hosea's insights and teachings. He also identified with Hosea because of the similarity of their names. The name Hosea (*hoshea*) is derived from the same Hebrew root as Isaiah (*yeshayahu*). While Hosea's name means simply "salvation," Isaiah's means "salvation of Jehovah" or "Jehovah is salvation."[1] True to these appellations, both prophets, in different styles, explain why Israel forfeited the Lord's salvation at that time. Both condemn the social evils and spiritual ignorance of the people. They denounce the fertility cults and ridicule idolatry while testifying that Jehovah lives and beside him there is no Savior. (Compare Hosea 13:2-4; 6:2 with Isaiah 43-45.) Finally, both prophets promise that the Lord's salvation will finally come to Israel.

Perhaps the primary difference between the messages of Hosea and Isaiah is that Isaiah develops his themes more extensively. Hosea may give a verse or two on a topic, while Isaiah employs an entire chapter or more to present the same concept. Of course Isaiah also expounds some themes Hosea does not address, such as his pronouncements to various nations, messianic prophecies, and promises of the last days.

In summary, Hosea was a prophet who typified a love for humanity. Separated from his wife and isolated from the wicked society of his age, he remained hopeful that the judgment and punishment of Jehovah would prompt both his wife and the people to repent and renew their covenants. His life and personality present a noble, sensitive father image to Israel. Isaiah, who followed Hosea, is not seen in an intimate fatherly role. His personality is more stern and his words

---

[1]The name Joshua is also derived from the same Hebrew root (Num. 13:16), while the name Jesus is an Aramaic derivation of the same word (Matt. 1:21).

more harsh as he builds upon Hosea's ideas and serves more as a teacher to Israel.

Micah

If Isaiah was Israel's teacher, then Micah was Isaiah's outstanding student and disciple. Micah began his ministry shortly after Isaiah received his first vision (Micah 1:1), and their prophetic callings paralleled each other for over three decades. Micah was Isaiah's younger, rural contemporary. He was raised in a village twenty-five miles southwest of Jerusalem. Neither a statesman nor an advisor to kings, as Isaiah was, he observed Israel and Judah from a common man's viewpoint. But, like Isaiah and the other contemporary prophets, Amos and Hosea, he mourned the greed, immorality, and idolatry of his age. He denounced these evils, and sounded a warning to both Israel and Judah. Like Isaiah, he also saw beyond his age and prophesied concerning the meridian of time and the last days.

Like Isaiah, Micah was a poet. Except for the first introductory verse, his whole short book has a poetic form, full of parallelism, word play, and imagery. His style is simple and forthright, and although his symbolism and phraseology are not as elaborate or eloquent as Isaiah's, he follows a similar pattern of grouping many smaller messages into larger, loose collections of writings. The smaller poems and segments of Micah are grouped into three collections now comprising chapters 1-2, 3-5, and 6-7. Each collection begins with an exhortation to his audience to "hear" the Lord's words. (Micah 1:2; 3:1; 6:1.) In each set, too, Micah gives a series of judgments or warnings before concluding with a promise of eventual blessings. (Micah 2:12-13; 4:1-5, 15; 7:14-20.) Isaiah uses a similar pattern of following a warning with a promise throughout his works, but his literary structure extends beyond individual poems, chapters, and collections of messages to encompass his entire book. The first thirty-five chapters of Isaiah are primarily warnings, while his great promises are found in the last twenty-seven chapters. It is possible that Micah used Isaiah's form as a model, but in any case, he develops a similar style and pattern in his three collections, as he first warns that God will send judgments for Judah's sins and then promises an eventual pardon and blessings.

In terms of the cyclical writing pattern (hear-warnings-blessings), the book of Micah is divided into three major sections:

Time Framework	Warning	Promise	Chapters
Contemporary	Judgment on Samaria and Jerusalem	Salvation of a remnant	1-2
Last days and messianic	Imminent destruction upon the wicked	Triumph of a remnant of Jacob	3-5
Universal (judicial contest)	Jehovah and Israel in controversy	Future restoration and glory	6-7

In summary, Micah was a representative prophet of the eighth century, for he shared Amos's passion for justice, Hosea's heart for compassion, and Isaiah's style for poetry. He denounced contemporary evils and promised a time of eventual restoration; he recognized the justice and mercy of Jehovah in present problems and future blessings; and he used moving poetry to depict the absolute holiness and majesty of the Lord. As a faithful disciple of Isaiah, he served as a noble servant and forceful prophet of the Lord becoming, as his name implies, "like unto the Lord."

Conclusion

Isaiah was not a solitary prophet. Other great prophets served before and during his ministry, influencing each other's ideas and messages. Together, these prophets warned Israel of her impending destruction and testified that the Lord would fulfill his plan with his children. Sharing contemporary problems and future hopes, each developed his own style to express the message he wanted the people to remember. By studying Isaiah in the context of these contemporary prophets, we can see that the Israelites received broad and varied messages that should have warned, taught, and comforted them. These eighth century B.C. prophets addressed the needs of their society as a body just as a group of any three or four apostles of this dispensation will speak out on a variety of themes, each in his own style; yet, together, they provide a comprehensive communication from the Lord to his children. Each of the ancient prophets (or modern apostles) usually stresses two or three main themes; by studying all of their writings, we can appreciate how God reveals many ideas through two or more witnesses.

The three prophets contemporary to Isaiah, Amos, Hosea, and Micah, not only addressed the same general themes, but they also borrowed ideas, words, and phrases from each other. Being led by the same source, they were able to share ideas and reinforce each other's message in the witnesses they provided the people.

In studying the writings of these prophets, it is important to remember that their messages were originally received and transmitted orally. They, therefore, preferred to give many short messages, which were often in allegorical and poetic form, so that people could more easily remember them. These messages were recorded on scrolls (or in books), and centuries later these writings were divided into the chapters and verses we have now. In the King James Version and many other translations, the verses are grouped by paragraphs (see ¶ markings) into units containing similar ideas and teachings. These paragraph and chapter divisions were established by medieval scribes who usually were able to distinguish and separate the individual messages and poems of the original prophetic writings. Thus, what had originally been three or four short discourses or poems of a prophet may now be found in a single chapter. The separate messages and literary units may still be distinguished if the reader carefully observes the paragraph markings and other features in the chapter.

The following suggestions will help you understand the many brief literary units found in most chapters:

1. Read the chapter quickly for an overall impression of its style and message.
2. Watch for key words and phrases, especially if they are repeated.
3. Separate the chapter into smaller literary units, paragraphs, and themes.
4. Study the individual verses and try to appreciate their more subtle meaning and poetic patterns.
5. Ponder the verses and ideas within the literary unit to understand how a particular message or theme is developed, and remember that these individual units were the building blocks of the prophet's writings.
6. Combine the separate units back into a general theme or message and see how your understanding of the whole chapter has been enriched by a deeper knowledge of its component parts.
7. Organize each verse, part, and chapter to see how the elements join together and reinforce each other; then a variety of integrating features will appear that will lead you from one unit to the next.

After such an exercise as this, you will be able to glean new insights and meaning from the passages each time you return to them. You will also increase your appreciation of prophetic and poetic writing styles and enrich your understanding of the various levels of spiritual meaning. Then the scriptures will always be a fresh, rich source of literary beauty and spiritual inspiration for you.

The words of Amos, Hosea, and Micah provide a strong theological foundation for Isaiah's teachings. Through Amos we learn that the Lord always gives adequate warnings through many prophets, thus enabling his followers to avoid impending destruction. The book of Hosea on the other hand, reflects the Lord's love for his children even when they break their covenants, and it promises a restoration if they will return to their Master. Micah condemns social abuse, hypocrisy, and false prophesying, while extolling the Lord's majesty and promising divine forgiveness to those who truly repent. Taken together, these prophetic writings complement Isaiah's words and provide inspired commentary about his time. Understanding them will help us understand the great culminating work of Isaiah.

MAJOR DOCTRINES TAUGHT BY ISAIAH

Isaiah is one of the major prophets of the Old Testament, both in terms of the length of his writings and the importance of his teachings. His work inspires every generation of readers because it contains basic religious truths and reveals profound latter-day prophecies in elevated, flowing poetry.

The truths Isaiah taught ancient Israel are still valuable today. His discourses on charity, morality, fasting, service, the Sabbath, and the true nature of worship still encourage people to live more righteous lives. Isaiah based most of his teachings upon the laws and discourses of Moses and the earlier prophets, but he also borrowed concepts and phraseology from the psalms. More than just a messenger, Isaiah recognized that he was a special witness for the Lord; along with teaching God's commandments, he testified concerning their truth and divinity. The "law" and "testimony"—these are the essence of Isaiah's teachings. (See Isa. 8:16-22.)

By teaching the laws of God and bearing his own witness concerning them, Isaiah served the Lord as a prophet, for a prophet serves the Lord both as a mouthpiece and a witness to the people. As a mouthpiece, or spokesman, he declares the truths, laws, and covenants that the Lord revealed to earlier prophets. (See Mal. 2:6; 2 Ne. 3:17-22; Ezek. 3:27; TG "Mouth.") As a witness, he testifies through the spirit of prophecy concerning the Lord and his mission, and concerning the peoples' responsibility to follow God's laws. (See Rev. 19:10; Num. 11:25-29; MD, pp. 602-9; BD "Prophet.")

Isaiah was a model prophet because he served as a lucid mouthpiece and an adamant witness. He taught and testified on many topics:

1. Basic principles and ordinances of the gospel (ch. 1).
2. The attributes of God (6-9, 40-46).

3. The role of covenants, oaths, and commandments (1, 30-31, 48, 52).

4. The laws of justice (blessings and punishments) and mercy (1, 24, 34, 35, 53, 57, 59).

5. The plan of salvation, including the spirit world and resurrection (24-26, 42, 49, 52, 53, 61).

6. Charity, stewardship, care for the oppressed (1, 56, 58, 63).

7. The value of studying the scriptures and learning truth (28, 29, 55).

8. The law of Moses, including sacrifices, festivals, etc. (1, 58).

As shown by this list, Isaiah instructed Israel how to truly worship Jehovah and fulfill their responsibilities as God's chosen people. If these teachings alone remained from all the writings of Isaiah, they would qualify him as one of the most comprehensive and eloquent spokesmen of the Lord.

Before we can understand the prophecies and teachings of Isaiah, or the doctrines taught by any prophet, we must first study his life and teaching techniques. Every prophet is unique, yet each prophet and his writings can be approached through ten basic categories, each of which can be applied to Isaiah:

1. *Preparation:* A prophet is prepared in the premortal existence and during his mortal existence for his calling. (Isa. 46:1-5, 9-10; 40:3; TG "Foreordination.")

2. *Calling:* A prophet is called of the Lord and given a divine commission to be God's spokesman. (Isa. 6:9-13; TG "Prophets, Mission of"; BD "Prophet.")

3. *Receiving the divine message:* A prophet receives the word of the Lord through revelation (visions, dreams, angels, manifestations) or inspiration (feelings, the "still small voice"). The communication may come spontaneously, though it usually comes in response to the pondering and petitioning of the prophet. (Isa. 1:1; 2:1; 6:1; TG and BD "Revelation.")

4. *Comprehending the message of the prophet:* A prophet knows when he has received communication from the Lord, though he may not always initially know its meaning or application. A prophet can even serve as the Lord's mouthpiece and articulate a divine message without comprehending it or knowing why he was called to deliver it. (Isa. 38:1, 4-5; TG "Understanding.")

5. *Delivering the message:* A prophet usually delivers God's message first in oral form, although occasionally he may use symbolism,

personal action, or other techniques to communicate it to the people. (Isa. 6:9-10; 8:1-4; 20:1-4; 51:16.) He sometimes indicates the source of his message ("thus saith the Lord"), though he often simply speaks in the first person as if the Lord himself were speaking. Also, as the prophet delivers an inspired message, he still often structures the message into his own vocabulary and style. (D&C 1:24; 18:33-36.)

In short, delivering a divine message is one of the most sensitive and important responsibilities of a prophet. He first has to be receptive and worthy to receive the communication from the Lord, and then he has to articulate that message clearly and precisely just as the Lord would desire it. Thus, the role of "mouthpiece" or "spokesman" is a crucial element in any prophet's calling. (See TG "Mouth," "Prophecy," "Spokesman.")

6. *Reception of the message by the people:* Numerous examples are recorded in the scriptures of how people accepted or rejected a prophet's words. Fewer examples are recorded of how the prophet himself felt about their attitudes. (Isa. 11:9; 29:9-10; 44:17; 53:1; TG "Rejoice," "Thanks," "Prophets, Rejection of," "Suffering.")

7. *Recording the message:* The word of the Lord was usually recorded personally by the prophet, though a scribe occasionally wrote down or made copies of it to be distributed as the prophet requested. (Isa. 8:1, 16; 30:8; TG "Record Keeping," "Write"; BD "Writing.")

8. *Transmission and translation of the message:* Copies of inspired writings were made, passed on, recopied, and translated throughout the centuries. The scriptures available in English today are far removed in time, language, and, unfortunately, even in content, since many records have been lost, edited, or confused through the transmission and translation process. (TG "Translate"; BD "Bible—Preservation of the Text of the Old Testament.")

9. *Meaning anciently:* The prophets taught, warned, and edified God's children through the message they delivered. The prophets' words, therefore, served as a special witness or testimony to their contemporary audience. (Isa. 8:16; 30:8, 13; TG "Witness.")

10. *Meaning today:* The value of the scriptures for us today is almost entirely dependent upon our own effort and spirituality. Before we can know the truth and value of scripture, we must study the

prophets' words and communicate with the same source that inspired the prophets, the Holy Spirit. (Isa. 8:20; TG "Scriptures, Value of"; BD "Scriptures.")

Isaiah was one of the major prophets and witnesses of the Lord for ancient Israel. However, he was also a *seer* who received and revealed important visions of the Messiah and the last days. His messianic and eschatological (referring to the last days) revelations have enlightened countless readers, including many prophets who succeeded him, such as the Book of Mormon prophets Nephi, Jacob, and Abinadi, who then understood more about God's plan for this earth and its inhabitants.

Isaiah's function as a seer is manifest at the outset of his writings. One Hebrew word for *seer* is *chozeh*, which comes from the root meaning "to perceive" or "to have a vision of." The introductions to both chapters one and two state that Isaiah literally "saw" (*chazah*) the vision that he later recorded. (See also Isa. 13:1.) He was a "see-er," one who sees, and he saw great visions.

In short, as a seer, Isaiah had spiritual insight beyond that of a prophet. (See Mosiah 8:15-17; MD, p. 315.) Isaiah was both a prophet and seer, for he envisioned events beyond his own time. His prophecies record that he perceived visions of at least two major events, the Messiah and the last days.

Isaiah's Messianic Prophecies

Isaiah's messianic prophecies are scattered throughout his writings, but are concentrated in chapters 6-9, 11, 61, and 63, and in the servant songs of chapters 42, 49, 50, and 53. Isaiah saw events and signs of both the first and second comings of Christ; his record stands not only as a witness of what Jehovah did for ancient Israel, but also as a prophecy of what Jesus Christ will do for all the inhabitants of the earth.

To fully understand the messianic prophecies, we must first realize that many of Isaiah's prophecies may have been fulfilled at more than one time throughout history. In other words, some of Isaiah's messianic prophecies describe events preceding the first advent of Christ as well as his second coming. As an example, the writers of the New Testament sometimes applied passages from Isaiah and the other prophets to the life of Jesus in an attempt to demonstrate that he really was the promised Messiah. Some of these same prophecies have been fulfilled, and will be fulfilled again during our day just prior to and during the second coming of Christ in his glory. (Compare Isa. 11:1 with Rev. 5:5; JS-H 1:40.) Simply stated, Isaiah spoke in such a manner that his words find application and fulfillment in many different ages and events in world history.

One example illustrates how a given prophecy can be fulfilled in different periods. In Joel 2:28-32, Joel utters a prophecy recognized by Latter-day Saints as a revelation regarding the second coming of Christ. He speaks of individuals receiving new visions and prophecies. He also speaks of the sun being darkened, the moon being turned to blood, and other events prior to the "great and terrible day of the Lord." On the night of September 21, 1823, while Joseph Smith conversed with the angel Moroni, Moroni quoted this prophecy from Joel 2:28-32 and said "that this was not yet fulfilled, but was soon to be." (JS-H 1:41.) Interestingly enough, this prophecy of Joel and a fulfillment of it had alrady been cited in the New Testament. On the day of Pentecost, Christ's followers had gathered at Jerusalem for this great Jewish holy day. A great sound from heaven arose, and the Lord's Spirit filled the people assembled there. Men began to prophesy and speak in tongues. People passing by the house stopped and wondered at what was happening. Some thought God was doing this great miracle; others mockingly said, "These men are full of new wine." Then Peter arose and spoke to those who had gathered and said that these men were not drunk, but that the event was the fulfillment of the prophecy in Joel 2:28-32. (See Acts 2:13-21.) Thus, through the examples of Peter and Moroni, both acting by the authority and inspiration of God, we see that a single prophecy can have more than one fulfillment.

A variety of resources are available to help us identify the particular Isaianic passages that might refer to the Messiah:

1. Review the synopsis of Isaiah's chapters in this book to see which chapters contain messianic references. (Pp. 57-69.)
2. Skim the chapter headings of Isaiah in the Latter-day Saint edition of the Bible and look for the words "Messiah" or "Messianically."
3. Study the footnote references in the Bible, especially those listing New Testament passages, to see how Isaiah's words were applied to Jesus.
4. Note the Topical Guide references in the footnotes that describe the life and mission of Christ. From reviewing the Topical Guide, it is obvious that Isaiah often prophesied concerning the Messiah. In

nearly every Topical Guide reference for Jesus Christ, Isaiah's words are noted.

Isaiah's Prophecies of the Last Days

The second major group of prophecies of Isaiah concern the last days. Since so many of his prophecies concern the period immediately before the Millennium, they were recorded by other prophets in their scriptures, particularly the Book of Mormon. These records were destined to come forth as special witnesses in the last days. For example, chapters 2-14 and 48-55 of Isaiah, which deal primarily with the house of Israel, are quoted in full in the Book of Mormon. In a new context and with additional commentary, they clarify important events concerning God's chosen people that are being fulfilled in these last days. In addition to the Isaiah chapters quoted in the Book of Mormon, Isaiah 27, 32-35, 54, and 60-66 provide additional insights into the great day just before the Lord's second coming and the creation of a new and glorious earth.

From Isaiah's 66 chapters, which are preserved for us in the Old Testament, Moroni, the angel-herald of the Restoration, singled out chapter 11 to quote to the boy prophet Joseph Smith on the night of September 21, 1823. It was as though the hidden roots of ancient recorded prophecy broke through the dry ground of intervening centuries to spring up in our day. Chapter eleven was of new yet venerable stock whose roots go deep in the soil of prophecy, a tree planted and preserved by God to bear him precious fruit.

The following list suggests some reasons why Isaiah's prophecies about the last days are so important:

1. Some fifty-three of the sixty-six chapters of the book of Isaiah, if they do not deal exclusively with the latter days, contain verses pointing to our time. (Those that do not are 7-9, 15-16, 20-21, 23, 36-39, and 46.) It would seem that the prophet spent more time envisioning our day than he did teaching in his own!
2. Nephi writes of Isaiah's prophecies, "I know that they shall be of great worth unto them *in the last days*; for *in that day* shall they understand them; wherefore, for their good I have written them." (2 Ne. 25:8; italics added.)
3. Nephi's brother Jacob writes, "And now, behold, I would speak unto you concerning things which are, and *which are to come*: wherefore, I will read you the words of Isaiah." (2 Ne. 6:4; italics added.)
4. As one scholar has described Isaiah, "Never perhaps has there

been another prophet like Isaiah, who stood with his head in the clouds and his feet on the solid earth, *with his heart in the things of eternity* and with mouth and hand in the things of time, with his spirit in the eternal counsel of God and his body in a very definite moment of history." (Robinson, *The Book of Isaiah,* p. 22; italics added.)

5. A latter-day apostle, Bruce R. McConkie, has said, "Much of what Isaiah . . . has to say is yet to be fulfilled. If we are to truly comprehend the writings of Isaiah, we cannot overstate or over-stress the plain, blunt reality that he is in fact the prophet of the restoration, the mighty seer of Jacob's seed who foresaw our day." (*Ensign,* Oct. 1973, p. 81.)

6. One clue to finding Isaiah's passages about the last days is to note his banner-phrase "in that day," for it occurs forty-two times throughout his work, almost always in conjunction with prophecies about our day.

7. Like the messianic prophecies, the prophecies of the last days in the writings of Isaiah are often written on many levels and find fulfill-ment in ages beyond those in which they were spoken or recorded. For this reason, some latter-day prophecies seem juxtaposed or out of place against fairly mundane historical background. But Isaiah is not alone in this prophetic style. In Revelation, John repeatedly moves backward and forward in time to make his point and strengthen his rhetoric, though in doing so he often confuses those who do not have the same prophetic insight as he does. For an Isaianic example, Isaiah launches forth in a declaration of the restoration of the gospel in chapter 5, verses 26-30 in the midst of what could be a call to repentance for any age.

8. Jews reading Isaiah miss the messianic references, which apply to Jesus Christ, while the traditional Christian readers usually over-look the glorious message of the Restoration. Latter-day Saints stand apart in their perspective of Isaiah because, with their fuller understanding of the gospel, they should be able to see how Isaiah's prophecies can find a full range of fulfillment and application.

As noted from the preceding list, most of the chapters in Isaiah contain important teachings and prophecies for us today. In addition, some chapters contain warnings and prophecies concerning other nations (13-23, 36, 37, 44, 45, 47), historical material (36-39), and limited autobiographical information (1, 6-9, 36-39). Obviously,

Isaiah's book is primarily a collection of his teachings and prophecies, not a record of his personal life.

As we study Isaiah's writings on various topics, five major themes soon become apparent (look up asterisked terms in the Bible Dictionary):

1. Prophecies about the northern kingdom of Israel* (in different chapters, especially 1-10).
2. Prophecies about the southern kingdom of Judah*, the Babylonian captivity, and the return to Judea (in twenty-five chapters, especially 1-10, 28-31, 36-39, and 44-48).
3. Prophecies about the first coming, mission, and return of the Messiah* (in twenty chapters, especially 53).
4. Prophecies concerning the last days: the restoration* of the gospel, the gathering of Israel, the destruction of the wicked, and the coming of the Messiah in glory (in 50 chapters scattered throughout).
5. Prophecies about other nations and the Gentiles* or the world at large (in twenty-six chapters, especially 13-23, 43-47, and 54-58).

The following synopsis indicates the Isaiah chapters in which these themes are highlighted, provides a brief introduction to each chapter, and suggests resources for helpful background information:

Chapter	Theme	
		Chapters 1-12: Israelites and Their Leaders
1		Isaiah's Invitation to the Gospel
	1, 2	The Lord is angry with Israel for her rebellion; he rejects her hypocritical feasts* and calls her to repentance. She is promised restoration: "I will restore thy judges as at first" (v. 26). A beautiful promise of forgiveness is in verse 18: "Be your sins like crimson, they can turn snow-white."
		See BD "Blood," "New Moon," "Sacrifices."
2		Fear and Exalt the Lord in That Day
	2, 4	The fall and restoration of Judah is prophesied, with emphasis upon the latter days: "And it shall come to pass in the last days, that the mountain of the Lord's house shall be established in the top of the mountains" (v. 2). The need for repentance and humility is also stressed (vs. 9, 11, 17). The day of judgment will humble all men (v. 12). Destruction of the wicked at Christ's coming is foretold (v. 19). Compare 2 Ne. 12 for

Chapter	Theme	
		important differences between Isaiah in the Old Testament and the Book of Mormon. See pp.89-98. See BD "Dead Sea Scrolls," "Italics," "Masoretic Text," "Septuagint," "Ship.")

king of Judah: "Don't fear Pekah* of Israel and Rezin* of Syria*." Isaiah prophesies that within sixty-five years Ephraim* will be scattered by Assyria* (vs. 1-9). The important Immanuel* sign to Ahaz and the prophecy about the coming of the birth of Christ is given: "Behold, a virgin shall conceive" (vs. 14-16; compare Matt. 1:23 for fulfillment in Jesus). Four signs given: (1) maiden shall bear a child; (2) it will be a son; (3) he will be called Immanuel; (4) before he is of an accountable age, the two invading kingdoms will be destroyed, and more animals than people will remain in the desolate land (vs. 20-25). (Review "History of Palestine Area" to 735 B.C., pages 27-30. Read 2 Kgs. 15-16. See BD "Fullers," "Jeroboam II," "Jonah," "Molech," "Symbolism." This chapter is quoted in 2 Ne. 17.)

8   Following a Singular Path

1, 2, 3   Trust in the Lord and not in foreign alliances. Judah is told not to be afraid of the impending war (vs. 17-25) or to unite with Syria and Assyria, but to repent and fear the Lord (vs. 10-13). Christ will be a stumbling block for Judah (vs. 13-14; see also Matt. 4:12-16). (See BD "Scroll." This chapter is quoted in 2 Ne. 18.)

9   His Arm Is Outstretched Still

1, 3   Israel will be devoured for her wickedness (v. 12), and she shall devour herself (vs. 19-20). There is also an important reference here to the Messiah*: "For unto us a child is born . . ." (vs. 6-7). (Compare Amos* 4-5. This chapter is quoted in 2 Ne. 19.)

10   The Proud Subjected to God's Rule

1, 2, 4, 5   Assyria is about to be sent against Israel (Samaria*) and then against Judah. She will march through the towns just north of Jerusalem (vs. 28-31), but will stop just outside the city (v. 32). Proud Assyria will later be destroyed by the Lord (vs. 15-16, 33-34). A righteous remnant of Israelites shall return (vs. 20-23). (Read 2 Kgs. 17. See BD "Samaritans," "Diaspora," "Dispersion," "Captivities of the Israelites." This chapter is quoted in 2 Ne. 20.)

11   Servants of the Last Days

3, 4   This chapter promises the restoration of Israel in the last days under great leaders. (Read JS-H 1:40; D&C 113:1-6; 101:26; 2 Ne. 30:9-15. See BD "Fear," "Jesse." This chapter is quoted in 2 Ne. 21 and in 2 Ne. 30:9-15.)

12   Praise the Lord

Chapter	Theme	

3, 4   A song of praise to Jehovah* (Christ) or the "Holy One of Israel"* at the time when his glory and mission shall be known over all the earth during the Millennium. (This chapter is quoted in 2 Ne. 22.)

Chapters 13-23: Prophecies to the Foreign Nations

13   The "Babylon" Pronouncement

2, 4, 5   Although Isaiah speaks directly of Babylon*, he also appears to be speaking about the world in the last days (see D&C 133:14). Verses 9, 10, and 13 indicate that a cosmic catastrophe will come. The actual downfall of the Babylonian kingdom is prophesied (vs. 15-22). (Read D&C 29, 45; Rev. 18. See BD "Dragon." This chapter is quoted in 2 Ne. 23.)

14   Victory over the Wicked

2, 4, 5   A continuation of chapter 13 that tells of the fall of Babylon and includes a "taunt song" against the king of Babylon (vs. 4-23). This king may be (1) an ancient political ruler, (2) Satan* or the Devil*, or (3) any leader of wickedness. Israel (house of Jacob) shall be restored and will rule over her oppressors (v. 2). There is also a reference to Lucifer's* fall (vs. 12-13), and his final ruin along with his followers in the last days (vs. 14-22). (Compare Moses 1:12-22; 4:1-4; Rev. 18. Note: the term *Satan* also means "earth-shaker," being derived from the Semitic term *satanah*. See BD "Hell," "Philistines," "War in Heaven." This chapter is quoted in 2 Ne. 24.)

15   The "Moab" Pronouncement

5   This is a prophecy against Moab* (now part of Jordan). (See Map 9.)

16   Moab's Depopulation

5   A continuation of chapter 15 that promises that only a remnant of no consequence shall be left (v. 14). (Compare v. 5 with Luke 1:32-33.)

17   The "Damascus" Pronouncement

1, 4, 5   This chapter contains a prophecy against Damascus* (Syria*) and Samaria*. The prophecy of a restoration is also suggested (vs. 7-8). (See Map 9.)

18   The "America" Pronouncement

Chapter   Theme

4, 5   Although this chapter is directed toward a land "which is beyond the rivers of Ethiopia*" (v. 1), it also appears that it pertains to the gathering of Israel (vs. 2-7), and perhaps even to America. This chapter is unusual also because of its placement as a prophecy of hope (to a certain people) among prophecies of destruction (to Israel's enemies). (See BD "Shechinah.")

19   The "Egypt" Pronouncement

4, 5   A prophecy against Egypt* that promises civil war, selfish and foolish leaders, drastic changes in society, despondent dam makers, and the powers of God creating chaos in Egypt. Judah will have power in Egypt, and an altar* or a temple* will be built (vs. 19-21). This temple could be the sixth century B.C. Jewish temple built on Elephantine Island at Syrene (see Map 12) or a modern temple (such as the recent smaller designs) of this dispensation. An alliance and highway between Egypt, Israel, and Assyria will be a blessing to the earth. Note how the recent Egypt-Israel peace treaty is not only a modern miracle, but also an important step toward the prophesied coalition between modern Egypt, Israel, and Iraq.

20   A Sign of Nakedness

1, 5   Isaiah is commanded to walk barefoot and without a sackcloth and outer garment (but probably still with a short, linen tunic) as a sign to Egypt and Ethiopia of an impending Assyrian conquest. He also gives a sign to Israel not to make a coalition with Egypt against Assyria. (See BD "Isles.")

21   The "Desert of the Sea" Pronouncement

5   This chapter has a prophecy of impending peril from the desert upon Babylon, Edom*, Seir* and Arabia* (perhaps from Assyria or Persia). (See Maps 2 and 10.)

22   The "Valley of Vision" Pronouncement

2, 3, 4   The first verses describe the lack of protection for Jerusalem* and how her people casually await destruction. Her leaders will fail. The last part (vs. 20-25) is perhaps a prophecy of the last days and the restoration of Judah, possibly Messianic, for a great leader will rule in Jerusalem (v. 21), and "the nail that is in the sure place shall be removed" (v. 25). This phrase could refer either to the crucifixion* or to the removal of political power from the house of David.

23   The "Tyre" Pronouncement

Chapter	Theme	
	5	This chapter is a prophecy of the fall of Tyre* and Sidon* in Phoenicia* (modern Lebanon). They are to be in captivity to Assyria for seventy years. (See Map 9; BD "Commerce.")

Chapters 24-27: Isaiah's Apocalypse

24		The Earth Suffers for the Sins of Mankind
	4	This is an apocalypse* (revelation*) concerning the last days. (See D&C 1.) The earth will mourn and fade away (v. 4; compare D&C 29:23-24; 88:26), and will "reel to and fro like a drunkard" (v. 20; see Rev. 16:18-20; D&C 133:23-24; D&C 88:87-91). The wicked in the spirit prison will be remembered (v. 22; see Isa. 42:6-7; 1 Pet. 3-4; D&C 138).
25		The Lord's Hand Will Descend
	4	A continuation or conclusion to chapter 24 that presents a song of praise to celebrate the Lord's victory over death (v. 8) and the redemption of his people. (See BD "Lees.")
26		Song of Judah
	3, 4	Judah's song of praise for her redemption*, restoration*, and exaltation. All men shall be resurrected* after the Lord.
27		The Wicked to Suffer More Than the Righteous
	4	This chapter refers to the gathering of the house of Israel (v. 6), with a possible reference to Assyria being synonymous with the world. (See BD "Leviathan.")

Chapters 28-35: Promises of Judgments and Blessings

28		The Crown, Wine, and Covenant of Ephraim
	1, 2, 4	Wickedness and judgment are to come upon Ephraim (v. 1) and Judah (v. 14), and yet there is an intimation that this prophecy applies to the last days, for "In that day shall the Lord of hosts be for a crown of glory" (v. 5). A childlike attitude and gradual process of learning are outlined (vs. 9-10, 12-13). (Read 2 Ne. 28, especially v. 30, and D&C 128:21. Compare Isa. 28:12 with Acts 3:19. See BD "Knowledge," "Cummin." [Fitches are either a forage herb, like tares, or a condiment, such as dill or blade cumin, whose seeds are beaten out with a staff.])
29		Ariel, Ariel—Speak from the Dust

Chapter	*Theme*	

	2, 4	This chapter concerns the restoration of the gospel and makes reference to the coming forth of hidden scriptures. It is interpreted by Nephi to include especially the Book of Mormon (vs. 4, 11-12). (Read 2 Ne. 26:14-22; 27, 29 for Nephi's additional insights. Read also JS-H 1:63-65. Note footnote 1a and read JST additions. See BD "Ephraim, Stick of," "Judah, Stick of.")
30		You Who Desire a False Prophet
	2, 4, 5	Isaiah prophesies against Judah; she has sought help from Egypt rather than relying upon the Lord. Later (vs. 19-33), Isaiah mentions events to occur in the last days: "Moreover the light of the moon shall be as the light of the sun, and the light of the sun shall be sevenfold" (v. 26). Verse 31 speaks of Assyria being beaten down, with Assyria meaning either the Assyrian kingdom or the "world." (See BD "Fiery Serpents.")
31		False Trust in Men
	2, 4, 5	A continuation of chapter 30 that warns Judah not to make an alliance with Egypt but to trust in the Lord, for the Assyrians will fall. Again, Assyria may also mean the world at the time of the Second Coming. (Read 2 Kgs. 18:1-16.)
32		Fruits of Righteous and Wicked Leaders Compared
	3, 4	This is a prophecy concerning the last days, for it refers to the desolate condition of the land "until the spirit be poured upon us from on high, and the wilderness be a fruitful field . . ." (v. 15). Finally the people will dwell in righteousness and peace. (Read carefully: 1 Ne. 19:13-17, especially v. 15; 2 Ne. 6:3-11, especially v. 11; 2 Ne. 10:3-9, especially v. 7 for three preconditions of gathering and restoration of Jews in the last days. Compare Zeph. 3:10-13, 19-20; Jer. 16; Morm. 5:14.)
33		Sinners Will Fear Zion
	4	A prophecy concerning the last days: the wicked will be destroyed and the Lord will be exalted (vs. 5, 10), the righteous will have their food supplies assured (v. 16), Jerusalem's tabernacle (temple) shall not be destroyed (v. 20), and there will be no illness (v. 24).
34		The Lord's Day of Retribution
	4, 5	Another prophecy concerning the last days: "The indignation of the Lord is upon all nations" (v. 2), "And all the host of heaven shall be dissolved, and the heavens shall be rolled

Chapter	Theme

together as a scroll" (v. 4), "they shall possess it (Jerusalem) forever, from generation to generation" (v. 17). Desolation is promised to Idumea (Edom, or "the world"). (Compare Isa. 13 [spiritual Babylon]; Isa. 24; D&C 1, 133. See BD "Brimstone.")

35

The Desert Shall Blossom as the Rose

4   Another prophecy concerning the last days (the desert shall blossom as the rose, v. 1) and the second coming of the Messiah (vs. 2, 4). The ransomed (Israel) shall also return (v. 10) and be gathered. (Compare D&C 133:21-25. See BD "Hart.")

Chapters 36-39: Historical Narrative

36

Assyrian Armies Surround Jerusalem

2, 5,   Sennacherib* of Assyria uses fear and subversive tactics to persuade Jerusalem to surrender. Review "History of the Palestine Area," pp. 27-30. (Read 2 Chr. 29-31; 2 Kgs. 18:13-37. See BD "Aram," "Aramaic.")

37

King Hezekiah Prays and Receives Deliverance

2, 5   Hezekiah* prays for deliverance from Assyria. His prayer is answered through Isaiah, and Jerusalem is miraculously saved by a destroying angel. The unstable condition in the land is prophesied to last until the third year (v. 30). (Read 2 Kgs. 19:1-37; 2 Chr. 32:1-23. See BD "Angels," "Hebrew," "Hezekiah's Tunnel.")

38

Extra Life to Hezekiah

2   Hezekiah is sick, but is promised an additional fifteen years of life and given a sign (v. 11). (Read 2 Kgs. 20:1-11; 2 Chr. 32:24-30.)

39

Temple Treasures Revealed

2, 5   Hezekiah's indiscretion brings the prophecy that Judah and her wealth would be taken to Babylon. (Read 2 Kgs. 20:12-21; 2 Chr. 32:31-33.)

Chapters 40-47: Affirmation of God's Power

40

Jerusalem Will Receive Strength through Sacrifice

3, 4   A very important chapter concerning our own dispensation and the second coming of Christ. It declares the power and might of

God and suggests how man can receive that strength (vs. 29-31). (Note the use of verses 3-5 and additional material in JST Luke 3:4-11. Ponder verses 29-31 carefully. Compare them with Ps.103, where many ideas of this chapter are stated.)

41   Trust in the Lord

4   This appears to be a continuation of chapter 40. Israel is told not to fear her oppressors (vs. 8-16). The poor will be comforted and the waste places renewed.

42   Hear My Servant (and Son)

3, 4   A continuation of chapter 41 that includes references to Christ (vs. 1-7). A "servant song" is given in vs. 1-9. Read Joseph Smith's translation of the last half of the chapter (vs. 18ff.) by noting footnote 19a and reading in the Appendix. (Read 2 Kgs. 21; 2 Chr. 33.)

43   I Am the Lord of This Earth!

3, 4, 5   A continuation of chapter 42, this discourse speaks of the overthrow of Babylon (vs. 14-17) and the gathering of the dispersed. The Lord will remember Israel's sins "no more" (vs. 5-9, 25). The Lord speaks of himself as the Savior (vs. 3, 11, 25). (See BD "Jacob," "Israel," "Christ, Names of.")

44   The Lord Is the Great Creator

2, 4, 5   A continuation from chapter 43, this chapter contains a reference to Cyrus* of Persia* as a shepherd of the Lord (v. 28) who will release the Babylonian captives.

45   The Lord Speaks to Cyrus

2, 3, 4, 5   The Lord again affirms his power and glory in this prophecy to Cyrus. There is also reference to the time when "every knee shall bow, every tongue shall swear" to Christ (v. 23). Also, it is not from idols (v. 20), but from God that will come victory, salvation, and the Savior ("Jeshua"* or "Jesus"*; see vs. 8, 15, 21-22).

46   God Is Not Found in Idols

2, 5   Because of the wickedness and idolatry of Babylon, she will be captured by a power (Persia) described as a "swooping bird from the East" (v. 11).

47   Babylon's Disgrace

Chapter	Theme

2, 4, 5   A song about Babylon's fall; perhaps a twofold prophecy about ancient and modern times. (Compare Rev. 18. See BD "Agriculture.")

Chapters 48-52: Different Types of Israelites Join Together

48   Listen to Me, O Jacob

2, 4   Israel* will be released from captivity and called to come out of Babylon and acknowledge the Lord as promised in the covenant of Abraham*. The house of Jacob (especially "covenant Israel") is called to repentance. (Read carefully 1 Ne. 20 for important changes. Also read 2 Ne. 30 for additional insights from Nephi. See BD "Adoption," "Birthright," "Covenant," "Jew.")

49   Listen, Scattered Israel

3, 4   An important chapter on the gathering of Israel. See 1 Ne. 21 for a number of textual changes. Also read 1 Ne. 22 (especially vs. 3-4) and compare D&C 133:21-22. Vs. 1-13 comprise a servant song. Israel will be adorned like a bride (v. 18).

50   Witness of a Prophet's Voice

2, 3, 4   This chapter on the restoration of the house of Israel contains a special reference to Christ in mortality (v. 6; compare Matt. 27:26). A servant song is developed in vs. 4-11. (See 2 Ne. 7 for a few textual changes.)

51   Hearken, O Jerusalem

3, 4   A continuation of chapter 50 on the last days. The Lord has not divorced Israel but suffers for his people. There is a reference to "two things" or "two sons" in vs. 19-20, which refer to the time just prior to the Millennium. (Read D&C 77:15; Rev. 11:8; 2 Ne. 9:1-3; 10. This chapter is quoted in 2 Ne. 8.)

52   Awake, Awake, O Zion

3, 4   Perhaps a continuation of chapter 51. (See D&C 113:7-10 for clarification of vs. 1-2). Christ's second coming as Messiah is suggested (vs. 6-10). There is some beautiful poetry in this chapter, including a servant song in vs. 13-15. Christ quotes this chapter in 3 Ne. 20, but groups the verses together in a different order as follows: 8-9-10, 1-2-3, 6-7, 11-12-13-14-15. Portions of this chapter are quoted in 2 Ne. 8:24-25; Mosiah 12:21-24; 3 Ne. 16:18-20; and 3 Ne. 21:29. (Read 3 Ne. 15:5–

17:3 and 20:10–23:5; note how Christ uses and testifies of Isaiah's promises of the Lord's covenant with the house of Israel. Also read Mosiah 15:13-18; Micah* 4-5; D&C 101; and Mor. 10:30-33 for further insights.)

Chapter 53: Servant Song of the Messiah

53   Suffering of the Son

       3   A continuation from chapter 52, this is a specific reference to the Savior while in mortality, including his life, mission, and atonement*: "He was smitten because of our sins" (v. 5). This chapter is "probably the greatest single Old Testament messianic prophecy." (Bruce R. McConkie, *Ensign*, Oct. 1973, p. 83.) This chapter is quoted by the prophet Abinadi in Mosiah 14. (Read Mosiah 15-16; 2 Ne. 31.)

Chapters 54-58: Discourses to Israel and the World

54   The Lord Promises His Loyalty to Israelites

       4, 5   Many Gentiles will join with covenant Israel in the last days. Zion will enlarge her stakes. Israel will be redeemed by Christ and be smitten no more. (See BD "Repentence." This chapter is quoted by Christ in 3 Ne. 22.)

55   My Ways Are Not Your Ways

       3, 4, 5   This is a beautifully written invitation bidding all to come and
and all   partake of the gospel. This chapter could be called Isaiah's
ages   "Sermon on the Mount," for it contains deep spiritual meaning and his personal testimony of God*, and describes how our Heavenly Father will help us return to his presence as an everlasting sign of the fulfillment of his plan. (Compare similar feelings of Nephi in 2 Ne. 26:23-28; 32-33; and Moroni in Moro. 10. See BD "Heaven.")

56   Sabbath Observers to Be Blessed

       4, 5   Primarily a chapter on keeping the Sabbath* and the blessings to the Gentile "outcasts" who come to the Lord and his house. There is also reference to the gathering of the "outcasts of Israel" (v. 8). (Read D&C 59. See BD "Eunuch," "Stranger.")

57   Repent, Wicked Children

       4   The people have forgotten the Lord. Therefore Isaiah calls Israel to repent, for "he that putteth his trust in me shall

Chapter	*Theme*	

possess the land, and shall inherit my holy mountain" (v. 13). The Lord forgives those who repent, but for the wicked there is no peace or safety. Isaiah denounces the twin sins of adultery and idolatry.

58		Remember the Fast, and the Lord Will Be Your Guard
	5 and all ages	An excellent chapter on fasting that emphasizes the attitudes, acts, and rewards of true fasts*. Isaiah seals the chapter with his witness "for the mouth of the Lord has spoken." (Read D&C 56:16-21; compare Isa. 58:8 with Isa. 52:12. See BD "Jubilee, Year of," "Sabbatical Year."

Chapters 59-66: The Great and Dreadful Day, and a New Earth

59		Christ Will Rectify
	3, 4	This chapter states why the Lord has withdrawn from Jacob (wickedness builds a barrier between us and the Lord). The Redeemer is promised, and this may refer to both the first and second comings of Christ. (See BD "Cockatrice.")

60		Ye Shall Know That I the Lord Am Your Savior
	4	A beautiful and descriptive chapter about the glory promised to Jerusalem and the Zion of the "Holy One of Israel"* in the Millennium. (Read D&C 106:30-32; 124:3-11; 45:59, 66-71 and compare with Isa. 40.)

61		Receive a Garment of Splendor
	4	Isaiah foretells the restoration of Jacob in the last days, the honor to be paid to her sons, and the rebuilding of the waste places. Jesus began his ministry as the Messiah (or the Anointed One*) with the first three verses of this chapter. (See Luke 4:16-21). Israel is referred to as a bride adorned for her husband (v. 10). Special robes or garments are promised the righteous (vs. 3, 10). (See Alma 5:7, 9-10; Eph. 6:11-12; 2 Ne. 2:23; 9:14 for other types of attire one could wear. See BD "Breastplate.")

62		Ye Shall Be Called by a New Name
	4	In this continuation of chapter 61, Zion and Jerusalem are promised restoration and honor in holiness*. All people will know the "bride and bridegroom" (Israel and the Lord). (Compare Hosea* 2-3.)

Chapter	Theme	
63		Dialogue between Isaiah and the Messiah
	3, 4	The atoning sacrifice of Christ is mentioned (vs. 2-3) and the destruction of the wicked is foretold. (Read D&C 133:46-53.)
64		Why Do You Let Us Suffer?
	4	A continuation of chapter 63 that includes Isaiah's prayer that the Lord will forgive the house of Jacob of their sins and no longer hide his face from them. (Read Isa. 13:9-12; D&C 133:41-45. In fact, read all of D&C 133 as a preview for the following chapter of Isaiah.)
65		I Am Creating a New Heaven and a New Earth
	4	In this continuation of chapter 64, the Lord answers Isaiah's prayer. The wicked will be destroyed (vs. 11-15) and a new heaven and a new earth will be created (v. 17). Jerusalem and its inhabitants will be blessed (vs. 18-25). (Read D&C 101:22-38, 101. Compare the message and spirit of this chapter with Isa. 1.)
66		All Flesh Shall Come to Worship Me
	4	This continuation of chapter 65 is a summary of the Lord's advice to his people. Jerusalem shall be a comfort to the faithful (vs. 10-14), and the Lord will destroy the wicked (vs. 15-18). In the last days, nations will bring Israel to Jerusalem in many conveyances (v. 20). Everyone will worship the Lord forever (v. 23). Compare vs. 14-21 with D&C 128:22-24. Note Isaiah's structural pattern in this chapter and in his entire book: (1) a warning of doom to the wicked; (2) a promise of blessings to the righteous; and (3) a word of caution to the faithful. In other words, repent, have God's Spirit* (the Holy Ghost*) with you, and endure to the end.

ISAIAH'S INVITATION TO THE GOSPEL
ISAIAH 1

Isaiah's introductory message reaches out to all Israel, inviting all of God's children to obey the Lord. It warns the Israelites that they will be scattered if they disobey, but still promises them an opportunity for divine cleansing and blessing if they repent. In this first chapter, Isaiah teaches the basic principles and ordinances of the gospel and prophesies concerning apostasy, restoration, and judgment. Chapter 1 of Isaiah is, therefore, a fitting introduction to his book, because it provides a broad preview of his gospel insights and essential teachings. Chapter 1 is also typical of Isaiah's writing style and poetry.

Most scholars agree that this chapter is not the first prophecy received by Isaiah, but that it heads his writings because of its profound, clear message. A renowned Isaiah scholar describes it in this way:

> The first chapter of the Book of Isaiah owes its position not to its date . . . but to its character . . . The prophecy . . . has been . . . placed in the front of the book, either by Isaiah himself or by an editor, as a general introduction to his collected pieces. . . . It is a clear, complete statement of the points which were at issue between the Lord and His own all the time Isaiah was the Lord's prophet. It is the most representative of Isaiah's prophecies, a summary, perhaps better than any other single chapter of the Old Testament, of the substance of prophetic doctrine, and a very vivid illustration of the prophetic spirit and method. (BOI 1:3-4.)

Latter-day Saint writers also compare Isaiah 1 with the first section of the Doctrines and Covenants, since this preface to modern scripture was received later in Joseph Smith's ministry, but was placed by him at the head of his revelations. Latter-day Saint scholar Sidney B. Sperry says of the first chapter of Isaiah, "It is one of the finest specimens of prophetic oratory in the Old Testament." (VIP, p. 20.)

The Great Arraignment

The first chapter of Isaiah is often called the "Great Arraignment," because it takes the form of a court scene with Jehovah as the plaintiff and judge, Israel as the defendant, Isaiah as an observer and occasional interlocutor, and heaven and earth as the witnesses. After a prologue (Isa. 1:1) comes the court scene, which can be outlined as follows:

Accusation: The Lord's charge of sin and sickness throughout Israel is given (vs. 2-6).

Immediate judgments: Physical and spiritual consequences are coming upon Israel because the people have not obeyed the Lord (7-15).

Promise of pardon: Conditions of cleansing, repentance, and blessing are presented (16-20).

Final sentencing: The Lord will purge the wicked and redeem the righteous through apostasy, restoration, and judgment (21-31).

Prologue (v. 1)

1 The prophecies of Isaiah son of Amoz, who prophesied concerning Judah and Jerusalem in the reigns of Uzziah, Jotham, Ahaz, and Hezekiah, kings of Judah. (NJV)

The first verse serves as a simple prose introduction to the entire book of Isaiah. Since most ancient Hebrew scripture was written on parchment scrolls, an introduction like this was valuable so that a reader would not have to unroll the entire scroll in order to identify its author and subject matter. This short verse contains all the essential identifying information: the type of writing ("vision," KJV, or "prophecies," NJV), the author or source of the material (Isaiah), the primary subject matter (Judah and Jerusalem), and the period of composition (c. 750-690 B.C., during the reigns of Uzziah, Jotham, Ahaz, and Hezekiah).

Accusation (vs. 2-6)

Beginning with verse 2, the rest of chapter 1 is written in poetic form rather than prose. The first few verses contain the Lord's charge against Israel as he decries her wickedness and sickness:

²Hear, O heavens, and give ear, O earth,
For the Lord has spoken:
"I reared children and brought them up—
And they have rebelled against Me!
³An ox knows its owner,
An ass its master's crib:
Israel does not know,
My people takes no thought."
⁴Ah, sinful nation!
People laden with iniquity!
Brood of evildoers!
Depraved children!
They have foreaken the Lord,
Spurned the Holy One of Israel,
Turned their backs (on Him).
⁵Why do you seek further beatings,
That you continue to offend?
Every head is ailing,
And every heart is sick.
⁶From head to foot
No spot is sound:
All bruises, and welts,
And festering sores—
Not pressed out, not bound up,
Not softened with oil. (NJV)

The beginning half of verse 2 contains two strong exhortations to Isaiah's audience. It begins with the command to "hear!" The Hebrew word (*shim'u*) is in the imperative form, meaning that the Lord insists that Isaiah's listeners or readers pay attention. The word also has the connotation of "obeying" or "following," in the sense of keeping the commandments. An alternate translation of this word is "give heed" or "hearken to act." Thus, Isaiah is not just politely asking for attention but is rather commanding adherence to his words.

The beginning phrase of verse 2 echoes the words of Moses as he begins the great psalm that was his last mortal discourse: "Give ear, O ye heavens, and I will speak; and hear, O earth, the words of my mouth." (Deut. 32:1; compare Deut. 31:28.) Moses' last sermon deals with God's greatness, his choice of Israel as his covenant people, Israel's rebellion, and God's final sovereignty over Israel and all nations. Isaiah expresses those same ideas and begins this chapter with a similar exhortation, indicating his familiarity with Moses' sermon. These words also serve as a reminder to Israel of the solemn covenants their ancestors made with the Lord before they entered the Promised Land. As in the past, willful disobedience to this covenant is sure to result in utter destruction. (See Deut. 4:25-26.)

Isaiah appropriately builds upon the Israelite covenant and the words of Deuteronomy, for he was the most profound prophet and teacher of Israel since Moses. Living halfway between the time of Moses and that of Christ, Isaiah forms a bridge between these two servants of Israel as he both testifies of the continued validity of Moses' dispensation and prophesies the promised redemption of Christ's. Isaiah's use of Mosaic phraseology and themes places him in the mainstream of Israel's prophetic tradition with the mantle of Moses resting firmly on his shoulders.

The second phrase of verse 2, "For the Lord has spoken," also confirms Isaiah's prophetic calling. Isaiah wants his listeners to know that he is not giving his own ideas or philosophy, but the words of the Lord. This phrase also catches his listeners' attention and alerts them to an important message to follow. In Isaiah (or any of the scriptures), phrases like "the Lord has spoken," and "hear the word of the Lord," "the mouth of the Lord has spoken," and "thus saith the Lord" are used as flags to attract our attention and to testify concerning the Lord's message. After using such a phrase in his opening exhortation, Isaiah is now ready to deliver the Lord's word to Israel.

The remainder of verse 2 and all of verse 3 testify that God's children have rebelled against their Lord and are worthy of death, the penalty allowed under Mosaic law for the deliberate disobedience by children. (Ex. 21:15, 17.) The Israelites have become less obedient than animals, who at least recognize their masters.

Verse 4 seems to warn of the dangers of disobedience, for it begins with the Hebrew exclamation *hoy*, which can be rendered simply as "ah!" although a more complete derivative would be "shame" or "alas." The Lord then elaborates upon Israel's corruption in a four-fold denouncement that describes four types of wickedness (sin, iniquity, evildoing, and depravity or corruption) among four groups (nation, people, brood or seed, and children). The description of the last group (depraved or corrupt children) demonstrates the seriousness of Israel's wickedness, for even her children are being taught to do evil.

In verses 5 and 6, the people contract sickness and open sores, which might be physical but are probably spiritual, because they result from the people's continued rebellion against the Lord. The sickness of the "head" and "heart" is most serious, because these organs are necessary both for physical health and for spiritual sensitivity. Intellectual and emotional faith, both necessary for true religious devotion, stem from the head and heart, respectively.

Sometimes a disease lies dormant within the body for a time, later manifesting itself through external symptoms like the open sores of verse 6. These festering wounds could be literal or figurative, representing either the nation's inability to care for her wounds in a time of chaos (or apathy), or her refusal to acknowledge her sins and heal herself spiritually. The verse might easily refer to both.

Immediate Judgments (vs. 7-15)

After presenting the Lord's accusation and opening remarks, Isaiah is ready to detail the imminent catastrophes coming upon Israel. These include desolation in the land, the loss of many people, and rejection by the Lord, as described in the following verses:

7Your land is a waste,
Your cities burnt down;
Before your eyes, the yield of your
    soil
Is consumed by strangers—
A wasteland as overthrown by
    strangers!
8Fair Zion is left
Like a booth in a vineyard
Like a hut in a cucumber field,
Like a city beleaguered.
9Had not the Lord of Hosts
Left us some survivors,
We should be like Sodom,
Another Gomorrah.
10Hear the word of the Lord,
You chieftains of Sodom;
Give ear to our God's instruction,
You folk, of Gomorrah!
11"What need have I of all your
    sacrifices?"
Says the Lord,
"I am sated with burnt offerings
of rams,
And suet of fatlings,
And blood of bulls;

And I have no delight
In lambs and he-goats.
12That you come to appear before
        Me—
Who asked that of you?
Trample My courts
13   no more
Bringing oblations is futile,
Incense is offensive to Me.
New moon and sabbath,
Proclaiming of solemnities,
Assemblies with iniquity,
I cannot abide.
14Your new moons and fixed
    seasons
Fill Me with loathing;
They are become a burden
    to Me,
I cannot endure them.
15And when you lift up your hands,
I will turn My eyes away from
    you;
Though you pray at length,
I will not listen.
Your hands are stained with
    crime. (NJV)

Verses 7-9 detail the destruction throughout the land and among the people. As a punishment for wickedness, strangers (foreigners or Gentiles) will occupy the land, and the fruits of the labor of Israelite hands will be consumed by strangers. The centuries Israel has spent developing the promised land will yield her nothing. This devastation came upon Israel and Judah during Isaiah's lifetime when the Assyrians destroyed Israel, took many captives, and repeatedly plundered Judah.

The imagery in verse 8 graphically portrays the extent of Israel's desolation. Isaiah emphasizes her condition through parallel phrases as he declares that fair Zion is left like a booth in a vineyard or a hut in the fields. During Isaiah's time, booths and huts were a common part of the agricultural landscape. Most Israelites lived in towns, villages, and fortified cities, while their fields and orchards lay among the valleys and surrounding hillsides. Usually the people would walk to and from the fields each day, but during the hectic harvest season, such traveling wasted precious daylight working hours. In addition, since the entire family was needed for a full day's work to gather, sort, dry, and store the harvested fruits and grains, they spent the season living in a hut, shack, or simple cottage in their fields. Huts were also available for other workers and for the watchmen who protected the harvest from straying livestock and thieves in the night.

When Isaiah prophesies that Zion will be left as a hut or lodge in the field, then, he is warning of a loss of people and productivity. This loss will be so great that only the empty huts and booths will remain, desolate reminders of former prosperity. They will serve as memorials of how the Lord once blessed Israel in the land but now curses her.

Verse 9 illustrates how close Israel comes to complete annihilation; if it were not for the Lord's intervention, she would be completely obliterated, like Sodom and Gomorrah. To compare Jerusalem with Sodom and Gomorrah was a dreadful indictment against Judah, and indicates the extremely depraved condition into which many Israelites had fallen.

Verses 10-15 demonstrate the complete division between Israel and the Lord. He rejects her external religious acts (sacrifices, festivals, and prayers) because she has rejected his counsel and stained her hands with sin. Actually, the Israelites were in many ways worse than the people of Sodom and Gomorrah, who were openly and blatantly wicked, while the Israelites hid their sins behind superficial symbols of religious devotion.

The most important theme of the Lord's pronouncement in chapter 1 is in verses 10-12. Note the verbal flags that direct attention toward this important section: *"hear* the word of *the Lord,"* *"give ear* unto the law of our *God,"* and, *"saith the Lord."* The passage between these declarations is a question to Israel from the Lord: "To what purpose is the multitude of your sacrifices unto me?" (KJV), or "What need have I of all your sacrifices?" (NJV). While a superficial reading of this passage may suggest the possibility that God is revoking his law of animal sacrifice, a more careful study reveals that God is not doing away with sacrifices but is rather rejecting the many perfunctory offerings of the wicked Israelites. He is weary of external signs—the smoke, fat, and blood of their sacrifices—that are not accompanied by true internal religious devotion.

Israelites, hearing these words of Isaiah, might have reflected upon two other occasions in their history when the Lord rejected burnt offerings. At the beginning of human history, God rejected Cain's sacrifices because Cain performed them only after Satan commanded him to. (Moses 5:18, 21.) Later in Israelite history, God rejected King Saul's offerings because he disobeyed the Lord by returning with large flocks captured from the Amalikites. (1 Sam. 15:21.) In each case, the Lord did not object to the law of sacrifice per se, but rather to the violation of the law of obedience, which must always precede an acceptable sacrifice. (1 Sam. 15:22.)

Latter-day Saints are also taught the relationship between these two laws, obedience and sacrifice.

In summary, verses 10-12 teach that though people may keep the letter of the law, thinking that pious acts alone will bring salvation, the Lord requires much more than mere outward performance. He wants internal commitment and integrity to precede the external ordinances. (See Moro. 7:5-11.) And knowing that the Israelites themselves recognize their hypocrisy, he asks them why they have assembled unrighteously before him in his temple courts. Don't they know better?

In reviewing the physical and spiritual judgments to come upon Israel, Isaiah is not just trying to scare the people into submission to the Lord. He is reminding them of their sacred covenants with God and their promises to obey him. If the people will listen to the promptings of the Spirit, they will remember the righteous attitudes that are expected of them before they can worthily appear at the Lord's temple courtyards with their sacrifices.

Promise of Pardon (vs. 16-20)

In the next five verses, God demonstrates his love for his children in a promise of cleansing, forgiveness, and blessing extended to Israel:

¹⁶Wash yourselves clean;
Put your evil doings
Away from My sight.
Cease to do evil;
¹⁷Learn to do good.
Devote yourselves to justice;
Aid the wronged.
Uphold the rights of the orphans;
Defend the cause of the widow.
¹⁸"Come, let us reach an
understanding"—says
the Lord

"Be your sins like crimson,
They can turn snow-white;
Be they red as dyed wool,
They can become like fleece."
¹⁹If, then you agree and give heed,
You will eat the good things of the
earth;
²⁰But if you refuse and disobey,
You will be devoured (by) the
sword.—
For it was the Lord who spoke.
(NJV)

Verse 16 is Isaiah's admonition to repent and be baptized. His terminology seems somewhat unfamiliar to us because some modern religious terms did not exist in the ancient Hebrew vocabulary. For example, *baptism* is derived from a Greek word, but the Greek civilization did not influence the Hebrew until centuries after Isaiah's time. Therefore, when Isaiah says "wash yourself," he could mean either a figurative cleansing or a literal washing, such as baptism. His references to repentance in verse 16, on the other hand, are more straightforward, suggesting that the washing he advocates is more spiritual than physical. His admonition continues in verse 17, as the people are told to use their heads (learning) and hearts (justice) for noble purposes. This is a direct contrast to the diseased heads and hearts of verse 5.

The Lord's beautiful and oft-quoted promise of forgiveness is found in verse 18. Although Israel may be stained red with sin, she can become pure white. Isaiah's use of these particular contrasting colors enriches the imagery. Where we might use black and white, he uses red and white to symbolize the purification process brought about by the cleansing blood of Christ's atonement. Blood plays an intrinsic part in the Mosaic law, which was instituted to prepare the Israelites for their Redeemer. (See Lev. 8:30; Isa. 63:3; Morm. 9:6.) Note how in Isaiah 1:16-18 acts of repentance and washing (or baptism) precede forgiveness. (See Moses 5:6-8; 2 Ne. 31:13, 17-18.)

Isaiah concludes this section with a twofold promise: the people will be either blessed in the land if they give heed to the Lord's word or destroyed if they rebel against him. The Doctrine and Covenants contains similar promises. (See D&C 59:1-3, 16-19; 64:34-38.)

Although the Lord warns the Israelites of some immediate consequences of their wickedness, he still offers a promise of cleansing, forgiveness, and blessing if the people will recognize and obey him as the Lord of this earth (compare v. 19 with v. 3). This promised pardon is conditional upon their attitude and actions, however. But as the next verses indicate, Israel does not change her behavior, becoming instead even further entrenched in apostasy and wickedness.

Final Sentencing (vs. 21-31)

Structurally, the last section of chapter 1 can stand alone as an independent pronouncement. The Lord first addresses a very wicked Jerusalem, threatening vengeance upon those who become his enemies. He then foretells a purging and a restoration of Zion, and concludes by prophesying the destruction of the wicked. This pronouncement is divided into three segments in the King James Version (note the ¶ markings) which follow a chiastic pattern of negative-positive-negative, that is: warning first of wickedness and vengeance (vs. 21-24), then promising cleansing and redemption (vs. 25-27), and finally burning the wicked and the worldly (vs. 28-31). The primary themes of these three segments also follow the common and easily remembered pattern of apostasy-restoration-judgment. These three segments of the pronouncement will be discussed in turn.

Apostasy (vs. 21-24)

²¹Alas, she has become a harlot,
  The faithful city
  That was filled with justice,
  Where righteousness dwelt—
  But now murderers.
²²Your silver has turned to dross;
  Your wine is cut with water.
²³Your rulers are rogues
  And cronies of thieves,
  Every one avid for presents
  and greedy for gifts;

They do not judge the case of the
  orphan,
And the widow's cause never
  reaches them.
²⁴Assuredly, this is the declaration
  Of the Sovereign, the Lord of
  Hosts,
The Mighty One of Israel:
"Ah, I will get satisfaction from
  My foes;
I will wreak vengeance on My
  enemies!" (NJV)

The Israelite society has become so wicked that Jerusalem is compared to a harlot, quite a contrast from the "daughter of Zion" in verse 8. From verses 21-24, it is obvious that the people of Jerusalem do not heed Isaiah's admonition to repent. Consequently, they find themselves out of favor with God and subject to his wrath. Their sins include adultery, murder, graft (adulterating the silver with alloys), deception (watering the wine),[1] rebellion, thievery, corruption (accepting bribes), and injustice (oppressing the needy). Small wonder, then, that they should be counted as the Lord's enemies and worthy of his vengeance (v. 24).

One immediate fulfillment of this prophecy upon Israel was the invasion by Assyria and the forced resettlement of many Israelites in the far reaches of the Assyrian Empire. Also, according to Oliver Cowdery, the angel Moroni quoted these verses to Joseph Smith and told him that they referred to the Ten Tribes, who were scattered because of their apostasy. Moroni indicated that the next verses predict a future restoration of Israel. (*Messenger and Advocate*, Apr. 1835, p. 110.)

Restoration (vs. 25-27)

25"I will turn my hand against you,
And smelt out your dross as with lye,
And remove all your slag:
26I will restore your magistrates as of old,
And your counselors as of yore.
After that you shall be called City of Righteousness, Faithful City."
27Zion shall be saved in the judgment;
Her repentant ones, in the retribution. (NJV)

After purging the imperfections of her inhabitants, the Lord will restore Jerusalem as a righteous city with trustworthy leaders. And as promised in verse 27, he will save Zion with justice and the repentant converts with retribution (or righteousness, KJV). It will be a marvelous time when the Lord and his people (Zion, or the pure in heart) will be established in judgment and righteousness upon the earth. It will be a time of peace and joy for many, though some will instead suffer the consequences described by Isaiah in the last verses of chapter 1.

---

[1]There is a slight possibility that this phrase is a euphemism for "mixing with urine," since Hebrew has an expression "to throw water," which means "to urinate" (just as we use the phrase "to pass water" for the same idea). The Hebrew term for water, *mai'm*, can mean almost any type of fluid.

Judgment (vs. 28-31)

28But rebels and sinners shall all be
crushed,
And those who forsake the Lord
shall perish.
29Truly, you shall be shamed
Because of the terebinths you
desired,
And you shall be confounded
Because of the gardens you
coveted.

30For you shall be like a terebinth
Wilted of leaf,
And like a garden
That has no water,
31Stored wealth shall become
as tow,
And he who amassed it a spark;
And the two shall burn together,
With none to quench. (NJV)

In verse 28 Isaiah describes an event before the second coming of
Christ when the wicked must be separated from the righteous, the
tares from the wheat, and be consumed. (See Matt. 13:30.)

As verse 29 indicates, the sinners will be ashamed of the trees and
gardens they coveted. The oaks (or terebinths) and gardens might
represent either the worldly acquisition of property or idolatrous
nature worship—sinners in groves of trees. The Canaanites usually
worshipped their pagan idols in the groves and on the high places, and
they even considered some trees sacred.[2] Isaiah foretells that the
wicked will be like trees and gardens that wither away (v. 30).

Isaiah concludes his pronouncement in verses 28-31 by warning of
consuming fire. The original Hebrew does not clearly define exactly
who will be burned by this fire, but the King James Version implies
that the powerful idol worshippers ("the strong") along with the
makers of idols ("the maker of it") will be like tow (or kindling), and a
spark will ignite one and it will consume the other with fire. The New
Jerusalem Version (quoted above) suggests another interpretation.
"Stored wealth" (worldly possessions or idols) and its owners (mate-
rialistic individuals or idol worshippers) will destroy each other. In
either case, idolatrous practices and selfishness will bring the downfall
of those who seek after idols and worldly treasures. The fire could be a
literal burning on earth or a figurative fire in the spirit, representing
either the consuming fire of the Lord's glory (D&C 29:12, 21; 63:34) or
the sufferings of the wicked in the fires of hell (D&C 29:29; 63:54).

As illustrated above, numerous possibilities of meaning can make
comprehension of this important first chapter a challenge. In order to

---

[2]Further information on these trees is found in the "Scriptural Notes and Commentary" on pp.
83-84.

improve the reader's understanding of how Isaiah's words and ideas are organized, a detailed outline of chapter 1 is given below. Both major segments of the chapter, the introductory discourse (vs. 2-20) and the pronouncement upon Israel (vs. 21-31), are presented in a chiastic pattern of introverted parallelism.

A. Introductory discourse (vs. 2-20)
   1. The Lord's accusation (2-6)
      a.   The Lord speaks—Israel has rebelled (2)
      b.   Animals know their master's crib (food supply) (3)
      c.   Sinful people! (4)
      d.   People stricken—every head and heart sick (5)
      e.   Open sores everywhere are not cared for (6)
   2. Immediate judgments (7-15)
      f.   Strangers consume the land (labor of hands yields nothing) (7)
      g.   Zion is desolate after the harvest (8)
      h.   People are like Sodom and Gomorrah (blatant wickedness) (9)
      i.   Hear the word of the Lord (10)

Pivot point: For what purpose are your sacrifices?
             Obedience is better than sacrifice! (See 1 Sam. 15:22.) (11)
      i'. Who asked you to come to the Lord? (Haven't you heard?) (12)
      h'. The Lord rejects sabbaths, religious assemblies
          (hiding wickedness) (13)
      g'. No more harvest feasts accepted by the Lord (14)
      f'. Sinful hands raised in prayer bring no results (15)
   3. Promise of pardon (16-20)
      e'. People wash themselves clean (16)
      d'. Noble learning (head) and justice (heart)— oppression ended (17)
      c'. Promise of forgiveness to people (18)
      b'. If people follow God, they will eat food of the earth (19)
      a'. Rebellious Israel will be devoured—the Lord has spoken (20)

B. Pronouncement upon Israel (21-31)
   1. Apostasy (21-24)
      u.   Jerusalem and wickedness together (21)
      v.   Watered wine (22)
      w.   Greed for wealth (23)
      x.   The Lord will send vengeance on his enemies (24)
   2. Restoration (25-27)
      y.   Wickedness will be purged out (25)

Pivot point: The LORD will restore proper leaders
             God will restore to righteousness! (See Jer. 33:7-9.)
      z.   Jerusalem will be the faithful city again (26)

      y'. Repentant ones will be redeemed (27)

3. Judgment (28-31)
   x'. The Lord will destroy sinners (28)
   w'. Coveting for property (29)
   v'. Gardens without water (30)
   u'. Selfish ones and their wealth burn together (31)

Though there are many productive ways to study the individual verses and smaller segments of prophetic writings, one helpful technique is to compare parallel verses on opposite sides of a chiasmus, that is, to match *a* (v. 2) with *a'* (v. 20), *b* (v. 3) with *b'* (v. 19), *c* (v. 4) with *c'* (v. 18), and so on.

Remember that two parallel verses usually contain similar ideas or concepts, and that sometimes words are even repeated. For example, in verses 2 and 20 of the King James Version (*a* and *a'* in the outline above) three words are repeated: "spoken," "Lord," and "rebel." You will not find any two of these words, let alone all three of them, together in any other verse of chapter 1. Another example: the word "water" appears only twice in the chapter, in parallel verses 22 and 30 (*v* and *v'* in the outline).

Some parallelisms can be translated only subtly and indirectly. For example, in verses 6 and 17 (*e* and *e'*), the first verse in the parallelism mentions open sores on the body, and its corollary commands the people to clean themselves, which is an obvious parallelism. However, verse 17 then goes on to admonish the people to repent and cease to do evil, to clean themselves spiritually as well as physically. Looking back at verse 6, one might conjecture that the open sores are not just physical, but might also be outward manifestations of spiritual ailments. Thus, parallel structures expand and clarify one another.

Verses 7 and 15 (*f* and *f'*) comprise another indirect parallelism. Verse 7 mentions strangers bringing physical destruction upon the land, while verse 15, seemingly unrelated, describes the Lord turning away from the people. By carefully comparing the verses in their contexts and with each other, though, we realize that the fruits of sin result ultimately in both physical and spiritual desolation. Although the invasion of verse 7 endangers lives and brings destruction, the spiritual death described in verse 15 is even more serious. Also, in comparing the two verses, we see in verse 7 that centuries of residence and manual labor in the land will not profit the Israelites, for strangers will enjoy the fruits of their labors (or work of their hands). Likewise, their hands raised in prayer (v. 15) bring no relief, for the Lord will not answer them because of their wickedness. Although the parallelism of these two verses is neither simple nor straightforward, a little study and reflection can produce helpful comparative insights.

Three major gospel themes are intertwined within chapter 1 of Isaiah.

First, Isaiah teaches the basic principles and ordinances of the gospel. Granted, he uses distinctive terminology that often differs from ours today, but he teaches the same concepts. For example, he uses words like "trust," "know," and "obey" to teach faith in the Lord (vs. 2, 10, 19-20). Concerning repentance, he talks about "returning" or "turning back to the Lord" and "ceasing to do evil" (vs. 16, 18, and 27). "Washing" is his word for baptism (v. 16). And the gift of the Holy Ghost is literally "listening to the Lord" or "hearing the word" (vs. 2 and 10). He also admonishes Israel to follow some basic gospel teachings, such as obedience and sacrifice (v. 11), charity (v. 17), morality (vs. 4, 18), and commitment (v. 19). Other fundamental gospel concepts can also be identified in the first chapter of Isaiah through careful reading and study.

Isaiah develops a second theme throughout chapter 1, which encompasses the opposing verities of good and evil, obedience and rebellion, and blessing and punishment. He likes to stress the opposites incorporated within the laws of justice and mercy. For example, he says that if we agree with the Lord and obey, we will be blessed, but if we disagree, we will be destroyed (see vs. 19-20). This theme will be amplified in Isaiah's later chapters.

The third theme taught by Isaiah in chapter 1 concerns the changing relationship between the children of men and their Lord. The Israelites go through different phases as they fulfill the Lord's plan for them—covenant-making, apostasy, restoration, and final judgment. All of these concepts are presented in chapter 1 and elaborated upon in following chapters.

In short, while the first chapter of Isaiah may appear initially to be just a simple introduction, it contains many profound gospel themes, which are expressed in a structured, elaborate, poetic style. This single chapter deserves hours of study so that its message can be fully comprehended; it will edify and inspire those who read, study, ponder, and pray about it.

SCRIPTURAL NOTES AND COMMENTARY

Isaiah 1:29: "Oak" or "Terebinth" trees

The "oaks" mentioned in verses 29 and 30 of the King James

Version are usually identified as "terebinth" trees in modern translations. (See footnote 29a.)

The terebinth is common in the eastern Mediterranean area and is used in landscaping either as a decorative windbreak or sunshield. It also yields a resinous sap from which turpentine is derived. Groves of terebinths were also used in pagan idol worship because, among other reasons, the pagans considered these evergreen trees to represent perpetual renewal and fertility. Thus, in Isaiah, groves of trees were often synonymous with idolatry.

Therefore, when Isaiah says that the Israelites covet the terebinths, he is referring to either their coveting and yearning to have their yards and estates landscaped with groves of terebinths, or their desiring to use terebinths for places of idol worship. In either case, their longing for materialism or idolatry will result in drought and death, as seen in verse 30.

THE MOUNTAIN OF THE
LORD'S HOUSE IN ZION
ISAIAH 2

The second chapter of Isaiah is significant for a number of reasons: it contains many prophecies of the last days and the Second Coming; it is quoted in the Book of Mormon with important changes in the text; and it introduces a great prophetic discourse, which continues into chapters 3 and 4.

Chapter 2 contains a vision of the future (vs. 2-4) and a rebuke with a promise of judgment (vs. 5-22). It promises an attainable ideal while chastising the present wickedness of the people. Using directional imagery, it contains a call to Israel to "come down" from the false and worldly heights of men and to "come up" to Zion, the mountain of the Lord. Indeed, the contrast between the "top of the mountains" (v. 2), where the Lord's house will be established as a center of worship and learning, and the "tops of the jagged rocks" (v. 21), where the idolators will flee for safety, reveals the seeming similarity and yet ultimate distinction between God's eternal glory and the world's vain and transitory pomp.

The chapter begins with a brief introduction:

2 The word which Isaiah the son of Amoz saw concerning Judah and Jerusalem. (NAS)

One interesting point in this verse is that Isaiah "saw" the word he delivered. It is difficult to know how he "saw the word," whether he saw it written out on an actual scroll or in a vision of a heavenly book (as Lehi did; 1 Ne. 1:11-14).

A Vision of "the Mountain of the Lord's House" (vs. 2-4)

Interestingly, the first words Isaiah records in verses 2-4 of chapter 2 are also found with only slight variations in Micah 4:1-4. It may be that Isaiah "saw" the words of Micah or that he "saw" his own vision and Micah borrowed his words. Or, both prophets may have read the prophecy of some earlier prophet. Scholars differ in their opinions on which of these possibilities best explains the textual similarities. There is yet a fourth possibility, however, that seems plausible, particularly to Latter-day Saints: Isaiah and Micah, by virtue of their prophetic callings, each "saw" the same heavenly vision and were inspired to record it in essentially the same words. Since Isaiah and Micah were contemporaries dealing with the same people and problems, it seems likely that they would share similar spiritual manifestations. Precedents for this explanation exist elsewhere in the scriptures, because several prophets far distant from each other have recorded the same inspired messages: compare the "charity" sermon in 1 Corinthians 13 with Moroni 7, and the discourse on gifts of the Spirit in 1 Corinthians 12 with Moroni 10 and Doctrines and Covenants section 46. Certainly it is possible for two prophets to use the same vocabulary in recording revelations if, as the Lord said, "these words are not of men, nor of man, but of me." (D&C 18:34.)

The important point here is that these verses have authority, regardless of their authorship. They are authentic and prophetic, and carry a beautiful message concerning the Lord's kingdom in the last days:

2Now it will come about that In the last days, The mountain of the house of the LORD Will be established as the chief of the mountains, And will be raised above the hills; And all the nations will stream to it. 3And many peoples will come and say, "Come, let us go up to the mountain of the LORD, That He may teach us concerning His ways, And that we may walk in His paths."

For the law will go forth from Zion, And the word of the LORD from Jerusalem. 4And he will judge between the nations, And will render decisions for many peoples; And they will hammer their swords into plowshares, and their spears into pruning hooks. Nation will not lift up sword against nation, And never again will they learn war. (NAS)

The varieties of interpretation of these verses usually depend upon the location and identification given to the "mountain of the Lord's house" (KJV) described in verse 2. Though the fulfillment of the prophecy is clearly set in "the last days," the implication is that a mountain of the Lord has been established before on this earth. (For example, see Ex. 3:1; Moses 7:2-3.)

A mountain is, both literally and symbolically, the highest reach of the earth toward heaven. As Latter-day Saints draw closer to heaven during their worship services, especially those conducted in the temples of the Lord, they are reaching new "mountains" or heights of spiritual growth. Modern temples have been erected, to which many people from all nations flow to learn the ways of the Lord; temples serve in many ways as "mountains of the Lord." The Salt Lake Temple, constructed of granite from the surrounding mountains, could very properly be termed "the mountain of the Lord's house" or, in other words, the Lord's house made of mountain.[1]

The Kirtland Temple serves as a type, as does the Salt Lake Temple, of the last great temple to be built in Jackson County, Missouri (D&C 84:2-4; 110:9) when, in the last days, the Jews flee to the "mountain of the Lord's house" while the Gentiles flee to Zion. This promise suggests that the temples to be built in the last days in both Old and New Jerusalem will serve as the Lord's "holy mountains." (See D&C 133:12-13.) In short, all temples stand as a type of the paradise lost in this world, of the place of contact between heaven and earth, and of the final temple that this earth will become—the abode of the Father and the Son and their sanctified ones.

Numerous prophets and apostles of this dispensation have quoted verses 2-4 of Isaiah and related how the prophecy has been fulfilled by the Latter-day Saints going to the Rocky Mountains, building temples, sending out missionaries, gathering converts, conducting general conference sessions, and presiding over the Lord's kingdom.[2]

Jewish readers of these verses will, of course, find ready application of the ideas to themselves as a people. In fact, the possibility of a double application is even suggested in the Doctrine and Covenants,

---

[1]See DWW, p. 337, where, in the dedicatory prayer of the Salt Lake Temple, President Woodruff mentions fulfillment of Isaiah's prophecy. A similar identification was made during the dedication of the Idaho Falls Temple. (*Improvement Era*, Oct. 1945, p. 564.)

[2]Some examples: John Taylor (JD 6:167; 11:345; 21:32; 23:333), Joseph Fielding Smith (CHMR 4:129-30), Harold B. Lee (CR Oct. 1945, p. 47; Apr. 1966, p. 68; Oct. 1972, p. 63; Apr. 1973, p. 5), Orson Pratt (JD 14:350; *Ensign*, Nov. 1971, p. 14), LeGrand Richards (CR Oct. 1962, p. 109; Apr. 1967, p. 22; Oct. 1970, pp. 61-62; Apr. 1971, p. 143; Oct. 1975, p. 77), and Bruce R. McConkie (CR Oct. 1967, p. 43; MD pp. 518, 690, 691, 781, 855).

where the Lord commands, "Let them who be of Judah flee into Jerusalem unto *the mountain of the Lord's house*." (D&C 133:13, italics added.)

Another more liberal application would even identify the "mountain of the Lord's house" with the entire earth. The blessings described would then portray the gospel going to all the Lord's children in their individual nations. It seems that the symbolism of these verses can take on a broader meaning than one might initially think.

In verse 3, Isaiah promises that the law will go out of Zion and that the Lord's word will go out of Jerusalem. Realizing that most of Isaiah's writings, including this verse, are written in poetic parallelism, we readily see some parallels in the structure of Isaiah's promise:

Object	*Place*
The law	Zion
The LORD's word	Jerusalem

Before one applies these parallels to his own people, especially if he is inclined to believe that they apply only to his group, he should first go beyond recognizing parallelism to ask: "What *type* of parallelism is this?"

If the two phrases are synonymous, and if the reader assigns narrow definitions to the terms, he might assume that Isaiah's words are applicable only to him and his people. For example, a Latter-day Saint might consider both "Zion" and "Jerusalem" to mean "America," while a Jew would believe both terms to mean "Israel." However, if the reader accepts a wider range of possibilities, he can apply this prophecy to other situations as well. He would probably consider the phrases to be composite and consider that "Zion" and "Jerusalem" could have a broad range of possible applications.

In summary, there is nothing wrong in taking the words of a prophet and seeing how they can be applied to oneself and one's people. Indeed, one of the most extensive prophetic commentators on Isaiah, Nephi, specifically states that one of his primary techniques for teaching Isaiah included "likening" or applying Isaiah's message to his own people. (2 Ne. 11:2, 8.) One of the apostles from this dispensation, LeGrand Richards, is also noted for his lively and creative applications of Isaiah's words to contemporary Latter-day Saint events.

On the other hand, one should not maintain an extremely narrow view of the meaning of Isaiah's words. Until the Lord or his prophets say that "this way and this way only is how Isaiah is to be understood," readers of Isaiah should seek application of his words both to their own lives and to other people and situations as well.

A Rebuke of the Proud, Worldly Idolators (vs. 5-22)

Beginning in verse 5, Isaiah's attention shifts from the future back to his own people. He rebukes them for their pride and idolatry and warns of the sure judgment of the Lord. (Since there are a number of significant changes in these verses as quoted in the Book of Mormon, the 2 Nephi 12 changes and additions will be included in this text within parentheses as the New American Standard translation is quoted.) While reading Isaiah's rebuke, notice that some words such as "gold," "silver," "idols," "proud," "humbled," "rocks," and "holes" are often repeated. Also recognize that three major themes are repeatedly stressed: the people's worldliness, the Lord's vengeance, and the wicked's humility and fear. The first theme is stressed in these verses:

⁵Come, house of Jacob, and let us walk in the light of the LORD; (yea, come, for ye have all gone astray, every one to his wicked ways.)
⁶For Thou (O Lord,) hast abandoned Thy people, the house of Jacob, Because they are filled with influences from the east, And they (hearken unto) soothsayers like the Philistines, And they strike bargains with the children of foreigners.

⁷Their land has also been filled with silver and gold, And there is no end to their treasures; Their land has also been filled with horses, And there is no end to their chariots. ⁸Their land has also been filled with idols; They worship the work of their hands, That which their fingers have made. (NAS)

These verses provide quite a contrast from the first verses of the chapter: instead of the word of the Lord going from Jerusalem to the entire earth (v. 3), worldly paganism comes to the house of Jacob (v. 6); instead of Israel being the light of the world, she is darkened with idolatry and worldliness (vs. 5-8). (See TG "Light," "Israel, Mission of.")

Beginning in verse 9, Isaiah introduces the two other major

themes in this pronouncement—the Lord's impending judgment and the people's humility and fear. Note particularly in verse 9 how the Book of Mormon clarifies what would otherwise be a very confusing verse. The Old Testament seems to suggest that one should not forgive those who repent and humble themselves. The account in 2 Nephi, on the other hand, explains that the people did *not* humble themselves, and therefore were not forgiven. These wicked people are destined to experience the following:

⁹So the common man has (not)
    been humbled,
And the man of importance has
    (not) been abased,
(therefore) do not forgive them.
¹⁰Enter the rock and hide in the
    dust
(O ye wicked ones,) the terror of
    the LORD and His majesty
    (shall smite thee.)

¹¹(And it shall come to pass that)
    the proud look of man will be
    abased,
And the loftiness of man will be
    humbled,
And the LORD alone will be
    exalted in that day. (NAS)

Isaiah next gives a list of those with high, proud, and worldly aspirations whom the Lord will bring down:

¹²For the LORD of hosts will have a
    day of reckoning (upon all
    nations; yea)
Against everyone who is proud
    and lofty,
And against everyone who is
    lifted up,
That he may be abased.
¹³(Yea, and the day of the Lord will
    come) and it will be against all
    the cedars of Lebanon that are
    lofty and lifted up,

Against all the oaks of Bashan.
¹⁴Against all the lofty mountains,
Against all the hills (and upon all
    the nations) that are lifted up,
¹⁵(And upon every people) against
    every high tower,
Against every fortified wall,
¹⁶(And upon all the ships of the
    sea,) against all the ships of
    Tarshish,
And against all the beautiful
    craft. (NAS)

The Book of Mormon adds five phrases in these few verses, four of which stress the universality of the judgment that will come upon "all nations" and "every people," even the high and lofty ones (the proud) as represented by tall trees, mountains, and towers (vs. 12-15). The fifth addition in verse 16 is also found in the early Greek version of the Old Testament, the Septuagint or LXX. (See BD "Septuagint.") The sixteenth verse in 2 Nephi 12 consists of three phrases, two of which are found in both the Septuagint and the Hebrew Masoretic text (which the KJV followed; see BD "Masoretic text"). However, the same two phrases are not in both the Greek and Hebrew texts. The structure of the three versions can be shown as follows:

Three phrases of verse 16	in KJV	in Septuagint	in B of M
And upon all the ships of the sea	−	+	+
And upon all the ships of Tarshish	+	−	+
And upon all pleasant ships	+	+	+

Thus, it appears that the Book of Mormon contains the most complete retention of the original structure of this verse. Since the prophet Joseph Smith did not know Greek, and since there is no evidence that he had access to a copy of the Septuagint when he completed his Book of Mormon translation in 1829, this addition supports the fact that Joseph Smith translated the Isaiah portion in the Book of Mormon from a more authentic ancient text.[3]

Verses 12-16 emphasize the status symbols of ancient times. The "cedars of Lebanon"—symbols of strength, splendor, and glory (v. 13)—provided beautiful, fragrant wood for major Israelite buildings such as Solomon's Temple. (IDB 1:545.) The "oaks of Bashan" (v. 13) came from the wooded areas east of the Sea of Galilee and were an important local source of hardwood, often a rare commodity in Palestine. The high mountains with their surrounding hills (v. 14) and the high towers with their surrounding walls (v. 15) represent man's false trust in natural and man-made defenses. The "ships of the sea" (v. 16) represent the people's commercial enterprises, especially the "ships of Tarshish," which were noted for their ability to travel long distances, their strength as war vessels, and their large storage capacity as commercial carriers. (IB 5:186; IDB 4:333, 517-18.) The "beautiful craft" (NAS) or "pleasant pictures" (KJV, v. 16) were apparently the pleasure crafts or ships in which the wealthy traveled throughout the Mediterranean. Isaiah prophesies that the Lord will abase all these superficial symbols of wealth and power.

---

[3]In studying the available texts, it is often noticeable that the Book of Mormon quotations from Isaiah conflict with the King James Version in the same verses in which the Septuagint and Masoretic texts conflict. This does not mean, however, that the Septuagint and Book of Mormon renditions agree, for they usually do not. It does seem to mean that neither the compilers of the Septuagint or the Masoretic texts had a clear text to work with. The text of the early scribes was apparently already corrupt, and the disagreements in the later texts do not show what the original said, but they do show that there is something wrong in their texts. The Book of Mormon thus proves to be a valuable resource in restoring a more correct version of the original material. Until older biblical documents that have not been corrupted come forth, the Book of Mormon will have to stand as its own witness to an inspired version of the Isaiah passages.

In verses 17-18, Isaiah directs his attention to the people who have relied upon these worldly symbols. Echoing verses 9-11, he foretells that the proud will be humbled and that their idols will vanish in the presence of the Lord:

17And the pride of man will be humbled,
And the loftiness of men will be abased,
And the LORD alone will be exalted in that day.
18But the idols will completely vanish.
19And men will go into caves of the rocks,
And into holes of the ground
(For) the terror of the LORD (shall come upon them),
And the splendor of His majesty (shall smite them),
When He arises to make the earth tremble. (NAS)

Isaiah concludes his pronouncement with another description of the final fate of the wicked and their idols when the Lord comes:

20In that day men will cast away to the moles and the bats
Their idols of silver and their idols of gold,
Which they made for themselves to worship,
21In order to go into the caverns of the rocks and the clefts of the cliffs,
(For) the terror of the Lord (shall come upon them), and the splendor of His majesty (shall smite them),
When he arises to make the earth tremble.
22Stop regarding man, whose breath of life is in his nostrils;
For why should he be esteemed? (NAS)

The imagery of verse 20 is striking: the people will throw their gold and silver idols to moles and bats, animals who are blind from living so long in darkness. The irony of this is that people who understood the material value of the precious metals, and should also have seen the spiritual impotence of the idols, will throw these precious items to animals who will not be able to see them at all.

The endpoint of Isaiah's pronouncement is verse 22, in which he reminds the people of man's insignificance when compared with God's glory. (See Moses 1:10.) The prophet exhorts Israel to cease placing confidence in man and his status symbols and idols. Instead of foolishly trusting in himself, man should exhibit wisdom, since he knows that someday he will stand accountable before the Lord.

ISAIAH IN THE BOOK OF MORMON

A strong scriptural foundation was a valuable element of the Book of Mormon society. Lehi sent his sons back to Jerusalem to acquire the brass plates of Laban, which contained the Old Testament records that were then extant. (1 Ne. 3-5.) These records were used to teach the people in the New World, and the Book of Mormon prophets often quoted from them, especially from the writings of Isaiah.

From his dream of the tree of life, Lehi records how important the rod of iron was in helping the people reach the tree, or salvation. (1 Ne. 8.) Yet Lehi did not define what the iron rod was. Nephi later saw the same vision, and was told that the rod of iron represented the word of God. (1 Ne. 15:23-24.) Since Isaiah's words were used by Nephi and others to teach the word of God, it appears from the context of Lehi's dream that the writings of Isaiah were a primary scriptural "iron rod" that the people could grasp.

The ancient American prophets quoted Isaiah so extensively that one-third of Isaiah is quoted directly, and at least another five percent is paraphrased, in the Book of Mormon. As Latter-day Saints read and compare the Isaiah portions in the Book of Mormon with those in the Old Testament, they should also study how they are used and why they are important for a better understanding of both Isaiah and the Book of Mormon. The following five ideas suggest some reasons *how* Isaiah was used and *why* it is important in the Book of Mormon:

Accuracy

Since the brass plates contain the earliest known version of Isaiah, it is likely that they are more correct than the version recorded in the Old Testament or Dead Sea Scrolls. Accordingly, there are over 70 verses with major changes (almost four changes per quoted chapter) in the Book of Mormon quotations of 433 verses of Isaiah. That there are not more implies the overall accuracy of the transmission of the book of Isaiah in the King James Version. The nature of the changes, however, makes clear the fact that, indeed, "many plain and precious things" have been lost. (See 1 Ne. 13:20-42.)

On the other hand, many Isaiah verses as quoted in the Book of Mormon have no changes at all when compared to the King James Version. Latter-day Saint scholar Daniel Ludlow discusses this so-called "Isaiah problem" of the Book of Mormon:

> Translation is frequently concerned with general ideas rather than specific words; even the best translators do not translate the same material from one

language into another word-for-word the same. There appears to be only one answer to explain the word-for-word similarities between the verses of Isaiah in the Bible and the same verses in the Book of Mormon. When Joseph Smith translated the Isaiah references from the small plates of Nephi, he evidently opened his King James Version of the Bible and compared the impression he had received in translating with the words of the King James scholars. If his translation was essentially the same as that of the King James Version, he apparently quoted the verse from the Bible; then his scribe, Oliver Cowdery, copied it down. However, if Joseph Smith's translation did not agree precisely with that of the King James scholars, he would dictate his own translation to the scribe. This procedure in translation would account both for the 234 verses of Isaiah which were changed or modified by the Prophet Joseph as well as the 199 verses which were translated word-for-word the same. Although some critics might question this procedure of translation, scholars today frequently use this same procedure in translating the Biblical manuscripts among the Dead Sea Scrolls. (CSBM, pp. 141-42.)

Contextual Meaning

Another dimension of meaning derives from the various contexts in which the Isaiah passages were quoted by Book of Mormon prophets:

Book of Mormon Reference	Use of Isaiah
1 Ne. 20-21	Nephi quotes Isaiah 48 and 49 to Laman and Lemuel as a plea for them to recognize God and the prophets and to repent of their rebelliousness. He seeks to "more fully persuade them to believe in the Lord their Redeemer." (1 Ne. 19:23; see also 1 Ne. 2:12-13; 7:8-15.)
2 Ne. 7-8	Jacob quotes Isaiah 50 and 51 so that his people "might know concerning the covenants of the Lord that he has covenanted with all the house of Israel." He uses the citations as a springboard for his discussion in 2 Nephi 9 on the atonement.
2 Ne. 12-24	Nephi records chapters 2-14 of Isaiah prior to his own prophecy "according to . . . plainness" (2 Ne. 25:7), which deals almost exclusively with the last days and speaks considerably of a certain "sealed book." (2 Ne. 27:6-22.)
Mosiah 12-15	In addressing King Noah's wicked priests who claimed to understand the law of Moses, the prophet Abinadi quoted most of Isaiah 52 and 53, echoing the teachings of king Benjamin, who said that "the law of Moses availeth nothing except it were through the atonement of [Christ's] blood." (Mosiah 3:15.) Like the Jews, Noah's priests claimed to be keeping the law of

Moses, though they didn't understand this "law of performances and ordinances" and that "all these things were types of things to come." (Mosiah 13:30-31.) In short, the wicked priests did not understand that the law of Moses foreshadowed the atonement. Abinadi's prophetic commentary makes the messianic interpretation of Isaiah 53 perfectly clear. (Mosiah 15.)

3 Ne. 16, 20-22   While among the Nephites, the resurrected Savior quoted at length from chapters 52 and 54 to prophesy of the final triumph of Israel and the foundation of Zion on this continent and commanded his disciple Nephi to include his addresses and accounts of other events in the sacred records. (3 Ne. 23:1-4.)

Prophetic Commentary

Because "the Book of Mormon prophets interpreted the passages they used," explains Elder Bruce R. McConkie, "*the Book of Mormon is the world's greatest commentary of the book of Isaiah.*" He continues, "No one, absolutely no one, in this age and dispensation has or does or can understand the writings of Isaiah until he first learns and believes what God has revealed by the mouths of his Nephite witnesses as these truths are found" in the Book of Mormon. (*Ensign*, Oct. 1973, p. 81; italics added.)

The following chapters contain specific commentaries on Isaiah's messages by the Nephite prophets and the Lord Jesus Christ: 1 Nephi 22 (Isa. 48-49); 2 Nephi 6, 9-11 (Isa. 50-51), 25-30 (Isa. 2-14, 29); Mosiah 15 (Isa. 52-53); 3 Nephi 16, 20-21, 23, 26 (Isa. 52, 54).

For example, as the capstone on his lengthy Isaiah citations, Nephi presents a case study of how to study Isaiah in his own chapters of inspired commentary. (2 Ne. 25-30.) Introducing his "plain prophecy" and saying that the words of Isaiah he has quoted are plain "to all those with the spirit of prophecy," Nephi draws together two broad themes found in the writings of Isaiah before closing his own testimony with his beautiful "Doctrine of Christ" discourse. These two themes become the dominant themes of the Book of Mormon as a whole and include an affirmation of belief in the Messiah and predictions of events to transpire in relation to the Restoration, the last days, and the Millennium. The following is a brief outline of five major topics introduced by Nephi and later developed in his six commentary chapters, followed by references showing the Isaiah passages Nephi may have drawn upon for his commentary.

ISAIAH: PROPHET, SEER, AND POET

1. The Jews are scattered and a Messiah is promised. (See 1 Ne. 11.)

2 Nephi		Isaiah
25:7-15	Scattering of the Jews after rejection of the Messiah	8:14
25:16-21	Convincing of the Jews	11:11
25:22-30	All judged in Christ	9:7

2. A remnant is destroyed, but its records will speak from the dust. (See 1 Ne. 12-13.)

2 Nephi		Isaiah
26:1-7	Destruction of the Nephites by internal	5:24-30;
	contention:	29:6
	words—law (26:1)	5:24
	stubble (26:4, 6)	5:24
	consume (26:6)	5:24
	cast out (26:3)	5:24
	blood cries/anger (26:3)	5:25
	earthquakes (26:6)	5:25
	streets torn (26:5)	5:25
	whirlwinds (26:5)	5:28
	anger kindled (26:6)	5:25
	pain and sorrow (26:7)	5:30
26:8-15	Seed smitten by Gentiles	
	camped against (26:15)	29:3
	destruction (26:11)	5:25
26:16-19	Speak from the dust	29:4
26:20-22	Problems of the Gentiles	3:15
	Leaders err (26:20)	3:15; 9:16; 8:14
26:23-33	Gospel is free (26:25)	55:1
	No need to stumble (26:20)	8:14
27:6-27	Sealed book	29:1-18
	sealed book (27:7)	29:11
	words from sealed books (27:15)	29:11
27:1-2	Abominations	10:23-27; 11:4
	signs (27:2-4)	29:6-9
	last days (27:25-34)	29:13-24

3. The ways of the devil; his destruction foretold. (See 1 Ne. 14.)

2 Nephi		Isaiah
28:12-32	Wickedness in the last days	
	pride of leaders (28:12-13)	3:15; 2:12
	destruction (28:16)	10:25
	repentance (28:17)	2:9
	abominable branch (28:18)	14:19
	fall of devil (28:19)	14:9
	brought down to hell (28:21)	14:15
	woes (28:24-32)	5:8-23

4. Righteousness will be established. (See 1 Ne. 22.)

2 Nephi		Isaiah
29:1-14	God speaks to all nations	11:10
	ensign (29:2)	11:10

second time (29:1)	11:11
remember isles of the sea (29:7)	11:11
all in all (29:13)	11:13
God's people (29:14)	14:32

5. People will be rejoicing in God's judgment. (See 1 Ne. 22.)

2 Nephi		Isaiah
30:1-18	Millennial joy	11:5-9
	great division (30:10)	5:24
	covenant/repent (30:2)	8:14-16
	gospel declared (30:5)	2:1-5
	rejoicing (30:6)	12:1-6
	gathering (30:7)	10:21
	commence work (30:8)	11:11
	judge poor (30:9)	11:4
	destroy by fire (30:10)	5:24
	blessedness and peace (30:11-15)	11:5-9

"One Isaiah" Affirmed

Because some disputed chapters of Isaiah (those after chapter 29) that belong to the "second Isaiah" are quoted in the Book of Mormon, the sectarian "deutero-Isaiah" theory and other theories of multiple authorship are disproved. Because the version from which most of the Isaiah passages were cited and recorded was itself produced no later than 600 B.C., and because the resurrected Lord quoted from the later chapters of Isaiah (52, 54) and attributed them to Isaiah, it seems reasonable to assume that the book of Isaiah as we have it is close to its original form and is the work of a single prophet-writer.

Editing and Compiling

The brass plates were had among the people. Copies of at least some of the writings (including Isaiah) were made and dispersed among the people. (See Jacob 7:23; Alma 13:20; 14:2, 8; 3 Ne. 20:11.) Why, then, did Nephi, for example, go to the trouble of copying so much of the book of Isaiah in his own records?

After Nephi had secured the brass plates of Laban and made his own plates, he recorded that "he received a commandment that . . . *the prophecies, the more plain and precious parts of them, should be written upon these plates* . . . and . . . kept *for the instruction of my people,* who should possess the land, *and also for other wise purposes,* which purposes are known unto the Lord." (1 Ne. 19:3, italics added.) Nephi's shortened account of his father's prophecies, the eight-year journey in the wilderness, the subsequent sea voyage, and the initial colonization of the promised land comprise only seventeen of the fifty-five chapters in Nephi's two books! (1 Ne. 1-8, 10, 16-18; 2 Ne. 1-5.) The remaining chapters deal with his reasons for writing his own record (2 Ne. 6, 9, 19); his own prophecies, visions, and interpretations of Lehi's dream (1 Ne. 11-15; 2 Ne. 25-33); his commentaries on the Isaiah passages he quotes (2 Ne. 25-30); and the *eighteen* chapters of Isaiah he or his brother Jacob quote in their entirety. (2 Ne. 12-24, 26-27; 1 Ne. 20-21.)

The Lord prompted the extensive quotation of the writings of Isaiah in the book that is a compilation of prophetic writings preserved specifically for our day and edited by prophets who have seen our day (several of whom said they could not write "the hundredth part" of what could have been written—see Jacob 3:13; W of M 1:5; Hel. 3:14; 3 Ne. 5:8; 26:6; Ether 15:33). Nephi, the most prolific commentator on Isaiah, wrote, "I know that they shall be of great worth unto them in the last days . . . wherefore, for their good have I written them." (2 Ne. 25:8.) Apparently, above all the ancient prophet-writers, Isaiah will be the best guide through the perilous last days of the dispensation of the fulness of times.

In conclusion, Latter-day Saints who accept the Book of Mormon as the word of God have a scriptural perspective unmatched in all the world. The writings of Isaiah contained in the Book of Mormon, when studied together with the Old Testament version, give a deep understanding of the words of the ancient prophet.

SCRIPTURAL NOTES AND COMMENTARY

Isaiah 2:2: Why is the "top of the mountains" significant?

A mountaintop is an exalted, high place, both literally and spiritually. Since the "top of the mountains" might apply to the site of the ancient temples in Jerusalem, a study of that site on Mount Moriah reveals that it is in fact lower than the surrounding hills. (See Map 17.) The only immediate area near Mount Moriah without a dominant ridge higher than the mount is to the south in the area of the ancient village of Salem and the early city of the Jebusites and David. During most of the Old Testament period, the major populace of Jerusalem lived south of the temple mount, and thus they would always "go up" to the temple. However, Mount Moriah still maintains a position of relative height, since valleys immediately surround it on three sides (east, south, and west) and since it is located in the middle of Jerusalem. It also retains importance because it is a sacred site revered by Christians, Jews, and Moslems alike.

Since the phrase "top of the mountains" can also apply to the Latter-day Saint temple sites in the Rocky Mountains, it is interesting that although the various Utah temples are built in valleys, their elevation still exceeds that of Mount Moriah in Jerusalem. That is, Jerusalem, on the top of the Judean Mountains, is more than one thousand feet lower than the cities in the valleys along the Wasatch Front of the Rockies. Therefore, the Latter-day Saint temples in Utah are even above "the top of the mountains" when compared to the site of the ancient Jerusalem temple.

And, of course, the Latter-day Saint temples in Utah and throughout the world represent the tops of the spiritual mountains, where God's children can rise closer to him than anywhere else on earth. They are the place where heaven and earth meet, and thus are extremely important for the full spiritual advancement of the children of God.

MEN AND WINE, WOMEN, AND SONG IN
THE LAST DAYS
ISAIAH 3-4

Seen in their proper context along with chapter 2, chapters 3 and 4 of Isaiah form the last half of a curve that begins in optimism, descends into despair, and ends with an upward surge of hope. In language unsurpassed in scripture, the beginning of chapter 2 describes the millennial condition of Judah and Jerusalem. The chapter concludes, however, by moving backward in time to an awesome description of the storm that must precede the calm. Chapter 3 continues and expands the theme of destruction until, in chapter 4, a future of God's blessings and protection is again foreseen.

This cyclical pattern is an integral part of Isaiah's prophecies, for over a span of many centuries they are fulfilled and refulfilled—destruction and regeneration repeat themselves throughout history. Though the Mesopotamian conquest of Israel and Judah is the watershed period of Israel's early history and the historical object of Isaiah's prophecies, the attending circumstances of this destruction accompany all the judgments of Israel throughout her history and are to eventually culminate in the great destruction prior to the second coming of the Messiah, Jesus Christ. Thus, the Assyrian invasion of Israel during Isaiah's time and the Babylonian exile of Judah a century and a half later are only the beginning of a series of prophetic fulfillments. Though there may be and probably are other instances of prophetic fulfillment for chapters 3 and 4, three in particular find adequate support in the text: first, the time of the Mesopotamian conquest; second, the meridian of time, Christ's mortal mission; and finally, the last days at the time of the Lord's second coming. Thus, in chapters 3 and 4, Isaiah's prophecies of chaos, destruction, and vanity within Israel could be describing any or all of these possible periods of fulfillment.

Chapters 3 and 4 divide themselves naturally into three sections: 3:1-15; 3:16–4:1; 4:2–4:6. The following discussion of these sections will cover the historical context while suggesting other prophetic possibilities, especially concerning the last days.

In the time of Isaiah, when society was still predominantly agricultural, fertility of the land was a foremost concern. The opening judgment of chapter 3 is therefore particularly poignant:

3 For behold, the Lord God of
 hosts is going to remove
from Jerusalem and Judah
Both supply and support, the whole
 supply of bread,
And the whole supply of water.
(NAS)

In ancient Hebrew, the words "supply" and "support" ("stay" and "staff" in the KJV) are the masculine and feminine forms of the same root, *masen* and *masenah*. By using both forms, Isaiah seems to suggest complete destruction—spiritual, social, and physical. Thus, the prophet's language and imagery carry many implications beyond the threat of physical famine.

The threat of physical famine is most obvious. Removing the staff or support from a nation is analogous to suddenly taking away the props or stakes of a tent—the tent collapses shapeless on the ground. "The whole supply of bread and the whole supply of water" might be taken literally, since at both the first and second desolations of Jerusalem, the city was besieged and was at the mercy of a devastating famine. Jeremiah records in the seventh century B.C. that "the famine was sore in the city, so that there was no bread for the people of the land." (Jer. 52:6.) The famine was probably even worse during a second siege in 70 A.D., for the ancient historian Josephus records the story of one woman, gone berserk from the ravages of war and famine, who roasted and ate her own child. *(Wars of the Jews* 6:3.)

The warning of a spiritual famine is also implied in verse 1, since the symbols of bread and water often represent Christ, his gospel, and the Atonement. He is also the "stay" and "staff" of ancient Israel. (See Amos 8:10-12.) Indeed, the Lord is referred to as the spiritual support or "stay" of Israel throughout the Old Testament. Note Isaiah 48:2: "For they call themselves of the holy city, and *stay* themselves upon the God of Israel." (See 1 Ne. 20:2; Micah 3:11; Isa. 26:3.) The Lord is also associated with the Good Shepherd in the twenty-third Psalm, verse 4: "thy rod and thy *staff* they comfort me" (italics added).

Verse 2 suggests that this spiritual famine will be thorough and far-reaching, since Judah is to be without not only the presence of the Lord but also his servants, the prophets and priesthood holders:

²The mighty man and the warrior,
 The judge and the prophet,
 The diviner and the elder. (NAS)

This verse attests that Israel's predicament is serious, especially as one recalls the promise of the Lord recorded by one of Isaiah's contemporary prophets: "Surely the Lord God will do nothing, but he revealeth his secret unto his servants the prophets." (Amos 3:7.) If there are no prophets remaining in Israel, who will warn the people and call them to repentance? Israel will be left as "blind leaders of the blind. And if the blind lead the blind, both shall fall into the ditch." (Matt. 15:14.)

Next, Isaiah lists the social "supports," which are destined to crumble:

³The captain of fifty and the
 honorable man
 The counselor and the expert
 artisan,
 And the skillful enchanter.
⁴And I will make mere lads their
 princes
 And capricious children will rule
 over them,

⁵And the people will be oppressed,
 Each one by another, and each one
 by his neighbor;
 The youth will storm against the
 elder,
 And the inferior against the
 honorable. (NAS)

The enumeration of various types of leaders suggests that Judah will be bereft of everyone who possesses any true leadership talent, whether it be military, social, or cultural. This is exactly what happened at the time of the Babylonian captivity. Josephus records that during the reign of Judah's young twenty-five-year-old King Jehoiakim, Nebuchadnezzar, the king of Babylon, came against Jerusalem. At first Jehoiakim served Nebuchadnezzar to avoid violence, but he later rebelled, whereupon Nebuchadnezzar "slew such as were in the flower of their age, and such as were of the greatest dignity. . . . He also took the principal persons in dignity for captives . . . among whom was the prophet Ezekiel." (AOJ 10:6.) After Jehoiakim's death, his son Jehoiachim, age eighteen, ruled only three months before the Babylonians struck again. The result was much the same:

And he [Nebuchadnezzar] carried away all Jerusalem, and all the princes, and all the mighty men of valour, even ten thousand captives, and all the craftsmen and smiths: none remained save the poorest sort of people of the land. (2 Kgs. 24:14.)

With the leaders of society killed or taken into captivity, only the poor, weak masses remained. Therefore, the warning in verse 4 that "capricious children" or "babes" (KJV) shall rule over Israel most likely refers to people with childish understanding who will unsuccessfully face the challenge of bringing order to anarchy.

The warning can also be understood literally, though, since many of the Jewish kings before the Babylonian captivity came to rule at a very early age. Ahaz, Hezekiah, Amon, and Jehoiakim were all in their early twenties. Manasseh was only twelve, Josiah a mere eight years old, and Jehoiachim either eighteen or eight, depending upon whether the age recorded in 2 Kings or 2 Chronicles is correct. (See 2 Kgs. 24:8; 2 Chr. 36:9.)

Still another interpretation of verse 4 is possible. The children mentioned might represent those outside the house of Israel who came to rule over the Jews. Jesus said that the Father was able "of these stones to raise up children unto Abraham" (Luke 3:8); Joseph Smith later identified the "stones" as the Gentiles who subjugated the ancient Jews. (WJS, pp. 234-36, 294-95.)

In the midst of ruin and "childish" rule, Isaiah prophesies that the people will accept any sort of credentials as a prerequisite for leadership:

6When a man lays hold of his
  brother in his father's house,
  saying,
"You have a cloak, you shall be
  our ruler,
And these ruins will be under your
  charge,"
7On that day will he protest,
  saying,
"I will not be your healer,

For in my house there is neither
  bread nor cloak;
You should not appoint me ruler of
  the people."
8For Jerusalem has stumbled, and
  Judah has fallen,
Because their speech and their
  actions are against the LORD,
To rebel against His glorious
  presence. (NAS)

These verses are important because they reemphasize both the social breakdown of the patriarchal order and the extreme physical poverty of the state. That the man mentioned here should "lay hold of his brother in his father's house" indicates, first of all, that the father has disappeared and left the family in upheaval, for the son (by custom, the eldest) refuses to fulfill the duty that is his by lineage. The cloak, or *simlah*, which is the brother's so-called claim to power, is not a rich robe but is itself a sign of extreme poverty. In other words, the petitioner is saying, "You have at least some sort of cloak and the provisions necessary for physical sustenance, food and clothing." Without either physical or social "stays," it is no wonder that the brother declines a position for which he might otherwise be ambitious.

Verse 8 concludes one segment of the first section and includes the same double appellation, "Jerusalem and Judah," found in verse 1. Also, the title "LORD" shows up only in verses 1 and 8, indicating a "book-end match" between the two verses. In fact, these verses begin and conclude a short chiasmus.

Theme	Outline	Verse	Quotation (KJV)
The LORD will judge and condemn his people	A	1	"The Lord doth take away from Jerusalem and from Judah . . ."
Loss of physical sustenance; no food	B	1	". . . the stay and the staff"
Loss of military defense; no soldiers	C	2	". . . the mighty man, and the man of war . . ."
Loss of social order; no leaders	D	3	". . . the honorable man, and the counselor . . ."
Incompetent youthful rulers; role reversed	E	4	". . . and babes shall rule over them . . ."
Social injustice and oppression	F	5	". . . the people shall be oppressed every one by another . . ."
Children rule adults; role reversed	E'	5	". . . the child shall behave himself proudly against the ancient . . ."
Desperate dearth of leadership in society	D'	6	". . . be thou our ruler, and let this ruin be under thy hand . . ."
No one to heal the soldier's wounds	C'	7	"I will not be a healer"

No physical sustenance	B'	7	". . . in my house is neither bread nor clothing"
The chosen people destroyed	A'	8	"Jerusalem is ruined and Judah is fallen . . . their doings are against the Lord . . ."

The pivotal point in verse 5 highlights the oppression that the people will inflict upon each other. Under the severe circumstances, the people both condemn and punish themselves; they bring condemnations as they oppress others, and they receive their own punishment or reward as they, in turn, are oppressed by others. But these wicked people have more to fear than punishment from others—they await the Lord's judgments. The following verses, 9-11 of chapter 3, record what the Lord will do. These verses are important, for they both explain the reason behind Judah's desolation and foreshadow her eventual restoration. They also promise justice for both the righteous and the wicked:

> [9]The expression of their faces
>   bears witness against them.
>   And they display their sin like
>   Sodom;
>   They do not even conceal it.
>   Woe to them!
> [10]Say to the righteous that it will go
>   well with them,
>   For they will eat the fruit of their
>   actions.
> [11]Woe to the wicked! It will go
>   badly with him,
>   For what he deserves will be done
>   to him. (NAS)

What is the reason for Judah's destruction? She had sinned openly and flagrantly before the eyes of God, just as the Sodomites did when they proclaimed their unnatural lust directly and unabashedly to Lot's face. (Gen. 19:5.) Also, Judah had degenerated to a condition of sin not unlike Sodom's (though not as depraved), in that she had perverted sexuality through misusing it in the idolatrous fertility rituals of the Canaanites. Though this was done to insure productivity in the land, Isaiah warns that the wicked participants will reap only destruction, while the righteous will "eat the fruit of their doings" (v. 10). Verse 10 is the only note of hope in this pronouncement (vs. 1-15), perhaps to signify that the only way for the people to save themselves is through righteousness.

In verses 12-15, Isaiah repeats his earlier warning of social upheaval, suggesting that the leaders will be as weak as or will actually be women, an insult in ancient Israelite culture. This implies a dissolution of the traditional patriarchal social structure that was the norm of the time. Isaiah reaffirms that since the weak and wicked leaders will not mete out justice to the poor, the Lord will judge them and mete out their deserved punishment:

¹²O My people! Their oppressors are children,
And women rule over them.
O My people! Those who guide you lead you astray,
And confuse the direction of your paths.
¹³The LORD arises to contend,
And stands to judge the people.
¹⁴The LORD enters into judgment with the elders and princes of His people,

"It is you who have devoured the vineyard;
The plunder of the poor is in your houses.
¹⁵"What do you mean by crushing My people,
And grinding the face of the poor?"
Declares the Lord GOD of hosts.
(NAS)

In recapitulating the primary points of his earlier pronouncement (vs. 1-8), Isaiah concludes in verse 15 an intricate chiastic pattern consisting of a third set of ideas that parallel the chiasmus developed earlier. Outlined according to the earlier pattern, the verses look something like this:

Theme	Outline	Verse	Quotation (KJV)
Oppression upon the people	F'	12	". . . children are their oppressors . . ."
Reversal of traditional leadership roles	E"	12	". . . women rule over them . . ."
Social and spiritual chaos	D"	12	". . . they which lead thee cause thee to err . . ."
The Lord will defend the oppressed	C"	13	"The Lord standeth up to plead . . ."

106

| Wicked leaders have robbed the poor of their sustenance | B" | 14 | "... for ye have eaten up the vineyard; the spoil of the poor is in your houses ..." |
| The chosen people are crushed | A" | 15 | "What mean ye that beat my people to pieces ... saith the Lord ..." |

The "triple repetition" of this pattern (A-E) serves to emphasize one of the primary sins of Israel, the abuse of the poor and weak by the rich and powerful. The intricate chiastic pattern also emphasizes the oppression that the people bring upon themselves (vs. 5, 12) and the Lord's impending judgment upon the wicked and the righteous (vs. 10-11).

A judgment particularly upon Judah's women is outlined beginning in verse 16. This segment actually fits better with chapter 4, since it begins anew a cyclical pattern of destruction and regeneration. The final restoration at the end of chapter 4 comprises the first truly Messianic prophecy recorded in Isaiah.

Isaiah records several verses at the end of chapter 3 that simply enumerate all of the vain women's bodily ornaments, which the Lord will replace with tokens of desolation and humiliation. Isaiah's cataloging of the ornaments stylistically mimics the excessive and vulgar fashions of the day:

16Moreover the LORD said,
"Because the daughters of Zion are proud,
And walk with heads held high and seductive eyes,
And go along with mincing steps,
And tinkle the bangles on their feet,
17Therefore the LORD will afflict the scalp of the daughters of Zion with scabs,
And the LORD will make their foreheads bare."
18In that day the Lord will take away the beauty of their anklets, headbands, crescent ornaments,
19dangling earrings, bracelets, veils,
20headdresses, ankle chains, sashes, perfume boxes, amulets,
21finger rings, nose rings,
22festal robes, outer tunics, cloaks, money purses,
23hand mirrors, undergarments, turbans, and veils.
24Now it will come about that instead of sweet perfume there will be putrefaction;
Instead of a belt, a rope;
Instead of well-set hair, a plucked-out scalp;
Instead of fine clothes, a donning of sackcloth;
And branding instead of beauty. (NAS)

In addition to creating an imaginative and convincing picture, the prophet intimates the conditions under which the finery will be removed. Verse 24, for example, includes several distinct consequences of invasion and destruction: the stink replacing sweet smells could refer to the decaying flesh of those slain by the enemy; a shaven or bald head, sackcloth, and branding traditionally mark those taken into captivity. In short, these women who delight in their immodest exposure are rewarded with indecent and rude exposure at the hands of the Babylonian conquerors, who molest and rape, thus discovering "their secret parts." (Isa. 3:17.) That the destruction outlined in these verses will come through invading armies is supported by the last verses of the chapter:

> 25Your men will fall by the sword,
> And your mighty ones in battle.
> 26And her gates will lament and mourn;
> And deserted she will sit on the ground. (NAS)

Since Jerusalem has been invaded so many times, it is difficult to identify which destruction best fulfills Isaiah's prophecy. Since the warning of destruction is prefaced in verse 18 with the phrase "in that day," Isaiah could be pointing to a fulfillment in the last days. Some students of Jewish history observe parallels in the Nazi Holocaust. Also, it seems that the last verses of Isaiah 3 might even describe the effects of a nuclear holocaust. (Recent statements by the First Presidency indicate an inspired concern about the dangers of nuclear proliferation; see Bruce R. McConkie, CR, Apr. 1979, p. 133.) Of course, other disasters, such as disease, plague, or famine, could fulfill these conditions in the last days. Regardless, it does seem certain that at the end of chapter 3, Isaiah could easily be talking about the last days, because in chapter 4 he has definitely made a transition from an ancient, historical context to a latter-day, visionary one. Oliver Cowdery claims a modern context for the last two verses of chapter 4 because the angel Moroni quoted these verses to Joseph Smith in September 1823 and said that they were soon to be fulfilled. (MA, Apr. 1835, p. 110.)

Having already examined some events that would happen "in that day" (Isa. 3:18), Isaiah returns to the latter-day time frame in verse 1 to continue the "fallen woman" motif:

> 4 For seven women will take hold of one man in that day saying, "We will eat our own bread and wear our own clothes, only let us be called by your name; take away our reproach!" (NAS)

In their humiliated state, the women have abandoned coquettish, alluring tactics for a direct, pragmatic approach befitting their desperate situation. The ratio of seven women for every man probably' indicates a markedly high death rate among men, perhaps a result of the war described in Isaiah 3:25-26. Or, a higher ratio of men might exist during that period, but because of increased sterility among the men (perhaps through radiation) only an average of one man for seven women would be capable of removing the women's "reproach." Barrenness, the reproach these women wish to escape, was the greatest curse that could befall women in ancient times, since bearing children was their only means of honor. (Gen. 30:22-24; Luke 1:24-25.)

Another prophet, Wilford Woodruff, on December 16, 1877, received a vision of the desolation that would come; his vision includes a specific reference to Isaiah 4:1:

> I had been reading the revelations . . . [when] a strange stupor came over me and I recognized that I was in the Tabernacle at Ogden. I arose to speak and said . . . I will answer you right here what is coming to pass shortly. . . . I then looked in all directions . . . and I found the same mourning in every place throughout the Land. It seemed as though I was above the earth, looking down to it as I passed along on my way east and I saw the roads full of people principally women with just what they could carry in bundles on their backs . . . It was remarkable to me that there were so few men among them. . . . Wherever I went I saw . . . scenes of horror and desolation rapine and death . . . death and destruction everywhere. I cannot paint in words the horror that seemed to encompass me around. It was beyond description or thought of man to conceive. I supposed that this was the End but I was here given to understand, that the same horrors were being enacted all over the country. . . . Then a voice said "Now shall come to pass that which was spoken by Isaiah the Prophet "That seven women shall take hold of one man saying &C." (*Journal of Wilford Woodruff*, June 15, 1878, Historical Department, The Church of Jesus Christ of Latter-day Saints, Salt Lake City.)

After the period of carnage and desolation, however, will come the final and greatest renewal of life, the culmination of the cyclical pattern of destruction and renewal repeated throughout history:

²In that day the Branch of the
LORD will be beautiful and glorious,
and the fruit of the earth will be the
pride and the adornment of the
survivors of Israel. (NAS)

In contrast to the barrenness described in verse 1, everlasting physical and spiritual fruitfulness will abound. In ancient Hebrew, the word for "branch" is also a symbolic name for the Messiah, who will spring forth from the line of Jesse and, at this second coming, appear in all his glory. He will be spiritual food (fruit) for the "escaped of Israel," or the scattered remnants of that royal house. (A more in-depth study of this image will be found in the chapter on Isaiah 11.) The "fruit of the earth" that blesses the survivors of Israel probably represents the blessings of the restored gospel. Centuries ago John Calvin saw in this verse a promise that "a New Church shall arise" created by Jesus Christ himself. (*Calvin Commentaries* 1:152-53.) The Church of Jesus Christ of Latter-day Saints was founded by the Lord and bears his name, and therefore should be the "pride of Israel."

When the promise of the ultimate restoration of Zion will be fulfilled, she will be a tower of strength and a fortress against harm or evil:

³And it will come about that he who is left in Zion and remains in Jerusalem will be called holy— everyone who is recorded for life in Jerusalem. ⁴When the Lord has washed away the filth of the daughters of Zion, and purged the bloodshed of Jerusalem from her midst, by the spirit of judgment and the spirit of burning, ⁵then the LORD will create over the whole area of Mount Zion and over her assemblies a cloud by day, even smoke, and the brightness of a flaming fire by night; for over all the glory will be a canopy. ⁶And there will be a shelter to give shade from the heat by day, and refuge and protection from the storm and the rain. (NAS)

In the images of this final passage we see a tying together of the old traditions and their new forms in the restoration that, again, closes the circle of history and the pattern of these chapters: "Washing away the filth of the daughters of Zion" and "purging the blood of Jerusalem" recalls the ancient sacrifices in which the burnt offerings were rinsed to remove impurities, the cleansing atonement of Christ, and washings and anointings. In finally bringing all these elements together, the Lord will create the New Jerusalem, Zion. The Hebrew word here, *bara*, connotes an absolute creation or salvation through him who is the "author of salvation." (Heb. 5:8-9.)

The all-encompassing nature of this restoration is also suggested by the cloud of smoke and pillar of flaming fire that will cover and protect "the whole area of Mount Zion." In ancient times, a single pillar of smoke and fire rested only over the Holy of Holies, which was approachable by the high priest alone. Now, under the tabernacle or wedding canopy, the remarriage of Yahweh and his people, promised and prophesied in Isaiah and throughout the Old Testament, will be consummated at last.

PARABLE OF THE VINEYARD
ISAIAH 5

In chapter 5, Isaiah combines parable, warning, and promise together with poetry and irony in order to portray the Lord's work with the children of Israel. Although a self-contained message, this chapter reflects the themes developed in the first four chapters of Isaiah and serves as a transition between these chapters and the prophet's record of his vision and calling in chapter 6. In the parable of the vineyard, Isaiah illustrates that although God has done everything possible for his people, they still reject him; this can be compared to the Lord's tender appeals in Isaiah 1. Isaiah then lists Israel's major sins and warns of destruction, desolation, and scattering; this echoes similar warnings in Isaiah 1 and 3. Chapter 5 concludes with the promise of an ensign to the nations, a gathering of Israel, and a mighty army of soldiers (or missionaries) bringing peace to Israel; similar expectations are found in Isaiah 2 and 4. In short, this chapter summarizes Isaiah's earlier teachings and completes the set of introductory chapters.

Chapter 5 is easily divided into three sections:
1. Isaiah's parable of the vineyard (vs. 1-7).
2. A series of six pronouncements upon wicked Israel (8-25).
3. Promises of an ensign, gathering, and army (26-30).

In each of these three sections, Isaiah follows a pattern of first calling upon his audience and introducing his subject matter, then describing the Lord's dealings with them, and finally highlighting how the outcome of events is usually contrary to earlier expectations. Since this pattern of "identification/description/contrast" appears at least a half-dozen times in this chapter, it will be pointed out as the individual verses are quoted. The three components of the pattern will therefore be identified in the left hand margin of the quotations with the following notation:

I = Identification: Isaiah introduces and defines the group to which the message will apply.

D = Description: The Lord's work, power, or judgments upon the group are described.

C = Contrast: The initial expectation of the Lord or the people does not come to pass; indeed, the opposite usually occurs.

Section 1: The Parable of the Vineyard (vs. 1-7)

Chapter 5 begins with Isaiah's famous "parable of the vineyard," the most striking example of this literary form in the Old Testament. This form is echoed throughout the scriptures. (Jer. 2:21; 12:10f.; Ps. 80:8f.; Jacob 5; Matt. 20:1-16; Matt. 21:28-32, 33-44; Mark 12:1-11; Luke 20:9-18; 13:6-9; John 15:1-8; Romans 11:17-24.) Isaiah's parable is described by various commentators as "a little masterpiece," "a passage of singular beauty and grace," and "the finest example of the prophet's art and skill in the whole book of Isaiah."

Its structure resembles that of the joyful oriental songs of the harvest or vintage festivals. It begins as a "love song" of the master of the vineyard and moves toward a description of a walled garden and fragrant orchard similar to the one described in the Song of Solomon. (Song 4:12–5:5.) The master's efforts, however, result not in sweet fruit, but in sour grapes. Therefore, after soliciting community approval, he destroys the vineyard. The parable concludes in verse 7 with Isaiah's identification of its major terms and a summary of how they apply to Israel:

5 Let me sing for my beloved
   a love song concerning his
     vineyard:
I My beloved had a vineyard
   on a very fertile hill.
D ²He digged it and cleared it of
     stones,
   and planted it with choice
     vines;
   he built a watchtower in the
     midst of it,
   and hewed out a wine vat
     in it;

C and he looked for it to yield
     grapes,
   but it yielded wild grapes.

I ³And now, O inhabitants of
     Jerusalem
   and men of Judah,
   judge, I pray you, between me
   and my vineyard.
D ⁴What more was there to do for
     my vineyard,
   that I have not done in it?
C When I looked for it to yield

> grapes,
> why did it yield wild
> grapes?

> and briers and thorns shall
> grow up;
> I will also command the clouds
> that they rain no rain upon it.

I   ⁵And now I will tell you
D   what I will do to my
       vineyard.
C   I will remove its hedge,
       and it shall be devoured;
     I will break down its wall,
       and it shall be trampled
       down.
     ⁶I will make it a waste;
       it shall not be pruned or
       hoed,

I   ⁷For the vineyard of the LORD
       of hosts
     is the house of Israel,
     and the men of Judah
D   are his pleasant planting;
C   and he looked for justice,
       but behold, bloodshed;
     for righteousness,
       but behold, a cry! (RSV)

The parable is divided into four segments, each with an Identification/Description/Contrast sequence. Also, in the first and last segment, Isaiah speaks about the Lord and his vineyard using third person narration, while in the middle segments he shifts to first person where the Lord himself assumes the narrative role. A shift in form such as this is fairly common in Isaiah and other prophetic writings and is employed in order to draw attention to key themes of the poem or message. By shifting to first person and using the direct voice of God, the prophet reminds his listeners that he is delivering the Lord's message, not just his personal philosophy. Also, a pattern of third person/first person/first person/third person is a form of grammatical parallelism and chiasmus, which assists the audience to remember the prophet's message.

In the first segment (vs. 1-2), Isaiah describes the preparations of his friend for the vineyard. The master of the vineyard follows five steps to ensure a productive harvest: (1) choice of fertile soil, (2) cultivation of the soil, (3) selection of good stock, (4) protection of the crop, and (5) preparation for harvesting and storing the crop. His extreme care is evidenced even more in the original language. In Hebrew, the hill chosen for the vineyard is literally translated as "a horn, the son of oil," indicating that the vineyard was located on the summit of a very fertile hill. Special grapevines (*soreq*) were used instead of the more common variety (*gephen*). The *soreq* grapes produce a red wine famous for its bouquet and taste.

Other indications of the vineyard master's efforts include the clearing out of stones and the building of walls and a watchtower. He obviously anticipates a plentiful harvest because he also "hews" a winepress or vat in the middle of the vineyard. Such a wine vat consists of two basins or pits carved out of the rocks. The upper pit, where the grapes are trodden out, is shallow and large enough to accommodate the workers. A trench carries the pressed-out juices to a lower, deeper pit, where the wine accumulates until it is stored in clay jars or skin bags. The construction of this type of press is usually undertaken by wealthy landowners or by those who press grapes for many farmers. Thus, the fact that the master of this vineyard builds a vat in the middle of his own field indicates that he expects his harvest alone to justify its construction. To his disappointment, however, his vines yield only wild, sour grapes.

In the second segment of the parable (vs. 3-4), Isaiah speaks for the master of the vineyard and asks the people of Judah to judge between him and his vineyard. These people, of course, knew about grapes, and many of them owned and cultivated grape vines themselves. They would have judged the master correct in all his efforts and empathized with his disappointment in the small, bitter grapes.

Finally, the master resolves that he will destroy the vineyard (vs. 5-6). Rather than uprooting the vines and planting new stock, however, he tears down the protecting walls and allows animals and travelers to trample the vines. He then stops tending the vines and commands the clouds to cease their rainfall, thus giving the first indication that he has more power than a normal, mortal landowner.

The master's true power and identity are disclosed by Isaiah in the last segment of the parable (v. 7). The Lord of Hosts is the owner, and his vineyard is the house of Israel. His process of abandoning the vineyard exemplifies the judgments of God, who usually does not destroy or severely punish a wicked person; God simply leaves him alone to face the challenges of life and buffetings of Satan without the protection of the Spirit, whose withdrawal is adequate immediate punishment.

The justification for God's action is found in the last part of the verse—the people receive a punishment commensurate with their sins. Isaiah uses striking word play to highlight the irony of the situation. Through similar sounds in words of opposite meaning, he accentuates the contrast between the expected "justice" (*mishpat* in the Hebrew) and resulting "bloodshed" (*mispach*). And instead of "righteousness" (*tsedakah*), the people bring forth a riotous "cry" (*tse'akah*). A similar play on words in English is illustrated by the following translation of the last part of verse 7. This translation uses antithesis and alliteration to convey Isaiah's message:

The Lord looked for true measures, but behold, massacres: the
right, but behold, riots.[1]

This type of literary device had a profound effect on the Hebrews, for they felt there was a power inherent in words that are mysteriously linked by similarity and contrast.

The style of this parable, in which the audience unknowingly condemns itself with an early judgment, is sometimes called a "Trojan horse" story, for the speaker disguises his intent until the end. By then, the unsuspecting listeners have already passed sentence on the characters in the parable before realizing that they, themselves, are the ones being spoken about. This technique was used by Nathan as he described an unjust man to King David, who assented to his own guilt as he rebuked the wicked selfishness of the man. (See 2 Sam. 12:1-8, 13.) Similarly, Jesus used this technique when he confronted the wicked chief priests and Pharisees and compared them to the wicked husbandmen. (Matt. 21:33-45.)

The precise setting and background of this particular parable is unknown, although many scholars believe that Isaiah delivered it as crowds of Israelites assembled in Jerusalem during the annual Feast of Tabernacles (*Sukkot*, meaning booths, or huts), for during this joyous autumn holiday, many harvest and vintage songs similar to the song beginning the parable were sung.

During the harvest season, most Israelite farmers and their families moved into huts in the fields and orchards. During the eight days of Sukkot, which usually fall during our month of October, they decorated the huts with flowers and vines to commemorate the use of tents by their ancestors during the exodus. They also brought tithes, offerings, and other gifts to the temple.

Ancient Israel was commanded to celebrate Sukkot each year to commemorate how the Lord brought them out of Egypt to Mount Sinai and gave them his laws during the autumn of their first wilderness year. (Lev. 23:39-43; see also the description of the Feast of Tabernacles under BD "Feasts," p. 673.) By Isaiah's time, almost seven centuries later, the Feast of Tabernacles was corrupted by

---

[1]Modified from an example in IB Isa. 5:198.

pagan ideas and practices in conjunction with excessive revelry and merrymaking. The riotous celebration prohibited the Israelites from properly observing the true spirit of Sukkot and distracted them from the fasting and rededication rites they had performed just a few days earlier during the Day of Atonement (*Yom Kippur*).

The Day of Atonement was a serious time of prayer and fasting. Observed five days before Sukkot, it provided an annual opportunity for recognition of sin and encouraged the Israelites to bring their transgressions before the Lord and seek his forgiveness. It was a somber time of recommitment and rededication as they renewed their vows with the Lord. (See the description of the Day of Atonement under BD "Fasts," p. 671.)

Unfortunately, the Israelites quickly forgot their vows and lost the spiritual benefits of prayer and fasting as they drank, sang, and danced to excess a week later during Sukkot. This condition seems to be the context for Isaiah's parable of the vineyard; his song and analysis of Judah's sins (following in vs. 8-25) fit very well in this setting. The vintage song beginning the parable is in the mood of the Sukkot festival, while the didactic lesson at the parable's conclusion would remind the people of the commitments they made on the Day of Atonement.

Section 2: Six Woes upon Israel (vs. 8-25)

Isaiah's parable of the vineyard condemns Israel for failing to serve the Lord. Isaiah presents evidence for this accusation by describing six "woes" that illustrate Israel's wickedness and hypocrisy. He also pronounces three major punishments that are to fall upon the wicked—the desolation of their land, their scattering throughout the world, and the hell of spirit prison. He follows the pattern established earlier in the parable by first identifying (I) different models of wickedness and then describing (D) dire consequences or results that are in contrast (C) to what the people expect.

His first pronouncement of "woe and judgment" is found in verses 8-10:

I   8Woe to those who join house to house,
who add field to field,
until there is no more room,
and you are made to dwell alone
in the midst of the land.

9The LORD of hosts has sworn in my hearing:
D   "Surely many houses shall be desolate,
large and beautiful houses,
without inhabitant.
10For ten acres of vineyards

> shall yield but one bath,
C   and a homer of seed shall
>   yield but an ephah."
> (RSV)

This judgment falls upon wealthy landowners who buy up all the property they can until their lands border one another. This results in a monopoly of property that should be divided among others, especially the poor. This practice violates the spirit of the Law of the Jubilee, the property law of ancient Israel, which states that "the land shall not be sold forever." (Lev. 25:23.) Instead, land was to remain within families and clans as a perpetual inheritance. (See 1 Kgs. 21, in which Neboth refuses to sell his ancestral lands to King Ahab.) The hoarding of land described in verse 8 was in violation of this law, for when all property was purchased by a few wealthy individuals, there was no place for the original families to dwell. Having no homeland, they were forced to move to the cities or live on the property of the owner as indentured servants or slaves. Although drought, sickness, or economic setbacks might require a farmer to sell his land or indenture himself and family to cover losses, the Year of Jubilee every fifty years was instituted to correct the perpetual loss of land and the slavery of people by guaranteeing the periodic return of land to the original owners. Obviously, this law was severely abused by the landowners of Isaiah's time. (See Young, *The Book of Isaiah* 1:207.)

Verse 10 describes the impending judgment upon the property of these selfish landowners. As the cursed land loses productivity and refuses to yield enough to support the population, "houses without inhabitants" will be found throughout the land. The empty "houses" might be either literal dwelling places or figurative representations of families and clans. The emptiness, in turn, might result from either the drought spoken of in verse 6 or the impending Assyrian invasion and destruction mentioned in verses 24-30. Still, even without external interference, farm productivity generally declines when the poor move to the cities or remain as oppressed tenants of absentee landlords.

The meager harvest is graphically portrayed in verse 10. The phrase "ten acres" is derived from the Hebrew phrase "ten yokes," meaning the amount of land ten yoke of oxen can plough in a day. Ten acres or "yokes" would equal about five acres. (ABC, p. 642.) A harvest of grapes from this much land would normally yield dozens of gallons of wine. For the cursed land of Israel, however, this large area produces only one "bath," or from four to eight gallons of wine.

Similarly, a "homer" of seed (about six bushels, also called a "donkey's load") yields only one ephah of harvest (four gallons or twenty-two litres). The complete irony of the situation can be seen in this last comparison, since ten ephahs equal one homer. Isaiah is promising that the harvest will be only one-tenth of the original planting. (See BD "Weights and Measures.") Instead of the soil yielding thirty, sixty, or one hundred fold, it produces only a fraction of the seed originally planted. This is such a drastic contrast from what is expected that if a farmer wanted food for the next year, he would be better off not to plant at all.

Isaiah turns from the selfish landowners and addresses drunkards and revelers in his second "woe" and judgment:

I ¹¹Woe to those who rise early in the morning,
     that they may run after strong drink,
who tarry late into the evening
     till wine inflames them!
¹²They have lyre and harp,
     timbrel and flute and wine
     at their feasts;
but they do not regard the deeds of the LORD,
     or see the work of his hands.

D ¹³Therefore my people go into exile for want of knowledge;
     their honored men are dying of hunger,
and their multitude is parched with thirst.
¹⁴Therefore Sheol has enlarged its appetite

and opened its mouth beyond measure,
     and the nobility of Jerusalem and her multitude go down,
     her throng and he who exults in her.
¹⁵Man is bowed down, and men are brought low,
     and the eyes of the haughty are humbled.
¹⁶But the LORD of hosts is exalted in justice,
     and the Holy God shows himself holy in righteousness.

C ¹⁷Then shall the lambs graze as in their pasture,
     fatlings and kids shall feed among the ruins. (RSV)

The Lord here condemns not only drinking, but the riotous lifestyle associated with it (v. 12; see also D&C 59:20-21). Verse 13 tells us that this type of behavior leads to captivity and thirst. It could be a pronouncement of a physical captivity and destruction to come upon the people, or of a spiritual captivity that leads to "hell," with the idea of "thirst" representing a lack of the Spirit. (See Amos 8:11-12; John 7:37-39.) Verse 14 then promises a definite spiritual punishment: the word *hell* in Hebrew is *sheol*, meaning "grave," "underworld," "spirit world," or "spirit prison."

Verses 13-17 describe the judgment coming upon the merrymakers who are the subject of this "woe." But while verses 13-16 are quite straightforward in describing the humiliation to come upon the drinkers, verse 17 is a bit confusing. The destruction portrayed in the earlier verses has now become so complete that where the "vineyard of the Lord" once stood, lambs now graze. The "waste places of the fat ones" (KJV) probably refers to the now desolate lands of the once rich and prosperous. Some translations describe "kids" (see translation quoted above) or goats eating in the land, while others record that "strangers" will feed in the area. The term used depends upon which early Old Testament version is followed—the Hebrew Masoretic text uses the word for "aliens" in this verse, while the Greek Septuagint has the word for "young goats." An interpretation differing from the verses quoted above is found in this alternate translation:

> Then the lambs will graze as in their pasture,
> And strangers will eat in the waste places of the wealthy. (ASV)

The warnings and judgments of this verse echo the words given by Isaiah in chapter 1 (v. 7), and by Moses in Deuteronomy. Moses told Israel that the Lord was giving them a bountiful land for which they did not need to work. Because it was a free gift, he warned them to "beware lest thou forget the Lord, which brought thee forth out of the land of Egypt, from the house of Bondage." (Deut. 6:12.) He later promised them that if they did forget the Lord, then:

> The Lord shall bring a nation against thee . . . And he shall eat the fruit of thy cattle, and the fruit of thy land, until thou be destroyed: which also shall not leave thee either corn, wine, or oil, or thy increase of the kine, or flocks of thy sheep, until he have destroyed thee. (Deut. 28:49, 51.)

This is the first time in the Old Testament that this warning and its attached curse is pronounced. In Isaiah, the ancient law is again pronounced upon the people: because of their wickedness, their food will be eaten by grazing flocks, strangers, and foreigners. In contrast to the Israelites enjoying their own vineyards, outsiders will eat and drink the fruits of Zion.

As Isaiah continues his woes and judgments in this section of chapter 5, he progresses from the covetousness or selfishness of the first woe to the mindless revelry of the second, and finally to the deliberate distortions and wickedness of the last four. He lists these last perverted woes together and then pronounces a series of severe punishments, which include desolation, scattering, and eternal judgment:

I ¹⁸Woe to those who draw
    iniquity with cords of
    falsehood,
  who draw sin as with cart
    ropes,
¹⁹who say: "Let him make haste,
  let him speed his work
  that we may see it;
  let the purpose of the Holy
    One of Israel draw near,
  and let it come, that we
    may know it!"
I ²⁰Woe to those who call evil
    good and
    good evil,
  who put darkness for light
  and light for darkness,
  who put bitter for sweet
  and sweet for bitter!
I ²¹Woe to those who are wise in
    their own eyes,
  and shrewd in their own
    sight!
I ²²Woe to those who are heroes
    at drinking wine,
  and valiant men in mixing
    strong drink,
²³Who acquit the guilty for a
    bribe,

and deprive the innocent of
    his right!
D ²⁴Therefore, as the tongue of
    fire devours the stubble,
  and as dry grass sinks down
    in the flame,
so their root will be as
    rottenness,
  and their blossom go up like
    dust;
for they have rejected the law
    of the LORD of hosts,
  and they have despised the
    word of the Holy One
    of Israel.
²⁵Therefore the anger of the
    LORD was kindled against
    his people,
  and he stretched out his
    hand against them and
    smote them,
  and the mountains quaked;
and their corpses were as
    refuse
  in the midst of the streets.
C For all this his anger is not
    turned away
  and his hand is stretched
    out still. (RSV)

Through the preceding analysis of Judah's sins, she learns that she has abandoned the Lord and deceived others. Through the announcement of doom, she finds she will be abandoned to the most severe judgments.

The promised judgments are introduced in verse 24. Isaiah uses imagery to describe them, moving quickly from the metaphor of "fire" to that of "rottenness" and then concluding with a justification for these punishments. This style vividly impresses upon the listeners the rapidity with which the judgments will come, one after another.

Isaiah's final analysis of Judah's sins is aptly summarized in the declaration that "Israel has rejected the word of the Lord." Ancient Israelites first rejected Isaiah's counsel, and later generations continued to ignore the warnings of Isaiah and the other prophets. Isaiah recognizes that the root of Israel's weakness is the spiritual rottenness of apostasy.

Isaiah concludes the drastic punishments and physical manifestations recorded in verse 25 with a twofold promise that the Lord's "anger is not turned away" and his "hand is stretched out still." These parallel warnings appear to be synonymous and thus stress the fact that the Lord's judgment remains over Israel. On the other hand, the two ideas could also be considered antithetic to each other, meaning that although the Lord's punishment or justice hangs over the people, his hand is always stretched out to help them out of their desperate situation. If Isaiah had described the Lord's hand more carefully and revealed whether it carries a sword of vengeance (see Isa. 34:5-6) or remains open to aid Israel (see Isa. 11:11; 48:13; 51:16; and especially 59:1), then we could more easily understand what the outstretched hand represents. (See Isa. 9:12; 17, 21; 10:4.) However, Isaiah may have wanted this verse to have a dual meaning—the Lord's hand of anger will stretch out to the people until they repent and then it will strengthen and protect them. In any case, the hand of the Lord will bring upon most Israelites consequences that they are not expecting.

Section 3: Promises of Ensign, a Gathering, and an Army (vs.26-30)

Chapter 5 of Isaiah concludes with the prophecy of the Lord raising an ensign or signal to a people who will quickly assemble in Zion. The speed of this gathering is described and the contrasting conditions of light and dark that surround these events are illustrated in the following verses:

I   26He will raise a signal for a
nation afar off,
and whistle for it from
the ends of the earth;
D   and lo, swiftly, speedily it
comes!
27None is weary, none stumbles,
none slumbers or sleeps,

not a waistcloth is loose,
not a sandal-thong broken;
28their arrows are sharp,
all their bows bent,
their horses' hoofs seem like
flint,
and their wheels like the
whirlwind.

²⁹Their roaring is like a lion,
  like young lions they roar;
  they growl and seize their
    prey,
    they carry it off, and none
    can rescue.
³⁰They will growl over it on
  that day,

C

like the roaring of the sea.
And if one look to the land,
  behold, darkness and
    distress;
and the light is darkened by
  its clouds. (RSV)

Taken in historical context, these verses probably describe Assyrian soldiers in all their terrible power. They come with speed, need no rest, and do not even pause long enough to take off their shoes. Their weapons are ready, their roar is like that of the lion, and, when they lay hold of their prey, none can stop them. The destruction is so swift and complete that even in daylight, darkness (perhaps from the smoke of burning cities) and gloom (or defeat) hangs over the people. If these verses describe the Assyrian army and the fear and destruction it inflicted upon its enemies, this judgment was fulfilled upon Israel and Judah during Isaiah's day. In 722-721 B.C. Assyria conquered Israel, carrying the Ten Tribes into captivity, and in 701 B.C. she destroyed most of Judah and besieged Jerusalem. (See Isa. 36-37.)

In addition, the raised signal or ensign may represent the assemblage of a future spiritual force rather than an ancient political army. The ancient American prophet Nephi placed this chapter in a latter-day context when he quoted it in 2 Nephi 15. Numerous references in modern scriptures also tell of an ensign in the last days that will be raised up in conjunction with the Restoration and the gathering of Israel.

Zion in the last days shall be known as "an ensign unto the people, and there shall come unto her out of every nation under heaven." (D&C 64:42.) The word *ensign* means a standard or flag, a rallying point. The gospel covenants and teachings are one rallying point in a metaphorical sense—"to be a standard for my people, and for the Gentiles to seek to it." (D&C 45:9.) In addition, the powers of the priesthood, including missionary work, serve in this dispensation as "an ensign, and for the gathering of my people in the last days." (D&C 113:6.) Also, the religious records of ancient American prophets have come forth as a signal in the last days—Nephi testifies that the Book of Mormon will "hiss forth unto the ends of the earth, for a standard unto my people, which are of the house of Israel." (2 Ne. 29:2; compare Isa. 5:26.) From these and numerous other scriptures, we see that an ensign in the last days can refer to Zion, the gospel, missionary work, the gathering, and the Book of Mormon. (See BD "Ensign.") In short, the term *ensign* encompasses the Lord's whole work, and all aspects of his Church serve as his "standard" to the world, as these verses testify:

> Verily I say unto you all: Arise and shine forth, that thy light may be a standard for the nations; and that the gathering together upon the land of Zion, and upon her stakes, may be for a defense, and for a refuge from the storm, and from wrath when it shall be poured out without mixture upon the whole earth. (D&C 115:5-6.)

These two verses describe a general setting of danger and wrath in which the gospel light comes forth and the gathering takes place. The same gloomy setting and glorious promises are found in Isaiah 5:24-30.

As promised in verses 26-30, the nation and people who are gathered to Zion will come so quickly that they will require neither rest nor a change of clothing. During Isaiah's day, any long journey required frequent rest stops and resulted in worn out clothing and sandals. Yet today, missionaries and converts can travel great distances without getting dusty or tired. Apostles of this dispensation have praised advances in modern transportation, and some have suggested how these advances might fulfill Isaiah's words in chapter 5. For example, Elder LeGrand Richards says:

> Since there were no such things as trains and airplanes in that day, Isaiah could hardly have mentioned them by name, but he seems to have described them in unmistakable words. How better could "their horses' hoofs be counted like flint, and their wheel like a whirlwind" than in the modern train? How better could "Their roaring . . . be like a lion" than in the roar of the airplane? Trains and airplanes do not stop for night. Therefore, was not Isaiah justified in saying, "none shall slumber nor sleep; neither shall the girdle of the loins be loosed, nor the latchet of their shoes be broken"? With this manner of transportation the Lord can really "hiss unto them from the end of the earth," that "they shall come with speed swiftly." (MWW, p. 236.)

Whereas verses 26-28 vividly describe nations (or missionaries) coming swiftly and powerfully from afar and verse 29 says that they will seize their prey (or converts) and take them safely away, verse 30 provides a perplexing conclusion to this section when interpreted in this way. It says that the nations will roar (or speak with authority) against their prey "in that day" (or in the last days), and as one looks upon the earth, there is "darkness and sorrow, and the light is darkened in the heavens thereof." (Isa. 5:30, KJV.) The "darkness and sorrow" might refer either to physical or spiritual conditions as destruction and apostasy rage upon the earth. The light "darkened in the heavens" seems to suggest the gospel or the Messiah himself coming forth out of obscure darkness. The verse describing the contrast between light and darkness follows the verse in which the ensign is raised by the Lord to the nations. Whereas one would expect that the ensign (v. 26), the manifestation of the Lord's army (vs. 27-29), and other events of the Latter-day dispensation would bring forth glory and brightness over the whole earth, instead much evil and darkness will shroud the light of God's work in the last days (v. 30).

Summary

Isaiah skillfully combines his prophetic gifts and poetic talents in this chapter.

He presents three messages:

> Parable of a vineyard (vs. 1-7).
> Pronouncements of woe (8-25).
> Promises of an ensign and the Lord's army (26-30).

Each follows a similar pattern:

> Identification of group being addressed.
> Description of the Lord's work with that group.
> Contrast of the final results with the earlier expectations.

He deals with three major themes:

> A. Zion, her land and people.
> B. The Lord's work with his children.
> C. Punishments coming upon Israel and the wicked.

These three themes follow each other in a chiastic pattern, A-B-C-B-C-B-C-B-A, with the second half of the parallelism (C-B-C-B-A) repeated for further emphasis. This pattern can be outlined as follows:

A. Zion prepared as a fruitful hill (vs. 1-2)
B. The Lord and his vineyard to be judged (3-4)
C. Destruction upon Zion (5-6)
B. The Lord's expected justice not received (7)
C. Woe to the selfish
   Emptiness in the land
   Woe to the drunkards (8-12a)
B. The Lord's works not considered (12b)
C. Scattering and spirit prison (13-15)
B. The Lord's sentence to be pronounced (16)
A. Zion desolated as grazing lands (17)

C. Woe to the sinners (18)
B. The Lord's second coming solicited (19)
C. Woe to the deceivers; destruction coming (20-24a)
B. The Lord's judgment and anger to come (24b-25)
A. Zion restored (or attacked) as missionaries travel (or armies invade) (26-30)

The last few verses also contain the three major themes:

A. Zion gathered through an ensign (the gospel) (vs. 26)
B. The Lord's army comes with speed and power (27-29)
C. Darkness in the land as the "light" shines forth (30)

In conclusion, Isaiah combines various modes and patterns of speech to instruct the Israelites concerning the Lord's efforts with them and other people upon the earth. And although a punitive mood dominates the chapter, Isaiah still conveys God's loving care for his children, promising a time of restoration and gathering when the light of the Lord's gospel will shine through the darkness.

A DELIBERATELY DIFFICULT PROPHET
ISAIAH 6

Perilous times faced Isaiah and his people as he began his prophetic ministry. Politically, the situation was unstable following the death of King Uzziah, who had ruled Judah for over fifty years, and Assyrian expansion threatened the peace in the area. Socially, poverty and oppression fell upon many Israelites as the wealthy increased their power. Spiritually, many Israelites continued to observe traditional religious practices but with their hearts turned away from the Lord. A prophet's role is challenging in the best of circumstances, but Isaiah's was particularly difficult because of the problems he faced.

In what is now chapter 6 of his writings, Isaiah records the foundation of his prophetic calling. He describes his vision of the Lord and the purpose of his mission to Israel. He testifies to the people concerning the holiness and glory of God and also explains why his prophetic role of speaking for the Lord to the people is so difficult.

There are many possible explanations as to why this sixth chapter of Isaiah is not placed at the head of his writings. Perhaps Isaiah wanted to introduce his message before he introduced himself; after delivering the important pronouncements found in the first five chapters, he wanted to provide a seal for his words by testifying concerning his prophetic authority. Or, it may even be that the vision and calling recorded in chapter 6 came to Isaiah after the visions of the first few chapters.

Or, chapter 6 may be where it is to bridge the two major segments of his opening chapters. The first section of Isaiah, chapters 1-12, contains two major themes: the unrighteousness of the Israelites, and the promise of a new Zion in the last days. The first five chapters emphasize Israel's separation from the "master of the vineyard," while chapters 7-12 promise deliverance and the millennial day. Both themes are epitomized by Isaiah himself in chapter 6; he fears the

Lord's judgment because of his own sins and yet is willing to serve the Lord because he knows that a latter-day remnant of Israel will believe and understand his prophecies.

Since Isaiah did not date most of his prophecies and pronouncements, we do not know the proper chronological placement of chapter 6 in relation to the other Isaiah chapters. Some scholars believe this was not Isaiah's original call into the prophetic ministry, but a calling to higher responsibilities. The examples of Elisha in the Old Testament (1 Kgs. 19:19; 2 Kgs. 2), Peter in the New Testament (Matt. 4:18; 16:13-20; 28:19; Acts 2:1-3), and Spencer W. Kimball in this dispensation (SWK, pp. 188, 237) illustrate how some of the Lord's servants have received new responsibilities or divine manifestations months and even years after they were first called.

Other scholars argue that chapter 6 records Isaiah's original call to his prophetic ministry. To them, Isaiah's feelings of unworthiness in verse 5 seem more appropriate to an inaugural call than to an additional, higher calling. For a modern example, compare Spencer W. Kimball's feelings when he was first called to the apostleship with his later feelings when he was given additional responsibility for the Lamanites. (SWK, pp. 189-95, 236-38.)

Whether the vision and calling recorded in Isaiah 6 highlight Isaiah's initial call or represent newer and higher responsibilities in his prophetic role, they attest to his importance as a servant of the Lord. If the events of this chapter did not begin Isaiah's ministry, they probably occurred early in his career. In any case, the full authority of a prophet did not accrue to Isaiah because of this vision. His actual power and authority as a prophet came through proper priesthood channels as he was ordained and set apart for his prophetic role. (See Deut. 34:9; Jer. 1:5; Acts 16:4; Heb. 5:4; Ex. 40:13.) Although Isaiah's actual ordination is not recorded in his own work, chapter 6 describes why he was worthy and willing and also foreshadows how the people would respond to his warnings.

Chapter 6 divides easily into two parts: Isaiah's vision of the Lord, and his prophetic commission. It can be outlined as follows:

I. The vision (vs. 1-7)
  A. The Lord's court (1-4)
    1. The Lord is seated upon his throne (1)
    2. The seraphim praise the Lord (2-4)
  B. Isaiah's cleansing (5-7)
    1. Isaiah shows humility in the divine presence (5)
    2. A seraph purges away Isaiah's guilt (6-7)

II. The call (8-13)
    A. Isaiah volunteers: "Here am I; send me" (8)
    B. Isaiah's prophetic commission (9-13)
        1. This people will not understand (9-10)
        2. His words will remain unclear until after Israel is emptied (11-12)
        3. A remnant shall return and understand his words (13)

According to verse 1, Isaiah received his vision of the Lord in the year of King Uzziah's death, around 740 B.C. Political conditions were unstable in both Israel and Judah at this time. For example, three men—Uzziah, Jotham (Uzziah's son), and Ahaz (Uzziah's grandson)—were all ruling Judah immediately prior to Uzziah's death.

But chapter 6 makes only brief mention of the political events of the time, concentrating instead upon Isaiah's experience with the Lord. In reading the account of Isaiah's vision, one should carefully note what he first sees and how his attention shifts to other beings and objects:

6 In the year that King Uzziah died, I beheld my LORD seated on a high and lofty throne; and the skirts of His robe filled the Temple. ²Seraphs stood in attendance on Him. Each of them had six wings: with two he covered his face, with two he covered his legs, and with two he would fly.

³And one would call to the other,
"Holy, holy, holy!
The LORD of Hosts!
His presence fills all the earth!"

⁴The doorposts would shake at the sound of the one who called, and the House kept filling with smoke. (NJV)

The first thing to attract Isaiah's attention is the Lord himself. Only later does Isaiah notice the interesting furniture, clothing, and seraphs.

Some commentators wonder whether Isaiah actually saw the Lord or just some evidence of Jehovah's presence, since Isaiah does not actually describe the Lord's person but talks about the hem of his garment, the seraphim, his voice, and so on. However, Isaiah himself simply declares, "I saw the Lord," and other ancient and modern prophets testify that Jehovah has appeared to many prophets. (See 2 Ne. 11:2; DS 1:27.)

Many similarities exist between the images of Isaiah's vision and the symbols of the temple service. The Lord's robe or train compares to the temple veil which separates us from God's direct glory. The seraphim are like temple attendants, calling to one another in a threefold petition (v. 2). The moving door posts (v. 4) suggest a stirring at the veil. Isaiah receiving a live coal from the temple altar (v. 6) reminds us of the eternal life promised to those who keep the covenants made at the temple altars. (See D&C 130:6-11.) If not during this vision of the Lord, at some time during his life Isaiah received the fullness of the priesthood and the temple blessings, including the assurance of eternal life, for he has become an "heir of the celestial kingdom" and enjoys eternity in the Lord's house. (D&C 137:7; 138:42, 51.)

After depicting the Lord in his glory, Isaiah describes special beings who attend the Lord. These seraphim (or seraphs[1]) are such unusual creatures that Isaiah carefully describes their three sets of wings and their manner of praising the Lord. The wings could be symbols of the ability of God's spirit children to move freely throughout his kingdom (see D&C 77:4; MD, pp. 702-3), though they are probably literal wings upon real animal-like entities that reside in God's presence. (See BD "Seraphim.") Many animals and plants live in God's kingdom, and some creatures communicate with God and man. John the Revelator saw and heard such animals in God's presence (Rev. 5:13), and Joseph Smith recorded how these animals praised and glorified God. (TPJS, pp. 291-92.)

Joseph Smith also describes seraphs in God's presence in the dedicatory prayer of the Kirtland Temple, and his record of them in Doctrine and Covenants 109:79 has some similarity to Isaiah's account:

> And help us by the power of thy spirit, that we may mingle our voices with those bright, shining *seraphs around thy throne,* with *acclamations of praise,* singing Hosanna to God and the Lamb! (Italics added.)

Both Isaiah and Joseph Smith envision the seraphs near God's throne, and both record that the seraphs give praise to God.

There are some differences between the two accounts as well. Isaiah says that the seraphs have wings and hands and that they move about. (Isa. 6:6.) Joseph records that they are bright, shining beings. This description fits very well with the Hebrew root of *seraph,* which means "burning." Thus *seraphim* would be the "burning ones," those who appear to be on fire; or, as Joseph describes them, "bright, shining seraphs."

---

[1]The KJV "seraphims" is a grammatical error, since it uses a double plural. The Hebrew plural is the *im* ending. To add the *s* is comparable to taking group plurals, such as *mice* or *geese* and making them double plurals, *mices* or *geeses.*

Joseph Smith also taught that God dwells in everlasting burnings and that righteous beings (animal and human) dwell with him in a place of continual burning or glory. (TPJS, pp. 372-73, 347, 361.) Other apostles of this dispensation have also taught that all celestial beings need to be able to endure eternal burnings. (See COR, p. 275; MD, pp. 116, 695-97.) The seraphs, celestial beings in God's presence, are therefore necessarily bright, shining, and burning beings. (See D&C 38:1.) In Isaiah's account, they are associated with an altar, burning coals, and a cleansing process. (Isa. 6:5-7.) Other than the descriptions mentioned above, however, very little is known about them.

Following his brief explanation of the seraphim, Isaiah describes a door whose posts (or foundations) moved as one seraph spoke. These could be the posts of the doorway leading into the Holy of Holies of the Jerusalem temple, or the heavenly doorway that leads into God's presence. In either case, that there is a door or gateway into the divine presence is a concept that is also suggested in other scriptures. (John 10; 2 Ne. 9:41; Isa. 22:22.)

Recognizing that he is in the presence of the Lord, the reality of his own mortal weaknesses strikes Isaiah, and he records:

⁵I cried,
"Woe is me; I am lost!
For I am a man of unclean lips
And I live among a people
Of unclean lips;
Yet my own eyes have beheld
the King LORD of Hosts."

⁶Then one of the seraphs flew over to me with a live coal, which he had taken from the altar with a pair of tongs. ⁷He touched it to my lips and declared,

"Now that this has touched your lips,
Your guilt shall depart
And your sin be purged away."
(NJV)

Isaiah's first response is fear: "Woe is me!" It is doubtful that Isaiah's earlier life was grossly sinful or corrupt. More likely, his confession of sin came from his deep humility resulting from suddenly finding himself in the divine presence. (See JS-H 1:28-29.) It is not unusual for people to experience such feelings of unworthiness, impending judgment, and possible destruction when they are visited by an angel, hear the Lord's voice, or see God in a vision. Often, the first message given them is either "Fear not" or "Peace be with you." After this, they usually feel free from guilt and soon realize that the visitation or vision is to be a blessing, not a condemnation. (See Ex. 3:6; Judg. 6:22-23; Moses 6:31-32; Hel. 5:43-48; JS-H 1:17.) Similarly, Isaiah's fear of unworthiness in the Lord's presence is quickly dispelled by a symbolic act of forgiveness.

The live coal (v. 6) that touches Isaiah's lips symbolizes the purging of his sins, just as our ordinances of baptism and the sacrament physically represent acts of spiritual power. (See Isa. 6, footnote 6a.) The coal could have come from the altar of burnt offerings outside the temple, but it could also have been the stone on the altar of incense inside the temple. The latter is more likely, since the Hebrew word for "live coal" is *ritzpah*, which is often translated as "stone," particularly as "glowing (incandescent) stone." In the ancient temple service, the incense was placed on a stone to be burned. (See Young, *The Book of Isaiah* 1:250.) Regardless of whether the coal (or stone) came from an altar outside or inside the temple, or whether the temple was in Jerusalem or in God's presence, the important fact is that the coal represents divine fire and the cleansing power of the Atonement. By touching Isaiah's lips, the cleansing object not only purges him from being "a man of unclean lips," but it also consecrates him to speak in righteousness as a mouthpiece of the Lord. (See Jer. 1:9.)

Now worthy to be with God, Isaiah hears God's own voice addressing an unmentioned audience, probably a celestial council:

8Then I heard the voice of my Lord
saying, "Whom shall I send? Who
will go for us?" And I said, "Here
am I; send me."

Isaiah volunteers for the calling even before it is directly offered to him; his acceptance echoes Jehovah's own response to a similar invitation in the heavenly councils of the premortal existence. (See Abr. 3:27.) Isaiah's answer to God's call is as simple as the call itself. The Lord asks, "Whom shall I send, and who will go for us?" Isaiah replies, "Here am I; send me." Although some great prophets, like Enoch, Moses, and Jeremiah, were initially reluctant to accept their prophetic calling, Isaiah responds without hesitation. (See Moses 6, Ex. 4, Jer. 1.) His willing attitude testifies to his greatness.

After Isaiah commits himself, God gives him further instruction about his calling (vs. 9-10). In contrast to the simplicity of the initial call, the Lord's directive raises many questions as to how Isaiah should preach to the people:

⁹And He said, "Go, say to that people:
  'Hear, indeed, but do not understand;
  See, indeed, but do not grasp.'
¹⁰Dull that people's mind,
  Stop its ears,
And seal its eyes—
Lest, seeing with its eyes
And hearing with its ears,
It also grasp with its mind,
And repent and save [heal]
  itself." (NJV)

The ambiguity of verse 9 is easily clarified if the additional pronouns in the Book of Mormon translation (2 Ne. 16:9) of this verse are combined with the modern punctuation and verb structure of the New Jewish Version:

Quotation	Details
And he [the Lord] said [to Isaiah],	introduction
"Go and tell this people:	charge to Isaiah
'Hear ye indeed,'	Isaiah's admonition
but they will not understand; and	people's response
'See ye indeed,'	Isaiah's admonition
but they will not perceive."	people's response

In other words, the Lord tells Isaiah that although he (Isaiah) will speak forthrightly to the people, they will not understand his message.

The complex charge given to Isaiah in verse 10 is more difficult to understand. In casual reading, it appears that Isaiah is told to deliberately confuse the people because the Lord does not want them to repent and be healed. Actually, Isaiah's words were to be incomprehensible not because the Lord desired the people to be ignorant, but because they, themselves, did not want to know the truth or to be converted and healed. The early Hebrew versions of this verse, and Christ's use of it in the New Testament, suggest this interpretation.

Lest That People Should Heal Itself

The earliest Hebrew versions of this verse, as found in the Dead Sea Scrolls and Masoretic texts, are translated quite correctly in the New Jewish Version quoted above. The New Jewish Version corresponds closely to the King James Version, although a slightly different vocabulary is used. An important difference between these two English versions, however, is that the New Jewish Version includes the word "itself" at the end of the verse ("lest that people . . . repent and save *itself*") while the King James Version simply states, "lest [this people] . . . convert, and be healed." The act of repenting (or converting) and being healed is the same in both versions, but the *source* of the healing differs. In the Hebrew and the New Jewish Version, the verse states that the people might try to heal themselves, which is impossible, especially in a spiritual context, since healing and forgiveness come only through Christ's atonement, after anything we can do for ourselves. With our free agency, we seek to avail ourselves of the saving power and healing power of the Atonement, but we do not have within us the capacity to completely cleanse ourselves. (See 2 Ne. 2:27; 25:23; D&C 58:28; Heb. 14:29-30; Alma 12:9-11; 1 Cor. 2:9-10, 12, 14; D&C 76:10.)

Speaking in Parables

Another explanation of why Isaiah's words are deliberately difficult is found in the New Testament. Both Jesus and the Apostle Paul used the language of Isaiah 6:10 to describe the Jews in their day who refused to hear and give heed to the gospel truths. (See Matt. 13:15; Acts 28:25-28.) Jesus' application of this verse is especially valuable, because with it he describes his own methods of teaching Israel.

Jesus used the parable as his primary teaching medium. On one occasion, when his disciples asked him why he taught in parables (Matt. 13:10), he responded that parables would enable his disciples to learn as much as they were prepared to understand, even the mysteries of the kingdom of heaven. But those who rejected the truth would not understand the true meaning of the parables and would thus avoid condemnation. (See Matt. 13:11-13; Matt. 13, footnote 12a.) Jesus then quoted from Isaiah, saying that Isaiah's words were fulfilled in the people of his day. The Jews did not understand the Lord's words because they closed themselves off from his message, "lest ... they ... should be converted and I [Jesus] should heal them." (Matt. 13:14-15; compare Mark 4:9-13; Luke 8:10; John 12:37-41.)

Isaiah and Jesus as Teachers

In many ways, Isaiah and Jesus faced comparable and extremely difficult teaching situations. Isaiah was the last great prophet to address assembled Israel. During his ministry, the Ten Tribes were taken captive; they later fled to the north and became lost. His words went with these Israelites, and later with Lehi and his people. Of course, Isaiah's messages also remained with the Jews in Jerusalem.

Furthermore, since so many of Isaiah's prophecies deal with the last days, his words are of particular value to those of covenant Israel who now read his book. Given this wide time period and recognizing the wide range of spiritual attitudes that the readers of his work would have, Isaiah was challenged to find the means to teach such a diversified audience.

Jesus faced a similar challenge during his earthly ministry. He needed to impart special knowledge to his "elect" apostles and disciples, while at the same time teaching the multitudes. Among the crowds were people of varying degrees of spirituality, some seeking the truth, others trying to entrap Jesus, and many simply satisfying their curiosity. Also, Jesus knew that his words would inspire countless generations of readers in varying cultures, languages, and spiritual conditions. Therefore, he spoke in parables so that the listener or reader would understand according to his individual level of spiritual sensitivity.

There are, however, at least two disadvantages in using parables. First, a listener or reader may miss the most important message of any parable if he lacks the background or keys necessary for understanding the story. Second, it is often too easy for a person to simply read a parable and quickly go through a mental checklist, saying, "Here is the simple meaning of the story, here is its moral application, and this is the spiritual meaning; now I understand this parable and am ready to read on." Someone who fails to seriously ponder the full *variety* of meanings in a parable may miss its most important application to him or his day.

Elder Bruce R. McConkie states that Jesus, the Master Teacher, chose to present many truths through parables in order to obscure his doctrine from those not prepared to receive it. (DNTC 1:283-84.) This is one of many reasons why Jesus used parables to teach his widely diversified audience.

Isaiah, when facing a difficult teaching situation, did not use the parable as a tool; instead, he veiled his message in clouds of symbolism, poetry, and complex terminology. In other words, instead of speaking at a simple level and letting his listeners build upon that foundation, Isaiah spoke at a high intellectual and spiritual level, thus challenging or even forcing his listeners to attain that level before they could begin to understand his words. Isaiah was not only difficult, he was deliberately difficult. We must study his words, wrestle with them, and ponder them at great length before his powerful, sublime teachings begin to emerge and inspire us. Because of this, it is easy to become discouraged and give up before we begin to understand his message. However, through serious and prayerful study, when we finally grasp the language and ideas of a particular chapter until they not only make sense, but enlighten and inspire as well, we realize that we have arrived at a profound level of understanding.

Why Is Isaiah Deliberately Difficult?

The following list suggests at least seven reasons, including those mentioned above, why the book of Isaiah is so difficult to understand. Some scriptures about other groups of people who experienced difficulty understanding Isaiah's words are included.

1. *Diversified audience.* Isaiah spoke to scattered Israel and to the Gentiles throughout many centuries, not just to the Israelites of his own time. People of any particular time period should try to recognize how his universal themes can apply to their own circumstances, since many of his prophecies find multiple fulfillment in later generations. (3 Ne. 23:2.)
2. *Uninterested audience.* Many ancient Israelites despised words of plainness and sought for things they could not understand; they desired intellectual, esoteric messages that tend to confuse us today. (See Jacob 4:14.) Also, some of Isaiah's "plain and precious" words may have been edited or deleted by later generations of Jewish scribes.
3. *Unworthy audience.* Many Israelites of Isaiah's age and later generations of readers were wicked and unworthy to have the truth revealed plainly to them. Similar barriers exist today. (See Isa. 1:3-4; 2 Ne. 25:2.)
4. *Teaching techniques.* Isaiah taught at a complex level and challenged us to rise up to it.
5. *Style.* Isaiah's prophetic style, particularly his use of symbolism, his use of poetic parallelism, and his command of the Hebrew language, is sophisticated and eloquent. Now, centuries later, his words are even more difficult when studied in different languages and cultures. (2 Ne. 25:1, 5.)
6. *Cultural contrasts.* Because of the drastic contrasts between his age and our own, Isaiah undoubtedly found it challenging to explain what he saw in his visions of the last days. For example, how would he describe modern travel by train or airplane? Would we, today,

be able to recognize his images (such as a great beast, or a bird carrying people off—Isa. 5:26-29; 40:31) as representations of contemporary transportation?

7. *Spiritual sensitivity.* Encompassing almost all the reasons listed above is the underlying premise that the amount of insight one gains from studying the scriptures (and especially Isaiah) is dependent upon one's spiritual development and readiness to receive greater truth and light. (2 Ne. 28:30.)

Isaiah's natural response to the conditions surrounding his call was to ask the Lord how long he would prophesy before his words would be understood. (Isa. 6:11.) He may have assumed that for at most a few months or maybe a few years his message would remain obscure, and thus he was probably surprised when the Lord answered that the prophecies would not be understood until after Judah was destroyed, her inhabitants scattered, and a remnant gathered (vs. 11-13). The answer itself includes a prophecy of the scattering and gathering, as well as a promise that Isaiah's words will finally be comprehended by a righteous remnant of Israel:

11I asked,"How long, my Lord?" And He replied: "Till towns lie waste without inhabitants And houses without people, And the ground lies waste and desolate— 12"For the LORD will banish the population— And deserted sites are many In the midst of the land.

13"But while a tenth party yet remains in it, it shall repent. It shall be ravaged like the terebinth and the oak, of which stumps are left even when they are felled: its stump shall be a holy seed." (NJV)

The righteous remnant that later returns to Jerusalem and sees the fulfillment of Isaiah's prophecies could be members of Judah who returned from the Babylonian captivity and witnessed the ministry of Jesus Christ. It could also refer to the righteous in Israel today who repent, return to the Lord, and receive the spiritual gifts necessary to understand Isaiah. In verse 13, this remnant is compared to the shoots of a tree stump. The symbol of the tree is found elsewhere in Isaiah (ch. 5) and other scriptures (especially Jacob 5), and is most appropriate to Israel; though the leaves are scattered, the limbs cut off or grafted into other trees, and the trunk burned up, the stump still has the potential for growth. Eventually, new buds and sprouts come forth which, though ravaged or afflicted by storm and pestilence, still carry on the life of the mother tree. The remnant or tenth (tithe) that returns and is called holy is one branch that will survive. Just as only one of ten cleansed lepers returned to thank the Lord (Luke 17:15-17) and as we still return a tithe to the Lord, so also in the last days a tenth of scattered Israel will return to him. Although the trials of men and the judgments of God may come upon this remnant of his chosen people, they will return to him in righteousness and become the seed (or vehicle) for carrying the Lord's message to the whole world.

Conclusion

The sixth chapter of Isaiah is short, yet it contains a number of profound teachings:

1. It testifies that God is a real being and a personal God who communicates with his servants and rules the whole earth.
2. The Lord of this earth is full of holiness. Indeed, Isaiah uses the terms "holy" and the "Holy One of Israel" to describe God more than any other prophet.
3. The importance of repentance and the reality of forgiveness are experienced by Isaiah, and they become a constant theme in his later teachings.
4. A prophet must be commissioned by God to enter into the Lord's service. We may desire to serve, but the Lord must call us before we become his authorized servants. (See Heb. 5:4.)
5. The path of service and growth is outlined in this chapter. The steps of Isaiah's call to the ministry parallel the path each must follow in order to enjoy God's full blessings: personal revelation (faith, vs. 1-4), contrition (repentance, v. 5), purification (cleansing or baptism, vs. 6-7), consecration (guidance of the Spirit, vs. 8-10), and justification (receiving a reward after enduring to the end, vs. 11-13).
6. The burden and challenge of serving the Lord is highlighted. Isaiah was told that the people would not understand his message. As discussed earlier, much of Isaiah's eloquence was born of the need to address the varied spiritual levels of the people.
7. The scattering and gathering of Israel is prophesied, along with the promise of a holy remnant returning and understanding Isaiah's (and the Lord's) words as they become the "seeds" of the gospel.

The challenge facing the readers of Isaiah is to understand and appreciate his message. As outlined by the Lord, his words are difficult, even deliberately difficult, to comprehend. Indeed, reading Isaiah may be especially frustrating for most Latter-day Saints; although they know many of his prophecies deal with these last days, they cannot understand them.

Although Isaiah is difficult, there are times when the Lord desires that we understand the timing and fulfillment of his prophecies concerning our dispensation. In keeping with the principle of "line upon line, precept upon precept" (Isa. 28:10; 2 Ne. 28:30), the Lord makes it possible for us to understand more and more Isaianic prophecies as we are spiritually prepared to receive them. Nephi, speaking of Isaiah's prophecies, said that "men shall know of a surety, at the times when they shall come to pass." (2 Ne. 25:7.) We now live during the time of the fulfillment of many Isaianic prophecies. We are therefore challenged to study his messages so as to be better prepared for the problems of our age.

Since many of Isaiah's prophecies are being fulfilled in these last days, we have a better opportunity to understand his writings than any other generation of Israelites. Also, we have the other scriptures and living prophets to enlighten us about Isaiah's words. Isaiah is not impossible to understand. If we study the scriptures, review contemporary events, listen to the living prophets, and, above all, heed our own spiritual promptings through the gift of prophecy, Isaiah's words will become clear to us as we open our eyes, ears, and hearts to the truths he proclaims.

IMMANUEL PROMISED TO KING AHAZ
AND THE HOUSE OF DAVID
ISAIAH 7-8

A new and distinct section of narrative begins in these chapters. Isaiah changes his writing from a personal memoir of his vision to a third-person, historical, prophetic account. He records both events in which he participates and records prophecies that he sees partially fulfilled during his lifetime. Most of his prophecies concern the Syro-Israelite War against Judah and the Assyrian encroachment into the area. However, the most significant of his prophecies in these chapters promises the presence of God with Israel through a child named Immanuel.

At the time the Immanuel prophecy was given (about 734 B.C.) the country of Judah was under threat of attack by Rezin, king of Syria, and Pekah, king of Israel. These kings had formed an alliance during the final part of the reign of Jotham, the predecessor of Ahaz, and had made war against Jerusalem but had not been able to prevail against it. (See 2 Kgs. 15:37; 16:5.) When Ahaz came to the throne in 735 B.C., the Syro-Ephraimite coalition made a renewed effort to take Jerusalem. The alliance had as its primary goal the unification of all the countries in the area into a solid anti-Assyrian block. When Ahaz refused to join, Rezin and Pekah decided to subjugate Judah and replace Ahaz with a leader more sympathetic to their anti-Assyrian policies. Syria and Israel made preparations for war and sent an invading army into Judah from the north. In a pitched battle, Pekah's army slew a hundred and twenty thousand men of Judah and took two hundred thousand captives in one day. (See 2 Chr. 28:6-15.) Although the alliance eventually released the Judean captives, it appeared that Judah would soon fall. Reports of further enemy success in the north caused Ahaz to fear greatly for the safety of Jerusalem (v. 2). He was apparently inspecting the city's water supply in the Kidron Valley when Isaiah came to him with a message of comfort:

7 When Ahaz son of Jothan, the son of Uzziah, was king of Judah, King Rezin of Aram and Pekah son of Remaliah king of Israel marched up to fight against Jerusalem, but they could not overpower it. ²Now the house of David was told, "Aram has allied itself with Ephraim"; so the hearts of Ahaz and his people were shaken, as the trees of the forest are shaken by the wind.

³Then the LORD said to Isaiah, "Go out, you and your son Shear-Jashub, to meet Ahaz at the end of the aqueduct of the Upper Pool, on the road to the Washerman's Field. ⁴Say to him, 'Be careful, keep calm and don't be afraid. Do not lose heart because of these two smoldering stubs of firewood—because of the fierce anger of Rezin and Aram and of the son of Remaliah.

⁵Aram, Ephraim and Remaliah's son have plotted your ruin, saying, ⁶"Let us invade Judah; let us tear it apart and divide it among ourselves, and make the son of Tabeel king over it." ⁷Yet this is what the Sovereign LORD says:

"'It will not take place,
    it will not happen,
⁸for the head of Aram is Damascus,
    and the head of Damascus is
        only Rezin.
Within sixty-five years
Ephraim will be too shattered to
    be a people.
⁹The head of Ephraim is Samaria,
    and the head of Samaria is only
        Remaliah's son.
If you do not stand firm in your
    faith,
you will not stand at all.'"
(NIV)

In order to properly associate all the various names of places and persons, remember that the same country often carried different names. Just as the United States of America and its government might be identified in the press by a number of terms (the administration; the president; Washington, D.C.; the Capitol; Congress; America; etc.), the ancient powers also had a variety of names. The names of the three countries involved in this incident are:

Country:	Judah	Syria	Israel
Capital city:	Jerusalem	Damascus	Samaria
Territory or tribe:	Judah	Aram	Ephraim
Leader:	Ahaz, of the House of David	Rezin	Pekah, son of Remaliah

Refer to Map 9 to identify the general geographical location of these nations, and note how the several names for the countries listed are variously repeated in verses 1-9.

In verse 3, one of Isaiah's two sons is introduced. His name is Shear-jashub, which means "a remnant shall return." His symbolic name refers to the literal return of a remnant of Israel to their land or a spiritual return of those who repent and return to the Lord. Actually, as will be seen in later chapters of Isaiah, both meanings apply simultaneously, since the physical return depends partially upon a spiritual return.

As Isaiah and his son meet with Ahaz, the prophet tells the king not to worry about Rezin and the "son of Remaliah" (v. 4). Isaiah does not hesitate to use scorn when he speaks of Pekah. Rather than mentioning him by name, the prophet expresses his disdain by continually referring to him only as "Remaliah's son" (vs. 5, 9).

As stated in verse 6, the goal of the Syro-Israelite alliance was to divide Judah and replace her king. In poetic prophecy, the Lord speaks through Isaiah to sooth the fears of Judah and promise a fate upon Israel that Israel sought to impose upon Judah—destruction and scattering. The divine pronouncement contains five segments alternating between prophecy and history.

Prophecy (or warning)	Verses	Historical statements
The alliance's goals will not come to pass	7	
	8a	For the head of Syria is Damascus and Rezin
Within sixty-five years Ephraim (Israel) will be scattered	8b	
	9a	For the head of Ephraim is Samaria and Remaliah's son
If you [Ahaz of Judah] do not believe, you will not be protected	9b	

The three prophetic segments in the lefthand column can be read without the historical segments to form one continuous prophecy. The combination of history and prophecy is characteristic of Isaiah's writings.

In this prophecy, Isaiah promises that the Syro-Israelite alliance will fail and that Israel will be scattered within sixty-five years. The fulfillment came about in successive stages. First, Tiglath-Pileser III (Pul) attacked Syria and Israel in 732 B.C. and took many Israelites captive to Assyria, especially those from the northern tribes. Secondly, in 730-727, Pul annexed the Transjordan area and deported large numbers of the Israelite tribes from that area to the far reaches of the Assyrian Empire. Third, in 726, Hoshea refused to pay Assyrian tribute, and Pul's successor, Shalmaneser, retaliated by attacking Israel and besieging Samaria, which fell in 722 B.C. Thus, within a dozen years of Isaiah's prophecy, the alliance had completely failed, and three major groups of Israelites had been deported. Finally, large groups of the Israelites fled from Assyria to the remote areas northward and became the lost Ten Tribes of Israel. Apparently, within

141

about fifty years of their leaving Assyria, they were scattered so widely that many of them no longer existed as a cohesive group. Thereby Isaiah's prophecy to Ephraim was completely realized.

In the last part of the prophecy, Isaiah warns Judah that she must remain firm in her trust of the Lord or she will not be able to stand. Unfortunately, Ahaz did not heed this warning and relied instead upon the Assyrians for deliverance. The Assyrians did hinder the Syro-Israelite attack by destroying Syria and large parts of Israel, but since the Assyrians desired more territory and wealth, Judah found herself paying tribute to avoid war. Knowing that the greatest danger to Judah came from Assyria and not Syria and Ephraim, the Lord would have helped Judah stand against both the Syro-Israelite attack and the Assyrians if her people had remained faithful.

Unfortunately for Judah, she had a difficult time in developing trust in the Lord at least in part because her king, Ahaz, lacked faith and trust. Even after Isaiah gave him an opportunity for a miraculous manifestation to strengthen whatever faith he may have had, Ahaz refused the sign and rejected the Lord's counsel. Isaiah gave him a sign and a promise anyway:

¹⁰Again the LORD spoke to Ahaz, ¹¹"Ask the LORD your God for a sign, whether in the deepest depths or in the highest heights."

¹²But Ahaz said, "I will not ask; I will not put the LORD to the test."

¹³Then Isaiah said, "Hear now, you house of David! Is it not enough to try the patience of men? Will you try the patience of my God also? ¹⁴Therefore the LORD himself will give you a sign: The virgin will be with child and will give birth to a son, and will call him Immanuel.

¹⁵He will eat curds and honey when he knows enough to reject the wrong and choose the right. ¹⁶But before the boy knows enough to reject the wrong and choose the right, the land of the two kings you dread will be laid waste. ¹⁷The LORD will bring on you and your people and on the house of your father a time unlike any since Ephraim broke away from Judah—he will bring the king of Assyria." (NIV)

In order to prove the authenticity of his words, Isaiah commands Ahaz in the name of the Lord to ask for a sign. This request is obviously different from the type of sign described in the Savior's statement that "an evil and adulterous generation seeketh after a sign" (Matt. 12:39; see also Isa. 5:18-19), for Ahaz had *not* sought a sign. Indeed, he refused to ask for a sign even when the prophet of the Lord gave him the opportunity. (See Deut. 6:16.) It is probable that

Ahaz refused to ask for a sign because he had no confidence in the Lord—he was secretly depending on the aid of the king of Assyria. Ahaz's hypocritical unbelief, however, so wearied God that Ahaz was no longer free to request any particular sign but had to receive whatever sign God chose to give. In this instance, therefore, what happens is in accordance with what the Lord has said in modern revelation: "Yea, signs come . . . not by the will of men, nor as they please, but *by the will of God.* (D&C 63:10; italics added.)

The Lord seems weary of the people's lack of faith (v. 13). It seems that he chose this situation to give a prophecy with various layers of meaning. The context of the pronouncement of the sign is almost as important, therefore, as the sign itself. The situation serves to emphasize man's complete, though often unwilling, dependence on God. The crux of the message is a call to faith; it is a type of the Lord's power to save one from a seemingly inescapable situation. In barest terms, though laden with meaning, the sign the Lord gives to signal the end of the threatening conspiracy is the birth of a male child.

The Immanuel Prophecy

There are several theories as to how this prophecy was fulfilled in the days of Ahaz. One theory proposes that the child to be born is Isaiah's own. This is based upon information in Isaiah 8:1-4, in which Isaiah names his new son. Although Isaiah already had a son, Shear-jashub (Isa. 7:3), it is still possible that the mother of the new son could be a virgin if Shear-jashub's mother was deceased and Isaiah was about to be remarried. (See Albert Barne, *Barne's Notes on Isaiah* [New York: Leavitt and Allen, 1847] 1:177.) One question asked about this theory is, "How could Isaiah have two new sons with different names in such a short period unless he had two wives?" However, it is possible that two names were given to the same child, specifically that Maher-shalal-hash-baz (Isa. 8:3) was also named Immanuel (Isa. 7:14). The practice of having two or more names is not unusual in the Bible, as shown in the cases of Joshua (see BD "Joshua"), Gideon (Judg. 6:11, 32), and Jesus (see BD "Christ, Names of"). This argument is disclaimed by many scholars, however. Some of them, such as Otto Kaiser, suggest a second possible fulfillment and state that Isaiah is promising such a rapid dissipation of the Syro-Israelite threat that any "women who are now with child will name their sons, in thankfulness for being saved, 'Immanuel,' 'God is with us.'" Kaiser goes on to say that the immediate fulfillment of the prophecy was necessary to show Ahaz that Isaiah's sign was given with God's authority and that to reject it is nothing other than apostasy from the living God. (Kaiser, *Isaiah 1-12*, p. 103.)

A third possible explanation is a variation of the one just mentioned: instead of the son of any woman fulfilling the promise, the son of one particular woman was designated. In the Hebrew, a definite article precedes the term translated as "virgin" or "young woman," indicating that she is *the* virgin and not just *a* virgin or any young woman. Isaiah identifies her as the first element of a fivefold prophecy:

1. Behold, the (that) young woman (virgin) will conceive (v. 14).
2. She will have a son.
3. She will call him Immanuel ("with us is El," or "with us is God").
4. Before the lad is old enough to choose good from evil, he will eat milk and honey as the land of the Syro-Israelite king is vacated (vs. 15-16).
5. The king of Assyria will come and vex Judah worse than she has been vexed in two centuries (v. 17).

Regardless of the precise identity of the woman and her child, it appears obvious that the circumstances of the child's birth and the conditions surrounding his early life were so much an evidence of divine protection as to make proper his name, Immanuel, for God was truly with the people of Judah.

Isaiah delivered the Immanuel prophecy when Jerusalem was threatened by the Syro-Ephraimite conspiracy from the north. As mentioned earlier, the sign given by the Lord of a son to be born signals the end of this threat. The naming of the son Immanuel shows that God was ultimately on the side of the people.

Given this brief background, it seems that this sign, or prophecy, can find fulfillment as a call to faith on three levels:

1. As mentioned earlier, Ahaz and the people of Judah needed to develop faith in the Lord to deliver them from the confederacy of Rezin and Pekah. A son was to be born and named Immanuel as a sign of the Lord's power of deliverance in the subsequent withdrawal and humiliation of the threatening alliance.
2. To the people at the time of the birth of Christ, it was a sign to know that Jesus Christ, the Messiah, was to come. Therefore, Isaiah was promised that God himself should "come down from heaven among the children of men and dwell in a tabernacle of

clay" (Mosiah 3:5) to free them from the threat of sin and spiritual bondage. (This level of fulfillment is the one usually stressed by General Authorities of this dispensation as they quote and apply the Immanuel prophecy.) (See Matt. 1:21-23.)

3. Isaiah's prophecy is a call to faith in the last days. The birth of Christ strengthens our faith that in the end of the world, against all odds, the Lord "shall bring again Zion." (See Isa. 52:9-10; D&C 84:99.) The memorial of Immanuel's birth is a sign of God's help in such extremity and is intended to build our faith today that indeed "God is with us."

Whatever Isaiah's understanding about his famous Immanuel prophecy, he knew that it was to be delivered to Ahaz and the house of David (v. 13). Isaiah also had further warnings to deliver to the people of Judah that were more clearly fulfilled during Isaiah's lifetime. Continuing with some terminology from the Immanuel prophecy, he warns about the impending Assyrian attacks upon Judah:

¹⁸In that day the LORD will whistle for flies from the distant streams of Egypt and for bees from the land of Assyria. ¹⁹They will all come and settle in the steep ravines and in the crevices in the rocks, on all the thornbushes and at all the water holes. ²⁰In that day the Lord will use a razor hired from beyond the River—the king of Assyria—to shave your head and the hair of your legs, and to take off your beards also. ²¹In that day, a man will keep alive a young cow and two goats. ²²And because of the abundance of the milk they give, he will have curds to eat. All who remain in the land will eat curds and honey. ²³In that day, in every place where there were a thousand vines worth a thousand silver shekels, there will be only briers and thorns. ²⁴Men will go there with bow and arrow, for the land will be covered with briers and thorns. ²⁵As for all the hills once cultivated by the hoe, you will no longer go there for fear of the briers and thorns; they will become places where cattle are turned loose and where sheep run. (NIV)

The humiliation and slavery that will befall the people is represented in verse 20 by the razor cutting off their hair. The Assyrians cut off all the hair from their captives for three reasons: humiliation, sanitation (especially while traveling under crude conditions to Assyria), and separation (if any slaves escaped while being moved from their homeland, they could not blend in with other peoples since their baldness would give them away; thus they usually were quickly recaptured, punished, and returned to their captors.)

The seriousness of the devastation in the land is expressed in verses 22-25. People will be able to retain only a fraction of their original herds and flocks (v. 22), yet the population will be so decimated that the limited livestock will provide plentiful milk and curds to the survivors. The relative losses of animals and people can be illustrated as follows:

Before the Invasion   *After the Invasion*

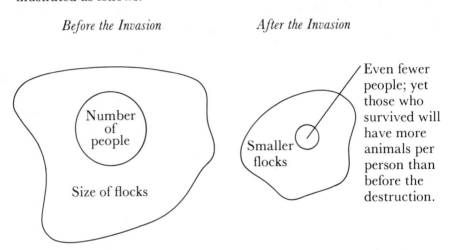

The abundance of honey in these devastating circumstances comes from the large land areas that are left uncultivated and quickly turn to wild flowers, weeds, and other blossom-producing plants. Thus, ironically, the few who remain in the land will enjoy milk and honey because of the relatively large numbers of food-producing animals. They will still have problems and dangers, however, since they must fight off the weeds, thorny bushes, and wild animals. All in all, Isaiah describes serious conditions that will beset the people.

A few years after his Immanuel prophecy, Isaiah elaborated upon his earlier warnings with a new set of prophecies. This time he spoke not to the king or a small body; he wrote a message in large letters witnessed by the leaders of Jerusalem as a promise of the impending Assyrian attack upon Syria and Israel:

8 The LORD said to me, "Take a large scroll and write on it with an ordinary pen: Maher-Shalal-Hash-Baz. ²And I will call in Uriah the priest and Zechariah son of Jeberekiah as reliable witnesses for me."

³Then I went to the prophetess, and she conceived and gave birth to a son. And the LORD said to me,

"Name him Maher-Shalal-Hash-Baz. [4]Before the boy knows how to say 'My father' or "My mother,' the wealth of Damascus and the plunder of Samaria will be carried off by the king of Assyria." (NIV)

The message Isaiah carried to the people was "Maher-Shalal-Hash-Baz" or, "quick to the plunder, swift to the spoil." (See Isa. 8, footnote 1d.) This message was written on a large tablet or parchment to warn the people that an Assyrian attack was imminent. The message was also embodied in Isaiah's son, who received the message as his given name.[1] The nearness of fulfillment was also to be seen in the son because before he could "call out" or speak to his parents, the invasion would come upon Damascus and Samaria, and their wealth would go to Assyria.

Since Pul's invasion of Syria and Israel took place in 732 B.C., this prophecy was probably given two years earlier. Isaiah had the warning witnessed by leaders of Jerusalem, and thus after his wife conceived and they named their son, the people waited for him to learn to speak. It appears that before he did, the attack came, and the Judeans received a confirmation of Isaiah's prophetic powers.

With a witness of Isaiah's prophecy about the Assyrian attack upon the northern countries, the people of Jerusalem could study his prophecy given about them and know that it was also to be fulfilled:

[5]The LORD spoke to me again:
[6]"Because this people has rejected
    the gently flowing waters of
        Shiloah
and rejoices over Rezin
    and the son of Remaliah,
[7]therefore the Lord is about to
    bring against them
the mighty flood waters of the
    River—
the king of Assyria with all his
    pomp.

It will overflow all its channels,
    run over all its banks
[8]and sweep on into Judah, swirling
        over it,
    passing through it and reaching
        up to the neck.
Its outspread wings will cover the
        breadth of your land,
    O Immanuel!" (NIV)

The gentle waters of Shiloah (v. 6) were the major water source for ancient Jerusalem. Located at the Gihon spring in the Kidron Valley

---

[1]His name is the longest word in the Bible.

147

east of the fortified city, they ebb and flow continually throughout the year. (See area D3 on Map 17.) During Isaiah's life, the waters were brought into a fortified area of the city when King Hezekiah, the son of Ahaz, built a tunnel through Mount Ophel, which still carries from eight to forty inches of running water. (See area C4 on Map 17.) This cool, flowing spring supplied more than enough water for the city of Jerusalem.

The "waters of Shiloah" also represent the continuous tender care that the Lord provided for his people as he sought to lead them with gentle promptings of the Spirit. The Judean leaders rejected the Lord's advice offered through Isaiah, who foretold how the raging floodwaters of the Euphrates River would replace the waters of Shiloah. Instead of gentle water around their knees, the raging torrent of the Assyrian army would gather around their necks (v. 8).

Having concluded his short warning to Judah with the expression "O Immanuel" or "Oh—God is with us!" Isaiah then addresses the nations rising against Judah and promises them, "God is with us":

9Raise the war cry, you nations,
    and be shattered!
Listen, all you distant lands.
Prepare for battle, and be
    shattered!
Prepare for battle, and be
    shattered!

10Devise your strategy, but it will
    be thwarted;
propose your plan, but it will
    not stand,
for God is with us. (NIV)

The repetition of phrases at the end of verse 9 accentuates the message and provides a form of the comparative. The comparative degree in Hebrew was formed by simply repeating a word or phrase. To repeat the item three or more times made it superlative. Whereas in English one would say "good," "better," and "best" to indicate comparative degrees, in Hebrew one could say "good," "good, good," and "good, good, good." Thus, in the verse above, Isaiah is warning the nations that if they prepare for battle, they will be devastated.

In chapter 8, Isaiah speaks to a variety of audiences: the leaders of Jerusalem, the Israelites and Syrians, the Judeans, and the enemy nations. Beginning in verse 11, he gives a rare personal discourse about his relationship with the people:

11The LORD spoke to me with his
    strong hand upon me, warning
    me not to follow the way of this
    people. He said:

12"Do not call conspiracy
    everything that these people
    call conspiracy;
do not fear what they fear,

and do not dread it.
¹³The LORD Almighty is the one
   you are to regard as holy,
   he is the one you are to fear,
   he is the one you are to dread,
¹⁴and he will be a sanctuary;
   but for both houses of Israel he
    will be
  a stone that causes men to
    stumble

and a rock that makes them
  fall.
And for the people of Jerusalem
  he will be
  a trap and a snare.
¹⁵Many of them will stumble;
  they will fall and be broken,
  they will be snared and
  captured." (NIV)

The Lord counseled Isaiah not to fear the people or teach what they wanted to hear. Instead of seeking public acceptance, Isaiah was to seek the favor and sanctuary of the Lord. (Compare similar counsel to Jeremiah and Ezekiel in Jer. 7:25-28; Ezek. 3:7-9.)

The Lord then told the prophet that while he (and the righteous) sought the Lord's presence, the wicked would stumble over the Lord's advent and teachings. Jehovah and his laws caused many Israelites who refused to follow him to stumble. (See Jacob 4:15.) Later, when the Lord lived among the Jews, he was still a stumbling block to those who rejected his divine mission. (See 1 Pet. 2:8; Rom. 9:33; 1 Cor. 1:23.) Using five verbs that develop a "downward" pattern, Isaiah describes the results befalling those who reject the Lord (v. 15)—they stumble—they falter in their faith; they fall—they commit sins; they are broken—they suffer consequences for their transgressions; they are snared—they are enticed by Satan's temptations; they are captured—they are turned over to Satan's buffetings.

The Lord commands Isaiah to record his testimony or witness (v. 16), and Isaiah responds with a promise to follow the Lord (v. 17):

¹⁶Bind up the testimony
  and seal up the law among my
    disciples
¹⁷I will wait for the LORD,
  who is hiding his face from the
    house of Jacob
I will put my trust in him. (NIV)

Other prophets have also been commanded to seal their witnesses and power to the people. (Jer. 32att. 16:19; 18:18; D&C 1:8; 68:12; 88:84.) Eventually, the records and testimonies of the prophets will help judge the people. (D&C 133:71-73.)

Isaiah concludes chapter 8 by comparing his role as witness and symbol with the false messages the people receive from evil sources:

¹⁸Here am I, and the children the LORD has given me. We are signs and symbols in Israel from the LORD Almighty, who dwells on Mount Zion.

¹⁹When men tell you to consult mediums and spiritists, who whisper and mutter, should not a people inquire of their God? Why consult the dead on behalf of the living? ²⁰To the law and to the testimony! If they do not speak according to this work, they have no light of dawn. ²¹Distressed and hungry, they will roam through the land; when they are famished, they will become enraged and, looking upward, they will curse their king and their God. ²²Then they will look toward the earth and see only distress and darkness and fearful gloom, and they will be thrust into utter darkness. (NIV)

In these concluding verses, Isaiah first holds up himself and his sons, with their symbolic names and lives, as special signs to the people. (See Isa. 7:3, 10-16; 8:1-4.) He then rebukes the people's attempts to receive signs and counsel from diviners (v. 19). Important guidelines follow verse 20, in which Isaiah tells Israel that if one does not speak according to the law and testimony (the discourses of Moses and the witnesses of the prophets in the scriptures), he is not of God.

In summary, Isaiah's discourse in chapter 8 is a collection of warnings sealed with his own special witness. Coupled with chapter 7, these two chapters provide a number of warnings, signs, prophecies, and witnesses to Israel. To the wicked, these words will be as a snare to demonstrate their true relationship with God when they reject his word. To the righteous, Isaiah's words provide insight, perspective, and the important eternal witness that "God is with us!"

SCRIPTURAL NOTES AND COMMENTARY

Isaiah 7: Chiasmus

Chapter 7 shifts from the Syro-Israelite invasion to God's signs and then to the Assyrian invasion. This develops a thematic pattern as follows:

A. Man vs. man (Judah vs. Syro-Israel) (vs. 1-10)
B. Man vs. God (Ahaz and a sign) (11-16)
A'. Man vs. God (Judah and prophecies) (17-20)
B'. Man vs. man (Judah vs. Assyria) (21-25)

WARNINGS TO ISRAEL AND ASSYRIA
ISAIAH 9-10

Chapters 9 and 10 of Isaiah are a natural continuation of chapters 7 and 8; the historical context still centers upon the Assyrian crisis of 734-701 B.C., although the situation worsens after Ahaz ignores Isaiah's counsel. In chapters 7 and 8, Isaiah told Ahaz that an Assyrian alliance would bring problems. Now, in chapters 9 and 10, with the alliance an accomplished fact, Isaiah prophesies more specifically about the Assyrian punishments coming upon Israel and Judah. He warns the ten tribes in the north of their impending captivity and foretells a later Assyrian attack upon the southern tribes.

The messianic prophecies of chapters 7 and 8 are also developed further in chapters 9 and 10. The Immanuel prophecy is amplified in chapter 9 as Isaiah promises a "new light" and a new leader for Israel. This promised child could be the young King Hezekiah, who would help deliver Judah from the Assyrians, but if Hezekiah is the object of Isaiah's prophecy, he is only a foreshadowing of Jesus Christ, the greater light and deliverer of all nations.

The material in chapters 9 and 10 divides easily into three major sections:

    I. The Prince of Peace (9:1-7)
   II. Four warnings to Israel (9:8-10:4)
      A. Pride and arrogance (9:8-12)
      B. Evil leaders (9:13-17)
      C. Selfishness and destruction (9:18-21)
      D. Unjust leaders (10:1-4)
  III. God sends Assyria against Judah (10:5-34)

The Prince of Peace (9:1-7)

Because of Canaan's location between Asia and Africa, it served as the crossroads for caravans and armies. Unfortunately for the

151

inhabitants, however, the armies usually did not pass through without plundering, destroying, and seeking to control the area. Egyptian and Mesopotamian powers often threatened the Israelites, but for over half a millennium no foreign power had established complete domination over them. With the encroachment of the Assyrians, however, it appeared that Israel's independence was finally ending and Judah's was likewise endangered. Isaiah's words seem to promise an immediate release from this threat:

9 But there will be no gloom for her that was in anguish. In the former time he brought into contempt the land of Zebulun and the land of Naphtali, but in the latter time he will make glorious the way of the sea, the land beyond the Jordan, Galilee of the nations. (RSV)

In this verse Isaiah immediately sets up a contrast before former and latter times. The former time refers to his own age when the Assyrians were punishing the Israelites in the lands of Zebulun and Naphtali, two tribes located near the Sea of Galilee; the latter time is a future period when God will "be heavy" (from the Hebrew root, *kaved*) with the land. Translators differ as to the meaning of this term, saying variously that God will "make glorious," "deal heavily" (NIV), or "grievously afflict" (KJV) the area. Besides the unsurety of what the Lord's actions will be, the precise time of this manifestation is not presented, and, for unknown reasons, the land area to be affected in the latter time is larger than that which was anciently attacked by the Assyrians. Also, the "way of the sea" is not identified, although the Book of Mormon includes a clarifying modifier, calling it the "way of the Red Sea." (2 Ne. 19:1.)

Verse 1 of chapter 9 bridges chapters 8 and 9, and its position might help clarify its meaning. In fact, it is included as the last verse of chapter 8 in the Hebrew versions of Isaiah but is made the beginning verse of chapter 9 in most English translations. Chapter 8 ends with a gloomy note of trouble and darkness, while, beginning in verse 2, chapter 9 speaks of light and joy. Therefore, it seems likely that chapter 9 verse 1 includes both a former time of darkness and a latter time when the Lord's "heaviness" will provide blessings.

A clearer promise is found in the second verse:

2The people who walked in darkness
have seen a great light;
those who dwelt in a land of deep darkness,
on them has light shined. (RSV)

Isaiah continues the contrast theme in this verse, shifting from a former-latter time contrast to a darkness-light comparison. He does not establish, however, whether the "darkness" and "light" refer to physical, social, or spiritual conditions. At least three explanations are possible:

1. The darkness represents Assyria; the light is the king who protects his people from Assyria. Since Hezekiah is victorious over the Assyrians, he is the natural candidate for this rescuing role. (Isa. 38-39.) This viewpoint is favored among Jewish scholars.
2. The darkness represents wickedness and the Lord's judgments; the light is the Israelites' recognition of earlier sins and their attempt at religious reforms. Both Hezekiah and Isaiah were very much involved in these reforms, especially after the Assyrian attack and captivity of Israel humbled the remaining Israelites, and the death of Ahaz gave Hezekiah full political power. This figurative interpretation is advocated by some Jewish and Christian commentators.
3. The darkness represents a period of wickedness and apostasy; the light is Jesus Christ, who comes to the earth to personally teach his gospel. This identification is, of course, preferred by many Christian scholars. (See Matt. 4:12-16.)

As Isaiah talks further about the conflict between the forces of darkness and light, notice how the three interpretations (Assyrians versus Hezekiah, a wicked versus a righteous people, and apostasy versus Christ) might apply:

³Thou has multiplied the nation,
thou hast increased its joy;
they rejoice before thee
as with joy at the harvest,
as men rejoice when they
divide the spoil.
⁴For the yoke of his burden,
and the staff for his shoulder,
the rod of his oppressor,
thou hast broken as on the
day of Midian.
⁵For every boot of the tramping
warrior in battle tumult
and every garment rolled in
blood

will be burned as fuel for the
fire.
⁶For to us a child is born,
to us a son is given;
and the government will be upon
his shoulder,
and his name will be called
"Wonderful Counselor, Mighty
God,
Everlasting Father, Prince of
Peace."
⁷Of the increase of his government
and of peace
there will be no end,
upon the throne of David, and

> over his kingdom,
> to establish it, and to uphold it
> with justice and with righteousness
> from this time forth and for
> evermore.
> The zeal of the LORD of hosts will
> do this. (RSV)

If Isaiah is prophesying about Hezekiah, then verse 3 describes the Israelites' joy at their deliverance; verse 4 portrays how the Assyrians were defeated in spite of their greater numbers, just as the many Midianites were by Gideon and his 300 men (Judg. 7); verse 5 describes the Assyrian casualties; and verses 6 and 7 tell about Hezekiah's titles and righteous, peaceful rule as king.

If the verses describe a righteous people fighting against wickedness, then verse 3 describes their joy at success, verses 4 and 5 portray the defeat of the enemy, and verses 6 and 7 describe a new age of millennial peace that may be assisted or ushered in by a messianic figure.

Finally, the identification of the ruler in verses 3-7 with Jesus Christ has a number of possibilities, as verse 3 talks about his many followers who rejoice at the spiritual blessings he has provided; verse 4 describes how he was able to overcome the temptations of Satan, break the yoke of sin, and maintain power over the legions of Satan's devils; verse 5 symbolizes his atonement and the cleansing powers of baptism and the Holy Ghost; verse 6 presents some of his titles and roles; and verse 7 describes his eternal position as the Lord and King of this earth. This last interpretation is amplified by a modern apostle, James E. Talmage, who said:

> Isaiah, whose prophetic office was honored by the personal testimony of Christ and the apostles, manifested in numerous passages the burden of his conviction relating to the great event of the Savior's advent and ministry on earth. With the forcefulness of direct revelation he told of the Virgin's divine maternity, whereof Immanuel should be born, and his prediction was reiterated by the angel of the Lord, over seven centuries later. Looking down through the ages the prophet saw the accomplishment of the divine purposes as if already achieved, and sang in triumph: 'For unto us a child is born, unto us a son is given: and the government shall be upon his shoulder: and his name shall be called Wonderful, Counselor, the mighty God, The everlasting Father, The Prince of Peace.'" (JTC, pp. 46-47.)

In verse 6, Isaiah prophesies that the promised deliverer will be born "unto us" (the house of Israel), and he gives four titles of the Redeemer: Wonderful Counselor, Mighty God, Everlasting Father, and Prince of Peace. Although the titles might apply to Hezekiah, they more naturally identify the Messiah, for each one describes an important role of Jesus Christ. Isaiah's use of symbolic titles is a very common technique of prophesying both in the Old Testament and the Book of Mormon. A brief study of this technique will help clarify Isaiah's literary and prophetic style.

A prophet contemporary with Isaiah records an important key to the prophetic technique: "I [the Lord] have also spoken by the prophets, and I have multiplied visions, and used *similitudes*, by the ministry of the prophets." (Hosea 12:10; italics added.)

This verse reveals that the Lord has spoken "by the prophets" through visions and used "similitudes" in the revelations in order to present his message to the people. (A similitude is an allegory or parable.) A natural question arising from the Hosea passage is, "What do the similitudes or parables represent?" The apostle Peter answers: "Yea, and all the prophets from Samuel and those that follow after, as many as have spoken, have likewise foretold of these days [of Jesus Christ]." (Acts 3:24; see also Acts 7:52; 10:43.)

A Book of Mormon prophet, Jacob, explains that all things are a "typifying" (an example or parable) of Christ. (2 Ne. 11:4.) This is what Hosea and Peter were saying: all the prophets have spoken and prophesied of Christ by using "all things" as a "typifying" of him. Ancient Israel understood this. The law of Moses with all its statues and rites existed expressly to prepare Israel for the coming of Christ. (See Deut. 18:15, 19; 2 Ne. 22:20; Acts 3:19-26.) Understanding the use of types as a technique of prophesying helps explain how Isaiah was able to use pious examples from his age as models for his messianic prophecies.

As stated earlier, some scholars believe that the leader promised by Isaiah in chapter 9 was Hezekiah. Hezekiah was indeed a righteous king, for he both helped bring Judah to a higher spiritual plane and brought a partial peace to the land. Hezekiah listened to the counsel of Isaiah and tried to follow it. He seems particularly righteous when contrasted with his father, Ahaz, and his son Mannaseh. Still, Isaiah was merely using Hezekiah as a type, a figure of the future Messiah. Isaiah's method was at least partially understood by the Jews, as evidenced in the above scriptures from New Testament times. When the Israelites heard of Isaiah's prophecy, they knew it applied to Hezekiah and that they would enjoy a period of peace, but some of them also knew that its full realization would come only in the birth and life of the Messiah, the perfect king.

Four Warnings to Israel (9:8–10:4)

Isaiah now turns his attention to the rebellious northern kingdom of Israel, whose ruling tribe is represented by Ephraim and whose capital is Samaria. The historical setting is the same as in verses 1-7: the northern tribes have already been placed under direct Assyrian control, and many leading citizens have been taken captive to Assyria. The campaign of Tiglath-Pileser III in 732 B.C. brought about the deportation of the major portions of the northernmost Israelite tribes, Zebulun and Naphtali. Still, the invasion and deportation did not bring the stubborn Israelites to the realization that the prophecies uttered against them would all surely come to pass unless they repented. They had had a taste of the Lord's judgment, but learned nothing from it, since Isaiah still levels four major accusations against them: pride, evil leaders, selfishness, and injustice.

This prophecy is written in four stanzas, each ending with the same refrain: "for all this his anger is not turned away, but his hand is stretched out still." As indicated earlier in the discussion of Isaiah 5:25, this same phrase implies both a warning of further punishment and an invitation to repent and yield to the Lord's mercy.

In the first stanza, Isaiah describes the people's arrogance in their response to the destruction around them. They respond with a boast, saying that they will build a civilization more glorious than the one destroyed:

8The Lord has sent a word against Jacob,
and it will light upon Israel;
9and all the people will know,
Ephraim and the inhabitants of Samaria,
who say in pride and in arrogance of heart:
10"The bricks have fallen,
but we will build with dressed stones;
the sycamores have been cut down,
but we will put cedars in their place."
11So the LORD raises adversaries against them,
and stirs up their enemies.
12The Syrians on the east and the Philistines on the west
devour Israel with open mouth.
For all this his anger is not turned away
and his hand is stretched out still. (RSV)

The second stanza or warning describes why the Lord has caused their leaders to be taken away and allowed universal suffering to occur:

156

13The people did not turn to him
who smote them,
nor seek the LORD of hosts.
14So the LORD cut off from Israel
head and tail,
palm branch and reed in one
day—
15the elder and honored man is the
head,
and the prophet who teaches
lies is the tail;
16for those who lead this people
lead them astray,
and those who are led by them
are swallowed up.
17Therefore the LORD does not
rejoice over their young men,
and has no compassion on their
fatherless and widows;
for every one is godless and an
evildoer,
and every mouth speaks folly.
For all this his anger is not turned
away
and his hand is stretched out
still. (RSV)

The third warning promises the consuming wrath of the Lord, yet the people are so selfish that they continue to grasp whatever they can in the chaos:

18For wickedness burns like a fire,
it consumes briers and thorns;
it kindles the thickets of the forest,
and they roll upward in a
column of smoke.
19Through the wrath of the LORD of
hosts
the land is burned,
and the people are like fuel for the
fire;
no man spares his brother.
20They snatch on the right, but are
still hungry,
and they devour on the left, but
are not satisfied;
each devours his neighbor's flesh,
21Manasseh Ephraim, and
Ephraim Manasseh,
and together they are against
Judah.
For all this his anger is not turned
away
and his hand is stretched out
still. (RSV)

The final stanza summarizes the northern Israelites' wickedness and describes their injustice toward the weak and needy. The Lord promises that since the oppressed have no one to help them, the Israelites will likewise be without a protector:

10 Woe to those who decree
iniquitous decrees,
and the writers who keep writing
oppression,
2to turn aside the needy from
justice
and to rob the poor of my people
of their right,
that widows may be their spoil,
and that they may make the
fatherless their prey!
3What will you do on the day of
punishment,
in the storm which will come
from afar?
To whom will you flee for help,

and where will you leave your wealth?	For all this his anger is not turned away
⁴Nothing remains but to crouch among the prisoners or fall among the slain.	and his hand is stretched out still. (RSV)

The Old Testament provides a limited account of the political events that led up to the destruction promised by Isaiah. Fortunately, some Assyrian records have been discovered and translated within the past century that give us a more complete history. Together, these two sources help us understand how the Lord used Assyria in an attempt to humble Israel and bring her to repentence. Israel, however, became progressively more wicked until she merited the complete destruction of her country, the loss of her independence, and the captivity of many of her citizens.

As prophesied, the Assyrians came and attacked Syria from the north. Pekah and Rezin were forced to lift their siege of Jerusalem and rush off to defend their lands. Here are the accounts as recorded in the Bible and the cuneiform tablets of Tiglath-Pileser III:

2 Kings

The king of Assyria went up against Damascus and took it, and carried the people of it captive to Kir, and slew Rezin (16:9).

In the days of Pekah, King of Israel came Tiglath-pileser king of Assyria, and took . . . Hazor, and Gilead, and Galilee, all the land of Naphtali, and carried them captive to Assyria (15:29).

And Hosea . . . made a conspiracy against Pekah . . . and slew him and reigned in his stead (15:30).

Cuneiform Text of Pul

His noblemen I impaled alive and displayed this exhibition to his land. All his gardens and fruit orchards I destroyed. I besieged and captured the native city of Reson [Rezin] of Damascus. 800 people with their belongings I led away. Towns in 16 districts of Damascus I laid waste like mounds after the flood.

Bet-Omri [Israel] all of whose cities I had added to my territories on my former campaigns, and had left out only the city of Samaria. The whole of Nephtali I took for Assyria. I put my officials over them as governors. The land of Bet-Omri, all its people and their possessions I took away to Assyria.

They overthrew Pekah their king and I made Hosea to be king over them. (Keller, *The Bible as History*, p. 245.)

By 732 B.C., as a result of this rebellion against the Assyrians, Israel was smashed to the ground, decimated by deportation, and beaten back into the southern corner of her kingdom. With the exception of Samaria, all her major cities were annexed by Assyria, and the countryside was divided into provinces over which Assyrian governors and officials exercised strict control.

The Assyrians controlled the whole of the Fertile Crescent from the Persian mountains to Asia Minor, and from the Mesopotamian plain through Lebanon to Palestine. Only Judah and a few other states remained independent, although they had to pay tribute or risk conquest. Samaria retained only a few square miles of farmland, and even though she was reduced to barely a city with her surrounding mountains and valleys, Samaria still boasted that she would rebuild and come to power again. (Isa. 9:10.)

With the death of Tiglath-Pileser III in 727 B.C., Hosea stopped paying annual tribute, conspired with Egypt, and rebelled against Assyria. Shalmaneser V, the next Assyrian king, attacked what remained of Israel and besieged Samaria. However, he soon died, and his successor, Sargon II, conquered Samaria. Sargon records:

> In the first year of my reign I besieged and conquered Samaria. . . . I led away into captivity 27,290 people who lived there. . . . People of the lands, prisoners my hand has captured, I settled there. My officials I placed over them as governors. I imposed tribute and tax upon them, as upon the Assyrians." (Keller, *The Bible as History*, pp. 246, 250; compare 2 Kgs. 17.)

The fall of Samaria in 722-721 B.C. was the beginning of exile for the lost ten tribes of Israel. The Assyrians deported the conquered nation's inhabitants to break their national spirit and assimilate them into Assyrian culture. Shortly thereafter, Samaria was inhabited by pagan people from other nations. These people mixed with the remaining Israelites, for not all of them had been taken into captivity. Through the mixing of these groups the Samaritans came about. As a result of this mixing, the Jews later felt that the Samaritans were no longer pure descendants of Abraham and therefore were not entitled to be remembered with the chosen people. The Samaritan Province, along with the other Assyrian provinces, is shown in the map on page 160.

The Assyrians could have been diverted from Israel if her people had only repented; instead, they persisted in boasting of their strength. Because they failed to heed the words of Isaiah and the other prophets, and ignored the earlier, minor judgments of the Lord, they were destroyed as a nation and taken captive to Assyria and Media. Later, they vanished from the stage of history, but the Lord has promised that a remnant will return again someday. (Jer. 16:14-15; D&C 133:23-28.) Isaiah gives a last warning to Israel along with a

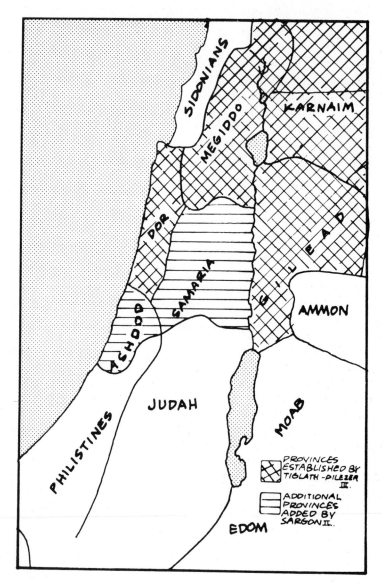

Assyrian Provinces in Palestine

promise concerning her redeemed remnant in the pronouncement in chapter 10.

God Sends Assyria against Israel (10:5-34)

After his fourfold warning to Israel, Isaiah continues his discourse in the form of a poetic prophecy. He gives warning to both Assyria and Israel in a poem structured in introverted parallelism (chiasmus). The poem encompasses the entire chapter and can be outlined as follows:

A. The wicked will bow down (vs. 1-4)
B. Assyria raised by the Lord (5)
C. The Assyrian king speaks against Jerusalem (6-11)
D. The Lord will punish proud Assyria (12-14)
E. An ax is used as a tool (15)
F. The Lord is a burning fire in the land (16-17)
G. Out of all the scrubs—only a remnant remains (18-19)
H. A remnant of Israel shall return to the Lord (20-21)
G.' Out of the "sands of the sea"—only a remnant returns (22)
F.' A divine consumption is in the land (23)
E'. A rod is used as an instrument (24-26)
D'. Assyria's yoke will be lifted (27)
C'. Assyrian army approaches Jerusalem (28-32)
B'. Assyria humbled by the Lord (33)
A'. The haughty will be cut down (34)

Isaiah records that the Lord allowed Assyria to become a strong nation to enable it to be the medium through which he would mete out his judgments upon various nations, especially the wicked northern kingdom of Israel. However, the Assyrian king thinks that he has been able to gain control over the western Fertile Crescent because of his armies' great power. In this he is sadly mistaken, and his people will themselves experience the Lord's punishment and lose many of their own numbers:

⁵Ah, Assyria, the rod of my anger,
the staff of my fury!
⁶Against a godless nation I send him,
and against the people of my wrath I command him,
to take spoil and seize plunder,
and to tread them down like the mire of the streets.

⁷But he does not so intend,
and his mind does not so think;
but it is in his mind to destroy,
and to cut off nations not a few;
⁸for he says:
"Are not my commanders all kings?
⁹Is not Calno like Carchemish?
Is not Hamath like Arpad?

Is not Samaria like Damascus?
[10]As my hand has reached to the
kingdoms of the idols
whose graven images were
greater than those of
Jerusalem and Samaria,
[11]Shall I not do to Jerusalem and
her idols
as I have done to Samaria and
her images?"
[12]When the Lord has finished all
his work on Mount Zion and on
Jerusalem he will punish the arrogant boasting of the king of Assyria and his haughty pride.
[13]For he says:
"By the strength of my hand I
have done it,
and by my wisdom, for I have
understanding;
I have removed the boundaries of
peoples,
and have plundered their
treasures;
like a bull I have brought down
those who sat on thrones.
[14]My hand has found like a nest
the wealth of the peoples;
and as men gather eggs that have
been forsaken
so I have gathered all the earth;
and there was none that moved a
wing,

or opened the mouth, or
chirped."
[15]Shall the axe vaunt itself over
him who hews with it,
or the saw magnify itself
against him who wields it?
As if a rod should wield him who
lifts it,
or as if a staff should lift him
who is not wood!
[16]Therefore the Lord, the LORD of
hosts,
will send wasting sickness
among his stout warriors,
and under his glory a burning will
be kindled,
like the burning of fire.
[17]The light of Israel will become a
fire,
and his Holy One a flame;
and it will burn and devour
his thorns and briers in one
day.
[18]The glory of his forest and of his
fruitful land
the LORD will destroy, both
soul and body,
and it will be as when a sick
man wastes away.
[19]The remnant of the trees of his
forest will be so few
that a child can write them
down. (RSV)

The extent of Assyrian power is described in verses 5-11, which include a list of the major Mesopotamian, Syrian, and Israelite cities that had already fallen (v. 9). Sargon records how he conquered and destroyed these cities:

> The king's throne would be set up before the gates of the city and the prisoners would be paraded before him, led by the monarch of the captured town, who would undergo the most agonizing torture, such as having his eyes put out or confinement in a cage, until the king of Assyria set a term to his long-drawn agony. Sargon had the defeated king of Damascus burned alive before his eyes.

The wives and daughters of the captured king were destined for the Assyrian harems and those who were not of noble blood were condemned to slavery. Meanwhile the soldiery had been massacring the population, and brought the heads of their victims in into the king's presence, where they were counted up by the scribes. Not all the male prisoners were put to death, for the boys and craftsmen were led into captivity, where they would be assigned to the hardest tasks on the royal building projects, where the swamps which cover so much of Mesopotamia must have caused an enormously high rate of mortality. The remainder of the population were uprooted and sent to the other end of the empire. (Quoted in A. Heschel, *The Prophets* [New York: Jewish Publ. Soc. of America, 1962], p. 163.)

The arrogant boasting of Assyria would eventually bring God's wrath upon her, but only after she had completed her task against Jerusalem.

In verse 12, Isaiah gives the first hint that Jerusalem will actually be attacked by Assyria as was Samaria. The Assyrian invasion no doubt fulfilled a purpose the Lord had in mind; he wanted to humble the Jews and awaken them to an awareness of him. The invasion referred to took place under Sennacherib in the year 701 B.C. During this invasion, many cities in Judah were destroyed, but Jerusalem miraculously held out against the Assyrian siege because the Lord sent a terrible sickness throughout the Assyrian camps, which caused many deaths. (2 Kgs. 19:35, 37; Isa. 36-37.)

The major point of these verses is that even though the Lord sent Assyria to carry out judgments on Israel and Judah, Assyria was sinful too, claiming victory because of her own strength and not rightfully giving the credit to God (vs. 12-14).

Starting with verse 15 and continuing through verse 19, the Lord pronounces the judgment coming upon Assyria for her undue pride. The ax, Assyria, is nothing without the one who wields it, the Lord; because Assyria has tried to take the credit, she will be smitten (v. 15). (As described earlier, sickness did break out among the Assyrian troops, causing them to lift their siege of Jerusalem.) Continuing the judgment upon Assyria, Isaiah says that they will be so completely destroyed that even a child could count the number of people left (v. 19). Indeed, the Babylonians and Persians later destroyed the Assyrian empire so completely that the Assyrians ceased to be a people.

A Remnant of Israel to Be Saved

Even though the country of Israel was destroyed by the Assyrians, and her people were scattered through the Assyrian Empire, Isaiah promises that a remnant of Israel will return to the Lord and their promised land:

> 20In that day the remnant of Israel and the survivors of the house of Jacob will no more lean upon him that smote them, but will lean upon the LORD, the Holy One of Israel, in truth. 21A remnant will return, the remnant of Jacob, to the mighty God. 22For though your people Israel be as the sand of the sea, only a remnant of them will return. Destruction is decreed, overflowing with righteousness. 23For the Lord, the LORD of hosts, will make a full end, as decreed, in the midst of all the earth. (RSV)

The concept of a remnant returning is a key theme in Isaiah's writings. It goes back to his initial vision (Isa. 6:13) and remains a thread of hope weaving throughout his darkest pronouncements of doom.

Isaiah uses the term *remnant* to describe two distinct groups of Israelites: he talks about a remnant that remains in the land after the Assyrian destruction and promises the return of a future righteous remnant. The two groups are called the *historical remnant* and the *eschatological remnant* respectively. The historical remnant is the group present from a past event (such as the Assyrian invasions), while the eschatological remnant is the group that will emerge from a future action of God and have the qualifications of a latter-day, millennial society. Isaiah's urgent hope is that the historical remnant of the eighth century B.C. will return to the Lord and become the community from which the eschatological remnant will emerge.

Isaiah concludes his pronouncement in chapter 10 by again addressing Israel and promising that the Lord will relieve her of the Assyrian oppression:

> 24Therefore thus says the Lord, the LORD of hosts: "O my people, who dwell in Zion, be not afraid of the Assyrians when they smite with the rod and lift up their staff against you as the Egyptians did. 25For in a very little while my indignation will come to an end, and my anger will be directed to their destruction. 26And the LORD of hosts will wield against them a scourge as when he smote Midian at the rock of Oreb: and his rod will be over the sea, and he will lift it as he did in Egypt. 27And in that day his burden will depart from your shoulder, and his yoke will be destroyed from your neck."
>
> He has gone up from Rimmon,
> 28he has come to Aiath;
> he has passed through Migron,
> at Michmash he stores his baggage;
> 29they have crossed over the pass,
> at Geba they lodge for the night,;

Ramah trembles,
  Gibe-ah of Saul has fled.
30Cry aloud, O daughter of Gallim!
  Hearken, O Laishah!
  Answer her, O Anathoth!
31Madmenah is in flight,
  the inhabitants of Gebim flee
  for safety.
32This very day he will halt
  at Nob,
  he will shake his fist
  at the mount of the daughter
  of Zion,
  the hill of Jerusalem.

33Behold, the Lord, the LORD
  of hosts
  will lop the boughs with
  terrifying power;
  the great in height will be
  hewn down,
  and the lofty will be brought
  low.
34He will cut down the thickets
  of the forest with an axe,
  and Lebanon with its majestic
  trees will fall. (RSV)

Although the Assyrian army will come close to Jerusalem (vs. 28-32), the Lord promises that he will finally cut down the Assyrian leaders in order to preserve Jersualem. The cities conquered during the Assyrian invasion are shown in the map on page 166.

The Assyrians did later invade Judah and came almost into Jerusalem. (Isa. 36-37.) However, the invasion Isaiah foretells may also be eschatological and refer to the future attack upon Jerusalem by forces from the north. (See Zech. 14:2; Rev. 11:1-13; JST Matt. 24.) Another reason for looking at the end of chapter 10 from a latter-day context is that chapter 11 is definitely a prophecy to be fulfilled after 1823, for Moroni told Joseph Smith in September of that year "that it was about to be fulfilled." (JS-H 1:40.)

In conclusion, chapters 9 and 10 present a blend of historical warnings, messianic promises, and latter-day prophecies. The people of Isaiah's time could have learned from his words and been blessed, especially as they heeded his counsel. We today can heed the same warnings, since similar conditions of wickedness and war appear in our society.

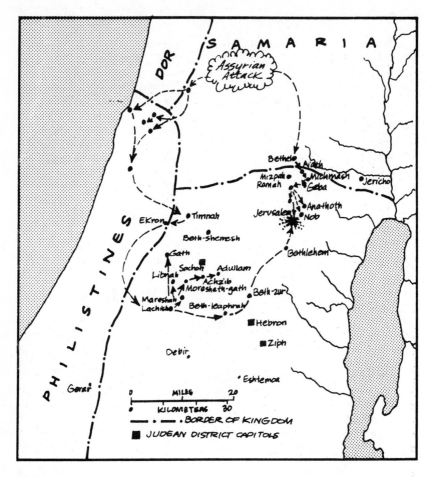

Assyrian Attack

LATTER-DAY SERVANTS OF POWER AND MILLENNIAL PEACE
ISAIAH 11-12

In sweeping panoramic visions, the Lord taught Isaiah remarkable truths about our time. Like Moroni (see Morm. 8), he saw our day—the last days; he foresaw the events and personalities of this dispensation in fulfillment of the Lord's designs to elevate this planet and its inhabitants to a more glorious millennial existence.

When Moroni visited Joseph Smith on the night of September 21, 1823, he quoted the eleventh chapter of Isaiah and told Joseph that "it was about to be fulfilled." (JS-H 1:40.) This important chapter describes people and events associated with the Millennium. It contains some classic verses about the wolf and the lamb dwelling together and how Israel will be gathered a second time. However, some of the terms and symbols in this chapter are extremely difficult to understand. Later revelations clarify some of the terms and identify leaders who would assume important roles in this dispensation. In 1838, Joseph asked the Lord about the meaning of three key terms in this chapter. The revealed answers were recorded in section 113 of the Doctrine and Covenants. These three terms are identified as separate personalities who would play important roles in the last days.

11 But a shoot shall grow
     out of the stump of Jesse
A twig shall branch off from his
  stock. (NJV)

This verse develops further the metaphor introduced in the previous chapter in which the Lord warned Assyria of her pride and eventual fall. The time would come when the oppressed of Israel would escape the power of the Assyrian yoke. Chapter 10 ends with Isaiah's promise that the mighty trees (or leaders) of Assyria would be hewn down (or humbled). Isaiah then begins his prophecy in chapter 11 speaking of *new* trees (or leaders) that would come forth out of Israel to rule and bless the earth.

Verse 1 appears to be an example of synonymous parallelism, a poetic device used by Isaiah in nearly every chapter. Apparently the reference to two separate individuals (rod = branch; stem = roots) is his way of saying the same thing twice, but in slightly different words:

A. And there shall come forth a *rod* out of the *stem of Jesse*,
B. And a *branch* shall grow out of *his roots*. (KJV)

In section 113 of the Doctrine and Covenants, the Lord identifies two key terms used in this verse: "rod" and "stem of Jesse." The "rod" is "a servant in the hands of Christ, who is partly a descendant of Jesse as well as of Ephraim . . . on whom there is laid much power." (D&C 113:3-4.) The "stem" is Christ himself. (See D&C 113:1-2.)[1] Therefore, the first part of verse 1 could be translated:

And there shall come forth a descendant of Jesse and Ephraim who shall be a powerful servant in the hands of Christ . . .

Continuing the parallelism, the second part of the verse ("and a branch shall grow out of his roots") could read:

. . . yea, a helper from among his children shall come forth.

The humble beginnings of this servant might be indicated by the use of the terms "rod" (twig) and "branch" instead of the more prominent images of "limb," "trunk," or "tree." It might also emphasize the barrenness of Israelite leadership at the time. At any rate, it is clear that this "rod" or "branch" would grow into a mighty tree and assume an important role in the last days.

The term *branch* in the King James text comes from the Hebrew word *natzar*, which appears in only one other prophetic book of the Old Testament—Daniel 11:7. In Daniel's vision of the last days, he mentions a "branch" coming from "roots." (See Dan. 11:7–12:1.) Many other scriptures mention the "branch" or leader who will build a temple and fight against the wicked king and stand witness of the Lord's final victory in the last days. He is called by many names and titles, including: "my servant, the BRANCH" (Zech. 3:8-9); "my servant David," a "king" over the Jews (Ezek. 37:21-28); "a righteous Branch and a King" in whose days Judah would be saved (Jer. 23:3-8); "a Branch of righteousness" (Jer. 33:15); "a leader and

---

[1]See also Rev. 22:16, where the Savior calls himself the "root and offspring of David." Also, in John 15, the branches (disciples) of the true vine (Christ) are described.

commander to the people" (Isa. 55:3-4); and "David their king in the latter days" (Hosea 3:4-5).

Modern prophets have also discussed this Jewish leader of the last days. Joseph Smith said, "The throne and kingdom of David is to be taken from him and given to another by the name of David in the last days, raised up out of his lineage." (HC 6:253.) In his dedicatory prayer on the Mount of Olives, Orson Hyde prophesied: "Raise up Jerusalem . . . and constitute her people a distinct nation and government, with David Thy servant, even a descendant from the loins of ancient David to be their king." (HC 4:457.)

In summary, the servant ("rod" and "branch") of Isaiah 11:1 appears to describe the great Jewish leader of the last days who will be called David. He will be an instrument (in somewhat the same manner as was Cyrus anciently—see Isa. 44:28) used by the Lord to fulfill his divine plan of events before the Millennium.

²The spirit of the Lord shall
    alight upon him:
A spirit of wisdom and insight,
A spirit of counsel and valor,
A spirit of devotion and reverence
    for the Lord.
³He shall sense the truth by his
    reverence for the Lord:
He shall not judge by what his
    eyes behold,
Nor decide by what his ears
    perceive.

⁴Thus he shall judge the poor with
    equity
and decide with justice for the
    lowly of the land.
He shall strike down a land with
    the rod of his mouth
and slay the wicked with the
    breath of his lips.
⁵Justice shall be the girdle of his
    loins,
And faithfulness the girdle of his
    waist. (NJV)

These verses describe some important characteristics of this great leader. The Spirit of the Lord will rest upon him and other spiritual gifts will be his. He will be led to reverence the Lord. He might not be a Christian or a member of Christ's true church, but he will respect the Lord and have concern for others. He will judge righteously through the power of discernment. Like the prophets Joshua (Deut. 34:9), Samuel (1 Sam. 16:7), and Jesus (John 7:24), he will not depend upon the physical senses of man, but upon the Spirit of God, and will be able to judge in righteousness and equity. (See 1 Cor. 2:10-16.) Indeed, verse 5 could be rephrased as "righteousness shall be the girdle [strength] of his loins, and faithfulness the girdle of his reins [sinews]."

These spiritual powers and promises also belong to Christ. (See D&C 113:2; 2 Ne. 30:9-11), as he is their giver. He, in turn, promises to share them with his endowed and faithful disciples as they live righteously and become more and more like him. (See Alma 20:4; D&C 113:8.) These verses therefore achieve a double fulfillment, as they describe both Christ and his servants. (Compare Ps. 22, 110.)

6The wolf shall dwell with the
   lamb,
The leopard lie down with the kid;
The calf, the beast of prey, and
   the fatling together,
With a little boy to herd them.
7The cow and the bear shall graze,
   Their young shall lie down
     together;
And the lion, like the ox,
   shall eat straw.
8A babe shall play
   over a viper's hole
And an infant pass his hand
   over an adder's den.
9In all of My sacred mount
   nothing evil or vile shall be done;
For the land shall be filled with
   devotion to the Lord
As water covers the sea. (NJV)

These well-known verses describe the millennial period of peace between wild and domesticated animals (wolf and lamb, leopard and goat, lion and calf) and between helpless people and deadly animals (children and poisonous serpents). Enmity between animals will cease and Satan will be bound as man's righteousness and knowledge increase. (D&C 101:26-34; 2 Ne. 30:16-18.) The earth will begin to fill the measure of her creation as righteousness prevails and the knowledge of the glory of God fills the world even as the waters cover the sea. (See Hab. 2:14.) The gospel will be spread to all nations until "all the inhabitants of the earth shall embrace it." (DS 3:64-65; see also Spencer W. Kimball, "Lamanite Prophecies Fulfilled," *BYU Speeches of the Year* [Provo: BYU Press], 1964-65, p. 11.)

10In that day,
   The stock of Jesse that has
     remained standing
   Shall become a standard to
     nations—
Peoples shall seek his counsel,
And his abode shall be honored.
(KJV)

Another major figure of the last days is introduced in this verse: a "root of Jesse," who shall stand as an ensign for the people to which the Gentiles shall seek. The Lord identifies this "root of Jesse" as a "descendant of Jesse, as well as of Joseph, unto whom rightly belongs the priesthood, and the keys of the kingdom, for an ensign, and for the gathering of my people in the last days." (D&C 113:5-6.)

This servant would hold the priesthood keys that would serve as an ensign for the Gentiles and result in the gathering of Israel in the last days. He is often identified as the Prophet Joseph Smith. (See VIP, pp. 34-38.) In comparing Joseph Smith with the "root of Jesse," each aspect of his calling will be analyzed:

1. A descendant of Jesse and Joseph.
2. A rightful heir to the priesthood.
3. A holder of the keys to the kingdom.
4. His work to be an ensign to the nations.
5. His role in the gathering of Israel in the last days.[2]

Joseph Smith: Descendant of Jesse and Joseph

The Book of Mormon contains an important prophecy about a descendant of the ancient Joseph who would also be named Joseph and who would do a great work of salvation among the Israelites to bring them to the knowledge of God's covenants in the last days. (2 Ne. 3:6-11, 14-15.) Joseph Smith, Jr., is this Joseph. His patriarchal blessing identifies him as the heir to the promises of Ephraim (son of

---

[2]In Romans 15:12, due to some mistranslations of "stem" and "root" in this chapter of the Greek Septuagint, Paul identified the root as Christ. See BMC, p. 223.

the ancient Joseph), and he is called a pure Ephraimite[3] by Brigham Young. (DS 3:250-54; WTP, pp. 125-27.)

There is not the same recorded evidence of Joseph Smith being a descendant of Jesse through the tribe of Judah. However, there were occasions in earlier Church history when a number of the brethren, including Joseph Smith, claimed that they shared lineage with Jesus in the tribe of Judah. (See *Life of Heber C. Kimball* [1888], p. 185; JD 4:248; *Journal of President Rudger Clawson*, pp. 374-75; *Ivins Journal*, p. 21.)

In short, Joseph Smith fulfills the requirements as a descendant of Joseph through his son Ephraim. He was also a descendant of Judah through Jesse, and he may have descended through the same lineage as Jesus.

Joseph Smith: Rightful Heir to the Priesthood

The early priesthood holders of this dispensation were lawful heirs to their power through their lineage. (D&C 86:8-11.) Indeed, Isaiah prophesied that the strength of Zion in the last days would be the authority of the priesthood to which Zion "has a right by lineage." (Isa. 52:1; D&C 113:8; see also 107:40-41, 56-57.) Joseph Smith held the priesthood and through it organized the Church of Jesus Christ in this dispensation. (See D&C 13; 20; 23; 84; 107; 124:123.)

Joseph Smith: Holder of the Keys of the Kingdom

With the priesthood, the Prophet also received certain keys. First, he received the office of an apostle under the hands of Peter, James, and John, who held the keys of "the kingdom of heaven." (See Matt. 16:19; D&C 27:12-13.) Later, through Moses, Elias,[4] and Elijah, he received the keys necessary for this dispensation and was told that thus the world would know that the "great and dreadful day of the

---

[3]This phrase could not mean that all of Joseph Smith's ancestors were descendants only of Ephraim, because Ephraim's immediate children could not marry each other but were probably married to other Israelites or at least to other Semites. Jesus is known as the rightful heir of Judah, yet even his ancestry contained non-Israelite blood (Ruth the Moabite). That Joseph Smith is a "pure Ephraimite" probably means that if he traced his genealogy back to the time of Jacob or Israel, his "pure" patriarchal line (that is, his father's-father's-father, etc.) would trace directly to Ephraim.

[4]See D&C 77:9, 14; HC 1:176, and HC 6:249-54 for ideas about the role of "Elias," messengers who were to come in this dispensation. See also Isa. 40:3, Mal. 3:1, and Mark 1:3 for scriptures about a messenger who was to come before the Messiah.

Lord" was near at hand. (D&C 110:11-16.) With these keys for the gathering of Israel, missionary work, the sealing powers of the temple, and other powers, Joseph Smith had the authority to usher in the dispensation of the fullness of times. (D&C 65:2; 107:8; 115:18-19; 128:10-14, 20-21.)

Joseph Smith: His Work to Be an Ensign to the Nations

In 1844, the Prophet Joseph Smith stated:

> The Savior said . . . the keys of knowledge, power and revelations should be revealed to a witness who should hold the testimony to the world. . . . The testimony is that the Lord in the last days would commit the keys of the priesthood to a witness over all people . . . a special messenger—ordained and prepared for that purpose in the last days. (HC 6:363-64.)

Joseph recorded that Moroni had told him "that God had a work for me to do; and that my name should be had for good and evil among all nations, kindreds, and tongues." (JS-H 1:33.)

After the Church was organized, the Prophet Joseph Smith became the rallying point and the source of God's knowledge and strength to the early Saints. (See D&C 5:10.) By the time of his martyrdom, the Church had grown so much that its leaders were ready to fulfill their purpose and continue the work Joseph began. The gospel (the everlasting covenant) has since spread worldwide, thereby becoming a *light* to the world, a *standard* (or ensign) for the Lord's people and for the Gentiles to seek and a *messenger*[5] to prepare the way before Christ's second coming. (See D&C 45:9; DS 3:254-62; D&C 135:3.)

Joseph Smith: His Role in the Gathering of Israel in the Last Days

On April 3, 1836, Joseph Smith received from the resurrected Moses the keys for the "gathering of Israel from the four parts of the earth, and the leading of the ten tribes from the land of the north." (D&C 110:11.)[6] A few years later, in 1841, the Prophet sent Orson Hyde to Palestine to dedicate the land for the return of the Jews, and since 1881, the Jews have returned to Israel from over a hundred

---

[5]See end of footnote 3.

[6]See also D&C 133:25-35; Amos 9:9; Isa. 10:20-22; 35:8-10; HC 4:456; 5:336-37; TPJS, pp. 17, 83, 308.

nations. Also, through missionary work, scattered remnants of Israel have joined the Lord's restored kingdom by the hundreds of thousands. The keys for this work have been passed down through succeeding presidents of The Church of Jesus Christ of Latter-day Saints, and the gathering that began with Joseph Smith is still in progress.

Joseph Smith's life and ministry easily demonstrate how he could be the "root of Jesse" spoken of in Isaiah 11:10. He was a priesthood leader and servant of the Lord who established a great work. The Church is an ensign to the world and now directs the gathering of Israel to spiritual Zion.

Still, Joseph Smith might not be the only "root of Jesse" in these last days. Many presidents of the Church have been related to him by blood, and all have held the priesthood and the keys of the kingdom that he held. For example, President Spencer W. Kimball is related to Joseph, and he has magnified the keys of missionary work, especially among the Lamanites and the Jews. The "root of Jesse" could also be that particular prophet who will hold the keys when Christ returns to preside personally over his kingdom. The term could even represent the office of the president of the Church. In any case, the "root of Jesse" designates a great leader in the Church of Jesus Christ in this dispensation.

[11]In that day, My Lord will apply His hand again to redeeming the other part of His people from Assyria—as also from Egypt, Pathros, Nubia, Elam, Shinar, Hamath, and the coastlands. [12]He will hold up a signal to the nations And assemble the banished of Israel, And gather the dispersed of Judah From the four corners of the earth. (NJV)

These verses elaborate on the gathering of Israel and the role of an ensign. The first gathering of Israel took place after the Babylonian captivity; during the second gathering, remnants will return from all directions (as symbolized by different countries)[7] and from various continents (islands of the sea). The Lord will also set up a church (or ensign) for the nations and the scattered outcasts of Israel. (A more detailed discussion of the gathering of Judah and Israel is on pp. 301-4, 414-17.)

[7]Assyria = Modern Iraq; Egypt and Pathros = Egypt; Cush (or Nubia) = Ethiopia; Elam = Iran; Shinar = Iraq; Hamath = Syria.

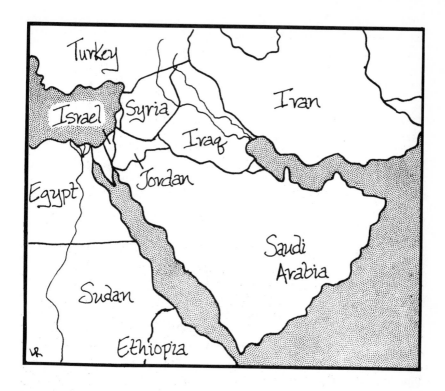

¹³Then Ephraim's envy shall cease
  And Judah's harassment shall
    end;
  Ephraim shall not envy Judah,
  And Judah shall not harass
    Ephraim.
¹⁴They shall pounce on the back of
    Philistia to the west,
  And together plunder the peoples
    of the east;
  Edom and Moab shall be subject
    to them
  And the children of Ammon shall
    obey them. (NJV)

After the dispersal of the Jews (Judah) and the remnants of Israel, including the Ten Tribes (Ephraim) return, they will work together and prevail over their earlier enemies to the east (Edom, Moab, Ammon = Modern Jordan) and west (Philistines = Gaza Strip). The ancient hostility between Israel (Ephraim) and Judah will cease as they unite their righteous efforts. Some scholars recognize a similar promise recorded in Ezekiel 37:16-17, where the stick of Judah (Bible) and the stick of Ephraim (Book of Mormon) will become one to testify to the world. (See Freehof, *Book of Isaiah*, p. 78.)

¹⁵The Lord will dry up the tongue of the Egyptian sea.—He will raise His hand over the Euphrates with the might of His wind and break it into seven wadis, so that it can be trodden dry-shod.

¹⁶Thus there shall be a highway for the other part of His people out of Assyria, such as there was for Israel when it left the land of Egypt. (NJV)

Various interpretations have been rendered for the term "tongue of the Egyptian sea" in verse 15. It might be the western arm of the Red Sea (or Gulf of Suez, for which the modern Suez Canal was named) and the narrow body of water that extended north from the Red Sea into the desert. Another possibility is the delta (or tongue) of the Nile, which protruded into the Mediterranean Sea along Egypt's north coast. The most likely explanation, however, is the large inland sea created late each spring as the Nile overflows its banks and floods a large part of the valley, like a tongue sticking far inland. Isaiah 19:5-10 describes the destruction of the Nile River in greater detail. If the Nile River is the "tongue of the Egyptian Sea," then this prophecy might have been fulfilled since the building of the Aswan Dam and the destruction of the traditional way of life along the Nile.

176

Verse 15 states also that the Lord will divert "the river" (usually understood to be the Euphrates River) into seven streams so that travelers can walk across without getting their feet wet. In addition, a highway will be prepared for the remnant of Israel coming from Assyria (the land on the other side of the Euphrates). Isaiah 19:23-25, too, prophesies of a highway all the way from Assyria (through Israel) to Egypt. Other prophecies describe a great highway for the righteous in the last days. (See Isa. 35:8-10; 51:9-11; D&C 133:27.)

Although this highway might be a literal, physical road, it could also be representative of any means of transportation, such as an airway or railroad. As indicated in verse 16, this will be a highway like there was for Israel when the Lord led them out of Egypt. The Lord did not create a literal road for ancient Israel, but he did prepare the way for them so they would reach their destination. (Compare Isa. 11, footnotes 15a, 15b; Rev. 16:12.) He will do the same for Israel in the last days and they will recognize his hand in their return. (Jer. 16:14-15; 30; 31.)

The eleventh chapter of Isaiah contains some marvelous prophecies of the last days. It enlightens modern Israelites about the roles of at least two great leaders who will prepare the way for the coming of Christ in power and glory. They may possibly be the two "saviors" or "messiahs" known in Jewish tradition as "Messiah ben David" (a redeemer descended from David) and "Messiah ben Joseph" (a redeemer descended from Joseph).[8]

Two brief psalms comprise the whole of chapter 12, and they provide a suitable conclusion to the messianic images of chapter 11. This short chapter is also a positive, inspirational capstone for the first dozen chapters of Isaiah's writings; in the beginning chapters, Isaiah sharply denounces Israelite follies and encourages the Israelites to repent (Isa. 1-5); in chapter 6, he reviews his calling and role as a prophet; in the next group he gives inspired political advice and subtle messianic prophecies (Isa. 7-9); and in his final section, he concludes with pointed warnings to Assyria and millennial promises to Israel (Isa. 10-11), with chapter 12 ending this section.

In the two psalms of chapter 12, Isaiah speaks for all Israel as he

---

[8]*Encyclopedia Judaica* 11:1411 states: "A secondary messianic figure is the Messiah son of [of the tribe of] Joseph (or Ephraim), whose coming precedes that of the Messiah, son of David, and who will die in combat with the enemies of God and Israel." Joseph Smith and his martyrdom could already be a fulfillment of this role. More detailed Jewish commentaries are recorded by Odeberg in *3 Enoch or The Hebrew Book of Enoch*, pp. 144-47.

gives thanks and praise to the Lord for providing salvation and millennial blessings.

12 In that day, you shall say: "I give thanks to You, O LORD! Although You were wroth with me, Your wrath has turned back and You comfort me, ²Behold the God who gives me triumph!

I am confident, unafraid; For Yah the LORD is my strength and might, And He has been my deliverance." ³Joyfully shall you draw water From the fountains of triumph. (NJV)

By comparing the punctuation, especially the quotation marks, with the King James Version, a major problem with this short psalm becomes apparent. Although the beginning of the psalm is clearly defined in verse 1, the conclusion of the psalm remains indefinite. Scholars agree that verse 3 is the most important verse in this set, but they disagree as to whether or not it should be included within the psalm. Unfortunately, the original Hebrew provides no help with this problem because it contains no punctuation at all. Indeed, most early Hebrew writings had no punctuation, since such symbols were not developed or even encouraged because space on writing materials (scrolls of parchment, clay tablets, metal plates, etc.) was at a premium, and most readers of the materials were familiar enough with it that they could supply the necessary breaks, pauses, and inflections. Therefore, context becomes the best clue for interpretation.

In analyzing the important role of verse 3 in this psalm, then, the first two verses need to be studied. In verse 1 Isaiah addresses the gathered remnants of Israel (see the end of chapter 11) and speaks as all Israel in giving thanks to the Lord for "turning away his wrath and comforting him," or forgiving his sins. Then, in verse 2, the Israelite turns to an unidentified audience and extolls the virtues of God. He could be speaking to the world at large or he might be bearing his testimony to fellow Israelites. If verse 3 is a continuation of this psalm, the speaker concludes by exhorting the listeners to come and join with him in these spiritual experiences. On the other hand, if the psalm ends with verse 2, then Isaiah himself would be the speaker in verse 3 as he encourages gathered Israel to enjoy these religious opportunities. In either case, those who have not yet enjoyed a close fellowship with the Lord are invited to receive that blessing. Other important concepts, including the basic gospel principles, are found in these three verses: justice and forgiveness, trust and faith, and an invitation to the waters of salvation (which are now symbolized by the waters of baptism and the sacrament) are the key themes of this psalm and exhortation. The speaker, be it Isaiah, an Israelite, or all those gathered to Zion, has much to be thankful for, and he beautifully expresses his gratitude in these few verses.

The second psalm is also one of thanksgiving. Technically, though, it is more of a "praise psalm" than a "thanks psalm," for in giving praise to the Lord one has a slightly different attitude than in giving thanks. In a praise psalm, attention is centered upon the person being extolled, but in a thanks psalm the viewpoint is focused on the person giving thanks and upon the blessing that he has received. The first psalm of chapter 12 is in the "thanks" category; the second is more of a "praise" type:

4And you shall say on that day:
   "Praise the LORD, proclaim His name.
Make His deeds known among the peoples;
Declare that His name is exalted.
5Hymn the LORD,

For He has done gloriously
Let this be made known
In all the world!
6Oh, shout for joy,
You who dwell in Zion!
For great in your midst
Is the Holy One of Israel." (NJV)

A natural pattern of spiritual growth is shown by Isaiah in these two short psalms. First, the individual gains his own faith in the Lord and the atonement (vs. 1-2). Second, he wants others to share in the blessings of baptism and salvation (v. 3). Then, his testimony manifests itself so strongly that he publicly exhorts others to make the Lord's deeds known to all (v. 4). Finally, his deep convictions are evidenced by his singing of praises and bearing witness of the truth (vs. 5-6). A pattern similar to this is developed in another millennial psalm as recorded by Joseph Smith in Doctrine and Covenants 84:99-102. First, the Lord's redemption is extolled and the principles of faith and covenant-making are enjoined (vs. 99-100). Then the Lord's deeds are recounted (vs. 100-101), and the hymn concludes with glorious praises to God (v. 102).

Isaiah and Joseph Smith yearned for the Millennium, and both prophets used short, powerful hymns to give sincere thanks and profound praise to the Lord for the blessings he would give the earth. In a few verses, they each expressed the gratitude all of us should feel as the Lord's works become manifest among men.

BABYLON AND HER KING
ISAIAH 13-14

Isaiah was first and foremost a prophet to the house of Israel, though he also spoke to others of God's children and gave inspired warning and promises to other nations. Most of these pronouncements to foreign nations are grouped together in Isaiah 13-23. Having laid the foundation of his teachings in the first dozen chapters of his writings, Isaiah turns to the nations who surrounded and often opposed Israel. Some of these nations had manifested themselves as enemies of God's people, while others had refused to aid their brothers and fellow Semites, the Israelites. In chapters 13-23 Isaiah prophesies concerning these nations in their contemporary settings, while often including promises of an eschatological nature. (See map, p. 181.)

In chapter 13, Isaiah first addresses Babylon, the ancient country that had ruled over the Middle East until displaced by the Assyrians. (See Map 2.) Although Babylon was subject to Assyrian rule during Isaiah's lifetime, she gradually regained power and independence until the New Babylonian Empire replaced Assyria as the major power in the Fertile Crescent at the end of the seventh century B.C. (Compare Maps 10 and 11.) But even during the so-called Assyrian period, Babylon still represented the best of culture, learning, literature, and religion (in the same way that Greek culture was sustained and imitated during the Roman period). Therefore, Isaiah often uses Babylon and her king as symbols of the world and its wickedness. (Isa. 13-14.)

Isaiah also speaks to Moab and Syria, both of which lie east of Israel. These peoples gloried in the downfall of Israel and the humiliation of Judah. Moab and Syria are warned of their impending destruction and promised a restoration in later times. (Isa. 15-17.)

Isaiah addresses some of the countries west of Israel. In chapter 18 he speaks of a strange land beyond Africa that thrives under the

180

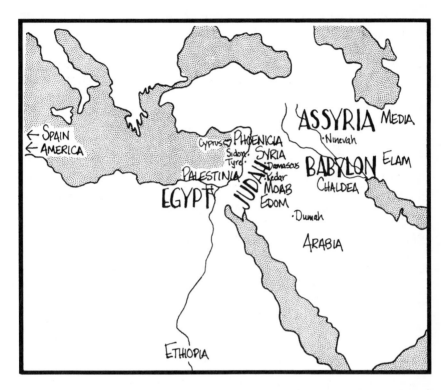

special protection of God. As Hyrum Smith indicated, this land represents America. (HC 6:322.) Chapters 19 and 20 contain special promises to Egypt.

Isaiah directs other pronouncements toward the Assyrians, Philistines, various nomadic desert people, Phoenicians, and even the inhabitants of Jerusalem. (Isa. 14:24-32; 21-23.) Isaiah 13-23 consists almost entirely of pronouncements upon the foreign nations, and as a section, it compares with Jeremiah 46-51 and Ezekiel 25-32, in which these prophets group their prophecies thematically rather than strictly chronologically.

This section of foreign pronouncements incorporates two major messages: first, that Jehovah's power and kingdom are worldwide, and second, that foreign oppression of Israel will end. The concept of the Lord's universal rule was somewhat peculiar to ancient Israel. Many ancient pagan religions taught that any given god could be worshipped properly in only one given place, and that he had no power outside certain boundaries.

Isaiah begins his prophecies against Babylon, since Babylon most clearly represents the hostility toward God's plan of salvation in the world. Although Babylon did not represent a military threat to Jerusalem during Isaiah's lifetime, Babylonian culture and its pagan ideologies spread throughout the Middle East. Babylon later became so great an enemy that in Revelation it represents the antichrist forces. (Rev. 17:1-5; 18.) This symbolism is sustained in modern scripture, in which Babylon is used as a name for Satan's kingdom, or "the world." (D&C 1:16; 133:14.)

Remembering that the term *Babylon* has both literal and spiritual meaning helps to clarify the awkward passages in chapters 13 and 14; as is the case with many of Isaiah's prophecies, there are dual fulfillments hidden in his words. This creates a "tension which results from the interviewing of prophecies of a local and a universal future event." (Kaiser, *Isaiah 18-39*, p. 9.)

In addition, Isaiah has some warnings to Assyria and Philistia in chapters 13 and 14, as shown by the outline below.

   I. The fall of Babylon (13:1-22, 14:1-23)
      A. Introduction (13:1)
      B. The Lord gathers his forces (13:2-5)
      C. The Lord brings his power against (spiritual) Babylon (13:6-13)
      D. The Lord brings the Medes against (physical) Babylon (13:14-22)
      B'. The Lord will be merciful to Israel (14:1-3)
      C'. A taunt song against the king of (spiritual) Babylon (14:4-21)
      D'. The destruction of (physical) Babylon (14:22-23)
  II. The fall of Assyria (14:24-27)
 III. The fall of Philistia (14:28-32)

Notice in the section "The Fall of Babylon" how Isaiah prophesies the nation's physical and spiritual downfall in a "double" pronouncement (BCD and B'C'D'). Though it appears that he warns "spiritual Babylon" first in each pronouncement, it is quite difficult to know whether Isaiah is talking about physical or spiritual Babylon. Thus, these verses should be studied in both a historical and eschatological setting. (See Isa. 13, footnote 1c.)

The Fall of Babylon

Isaiah introduces his vision of Babylon with a short verse:

13 This is a message about Babylon, which Isaiah son of Amoz received from God. (TEV)

The "message" (or "burden" [KJV]) that Isaiah delivers to Babylon is a prophetic oracle or divine declaration. The term comes from the Hebrew word *massa*, which becomes a superscription throughout Isaiah's prophecies to the foreign nations. (See Isa. 14:28; 15:1; 17:1; 19:1; 21:1, 11, 13; 22:1; 23:1.) Whereas some translators follow the King James Version and render this term as "burden," others follow the more literal meaning of the Hebrew ("raise up") and translate it as "oracle" or "message." The meanings complement each other, because when a prophet "raises his voice" for God, he delivers an "oracle," which can become a "burden" for the people, since additional knowledge and responsibility is placed upon them. (See Isa. 13, footnote 1b.)

The means by which Isaiah received his message is clearly expressed in the Hebrew: he "saw" (*chazah*) the oracle of Babylon. Since *chazah* is the root for "seer," Isaiah did not just see (*ro'eh*) the vision physically, but he saw it as inspired in his calling as a prophet or seer.

Isaiah begins his pronouncement with the Lord's summoning of his forces from the ends of the earth in preparation for a "holy war":

2On the top of a barren hill raise the battle flag! Shout to the soldiers and raise your arm as the signal for them to attack the gates of the proud city. 3The LORD has called out his proud and confident soldiers to fight a holy war and punish those he is angry with. 4Listen to the noise on the mountains—the sound of a great crowd of people, the sound of nations and kingdoms gathering. The LORD of Armies is preparing his troops for battle. 5They are coming from far-off countries at the ends of the earth. In his anger the LORD is coming to devastate the whole country. (TEV)

The "battle flag" could be used to rally the forces of the world against Jerusalem (see Isa. 10), or it might serve as an "ensign" (KJV) around which the Lord's servants and saints gather against the evil forces of the world. (See Isa. 11:10; 62:10, where the same word is used.) In either case, it will assemble a mighty force that will fulfill some of the Lord's judgments against the wicked.

Isaiah next describes the destruction that the "day of the Lord" will bring upon the world:

6Howl in pain! The day of the LORD is near, the day when the Almighty brings destruction. 7Everyone's hands will hang limp, and everyone's courage will fail. 8They will all be terrified and overcome with pain, like the pain of a woman in labor. They will look at each other in fear, and their faces will burn with shame. ⁹The day of the LORD is coming—that cruel day of his fierce anger and fury. The earth will be made a wilderness, and every sinner will be destroyed. ¹⁰Every star and every constellation will stop shining, the sun will be dark when it rises, and the moon will give no light.

¹¹The LORD says, "I will bring disaster on the earth and punish all wicked people for their sins. I will humble everyone who is proud and punish everyone who is arrogant and cruel. ¹²Those who survive will be scarcer than gold. ¹³I will make the heavens tremble, and the earth will be shaken out of its place on that day when I, the LORD Almighty, show my anger. (TEV)

The phrase "day of the Lord" first appears in the writings of the eighth-century prophets Amos and Isaiah (Amos 5:18-20; Isa. 2:6-22) to refer to a day of judgment that is so extremely severe that the people will howl with fear. Isaiah compares the trembling fear and shaking terror of the men to the anguish of a woman in labor: "But whereas a woman in labour cries, men will only stare at each other aghast in horror and begin to sweat from fear." (Kaiser, *Isaiah 13-39*, p. 16.) The fear of the people described in these verses compares with the fear portrayed earlier by Isaiah in chapter 2 (especially vs. 1-21; see Rev. 6:15-17, in which John writes of a fear that will come upon all the wicked).

Verses 9-13 describe the purpose and results of the Lord's day of vengeance. Verse 9 explains that the purpose of the day of the Lord is to purge the earth of all sinners. (See D&C 133:50-51; Joel 2:1-2; Mal. 4:1; 2 Thes. 1:7-9.) In his later writings, Isaiah elaborates upon the intensity and completeness with which the Lord will cleanse the earth. (Isa. 24:1-6; 34:2-8; 63:4; 64:1-2; 66:15-16.) The cleansing upon the earth parallels manifestations upon the earth and in the heavens (vs. 10, 13). The earth will shake and the heavens turn dark as signs of the day of the Lord. (See Rev. 6:12-14; D&C 133:21-24, 49.) The few who remain upon the earth will be humble and righteous people (vs. 11-12). As a remnant surviving the destruction, they will form the nucleus for a new generation living in a new millennial age. (See Isa. 6:13; 43:1-7, 14-21.)

Isaiah concludes his first pronouncement upon Babylon by graphically describing the physical consequences that will befall the land and its inhabitants:

¹⁴"The foreigners living in Babylon will run away to their homelands, scattering like deer escaping from hunters, like sheep without a shepherd. ¹⁵Anyone who is caught will be stabbed to death. ¹⁶While

they look on helplessly, their babies will be battered to death, their homes will be looted, and their wives will be raped."

[17]The LORD says, "I am stirring up the Medes to attack Babylon. They care nothing for silver and are not tempted by god. [18]With their bows and arrows they will kill the young men. They will show no mercy to babies and take no pity on children.[19]Babylonia is the most beautiful kingdom of all; it is the pride of its people. But I, the LORD, will overthrow Babylon as I did Sodom and Gomorrah! [20]No one will ever live there again. No wandering Arab will ever pitch his tent there, and no shepherd will ever pasture his flock there. [21]It will be a place where desert animals live and where owls build their nests. Ostriches will live there, and wild goats will prance through the ruins. [22]The towers and palaces will echo with the cries of hyenas and jackals. Babylon's time has come! Her days are almost over." (TEV)

The Medes (v. 17) came from Persia and easily conquered Babylon in 538 B.C.. The walls were destroyed twenty years later, after which the city never again became the capital of an independent, strong Mesopotamian power. Two centuries later, after the Greeks, under Alexander the Great, conquered the Persians, Babylon rapidly declined in commercial and cultural importance as Seleucia became the major city in the area. By the time of Christ, only a few astronomers and mathematicians continued to live in the ancient, sparsely populated city. After they left, Babylon remained a deserted *tell* (mound), which sand and brush gradually covered until it became a hill used only by wild animals and as grazing land for nomadic flocks. (IDB 1:335; compare vs. 20-22 above, and Isa. 13, footnote 19a.)

Isaiah begins his second Babylonian pronouncement with another gathering of the Lord's forces. Having proclaimed the destruction of Babylon, he anticipates a time when Israel will return from her exile (physical and spiritual) as other peoples assist her and even become subject to her. Israel will finally rest from her hard centuries of subjugation and service to foreigners:

14 The LORD will once again be merciful to his people Israel and choose them as his own. He will let them live in their own land again, and foreigners will come and live there with them. [2]Many nations will help the people of Israel return to the land which the LORD gave them, and there the nations will serve Israel as slaves. Those who once captured Israel will now be captured by Israel, and the people of Israel will rule over those who once oppressed them.

[3]The LORD will give the people of Israel relief from their pain and suffering and from the hard work they were forced to do. (TEV)

Historically, these verses were fulfilled when Cyrus the Great of Persia issued an order allowing all captive peoples in Babylon to return to their place of origin. The first group of Jews returned in 538 B.C. and started to rebuild Jerusalem and Judea. Another great exodus of Jews began in 520 B.C., and the group eventually was able to rebuild the walls of Jerusalem, the city itself, and the temple. Later, under the Maccabees (167-70 B.C.), the Jews enjoyed autonomy and prosperity, being so successful that they began to proselyte other people in the area and to grow in numbers. Indeed, the body of Jews grew into the millions by the time of Christ; while Babylon became desolate, Judea flourished.

Taken in an eschatological sense, these verses can also find two fulfillments in the latter days. First, they may refer to The Church of Jesus Christ of Latter-day Saints, whose missionary work spreads to all nations and prepares for the peaceful conditions under which the Savior will establish his kingdom at the time of his second coming. Second, these verses may refer to the modern-day return of the Jews to the Holy Land and their building of the modern state of Israel. However, the full blessings of these verses will not be realized until the second coming of Christ, when the Jews will accept him as their Savior.

Isaiah foretells that the Israelites in their homeland will eventually recite a taunt-song about the king of Babylon. Structured in flowing poetry, "this taunt, in the form of a lament, upon the death of a world ruler and the fall of his empire, is one of the most powerful poems not only of the Old Testament, but of the whole literature of the world." (Kaiser, *Isaiah 13-39*, p. 29; Isa. 14, footnote 4a.) In its historical context, the taunt song refers to the fall of the king of Babylon; in an eschatological context, it symbolizes any leader of wickedness, especially Satan:

4When he does this, they are to mock the king of Babylon and say:
"The cruel king has fallen! He will never oppress anyone again! 5The LORD has ended the power of the evil rulers 6who angrily oppressed the peoples and never stopped persecuting the nations they had conquered. 7Now at last the whole world enjoys rest and peace, and everyone sings for joy. 8The cypress trees and the cedars of

A. *On earth.* (See Rev. 17:5; D&C 43:31; Isa. 55:12; Zech. 11:2; the trees also represent people; see Isa. 2:13; 37:24 as discussed in this book.)

186

Lebanon rejoice over the fallen king, because there is no one to cut them down, now that he is gone!

⁹"The world of the dead is getting ready to welcome the king of Babylon. The ghosts of those who were powerful on earth are stirring about. The ghosts of kings are rising from their thrones. ¹⁰They all call out to him, 'Now you are weak as we are! ¹¹You are one of us! You used to be honored with the music of harps, but now here you are in the world of the dead. You lie on a bed of maggots and are covered with a blanket of worms,'"

¹²King of Babylon, bright morning star, you have fallen from heaven! In the past you conquered nations, but now you have been thrown to the ground. ¹³You were determined to climb up to heaven and to place your throne above the highest stars. You thought you would sit like a king on that mountain in the north where the gods assemble. ¹⁴You said you would climb to the tops of the clouds and be like the Almighty. ¹⁵But instead, you have been brought down to the deepest part of the world of the dead.

¹⁶The dead will stare and gape at you. They will ask, "Is this the man who shook the earth and made kingdoms tremble? ¹⁷Is this the man who destroyed cities and turned the world into a desert? Is this the man who never freed his prisoners or let them go home?"

¹⁸All the kings of the earth lie in their magnificent tombs, ¹⁹but you have no tomb, and your corpse is thrown out to rot. It is covered by the bodies of soldiers killed in bat-

B. *In the spirit world.* (See Ezek. 32:21.)

C. *In heaven.* (See Moses 4:1-4; D&C 76:25-27; D&C 29:36-38; Rev. 9:11.)

B'. *In the spirit world.* (See Moses 1:19-21; 4:6; 2 Ne. 2:18-19; 9:9.)

A'. *On earth.* (See Jude 1:6; Jac. 5:73-75; Rev. 12:4, 7-9; 19:21; D&C 29:27-29; 88:85, 101.)

187

tle, thrown with them into a rocky
pit, and trampled down. [20]Because
you ruined your country and killed
your own people, you will not be
buried like other kings. None of
your evil family will survive. [21]Let
the slaughter begin! The sons of
this king will die because of their
ancestors' sins. None of them will
ever rule the earth or cover it with
cities. (TEV)

As highlighted in the chiastic outline in the right margin, the song
contains five stanzas, each with a variation of scene—earth/spirit
world/heavens/spirit world/earth. The scriptural references listed
afterward indicate just a few of the many sources that describe the
same events, though nowhere else are they portrayed in such moving
poetry.

The pivotal point and most important scene lies in verses 12-15, in
which Isaiah identifies the king of Babylon as Lucifer (KJV, "bright
morning star" in the Hebrew and in the TEV quoted above). Most
scholars identify the "morning star" or Lucifer as a mythical figure or
as a figurative representation of a Babylonian king. Latter-day Saints
are fortunate to have modern scripture that explains who Lucifer is.
Additional modern scripture explains his actions and attitude in
greater detail. (Compare Isa. 14:12-14 with D&C 76:25-27; 29:36-37;
Moses 4:1-4.)

Lucifer's attempt to usurp God's power and glory "transgresses
the limits laid down for both mortal and heavenly beings, for he is
trying to take the place reserved for the highest God alone, and is
consequently punished by a fall into the deepest and darkest depths of
the underworld." (Kaiser, *Isaiah 13-39*, p. 41.)

The last two stanzas of the song demonstrate that Lucifer will not
have any honor such as the mortal kings of earth have, though he will
have some temporary power on the earth, even enough to control the
elements (v. 16; see Moses 1:19-21). He did not want the doors of the
(spirit) prison to be opened (v. 17), but he was powerless against
Christ's atoning power. The free gifts of salvation and resurrection are
given to all mortals; even the most wicked kings on earth will still "lie
in glory, every one in his own house" (or "degree of eternal glory"; see
KJV, v. 18). But Lucifer will have no tomb ("house" [KJV] or body,
v. 19), and he will be thrown into a pit (of outer darkness) without any

posterity (v. 20). Finally, he and his sons of perdition will be cast off the earth when it receives its celestial glory (v. 21). The ultimate humiliation is that they will never be renowned (KJV) or named (NJV), but will fade into oblivion (v. 20).

Isaiah concludes his second Babylonian pronouncement by simply stating the Lord's intentions against temporal, physical Babylon:

> ²²The LORD Almighty says, "I will attack Babylon and bring it to ruin. I will leave nothing—no children, no survivors at all. I, the LORD, have spoken. ²³I will turn Babylon into a marsh, and owls will live there, I will sweep Babylon with a broom that will sweep everything away. I, the LORD Almighty have spoken." (TEV)

Babylon will remain an empty, desolate memorial to wickedness because the Lord in his universal power has spoken it. (See Isa. 34, where a similar desolation is promised to Edom.)

After delivering his "double" Babylonian pronouncements, Isaiah continues with two short warnings, one to Assyria and the other to Philistia.

The Fall of Assyria

Isaiah promises that the Lord will "bring" (JST) or "break" (KJV) the Assyrians in the land of Israel. They will feel the measure of his wrath:

> ²⁴The LORD Almighty has sworn an oath: "What I have planned will happen. What I have determined to do will be done. ²⁵I will destroy the Assyrians in my land of Israel and trample them on my mountains. I will free my people from the Assyrian yoke and from the burdens they have had to bear. ²⁶This is my plan for the world, and my arm is stretched out to punish the nations." ²⁷The LORD Almighty is determined to do this; he has stretched out his arm to punish and no one can stop him. (TEV)

It is difficult to determine whether Isaiah is prophesying about the destruction of Sennacherib's Assyrian army in 701 B.C. or the defeat of the army of the nations led by King Gog in the last days. (Compare Isa. 36-37 with Ezek. 38-39.) In both cases, the Lord's punishment is felt by the wicked nations of the earth.

The Fall of Philistia

In one of the rare Isaianic prophecies or "burdens" that are dated, Isaiah speaks to Philistia around 720 B.C.:

²⁸This is a message that was proclaimed in the year that King Ahaz died.

²⁹People of Philistia, the rod that beat you is broken, but you have no reason to be glad. When one snake dies, a worse one comes in its place. A snake's egg hatches a flying dragon. ³⁰The LORD will be a shepherd to the poor of his people and will let them live in safety. But he will send a terrible famine on you Philistines, and it will not leave any of you alive.

³¹Howl and cry for help, all you Philistine cities! Be terrified, all of you. A cloud of dust is coming from the north—it is an army with no cowards in its ranks.

³²How shall we answer the messengers that come to us from Philistia? We will tell them that the LORD has established Zion and that his suffering people will find safety there. (TEV)

In verses 28-30, Isaiah warns the Philistines against prematurely rejoicing either in the death of Shalmaneser V (727-722) or the freedom Philistia maintained after Sargon's conquest of Samaria and Israel (722-721). For although the king was dead and the threat diminished (one snake had died, v. 29), a worse danger ("out of the serpent's root" [KJV]) would come forth (Sennacherib). (The destruction of Philistia is described later in this book as chapters 36 and 37 of Isaiah are examined.)

Isaiah concludes in verses 30-32 with a promise of help and protection to the Philistines. The Lord is also their shepherd, and if they will come and be a part of Zion, they can find refuge and peace with the children of Israel.

In summary, Isaiah concludes his first series of pronouncements upon foreign nations with a picture of refugees from the nations gathered safely within Zion. In spite of the judgments and destructions that he describes, Isaiah recognizes the source for security and peace, the Lord's kingdom of Zion here upon the earth. Those who seek for Zion will find that peace both physically and spiritually, while those who follow the ways and king of Babylon will find only the eternal judgments of God.

WOES UPON MOAB AND SYRIA
ISAIAH 15-17

Having spoken to distant Gentile nations in chapters 13 and 14, Isaiah turns his attention to his fellow Semites and delivers the Lord's pronouncements upon them. He speaks primarily to Moab and Syria, neighboring nations immediately east of the Jordan Valley. The Syrians to the northeast of Israel were distant Semitic relatives, while the Moabites to the southeast were more closely related, as they were descendants of Abraham's nephew, Lot. Some Israelite tribes, Gad, Reuben, and part of Manesseh, occupied the territories east of the Jordan River (the Transjordan), and Isaiah also included some promises for them.

Moab (ch. 15-16)

Moab lies in the region east of the Dead Sea. Her inhabitants descended from Moab, the son of Lot and his eldest daughter. (See Gen. 19:31-37.) In chapters 15 and 16, Isaiah pronounces a two-part "burden" upon Moab. Chapter 15 describes the destruction of the cities of Moab and the mourning of its inhabitants, and chapter 16 gives an allusion to the future Messiah while continuing the description of woe. This allusion to the Messiah helps us to see these chapters not only in their historical context but also in their eschatological setting and fulfillment. The eschatological setting of this Moab prophecy is in keeping with this section of prophecies to the nations (Isa. 13-23) and their dual fulfillment—anciently and in the last days. In a latter-day context, Moab can be viewed as representing the enemies of God, with her destruction typifying the consequences coming upon those who oppose Israel at Christ's second coming. A survey of Moabite history preceding Isaiah will help us understand Moab's relationship with the ancient Israelites and how their hatred resulted in wars and came to represent opposition to the Lord's chosen people.

During Isaiah's lifetime, Moab lost her independence, becoming a vassal state to Assyria at least as early as the reign of Tiglath-Pileser III (754-727 B.C.), who destroyed Syria, invaded Israel, annexed large territories east of the Jordan Valley, and deported many Israelites to Assyria. Although the dates of Isaiah's pronouncements upon Moab are not given, it is assumed that they were delivered a few years before the massive Assyrian invasion and conquest of the Transjordan area in 730-727 B.C. (See Map 9 and note the places on the parallel map on page 193 as you read Isaiah's account of the great destruction coming upon Moab.)

15 The Burden of Moab
For in the night that Ar of
    Moab is laid to waste,
He is brought to ruin;
For in the night that Kir of
    Moab is laid waste,
He is brought to ruin.
²He is gone up to Bajith, and to
    Dibon
To the high places, to weep;
Upon Nebo, and upon Medeba,
    Moab howleth;
On all their heads is baldness,
Every beard is shaven.
³In their streets they gird
    themselves with sackcloth.
On their housetops, and in their
    broad places,
Every one howleth, weeping
    profusely.
⁴And Heshbon crieth out, and
    Elealeh;
Their voice is heard even unto
    Jahaz;
Therefore the armed men of Moab
    cry aloud;
His soul is faint within him.
⁵My heart crieth out for Moab;
Her fugitives reach unto Zoar,

A heifer of three years old;
For by the ascent of Luhith
With weeping they go up;
For in the way of Horonaim
They raise up a cry of destruction.
⁶For the Waters of Nimrim shall be
    desolate;
For the grass is withered away, the
    herbage faileth,
There is no green thing.
⁷Therefore the abundance they
    have gotten,
And that which they have laid up,
Shall they carry away to the brook
    of the willows.
⁸For the cry is gone round about
The borders of Moab;
The howling thereof unto Eglaim,
And the howling thereof unto
    Beerelim.
⁹For the waters of Dimon are full of
    blood;
For I will bring yet more upon
    Dimon,
A lion upon him that escapeth of
    Moab,
And upon the remnant of the land.
(JPS)

Isaiah begins by telling us that destruction will come upon Moab "in the night," probably meaning that it will be sudden and unexpected. It will come first to Ar and Kir, ancient cities of Moab (Kir

was probably Moab's capital at this time). The high places in verse 2 undoubtedly represent the pagan temples, since shrines for idolatrous worship were built on the mountaintops. Isaiah foretells that, eventually, the people will go up not for worshipping, but for weeping and lamentation because their idols cannot protect them from destruction. It follows, then, that their baldness and shaven beards are signs of mourning and perhaps even slavery. Verse 3 supports this idea by saying that the people will wander through their towns girded with sackcloth.

Verse 5 contains a puzzling phrase translated as "an heifer of three years old." The Jewish commentators Rashi and Drauss explain that at three years a heifer is at its best in health and beauty. So, Isaiah may be saying that Moab was to be destroyed at its most prosperous period. (Freehof, *Book of Isaiah*, p. 95.) Other commentators consider the place of refuge, Zoar, to be represented through this phrase as a young and vigorous city. (See Isa. 15, footnote 5b.) Some, too, simply transliterate the phrase directly into English and consider it to be a name for some area near Zoar. For example, the Revised Standard Version translates the first half of verse 5 as follows:

My heart cries out for Moab;
her fugitives flee to Zoar,
to Eglath-shelishiyah.

Regardless, in the context of verse 5, wherever (to Eglath-shelishiyah) or however (as a heifer of three years), the Moabites are wandering, their travels marked with weeping and crying.

The next verses (6-9) describe the drought, plundering, mourning, and slaughter that will fall upon Moab. Afterward, however, Isaiah changes the context and mood of his pronouncement to describe a period of harmonious relations between Moab and Judah when the Moabites will come under the protection of a righteous king of David.

16 Send ye the lambs for the ruler of the land
Unto the mount of the daughter of Zion.
2For it shall be that, as wandering birds,
As a scattered nest,
So shall the daughters of Moab be
At the fords of Arnon.

3"Give counsel, execute justice;
Make thy shadow as the night in the midst of the noonday;
Hide the outcasts, betray not the fugitive.
4Let mine outcasts dwell with thee;
As for Moab, be thou a covert to him from the face of the spoiler."
For the extortion is at an end,

spoiling ceaseth,
They that trampled down are
   consumed out of the land;
⁵And a throne is established
   through mercy,

And there sitteth thereon in truth,
   in the tent of David,
One that judgeth, and seeketh
   justice, and is ready in
   righteousness. (JPS)

Sending lambs to the ruler (v. 1) apparently alludes to an earlier time when Mesha, King of Moab, sent the wool of lambs as a gift to the king of Israel. (2 Kgs. 3:4.) Isaiah says here that the time will come when the lambs will be sent as tribute to a king of Jerusalem, who will represent the Davidic dynasty as the ruler of Israel.

In verse 2, Isaiah gives Judah an unusual command: "Make thy shadow as the night in the midst of the noonday." Like the cloud that covered Israel by day during the exodus, the "shadow" is symbolic of protection and help. Thus, to come under the shadow of the Lord's wings means to receive his divine protection. It appears that Judah's shadow, like night in midday, will hide and protect Moab from her enemies. This relationship strongly contrasts their earlier attitude; the two often fought and rarely protected each other.

The Davidic ruler of verse 5, protector of Moab, can also be interpreted as a messianic figure. Before Christ returns at his second coming and fulfills such a role (see Luke 1:32-33), there will be another "king of the Jews" who will be just and righteous and who might provide aid to the descendants of Moab. (Compare Isaiah 11:1-5.)

The last verses of Isaiah 16 abandon the promise of aid from Israel and return to a straightforward description of the catastrophe and physical desolation to come upon Moab:

⁶We have heard of the pride of
   Moab;
He is very proud;
Even of his haughtiness, and
   his pride, and his arrogance,
His ill-founded boastings.
⁷Therefore shall *Moab* wail   a, a
   for *Moab*,
Every one shall wail;
For the sweet cakes of *Kir-*
   hareseth shall ye mourn,   b
Sorely stricken.
⁸For the fields of *Heshbom*
   languish   c

And the vine of *Sibmah*,   d
   Whose choice plants did
   overcome
The lords of nations;
They reached even to *Jazer*,   e
They wandered into the
   wilderness;
Her branches were spread
   abroad,
They passed over the sea.
⁹Therefore I will weep with the
   weeping of *Jazer*   e'
For the vine of *Sibmah*;   d'
I will water thee with my tears,

195

O *Heshbon*, and Elealeh;   c'
For upon thy summer fruits
  and upon thy harvest
The battle shout is fallen.
¹⁰And gladness and joy are
  taken away
Out of the fruitful field;
And in the vineyards there
  shall be no singing,
No treader shall tread out wine
  in the presses;
I have made the vintage
  shout to cease.
¹¹Wherefore my heart moaneth
  like a harp for *Moab*,   a'
And mine inward parts of
  Kir-heres.   b'

¹²And it shall come to pass, a'
when it is seen that *Moab* hath
wearied himself upon the high
place, that he shall come to his
sanctuary to pray; but he shall
not prevail.
  ¹³This is the word that the
Lord spoke concerning Moab in
time past. ¹⁴But now the Lord
hath spoken, saying: "Within
three years, as the years of hire-
ling, and the glory of Moab shall
wax contemptible for all his
great multitude; and the remnant shall be very small and
without strength." (JPS; italics
added)

Notice the chiastic pattern of the primary cities and areas mentioned in these verses as outlined in the right hand column. You might want to locate these places on the map on page 193 and note how the vine-producing areas (vs. 8-9) all lie in the northernmost territories controlled during Isaiah's time by Moab. These rich vineyards were easily destroyed by the invading Assyrian armies. The vineyards were located primarily on the terraced hillsides between the desert wilderness on the east and the Dead Sea on the west (v. 8). As the Assyrians marched through them, each soldier would remove a stone from the terrace walls and throw it into the fields. In this way, the walls were quickly dismantled and strewn about. If the original landowners were still in the area and if it was safe for them to work in their fields, only great effort could restore the walls. However, if such restoration was not possible before the next winter rainy season, much of the fertile soil would wash off the hillsides, and it would take many years before fertility could be restored. Small wonder, then, that the loss of vineyards would result in the weeping and wailing Isaiah describes, especially if the people not only mourn the loss of their fields but also regret the lack of wine to drink and enjoy.

Verses 13 and 14 conclude the chapter with two interesting time references. First, verse 13 states that "this is the word that the Lord spoke concerning Moab in time past," probably indicating that the previous verses of the Moab pronouncement were originally given at some earlier time. Isaiah does not indicate whether he or someone else gave the first prophecy. Some scholars wonder if these might be the words of Jonah spoken during the reign of Jeroboam II, who expanded Israel's borders as he invaded and conquered Moab. (2 Kgs. 14:25.) Still, any earlier prophet might have given the prophecy which Isaiah, in turn, quotes without indicating its exact sources, just as Jeremiah does over a century later. (Jer. 48:2-5, 29-40; see also Amos 2:1-3.)

But, regardless of who originally gave the Moab prophecy and when it was pronounced, Isaiah acknowledges in verse 13 that it had been revealed earlier, and he then shifts to a second time frame in verse 14 to promise that the warning will finally be fulfilled within three years. This would be analogous to a prophet speaking in a general conference and saying: "The Lord has warned us through earlier prophets that we need to have a year's supply of food, and now I tell you that this food supply will be required within three years." As far as Moab is concerned, there is no indication that she heeded either the earlier prophecy or Isaiah's specific warning.

Since part of this prophecy was later repeated by Jeremiah and, as mentioned earlier, because much of the pronouncement might refer to the last days, it is difficult to pinpoint how this prophecy has been or might be fulfilled. Indeed, these chapters, 15 and 16, have so perplexed scholars that one has written: "There are few passages in the Old Testament which convey so little meaning to the modern reader as do these two chapters." (IB 5:267.)

As indicated above, however, the warnings and promises of these chapters do suggest some events between Moab and Judah in the last days. It seems here, as in chapters 13 and 14, that Isaiah uses the historical situation of his own day to prophesy of future events in the same area. His words allude to latter-day events and contain some messianic expectations that may only be more clearly understood when they are finally fulfilled.

Syria (and Israel) (ch. 17)

As seen in the previous prophecy to Moab, which also contained promises to Judah, Isaiah often weaves prophecies to the house of Israel into his discourses to foreign nations. Thus, it is not surprising that his pronouncement concerning Damascus (the capital of Syria) also includes warnings to Israel as well. His words to the Gentiles are not just a witness to them, but also contain warnings and promises concerning their relationship with Israel.

To those Israelites who live east of the Jordan Valley with Syria on the north and Moab to the south, Isaiah's words to their neighbors are obviously of some consequence, though they probably did not want to hear his warnings to them. His pronouncement to Syria and the eastern Israelites can be easily divided into five parts:

1. Syria (the ancient rival of Israel) will be emptied (vs. 1-3).
2. Israel will dwindle (4-6).
3. The people will eventually turn to God (7, 8).
4. Harvests will cease (9-11).
5. Those who threaten God's children will be suddenly destroyed (12-14).

These five elements are in a clear chiastic pattern that spans the entire chapter. It will simply be highlighted in the right-hand column as the applicable verses are quoted.

Syria Will Be Emptied (vs. 1-3)

Isaiah first addresses Syria's capital, Damascus, and delivers a warning for the whole Transjordan territory:

17 An oracle concerning Damascus:
"See, Damascus will no longer be a city
but will become a heap of ruins.
A. Israel's rival is destroyed.

²The cities of Aroer will be deserted and left to the flocks, which will lie down,
with no one to make them afraid.
B. Her people are gone.

³The fortified city will disappear in Ephraim,
and royal power from Damascus,
the remnant of Aram will be
like the glory of the Israelites,"
declares the Lord Almighty.
(NIV)
C. Fortified places and powers will cease.

The cities of "Aroer" (v. 2) are also known as the cities of the "junipers." At least four places have this name in the Old Testament. One is in Moab (see map earlier in this chapter), although the Aroer mentioned here is in the territory of Damascus. "Aram" (v. 3) is another name for Syria. (See BD "Aram, Aramaeans"; "Syria.") It is the valley wherein Damascus lies.

Israel Will Dwindle (vs. 4-6)

After highlighting the desolation coming upon Syria, Isaiah changes topics and addresses the house of Israel, talking about the losses coming to them:

4"In that day the glory of Jacob will fade;
    the fat of his body will waste away.

D. Jacob becomes thin.

5It will be as when a reaper gathers the standing grain
  and harvests the grain with his arm—
as when a man gleans heads of grain in the Valley of Rephaim.

E. A harvesting takes place.

6Yet some gleanings will remain,
  as when an olive tree is beaten,
leaving two or three olives on the topmost branches,
  four or five on the fruitful boughs,"
declares the Lord, the God of Israel. (NIV)

F. Only a little fruit (Israelites) remains on the branches.

The Valley of Rephaim spoken of in verse 5 is a fertile vale northwest of Jerusalem noted for harvests so fruitful that it was the camping place and grazing area for the Philistine armies as they attacked Israel during the days of Saul and David. (See 2 Sam. 5:18, 22; 23:13.)

The warning to Jacob in verse 4 parallels the earlier one to Damascus, in that both warnings include four similar elements:

1. The head will be weakened (Damascus, Jacob).
2. The people will be destroyed.
3. Only a remnant will remain.
4. Thus declares the Lord!

The People Will Eventually Turn to God (vs. 7-8)

Isaiah now speaks to both groups and perhaps even the world at large as he prophesies concerning a time ("in that day" meaning, most likely, the last days) when all people will turn to the Lord:

7In that day men will look to their Maker
  and turn their eyes to the Holy One of Israel.

G. The people look to God.

⁸They will not look to the altars,
    the work of their hands,
and they will have no regard for
    the Asherah poles
and the incense altars their fingers
    have made. (NIV)
	G'. They look away from
	idols.

The Asherah poles of verse 8 are the idols, images, or symbols of the pagan fertility goddess, Asherah. The female counterpart to Baal, she was notorious for the prostitution cults associated with her temples. It is also possible that the "poles" mentioned above were phallic symbols with her figure carved upon them. Despite the widespread influence of idolatry in Isaiah's day and the great work ("the work of their hands") in constructing the objects for pagan worship and fertility rituals, Isaiah foresees a time when mankind will eventually be spiritually mature enough to turn away from pagan polytheism and embrace the one Lord of the earth. This trend has been the case historically as monotheistic religions have gradually won out over paganism.

Harvests Will Cease (vs. 9-11)

Isaiah again reverses direction and repeats some earlier themes concerning the empty cities (compare vs. 1-3) and fields (compare vs. 4-6):

⁹In that day their strong cities, which they left because of the Israelites, will be like places abandoned to thickets and underbrush. And all will be desolation.	F'. Wild brush is everywhere (no fruit on their limbs).
¹⁰You have forgotten God your Savior; you have not remembered the Rock, your fortress. Therefore, though you set out the finest plants and plant imported vines,	E'. A planting takes place.
¹¹though on the day you set them out, you make them grow, and on the morning when you plant them, you bring them to bud,	D'. No fruit is harvested.

> yet the harvest will be as nothing
>   in the day of disease and
>   incurable pain. (NIV)

These three verses parallel verses 5 and 6. The correspondence between verse 6 (F on the outline) and 9 (F') is more clear in the King James Version, where the words "uttermost," "bough," and "branch" are repeated in both verses. Similarly, an exact parallelism exists in the original Hebrew.

The phrase "finest plants" in verse 10 is translated as "pleasant plants" in the King James Version and as "plants of pleasantness" in the Jewish Publication Society translation. Some authorities see in this phrase an allusion to the pagan "gardens of Adonis." Adonis is the Greek name for the Syrian pagan god Naaman, meaning "pleasantness." Thus the "plants of pleasantness" might be the "plants of Naaman" (or Adonis), which were important symbols of regeneration in the fertility rituals. In fact, a widespread custom in the eastern Mediterranean area was to plant little seed boxes (gardens of Adonis) at special times in the religious seasonal calendar. Germination of the seeds and plants indicated the revitalized virility of the pagan gods, who would then bring fertility to the people's fields. As prophesied in the verses above, these plants would someday not grow or produce fruit as a sign of the impotence of false gods.

The term "imported vines" in verse 10 probably alludes to the same or a similar ritual. The association of this phrase with pagan worship is more apparent in the King James Version, where it is translated as "strange slips." Slips are small cuttings, also known as *scions*, grafted into fruit trees or vines. Isaiah is saying here, then, that though faithless people may plant the finest stock and graft the best cuttings, both in full budding growth, they will receive no harvest, especially if the plantings are part of pagan worship. In short, regardless of the people's best efforts in the fields and orchards, God's aid is ultimately necessary to produce a bountiful harvest.

Those Who Threaten the Lord's Children Will Be Suddenly Destroyed (vs. 12-14)

In the beginning of this chapter, Isaiah promises that the ancient enemy of Israel, Syria, will become a ruin. He now concludes the pronouncement with a promise—any nation that speaks out (roars) against the Lord and seeks to plunder his children will be suddenly removed out of its place:

¹²Oh, the raging of many nations—
    they rage like the raging sea!
Oh, the uproar of the peoples—
    they roar like the roaring of
    great waters!
¹³Although the people roar like the
    roar of surging waters,
  when he rebukes them they flee
    far away,
driven before the wind like chaff
    on the hills,
like tumblewood before a gale.
¹⁴In the evening, sudden terror!
  Before the morning, they are
    gone!
This is the portion of those who
    loot us,
  the lot of those who plunder us.
(NIV)

C'. Nations and people rage and roar (but they are a vain threat).

B'. The people flee before the Lord.

A'. Those who threaten are suddenly swept away.

By comparing these verses with the first verses of the chapter, one can see how the population of Damascus and the other cities and fortified places will be emptied. The parallelism in verse 13 indicates that it is not the powers or armies of men that will send the people fleeing away, but the power of the Lord.

Thus, for Israel at least, the chapter concludes with the promise of special protection. Though thieves, powers, or armies may threaten God's people as night approaches, the enemy will have vanished by morning, leaving the people unharmed.

In reviewing chapter 17 of Isaiah and studying the five separate sections and how they parallel each other, be careful not to lose sight of the message Isaiah is teaching in this passage. Although the pronouncement generally has a negative tone as Isaiah foretells desolation, emptiness, famine, and scattering, it also contains a positive undercurrent as he declares the sovereignty of God and the divine protection God's children will receive. Later in his writings, Isaiah stresses and builds upon these positive themes, though here he remains rather gloomy. For now he gives a cry of warning; later he will raise a voice of hope.

MESSENGERS FROM
A SHELTERED LAND
ISAIAH 18

Isaiah 18 has perplexed scholars and translators as much as any other Isaianic chapter. In this chapter, the unnamed land, its messengers, their purpose, the people they visit, their relationship, and the historical context are all obscure. Various scholars identify several lands and peoples throughout Africa and Asia as the subject matter, but their speculations differ greatly concerning when and how this prophecy is fulfilled.

If any semblance of a historical consensus does exist, it centers around an African delegation representing a new dynasty in Egypt that sought support from King Hezekiah of Judah. The best guess for the date of their visit is about 705 B.C., just after the death of King Sargon of Assyria when Hezekiah and other neighboring states established an anti-Assyrian confederation. Shabako, the Ethiopian pharaoh of the twenty-first or Nubian Dynasty, apparently sent a delegation to Judah in order to discuss a united effort against the disorganized Assyrians. Isaiah's message to this delegation was that the Lord would subdue Judah's enemies, implying that political measures against the Assyrians were unnecessary and futile. Therefore, Judah did not need to make an alliance with the Egyptians, her former oppressors. Indeed, Isaiah promises a time when gifts from a distant land (perhaps Assyria or Africa) will be brought to Mount Zion, indicating a somewhat universal sovereignty of the Lord's people in Jerusalem.

The positive tone of the chapter has motivated some biblical authorities such as H. L. Ginsberg to suggest that the chapter really belongs with chapters 32-35, which refer to the latter-days and the restoration and glory of Zion. (*The Book of Isaiah*, p. 17.) The chapter is unusual because of its placement as a prophecy of hope (to a certain people, probably the Israelites) among prophecies of destruction (to Israel's neighbors and enemies.)

Nearly all scholars accept Isaiah's authorship of chapter 18, and some even recognize it as the "noblest of Isaiah's utterances," with a "magnificence of language and imagery" and "depth of perception and faith." They also recognize, however, the "many perplexities which beset the interpreter" of this chapter. (IB 5:275-76.)

One solution to the chapter's obscure message comes from modern prophets and apostles whose inspired commentaries provide an entirely new dimension to the pronouncement. They move the chapter's locale to the new world (America) in the last days. The ambassadors going forth are interpreted as missionaries who gather the scattered remnants of Israel and bring them back to Zion as a gift to the Lord.

The chapter begins with Isaiah's address to an unspecified nation:

18 Oh, land shadowed by wings
    [the divine Spirit],
Which land is [far] beyond the
    rivers of Cush [Africa].
[2]He sends out envoys by sea
    And in swift vessels of reeds
        over the face of the waters.
    (VLL[1])

Complex questions can be asked about each of these lines such as: What land is Isaiah addressing, how is it divinely protected, how far away is it, who are its envoys, how do they travel? Since these lines introduce the entire pronouncement, they merit special study.

The opening word is a simple interjection or form of address without the negative tone of the "woe" in the King James Version. Other possible translations are "ho," "ah," "hail," "hark," or "behold." As Joseph Fielding Smith says, the opening word "shows clearly that no woe was intended, but rather a greeting." (SOT, p. 51.)

It is harder to clarify exactly what land is addressed. The Hebrew phrase probably means "land of ships (or shadows) like wings," while the Greek Septuagint refers to it as a land with the "wings of the ships."

Fortunately, an important key to identifying this mysterious land was provided by a Latter-day Saint leader of this dispensation.

---

[1]Since Isaiah 18 is so ambiguous, the author has prepared a translation of the chapter that remains true to the Hebrew original while using English terminology including a range of associations familiar to most Latter-day Saints.

Hyrum Smith, brother of the Prophet Joseph and patriarch to the Church, clarified this portion of Isaiah in the general conference of April 1844. In speaking of the gathering from all the nations to America, the land of Zion, Hyrum Smith said that "North and South America are the symbols of the wings." (HC 6:322.)

This brief statement by Hyrum clarifies a number of verses in Isaiah 18. If the wings represent America, then the obscure land of verse 1 has been identified. And if the dominant theme of the chapter is the gathering of people to Mount Zion, later phrases in the chapter become more clear. Although other interpretations of Isaiah 18 are possible, the remarks of this mouthpiece of the Lord provide a basis for the view that this pronouncement is directed to America and deals with missionary work and the gathering of Israel.

Many reasons exist for identifying America as the "land shadowing with wings." For one, Joseph Fielding Smith calls it a land literally "in the shape of wings." (SOT, p. 51). Also, Christian and Jewish Bible commentators use a variety of phrases to describe the land Isaiah refers to, many of which can be applied to America. Some examples are:

A land whose extreme parts are shaded by mountains or hills. (America is a land of everlasting hills and mountains. [Gen. 49:26; D&C 49:25; 133:31.] A single mountain range extends from north to south.)

A land whose sails are spread out as an eagle. (The eagle is the national symbol of both the United States and Mexico.)

A land on the wings or extremities of the world. (From Jerusalem, America is the farthest country to either the east or west.)

A land under the expanding rays of the morning sun. (Many Indians claim that their ancestors or their great white god "came out of the east.")

A land that is most sheltered. (America is a land protected by the Lord [1 Ne. 13:12-19.].)

A land furnishing protection, as a hen's wings are a shelter for young chicks. (America has a tradition of defending the oppressed.)

There are many ways in which America is a "land shadowing with wings." (Most of these suggestions are found in Barnes, *Notes on Isaiah* 1:335-36.)

The symbol of wings is also very prevalent in the scriptures and usually represents shelter (Ps. 57:1; 17:8; 91:4; Matt. 23:27; Ruth 2:12; 3 Ne. 10:4-6), movement (Ex. 19:4; Ps. 18:10; D&C 77:4; 88:45; 2 Ne.

4:25) or power (2 Ne. 25:13; Ezek. 17:3, 7; Isa. 40:31; D&C 124:18, 99; Mal. 4:2). In Jewish literature, the presence and protection of the Lord for his chosen people is often represented by a wing and is called the *shechinah*. (See BD, "Shechinah.") It is clear that "the land in the shadow of wings" recorded in Isaiah 18 must be a land of refuge, shelter, and power. The phrase connotes the special protection promised America by the Lord (Ether 2:7-12; 2 Ne. 1:5-11), and thus can be the land shadowed by "the divine spirit" (VLL).

One may question how much Isaiah could have known about America in 700 B.C., since its existence was unknown to most people in the Middle East at that time, although some scholars believe that the Phoenicians had already established trade routes across the Atlantic with America decades before Isaiah's birth. Furthermore, one should remember that, as a prophet and seer, Isaiah was not restricted to man's knowledge of other lands, and that the Lord could easily have revealed much about America to him. (See 1 Ne. 13; Mosiah 8:17.)

It may even be that the vision or inspiration that prompted Isaiah's pronouncement in chapter 18 was not fully understood by the prophet himself. He may have been like Daniel, who had visions and recorded them even though he did not altogether comprehend their meaning. (See Dan. 12:8-9.) In any case, the identification of the "land shadowing with wings" with America gives us a basis for studying the rest of the chapter.

The remainder of verse 1 and the first part of verse 2 can be translated as follows:

Which land is [far] beyond the rivers of Cush [Africa].
He sends out envoys by sea
And in swift vessels of reeds over the face of the waters. (VLL)

Obviously, the land of America is beyond the rivers of Africa; indeed it is beyond the ocean surrounding Africa. In biblical Hebrew, a term for *ocean* does not exist, but particularly large bodies of water are called rivers or seas, so that the land beyond the "rivers" of Africa might also mean beyond the oceans of Africa. Also, the envoys being sent out could represent the missionaries going forth, leaving the center of the Church in North America and traveling over the seas to foreign fields of labor. Note the emphasis Isaiah places upon the separation by water between the homeland of the messengers and the land where they go. How else could Isaiah have explained the methods of modern-day missionary travel, given the limited knowledge of his audience?

The "vessels of bulrushes" (KJV), "vessels of speed" (SOT, p. 51), or "swift vessels of reeds" (VLL), are literally the papyrus boats that sailed the Nile, the Great Sea, and even the Atlantic (Thor Heyerdahl's *Ra II* duplicated such travel). But reed-shaped or hollow vessels still ply the seas in the form of ocean liners, and long, hollow vessels "sail" or fly over the waters in the form of airplanes. Again, how else could Isaiah have described modern modes of transportation seen in vision? His imagery is very descriptive, considering his limitations.

Verse 2 continues:

Go swift messengers
To a nation scattered and shining
To a people terrible from the
  beginning onward,
A nation measured together and
  trampled,
Whose land is cut off by rivers.
(VLL)

This verse also perplexes translators, since many of the terms are used by Isaiah only in these phrases. The nation "scattered and shining" could also be described as "scattered and peeled" (KJV), "far and remote" (NJV), "tall and smooth" (RSV), "tall and smooth-skinned" (NEB), or "tall and bronzed" (JB). It seems very likely that this people is the scattered remnants of Israel throughout many continents. Their many homelands are "cut off by rivers" or separated by oceans and seas. Also, their physical appearances now vary greatly because as the Israelites scattered, they often intermarried with other peoples until they assumed a variety of physical characteristics.

Although Israel was once the Lord's chosen people, whose power brought fear into the hearts of neighboring peoples, they have since been scattered and oppressed. The phrase in verse 2 describing them as "terrible from the beginning" probably refers more to their spiritual weakness than their political power. They have been an obstinate people who needed to be constantly reminded of their covenant relationship with God. Yet they have remained "measured together" (VLL), "meted out" (KJV), or joined together in large enough segments that they have maintained some cohesiveness and identity as a people.

America plays an important role in the gathering of all the remnants of Israel. Already, more Jews and Lamanites reside on the American continents than anywhere else on the earth. And, apparently, when the remnant of the Ten Tribes returns, it will travel through America. (D&C 45:43; 110:11; 133:26-32.) Considering the important role America has in the last days for Israel, it is not surprising that the Lord would reveal insights concerning it to Isaiah. (See Isa. 33:13-20.)

In verse 3 of chapter 18, Isaiah turns from Israel and addresses the whole world. He extends to all an invitation to heed God's word and a warning of the Lord's judgment. At that judgment, the wicked, those who are pruned out of the true vine, will become food for the beasts of the earth:

³All you who live in the world
And inhabit the earth,
When an ensign is raised on the
mountains, take note,
When a ram's horn is blown, give
heed!
⁴For thus said the Lord to me:
"I rest calm and confident in my
dwelling place
Like a clear heat in the sunshine,
Like a dewy mist in the heat of the
harvest."
⁵For before the harvest and after
the budding

When the blossom is turning into a
ripening grape,
He will cut off the twigs with
pruning hooks,
And the branches he will lop off.
⁶They will be left together
For the birds of the mountains,
And for the beasts of the earth.
And the birds will summer on
them,
And all the beasts of the earth will
winter on them. (VLL)

The "ensign" of verse 3 can be interpreted as a symbol of the gospel going forth to the world. (See D&C 64:42; TG "Ensign"; and the commentary on Isa. 11:10 in chapter 15 of this book for further ideas.) The blowing of a ram's horn or trumpet (KJV) is also mentioned in Joel 2:1, and the same Hebrew word is used in both prophecies. Since the second chapter of Joel undoubtedly refers to the last days (Moroni quoted the latter portion of it to Joseph Smith [JS-H 1:41]), the blowing of the horn can also refer to the gospel going forth from America in the last days.

Verse 4 explains that, as the gospel goes forth, the Lord will calmly remain in his dwelling place like a "clear heat" or a "dewy mist" during the harvest season. Both heat and moisture are necessary in the weeks just before the harvest in order to fully ripen the grapes. On the other hand, too much heat or cold weakens the crop, while drought or heavy rains can easily destroy them. Like the delicate balance of warmth and moisture needed to fully ripen the grapes, God attends to the harvest of souls by providing the proper light (truth) and water (cleansing powers) to ensure the full development of each person.

208

In verse 5, Isaiah describes a special vine-pruning. A vineyard must be pruned twice each year. The more severe pruning comes late in winter, just before the dormant limbs develop their spring growth. The non-producing branches from the previous season and most of the vines are then cut off. The second and less severe pruning occurs after the grapes have formed, when the vine dresser cuts off the nonbearing branches and those with small, green, bitter fruit. The result is a vine whose remaining branches are stronger, are in full sunlight, and are able to produce more ripe fruit. (See IDB 3:941; 4:785.)

In a similar fashion, just before the harvest of the Millennium, the Lord of the vineyard will prune out the non-productive, bitter limbs of the house of Israel so that the strong branches can produce a full, sweet fruit. (See Matt. 13:24-43; Jacob 5.)

Verse 6 portrays what happens to the trimmings as birds and beasts feed on them year round. This same image is found in modern revelation: "And it shall come to pass that the beasts of the forest and fowls of the air shall devour them up." (D&C 29:20.) But where Isaiah uses the vine as a metaphor, the Doctrine and Covenants describes the Lord's literal destruction of the wicked. The latter-day revelation also provides additional details, such as manifestations in heaven and on earth, a great hailstorm, flies destroying the wicked, and bodies left for the birds and beasts to feed upon. (D&C 29:14-20.)

Not all people on the earth in that day will become carrion for devouring beasts, however. The righteous will be gathered to Zion and unto the Lord:

7And in that day,
A gift shall be brought to the Lord of Hosts—
[Namely] a people scattered and shining;
And from a people terrible from the beginning onward—
A nation measured together and trampled,
Whose land is cut off by rivers,
To the place of the name of the Lord of Hosts—
Mount Zion. (VLL)

Repeating phrases from verse 2, Isaiah concludes the chapter with a promise that the representatives from the land shadowed by wings will bring a special gift to the Lord—the remnants of Israel gathered to Mount Zion.

In summary, the land beyond the rivers of Ethiopia is a particularly blessed land that will assist in Israel's gathering to Zion. The gathering can be taken either as a literal returning of the Jews to

209

Jerusalem or as a figurative spiritual gathering of covenant Israel to the stakes of Zion. Joseph Fielding Smith said:

> This chapter is clearly a reference to the sending forth of the missionaries to the nations of the earth to gather again this people who are scattered and peeled. The ensign has been lifted upon the mountains, and the work of gathering has been going on for over one hundred years. No one understands this chapter, but the Latter-day Saints, and we can see how it is being fulfilled. (SOT, pp. 54-55.)

In conclusion, chapter 18 expresses in unique images the theme of gathering the Lord's chosen. A major element of this prophecy is the role of America in bringing the gospel message to all who will listen.

EGYPT AHD JUDAH
ISAIAH 19-20

The nineteenth chapter of Isaiah contains the most important prophecies concerning Egypt in the entire Old Testament. Again, in this chapter, Isaiah skillfully uses the historical events of his day to prophesy of events in the last days. His pronouncement warns Egypt of contemporary dangers and promises future blessings that will finally occur "in that day," the last dispensation. The prophecy as a whole, then, finds complete fulfillment only in the latter days. Indeed, many of the events promised in Isaiah 19 seems to have been fulfilled in the events of the 1970s.

Isaiah 19 begins by describing several calamities that will befall Egypt—internal disorder, disruption of the flow of the Nile River, and inept, ruthless leadership. Conditions will become so serious that Egypt will be greatly afraid of Judah. Still, the chapter concludes with the promise of blessings—when Egypt follows the Lord, he will heal her and enable her to join with other nations in blessing the earth.

Chapter 19 falls into distinct halves—verses 1-15 threatening destruction and verses 19-25 promising redemption. Verses 16-18 serve as a bridge between the two sections. A close study of the chapter also reveals a chiastic pattern between the two sections as outlined below:

  I. God's judgments upon Egypt (vs. 1-15)
    A. Man versus man—internal chaos in Egypt (1-4)
    B. Man versus nature—life along the Nile River destroyed (5-10)
    C. Man versus his leaders—anarchy and confusion (11-15)
 II. Egypt is full of fear, for Judah terrorizes her (16-18)
III. The Lord's healing of Egypt (19-25)
    C'. Man turns to God—the Egyptians serve the Lord (19-21)
    B'. Man in harmony with the land—the Lord heals Egypt (22)
    A'. Man serves others—Egypt joins Assyria and Israel (23-25)

Man versus Man—Internal Chaos in Egypt (vs. 1-4)

19 The "Egypt" Pronouncement.
Mounted on a swift cloud,
The LORD will come to Egypt;
Egypt's idols shall tremble before
Him,
And the heart of the Egyptians shall
sink within them.
2"I will incite Egyptian against
Egyptian:
They shall war with each other,
Every man with his fellow,
City with city
And kingdom with kingdom.

3Egypt shall be drained of spirit,
And I will confound its plans;
So they will consult the idols and
the shades
And the ghosts and the familiar
spirits.
4And I will place the Egyptians
At the mercy of a harsh master,
And a ruthless king shall rule
them"
—declares the Sovereign, the
LORD of Hosts. (NJV)

"The Lord riding on a swift cloud" (v. 1) is a figure of speech describing the Lord's imminent judgment, which will destroy Egypt's false religion and bring fear into the hearts of her people. (Compare Nahum 1:3.) Civil war results (v. 2) and brings terror to the hearts of the people, with kingdom warring against kingdom (or better said, district against district, since ancient Egypt was comprised of forty-four small kingdoms, called *nomes*). In their desperation, the Egyptians will seek "familiar spirits" or sorcerers to save themselves (v. 3), but they will inevitably be placed under the yoke of a harsh ruler (v. 4.)

Opinions vary greatly as to who this ruthless king might be. No pharaoh ruling Egypt during Isaiah's time seems to fit this role, so scholars usually point to various later Assyrian, Babylonian, Persian, Greek, or Roman surrogate rulers who conquered Egypt. No consensus has been reached, however, and some scholars speculate that the fulfillment of this prophecy may still lie in the future.

Man versus Nature—Nile River Life Destroyed (vs. 5-10)

5Water shall fail from the seas,
Rivers dry up and be parched,
6Channels turn foul as they ebb,
And Egypt's canals run dry.
Reed and rush shall decay,
7And the Nile papyrus by the
Nile-side

And everything sown by the Nile
Shall wither, blow away, and
vanish.
8 The fishermen shall lament;
All who cast lines in the Nile
shall mourn,
And those who spread nets on

the water shall languish.
⁹The flax workers, too, shall be
  dismayed,
Both carders and weavers

chagrined.
¹⁰Her foundations shall be crushed.
And all who make dams shall be
  despondent. (NJV)

The Nile River has supplied, from the beginning of civilization, the lifeblood of Egypt. Most of the Egyptian population has always clustered on the river's floodplain, where the waters systematically and gradually rise, overflow the banks, and inundate and irrigate the rich fields that would otherwise become desert. The Nile, with a watershed that drains half a continent through a four-thousand mile river-course, annually carries millions of tons of sediment toward the Mediterranean Sea, providing nutrients for many ecological life-systems along its way. At its height in August, the river usually rises twenty-five to thirty feet above its normal course:

> The annual flood was one of nature's exquisitely balanced wonders. Sometimes it brought too much water, engulfing villages, and sometimes it brought too little; even in normal years about 30,000,000,000 tons flowed unused to the sea. But the water was not wasted. Every sediment laden drop that emptied into the Mediterranean strengthened the aquatic food chain, nourishing marine life, and maintained an exact balance of salinity. . . . that has made the Nile Valley the agricultural marvel it is. (Sterling, "The Trouble with Superdams," *Britannica Yearbook of Science and the Future, 1974,* p. 115.)

In verses 5-10, Isaiah, warns that this natural agricultural marvel would someday be disrupted, and the waters of the "sea," the flooded valley, would fail. Various events could cause such a drastic disruption. In ancient times, social disorder (like that described in vs. 1-4) so disrupted normal life along the river that canals and ditches could not be cleaned or maintained. Neither could the fields be properly prepared, planted, and cultivated; therefore, the Nile Valley's productivity would drastically decline until social order was restored.

Another cause could be meager snowfall and rains in the African highlands that provided the Nile waters. This highland water is vital, since Egypt receives an average of only one hour of rain per year. When snow and rains failed in the south, then, the northern Egyptians had only limited flooding and irrigation for their crops until the next year.

The adverse social and weather conditions described above rarely lasted more than a decade, though, and fertility along the Nile was usually quickly restored. In modern times, however, a new kind of social phenomenon arose that changed conditions on the Nile so drastically that its consequences will continue for at least a century.

In 1960, construction began on the Aswan Dam, an engineering wonder but ecological and social nightmare. Built to provide abundant, cheap, clean hydroelectric power, to store water for irrigation, and to control flooding, the dam was to help fulfill President Nasser's dream of bringing Egyptian society out of the "dark ages" and into a powerful position among third world countries. Within a decade, Nasser hoped to deliver the country from poverty and famine, and to double its income through industrialization. Yet more than a decade after the dam's completion in 1971, poverty is still rampant (the average Egyptian worker's daily salary is only three dollars, the nation is deep in debt, and progress toward modernization is very slow).

Countless other problems have resulted from building the dam. Though some problems were anticipated, their magnitude was never even imagined:

1. Billions of tons of silt, which had enriched Egyptian fields for centuries, are now piled up behind the dam and quickly filling massive Lake Nasser, the dam's two-thousand-square-mile reservoir. Egyptian engineers fear that the lake may be completely filled within a few decades instead of two centuries as originally anticipated.

2. Underground seepage and reversed underground flows in the dam area claim up to one-third of the water coming into the lake. Apparently, these underground rivers are flowing into the Mediterranean Sea without any benefit to agriculture or society.

3. Extreme evaporation loss (fifteen billion cubic meters of water per year) is being caused by high desert temperatures and wind velocity in the area. This figure is at least fifty percent more than planners expected.

4. Water weeds, such as the hyacinth, proliferate in the warm waters, robbing nutrients and oxygen from the fish and food chains, menacing the dam's turbines through clogging, and depleting water resources through transpiration (using up to ten times more water, meter for meter, than Lake Nasser's evaporation rate).

5. Ninety thousand Egyptian and Sudanese peasants who formerly lived on the rich bottomlands of the Upper Nile have been uprooted and moved to the hot, rocky, barren hills above Lake Nasser.

214

6. At the cost of millions of dollars, great archaeological treasures, such as the Abu Simbel temple statues of Ramses II, were cut from the solid rock, moved, and reconstructed on higher ground. Other unknown sites and treasures may still lay buried under the lake.
7. Immense water pressure has increased the potential for seismic disturbances and even major earthquakes.

Further complications have developed downstream:

8. Although there is less water flowing downstream from Aswan today than before the dam was built, the silt-free water flows much faster and is scouring and eroding the riverbeds, thus undermining bridge and wharf foundations. To prevent their collapse and to slow the river, Egypt now plans to build ten additional dams between Aswan and the sea.
9. The clear river water is void of most nutrients and therefore no longer supports the fishing, flax, papyrus, and other ancient industries. (See Isa. 19:7-9.)
10. Without Nile sediment, the land requires millions of tons of artificial fertilizer, which increases productivity (especially in areas of double cropping) but cuts the average income per acre by about a fifth due to the extra cost. (Ironically, the world's largest resource of mineral fertilizers is the Dead Sea basin, located 250 miles northeast of the Nile Valley. Egyptian water coupled with Israeli fertilizer could improve the productivity of both countries.)
11. Without the floods to wash salts away, soil salinity is reaching ominous levels, requiring ambitious leeching and drainage projects.
12. The population of water snails has boomed, increasing the number of hosts of blood flukes, which carry schistosomiasis (bilharzia), the scourge of Egypt. This disease afflicts approximately every other Egyptian and causes one out of every ten deaths in the country. Also, increased outbreaks of malaria have resulted from enlarged breeding areas for mosquitoes.

As if these problems along the river were not enough, further disruptions have occurred at the mouth of the Nile:

13. Strong west-to-east currents in the Mediterranean Sea are eroding the delta coastline, since no new sediment comes out of the Nile to maintain coastal sandbars and dunes.
14. Sea water is beginning to intrude into five big freshwater lakes of the delta, which are indispensable to the cultivation of a million acres of delta lands reclaimed at great expense.

15. The aquatic food chain in the eastern Mediterranean has been broken along a continental shelf 12 miles wide and 600 miles long. For example, the eighteen thousand tons of sardines that once supplied one-fifth of Egypt's annual fish catch have disappeared.
16. The salinity of the eastern Mediterranean Sea is rising, since the salty Red Sea waters pour through the Suez Canal without the sweet Nile floodwaters to counteract them.

(The sources for this list are Sterling, "The Trouble with Superdams," *Britannica Yearbook of Science and the Future, 1974*, pp. 115-27, and Lytle, *The Aswan High Dam*, pp. 2-3.

After reviewing these facts, reread Isaiah 19:5-10 to appreciate why Egyptians "who make dams shall be despondent" (v. 10, NJV). Many Egyptian leaders, in discussing the Aswan Dam, admit privately that "probably they would not build it if they had it to do over again." (Sterling, p. 127). Some even think that the dam should be destroyed before additional problems develop. Undoubtedly, no event in Egyptian history has so completely disrupted the way of life along the Nile River as the Aswan Dam. It therefore appears that no other event has a better claim to fulfilling Isaiah's prophecy in verses 5-10.

Man versus Leaders—Anarchy and Confusion (vs. 11-15)

11Utter fools are the nobles of
Tanis;
The sagest of Pharaoh's advisers
[Have made] absurd predictions.
How can you say to Pharaoh,
"I am a scion of sages,
A scion of Kedemite kings"?
12Where, indeed, are your sages?
Let them tell you, let them
discover
What the LORD of Hosts has
planned against Egypt.
13The nobles of Tanis have been
fools,

The nobles of Memphis deluded;
Egypt has been led astray
By the chiefs of her tribes.
14The LORD has mixed within her
A spirit of distortion,
Which shall lead Egypt astray in
all her undertakings
As a vomiting drunkard goes
astray;
15Nothing shall be achieved in
Egypt
By either head or tail,
Palm branch or reed. (NJV)

In verse 11, the foolish nobles of Tanis (or of Zoan in KJV, the ancient capital of the delta) are absurd enough to claim to be sons of the Kedemite kings, who lived east in the Arabian desert and were renowned for their wisdom. (See 1 Kgs. 4:30-31.) The nobles of Memphis (or Noph, KJV; the traditional capital of all northern or lower Egypt) are also deluded and lead all of Egypt astray (v. 13). Indeed, the whole society, whether of high station or low (symbolized by the palm branch and papyrus reed, respectively), will achieve nothing (v. 15).

As with earlier parts of this chapter, it is difficult to establish a precise historical context for the fulfillment of these words. By the time of Isaiah, Egypt was well into a period of political decline that later resulted in repetitive conquests by various empires. Not until the twentieth century did the Egyptians completely regain their lost independence, but even now they require foreign aid for the people and expertise for the industries. Sometimes the foreign powers and their advisors have hindered more than helped Egypt. Perhaps, again, a modern fulfillment of this prophecy is as likely as any other.

Egypt Is Full of Fear, for Judah Terrorizes Her (vs. 16-18)

¹⁶In that day, the Egyptians shall be like women, trembling and terrified because the LORD of Hosts will raise His hand against them. ¹⁷And the land of Judah shall also be the dread of the Egyptians; they shall quake whenever anybody mentions it to them, because of what the LORD of Hosts is planning against them. ¹⁸In that day, there shall be several towns in the land of Egypt speaking the language of Canaan and swearing loyalty to the LORD of Hosts; one shall be called Town of Heres. (NJV)

An important stylistic and thematic transition occurs in verse 16. Isaiah shifts from poetry to prose and begins this section with the phrase "in that day." This phrase is repeated five additional times in the second part of the chapter, but it is not found at all in the first. Since, for Isaiah, the phrase "in that day" is almost always his way of saying "in the last days" or "in that day just before the Millennium," it is likely that at least the last portion of chapter 19 finds its fulfillment in modern times.

The verses above describe the frenzied fear that overcomes the Egyptians. The Egyptians not only generally lack courage, but specifically fear the Jews, their former slaves. In their male-centered society, the accusation that they have become "like women" is the lowest insult.

Until the time of modern wars between Israel and Egypt—which began in 1948 and included conflicts in 1956, 1967, and 1973—Egypt has historically had no hesitation in carrying on battles in Palestine.

Egypt was also so large and strong that she never had reason to fear invasion from any military power of Judah. Although Jewish traders, travelers, and refugees often entered Egypt, Jewish armies never advanced into Egyptian soil until very modern times.

The low point of Egyptian military power in comparison to that of Israel was the Six Day War of June 1967. Dozens of books have been written and countless stories told of how, within hours on June 5, the Israeli air force devastated all Egyptian air bases and two-thirds of her air force. In four days of fighting, Israel destroyed the bulk of the Egyptian army and overran an area of Egyptian territory six times the area of the entire country of Israel.

With control of the Sinai Peninsula, Israel later established some settlements (this could be a fulfillment of verse 18), although many of these areas were evacuated after the 1973 Yom Kippur War agreements. Therefore, the time of more permanent Jewish communities in Egypt is probably still future. Some progress in that direction has been made, though, through recent treaties opening the borders between Israel and Egypt.

One other phrase in verse 18 requires brief explanation: "the language of Canaan." Isaiah's prophecy that "the language of Canaan" will be spoken in "several" (translated "five" in KJV) Egyptian towns has caused much debate. Scholars debate whether these cities will become Jewish possessions, or whether Jews will simply live abroad there, bringing their language with them. However, though the "language of Canaan" most likely means the Hebrew language, it might also imply that the system of thought, custom, and theology indigenous to Canaan will become a part of Egyptian society. In this case, the ideas and ideals of Judaism may become firmly entrenched and practiced in some Egyptian cities.

In short, as illustrated in verses 16-18, one important sign concerning Egypt in the last days will be her greatly improved relationship with Judah. Verses 19-21, in turn, describe a new Egyptian relationship with the Lord.

Man Turns to God—the Egyptians Serve the Lord (vs. 19-21)

¹⁹In that day, there shall be an altar to the LORD inside the land of Egypt and a pillar to the LORD at its border. ²⁰They shall serve as a symbol and reminder of the LORD of Hosts in the land of Egypt, so that when [the Egyptians] cry out to the LORD against oppressors, He will send them a savior and champion to deliver

them. ²¹For the LORD will make
Himself known to the Egyptians,
and the Egyptians shall acknowledge the LORD in that day, and

they shall serve [Him] with sacrifice and oblation and shall make
vows to the LORD and fulfill them.
(NJV)

Beginning with these verses, Isaiah promises great blessings to Egypt. The Egyptians will serve the Lord "in that day" (v. 21), and build a pillar and altar to the Lord (vs. 19, 21). Scholars generally agree that the pillar and altar represent a temple to be built in Egypt.

Some historians feel that this promise was fulfilled by the Jewish colonists living at Elephantine Island from the seventh to fourth centuries B.C. (This island is located at the southern border of Egypt, near Aswan and the first cataract.) About the same time that Lehi left Jerusalem for America, a number of Jews fled from the invading Babylonians and settled at this border post in upper Egypt. Correspondence and other records from this community indicate that they constructed a temple before 525 B.C. which remained standing for at least a century. It was apparently destroyed around 410 B.C. and then later rebuilt. ("Elephantine Papyri," IDB 2:83-85.)

The Roman-Jewish historian Josephus records that another Jewish temple was built centuries later by refugees who fled to the delta area in the second century B.C. (*Antiquities*, XIII. iii. 1-2.) Very little is known about their settlements and temple at Leontopolis, including whether or not they were an "official" or orthodox Jewish religious community.

It is interesting that Jewish historians traditionally discounted the Josephus account; they did not believe he could be describing a group of orthodox Jews. Most historians believed that "true" Jews would build a temple only in Jerusalem. After all, they did not build one in Babylon during their captivity, so why should they build one anywhere else. With this same argument, some critics have discounted the Book of Mormon, for the Nephites (uprooted Jews) built temples in the new land. (See 2 Ne. 5:16.) Following the discovery of the Elephantine Papyri in 1893 and recent Israeli archaeological findings in the Holy Land, however, many scholars now acknowledge the legitimate existence of many other Israelite temples. (For example, see "Hebrew sanctuaries and temples—those besides Jerusalem," IDB 4:566-68.) Now, some Israeli archaeologists will assert that if a group of ancient religious, practicing Jews were to be isolated from Jerusalem, one would expect them to build their own temple. This is exactly what the Book of Mormon indicates and, apparently, what Isaiah promises for Egypt.

It should not be overlooked, however, that the temple to be built in Egypt does not necessarily have to be a Jewish one. One Latter-day Saint temple is already being built in South Africa, and it is not improbable that one could be erected in northern Africa or even in Egypt at some future time.

Man in Harmony with the Land—the Lord Heals Egypt (v. 22)

22The LORD will first afflict and then heal the Egyptians; when they turn back to the LORD, He will respond to their entreaties and heal them. (NJV)

In this verse, Isaiah explains the Lord's plans for Egypt, plans that the sages were unable to discover or reveal (vs. 12-13). This verse needs to be viewed in a religious context through the terminology Isaiah uses. He implies that the Egyptians are "wicked" and that the Lord will afflict them and bring them to humility. (Compare Alma 32:13.) Also, Isaiah says that they will "turn back" (or repent), meaning that they must have sinned earlier. After they repent, the Lord will respond to their entreaties (prayers) and heal (forgive) them. This promise is among the greatest that any people can receive from the Lord.

Man Serves Others—Egypt Joins Assyria and Israel (vs. 23-25)

23In that day, there shall be a highway from Egypt to Assyria. The Assyrians shall join with the Egyptians and Egyptians with the Assyrians, and then the Egyptians together with the Assyrians shall serve [the LORD]. 24In that day, Israel shall be a third partner with Egypt and Assyria as a blessing on earth; 25for the LORD of Hosts will bless them, saying, "Blessed be My people Egypt, My handiwork Assyria, and My very own Israel." (NJV)

There were various times during the Persian, Greek, and Roman occupations when the areas of Egypt, Israel, and Assyria (Mesopotamia) were joined together through a common means of transportation and communication. In times past, however, the three areas did not ever unite to "bless the nations of the earth." The fulfillment of this Isaianic promise remains in the future. Indeed, most readers of the scriptures who understand the history of the area find it incredible that these peoples could ever come together before a millennial era is established upon the earth.

Still, recent developments in the Middle East have significantly altered the relationship between Israel and her neighbors such that the possibility of unification seems a bit more probable. In fact, diplomatic developments have altered so rapidly, especially between Israel and Egypt, that political scientists are amazed at the drastic change of events. If, in the summer of 1977, experts on the Middle East had been polled and asked if they thought Israel and Egypt would sign a peace treaty before the summer of 1979, scarcely any would have thought it possible. But events beginning in the fall of 1977 started a process that miraculously culminated in the signing of a formal peace treaty between Egypt and Israel on March 26, 1979.

The road to peace between Egypt and Israel was not without its stumbling blocks, however, although President Jimmy Carter and his Camp David talks were helpful in removing those obstacles. Also, each major party involved in the negotiations—President Answar Sadat, Carter, and Prime Minister Menachem Begin—agreed that a fourth party had helped them travel the road to peace. They used different names to describe him—*Allah, Adonai,* or the Lord—but all acknowledged the divine help they received. In fact, Carter was strengthened by the words of Isaiah, and Sadat and Begin quoted them in reference to the peace settlement. The night before the treaty was signed, Carter "read from the fifth chapter of Isaiah, a Prophet who seemed to walk with the peacemakers the entire week. Isaiah's stern admonition to practice humility and diligence seemed to stay with Carter through the celebration of 'the miracle.'" Sadat and Begin quoted Isaiah 2:4 when they as "two of the world's most implacable antagonists signed a formal treaty of peace and eloquently pledged their determination as men of God to heed the plea of Isaiah to 'beat their swords into plowshares, and their spears into pruning-hooks.'" (*Time,* Apr. 9, 1979, pp. 30-31.)

However, the open dialogue of peace between Egypt and Israel has not been well received in most of the Arab world. In Iraq, for example, (the modern name for the ancient territory of Assyria), the peace treaty was protested in Baghdad by half a million Iraqis marching in mass demonstration. Iraq's long-time hatred of Israel now extends to Egypt, especially after Egypt's mild rebuke of Israel after Israeli bombs destroyed Iraq's largest nuclear reactor on June 7, 1981.

Iraq would probably be much more actively involved in fighting Zionism were she not so entrenched in her own conflict with Iran.

And, considering Iraq's strong ties with Russia and the fierce anti-Zionist attitudes of the Iraqi leaders, it seems highly unlikely that Iraq will ever be pro-American, let alone pro-Egyptian or pro-Israeli, within the next few decades. In fact, if experts on the Middle East had been polled in the summer of 1981 about the possibility of peace between Iraq and Israel before 1990, it is unlikely that a very few, if any, would believe that it could occur. But remember that the Lord's efforts between Egypt and Israel wrought a political miracle within two years. Perhaps the future will see a similar miracle and change of heart in Iraqi-Israeli relations.

Whenever it happens, but at some time before the Millennium, it seems quite certain that Iraq will join Israel and Egypt, becoming a third partner with them. These three nations will then be blessed by the Lord and will, in turn, bless the whole earth.

Unlike chapter 19, chapter 20 seems to fit entirely within the historic framework of ancient Egypt, for it provides a warning to the contemporary political powers, although it raises questions about Isaiah's public actions. This short prophecy promises Egypt that she will be conquered by Assyria and that many of her people will become Assyrian slaves. However, the means by which Isaiah gives this warning is most unusual; he emphasizes the impending slavery by walking around without his clothes and sandals. By actually demonstrating to Judah what was to happen to Egypt, Isaiah taught the Jews that they could not trust Egyptian power to rescue them from Assyria. This lesson holds true today; no nation can depend entirely upon its own military power or alliances to preserve it from invasion and destruction. In the end, the Lord's protection, earned through righteousness, is the only guarantee of security. (See Spencer W. Kimball, "The False Gods We Worship," *Ensign*, June 1976, pp. 3-6.)

The historical setting of this chapter is around 715 B.C., when the Ethiopian Pharaoh Shabako conquered Egypt and seemed likely to establish a powerful dynasty. The princes of various states near Egypt and Judah were given fresh hope of liberation in this new Ethiopian dynasty, a hope that they could now break the yoke of the Assyrian King Sargon II. The northern Philistine city of Ashdod became the center of the resistance. Its king, Azuri, withheld tribute payments from the Assyrians and then sent envoys to encourage the kings of neighboring kingdoms to rebel. But Azuri's revolt was crushed when

Sargon deposed him in 713 B.C., replacing him with his brother, Achimiti. The people of Ashdod, in turn, rebelled against Achimiti, replacing him with an Ionian Greek named Jaman. Jaman, too, hoped to create a coalition between other Philistine cities and Edom, Moab, and Judah, with additional support to come from the newly founded Ethiopian-Egyptian empire. But the hoped-for Egyptian help did not materialize. Pharaoh Shabako did not feel that a rebellion against his strong Assyrian enemy was of any value to him. So, in 711 B.C., when the Assyrian army drew near to Philistia and the Ionian ruler fled to Egypt, the pharaoh arrested Jaman and turned him over, bound hand and foot, to Sargon. The revolt in Ashdod was crushed with the aid of an Egyptian army, and the inhabitants of Ashdod, many Egyptians, and others in the surrounding area were taken as Assyrian slaves.

It is not known how much Hezekiah, ruling at the time in Jerusalem, became involved in the movement for revolt. It is assumed that he went no further than conspiracy or else submitted in time to save Judah from an Assyrian invasion.

It is in the midst of this rebellion that Isaiah was commanded to give a sign of the impending slavery. And it was about 711 B.C., as the revolt drew to an end, that Tartan went to Ashdod and Isaiah delivered his prophecy in Jerusalem:

20 It was the year that the Tartan came to Ashdod—being sent by King Sargon of Assyria—and attacked Ashdod and took it. ²Previously, the LORD had spoken to Isaiah son of Amoz, saying, "Go, untie the sackcloth from your loins and take your sandals off your feet," which he had done, going naked and barefoot. ³And now the LORD said, "It is a sign and a portent for Egypt and Nubia. Just as My servant Isaiah has gone naked and barefoot for three years, ⁴so shall the king of Assyria drive off the captives of Egypt and the exiles of Nubia, young and old, naked and barefoot and with bared buttocks—to the shame of Egypt! ⁵And they shall be dismayed and chagrined because of Nubia their hope and Egypt their boast. ⁶In that day, the dwellers of this coastland shall say, 'If this could happen to those we looked to, to whom we fled for help and rescue from the king of Assyria, how can we ourselves escape?'" (NJV)

While this chapter is short and fairly easy to understand once the historical background is known, a few terms and concepts need further explanation.

The Assyrian representative sent by Sargon to the city of Ashdod

223

is known only by his title, Tartan. A tartan was a general, probably the general second in command to the king. (See 2 Kgs. 18:17.) In other words, Sargon himself did not attack Ashdod, but left that and the suppression of the revolt to his general, the tartan.

The most unusual segment of the chapter is verses 2 and 3, in which the Lord commands Isaiah to go "naked and barefoot" as a sign of Egypt's impending humiliation and captivity. Actually, Isaiah was probably not completely naked, but simply without his tunic and outer robes, (Isa. 19, footnote 2a.) In Isaiah's time, men usually wore a loincloth, tunic, and robe when they were in public; while working in the fields or at home, the robe was probably put aside and the tunic remained the main item of attire (the tunic was a loose-fitting linen garment, short-sleeved or sleeveless, that extended to the knees). Slaves, captives, and the lowest manual workers in the society would often not even wear a tunic, but labored in a loincloth. However, it was considered embarrassing for one to be seen in public with only his loincloth, just as today one would be utterly humiliated to be seen in public in his underwear. As evidenced by the end of verse 4, the sign of shame or "nakedness" in Isaiah's time was the exposure of the upper thighs or buttocks.

Even so, one might ask why the Lord would request the prophet to show himself in such humble and improper attire in public. It was probably intended as a graphic sign to the people, one they could not forget or ignore. It was similar to some of the signs Ezekiel gave the Jews during the early stages of their Babylonian captivity, such as cutting his hair, crawling under a wall, and so on. (See Ezek. 4-5.) Isaiah's bizarre behavior and dress was an unusual sign repeated over a three-year period.[1]

The Israelites' attitude to the fulfillment of Isaiah's prophecy is recorded in the last verse of chapter 20. They recognized that if Egypt, powerful as she was, gave in so easily to Assyria, then Judah was in a very vulnerable position. Their situation is summarized in the final desperate question of "How can we escape?" The only answer, even today, is: "Through the help of the Lord."

Isaiah waits awhile before giving his own answer to that question. First he concludes his pronouncements to the other nations and then in chapters 24-27 records how the Lord's hand will be manifest upon the earth, allowing some to escape the coming destruction.

---

[1] It is indefinite whether Isaiah was so dressed during the whole period or only at specific occasions, perhaps annually or at the pilgrimage festivals over the course of the three years.

DESERT CARAVANERS, CITY DEFENDERS, AND SEA TRADERS ISAIAH 21-23

Chapters 21-23 comprise one of the most varied and obscure sections of Isaiah. This section contains seven separate pronouncements, five "burdens," and two "personal" prophecies: the burden of the desert of the sea (21:1-10), the burden of Dumah (21:11-12), the burden upon Arabia (21:13-17), the burden of the valley of vision (22:1-14), and the burden of Tyre (23:1-18); and a personal prophecy to Judah's national treasurer, Shebna (22:15-19), and a prophecy to his successor, Eliakim (22:20-25). The seven pronouncements vary not only in subject matter and length, but also in mood, style, and structure: often passages of revelry and despair are randomly rendered side-by-side in prose or poetry to depict contemporary events and future, messianic incidents. This set of seven pronouncements comprises the final three chapters of the collection of Isaiah's prophecies directed to the foreign nations (Isa. 13-23), and precedes the "Apocalypse of Isaiah," his visions of the judgment of the world (Isa. 24-27). Some of the language and imagery in these three chapters was later used by John the Revelator to describe his own apocalypse (the book of Revelation). The similarity suggests the question, "Are the substance and subject of the two seers' visions similar, or did John simply borrow Isaiah's phraseology?" (Compare Isa. 21:9 with Rev. 14:8; Isa. 22:22 with Rev. 3:7; and Isa. 23:8 with Rev. 18:23.) It appears that John merely uses some of Isaiah's terminology, since he comes later historically, but answers to this question and several other questions about the meaning of these chapters will become more obvious as the seven pronouncements are analyzed.

First Pronouncement: The Burden of the Desert of the Sea (21:1-10)

Isaiah's vision opens with a description of a violent desert storm, which represents an unidentified invader coming against an unnamed force in a land known simply as the "desert by the sea":

21 An oracle concerning the Desert by the Sea:

Like whirlwinds sweeping through
the southland,
an invader comes from the
desert,
from a land of terror.
²A dire vision had been shown to
me:
The traitor betrays, the looter
takes loot.
Elam, attack! Media, lay siege!
I will bring to an end all the
groaning she caused.

³At this my body is racked with
pain,

pangs seize me, like those of a
woman in labor;
I am staggered by what I hear,
I am bewildered by what I see.
⁴My heart falters,
fear makes me tremble;
the twilight I longed for
has become a horror to me.

⁵They set the tables,
they spread the rugs,
they eat, they drink!
Get up, you officers,
oil the shields! (NIV)

In this oracle (or "burden," KJV) upon the "Desert by the Sea," Isaiah records a vision (v. 2) so vivid and terrifying that he himself trembles and fears (vs. 3-4). Isaiah's pain is like that of a "woman in labor" (compare Isa. 13:8) and causes intense emotional sorrow (compare Isa. 15:5; 16:9, 11; Dan. 10:16; Jer. 6:24; Ezek. 30:4, 9; Isa. 21, footnote 3a). Those people actually in the vision, though, seem unaware of the impending disaster as they sit at their banquet. Isaiah must interrupt their festival to warn them to arm and prepare themselves against an attack (v. 5).

Although those under attack remain unidentified, two peoples of the attacking force are identified as Elam and Media (v. 2; see areas G3 and G4 on Map 2). The Elamites were Semites; the Medes descended from Japheth. (Gen. 10:2.) At times these two nations warred against each other, but during Isaiah's age they joined together against the Assyrian Empire. From 850 to 690 B.C. Elam and Media each fought a number of battles with the Assyrians and managed to maintain their independence in spite of the eastern Assyrian expansion. (See 824 B.C. Assyrian boundaries on Map 10.) Shortly after Isaiah's death, however, Assyria gradually expanded into Elamite and Median territories until the two nations lay almost completely within her empire. (See 640 B.C. Assyrian boundaries on Map 10.) The Medes later gained dominion over their own territories and incorporated part of Elam as they pushed back the Assyrians. Indeed, the Medes became so powerful that they eventually attacked the

Assyrian heartland and destroyed Nineveh in 612 B.C.. (See Map 11.) Almost a century later they and the Persians, Elamites, and other peoples conquered Babylon in 539 B.C., thereby forming the greatest empire the ancient world had ever known. (See Map 12.)

Since Elam and Media united in so many ventures, it is difficult to distinguish which "joint attack" the prophet records in chapter 21. Some scholars feel that the joint effort described was one aimed against the Assyrians during Isaiah's lifetime, about 700 B.C., while others believe that Isaiah foresaw the Elam-Media attack to come upon Babylon in 539 B.C. (See Isa. 21, footnote 2b.)

Limited additional information about the historical context and fulfillment of Isaiah's oracle is given in the last half of his pronouncement. While the first half of the oracle describes Isaiah's intense emotion as he glimpses the siege, the second depicts his wait for the news of the outcome:

⁶This is what the Lord says to me:
"Go, post a lookout
    and have him report what
    he sees.
⁷When he sees chariots
    with teams of horses,
    riders on donkeys
    or riders on camels,
let him be alert,
    fully alert."

⁸And the lookout shouted,

"Day after day, my lord, I
    stand on the watchtower;

every night I stay at my post.
⁹Look, here comes a man in a
    chariot
    with a team of horses.
And he gives back the answer:
    'Babylon has fallen, has fallen!
All the images of its gods
    lie shattered on the ground!' "

¹⁰O my people, crushed on the
    threshing floor,
    I tell you what I have heard
from the LORD Almighty,
    from the God of Israel. (NIV)

A historical context is identified in verse 9, in which the messengers record that Babylon is fallen and her idols shattered.

As noted earlier in this book (in the discussion of Isaiah 13-14) Babylon fell to the Persians in 539 B.C. At that time, however, her idols and pagan temples were *not* destroyed because of the beneficence of the Persian king, Cyrus. Babylon's idols were destroyed earlier, though, when the Assyrians attacked her in 689 B.C. A long chain of disputes between Elam, Babylon, and Assyria spanned most of Isaiah's life and led to this destruction.

Thus, the Babylonian downfall that Isaiah foresaw seems to be the result of the Assyrian attack in 689 B.C.

Isaiah foresaw that although Assyria was the greatest threat to God's chosen people in Judah, the combined Elam-Media-Babylonian opposition to Assyria would not succeed. Assyria remained a strong empire for almost a century after Isaiah received this vision of the "desert of the sea." It must have discouraged the prophet to know that Assyria would retain its power for so long, especially since the Assyrians had so brutally attacked Israel and Judah.

The concluding verse of Isaiah's oracle leaves the reader anticipating further details:

> Full of compassion, he addresses himself to his people, so often put to shame and mistreated in the course of history. . . . Even the poet's concluding words do not remove the doubt as to whether he is foretelling merely the fall of Babylon or going beyond it to the subsequent horrors. (Kaiser, *Isaiah 13-39*, p. 128.)

Ancient Israel experienced great suffering at the hands of both the Assyrians and Babylonians. And just as Babylon forcibly and physically oppressed ancient Israelites and Jews, God's children continue to suffer spiritually as long as they submit themselves to the enticing of wickedness or "spiritual" Babylon. Isaiah seems to have foreseen all the types of suffering that Babylon would bring upon his people, and thus is grieved as he delivers his oracle. The prophet experienced actual pain from this vision; it was, in a very real sense, a "burden" to him.

Second Pronouncement: The Burden of Dumah (21:11-12)

Isaiah's next oracle is one of the shortest and most enigmatic in his entire book:

11An oracle concerning Dumah:

Someone calls to me from Seir,
"Watchman, what is left of the night?
Watchman, what is left of the night?"

12The watchman replies,
"Morning is coming, but also the night.
If you would ask, then ask;
and come back yet again."
(NIV)

Dumah is a desert oasis approximately two hundred and fifty miles southeast of the Dead Sea. (See area E4 on Map 2.) Dumah was also the name of a son of Ishmael who founded an Arabian tribe. (Gen. 25:14.) Seir is the chief mountain range immediately southeast of the Dead Sea in the area of Sela, the home of Esau and his descendants, the Edomites. (See area D4 on Map 3.)

The oracle recounts a nighttime episode in which someone asks a watchman how much of the night has passed. He responds that morning is coming, but that night will inevitably fall again. Morning is symbolic of salvation and deliverance, while night represents distress, misery, and evil. In other words, the watchman implies that although redemption is coming, it will be followed by a period of disaster, oppression, or wickedness. (Compare Isa. 8:22; 9:1.) Or, more broadly, he may be saying that "morning" is coming for the righteous and "night" for the wicked.

Spiritually, Edom symbolizes "the world" (D&C 1:36) and the watchman represents a prophet (Jer. 6:17; Ezek. 3:17). Thus, a prophet's saying "morning and darkness are coming, inquire later when the night will end" could be a manner of prophesying about an apostasy and restoration. The "night" in the question asked the watchman seems to symbolize the night of apostasy or spiritual darkness. The watchman, in reply, says that "the morning cometh" (the Millennium, the Lord at his coming, hope for a benighted world) "and also the night" (wherein there can be no labor performed; the end of probation, mortality [Alma 34:32]). The prophet's cryptic reply seems to mean that time is passing; if you want to ask, come later and ask when the time is closer for these events to be fulfilled. Like John the Revelator, Isaiah saw the glorious, triumphant return of the Lord and the end of the earth. One cannot but hear an echo of this in the final words that seal John's revelation: "Come . . . even so, come, Lord Jesus." (Rev. 22:20.)

Third Pronouncement: The Burden upon Arabia (21:13-17)

Without giving any information to explain the situation of this oracle, Isaiah warns a desert people to provide water and food for the refugees who will soon be coming to their towns:

13An oracle concerning Arabia:

You caravans of Dedanites,
who camp in the thickets of Arabia,
14 bring water for the thirsty;
you who live in Tema
bring food for the fugitives.
15They flee from the sword,
from the drawn sword,
from the bent bow
and from the heat of battle.

16This is what the Lord says to me: "Within one year, as a servant bound by contract would count it, all the pomp of Kedar will come to an end. 17The survivors of the bowmen, the warriors of Kedar, will be few." The LORD, the God of Israel, has spoken. (NIV)

Apparently, an Assyrian military expedition into the Syrian desert forced many people of Kedar to move south to the towns of Tema and Dedan. (See areas D3, 4, 5 on Map 2.) Kedar was the second son of Ishmael and, according to some Arab genealogists, an ancestor of the prophet Muhammed. Kedar's descendants were desert dwellers and herdsmen comparable to the modern Bedouin. (IDB 3:3.) The Dedan-ites, on the other hand, were an important commercial people who lived in northwest Arabia. (See Ezek. 27:20.) Their ancestry is uncertain, although they are thought to have descended either from Cush (Gen. 10:7) or from Abraham through his third wife, Keturah (Gen. 25:3). They apparently settled in parts of Edom. (IDB 1:812.) Tema was another son of Ishmael, and the oasis named after him was located on the main routes stretching from the Red Sea east to the Persian Gulf and north to Damascus. The Temanites were caravaners who, although they paid tribute to the Assyrians, remained secure in the desert until the Babylonians destroyed their city in 552 B.C. (Job 6:19; Jer. 25:23; compare Jer. 29:28-32.)

Isaiah's pronouncement upon this desert people is quite straightforward, strongly admonishing them to provide refuge and supplies for the Kedarites who are to be invaded and exiled within a year. There is also a slight possibility that the oracle foretells events of the last days, with the unnamed enemies coming from the north representing an eschatological threat and the "food" and "water" symbolizing spiritual as well as physical sustenance to be provided for the influx of refugees.

Fourth Pronouncement: The Burden of the Valley of Vision (22:1-14)

Isaiah harshly rebukes the inhabitants of Jerusalem for their selfish attitude in a time of distress. He also denounces the pride and insensitivity they continue to maintain even under divine chastisement. Although calamities are about to befall Jerusalem because of Sennacherib's invasion, the Judeans' only thoughts are for pleasure.

Isaiah's pronouncement can be separated into four segments:

1. The prophet compares their attitudes with his own (vs. 1-4)
2. He warns that the Lord will send enemies instead of allies into their land (5-7)
3. He warns that they are ignoring God in their reliance upon physical means of defense (8-11)
4. He compares their behavior with what the Lord desires (12-14)

Into each segment Isaiah incorporates antithetic parallelism to emphasize how Judah's attitudes, expectations, plans, and behavior oppose that which the Lord desires. In the end, however, Judah will experience the opposite of what she desires when she receives the full rewards of her wickedness.

Isaiah begins the oracle by comparing the people's attitudes in the face of the Assyrian invasion with his own:

22 An oracle concerning the Valley of Vision:

What troubles you now,
 that you have all gone up on
  the housetops,
²O town full of commotion,
 O city of tumult and revelry?
Your slain were not killed by the
  sword,
 nor did they die in battle.
³All your leaders have fled together;
 they have been captured
without using the bow.
All you who were caught were
  taken prisoner together,
 having fled while the enemy
  was still far away.
⁴Therefore I said, "Turn away
  from me;
 let me weep bitterly.
Do not try to console me
 over the destruction of my
  people." (NIV)

While the people of Jerusalem rejoice because they have not been killed or captured, Isaiah mourns for the losses already incurred and those that will follow. Although the Assyrians have already destroyed dozens of Judean cities and taken thousands of Jewish captives, the people in Jerusalem celebrate their freedom. Isaiah sorrows not only for the impending disaster, but also for those who do not understand or seem concerned about the problems Judah faces.

The "valley of vision" in verse 1 refers to Jerusalem, for this holy city is the place where revelation is given. (See Isa. 22 chapter heading and footnote 1a.) Although built on the tops of the rolling Judean mountains, Jerusalem is laced with hills and valleys. Mount Moriah, the site of the temple, is lower in elevation than most of the hills of Jerusalem that surround it. It is nestled in a valley between Mount Zion to the west and the Mount of Olives to the east.

Isaiah then describes the destruction that the Lord will bring to the "valley of vision." Enemy soldiers and chariots replace revelations and prophecies:

⁵The Lord, the LORD Almighty, has
  a day
 of tumult and trampling and
terror
 in the Valley of Vision,
 a day of battering down walls

and of crying out to the
mountains.
⁶Elam takes up the quiver,
with her charioteers and
horses;
Kir uncovers the shield.

⁷Your choicest valleys are full of
chariots,
and horsemen are posted at
the city gates;
⁸the defenses of Judah are stripped
away. (NIV)

When the Lord's day finally comes to Jerusalem, the people will not celebrate, for their defense will fail. Although the people think the soldiers of Elam and Kir will be able to defeat the Assyrians before they reach Jerusalem (v. 6), the enemy will come to the city gates. (Kir was on the main road between Elam and Babylon, and its inhabitants joined the Elam-Babylonian confederation in opposing Assyria.)

Jerusalem's defenses were immense, but not strong enough to withstand the Assyrians. Isaiah reviews Jerusalem's defenses, telling why the people lack the most important element of defense—the protection of God:

And you looked in that day
to the weapons in the Palace
of the Forest:
⁹you saw that the City of David
had many breaches in its
defenses;
you stored up water
in the Lower Pool.
¹⁰You counted the buildings in
Jerusalem

and tore down houses to
strengthen the wall.
¹¹You built a reservoir between the
two walls
for the water of the Old Pool,
but you did not look to the One
who made it,
or have regard for the One
who planned it long ago.
(NIV)

A modern scholar described the same defenses:

> The carefully thought out policy of Hezekiah is discernible not only in his patient waiting for the opportune moment to rebel against Assyria and in the extensive diplomatic maneuvers which created an association of allies far and near, but also in his efforts to fortify Judah itself against the inevitable struggle against the Assyrians. In a major engineering feat, Hezekiah devised the means for transferring the water from the spring of Gihon, located outside the Jerusalem walls, through an underground tunnel to the pool of Siloam located within the city walls. Monumental evidence for the digging of Hezekiah's tunnel has been preserved in the 'Siloam Inscription'. Furthermore, Hezekiah strengthened the walls of Jerusalem and fortified numerous Judean cities. He reorganized the army, prepared military weapons, and it seems also that he brought mercenary troops into Jerusalem. The reorganization of the army was no doubt associated with the census carried out by Hezekiah in southern Judah. He built store cities of warehouses for agricultural supplies. There is

also the possibility that Hezekiah restructured the royal administrative system. Evidence for this political reorganization may be seen in the transference of the office of 'the royal steward' from Shebnah to Eliakim. (Isa. 22:15-25: Hayes, *Israelite and Judean History*, p. 447.)

Isaiah concludes his oracle upon Jerusalem by comparing the Lord's anticipations with those of the people, noting how they reacted to the threatening situation:

12The Lord, the LORD Almighty, called you on that day
to weep and to wail, to tear out your hair and put on sackcloth.
13But see, there is joy and revelry, slaughtering of cattle and killing of sheep,
eating of meat and drinking of wine!

"Let us eat and drink," you say, "for tomorrow we die!"

14The LORD Almighty has revealed this in my hearing: "Till your dying day this sin will not be atoned for," says the Lord, the LORD Almighty. (NIV)

To describe the people eating and drinking, Isaiah uses the Hebrew infinitives "to eat" and "to drink," thus implying continuous and excessive indulgence in revelries and orgies. The sentence "Let us eat and drink for tomorrow we may die," could be the slogan of the reckless revellers, although it might also be the prophet's scornful thrust hinting at their impending doom. (Israel Slotki, *Isaiah*, p. 102; compare 2 Ne. 28:7.)

In comparing Isaiah's feelings with Jerusalem's, it is obvious that Isaiah mourns not only for the physical hardships descending upon Jerusalem, but also for the spiritual gulf separating God from his chosen people. The people may think that their troubles are over when the Assyrians finally depart, but they must still face the Lord and the consequences of their sins (v. 14).

Fifth Pronouncement: A Prophecy of Shebna (22:15-19)

After portraying the unconcerned and sinful condition of Jerusalem's inhabitants, Isaiah singles out a leading citizen and describes his selfish, vain actions. The individual selected is Shebna, the leader of the king's court, a position similar to a present-day secretary of state. Isaiah apparently confronts Shebna in the Kidron Valley near the tombs of the kings:

15This is what the Lord, the LORD Almighty, says:

"Go, say to this steward,

to Shebna, who is in charge of the palace:
16What are you doing here and who gave you permission

to cut out a grave for yourself here,
hewing your grave on the height
and chiseling your resting place in the rock?

[17]"Beware, the LORD is about to take firm hold of you
and hurl you away, O you mighty man.
[18]He will roll you up tightly like a ball

and throw you into a large country.
There you will die
and there your splendid chariots will remain—
you disgrace to your master's house!
[19]I will depose you from your office,
and you will be ousted from your position. (NIV)

Like the dashed expectations of those in Jerusalem, Shebna's hope for a magnificent tomb in Jerusalem is destined to come to naught. Indeed, Shebna was eventually disgraced in office and demoted to the office of secretary or scribe of the king's court. (Isa. 36:3.) This position was still influential, however, being the post second only to the head of the court.

According to some scholars, Shebna was actually a foreigner who rose to power in Jerusalem. They give three primary reasons for this supposition: (1) his father is never mentioned, although other officials are identified by their families (see Isa. 22:20; 36:3); (2) his name is not Hebrew; and (3) Isaiah makes a strong contrast between "here" in Jerusalem where Shebna hews out his tomb and "there" where he will die. (Young, *The Book of Isaiah* 2:106; Slotki, *Isaiah*, p. 103.)

Many scholars also believe that Shebna favored a strong pro-Egyptian policy, and that Jerusalem's immunity from Sargon's campaign of 711 B.C. resulted from a shift in Judean policy at the time when Shebna was removed from office. In short, the Jewish government became more submissive to Assyria. (IDB 4:312.)

In any case, Isaiah presents two strong contrasts in this short discourse: Shebna planned a glorious tomb for himself in Jerusalem, but the Lord has planned another burial in a foreign land; Shebna, indifferent to Jerusalem's fate, builds himself a permanent tomb while Isaiah weeps over the fate of his people.

Sixth Pronouncement: A Prophecy to Eliakim (22:20-25)

Here Isaiah continues speaking to Shebna, but prophesies about the person who will replace him: Eliakim is to be invested with the keys and authority of Shebna's office. Isaiah has a warning for

Eliakim, however, concerning the way in which his family will rely upon Eliakim's position and influence for protection:

20"In that day I will summon my servant, Eliakim son of Hilkiah. 21I will clothe him with your robe and fasten your sash around him and hand your authority over to him. He will be a father to those who live in Jerusalem and to the house of Judah. 22I will place on his shoulder the key to the house of David; what he opens no one can shut, and what he shuts no one can open. 23I will drive him like a peg into a firm place; he will be a seat of honor for the house of his father. 24All the glory of his family will hang on him; its offspring and offshoots —all its lesser vessels, from the bowls to all the jars.

25"In that day," declares the LORD Almighty, "The peg driven into the firm place will give way; it will be sheared off and will fall, and the load hanging on it will be cut down." The LORD has spoken. (NIV)

In hanging all their hopes upon Eliakim's position as a "peg in a firm place," Eliakim's family will be disappointed, for when he loses his position of influence they will fall with him.

Some of the terminology of this warning also seems to refer to the priesthood keys and atoning powers of Jesus Christ. First of all, the name Eliakim means "God shall cause to arise," a messianic title pointing to the Resurrection. (See Isa. 22, footnote 20a.) Secondly, Eliakim is called as a servant of God (v. 20). Third, he holds the physical keys to the king's storerooms. Fourth, Eliakim serves as a "nail in a sure place" (KJV) for his family, meaning that they depend upon him for security. Similarly, Christ was crucified by a "nail in a sure place," thus fulfilling the demands of the Atonement under the law of justice. (See Ezra 9:8; Zech. 12:10; 13:6; John 20:25; D&C 45:51-53; TG "Jesus Christ, Crucifixion of"; BD "Crucifixion.")

Important differences remain between Eliakim and Christ, however. Eliakim's office was temporal, temporary, and unsuccessful, while Christ's mission is heavenly, eternal, and triumphant. Eliakim failed as a "nail in a sure place" but Christ's "nail in a sure place" (crucifixion) secured the eternal blessings of the Atonement.

Seventh Pronouncement: The Burden of Tyre (23:1-18)

It is appropriate that the concluding prophecy in Isaiah's pronouncements upon the foreign nations (chs. 13-23) be an oracle against Tyre. Tyre had much in common with Babylon (to whom

Isaiah had directed his first foreign pronouncement), although the two came into prominence by contrasting means: Babylon was at the heart of political kingdoms, Tyre was the central commercial city; Babylon was the traditional center of land power, Tyre was the leading sea power; Babylon extended her empire by war, Tyre expanded her influence through trade; Babylon tore down and destroyed other cities, Tyre planted colonies and built new cities. (See Young, *The Book of Isaiah* 2:121.)

The name of Tyre is also a symbol of the ways of the world: while Babylon represents wickedness and idolatry, Tyre symbolizes worldliness and materialism. Isaiah first foretells how Tyre's commercial power will be broken:

23 An oracle concerning Tyre:

Wail, O ships of Tarshish!
For Tyre is destroyed
  and left without house or
  harbor.
From the land of Cyprus
  word has come to them.

²Be silent, you people of the island
  and you merchants of Sidon,
  whom the seafarers have
  enriched.
³On the great waters
  came the grain of the Shihor;
the harvest of the Nile was the
  revenue of Tyre,
  and she became the
  marketplace of the nations.

⁴Be ashamed, O Sidon, and you, O
  fortress of the sea,
  for the sea has spoken:
"I have neither been in labor nor
  given birth;
I have neither reared sons
  nor brought up daughters."
⁵When word comes to Egypt,
  They will be in anguish at
  the report from Tyre.

⁶Cross over to Tarshish;
  wail, you people of the island.
⁷Is this your city of revelry,
  the old, old city,
whose feet have taken her
  to settle in far-off lands? (NIV)

The oracle begins with four parallel couplets that mention important Phoenician trade cities:

Tarshish and Cyprus (Chittim, KJV) (v. 1)
Sidon, Shihor, and the Nile (2-3)
Sidon and Egypt (4-5)
Tarshish and "people of the island" (Tyre and Cyprus?) (6-7)

Most of these sites are identified on Map 2, and each is important for different reasons:

Tyre is in southern Phoenicia with the oldest settlements on the mainland and the important seaport located on a small island. Tyre was usually the strongest of the Phoenician city-states and was noted for its purple dye, the most famous and precious of the dyes in ancient times (area D3 on Map 2; this area is part of modern Lebanon).

Tarshish is west of Phoenicia either in Asia Minor (Tarsus, in modern Turkey) or, more likely, on the Iberian Peninsula (Tartessus, in modern Spain). The "ships of Tarshish" were noted for their long travel, power, and heavy loads. In addition to dyed clothes, they delivered timber, grain, oil, wine, metal, slaves, and horses. (See Isa. 2:16 and pp. 90-91 in this book where they are also discussed.)

Cyprus, identified as Chittim in the King James Version, is a large island west of Phoenicia. It was controlled by Tyre during most of Isaiah's lifetime. It later came under the control of the Assyrians after the subjugation of the Phoenician city-states by Sargon and Sennacherib. It was an important seaport and trade center for the Phoenicians (area C3 on Map 2; today the island is controlled by both the Greeks and the Turks).

Sidon, called Zidon in the King James Version, was located along the central Phoenician coast about twenty-five miles north of Tyre. At times a rival with Tyre, it was usually subject to the kings of Tyre. It was noted for its fishing and industries, such as producing purple dye (area D3 on Map 2; also part of modern Lebanon).

Shihor, called Sihor in the King James Version, was probably located in the swamps of northeastern Egypt. Its precise location is unknown, but it is sometimes mentioned with Ramses or Zoan, which is located in the eastern delta; much of Egypt's grain was shipped from this area (area C4 on Map 2; part of modern Egypt). (See IDB 1:753-54; 4:328, 343-44, 517-18, 721-22; see also BD "Tyre," "Sidon," "Phoenicia.")

As shown by the description of these cities, the Phoenician trade empire extended throughout the Mediterranean Sea and encompassed areas that are today located in at least a half dozen different countries.

Isaiah promised Tyre, however, that she would lose her dominion of the sea and that the effects of the loss would be felt throughout her empire. He then told why and through whom this humiliation was coming:

[8]Who planned this against Tyre,
   the bestower of crowns,
whose merchants are princes,
   whose traders are renowned
     in the earth?

[9]The LORD Almighty planned it,
   to bring low the pride of all
   glory
and to humble all who are
   renowned on the earth. (NIV)

237

Although the Lord used the Assyrians to subdue Tyre, he did it primarily to humble the proud Phoenicians.

Isaiah repeats his warning, listing the major Phoenician cities and colonies once again, thus emphasizing the inevitability of the impending destruction:

10Go through your land;
the Daughter of Tarshish,
like the Nile,
will no longer be a haven
for you.
11The LORD has stretched out his
hand over the sea
and made its kingdoms
tremble.
He has given an order concerning
Phoenicia
that her fortresses be
destroyed.
12He said, "No more of your
reveling,
O Virgin Daughter of Sidon,
now crushed!

"Up, cross over to Cyprus;
even there you will find
no rest."
13Look at the land of the
Babylonians,
this people that is now of no
account!
The Assyrians have made it
a place for desert creatures;
they raised up their siege towers,
they stripped its fortresses
bare
and turned it into a ruin.

14Wail, you ships of Tarshish;
your fortress is destroyed!
(NIV)

In his second warning, Isaiah singles out the Assyrians as the instruments of God's judgment. As seen in the discussion and maps concerning Isaiah 36 and 37 in this book, Sennacherib gained absolute control of Phoenicia, thus initiating Tyre's humiliation.

Isaiah concludes his pronouncement upon Tyre with a note of hope, promising an end to the Lord's punishment and a time when Phoenician profits will benefit the Lord's righteous children:

15At that time Tyre will be forgotten for seventy years, the span of a king's life. But at the end of these seventy years, it will happen to Tyre as in the song of a prostitute:

16"Take up a harp, walk through
the city,
O prostitute forgotten;
play the harp well, sing many a
song,
so that you will be
remembered."

17At the end of seventy years, the LORD will deal with Tyre. She will return to her hire as a prostitute and will ply her trade with all the kingdoms on the face of the earth. 18Yet her profit and her earnings will be set apart for the LORD; they will not be stored up or hoarded. Her profits will go to those who live before the LORD, for abundant food and fine clothes. (NIV)

238

The term "seventy years" seems to have a double meaning. About seventy years after Sennacherib humiliated Tyre and placed his own ruler on the throne, the Assyrians quickly declined in power. The small countries in the Mediterranean area were thereby able to reestablish some independence (701 B.C.). Tyre later fell to the Babylonians about the same time as Jerusalem did (587-586 B.C.) and thereafter never regained any real power as a nation. Although Tyre was freed after seventy years of bondage, she did not set apart her riches to the Lord. Therefore, since the numbers seven and seventy can also represent completeness, perfection, and wholeness, perhaps Isaiah is also promising that after an appropriate period of time the riches of Tyre will be dedicated to the Lord. (IDB 4:295.)

The destruction of Tyre also parallels the destruction of spiritual Babylon in the last days. John the Revelator used a number of Isaiah's descriptive terms to portray Babylon as a symbol of wickedness. (See Rev. 14:8; 16:19; 17:1-5, 15, 18; 18:3, 11, 15, 17-19, 23.) Both Isaiah and John denounced the worldly wealth of the two cities, and both visions of destruction serve as a warning to the entire world to avoid the bondage of wealth and pride. (See 2 Ne. 28:17-19; D&C 132:12-14.)

In conclusion, the seven pronouncements of Isaiah in chapters 21-23 deal with a variety of countries, people, historical contexts, and possibilities of prophetic fulfillment. The dominant theme throughout them all, however, is that worldly aspirations, wickedness, selfishness, and pride will eventually be thwarted. Generally given in a punitive tone, these oracles warn the wicked of the Lord's sure judgments upon the world. In the following chapters (24-27), Isaiah elaborates upon this theme and expands it to describe a universal judgment to come upon all mankind. He also encourages hope, however, as he promises the Resurrection and a new life of righteousness.

ISAIAH'S APOCALYPSE
ISAIAH 24-25

A seer can know of things which are past, and also of things which are to come, and by them shall all things be revealed, or, rather, shall secret things be made manifest, and hidden things shall come to light, and *things which are not known shall be made known by them, and* also *things* shall be made known by them *which otherwise could not be known.* (Mosiah 8:17; italics added.)

Isaiah was a great seer because things that were not known and recorded in other writings of his time were made known to him.

Isaiah's seership becomes fully evident in chapters 24-27. He records a cycle of prophecies that has no parallel in the writings of earlier Old Testament prophets, although it is echoed in the later writings of Daniel (ch. 7-12), Zechariah (ch. 9-14), and John (Rev. 7-22). He sees the judgment, Christ's second coming, the establishment of Zion, the resurrection, and the glory of the millennial and celestial periods. He records so many profound insights in these four chapters that they are often called the "apocalypse of Isaiah." (See Kaiser, *Isaiah 13-39*, p. 173; IDB 1:157.) Although a fitting capstone to the preceding chapters, Isaiah's apocalypse also advances new concepts that will lead into the new insights and prophecies recorded in Isaiah's later writings.

Chapters 24 and 25 introduce Isaiah's apocalypse (revelation), each developing contrasting themes and moods: chapter 24 ominously foretells destruction and sadness, while chapter 25 auspiciously promises new life and gladness. In these two chapters Isaiah speaks as prophet, seer, and poet: as a prophet he warns and testifies of the consequences of wickedness; as a seer he reveals future events upon this earth and spiritual developments in the post-earthly spirit world; as a poet he combines semantic parallelism, sound, repetitions, and symbolism to memorably portray the condition of the earth in the last days.

Characteristically, Isaiah begins chapter 24 with the bold interjection "behold," thus emphasizing the importance of the message that follows. He describes a catastrophe that will afflict all classes of society:

24 Behold,
The LORD will strip the
    earth bare,
And lay it waste,
And twist its surface,
And scatter its inhabitants.
²Layman and priest shall fare alike,
Slave and master,

Handmaid and mistress,
Buyer and seller,
Lender and borrower,
Creditor and debtor.
³The earth shall be bare, bare;
It shall be plundered, plundered;
For it is the LORD who spoke this
    word. (NJV)

A quick review of Isaiah's poetic technique as illustrated by these verses reveals the variety of form at his command. The first three verses are chiastic, following a sequence of (a) Lord, (b) bare earth and disaster, (c) people affected, (b') bare earth and disaster, (a') Lord. Furthermore, these verses contain antithetic, and climactic parallelism. In verse 3 Isaiah employs direct repetition in order to emphasize the extent of "barrenness" and "plundering."

In biblical Hebrew, the repetition of a word, for example, "bare, bare" makes the word comparative ("more bare") or superlative ("most bare"). By repeating "bare" three times in verses 1-3, Isaiah stresses his point—the earth will be extremely bare! Isaiah also uses assonance in verse 1 (*boqeq* "empty" and *boleqah* "waste") and alliteration in verse 3 (*hiboq-tiboq* "empty-empty" and *hiboz-tiboz* "spoiled-spoiled") to further tighten his poetic form. Thus, through structure, sound, and meaning, Isaiah combines many forms of parallelism in just three verses.

In contrasting different classes of people (v. 2), Isaiah first indicates that both priests and laity will suffer. As a representative of God, the ancient priest occupied an exalted position of authority. But similar to the Israelites as a chosen people, the priest as God's representative has strayed into wickedness and will no longer live worthy of God's blessings; indeed, the people and priest together will experience God's judgments. (Compare Spencer W. Kimball's similar feelings about religious leaders and "priests who encourage the defilement of men and wink at the eroding trends and who deny the omniscience of God." [CR, Apr. 1971, p. 9.])

Isaiah testifies concerning the certainty of the Lord's judgment in verse 3, which concludes with one of Isaiah's favorite insertions: "the Lord has spoken. " This short clause characterizes Isaiah's prophetic authority and strengthens the majestic force of his prophecies.

After testifying briefly about what is coming to whom, Isaiah explains why God's judgments are coming:

⁴The earth is withered, sear;
The world languishes, it is sear;
The most exalted people on earth
   languish.
⁵For the earth was defiled
Under its inhabitants;
Because they transgressed
   teachings,
Violated laws,
Broke the ancient covenant.
⁶That is why a curse consumes the
   earth,
And its inhabitants pay the
   penalty;
That is why earth's dwellers have
   dwindled,
And but few men are left. (NJV)

The "most exalted people on earth" could be those who exalt themselves and thus become the proud or haughty (v. 4, KJV). They might also be the ancient Israelites or members of Christ's latter-day church who have been called and ordained to great callings but who "languish" and fail to fulfill their stewardship. Whoever they are, their primary sin is that they have changed the teachings, laws, and covenants of the Lord (v. 5). Each gospel principle, commandment, and ordinance was designed by God to help his children grow spiritually. Isaiah emphasizes that their changes have occurred upon three levels of the gospel: the knowledge level (teachings, instruction, or understanding), the action level (laws, commandments, or guidelines), and the contractual level (covenants, ordinances, or promises). In other words, complete apostasy among the people necessitates the Lord's curse upon the whole earth. These people must suffer until only a few of them remain upon the earth.

Isaiah continues to describe in greater detail the effects of God's judgments:

⁷The new wine fails,
The vine languishes;
And all the merry-hearted sigh.
⁸Stilled is the merriment of
   timbrels,
Ended the clamor of revelers,
Stilled the merriment of lyres.
⁹They drink their wine without
   song;
Liquor tastes bitter to the drinker.
¹⁰Towns are broken, empty;
Every house is shut, none enters;
¹¹Even over wine, a cry goes up in
   the streets:
The sun has set on all joy,
The gladness of the earth is
   banished.
¹²Desolation is left in the town
And the gate is battered to ruins.
(NJV)

Before elaborating further upon the disastrous consequences of God's judgment upon the world, Isaiah interjects some positive results of the period of chastisement:

[13]For thus shall it be among the peoples
In the midst of the earth:
As when the olive tree is beaten out,
Like gleanings when the vintage is over.
[14]These shall lift up their voices,
Exult in the majesty of the LORD.
They shall shout from the sea:
[15]Therefore, honor the LORD with lights
In the coastlands of the sea—
the name of the LORD, the God of Israel.
[16]From the end of the earth
We hear singing:
Glory to the righteous!
And I said:
I waste away! I waste away! Woe is me!
The faithless have acted faithlessly;
The faithless have broken faith!
(NJV)

Some of God's children will be gleaned in righteousness out of the world's wickedness. These will praise the Lord throughout the earth.[1] They are:

A new group of persons, distinguished by an emphatic pronoun [therefore] from the rest of mankind, which was treated as a whole in the previous prophecy [vs. 1-12]. . . . This group is to rejoice at the majesty of Yahweh, and . . . it is obvious to suppose that they are members of the people of God. (Kaiser, *Isaiah 13-39*, p. 187).

The chosen few do not sing a taunt song against their destroyed brothers and sisters, nor do they praise their own righteousness, but they praise their Savior and the light and glory he brings to the earth. These verses of praise bring hope to an otherwise gloomy revelation of judgment.

Despite the prospect of a glorious future, Isaiah cannot remain hopeful in the midst of the wickedness that surrounds him. In verse 16, he bemoans his ineffectual capacity to change the people's behavior as he contrasts the contemporary state of wickedness around him with the future age of righteousness.

Isaiah expresses his grief in six short Hebrew words that all end

---

[1]Jewish tradition applies the "gleanings" to the remnants of Israel among the Gentiles. (Slotki, *Isaiah*, p. 112.) Latter-day Saints recognize that remnants of Israel will be among the Lord's "gleanings" but that other people will also become part of God's harvest in the last days.

with the same sound. They are transliterated and translated as follows:

razi	*li*	*razi*	*li*	*oi*	*li*
(leanness to me)		(leanness to me)		(woe is to me)	

Isaiah's expression in English would be similar to "Skinny me, skinny me—pity me!"

He concludes verse 16 by repeating the same root, *beged*, five times, twice as a participle, twice as a perfect verb, and once as a noun. It would have sounded like this: *bodgim bagadu, uveged bogdim bagadu.* In order to retain a sense of the sound and meaning of these words, one scholar has rendered them as "Plunderers plunder, even with plunder do plunderers plunder." (Young, *The Book of Isaiah* 2:174.)

Isaiah continues his discourse by portraying the helplessness that will befall people on the earth, the earth itself, and people in the spirit world. First, the people on the earth:

¹⁷Terror, and pit, and trap
  Upon you who dwell on earth!
¹⁸He who flees at the report of the
    terror
  Shall fall into the pit;

And he who climbs out of the pit
Shall be caught in the trap.
For sluices are opened on high,
And earth's foundations tremble.
(NJV)

The wicked will futilely attempt to avoid God's many judgments. Although they may escape from one, they will fall into another, and if they escape from the second judgment, they will be ensnared in a third.[2]

Isaiah indicates that the earth will also be in a helpless condition:

¹⁹The earth is breaking, breaking;
  The earth is crumbling,
    crumbling.
²⁰The earth is swaying like a
  drunkard;

It is rocking to and fro like a hut.
Its iniquity shall weigh it down,
And it shall fall, to rise no more.
(NJV)

The climactic parallelism of verse 19 leads into the severe consequence portrayed in verse 20. The progressive steps in verse 19 are explained by one scholar as follows:

---

[2]Strong assonance helps convey the meaning of this verse. All three dangers (terror, pit, and trap) begin with the same two letters in the Hebrew; *pachad* and *pachat* and *pach* are befalling the people.

244

In the description there appears to be an ascending gradation of thought. The first verb implies a breaking or shattering, as though pieces of the earth were broken off; it is probably onomatopoeic. The word is suitable for describing an earthquake or some great convulsion that breaks the earth in pieces. The second verb is probably stronger, and suggests that the earth is actually divided by being split through; while the last verb denotes a violent or great shaking of the earth. Quite possibly the imagery or figure of the earthquake lies at the basis of the portrayal, but Isaiah's purpose is not to describe an earthquake; rather he is pointing to a tremendous shaking of the earth that will come when the punitive judgment of God strikes. (Young, *The Book of Isaiah* 2:176.)

The eventual fulfillment of these verses is also promised in modern scripture, which says that "not many days hence" the earth will "tremble and reel to and fro as a drunken man." (D&C 49:23; 88:87.)

Apparently, people other than those living upon the earth will be involved in the events described by Isaiah. Spirit beings from above the earth (the "hosts of heaven") and those still bound to this earth ("captives" in a spirit "prison") will also be affected:

> ²¹In that day, the LORD will punish The host of heaven in heaven And the kings of the earth on earth. ²²They shall be gathered in a dungeon As captives are gathered; And shall be locked up in a prison. But after many days they shall be remembered. (NJV)

The "hosts of heaven" that the Lord punishes are most likely the original followers of Satan who were cast out of God's presence. They will suffer with the spirits of the wicked who lived on this earth. Yet after a time, the spirits of this earth will be remembered and "visited" (KJV) by messengers teaching the gospel of Jesus Christ. (See D&C 138; DS 2:155; MD, p. 755.)

Isaiah concludes his prophecy with a promise that the Lord himself will come to the earth in such radiant glory that the sun and moon will pale in comparison:

> ²³Then the moon shall be ashamed, And the sun shall be abashed. For the LORD of Hosts will reign On Mount Zion and in Jerusalem, And the Presence will be revealed to His elders. (NJV)

The "elders" who will receive the Lord upon the earth might be those who hold his priesthood in the latter days, although they could also be the "elders" or ancient ones who lived upon this earth in earlier dispensations who "shall come to visit" their descendants (D&C

116:1) and will help usher in the Lord's rule. (See BD "Adam"; D&C 133:49.)

In chapter 24, Isaiah answers many questions about God's judgments upon this earth and its inhabitants. He foretells primarily *what* will happen (vs. 1-3, 7-12, 17-23), although he also describes to *whom* the judgments will come (v. 2), *where* they will come (vs. 17, 21-22), and *why* they will come to both the wicked (vs. 4-6) and the righteous (vs. 13-16). One important question Isaiah does not answer is *when* they will occur.

From Isaiah's time and perspective, he could be describing any one of three important periods in the earth's history. First, the earthquakes, the helplessness of the people, and a visiting of the spirits in prison might describe the disaster in the Americas at the time of Christ's crucifixion and his visit to the spirit world. (See 3 Ne. 8-9; D&C 138.) Second, similar events will affect this earth prior to Christ's second coming, and many spirits will be "remembered" and rise up from the dead. (See D&C 45:33; 88:89; 63:49.) Third, at the end of the Millennium, there will be a great cleansing of the earth prior to the last reuniting of spirits to their bodies, the resurrection of the unjust. (D&C 76:71-112; 88:99-102.) The earth will then be celestial, a body of light that will cause the sun to be "abashed" and the moon (which is lit by the sun) to be "ashamed" (v. 23; compare D&C 29:22-25; 130:7; 77:1-2).

Isaiah's use of imagery in this poem makes this prophecy a truly great piece of literature that would be repeated and remembered by generations of Israelites even though they might not enjoy its sober message of judgment. Isaiah's beautiful prophecy promises divine justice and carries some hope for those who are righteous (vs. 14-16) and await the Lord's reign on this earth (v. 23).

Isaiah becomes even more hopeful as his apocalypse unfolds. In chapter 25, he breaks forth into an exulting hymn, declaring a time of feasting, closeness to God, resurrection, joy, and victory.

He begins with praise for the Lord's power over the unrighteous and protection of the needy:

25 O Lord, You are my God;
I will extol You, I will
praise Your name.
For You planned graciousness of
old,
Counsels of steadfast faithfulness.

²For You have turned a city into a
stone heap,
A walled town into a ruin,
The citadel of strangers into
rubble,
Never to be rebuilt.

³Therefore a fierce people must honor You,
A city of cruel nations must fear You.
⁴For You have been a refuge for the poor man,
A shelter for the needy man in his distress—
Shelter from rainstorm, shade from heat.
When the fury of tyrants was like a winter rainstorm,
⁵The rage of strangers like heat in the desert,
You subdued the heat with the shade of clouds,
The singing of the tyrants was vanquished. (NJV)

God's pre-earthly councils in heaven are alluded to in verse 1, in which Isaiah thanks God for fulfilling his foreordained plans. The prophet also portrays the range of God's emotions by describing both God's anger against the tyrants and his concern for the poor and needy.

Isaiah describes how and why the righteous people will rejoice:

⁶The LORD of Hosts will make on this mount
For all the peoples
A banquet of rich viands,
A banquet of choice wines—
Of rich viands seasoned with marrow,
Of choice wines well refined.
⁷And He will destroy on this mount the shroud
That is drawn over the faces of all the peoples
And the covering that is spread
Over all the nations:
⁸He will destroy death forever.
My Lord God will wipe the tears away
From all faces
And will put an end to the reproach of His people
Over all the earth—
For it is the LORD who has spoken. (NJV)

Finally, after the days of tribulation, the earth's inhabitants will rejoice, feast, and celebrate together with the Lord (v. 6; see D&C 58:3-12). The veil of spiritual darkness and separation from the Lord will be taken away (v. 7; see D&C 38:8; 67:10; 110:1). Death will be destroyed and the reproach of sin will be removed through the power of the Atonement and Resurrection (v. 8). These promises of eternal life and happiness with God stand in sharp contrast to the mood of the preceding prophecy of judgment and destruction.

Isaiah continues to briefly describe what the people will say in that day:

⁹In that day they shall say:
  This is our God;
  We trusted in Him, and He
    delivered us.

This is the LORD, in whom we
  trusted;
Let us rejoice and exult in His
  deliverance! (NJV)

He concludes his hymn with sober words of warning for the proud people who live on this "mountain" or this earth:

¹⁰For the hand of the LORD shall
    descend
  Upon this mount,
  And Moab shall be trampled
    under Him
  As straw is threshed to bits at
    Madmenah.
¹¹Then He will spread out His
    hands in their homeland,
  As a swimmer spreads his hands

  out to swim,
  And He will humble their pride
  Along with the emblems of their
    power.
¹²Yea, the secure fortification of
    their walls
  He will lay low and humble,
  Will raze to the ground, to the
    very dust. (NJV)

As the Lord sweeps his hand through the land (like a swimmer spreads his hands through the water), he will humble the proud and haughty ones (like those of Moab; see Isa. 15-16; Madmenah is a village north of Jerusalem; see Isa. 10:31).

Reviewing Isaiah 24 and 25, one sees a pattern that is very common in Isaiah's writings; Isaiah often delivers a pronouncement of serious warnings mingled with a note of optimism (as in chapter 24) and then follows it with a prophecy of joyful promises, concluding with a somber tone of caution (as in chapter 25).

One also sees in Isaiah's writings the unique way in which he combines his gifts as prophet, seer, and poet. He was a mighty seer, one of those whom Joseph Smith described when he said,

> Search the revelations of God; study the prophecies and rejoice that God grants unto the world Seers and Prophets. They are they who saw the mysteries of godliness; . . . they saw the glory of the Lord when he showed the transfiguration of the earth on the mount; . . . they saw the day of judgment when all men received according to their works, and they saw the heaven and the earth flee away to make room for the city of God, when the righteous receive an inheritance in eternity.

Joseph then added a challenge to those who read the words of Isaiah and the other seers: "Fellow sojourners upon earth, it is your privilege to purify yourselves and come up to the same glory, and see for yourselves and know for yourselves." (TPJS, pp. 12-13.) As we improve our gifts of prophecy, inspiration, and expression, we will come to understand the words of Isaiah, the great prophet, seer, and poet.

A SONG OF JUDAH AND THE DELIVERANCE OF ISRAEL
ISAIAH 26-27

Beginning with chapter 13 and continuing through chapter 27, Isaiah prophesies the destruction of the enemies of God's people and the glorious salvation that awaits the righteous. Isaiah begins his pronouncements to specific nations in chapter 13, which portrays the downfall of the Babylonian kingdom, representing the center of land power, and concludes with chapter 23 on Tyre, representing the center of sea power. Moving from the particular judgments that God gives the various nations of the earth, Isaiah portrays in chapter 24 the whole world under the judgment of God. But God's purpose is not just to condemn the world; Isaiah's single chapter on judgment is followed by three chapters on God's glorious salvation.

Chapter 25 begins with Isaiah's song of praise to the Lord for God's concern for the week and helpless, and then describes the joy awaiting the covenant people after judgment. Moab is singled out as a representative of the proud heathen nations that receive God's harsh judgment.

Chapter 26 is the song of rejoicing and thanksgiving that Judah will sing in the last days when Zion has been ultimately defended and her enemies humiliated. In praising the Lord, Judah expresses her trust in him, for even though she long endured sufferings and waited many centuries to see his judgments, she knows that he will remember his covenants and redeem his people. The chapter concludes with a description of the Lord's vengeance upon the wicked. This theme carries over into chapter 27, which begins with a promise of the Lord's power over Leviathan, the symbol of Satan.

Chapter 27 continues with a song of the vineyard, which celebrates the day of Israel's deliverance. The chapter also promises better days when God's purposes for his people will be fulfilled after they are chastised and return to him. It concludes with a prophecy of the gathering and restoration of Israel in the last days.

249

As chapters 25-27 develop the theme of salvation through the three songs of Isaiah, Judah, and the vineyard, the mood is obviously hopeful and joyful. The last two chapters in this set can be outlined as follows:

I. Song of Judah (26:1-19)
    A. A hymn of thanksgiving and victory (26:1-6)
    B. A prayer of entreaty and faith (26:7-19)
II. The Lord's slaying of Leviathan, Satan (26:20–27:1)
III. Deliverance of Israel (27:2-13)
    A. A song of the Lord's vineyard (27:2-6)
    B. The meaning of Israel's suffering (27:7-11)
    C. A day of harvesting the Lord's people (27:12-13)

At the end of chapter 25, the Moabites had been brought into shameful disgrace. In chapters 26 and 27 (as shown in the outline above) the people of Zion are brought forth to joyful restoration. Some warnings of punishment are found in these chapters, but they are usually found alongside affirmations of peace and blessings.

A Song of Judah (26:1-19)

Isaiah begins his prophecy with the phrase "In that day," placing this section in an eschatological setting. The song in verses 1-6 will be sung "in the land of Judah" during the last days:

26 In that day this song will be sung in the land of Judah:

We have a strong city;
    God makes salvation
    its walls and ramparts.
²Open the gates
    that the righteous nation may enter,
    the nation that keeps faith.
³You will keep in perfect peace
    him whose mind is steadfast,
    because he trusts in you.

⁴Trust in the Lord forever,
    for the Lord, the Lord,
    is the Rock eternal.
⁵He humbles those who dwell on high,
    he lays the lofty city low;
    he levels it to the ground
    and casts it down to the dust.
⁶Feet trample it down—
    the feet of the oppressed,
    the footsteps of the poor. (NIV)

This song contrasts two cities. The first, apparently Jerusalem, is a city of peace and security; her gates can be opened with no fear of attack. The description implies that the people had been previously in distress, either physically or spiritually. The opened gates represent peace in the land. Upon entering the gates, the righteous nation may be entering an actual city—either old or new Jerusalem—or the celestial city of the Lord through the gateway of baptism, forgiveness, and cleansing by the Holy Ghost. (Compare Ps. 24 with 2 Ne. 9:41; 31:17-21.) Thus, Judah's song in the last days could result in either thanks for the literal, physical deliverance of Jerusalem or praise to God through those who join the Lord's church and kingdom upon the earth. The "perfect peace" they enjoy is emphasized in the original Hebrew by the repetition of "peace, peace."

The second city Judah will sing of is a city of wickedness, perhaps representing Babylon (vs. 5-6). This proud city will be brought to the dust while the Lord's city is protected; the feet of those formerly oppressed will trample the wicked oppressors into the dust. Therefore, the chosen people will sing first for their own redemption and then for the Lord's power over their enemies.

Isaiah next turns to a prayer in which the people of God are portrayed as an offering to the Lord. This prayer contains several stages. First, the Lord blesses the righteous (v. 7). Next, the people explain that they wait for the Lord to bring judgments upon the wicked and salvation to the righteous (vs. 8-11). Verses 12-15 appear to describe the Millennium, and verses 16-18 portray the events immediately preceding it. Verse 19 concludes with a beautiful promise of the Resurrection. The entire prayer begins with Isaiah's petition for all Israel:

7The path of the righteous is level;
O upright One, you make the
way of the righteous smooth.
8Yes, LORD, walking in the way of
your laws,
we wait for you;
your name and renown
are the desire of our hearts.
9My soul yearns for you in the
night;
in the morning my spirit
longs for you.
When your judgments come upon
the earth,
the people of the world learn
righteousness.

10Though grace is shown to the
wicked,
they do not learn
righteousness;
even in a land of uprightness they
go on doing evil
and regard not the majesty of
the LORD.
11O LORD, your hand is lifted high,
but they do not see it.
Let them see your zeal for your
people and be put to shame;
let the fire reserved for your
enemies consume them. (NIV)

In contrast to verse 9, verse 10 explains that even though the wicked are taught the truth, they do not learn righteousness. The point to be taken from these statements is that certain people are wicked, not just because they were raised by wicked parents, but because they choose wickedness over righteousness, though the Lord himself is their teacher. The judgments to come upon the wicked are just indeed. Verse 11 carries this idea even further: the wicked are shown miracles, but still do not see. Finally, their end is consumption by the fire set aside for the enemies of God. The whole judgment here described hints at the second coming of Christ, when the Lord will destroy the wicked and bless the righteous.

Verses 12-15 seem to describe the Millennium, since the Lord has already established peace in the land:

> ¹²LORD, you establish peace for us;
> all that we have accomplished
> you have done for us.
> ¹³O LORD, our God, other lords
> besides you have ruled over us,
> but your name alone do we
> honor.
> ¹⁴They are now dead, they live no
> more;
> those departed spirits do not
> rise.
> You punished them and brought
> them to ruin;
> you wiped out all memory of
> them.
> ¹⁵You have enlarged the nation, O
> LORD;
> you have enlarged the
> nation.
> You have gained glory for
> yourself;
> you have extended all the
> borders of the land. (NIV)

Israel has had problems and persecutions, but Isaiah recognizes that she will be remembered by the Lord. Though Israel has been ruled by other Lords (or masters, v. 13), only the one true master will eventually reign as Lord over Israel.

Isaiah next seems to describe the situation of the people of God, especially the Jews, during their long absence from the lands of their inheritance:

> ¹⁶LORD, they came to you in their
> distress;
> when you disciplined them,
> they could barely whisper a
> prayer.
> ¹⁷As a woman with child and about
> to give birth
> writhes and cries out in
> her pain,
> so were we in your presence, O
> LORD.
> ¹⁸We were with child, we writhed in
> pain,
> but we gave birth to wind.
> We have not brought salvation to
> the earth;
> we have not given birth to
> people of the world. (NIV)

Scattered Israel travailed and yet gave birth to wind or nothingness. They, as the covenant people, were supposed to bring the gospel of God to the world, but because they themselves were led astray, they did not fulfill their purpose. Still, even though many perished, the Lord will not forget them. He will call them forth from the dead:

¹⁹But your dead will live;
their bodies will rise.
You who dwell in the dust,
wake up and shout for joy.

Your dew is like the dew of the
morning;
the earth will give birth to her
dead. (NIV)

Scholars are usually very confused over this verse, stumbling over the grammar and wondering at the meaning of the promise.

Grammatically, the verse is difficult because of the inexplicable changes in pronouns in the first part. One scholar, Otto Kaiser, describes the verse as follows: "One has to read this short passage several times in order to become really aware of the irritation caused by the change of possessive pronouns. The attempt to work out who is speaking and to identify the literary category is like solving a puzzle." (*Isaiah 13-39*, p. 215.)

In the Hebrew, the first two phrases are literally, "shall live your dead ones," and "my corpse [that] shall arise." Another scholar, Edward Young, explains them as follows:

In thus speaking the prophet identifies himself with the Lord's purposes. The dead are those who belong to the Lord, but the nation is Isaiah's. He is concerned over its downfall as is the Lord, for he speaks as a prophet of the Lord. To be noted also is the chiastic arrangement of words, an arrangement which lends strength to the description; thus, *there will live* (A) *thy dead ones* (B), *and my corpse* (B) *they will arise* (A).

By means of this additional statement, *my corpse they will arise*, the prophet clearly introduces the doctrine of the resurrection of the body.

Isaiah contrasts this verse and verse 14: the death of the righteous is filled with the hope of the Resurrection, while the death of the wicked results in oblivion.

Isaiah also gives an interesting analogy between the earth's dew and the Resurrection. Scholar George A. Smith beautifully explains the comparison:

The wonder of dew is that it is given from a clear heaven, that it comes to sight with the dawn. If the Oriental looks up when dew is falling he sees nothing to thank for it between him and the stars. If he sees dew in the morning, it is equal liquid and lustre; it seems to distil from the beams of the sun—the sun, which riseth with healing under his wings. The dew is thus doubly 'dew of lights.' But our prophet ascribes the dew of God, that is to raise the dead, neither to stars nor dawn, but, because of its Divine power, to that higher supernal glory which the Hebrew conceived to have existed before the sun, and which they styled, as they styled their God, by the plural of majesty: A

253

dew of lights is Thy dew. As when the dawn comes, the drooping flowers of yesterday are seen erect and lustrous with the dew, every spike a crown of glory, so also shall be the resurrection of the dead. (*The Book of Isaiah*, pp. 468-69.)

In short, verse 19 seems to promise a resurrection both to the individuals and nation of Israel. (Compare verses 15 and 19 with Young's quotation and Joseph Fielding Smith's statement that this verse refers especially to Israel; CR, Apr. 1924, p. 44.) A full understanding of the postmortal spirit world easily explains how people whose bodies are dead can still live on (as postulated in the first phrase of the verse). Also, a knowledge of Christ's resurrection elucidates the fact that when the Lord's body rises, the bodies of the dead will be resurrected (second phrase in the verse). Thus, those whose bodies have laid in the earth will be born again into a new life and will be able to shout for joy (remainder of verse 19). Isaiah's words do complement a more complete understanding of the spirit world and Resurrection, although they may confuse secular scholars who lack revelation concerning these teachings.

The LORD's Slaying of Leviathan, or Satan (26:20–27:1)

Before the resurrection can become a reality, the power of death must be overcome, and before the gates of a heavenly Jerusalem can be opened to a righteous nation (v. 2), the power of sin must be defeated. Isaiah describes the Lord's power over the "author of death" in the next few verses:

[20]Go, my people, enter your rooms and shut the doors behind you;
hide yourselves for a little while until his wrath has passed by.
[21]See, the LORD is coming out of his dwelling
to punish the people of the earth for their sins.
The earth will disclose the blood shed upon her;
she will conceal her slain no longer.

27 In that day,
the LORD will punish with his sword,
his fierce, great and powerful sword,
Leviathan the gliding serpent,
Leviathan the coiling serpent;
he will slay the monster of the sea.
(NIV)

This whole section alludes to the symbols of the passover in its description of the Lord's war with the wicked. For example, in verse 20, the Lord's people are told to flee from the coming disaster, enter their homes, shut their doors, and hide until the Lord's destruction passes over. This means of protection hardly seems adequate if the destruction described here is a military invasion or some large-scale natural catastrophe. It should be remembered, though, that when the Lord killed the firstborn of Egypt by the tenth plague, the only protection the Israelites had was the closed doors of their homes and lamb's blood on the doorposts. In other words, rather than destroying everyone, the Lord will punish only those who merit his judgments, just as at the time of the passover.

Leviathan represents the forces of chaos that originally opposed the creator of this earth. (See Isa. 27, footnote 1c.) The serpent or sea monster (or dragon, KJV) also represents the personification of chaos, Satan himself. (See Rev. 12:9; 20:2.) Leviathan probably includes not only Satan, but all who serve him. Some scholars believe that Isaiah simply borrowed the term from a Canaanite myth, but more likely the Canaanite myths about Leviathan are apostate versions of an earlier record about the earth's creation out of a state of disorder. (Compare Kaiser, *Isaiah 13-19*, p. 221 with Abr. 4:1-2.)

Isaiah knew that the Lord would have at least one major confrontation with Satan or Leviathan and his forces. Since three epithets are given—the gliding serpent, the coiling serpent, the monster of the sea—some scholars believe that the Lord has three enemies to slay. (Young, *The Book of Isaiah* 2:233.) However, it is also likely that the threefold enemy represents three major conflicts the Lord Jesus Christ has to wage with Satan. First, Christ was the advocate of the Father's plan and helped cast Satan out of heaven. Second, the Savior had to overcome temptation, sin, and death through his exemplary life, the Atonement, and the Resurrection. Finally, before the earth can progress from a telestial to a terrestrial or finally a celestial state, Christ and his forces must battle the forces of sin, and Christ will again overpower Satan, who will finally be banished to outer darkness.

The Deliverance of Israel (27:2-13)

After Leviathan has been overcome, a song will be sung "in that day." Isaiah describes the song that will be sung about the Lord's vineyard:

²In that day—

"Sing about a fruitful vineyard:
³ I, the LORD, watch over it;
  I water it continually

I guard it day and night
  so that no one may harm it.
⁴ I am not angry.
If only there were briers and

thorns confronting me!
I would march against them in
battle;
I would set them all on fire.
⁵Or else let them come to me for
refuge;
let them make peace with me,
yes, let them make peace
with me."

⁶In days to come Jacob will take
root,
Israel will bud and blossom
and fill all the world with fruit.
(NIV)

Isaiah then poses a rhetorical question (expecting a negative answer) about the Lord's judgments with Israel; he questions whether God has been as harsh with Israel as with her oppressors. Isaiah continues by elaborating upon the consequences to befall Israel:

⁷Has the LORD struck her
as he struck down those who
struck her?
Has she been killed
as those were killed who killed
her?
⁸By warfare and exile you contend
with her—
with his fierce blast he drives
her out,
as on a day the east wind
blows.
⁹By this, then, will Jacob's guilt be
atoned for,
and this will be the full fruitage
of the removal of his sin:
When he makes all the altar stone
to be like chalk stones crushed
to pieces,

no Asherah poles or incense altars
will be left standing.
¹⁰The fortified city stands desolate,
an abandoned settlement,
forsaken like the desert;
there the calves graze,
there they lie down;
they strip its branches bare.
¹¹When its twigs are dry, they are
broken off
and women come and make
fires with them.
For this is a people without
understanding;
so their Maker has no
compassion on them,
and their Creator shows them
no favor. (NIV)

The east wind (v. 8) is probably the hot sirocco that blows out of the Arabian desert and destroys vegetation. Usually arriving in the early summer months while the plants are still young and tender, the sirocco destroys crops and brings chaos to the seas as it carries sand and debris before it. (See Isa. 14:7; Hosea 13:15; Ezek. 27:26; Jer. 18:17.) It is clear that Isaiah is promising severe treatment for Israel.

The unnamed fortified city that is described as desolate in verse 10 may refer to a specific city, such as old or new Jerusalem, Samaria, or Babylon, but more likely represents the community of the children of

Israel as a whole (see 26:2). But, finally, a new community and a new Jerusalem will be built which will be the home of the gathered remnants of Israel:

¹²In that day the LORD will thresh from the flowing Euphrates to the Wadi of Egypt, and you, O Israelites, will be gathered up one by one. ¹³And in that day a great trumpet will sound. Those who were perishing in Assyria and those who were exiled in Egypt will come and worship the LORD on the holy mountain in Jerusalem. (NIV)

In these two short verses the whole prophecy is put into perspective. Although the children of Israel have strayed from the path of God, "in that day" the Lord will gather them from the entire earth. And although the gathering of Israel in a general sense refers to the gathering of all believers, the gathering here refers to the particular gathering of scattered Israel. The gathering that begins just prior to the second coming of Christ is made complete at the sound of the last trumpet, which ushers in the millennial reign of Christ. At the sounding of the trumpet, all the exiled Israelites will return to the lands of their inheritance, either in old or new Jerusalem, and will there worship the Lord at his holy mountain, the temple.

SCRIPTURAL NOTES AND COMMENTARY

Isaiah 27: A chiastic pattern
The entire twenty-seventh chapter of Isaiah is structured into a neat chiasmus that is more easily recognized in the Hebrew but is also clear in the following English outline:

A.   In that day the Lord will conquer Satan (v. 1)
B.   The house of Israel (vineyard) is sung about (2)
C.   The Lord watches over the people (3)
D.   The Lord consumes his enemies with fire (4)
E.   The strength and friendship of the Lord for his followers (5)
F.   Jacob will grow and prosper (6)
G.   Israel has not suffered as much as her oppressor (7-8)
F'. Jacob will be purged (9)
E'. The strength and power of the Lord against his enemies (9)
D'. Animals consume the branches and women make fires with them (10-11)
C'. The Lord knows the people lack understanding (or obedience; see Job 28:28) (11)
B'. The house of Israel gathered one by one (12)
A'. In that day the righteous will worship the Lord together (13)

TEACHING THE CHILDREN
OF THE LORD
ISAIAH 28

God sincerely desires to provide peace and rest for everyone, especially for the children of Israel. In his wisdom, however, he realizes that his love, care, and protection should not be forced upon anyone. In chapter 28, Isaiah extends an invitation for peaceful rest to God's children (v. 12). He also reminds Israel that God the Father teaches only the truth and instructs the people precept by precept, line upon line, and little by little (vs. 11, 13).

Having previously pronounced woes upon the whole world (chs. 13-23) and predicted the events of the Lord's great and dreadful day (chs. 24-27), Isaiah begins in chapter 28 to condemn the condition of the people of his own time. He issues warnings first to Samaria and then to Jerusalem. His discourse was probably given after Assyria cut down the Syro-Israelite alliance in 732 B.C. and before the Assyrian army destroyed Israel in 722 B.C. The most likely date is 724 B.C., for it was then that King Hoshea of Israel began to resist Shalmaneser V of Assyria. While only the capital, Samaria, and the immediate surrounding territories remained out of Assyrian control, the remaining "free" Israelites rejoiced in their independence and boasted in the invincibility of their defense.

Isaiah therefore addresses the proud Israelites in Samaria as the "haughty crown" of Ephraim and prophesies their impending judgment:

28 Woe to the haughty crown of the drunkards of Ephraim, and to the fading flower of its ornament of beauty, which is on the head of the fertile valley of those overcome with wine! ²Behold, the LORD has a strong and mighty agent; like a tempest of hail and a destroying storm, like a flood of powerful, overwhelming waters, He will cast down to the earth with the [clenched] hand. ³The proud crown of the drunkards of Ephraim shall be trodden under foot; ⁴and the fading flower of its ornament of beauty, which is at the head of the fertile valley, shall be like a first ripe fig before summer; when a man sees it, he eats it as soon as he has put it in his hand. (MLB)

The prophet contrasts Israel's present condition with the time when the Lord will be a "crown of glory" for a just, righteous remnant:

⁵In that day the LORD of hosts shall be a crown of glory and a diadem of beauty to the remnant of His people, ⁶a spirit of justice to him who executes justice, and of valor to those who turn back the battle to the gate. (MLB)

Isaiah makes several other interesting comparisons in these two sets of verses. First he tells proud Israel that when she raises herself as a "crown" and is overcome with wine, she will be humbled by the Lord. However, when she finally recognizes the Lord as her "crown" or ruler, he will give Israel justice and courage so that her warriors can push back any threatening danger to the place (or "gate") from which it came (v. 6).

Isaiah returns to a discussion of the drunken condition of the leaders in his own day in the next two verses:

⁷These also reel with wine and wander about because of strong drink; [both] priest and prophet reel because of strong drink; they are victims of wine; they wander about due to strong drink; they err in vision and stumble in giving judgment; ⁸for all their tables are covered with vomit; there is not a place without filth. (MLB)

The priests and prophets that Isaiah identifies are probably the corrupt and apostate Israelites who have either abused their priestly roles or falsely claimed to be prophets of God. (See Isa. 28, footnotes 7a and 7d.) On the other hand, even true, honorable priests and prophets can be "victims of wine" when their message is misunderstood or rejected because of spiritual "drunkenness" or wickedness among the people. (See 2 Ne. 27:1-5.)

Isaiah portrays the drunkenness of Israel through assonance. In choosing his words, he imitates the staggering and stumbling of the drunkards with a threefold repetition of *shagu-taghu, shagu-taghu, shagu-paqu* (*Shagu* is usually translated as "err" or "reel," *taghu* as "wander" or "stagger away," and *paqu* as "stumble.") The prophet places all these verbs "in the preterite completed action, thus implying that drunkenness was a habit long entrenched." (Young, *The Book of Isaiah* 2:272.)

Since Israel's leaders are unable to receive or understand the Lord's message, Isaiah asks a rhetorical question: "Whom then can the Lord teach?" He then answers his own question:

⁹Whom will He teach knowledge, and who shall be made to understand the message? [Babes just] weaned from the milk, [just] drawn from the breasts? ¹⁰For [it is] pre- cept upon precept, precept upon precept, line upon line, line upon line, here a little, there a little. (MLB)

The "message" or "doctrine" (KJV) that Israel is to understand is one given by divine revelation to a prophet and then through him to the people in a manner commensurate with their spiritual development. (See 2 Ne. 28:30-31; compare Isa. 53:1.)

Such disciplines as reading, speaking, mathematics, and foreign languages are not mastered at first exposure, but require gradual growth and constant study. Similarly, spiritual growth is a gradual learning process that requires constant effort. Spiritual development is gradual both because of its complicated nature and because of its elusiveness in a temporal world, although one of the purposes of mortal existence is to learn spirituality.

Isaiah teaches us in the same way the Lord does. The development of spirituality "precept upon precept," "line upon line," and "here a little, there a little" is also mentioned in modern scripture (D&C 98:11-12; 128:21) and by modern prophets (Brigham Young in JD 7:143; 9:167; 10:350; Joseph F. Smith in JD 18:276). A contemporary apostle, Bruce R. McConkie, suggests how one can learn spiritual truths, especially those taught by Isaiah:

> Read, ponder, and pray—verse by verse, thought by thought, passage by passage, chapter by chapter! As Isaiah himself asks: "whom shall he teach knowledge? and whom shall he make understand doctrine?" His answer: "them that are weaned from the milk, and drawn from the breasts. For precept must be upon precept, precept upon precept; line upon line, line upon line; here a little, and there a little." (*Ensign*, Oct. 1973, p. 83.)

Three descending levels of learning are stressed by Isaiah in the phrases "precept upon precept," "line upon line," and "a little" at a time. The highest level, "precept" is a "principle imposing a particular standard of action" (*American Heritage Dictionary*, 1969, p. 1030) or "an instruction intended as a rule of conduct" (*Webster's Dictionary*, New American Edition, p. 289). Latter-day Saint beliefs expand the meaning to include "eternal principle" or "higher law."

Eternal principles based upon unconditional love form the framework for God's actions with his children. For example, the concept that "life is sacred" is an eternal precept.

The word Isaiah uses to describe the second level of learning, translated as "line upon line," refers to a plumb line, the means of measuring vertical and horizontal relationships. Literally, the word is equivalent to "rule upon rule" (Young, *The Book of Isaiah* 2:276) and can be considered as a course of conduct, thought, or policy (*Webster's Dictionary*, New American Edition, p. 219). Further emendation based upon Latter-day Saint perspective yields "commandment" or "lesser law"; it is God's direction to us on how to fulfill the higher law. A commandment is usually given to us by the Lord through the prophets, although the individual conscience can and should provide guidelines for conduct without direct instruction from a prophet. An example of a "line upon line" or "lesser law" within the framework of the precept "Life is sacred" would be the commandment "Thou shalt not kill."

The third level of learning, "here a little, there a little," is more difficult to identify. As bits of information are learned about any new subject, a gradual, more complete understanding develops. Repetition is a tool used by effective teachers; it reinforces the learning just a "little" until the concept or term is finally mastered. Similarly, the Lord expects us to learn his truths a little at a time as we grow spiritually until we come to an "understanding in all things" and even a knowledge of "the mysteries of God." (2 Tim. 2:7; 1 Ne. 10:19; compare Matt. 13:11 and TG "Mysteries of Godliness.") The "little" means by which we learn and apply God's instructions and commandments are the personal resolutions we make to help us draw nearer to God. These allow us to apply God's directions in a manner best suited to our own spiritual level.

In Jewish tradition, the personal application of the laws is called the "fence" around the law that protects one from accidentally or inadvertently breaking any commandment. As one applies a commandment in his own life, he establishes for himself how he will interpret the Lord's law and put it into practice. If he is unsure of his capacity to fully obey the law, he may also need to put a fence around the law to protect himself. Considering the examples given earlier of "life is sacred" and "thou shalt not kill," a "little" personalized law or fence that could help someone follow the higher precept and commandment would be "Do not lose your temper."

The relationship between the three levels of learning presented by Isaiah and discussed above can be outlined as follows:

Isaiah's Term	Ludlow's Emendation	LDS Synonym	Definition	Meaning	Example: Law of Life
precept	principle	higher law	framework for God's actions	*Why* God acts as he does	Life is sacred
line	command-ment	lesser law	God's directions to us	*What* God wants us to do	Thou shalt not kill
here a little	fence	personal law	individual application	*How* we live God's laws	Do not lose temper

Before repeating the three levels of learning, Isaiah gives a few rather enigmatic details concerning how the Lord speaks to the people and lists some puzzling reasons why the Lord teaches as he does:

[11]But with stammering lips and in a foreign language, He will speak to this people, [12]to whom He said: This is the rest you shall give to the weary, and this is the refreshing. Yet they would not listen. [13]However, the word of the LORD shall be to them, precept upon precept, precept upon precept, line upon line, line upon line, here a little, there a little; that they may go and stumble backward, be broken, snared, and taken. (MLB)

The "foreign" language in which the Lord speaks (v. 11) is only foreign to those who lack enlightenment by the Holy Ghost. On the other hand, God's message will relieve and refresh those "who have ears to hear." It will undoubtedly free them not only from physical worries but from emotional concerns and spiritual doubts. (See Isa. 33:19; Acts 3:19.) Unfortunately, however, the people generally will not listen to the Lord's word.

Still, the Lord attempts to instruct such people "precept upon precept," "line upon line," and a "little" at a time. But instead of leading them to a full knowledge of truth, this knowledge only condemns the insensitive people who refuse to heed God's counsel. (See Isa. 28, footnote 13b.) For them, his word is a snare in which they trap themselves, and because they refuse to receive more direction from the Lord, they lose the spiritual insights they have already received. (See 2 Ne. 28:30; compare D&C 50:24; 93:20.)

Sensing that the people in Jerusalem were falling into the same pitfalls as the northern Israelites, Isaiah turned his attention to the Judeans and repeated some warnings found in Isaiah 7 and 8, structuring his words in chiastic parallelism:

[14]Therefore, hear the *word* of the LORD, you scoffers, who rule this people in Jerusalem! [15]Because you have boasted, "We have made a *covenant* with *death*, and with *Sheol* we have an *agreement*; when the *overwhelming scourge* passes through, it shall not reach us, for we have made falsehood our *refuge*, and in fraud we *hid* ourselves"; [16]therefore, thus says the LORD God, "Behold, I lay in Zion a foundation *Stone*, a tested Stone, a precious *cornerstone*, a sure foundation; he who believes will not be hurried. [17]I will make justice the *measuring line* and righteousness the *plummet*; hail will sweep away your *refuge* of lies, and waters will flood your *hiding* place. [18]Your *covenant* with *death* will be annulled, and your *agreement* with *Sheol* will be cancelled. When the *overwhelming scourge* passes through, you shall be trampled down by it. [19]As often as it passes through, it will carry you away, for morning by morning will it pass, by day and by night. It will be unmixed terror to understand the *message*." (MLB, italics added)

A. Word

B. Covenant with death, agreement with hell, overwhelming scourge.

C. Refuge and hiding

D. Stone and cornerstone

D'. Measuring line and plummet

C'. Refuge and hiding

B'. Covenant with death, agreement with hell, overwhelming scourge

A'. Message

The people of Jerusalem obviously believed that they could avoid the "overwhelming scourge" (vs. 15, 18) that would sweep over the earth. Although the scourge is not specifically identified in Isaiah, it is described in modern scripture as something that will come forth in "waves," that is, from time to time. (D&C 5:19.) Also, it is listed parallel with a "desolating sickness" in Doctrine and Covenants 45:31, and Doctrine and Covenants 97:23 promises that the Lord's scourge shall pass over by night and by day," not ceasing until the

Lord comes. (Compare Isa. 28:19, especially the KJV.) Joseph Smith adds that this act of divine punishment will come before the servants of God have carried this warning voice to all the Gentiles, and that it will be initiated by the destroying angel, who will "waste the inhabitants of the earth, and as the prophet [Isaiah] hath said, 'It shall be a vexation to hear the report.'" (TPJS, p. 87; compare Isa. 28:19.)

Some people, however, will not be "hurried," confounded, or overly concerned (v. 16; compare 1 Pet. 2:6; Rom. 9:33). These people will believe in a "stone" or "cornerstone" that the Lord himself will provide. Although the stone undoubtedly refers to the Messiah (see Isa. 28 chapter heading and Isa. 8:14-15), this interpretation is only one of five advocated by most scholars: Jerusalem, Hezekiah, a remnant of Israel, confidence or faith in the Lord, and Jesus Christ. (Young, *The Book of Isaiah* 2:301-3.) The Bible contains other allusions to a stone rejected by the people. (See Ps. 118:22; Matt. 21:42.) The Book of Mormon also explains how the rejected stone (Christ) will become the "head of the corner" or cornerstone. (Jacob 4:14-18; compare Eph. 2:20.)

Continuing his warnings to the people of Judah, Isaiah compares their dilemma to that of people sleeping on short beds with small blankets:

> 20For the bed is too short to stretch one's self upon it and the covering too narrow for him to wrap himself in it. 21For the LORD shall arise as on Mount Perazim and be indignant as in the valley of Gibeon, to do His work, His strange work, and to perform His task, His unusual task. 22Now therefore, scoff no more, lest your bondage be aggravated; for of a determined annihilation upon the whole earth have I heard from the LORD God of hosts. (MLB)

Besides illustrating God's punitive judgment in verse 21, Isaiah also compares two earlier events in Israelite history. Around 1000 B.C. David's army smote the Philistines at Mount Perazim, so named because it was the place where "the Lord hath *broken forth* upon mine enemies before me as the *breach* of waters." (2 Sam. 5:20; italics added.) At Perazim, or "breaking forth," the Lord assisted David in his victory. In chapter 28, Isaiah also refers to waters and scourges that will "break forth" and overflow the wicked (vs. 2, 15, 17-18). This comparison is carried through to verse 21, in which the Lord's work in the last days is described as his "breaking forth" at Perazim. The second point of comparison occurred even earlier in Israelite history when the Lord assisted Joshua in his victory over the Canaanites in the valley of Gibeon. (Josh. 10:8-14.) Here the Lord destroyed more of the enemy through hailstones than were killed by all the Israelites in battle. If the Lord works again as he did in Gibeon, a violent hailstorm may be one means of punishing the wicked in the last days (compare v. 17 with D&C 29:16; 43:25; 109:30).

The purpose of the Lord's punishment is to do his "strange work" in separating the righteous from the wicked as his Spirit eventually pours out upon all flesh. (D&C 101:95; 95:4.) Apparently, then, the scourges and judgments that will come upon the earth will not only punish many of the wicked, but also separate those who will follow the Lord from those who will be unworthy to remain upon the earth in a millennial condition. Thus, the punishments that come upon all the earth will *result from* the general wickedness of the people and *result in* the preparing of the earth's inhabitants for the Lord's second coming.

The means by which the Lord prepares the earth for his coming might be questioned by some people, but Isaiah answers their concerns in the last verses of chapter 28. Verses 23-29 deal with a "parable of the farmer" written in poetry. They can be divided into two segments: Isaiah first describes the method of sowing grain and then carefully distinguishes the methods used for threshing different crops:

²³Give ear and hear my voice; listen and hear my words. Does he who plows for sowing plow continually? ²⁴Does, he [continually] tear up and harrow his land? ²⁵Does he not rather, after leveling the surface, scatter dill and sow cummin, put the wheat in rows, barley in the appointed places and rye around its border? ²⁶His God correctly instructs and teaches him. ²⁷Dill is not threshed with a threshing sledge, neither does a cart wheel roll over cummin; but dill is beaten out with a rod and cummin with a flail. ²⁸Grain is crushed; he will not continually thresh it, but he rolls the wheels of his cart over it, since with his horses he cannot crush it. ²⁹Even this comes from the LORD of hosts, who is wonderful in counsel and excellent in wisdom. (MLB)

In verse 23, Isaiah uses four imperatives—give, hear, listen, and hear—to alert his listeners to this important parable, which portrays why the Lord acts as he does in preparing the children for their final state. (Compare Isa. 1:2 where some of the same imperatives are used.) Verse 26, inserted between the "sowing" and "threshing" sections, provides an important key for understanding the parable. Verse 29 provides a concluding key and witness about the Lord's wisdom in all his doings.

Sowing requires preparation. The farmer must plow, harrow, and level the ground before planting, and yet must not spend too much time in these tasks or he will not have enough growing season left for the seeds to mature (vs. 23-25). After preparing the soil, he is ready to plant each seed in its proper place. The comparatively abundant seed of the dill (or black cummin, "fitches" in the KJV) and the common cummin are used as a spice and on the crust of breads. This seed is scattered carelessly in the fields while the more valuable grain seeds, wheat and barley, are sown more carefully in the middle of the fields. Finally, the coarse, inferior rye seed is sown on the edges of the fields, which give a much lower yield. The farmer does his work carefully, using different methods for the different crops he grows. (Kaiser, *Isaiah 13-39,* p. 260; IDB 1:843; 2:274.)

The threshing process also requires careful planning and the correct choice of tools and technique. The dill and cummin seeds are so small that a threshing sledge or cart is inappropriate, since the seeds would be crushed or lost. A stick is used to thresh them (v. 27). The larger and coarser grains require a heavy cart pulled by oxen, horses, or donkeys to separate the seeds from the stems and husks. The cart should not roll over the grain too long, however, or the seeds will be crushed to powder. After the threshing, a mill will eventually be used to grind the grain into flour (v. 28).

In both the sowing and the threshing, the farmer acts with wisdom taught to man by God (vs. 26, 29). God instructs man correctly through divine counsel and wisdom, which is "wonderful" and "excellent." In other words, the Lord provides the proper instruction so that the farmer may have a successful harvest.

The key to understanding this parable is the analogy between the farmer's technique and God's plan for "harvesting" souls. God's activities are similarly purposeful, orderly, and discriminating. He cannot spend all of his time preparing the earth for his children; finally he must send them there. As people grow, they must have "threshing" or testing, which differs from person to person. The threshing process suggests three elements about God's plan: (1) sifting the grain from the chaff suggests the separation of the righteous from the wicked; (2) the harshness of the threshing process suggests suffering as a necessary condition for the emergence of good, worthy souls (good, clean grain); and (3) the care of the divine Harvester in dealing with the more precious kinds of grain suggests the particular attention the Lord would give to the house of Israel and those foreordained to special callings. (IB 5:321.) God will not punish (thresh) his children beyond what they deserve. Isaiah emphasizes God's perfect wisdom in sowing and threshing his children until he achieves a full, complete harvest. (See Rom. 11:33; Jacob 4:8-10.)

RECORDS FROM THE DUST
ISAIAH 29

Many visions from the Lord have been recorded as scripture for all to read and study. Yet these scriptures often seem to be sealed, in that although we can read the words, we often don't understand them. Chapter 29 of Isaiah is one such vision; it often confuses readers with its promises of records and sealed books that will come out of the ground and perplex both the wise and the ignorant. Fortunately, later prophets have received additional revelation about this prophecy, and their insights help to illuminate the words of Isaiah.

Most Latter-Day Saints associate the promises of Isaiah 29 with the Book of Mormon, its coming forth out of Hill Cumorah and its translation, mainly because Nephi quotes most of the chapter in the Book of Mormon; he likens Isaiah's prophecy to his own plates and to the Book of Mormon. Furthermore, as Nephi quotes Isaiah 29:3-24 in 2 Nephi 26-27, he adds additional information about Isaiah's prophecy. Whereas Isaiah 29 consists of twenty-four verses, Nephi's record contains fifty-four verses. (See Ne. 26:15–27:35.)

There are several possible explanations as to why the material of Isaiah 29 is so much longer in 2 Nephi. Among them are the following:

1. Isaiah's record was originally much larger, but editing and the loss of plain and precious parts shortened it to its present twenty-four verses. However, Nephi had access to a more complete version of Isaiah from the Brass Plates of Laban, and thus his Isaiah material is longer.
2. Isaiah's record was originally the same basic size and format that it is now, but Nephi expounded upon the material and added many verses of his own commentary.

Since we lack the Brass Plates of Laban, we do not know how the record that we have compares to the record of Lehi's time, which probably closely resembled the original prophecy recorded by Isaiah.

Also, since Nephi does not separate Isaiah's words from his own additions in his record, it is difficult to distinguish Isaiah's text from Nephi's commentary. The inspired efforts of a third prophet, who has also dealt with this same Isaiah material, can help to shed further light on the meaning of Isaiah's vision.

This third prophet is Joseph Smith. In March 1833, four years after he completed his translation of the Book of Mormon, Joseph was translating the Isaiah chapters of the Old Testament as he prepared his Inspired Version of the Bible (now known as the Joseph Smith Translation). Although he had access to both the King James Version and his earlier Book of Mormon translation of Isaiah 29, his new translation differs somewhat from both. The content of the Joseph Smith Translation is very similar to that of the Book of Mormon version, although some of the Book of Mormon additions are lacking from the Joseph Smith Translation, and there are some differences in punctuation. The inclusion of some phrases from the King James Version that are not in the Book of Mormon account indicates that Joseph did not simply "lift" the Isaiah material from the Book of Mormon and place it in his inspired translation.

The Joseph Smith Translation stands partway between the King James and Book of Mormon translations in size, phraseology, and content, and seems to present the most correct text available of the original Isaiah 29. Its size, thirty-two verses, is larger than the King James Version's twenty-four verses, but smaller than the Book of Mormon's fifty-four verses. Although all of its phrases are found in either the King James Version or the Book of Mormon, many are found in one but not in both, which makes it a distinct document.

In order to appreciate the relationship between the three versions of Isaiah 29, careful study and comparison is necessary. To facilitate such a study, all three versions are compared in the following chart:

Isaiah	JST	2 Nephi
29:1-2	29:1-2	26:15-16
29:3-4	29:3-4	26:17
29:5	29:5	26:18

Note: Shaded areas indicate major additions to the text.

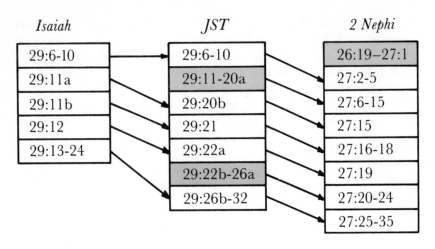

	Isaiah	JST	2 Nephi
	29:6-10	29:6-10	26:19–27:1
	29:11a	29:11-20a	27:2-5
	29:11b	29:20b	27:6-15
	29:12	29:21	27:15
	29:13-24	29:22a	27:16-18
		29:22b-26a	27:19
		29:26b-32	27:20-24
			27:25-35

King James Version of Isaiah 29

As the major points of the King James Version are described, you can read from your own Bible (especially the new Latter-day Saint edition if you have one).

Isaiah 29 contains five major themes or discourses:

1. Warnings to Ariel (Zion) (vs. 1-4).
2. Judgments upon the wicked (5-10).
3. Words of a sealed book (11-12).
4. A marvelous work to come forth (13-21).
5. Blessings to Israel (22-24).

These five sections are in a rough chiastic pattern: Isaiah directs the Lord's words to the house of Israel at the beginning and end of the prophecy (1, 5); the next two sections (2, 4) tell the wicked how the Lord's work will be accomplished; and the center, pivot section (3) contains the ambiguous promise of a sealed vision or book.

Warnings to Ariel (vs. 1-4). Isaiah's prophecy is initially directed to Ariel, a term that appears only five times in Isaiah's writings, all five in this chapter. The name *Ariel* is applied to Jerusalem and is usually interpreted to mean "lion of God," although a more exact translation would be "altar of God." The Hebrew word *ariel* actually means "altar hearth," the highest tier of the altar of Solomon's Temple on which the wood and sacrifices were consumed by fire. (See Isa. 29, footnote 1b.) Since the term is used to describe Jerusalem in her distressed condition (the word "Zion" replaces this term in 2 Ne.

27:3), it implies that Judah will need to be humbled and that God's fire of judgment will refine her. This implication can be illustrated in verse 3 by substituting the term "sacrificial hearth" for the second use of the word *Ariel* so that the verse reads: "I [the Lord] will distress Ariel, and there will be moaning and sorrow and she will be like a sacrificial hearth."

Verses 3 and 4 further describe how the Lord will come against Zion until the Israelites are brought low in humility, so that their fallen nation speaks "out of the ground" and "out of the dust." Israel speaking to the world from "low out of the dust" can be understood figuratively to mean that she will deliver her message from the depths of her humiliation. The remnants of Israel in their scattered condition have often been taught by the Lord how disobedience to divine law brings punishments, while obedience brings blessings. Because of this, the sad experiences of the Jews and the Lamanites serve as a witness to the world of what will happen to everyone who turns away from God.

Israel's words speaking "out of the ground" can also be interpreted more literally to mean that her written prophetic records would be preserved in the earth for a time before coming forth as a witness to the world. Of course, the Book of Mormon fulfills such a role. (See 2 Ne. 26:15-17; compare LeGrand Richards, CR, Apr. 1963, p. 118.) Also, the Dead Sea Scrolls provide an ancient record of the importance given to Old Testament texts; they reveal a Jewish religious community that maintained many teachings, ordinances, and practices that were not followed by orthodox Jews and Catholics. Yet other records that are now hidden in the earth will undoubtedly come forth from Israel to bear witness of the Lord's gospel. (See 2 Ne. 29:7-14.) They also will be speaking forth "out of the dust."

Judgments upon the wicked (vs. 5-10). In this portion, Isaiah tells about the multitude of the Lord's judgments that will fall upon the strangers (or Gentiles) and the terrible ones (the wicked) who fight against Ariel. They, with their expectations of power over Zion, will be as frustrated and empty as a sleeper who dreams of food and drink but awakens still hungry and thirsty. These people, who are full of iniquity, will be lost and confused because they have rejected their rulers, the seers, and the Lord's prophets. They will live in a time of spiritual darkness and apostasy because of their wickedness. (See Orson Pratt, JD 15:185-86.)

Words of a sealed book (vs. 11-12). Latter-day Saints understand how the words of a sealed book (the Book of Mormon) at one time went to a learned man who claimed he was unable to translate from such a record. The well-known visit of Martin Harris to the scholar Charles Anthon is recorded in modern scripture. (JS-H 1:63-65.)

Verse 12 describes the words of a sealed book going to an unlearned man. Joseph Smith was such a man; in spite of his lack of higher education, he eventually was able to read and translate the sacred records. (See JS-H 1:59; D&C 1:29; compare Orson Pratt, JD 15:186.)

A marvelous work to come forth (vs. 13-21). The verses of this section build upon the themes of the previous two sections. Warnings similar to those in section 2 (vs. 5-10) are given, along with promises of marvelous events similar to those promised in section 3 (vs. 11-12).

Verses 13 and 14 are familiar to Latter-day Saints because the Lord quoted to Joseph Smith the pronouncement in verse 13 about apostasy and the precepts of men (JS-H 2:19); the promised "marvelous work and wonder" of verse 14 has become a motto of the Restoration (especially because of Elder LeGrand Richard's book of that title; see especially pp. 34-35 of *A Marvelous Work and a Wonder*).

Verses 15 and 16 warn the earth's inhabitants against ignoring the omniscience of the Creator, and verses 17-19 promise his physical and spiritual blessings to those who seek and accept the gospel truths. The next two verses (20-21) echo some of the phrases found earlier in the chapter and are directed back to the wicked and to the "terrible one" (perhaps Lucifer), who will be brought to naught (compare v. 5). Scorners, those who deliberately lie about others ("make a man an offender for a word"), and those who seek to persecute the righteous will be cut off from the Lord. In summary, this section combines positive and negative promises as the Lord speaks through Isaiah to both the righteous and the wicked of the last days.

Blessings to Israel (vs. 22-24). Isaiah's prophecy concludes on a warm, positive note, promising an intimate relationship between the Lord and his children. Jacob will no longer be ashamed of his descendants nor will his face pale any longer as it did earlier when he observed their offenses. Many of the children of Israel who have rejected the Spirit and murmured against God will eventually come to understand the truth and receive forgiveness (v. 24). One need not wait until the world at large or the whole house of Israel receives these blessings, however, because each one of us can obtain these promises for himself just as soon as he turns to the Lord and sanctifies him (v. 23).

Joseph Smith Translation Additions to Isaiah 29

The additional insights and verses provided by Joseph Smith's translation are centered in five areas of Isaiah 29:

1. Additions to verses 9-10.
2. Ten verses added between verses 10 and 11.
3. Additions to verses 11-12.
4. Four verses added between verses 12 and 13.
5. Minor additions to other verses (especially vs. 16, 17, and 20).

Additions to verses 9-10. The audience being addressed in these verses remains ambiguous in the King James Version. The Joseph Smith Translation and Book of Mormon amplify the verses, indicating that they are directed only to those who "do iniquity." The Joseph Smith Translation also makes it clear that the Lord has not retracted his prophets, but that the people themselves have closed their eyes to his word. The apostasy that results comes not because of the Lord's prophets but because of the people's iniquities.

Ten verses added between verses 10 and 11. The ten verses added after verse 10 in the Joseph Smith Translation describe the contents of the sealed book. The words of the sealed book reveal God's work with this earth from its foundation to its final state. The sealed book will eventually be delivered to a man (Joseph Smith) who will show it to a few select witnesses. Through the words of the book and through the special witnesses, God will establish his word (the gospel) upon the earth.

The existence of sealed books is mentioned in the writings of other apocalyptic and eschatological prophets, including Daniel (Dan. 12:1, 4), John the Revelator (Rev. 5:1-14; D&C 77:6-7; D&C 93:18), the brother of Jared (Ether 3:21–4:19), Ether (Ether 1:1-5; 13:1-14; 15:33-34; see also Mosiah 8:9; 21:27; 28:11-20; Alma 37:21-31), and Nephi (1 Ne. 14:19-28). A common trademark of these sealed books is that they are sealed because of the wickedness of the people, as is described in Joseph Smith's translation of Isaiah 29. Because of the sacred material contained in these inspired books, "the things which are sealed shall not be delivered in the day of the wickedness and abominations of the people." (JST Isa. 29:13.) The sealed books will not come forth while the people are unworthy to receive them. Also, since the transmission of sacred records is often faulty, as texts are easily corrupted when left in secular hands, Nephi tells us that some inspired books and records "are sealed up to come forth in their purity." (1 Ne. 14:26.) The Lord

273

is waiting until he can restore these pure records to a people faithful and ready to receive them. Apparently, the additions to Isaiah 29 found in the Book of Mormon and the Joseph Smith Translation concerning sealed visions refer to the sealed portion of the Book of Mormon plates, which contains the visions of the brother of Jared and the "revelation from God, from the beginning of the world to the ending thereof," which will be translated in the "due time of the Lord." (2 Ne. 27:7, 10; see also Ether 3:21-28; D&C 17:6.)

Isaiah 29 is an interesting example of a prophecy within a prophecy. Isaiah 29 contains a prophecy about a sealed book. This prophecy is amplified in the Joseph Smith Translation, which contains a more pristine text of the prophecy and makes it clear that the sealed book will itself contain an apocalyptic and eschatological sealed portion. (See JST Isa. 29:14-15.) The Book of Mormon thus fulfills the conditions of the sealed book prophecy of Isaiah 29, although it may not be the only hidden, sealed record to do so.

With the rebirth of the spirit of prophecy in the spring of 1820, Latter-day Saints have been able to witness through the Book of Mormon a literal fulfillment of the prophecy contained in Isaiah 29. Furthermore, the Book of Mormon mentions a time when the Lord will see fit to reveal even more sacred instruction to those who accept the scriptures and teachings of the living prophets. (See 2 Ne. 27-29.) Indeed, this sequence of revelation seems to fulfill the prophetic statement in the chapter directly preceding Isaiah 29 (as quoted by Nephi in the chapter following his text of Isa. 29): "I will give unto the children of men line upon line, precept upon precept, here a little and there a little; and blessed are those who hearken unto my precepts, and lend an ear unto my counsel, for they shall learn wisdom; for unto him that receiveth will I give more; and from them that shall say, We have enough, from them shall be taken away even that which they have." (2 Ne. 28:30; compare Isa. 28:10.)

It becomes clear, then, that to scholars who reject prophecy (especially in our time), and with it the divine calling of the Prophet Joseph Smith and the authenticity of the Book of Mormon, the prophecy in Isaiah 29 is itself a "sealed book." In the words of Jacob, "The things of the wise and the prudent shall be hid from them forever" and they will not understand or enjoy "that happiness which is prepared for the saints." (2 Ne. 9:43.) The saints, meanwhile, will not only understand the words of Isaiah 29, but they will also be better prepared to receive the full sealed vision that is promised in this prophecy.

The ten verses in the Joseph Smith Translation that describe the sealed book and its vision are missing from the King James Version, but they are briefly summarized in the first part of verse 11 of that text: "And the vision of all is become unto you as the words of a book that is sealed." The next verses describe how some words of the sealed book will be taken to and received by different types of men.

Additions to verses 11-12. The basic contents of the King James Version of verses 11 and 12 are found in the Joseph Smith Translation (vs. 21-22), along with additional phrases that give more details about how words from the unsealed portions of the sealed book will be taken to both the learned and unlearned. As indicated earlier, the learned man is Charles Anthon and the unlearned man is Joseph Smith. The Joseph Smith Translation gives a few additional details about how the words of the book are received by these men.

Four verses added between verses 12 and 13. The next few verses of the Joseph Smith Translation (end of v. 22 to the first part of v. 26), which are not in the King James Version, contain direct instructions to the unlearned man who will receive the sealed book. He is charged to follow the Lord's directions with the sealed book and then to hide it up unto the Lord. Later, God will again bring forth the book, revealing all its contents to his faithful children.

Minor additions to other verses. The rest of the Joseph Smith Translation (vs. 26-32) has the same basic content as the King James Version (vs. 13-24), although the versification differs slightly.

Book of Mormon Additions to Isaiah 29

The Book of Mormon version of Isaiah 29, found in 2 Nephi 26-27, contains all the additions of the Joseph Smith Translation, although it lacks some phrases found in the King James Version. The 2 Nephi account also contains some verses that are not duplicated in the King James Version or Joseph Smith Translation. These verses appear to be Nephi's commentary on how the first part of Isaiah 29 (vs. 1-5) could be applied to his own people. This commentary consists of about eighteen verses, primarily in 2 Nephi 26:15-33.

Summary

What is the message of Isaiah 29 and how has it been fulfilled, especially as it discusses special hidden records? Some possible interpretations might be:

1. Isaiah was talking only to the Jews of Jerusalem about the Bible

and other records that would come forth in the last days in Judea. Such records could be the Dead Sea Scrolls or some other sacred, sealed works yet to come forth.

2. Isaiah was not addressing the Israelites in the Old World. Rather, he was talking to the branch of Joseph that would cross the sea, and Nephi recognized this, recording Isaiah 29 in 2 Nephi 26-27. Nephi's record differs from the King James Version, but it is hard to say whether Nephi was expounding upon the text by giving his additional insights or whether he was reading from a more correct text.

3. Isaiah was addressing the Jews about their records, but Nephi applied this material to his own record, the Book of Mormon. In other words, he likened the Isaiah description of Old World records to his New World witness, amplifying the description and giving more specific details about the Book of Mormon in his inspired interpretation.

4. Isaiah was talking to us in the last days about any number of records, sacred writings, and scriptures that would miraculously appear, confounding the "wise" and confusing the "unlearned." The sealed words of any of these hidden books would be delivered to prophets who, although they were "unlearned" in that they were not language scholars, would be able to translate these sacred records through the power and inspiration of God.

A review of the above possibilities coupled with a comparison of the three versions of Isaiah 29 strongly supports the common Latter-day Saint viewpoint that Isaiah's vision of the sealed book applies to the Book of Mormon. However, students of the scripture should not ignore the possibility that Isaiah's prophecy may yet be fulfilled by still other hidden records. In any case, Isaiah prophesies that the Lord will perform marvelous works in the last days, even revealing new scriptures.

Isaiah also tells us that faithful readers of the scriptures that are now available will come to understand the words of the new sealed books as they are revealed (v. 24). There appear to be at least three types of people who receive and attempt to understand the words from a religious record:

1. The unlearned, who cannot read the language or words of the book, and who make no attempt to understand them.

2. The learned, who can read the book but cannot understand it because it is "sealed" to those without the spirit of inspiration.

3. Those who can read and understand the words of the book. Even though they may lack a knowledge of the language of the work, God's revelation can help them translate it, and after they know the words, his Spirit will help them understand the meaning of the "sealed" book.

Hopefully we will become this third type of person who is able to understand not only the words of Isaiah, but also the other scriptures that the Lord has given us and the "sealed" books that he will yet reveal to us according to our faithfulness.

FALSE TRUST IN EGYPT
ISAIAH 30-31

Historical Setting

King Hezekiah's rule over Judah was constantly threatened by the Assyrian Empire. After the Assyrians, under Sargon II, had conquered the northern kingdom, Israel, and deported her leading citizens to the far northeastern Assyrian territories, Judah remained one of the few independent countries in the western Fertile Crescent. Sargon II attempted to encircle Judah with his armies as he had established dominion over the coastal states Phoenicia and Philistia and had forced Egypt to open trade relations with her.

King Hezekiah knew that any offensive action by Judah would immediately bring the Assyrian army upon his country. However, after Sargon II's death in 705 B.C., a number of political conditions seemed to favor a move away from Assyrian domination:

1. With Sargon's death on the Hittite battlefield of Tabal (now part of southern Turkey), internal dissension and questions over the power of his successor encouraged numerous vassal states to revolt against Assyrian power and taxation.
2. Egypt seemed to be growing more powerful as the Nubian pharaoh, Shabako, developed the twenty-fifth (or Ethiopian) dynasty into a strong threat against Assyrian expansion in the west.
3. In the east, Babylon showed signs of resurgent power, as a new leader, Merodach-baladan, received support from neighboring states.
4. Closer to Judah, other states were exerting increased independence.

Taking advantage of these circumstances, Judah joined a coalition of states in Philistia and Phoenicia in their rebellion against Assyria. She also entered into a treaty with Egypt, with the Egyptians promising military aid against any Assyrian attack.

278

Isaiah strongly opposed this whole series of events as they developed from 705 to 701 B.C. and renounced Judah's reliance upon Egyptian power. He desired the people to seek counsel and strength from the Lord instead of turning to Egypt, the land of their former bondage and affliction. Isaiah prophesied that, because the Judeans rejected the prophets and relied upon the power of men, Judah would fall along with her guardian, Egypt, and her inhabitants would be scattered until the Lord's judgments upon them were complete.

Primary Message

The alliance with Egypt was condemned not only as a political mistake, but because it represented a national frame of mind that feared men more than God. Previous to Hezekiah's reign, King Ahaz had made a similar pact with Assyria during the 730s B.C., which had ultimately produced the current threat. (Isa. 7-8.) Now, to avoid the threatened Assyrian bondage, Ahaz's son, Hezekiah, sought deliverance through Egyptian help. In both cases, the Judean kings attempted to avoid danger by turning to other political powers rather than relying upon God. Isaiah exhorted Judah to break out of this vicious circle through trust in the Lord. He told the children of Israel to be quiet and confident with God—in other words, to build their faith. Also, they should turn away from their sins (30:1) and return to the Lord (30:15) so that he might bless them in righteousness (30:18-25, 29).

Four major topics are presented by Isaiah in these two chapters:

1. Dependence upon Egypt will result in disappointment.
2. As the children of Israel reject God's word they will be punished, and as they return to the Lord they will be blessed.
3. Blessings will be given righteous Israel in a latter day.
4. Judgments will come upon the wicked world.

These four themes are intertwined throughout the chapters and are developed as follows:

Dependence upon Egypt results in disappointment. Isaiah uses five examples to illustrate this theme. The most detailed example begins chapter 30:

30 Alas for you, rebellious children, says the LORD, who formulate a policy that is not Mine; who make an alliance contrary to My Spirit, thus adding sin to sin; ²who set out to go down to Egypt without asking for My counsel, to take refuge in the protection of Pharaoh and to seek shelter in the shadow of Egypt. ³The protection of Egypt shall end in shame, and the protection you seek in the shadow of Egypt shall be to your reproach. ⁴His princes are in Zoan, and his messengers have arrived in Hanes. ⁵All shall come to shame because of a people who will bring them no benefit, that are of no help or profit, but bring shame and disgrace. (MLB)

In these verses, Isaiah warns the Israelites that they are following their own whims and not God's Spirit as they send a delegation down to Egypt. Instead of strength they will receive shame from their alliance.

The second illustration (vs. 6-7) is less detailed but more subtle and powerful, for it equates their present situation with the earlier Israelite bondage in Egypt and their tribulations in the desert south of their promised land:

⁶A message concerning the beasts of the southland. Through a land of trouble and anguish, the home of the lioness and the lion, the viper and the flying serpent, they carry their riches on the backs of donkeys and their prized treasures on the humps of their camels to a people who cannot help them. ⁷As for Egypt, its assistance is empty and vain; therefore I have called her "Rahab who sits still." (MLB)

Generations earlier, the Israelites had been led by the Lord through these same dangerous deserts as they escaped with gifts and treasures from Egypt. (Ex. 11:2; 12:35-36). Now, against God's command (Deut. 17:16), they were returning to Egypt, laden with treasure to repurchase their bondage in the form of a military alliance. Furthermore, the lions, poisonous snakes, and fiery serpents that had tormented Moses' party also threatened Hezekiah's Judean delegation as it traveled the inland desert route instead of the major highway to avoid Assyrian spies along the sea. By suggesting with these similarities that history would repeat itself, Isaiah warned that instead of support from Egypt, the Israelites would receive renewed suffering.

The third example (vs. 12-14) presents an analogy concerning Israel and her Egyptian alliance, which is doomed to destruction:

¹²Therefore thus says the Holy One of Israel: Because you have spurned this word and have trusted in oppression and crookedness and have relied on them, ¹³therefore this iniquity shall be to you as a broken section ready to fall, bulging out from a high wall, whose crash shall come suddenly at any instant. ¹⁴It shall be broken like the smashing of a potter's vessel smashed intentionally in pieces, so that among the fragments there shall not be found a piece with which to carry a coal of fire from the hearth or to dip water from a cistern. (MLB)

Turning away from Yahweh to Egypt is a "breach" in the ancient covenant represented by a break in the protecting wall around Israel. The crack, initiated by the military alliance, will someday suddenly break the wall in pieces, leaving Israel exposed to external dangers. Likewise, Israel's faithless attitudes toward God weaken her until she becomes fragile like a pottery jug that is shattered and then spills its contents. Instead of being protected by the strength guaranteed through Egyptian might, Judah will find herself defenseless. Instead of being walled in and protected by the Lord, she will be broken and scattered.

In the fourth illustration (vs. 16-17), Isaiah ironically promises the people both horses and swift speed, but not for the purposes they originally desired:

16But you answered, "No! we will flee upon horses"; therefore you shall flee—"upon the swift shall we flee"; therefore your pursuers shall be swift. 17At the threat of one, a thousand of you and at the threat of five [all of you] shall flee, till you will be left like a flagstaff on the peak of a mountain, and as a beacon on a hill. (MLB)

The horses would not be needed to fight against the Assyrian forces but to flee from them; the swift speed would come not to the Israelites, but to those who pursued them. Indeed, a few of the enemy would send multitudes of Israelites running, and Judah would find herself fleeing until she would be scattered across the hills of the earth.

The last example begins chapter 31 (vs. 1-3) and summarizes the four earlier illustrations:

31 Alas for those who go down to Egypt for help, who rely on horses and trust in chariots because they are many and in horsemen because they are powerful; but they do not look to the Holy One of Israel; they do not seek the LORD. 2Yet He who brings calamity is also wise, He shall not retract His words; He will arise against the house of evildoers and against the helpers of those who work iniquity. 3The Egyptians are men and not God; their horses are flesh and not spirit. For, when the Lord stretches out His hand, he who helps falls and he who is helped stumbles; they shall all perish together. (MLB)

The horses, men, or power of Egypt will not be able to help Judah when the hand of the Lord is raised against her. Indeed, both Egypt and Judah will fall together. Judah's lack of trust in the Lord and her attempt to go her own way with Egypt will result in great tragedy for both nations.

These five examples demonstrate Isaiah's awareness of the political situation. But he was more than a political observer—he was an inspired prophet who knew the future consequences of political actions. Hezekiah and the Jewish leaders may have thought their actions would lead to political independence, but the Lord and Isaiah knew otherwise—political subservience and the scattering of the Jews would be the result.

Israel's rejection or reception of God's word. As a sign of his prophetic foreknowledge and a seal upon his warning to Judah, Isaiah was commanded to record his message as a witness to the people (30:8). He also chastised the people for their unwillingness to hear God's word (v. 9). In fact, their rejection of the Lord was so advanced that they wanted the prophets to cease their warning and leave the people alone (vs. 10-11):

> [8]Go now, write it in their presence on a tablet, and inscribe it in a book, that it may be for the time to come [as a witness] for ever and ever: [9]that they are a rebellious people, lying children who will not listen to the LORD's instruction, [10]who say to the seers, "See not," and to the prophets, "Do not prophesy to us right things! Speak smooth things to us; predict delusions! [11]Forsake the way, swerve from the path, and cease holding up before us the Holy One of Israel." (MLB)

Here, Isaiah does more than just rebuke the people because of their attitudes and their reliance upon their own counsels. He shows them the true solution to their problems both as a people and as individuals. Recognizing that national problems will be solved only after individual spiritual weaknesses are overcome, he gives a few suggestions as to how the children of Israel can reestablish their relationship with God.

The first and most powerful solution is suggested in 30:15:

> [15]For thus says the Lord God, the Holy One of Israel: In conversion and rest you shall be saved; in quietness and confidence shall be your strength. Yet you would not. (MLB)

In his own way, using vocabulary common to the Hebrew Old Testament period, Isaiah challenges the people to develop the first two principles of the gospel—faith and repentance. As their relationship with the Lord becomes calm and confident, this development will be a measurement of the faith and trust they have developed in God, and, as they return to the Lord and rest in the companionship of his Spirit, their repentance and spiritual development will guarantee them the guidance and power of God.

A further suggestion and promise is given in verse 18. If the people exalt the Lord and wait for him (trust in him) they will be blessed:

¹⁸Nevertheless the Lord longs to be gracious to you! Therefore He shall rise up to bestow mercy on you: for the LORD is a God of justice. Blessed are they who wait for him. (MLB)

Specific promises of leadership and guidance are given in verses 20 and 21. The Israelites are told to listen to the voice of the Lord (v. 21) and to cast aside their idols and pagan images (v. 22):

²⁰Though the LORD gave you the bread of adversity and the water of affliction, yet your Teacher will not hide Himself any more, for with your eyes you will see your Teacher. ²¹When you turn, whether to the right or to the left, your ears will hear a voice behind you, saying, "This is the way; walk in it!" ²²Then you will consider unclean your graven images overlaid with silver and your molten images plated with gold; you will cast them aside as an unclean thing, and you will say to them, "Be gone!" (MLB)

The final command to Judah is issued in 31:6-7. Isaiah repeats the exhortations to turn to the Lord and to cast aside all idols:

⁶Return, O children of Israel, to Him from whom you have so gravely revolted! ⁷For in that day each man will cast away with con- tempt his idols of silver and his idols of gold, which your sinful hands have made for you. (MLB)

The common theme of these four sets of verses is an admonition to turn to the Lord and to heed his word. A sign of adherence to this admonition would be demonstrated by the people rejecting their idols and listening to the Lord's prophets and his Spirit.

Future blessings to Israel. When Israel follows the Lord, she is ready to receive his blessings. Isaiah illustrates this relationship between action and reward in 30:18-26:

	Chiastic Outline
¹⁸Nevertheless *the LORD longs to be gracious* to you! Therefore He shall rise up to bestow mercy on you; for the LORD is a God of justice. Bless-ed are they who wait for Him. ¹⁹*O people in Zion,* who dwell in Jerusa-lem, you shall weep no more. *He shall surely be gracious to you* at the	A. Lord's blessings
	B. Blessed people

sound of your cry! He will answer you when He hears you. ²⁰Though *the LORD gave you* the *bread* of adversity and the *water* of affliction, yet *your Teacher will not hide Himself* any more, for with your eyes you will see your Teacher. ²¹When you turn, whether to the right or to the left, *your ears will hear a voice* behind you, saying, "This is the way; walk in it!" ²²Then you will consider unclean your graven images overlaid with silver and *your molten images* plated with gold; *you will cast them aside* as an unclean thing, and you will say to them, "Be gone!"

²³*He shall then give you rain* for the seed with which you sow the soil, *and food*, the produce of the soil which is rich and plenteous; your cattle in that day will graze in large pastures. ²⁴*The oxen and the donkeys* that till the ground *will feed* on salted provender winnowed with sieve and fan. ²⁵On every lofty *mountain* and on every high *hill* there *will flow* brooks, copious streams in the day of the great slaughter when the towers fall. ²⁶Then the light of the moon will be as the light of seven days, at the time *the LORD binds* up the fractures of His people *and heals* the severe wounds of his blows. (MLB, italics added to show chiasmus)

C. Bread and water

D. Your true teacher

E. Spiritual guidance

D'. False idols

C'. Rain and food

B'. Blessed animals

A'. Lord's blessings

While reading verse 20 of this optimistic poem, one might ask why Isaiah would use the terms *bread* and *water* to represent types of suffering, "adversity" and "affliction." Bread and water usually symbolize sustenance, both physical and spiritual. Sometimes, however, bread and water are the only food and drink provided poor people or captives. Thus, one possible meaning of these phrases is that the people will become slaves or prisoners. (For an earlier example of these terms in this context, see 1 Kgs. 22:27.)

Another possible meaning comes from a more literal translation of *bread = adversity* and *water = affliction*. In the Hebrew scriptures, these terms are in apposition to each other so that they read "bread which is adversity" and "water which is affliction." By combining these phrases with the rest of verse 20, the following more literal translation develops:

And the Lord gives you bread
  (which is adversity)
  and water (which is affliction)
And your teacher will not hide
himself anymore
And your eyes shall see your
  teacher.

If the teacher in this verse is the "teacher of all teachers," or the Messiah, Jesus Christ, then this verse may be a promise to ancient Israel of the eventual presence and atonement of Christ using the symbolism of the bread and water of the sacrament. Thus, the bread-adversity and water-affliction could easily represent his suffering for sin and the subsequent resurrection. Also, without this type of bread and water, there would be a spiritual famine, such as the one described by Isaiah's contemporary, Amos. (Amos 8:11.)

We who partake of the bread and water of the sacrament should not only remember the adversity and affliction that Christ suffered, but also realize that as we take his name upon ourselves, we too become subject to adversity and affliction from Satan and his followers. Thus, for the children of Israel or us today to receive "bread of adversity" and "water of affliction" from the Lord should not always be considered a punishment. It often gives us an opportunity to remember the Atonement and to share the burdens of furthering God's work against those forces that oppose it.

In addition to the prophesied blessings in the chiasmus above, Isaiah tells in 31:4-5 that the Lord promises he will come to Zion to defend and deliver it:

⁴For thus the LORD said to me: As the lion or the young lion growls over his prey and, though a full band of shepherds be called out against him, is neither terrified at their shouting nor daunted at their noise, so the LORD of hosts will come down to fight upon Mount Zion and upon His hill. ⁵Like hovering birds, [so] will the LORD of hosts protect Jerusalem, protect and deliver it; [by] passing over, He will preserve it. (MLB)

The lion probably represented one of two symbols for Israelites of Isaiah's time. On one hand, the lion is the ancient symbol of Assyria. Therefore, if the Lord is like a lion, fearless against the shepherds of

285

the land, Isaiah must be saying that the local inhabitants will be powerless against Assyrian might. Thus, the Lord will allow the lion (Assyria) to make war *against* the mount of Zion.[1]

On the other hand, the lion was also the symbol of the tribe of Judah, and if the lion in this verse represents Judah, then Isaiah is saying that Judah will have power over those who come *against* her. This interpretation seems more likely, especially in light of Isaiah's ideas in verse 5. There he compares the Lord of Hosts to birds and explains that the Lord will protect Jerusalem as the birds defend their nests. In short, the Lord will help the lion (Judah) to defend her property (Jerusalem) from conquest.

Historically, although the lion of Assyria did come against Judah with great power and arrogance as a tool of chastisement in the Lord's hand, (Isa. 10:5-6, 24-25), the Lord defended Jerusalem and ensured that the lion of Judah was able to retain its independence. (Isa. 36-37.)

God's judgment upon the wicked. Isaiah combines powerful vocabulary with the poetic structure of a double climactic parallelism in 30:27-33 as he prophesies concerning the Lord's punishments upon the wicked:

27Behold, the Name of the LORD is coming from afar, in burning anger, amid thick rising smoke; His lips are filled with fury; His tongue is like consuming fire. 28His breath as an overflowing torrent shall reach the neck, to sift the nations with the sieve of destruction [and to place] on the jaws of the people a bridle that will mislead them. 29But you shall have a song as in the night consecrated for feasting; and you shall [have] gladness of heart as when men march with flutes to come to the mountain of the LORD, the Rock of Israel. 30For the LORD will cause His powerful voice to be heard and will show His arm descending with furious anger, [with] a flame of devouring fire, a cloudburst, a tempest, and hailstones. 31The Assyrians will be terror-stricken at the voice of the LORD when he smites with the rod; 32but every stroke of the rod of chastisement which the LORD lays upon them shall be accompanied by the timbrel and harp, when, in battles, He assails them with a brandishing arm. 33For Topheth has already been prepared; yes, for the king it has been made ready, made deep and wide piled high with fire and logs in abundance. The breath of the LORD, like a stream of brimstone, is setting it on fire. (MLB)

---

[1]The Hebrew preposition *al* could be translated "for" (KJV), "against" (JPS), or even "upon" (RSV).

These parallel messages can be outlined as follows:

First Message	Second Message
A. The Lord's anger, indignation, and devouring fire (v. 27)	A'. The Lord's anger, indignation, and devouring fire (v. 30)
B. The Lord's breath will control the vain nations (28)	B'. The Lord's voice will beat down Assyria (31)
C. The people will sing songs of gladness as they come to the Lord (29)	C'. Instruments of music follow the Lord's path (32)
	D. A place of judgment and fire near Jerusalem has been prepared by the Lord for the wicked (33; climax of this parallelism)

This idea is repeated in 31:8-9, where Assyria's fall is predicted and a place of fire at Jerusalem is promised:

8The Assyrian shall fall by the sword of no man; no human's sword shall devour him. He shall flee from the sword, and his young men shall be put to bond service. 9His rock will pass away in terror and his princes will desert the standard in panic, says the LORD, whose fire is in Zion and His furnace in Jerusalem. (MLB)

Although on one level these chapters are a warning to Judah to avoid any alliance with Egypt, they also contain Isaiah's deep pleading with Israel to hear the word of the Lord and to have faith and trust in his word. The Israelites are promised that if they repent and return to God, they will receive marvelous blessings; if they continue in their present path, they will be numbered among the wicked, who will suffer divine punishment.

The same message should be understood by God's children who live now on the earth. Neither treaties among nations nor the powers of men will bring peace and security; they eventually bring only frustration and disappointment. If we hear and follow God's counsel, we can find rest and peace as we receive his blessings. Otherwise, we will join the wicked in their sufferings.

SCRIPTURAL NOTES AND COMMENTARY

Isaiah 30:4: "Zoan" and "Hanes"

When Isaiah states that the Judean messengers were at "Zoan" and at "Hanes," he is referring to Egyptian places. He referred to Zoan earlier in 19:11, 13. (See also Ps. 78:12, 43.) It was a northern Eygptian city, the regional center of the delta, and was located near the border of the Sinai toward Palestine. It was also known as Tanis.

Hanes is mentioned nowhere else in scripture and is thought to be either a city known as Anusis in middle Egypt or the name of the pharaoh's palace in Zoan. If Hanes is a city in southern Egypt, then the idea of having messengers "in Zoan and in Hanes" could mean "from one end of the kingdom to the other." If Hanes comes from the Egyptian word meaning "mansion of the king," then the messengers "in Zoan and in Hanes" would mean "in the city and in the palace." In either case, the idea is conveyed that a large, official delegation of Egyptians was going to meet with the Judeans in order to effect the treaty between the two countries.

Isaiah 30:17: "Beacon upon a mountain" or "ensign upon a hill"

In the context of verse 17, the fact that the people are to be left as a beacon or ensign means that, instead of being a numerous people in the land with many cities and towers, they will be scattered and left alone as small, lonely remnants upon the hilltops.

The symbolism of a beacon or ensign also implies that Israel will serve as a signal bearer or rallying point for those who might desire to unite with her. The fact that the children of Israel remain as a beacon or ensign (sources of light and truth) means that they still have the potential to attract others toward their prophesied destiny. Note in 31:9 that the "ensign" (the gospel) will eventually bring fear unto Assyria (or the world).

Isaiah 30:26: Light of the moon and the sun increased sevenfold

The great increase of light promised in these verses could be either a literal magnification of light from the moon and the sun (as is stressed in the apocalyptic works *Jubilees* 1:29; 19:25 and *First* or *Ethiopic Enoch* 91:16) or the great light of Christ's glory when he returns to the earth. (Compare Rev. 21:23 and Isa. 24:23 with D&C 133:49.) Other symbolic meanings of light during and after the Millennium can be found in this verse, since the moon and the sun represent terrestrial and celestial glories. The seventh or sevenfold light could

represent the seventh gospel dispensation (or a "sabbath" dispensation) or the seventh thousand-year period (millennium) of the earth's
history. A sevenfold increase of the Lord's Spirit or of missionary work
and the light of the gospel might also be implied. Numerous other
interpretations might also apply. Whatever the case, great blessings
will come to the people during this period of great light, when they
will be healed from their physical and spiritual wounds.

DAYS OF GATHERING, RESTORATION, AND JUDGMENT
ISAIAH 32-33

One characteristic of Isaiah's writings is that a pronouncement of judgment is often followed by a promise of a blessed, ideal life. Therefore, having outlined the conditions of wickedness and false trust in chapters 30-31 by warning the people of punishment for their sins, Isaiah naturally proceeds in chapters 32-33 to portray the condition of men and society under the influence of the Spirit of God. He states that although the wicked condition of the people currently warrants punishments, great blessings will follow as their behavior improves. He also describes the ever-increasing polarity between good and evil, contrasting the burning of the wicked with the quiet peace of the righteous.

32 Behold, a king will reign in righteousness,
and princes will rule in justice.
²Each will be like a hiding place
from the wind,
a covert from the tempest,
like streams of water in a dry
place,
like the shade of a great rock in a
weary land.

³Then the eyes of those who see will
not be closed,
and the ears of those who hear
will hearken.
⁴The mind of the rash will have
good judgment,
and the tongue of the
stammerers will speak readily
and distinctly. (RSV)

Chapter 32 begins with the promise of a righteous king and just leaders for Israel. This king could be either the Messiah or a righteous man who rules over Israel under the Lord's direction. Likewise, the princes mentioned could be either religious ministers or political administrators. Whatever the case, Isaiah promises that these leaders will protect the people (v. 2) and that all in Israel will be blessed with an understanding of what they see and hear, a spirit of discernment, and an improved ability to communicate (vs. 3-4). With such enlightenment, the chosen people will be able to recognize a person for what he actually is and not for what he appears to be:

⁵The fool will no more be called noble,
nor the knave said to be honorable.
⁶For the fool speaks folly,
and his mind plots iniquity:
to practice ungodliness,
to utter error concerning the LORD,
to leave the craving of the hungry unsatisfied,
and to deprive the thirsty of drink.

⁷The knaveries of the knave are evil;
he devises wicked devices
to ruin the poor with lying words,
even when the plea of the needy is right.
⁸But he who is noble devises noble things,
and by noble things he stands.
(RSV)

In these verses, Isaiah distinguishes four types of people whose identities are sometimes confused by the world. In the several Bible translations, a variety of English terms are used to describe these four categories. Using the Revised Standard Version of verse 5 above as a starting point and comparing it with ten other major English translations, these four types of people can be identified as follows:

1. Fool (usually translated as fool; also as villain, ungodly, unbeliever, or scoundrel).
2. Noble (almost always translated as noble; also hero, honorable, or liberal [KJV]).
3. Knave (churl [KJV], scoundrel, villain, rogue, cheater, or crafty).
4. Honorable (generous, bountiful [KJV], princely, honest, respected, liberal, or gentleman).[1]

In verses 6-8 Isaiah portrays some characteristics of the first three types of people by using alliteration and verb repetition. For example, each verse begins with assonance: *naval-nevalah* (6), *caylai-kaylaiw* (7), *nadeev-nedeevot* (8). Some verbs of action (such as "speaking," "devising") are repeated and are used in both negative and positive contexts. Isaiah especially denounces the wickedness of the two negative personalities (the fool and the knave), for they oppress the hungry and thirsty, the poor and the needy. On the other hand, he commends the

---

[1]Compare also Isa. 32, footnotes 5a, b, and c.

one positive personality (the noble) because he thinks and does good deeds. As Isaiah commends the noble (v. 8), one must assume that the same characteristics of generosity and concern would apply to the fourth person (the honorable one, who is not described in detail). Thus, Isaiah recommends that in order to discern the true character of a person, one should measure the charity he has for those in need. (Compare Isaiah's ideas on charity with 1 Cor. 13., Morm. 7, and TG "Charity.")

In the rest of what is now chapter 32, Isaiah contrasts the destruction soon to come upon the unsuspecting Israelites with the peaceful conditions of a later period. Note the parallel ideas of verses 9-14 in comparison to verses 15-20. To make plain the instances of comparison and contrast, similar words or ideas have been underlined in each verse:

⁹*Rise* up, you women who are   a, b
     at ease, hear *my voice*;
you complacent daughters, give
     ear to my speech.
¹⁰In a little more than a year
     you will shudder, you
     complacent women;
for the vintage will fail,
     the *fruit* harvest will not
     come.   c
¹¹*Tremble*, you women who are   d
     at ease,
     shudder, you complacent
     ones;
strip, and make yourselves
     bare,
and gird sackcloth upon
     your loins.
¹²*Beat* upon your breasts for the   e
     pleasant fields,
for the fruitful vine,
¹³for the soil of my people
     growing up in thorns and
     briers;
yea, for all the joyous houses
     in the joyful *city*.   f
¹⁴For the palace will be
     forsaken,

     the populous city deserted;
the hill and the watchtower
     will become dens for ever,
a *joy* of wild *asses*,   g, h
     a pasture of flocks;
¹⁵until *the Spirit* is poured   b', a'
     upon us from on *high*
and the wilderness becomes
     a fruitful field,
and the fruitful field is
     deemed a forest.
¹⁶Then justice will dwell in the
     wilderness,
     and righteousness abide in   c'
     the *fruitful* field.
¹⁷And the effect of righteousness   d'
     will be *peace*,
and the result of righteous-
     ness, quietness and trust
     for ever.
¹⁸My people will abide in a
     peaceful habitation,
     in secure dwellings, and   e'
     in *quiet* resting places
¹⁹And the forest will utterly
     go down,
     and the *city* will be utterly   f'
     laid low

²⁰*Happy* are you who sow beside   g'   the *ass* range free. (RSV,   h'
    all waters,   italics added)
    who let feet of the ox and

The major idea of these two contrasting conditions is found in verses 9 and 15: although Israel deserves the severe pronouncement of doom at that time, she will receive the full blessings of God's Spirit in the latter days. Some blessings are already being enjoyed by some Jews who have returned to their homeland and have turned desolated hills and valleys into the productive country described in verses 15-20.

The Jews have recently been gathering to their homeland of Israel from over one hundred nations of the earth. These Jews, who automatically and immediately are accepted as Israeli citizens under the "law of the return," have returned from many countries, such as New Zealand, Lithuania, Argentina, India, Canada, and South Africa. Most of them, however, have come to Israel from middle eastern or eastern European countries. For example, shortly after Israel became independent in 1948, over 120,000 Jews immigrated from Rumania; 100,000 from Russia, Poland, and Iraq; and 30,000 from Czechoslovakia, Hungary, Bulgaria, Turkey, Syria, and Iran. (Gilbert, *Jewish History Atlas*, pp. 97-99.)

As Isaiah, Jeremiah, and others prophesied, these Jews have returned from "the north" and from the countries to which they had been driven. They now dwell in their own land in the state of Israel. However, most of the Jews now living in Israel do *not* identify the Lord, Jehovah, as the cause of their gathering. When asked why and by what means they have returned, most Israelis maintain that their country came into existence through political, military, social, and monetary means, not through any divine guidance. For them, the "holocaust complex," a desire for freedom, or better trained armies have maintained their independence. This appears to be a contradiction of those prophecies to be discussed later in a special topic, "The Return of the Jews in the Last Days." These scriptures promise that righteous Israelites will return to their land in the last days and identify their Lord as the force behind their return. It seems that presently irreligious Jews, trusting in their own power, have returned to their promised land and established a strong modern state.

The reader who approaches chapter 33 for the first time without any experience in reading the Psalms and the other eschatological portions of the prophetic books will undoubtedly struggle to comprehend much more than the main outline of its content:

He will understand that it speaks of a powerful enemy who has risen up against Jerusalem, and of the ultimate destruction of that enemy, to be followed by the glorification of Jerusalem. But he will nevertheless be confused by the changing aspects and speakers, and will be irritated by the partial obscurity which is found in some of the statements. But even an experienced reader, well acquainted with the Old Testament, will find constant difficulties, and will wonder whether he has understood correctly what he has read, whether the received text is reliable and whether individual themes have been accurately interpreted. (Kaiser, *Isaiah 14-39*, p. 339.)

Moving from a theme of general destruction and restoration in chapter 32, Isaiah becomes more symbolic as he prophesies in chapter 33 about the sources of destruction and deliverance. This chapter follows a pattern of chiasmus or introverted parallelism:

Introduction (v. 1)

A. Prayer to the Lord (2-6)
B. Power of the destroyer (7-9)
C. Results upon the wicked (10-12)
D. The Lord will reveal his works (13)
C'. Rewards of the righteous (14-16)
B'. The enemy is gone (17-19)
A'. The Lord's many blessings (20-24)

The first verse of this prophecy contains a pronouncement of woe against an enemy of God's people:

33 Woe to you, destroyer,
who yourself have not
been destroyed;
you treacherous one,
with whom none has dealt
treacherously!

When you have ceased to destroy,
you will be destroyed;
and when you have made an end
of dealing treacherously,
you will be dealt with
treacherously. (RSV)

The person Isaiah refers to in this warning is unnamed, but is most often identified as Sennacherib, the king of Assyria who attacked Jerusalem in 701 B.C. Whoever he is, his power will undoubtedly end through destruction as severe as that which he heaped upon others. As seen in Isaiah 16:4 and 21:2, Isaiah uses similar terms to describe the leader of the nations in the last days who will rage over the earth, destroy the nations surrounding Israel, and finally storm against Zion. (Compare Hab. 2:5-8.) This awesome leader, perhaps Gog from the land of Magog (Ezek. 38), would easily generate the destruction that Isaiah prophesied in chapter 32.

Prayer to the Lord

In contrast to the sharp warning of the introduction, the next few verses record Isaiah's fervent prayer and the Lord's promise for his people:

²O LORD, be gracious to us; we wait for thee.
Be our arm every morning, our salvation in the time of trouble.
³At the thunderous noise peoples flee,
at the lifting up of thyself nations are scattered;
⁴and spoil is gathered as the caterpillar gathers;
as locusts leap, men leap upon it.

⁵The LORD is exalted, for he dwells on high;
he will fill Zion with justice and righteousness;
⁶and he will be the stability of your times,
abundance of salvation, wisdom, and knowledge;
the fear of the Lord is his treasure. (RSV)

Isaiah first expresses trust in the Lord and his salvation. He then describes chaotic times during which the people will flee and scatter as the Lord is lifted up (v. 3). The lifting up of the Lord could refer to Christ's role as a bearer of light or an ensign of power, or it might be a prophetic reference to his being lifted up on the cross, after which the Jews were scattered by the Romans in A.D. 70. Verse 4 is even more difficult to understand, since the major terms are not easily identifiable. A literal translation of this verse is:

And [as] is gathered your spoil
gathers the caterpillar
Like leaping [running] locusts
do they leap [run] upon it

Or, if this prophecy refers to the last days, it might read as follows:

And the spoil [or reward of the Lord, that is, the House of Israel] shall be gathered [by his servants and missionaries] as the caterpillar gathers; and as locusts run to and fro shall they [the missionaries] run about [or attach themselves] upon it [the house of Israel].

The restoration will continue as the Lord's presence fills the high places throughout Zion, and stability and enlightenment fill the land (vs. 5-6). First a "stability of . . . times" is promised. During Isaiah's ministry, the milieu or "times" underwent many drastic revolutions and changes: war, chaos, and confusion characterized this period. Isaiah promises, however, that the Lord will eventually provide Israel a period of peace, a "stability of . . . times."

The "abundance of salvation" or deliverance prophesied by Isaiah could be either political or spiritual: the Israelites could be saved from war and physical destruction or from sin and spiritual desolation. In either case, the salvation that Isaiah promises refers to gifts bestowed from without.

Isaiah further promises some gifts found within an individual—wisdom and knowledge. The wisdom and knowledge Isaiah refers to encompasses more than the intellectual and educational processes we usually associate with these terms. Many kinds of "wisdom" literature, which stressed a spiritual devotion along with factual understanding, was already a part of Israelite heritage by Isaiah's time. This type of literature can best be elucidated through a selection of verses from each of the three major wisdom books of the Old Testament:

The fear of the Lord is the
  beginning of knowledge:
but fools despise wisdom and
  instruction. (Prov. 1:7.)

Be not wise in thine own eyes:
  fear the Lord,
and depart from evil.
(Prov. 3:7.)

Behold, the fear of the Lord,
  that is wisdom;
and to depart from evil
  is understanding. (Job 28:28.)

The fear of the Lord is the
  beginning of wisdom:
a good understanding have all they
  that do his commandments.
(Ps. 111:10.)

In all these verses, "fear of the Lord" means an acknowledgment of his preeminence. This is the same term and meaning used in Isaiah 11:2, where the prophet describes a righteous leader of the last days as having "the spirit of wisdom and understanding," "the spirit of knowledge and understanding," and "the spirit of knowledge and of the fear of the Lord."

Thus, the final and most important gift promised by Isaiah in verse 6 is "the fear of the Lord." Using climactic parallelism, Isaiah moves from the broad universal gifts of God to more specific ones. Finally, he promises the most important gift a wise child of God could request—fear of the Lord. This gift goes beyond a sense of awe and the beginnings of faith to include entire devotion to God. Indeed, this gift is God's special treasure. On the one hand, he shares it with us as he encourages us to respect his glory, develop faith, and strengthen our testimony of him, his Son, and his gospel. On the other hand, we can share this gift with him as we serve him well and bring honor and glory to his name. As we fear the Lord, we honor him and set an example for others so that they can improve their relationship with our Heavenly Father.

Power of the Destroyer

In verse 7 of Isaiah 33, the narrative moves from a future of well-being back to the conflicts and struggles with the enemy of Israel. Isaiah describes the disastrous results of this destroyer:

7Behold, the valiant ones cry
   without;
   the envoys of peace weep
   bitterly.
8The highways lie waste,
   the wayfaring man ceases,
Covenants are broken,
   witnesses are despised,
there is no regard for man.
9The land mourns and languishes;
   Lebanon is confounded and
   withers away;
Sharon is like a desert;
   and Bashan and Carmel shake
   off their leaves. (RSV)

Results upon the Wicked

The Lord finally responds to Isaiah's prayer and counters the powers of wickedness as he speaks to the destroyer and his followers:

10"Now I will arise," says the
   LORD,
"now I will lift myself up;
   now I will be exalted.
11You conceive chaff, you bring
   forth stubble;
your breath is a fire that will
   consume you.
12And the peoples will be as if
   burned to lime,
like thorns cut down, that are
   burned in the fire." (RSV)

The Lord Will Reveal His Works

God then foretells the time that the whole world will know of his works and glory:

13Hear, you who are far off, what
   I have done
and you who are near,
   acknowledge my might.
   (RSV)

This important promise in verse 13 becomes the pivot point of this chapter and a key theme for the following verses in which the Lord (or Isaiah) comforts those in Zion who fear their weaknesses and wonder how they can abide the presence of the Lord in all his glory.

Rewards of the Righteous

In contrast to the burnings of the wicked (vs. 10-12), Isaiah describes the "burnings" or glory of the righteous and the Lord's blessings for such people:

14The sinners in Zion are afraid;
trembling has seized the
    godless:
"Who among us can dwell with
    the devouring fire?
Who among us can dwell with
    everlasting burnings?"
15He who walks righteously and
    speaks uprightly,
who despises the gain of
    oppressions,
who shakes his hands, lest they
    hold a bribe,
who stops his ears from hearing
    of bloodshed
and shuts his eyes from
    looking upon evil,
16he will dwell on the heights;
his place of defense will be the
    fortresses of rocks:
his bread will be given him, his
    water will be sure. (RSV)

The beautiful composite parallelism of verse 15 equates different body parts with certain spiritual qualities in order to describe the type of person who can dwell in God's celestial glory. The following chart highlights these comparisons:

Part of body	Action	Spiritual quality
feet	walking	righteousness
mouth	speaking	morality
head?	wagging "no"	integrity
hands	shaking	honesty
ears	closing	justice
eyes	shutting	virtue

The promise of verse 16 is also noteworthy in the context of the historical setting of this message. Although Israel relied upon physical means for shelter, food, and water, the Lord's guarantee for protection and necessities of life come only to those whose righteousness warrants such blessings. This counsel is applicable today in relationship to our food storage. We ought not to rely upon a rifle or shotgun to protect these supplies, but should be willing to share them with those in need and have faith that the Lord will protect and nourish us.

Another prophet of the Lord has given some commentary on verses 14-16 of Isaiah 33. In general conference of October 1973, Elder Bruce R. McConkie said:

> Now if I may, I shall take these words of Isaiah, spoken by the power of the Holy Ghost in the first instance, and give some indication as to how they apply to us and our circumstances.
>
> First, 'He that walketh righteously, and speaketh uprightly.' That is, building on the atoning sacrifice of the Lord Jesus Christ, we must keep the commandments. We must speak the truth and work the works of righteousness. We shall be judged by our thoughts, our words and our deeds.
>
> Second, 'he that despiseth the gain of oppressions.' That is, we must act with equity and justice toward our fellowmen. It is the Lord himself who said that he, at the day of his coming, will be a swift witness against those that oppress the hireling in his wages.
>
> Third, ' . . . he that shaketh his hands from holding of bribes.' That is, we must reject every effort to buy influence, and instead deal fairly and impartially with our fellowmen. God is no respecter of persons. He esteemeth all flesh alike; and those only who keep his commandments find special favor with him. Salvation is free; it cannot be purchased with money; and those only are saved who abide the law upon which its receipt is predicated. Bribery is of the world.
>
> Fourth, he ' . . . that stoppeth his ears from hearing of blood, shutteth his eyes from seeing evil.' That is, we must not center our attention on evil and wickedness. We must cease to find fault and look for good in government and in the world. We must take an affirmative, wholesome approach to all things. . . .
>
> We have the promise that if we seek him with full purpose of heart, keeping his commandments and walking uprightly before him, we shall indeed see his face and eventually be inheritors with him of eternal life in his Father's kingdom.

President Harold B. Lee then said of Elder McConkie's remarks:

> We have heard from Elder Bruce R. McConkie of the Council of the Twelve, who has given us *the key* by which we can continue to spiritualize ourselves. May we follow his counsel. (Bruce R. McConkie and Harold B. Lee, CR, Oct. 1973, pp. 55-56; italics added.)

The Enemy Is Gone

Isaiah prophesies further to the children of Israel in verses 17-19 of chapter 33. He tells them of their future king or Messiah and of how their enemy will be vanquished:

17Your eyes will see the king in his
    beauty;
  they will behold a land that
    stretches afar.
18Your mind will muse on the
    terror:

"Where is he who counted,
  where is he who weighed the
    tribute?
Where is he who counted the
    towers?"
19You will see no more the insolent

people,
the people of an obscure speech
which you cannot
comprehend,

stammering in a tongue which
you cannot understand.
(RSV)

The Lord's Many Blessings

Isaiah concludes the messages by recording a variety of blessings that will come upon Zion in the last days:

20Look upon Zion, the city of our
appointed feasts!
Your eyes will see Jerusalem,
a quiet habitation, an
immovable tent,
whose stakes will never be
plucked up,
nor will any of its cords be
broken.
21But there the LORD in majesty
will be for us
a place of broad rivers and
streams,
where no galley with oars can go,
nor stately ship can pass.
22For the LORD is our judge, the

LORD is our ruler,
the LORD is our king; he will
save us.[2]
23Your tackle hangs loose;
it cannot hold the mast firm in
its place,
or keep the sail spread out.
Then prey and spoil in
abundance will be divided;
even the lame will take the
prey.
24And no inhabitant will say, "I am
sick;"
the people who dwell there will
be forgiven their
iniquity. (RSV)

The symbols and ideas in these last verses are more easily understood when they are compared with earlier ideas in the chapter (vs. 2-6, Isaiah's prayer to the Lord).

Conclusion

Isaiah's warnings of a coming desolation (ch. 32) and the "destroyer" (ch. 33) not only portray the impending Assyrian invasion but also (and more importantly) foreshadow the chaotic conditions and the power of God over Israel in the last days. Both chapters contain promises of spiritual and material blessings, including a gathering to the promised land of *righteous* Israel. Both the Israelites of Isaiah's time and those who claim to be of the house of Israel today can claim these blessings as they honor the Lord in righteousness.

---

[2]According to the Prophet Joseph Smith, this verse should be the "political motto of Israel." (TPJS, p. 252.)

RETURN OF THE JEWS IN THE LAST DAYS

A seeming contradiction is present in some Book of Mormon prophecies concerning the return of the Jews to the Holy Land. These prophecies state that *after* the Jews begin to believe in Christ, *then* they will be gathered in from their long dispersion. Obviously, the Jews in Israel today do not believe in Jesus Christ as their messiah. Are they, then, fulfilling these prophecies of Isaiah, Jeremiah, Jacob, Nephi, Mormon, and others? Probably not. They are, however, fulfilling some of the lesser-known prophecies of Jeremiah and the Book of Mormon prophets.

The Book of Mormon explains in greater detail the relationship between the gathering of the Jews and their attitude toward Jehovah. Lehi prophesied that after their scattering, the Jews would be gathered in with the house of Israel and come to a knowledge of the true Messiah, their Lord and Redeemer. (1 Ne. 10:14.) This statement is in harmony with the teachings of Jeremiah. Indeed, being contemporaries, Lehi and Jeremiah may have known one another in Jerusalem. Even if not, both had access to the Old Testament scriptures compiled up to that time, Lehi's canon being contained in the Brass Plates of Laban. (1 Ne. 5:13.) In addition, Lehi possessed other records not later incorporated into our Old Testament, such as the prophecies of Zenos. (See 1 Ne. 19:10.)

Zenos prophesied specifically about the Jews, not the whole house of Israel. He stated that the time will come when the Jews would *"no more turn aside their hearts* against the Holy One of Israel." (1 Ne. 19:15; italics added.) Then, the Lord will remember the covenants which he has made with their fathers and *gather* them from the corners of the earth back to their land. (1 Ne. 19:16.) This important Book of Mormon prophecy concerning the Jews has been fulfilled only within the past one hundred years. Before then, even back to the time of Paul the apostle, the Jews did not recognize Jesus Christ as their messiah, the Holy One of Israel. And while Jesus himself lived on the earth, the majority of the Jews did not identify him as their messiah. One reason for this was that they expected the Messiah to come in a display of power and glory. They did not realize that he would not come in such glory until a later period when remnants from all of Israel have returned to their lands of inheritance in righteousness.

During the nineteenth century, however, Jewish attitudes toward Jesus and their messiah changed drastically, especially in America. By 1885, one major segment of American Jewry, the Reform Jews, had gone so far as to accept Jesus as a great teacher and prophet, although

301

not as the Savior or the Messiah, since they no longer believe in a messiah, past or future. Most Jews in the world today are no longer offended simply by the mention of Jesus' name. Christian missionaries (including Latter-day Saints) are now often allowed to present their messages, whereas a century ago they would have been turned out of almost all Jewish homes.

This change in Jewish attitude is also evident within the Jewish communities and synagogues. Not only do they mention the name of Jesus, but they also talk about his life and teachings in their schools and literature. This change fulfills another important Book of Mormon prophecy recorded by Jacob, the son of Lehi. He received a special vision about the Jews that indicated that after they were scattered, smitten, and hated, they would "come to the *knowledge* of their Redeemer" and then be "*gathered* together again to the lands of their inheritance." (2 Ne. 6:11, italics added.)

Many Jews have come to a "knowledge" of Jesus. Some have read the New Testament more often than many Christians and know a great deal about his life and teachings. Though they may not yet accept him as their messiah (this is why they always refer to him as Jesus and not as Christ), they accept him as a great prophet.

A third important Book of Mormon prophecy concerning the return of the Jews was recorded by Jacob as he quoted a message from the Lord:

> When the day cometh that they shall *believe* in me, that I am Christ, then have I covenanted with their fathers they they shall be *restored* in the flesh, upon the earth, unto the lands of their inheritance. (2 Ne. 10:7, italics added; compare Deut. 30:1-10.)

This Book of Mormon prophecy has not yet been fulfilled, even though hundreds of Latter-day Saint missionaries throughout the world are now working specifically within Jewish communities.

It is interesting to note that Zenos and Jacob state that when the Jews (1) "*no more turn aside* their hearts against the Holy One of Israel" or (2) "*come to the knowledge* of their Redeemer," they would be *gathered* in again to the lands of their inheritance. However, Jacob later said (in the scripture quoted above) that when the Jews would finally come to *believe* that Jesus is Christ, then they would be *restored* unto the lands of their inheritance. What we are witnessing in Israel today is a "gathering" and not a "restoration" of the Jews. Physically they are turning, but they will not be fully secure in the land until they are spiritually strong.

As a resurrected being, Jesus Christ delivered similar teachings about the Jews' belief and their gathering when he visited the Book of Mormon people. (3 Ne. 16, 20.) About three hundred years after Christ instructed the Nephites, the prophet Mormon taught these same principles in connection with the effect his record (the Book of Mormon) would eventually have on the Jews. This record is destined to go to the unbelieving of the Jews, that they might be persuaded to believe in Chirst. The Lord's purpose will be fulfilled when the Jews believe in him and he can then restore them and all the house of Israel to the lands of their inheritance. (Morm. 5:14.)

Summary

When one initially reads Isaiah, Jeremiah, or the Book of Mormon prophets and their prophecies concerning the gathering of Israel in the last days, he will probably remember the oft-repeated promise that when Israel accepts the Lord (or recognizes Christ as Messiah) they will be gathered in. This general understanding is basically correct.

A more precise study of the scriptures reveals, however, that certain important details exist concerning the relationship of the Israelites to their Lord and their gathering to their lands. This is particularly true for one branch of the Israelites, the Jews. In short, one of three conditions must precede any gathering of the Jews: (1) they no longer rebuke Christ, (2) they come to a knowledge of Christ, or (3) they begin to believe in Christ as their messiah.

Although any of these conditions could precede a "gathering" of the Jews, the Lord will not fully accept the inhabitants of Israel as his people until they believe on him as their God. When they become righteous and God-fearing, he will "restore" them to the lands of their inheritance and protect them from their enemies. In other words, although the Lord might lead the Jews back to their land under various conditions, he will not recognize them as fully legitimate heirs of the land until they properly worship him.

Understanding this fact helps answer two questions that Latter-day Saints have as they attempt to understand the events of the last days: (1) Why are most Jews who are returning to Israel essentially non-religious Israelites who do not recognize the Lord or his hand in their gathering? and (2) Why will great punishments still come upon the Jews in the "great and dreadful day" of the Lord if they are his chosen people? The truth is that, along with righteous and honorable people, other non-religious, non-believing, and even wicked Jews are today fulfilling some prophecies of the gathering. The Jews who take the credit for themselves and reject the Lord and his laws will be punished in the future. Knowing this, Latter-day Saints can better understand how the many different prophecies concerning the return of the Jews are being fulfilled.

These prophecies should also motivate Latter-day Saints to be righteous in their own lives, so as to be effective in bringing the gospel truths to scattered Israel and Judah. As the Jews and all the children of Israel begin to believe in Christ as their messiah, they can be gathered to their promised land in righteousness, and they and the whole earth will be blessed.

BURNING PITCH AND
A BLOSSOMING ROSE
ISAIAH 34-35

These two chapters provide a capstone for chapters 28-33 of Isaiah and epitomize his message to the world. Earlier, Isaiah had prophesied to Israel (in chs. 1-12) and to the Gentile nations (chs. 13-23), and he followed these messages with an apocalyptic vision for the whole world (chs. 24-27). In a similar pattern, after giving warnings and promises to Judah (chs. 28-33), Isaiah again speaks to the whole world in a profound revelation (chs. 34-35).

In these two chapters his message is universal and his poetic style superb. The warnings and judgments of chapter 34 recapitulate many pronouncements given in his earlier chapters, and the hopes and promises of chapter 35 become favorite themes in his later writings, where he repeats its ideas, words, and entire verses. His visions of a blossoming desert, a crippled people becoming whole, and a righteous remnant returning to Zion have inspired countless generations of Bible readers.

Throughout his writings, Isaiah longs for the time when God's justice and mercy will be vindicated. He loves to stress the contrasts between the wicked and the righteous. In order that his listeners will more easily remember the messages he delivers for the Lord, he arranges his writings into thematic patterns and poetry. These two chapters are good examples of this.

Chapter 34 contains Isaiah's harshest pronouncements against the wicked. Echoing the warnings of chapter 13 against Babylon, it graphically portrays the Lord's sword of wrath upon the evil nations. Isaiah's imagery and poetry intensify this picture of dark desolation as he describes death, burning, and wild desert life. The literary excellence continues into the next chapter, but in sharp contrast to chapter 13. Green, watered valleys replace the desolation. Righteous Israelites are protected under the arm of the Lord as they gather to Zion. Songs of rejoicing overcome the shrieks of the desert night-creatures, and the blessings of the righteous take precedence over the remembrance of the wicked.

Isaiah introduces his prophecy by addressing the earth and its inhabitants with two synonomous parallelisms:

34 Come near, you nations,
and listen;
pay attention, you peoples!
Let the earth hear, and all that

is in it,
the world, and all that comes out
of it! (NIV)

He tells the world that the Lord's devastating anger will be upon all nations and that the hosts in heaven will also be affected in judgment (vs. 2-4). Vivid descriptions of destruction, blood, and death follow (vs. 5-7) before Isaiah concludes this section with a promise for Zion (v. 8).

²*The LORD is angry with all
nations;
his wrath is upon all their
armies.
He will totally destroy them,
he will give them over to
slaughter.
³Their slain will be thrown out,
their dead bodies will send up a
stench;
the mountains will be soaked with
their blood.
⁴All the stars of the heavens will be
dissolved
and the sky rolled up like a
scroll;
all the starry host will fall
like withered leaves from the
vine,
like shriveled figs from the fig
tree.

⁵*My sword has drunk its fill in the
heavens;
see, it descends in judgment on

Edom,
the people I have totally
destroyed.
⁶The sword of the LORD is bathed
in blood,
it is covered with fat—
the blood of lambs and goats,
fat from the kidneys of rams.

*For the LORD has a sacrifice in
Bozrah
and a great slaughter in Edom.
⁷And the wild oxen will fall with
them,
the bull calves and the
great bulls.
Their land will be drenched with
blood,
And the dust will be soaked with
fat.

⁸*For the LORD has a day of
vengeance,
a year of retribution, to uphold
Zion's cause. (NIV)

*At the beginning of verses 2, 5, 6b, and 8, Isaiah uses the Hebrew conjunction *kee* (usually translated as "for" or "thus") to introduce and connect four pronouncements of the Lord's vengeance.

The first pronouncement goes beyond the graphic description of destroyed armies; it includes, in verse form, promises of heavenly manifestations. Though the signs are difficult to interpret, some alternate translations suggest various possible meanings:

All the host of heaven shall molder. The heavens shall be rolled up like a scroll, And all their host shall wither, Like a leaf withering on the vine Or shriveled fruit on a fig tree. (NJV)

All the host of the heavens shall be dissolved and crumble away, and the skies shall be rolled together as a scroll; and all their host (the stars and the planets) shall drop like a faded leaf from the vine, and as a withered fig falls from the fig tree. (AB)

The sun, moon, and stars will crumble to dust. The sky will disappear like a scroll being rolled up, and the stars will fall like leaves dropping from a vine or a fig tree. (GNB)

The first phrase of verse 4 reads as follows in the King James Version: "And all the host of heaven shall be dissolved." The "host of heaven" could refer either to heavenly bodies (sun, moon, stars, etc.) or to celestial beings (spirits, angels, etc.) in God's presence. The phrase "shall be dissolved" comes from a Hebrew word that also means "to dwindle" or "to decompose." Thus the hosts of heaven dissolving could mean either that stars and planets will be destroyed or that there will be fewer beings in the Lord's presence (since his spirit children come to earth to acquire mortal bodies and some do not return to him). Of course, other possibilities exist, but by combining the two suggestions above with verses 2 and 3, we end up with a more encompassing interpretation composed of two main concepts:

1. Both earthly nations and heavenly orbs will be destroyed or disrupted.
2. The earth's population will be decimated (as armies are destroyed), and the heavenly population will decrease (as spirits leave and do not return).

Joseph Smith prophesies of similar signs in the heavens and the earth in Doctrine and Covenants 29:15-16 and 45:39-43.

The second phrase of verse 4, "and the heavens shall be rolled together as a scroll" (KJV), is echoed in many other scriptures.[1] (See Morm. 5:23; 9:2; 3 Ne. 26:3; Rev. 6:14; D&C 88:95.)

---

[1] This idea of the heavens as a scroll or a curtain is presented by Isaiah a number of times (40:22; 42:5; 44:24; 45:15; 51:13).

Three possible interpretations of this phrase can be supported by modern revelation recorded in the Doctrine and Covenants:

1. The signs of the times preceding the Millennium will include manifestations in the heavens, such as thunder and lightning, darkness, darkened sun, red moon, and falling stars. (D&C 43:25; 133:69; 88:87.)
2. The records (or scrolls) of heaven will be sealed (or opened up) as the earth's inhabitants are judged from the heavenly records (some don't return to heaven). (D&C 77:8 and 128:7, 14.)
3. The work of this telestial world will be completed, the veil over the earth will be removed, and the earth's inhabitants who have kept a terrestrial law will see Christ at his second coming. (D&C 88:95; 101:23; see also *Hymns*, no. 123.)

Interpretations 1 and 2 above parallel concepts 1 and 2 in the earlier part of the verse.

It seems that Isaiah is prophesying about apocalyptic signs that will occur in the heavens during the last days. Though astounding, these phenomena will come about through such natural means that he portrays the events by comparing them to falling leaves and fruit. In his other writings, he mentions more of these cataclysmic events and gives further details. (See Isa. 13:10; 24:23; 30:26; 50:3; 60:19-20; 65:17.)

After describing the universal signs upon the earth and in the heavens, Isaiah narrows his scope and gives two pronouncements on Edom and its capital, Bozrah. Using synonymous parallelism, he gives a double warning—the first is found in verse 5 and the first half of verse 6 and the second is in the second half of verse 6 and in verse 7 as outlined below:

First Pronouncement		Second Pronouncement
v. 5	judgment will come to Edom Idumea	v. 6b
6a	sacrifice of lambs, goats, and rams sacrifice of oxen, calves, and bulls	7
6a	blood and fat on the Lord's sword blood and fat over the whole land	7

The term "Edom" has a double meaning here. In addition to denoting the country located east of the Dead Sea, it means "the world" and especially "the wicked world." This second definition can be supported by modern revelation (D&C 1:36) and a linguistic evaluation of the term. The Hebrew word Edom also means "red" or "earth" and is the root for the words *Adam* and *man*. Therefore, it often connotes human or worldly qualities. As one scholar defines it, "Edom is always figurative of the natural state of man in his antagonism against God." (Vine, *Isaiah*, p. 84; see also Mosiah 3:19.)

The last pronouncement in this set is found in verse 8, where Isaiah promises "a day of the Lord's vengeance" and "a year of recompences" for the cause of Zion.

The events that Isaiah describes in these first eight verses of chapter 34 are also mentioned in three other standard works. All of these sources should be studied carefully (as well as those cross-referenced in their footnotes):

Rev. 6:12-17: John's vision, which includes many terms similar to those in Isaiah's prophecy, including stars of heaven, figs and fig tree, heaven, scroll, mountains, great day of the Lord's wrath, etc.

3 Ne. 26:1-5: Christ's brief summary of events prior to his return in glory, with mention of the earth, heavens, a scroll, peoples, and nations.

D&C 88:84-98: Joseph Smith's marvelous revelation of key signs before the Lord's second coming. He also uses many ideas found in the first verses of Isaiah 34: day of wrath, judgments, vine (vineyard), blood, earth, bodies in heaven, figs and fig trees, peoples and nations, a scroll or curtain in heaven, etc.

Beginning with verse 9, Isaiah describes the physical conditions of the land of Edom:

⁹Edom's streams will be turned
  into pitch,
her dust into burning sulfur;
her land will become blazing
  pitch!
¹⁰It will not be quenched night and
  day;
its smoke will rise forever.
From generation to generation
  it will lie desolate;
no one will ever pass through
  it again.
¹¹The desert owl and screech owl
  will possess it;
the great owl and the raven will
  nest there.
God will stretch out over Edom
  the measuring line of chaos
  and the plumb line of
  desolation.

¹²Her nobles will have nothing
  there to be called a kingdom,
all her princes will vanish
  away.
¹³Thorns will overrun her citadels,
  nettles and brambles her
  strongholds.
She will become a haunt for
  jackals,
a home for owls.
¹⁴Desert creatures will meet with
  hyenas,
and wild goats will bleat to
  each other;
there the night creatures will also
  repose
and find for themselves places
  of rest.
¹⁵The owl will nest there and lay
  eggs,

> she will hatch them, and care
>   for her young under the
>   shadow of her wings;
> there also the falcons will gather,
>   each with its mate. (NIV)

Unusual birds and strange animals are mentioned in verses 11 and 14. Their exact identity is ambiguous, as can be demonstrated by comparing the New International Version above with the King James and other versions. Although the exact meaning of the Hebrew terms is unknown, the picture Isaiah presents is graphic and symbolic.

In these verses, we see before us not only a desert wilderness, but also a dreadful desolation where sights and smells of burning sulfur and smoke offend our senses. Thorns and weeds inhibit movement, and strange creatures of the air and night bring foreboding to the heart. It is no wonder humans do not travel through the area (v. 10). Indeed, the destruction is so complete in this land that Isaiah borrows two rhyming terms (*tohu* and *bohu*) from Moses' story of the earth's desolate condition before it was organized: without form (confusion) and void (emptiness) (compare v. 10 with Gen. 1:2).

The land is not devoid of all life, however, only of human inhabitants. Having banished men from the area, the Lord transforms their cities and dwellings into nests for birds and dens for animals so that instead of these cities standing as monuments of human achievement, they become memorials of foolish ambition. The homes of men are occupied by animals whose wild dispositions resemble those of the original occupants. As John Calvin said of this series of events:

> This overthrow of order is likewise a sad token of the wrath of God, where the earth, which was created for the use of man, beholds its natural lords banished, and is compelled to admit other inhabitants; . . . yet this is also a punishment threatened against the cruelty of a wicked nation, which was eagerly bent on the oppression of neighbors and brethren. (*Calvin's Commentaries*, Isaiah 3:55-56.)

After prophesying the destruction upon Edom, Isaiah next addresses those who will witness the fulfillment of his predictions as recorded in the scriptures:

16Look in the scroll of the LORD and read:

None of these will be missing, not one will lack her mate. For it is his mouth that has given the order,

and his Spirit will gather them together.

17He allots their portions; his hand distributes them by measure. They will possess it forever

and dwell there from
   generation to generation.
(NIV)

The simple, obvious meaning of these two verses would be the animals described in earlier verses—they will be gathered together with their mates and given their inheritances. A deeper meaning is that if the Lord will provide such order and inheritance for these strange desert creatures, all of which were considered to be unclean by the law of Moses (Lev. 11), how much more must he surely provide for his pure and faithful children! Their names will also be called out from the book of the Lord, and they, with their mates, will be given their lands of eternal inheritance. But their inheritance will not be desert waste places; they will be garden paradises as described by Isaiah in the first verse of chapter 35:

35 The desert and the parched land will be glad;
the wilderness will rejoice and blossom.
Like the crocus,[2] it will burst into bloom;
   it will rejoice greatly and shout for joy.

The glory of Lebanon will be given to it,
   the splendor of Carmel and Sharon;
they will see the glory of the LORD, the splendor of our God. (NIV)

Isaiah's promise of the "desert blossoming as a rose" (v. 1, KJV) has inspired many people to work toward its fulfillment. The Jews returning from Babylon restored the desolate countryside to productive fields and orchards, as witnessed by the many places recorded in the New Testament. Also, Jews who have returned to the Holy Land during the past century have restored much of that neglected area into fields, groves of fruit trees, and forests. Likewise, the great western desert of North America has blossomed as the Mormon pioneers and their followers, prospective builders of the New Jerusalem, have developed that land. But, more than the increased productivity of the land, Isaiah predicts curative blessings upon the people:

[3]Strengthen the feeble hands,
   steady the knees that give way;
[4]say to those with fearful hearts,
   "Be strong, do not fear;
your God will come,
   he will come with vengeance,
with divine retribution
   he will come to save you."

[5]Then will the eyes of the blind be opened
   and the ears of the deaf unstopped.
[6]Then will the lame leap like a deer,
   and the tongue of the dumb shout for joy. (NIV)

Just as the earth must be blessed to bring forth its fruits, so also the inhabitants of the land must be strengthened to fulfill their destiny. In verses 3-6, an unnamed being is commissioned to strengthen their limbs and to alleviate their fears. The source of the people's weaknesses or fears is also unnamed, though it could result from the horror of their life in the desert. Desert life for the Hebrew usually symbolizes one of two conditions: either a place of refuge and asylum, or a place into which one is forced as a trial and tribulation. In either case, the desert is where God segregates and tests his people. (See Nibley, *An Approach to the Book of Mormon*, p. 115.) Regardless of the source or purpose of their fears, Isaiah promises the people that the Lord will save them (v. 4).

Before the Israelites can become productive on the blossoming land, they need strong, healthy bodies. Included in the Lord's blessings are cures for their ailments:

The blind shall see,
the deaf shall hear,
the lame shall jump, and
the dumb shall sing (vs. 5-6).

The cures listed might be either literal or figurative. That is, their physical handicaps will be healed or their spiritual weaknesses overcome. These blessings might even be a combination of the two; the people may remain, for example, physically blind, but they could still be spiritually blessed by "seeing" the gospel truths as they study the scriptures through tapes or braille. (Elder LeGrand Richards has suggested that such modern technological advancements for the blind, deaf, and handicapped are a type of fulfillment for these Isaianic prophecies. See *Ensign*, May 1976, p. 84.) Indeed, the two may go together, for often after the Lord heals someone physically, he sometimes adds "thy sins are forgiven thee," indicating a double healing process. (Matt. 9:2-8.)

A literal, physical fulfillment of these healing promises will undoubtedly occur as the Lord visits the earth at his second coming. In his earlier appearances to the multitudes of the Old and New Worlds, he healed many of the physically ill. He will surely do likewise when he returns in glory.

Still, the figurative applications of these verses should be understood, for they will also come to pass. Isaiah records earlier that he was told that the people would physically hear and see but would not spiritually understand or perceive the Lord's messages. (Isa. 6:9.) He

312

also promises that some will eventually and completely see and hear his message. (Isa. 6:11-13; 29:18; 32:2-4.) They will see the signs and perceive what the fulfilled prophecies mean. They will hear God's word and understand it. They will burst forth with new spiritual life just as the desert will burst forth with life-giving waters. These waters are promised by Isaiah in the following verses:

6bWater will gush forth in the wilderness
and streams in the desert.
7The burning sand will become a pool,
The thirsty ground bubbling springs.
In the haunts where jackals once lay,
grass and reeds and papyrus will grow. (NIV)

As with the first two verses of chapter 35, these verses have already seen some fulfillment in the deserts of North America and in Israel as irrigation ditches, water pipelines, sprinklers, and drip-irrigation tubes carry life-giving moisture across the land. (See MWW, pp. 10, 237-40.)

Isaiah concludes chapter 35 with prophecies about a special highway. This path may be a literal road, but could also be a "way of holiness" for the remnants of Israel returning to Zion:

8And a highway will be there;
it will be called the Way of Holiness.
The unclean will not journey on it;
it will be for those who walk in that Way;
wicked fools will not go about on it.
9No lion will be there,
nor will any ferocious beast get up on it;
they will not be found there.
But only the redeemed will walk there,
10 and the ransomed of the LORD will return.
They will enter Zion with singing;
everlasting joy will crown their heads.
Gladness and joy will overtake them
and sorrow and sighing will flee away. (NIV)

Verse 8 is incomplete in the Hebrew, and scholars disagree on how to translate it, the second half of the verse being especially challenging. To clarify this verse, Joseph Smith added a number of words to it in his inspired translation. With his additions underlined, the King James translation reads as follows:

And a highway shall be there; *for a way shall be cast up* and it shall be called the way of holiness.

313

The unclean shall not pass over
    upon it;
but it shall be *cast up* for those *who
are clean*,

And the wayfaring men,
Though *they are accounted* fools,
shall not err therein.

By reading this verse without the underlined portions, one can easily see that it is incomplete and how varied interpretations would arise. The highway mentioned in this verse could be a literal road, such as the one Isaiah promises in 11:16, because the next verse (9) says that wild animals will not be allowed on it. However, these wild animals might represent evil forces, and the highway could also symbolize a spiritual path that will lead some of God's children back to Zion, where the pure in heart dwell. (D&C 97:21; 133:17-18.) Verses 9 and 10 also suggest a spiritual symbolism for this highway. In short, there are at least three figurative ways in which this highway might represent Israelites returning to Zion in the last days:

1. The highway might be Isaiah's way of describing the Zionist movement and other political events that encouraged the return of the Jews to Israel within the past century.
2. The highway might symbolize the "straight and narrow path," the basic principles and ordinances of the gospel, which God's children follow in order to become part of spiritual Zion.
3. More specifically, the highway might refer to the exact procedures required of the members of Christ's Church as they enter the temple and receive the instruction and ordinances necessary to return to our Heavenly Father's presence.

Even though we do not understand the exact meaning of the "way to holiness" by which the redeemed of the Lord will return to Zion, Isaiah describes it well enough that we know it is one of the great blessings the Lord will provide in these last days. Whether it is a literal, physical road or a figurative, spiritual path, or both, we know the Lord is preparing a way for his righteous children to return to their rightful places of inheritance.

Personally, Isaiah probably preferred to deliver such messages of promise and hope, but, like most prophets, he was required to deliver many specific warnings and to teach the Israelites about their covenant relationship with God. But, when given the opportunity, he, more than any other Old Testament prophet, excels in elevating Israel's hope for an age of paradisiacal glory. He develops this theme in the last half of his book, in which he extols the qualities of spiritual life and describes the proper role of a servant of the Lord. He also helps later Israelites to anticipate and to prepare for a new earth by encouraging a new relationship with heaven so that God and his children can work harmoniously together.

SCRIPTURAL NOTES AND COMMENTARY

Isaiah 35:2: The "Glory of Lebanon" and the "excellency of Carmel and Sharon"

Lebanon, Carmel, and Sharon were beautiful and productive places during Isaiah's time. All three areas were near the Mediterranean Sea, where they received abundant rain and enjoyed moderate climates. Lebanon is northwest of Israel, Carmel juts into the sea along Israel's western coastline, and Sharon extends along the coast south of Carmel.

Lebanon's glory consisted in her beautiful trees (especially cedars) and magnificent vegetation. The excellency of Carmel was (and still is) in her productive vineyards. The plains of Sharon excelled in all types of fruits and vegetables.

Note how Isaiah transferred the glory and excellency of these areas over to the Lord in the second half of the verse. These areas were bountiful only because of the Lord's favor. If he so desired he could also bestow such blessings upon the deserts. The glory or credit for the productivity of a place did not belong to the area itself, but to the Lord.

JUDAH AND ASSYRIA
ISAIAH 36-37

Hezekiah was an experienced ruler and a seasoned diplomat when the Assyrian armies approached his territory in 701 B.C., but he had never faced a more serious crisis. He had ruled Judah for almost three decades and faced much opposition when he initiated his religious reforms. He had organized Judean resources to fortify Jerusalem and many other cities. He had negotiated with Egyptian, Philistine, Phoenician, and Babylonian leaders, especially during the few years preceding 701 B.C. But all these experiences and negotiations did not prepare him for the massive Assyrian invasion.

In 701 Sennacherib, King of Assyria, launched the third military campaign of his reign, directing his armies toward the Mediterranean. His first objective was to reestablish the taxing of his rebellious tributaries, but he also hoped to bring them completely within the Assyrian Empire and to invade and subdue Egypt. To be successful, he had to achieve control over four areas: the Phoenician city-states, the Philistine city-states of Ashkelon and Ekron, Judah and her fortified cities, and Egypt. None of these areas had earlier been incorporated within the Assyrian Empire by Sargon and they were centers for insurrection and anti-Assyrian movements. (See map , p. 317.)

Assyria easily reestablished control over Phoenicia. Sennacherib moved south along the seashore toward Ashkelon and Ekron, where he met stiffer opposition. Egyptian and Judean support encouraged the Philistine leaders, but Sennacherib quickly defeated the Egyptian garrison, captured the cities, and executed the rebels. The defeats of Phoenicia, Philistia, and the Egyptians all fulfilled earlier prophecies of Isaiah. (Isa. 23; 14:29-32; 20.)

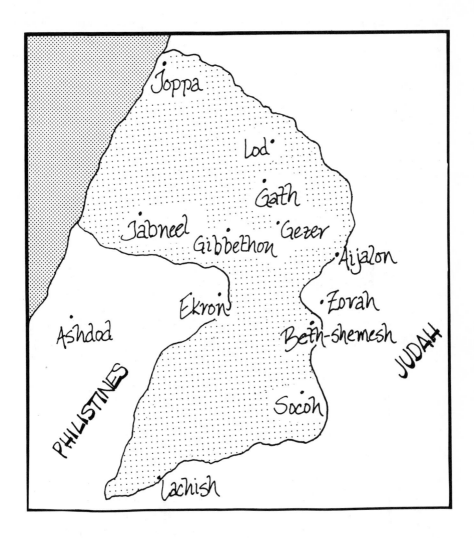

With control of the important cities and trade routes along the sea now secured, Sennacherib was ready to move into the Judean hills toward Jerusalem. He conquered as many as forty-six walled cities throughout the Judean countryside. Assyrian records and carvings portrayed with pride their techniques of conquest: hands and heads cut off, rebels impaled upon stakes, soldiers flung off walls, generals skinned alive, and multitudes led away as captives. Such a fate threatened the Jews in Jerusalem as Sennacherib prepared to conquer Hezekiah's capital city. (See map on page 166 in this book for the possible route of Sennacherib's invasion.)

Anticipating just such an attack, Hezekiah had begun years earlier to fortify and strengthen his city. Performing what was for his time a major engineering feat, he had a special tunnel built to bring water from the spring of Gihon to within the city walls (see map below). He strengthened the walls and built new fortifications. Supplies were placed in giant new storehouses, and new armaments were prepared for all his soldiers. He did all that was physically possible to prepare his city for the inevitable Assyrian siege. (See 2 Chr. 32:1-8, 30.)

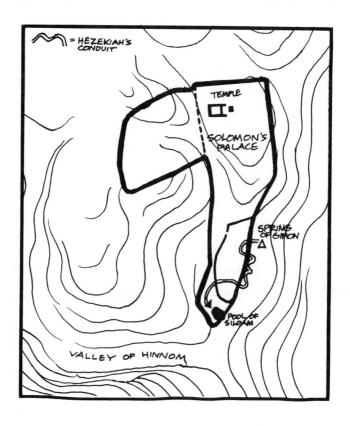

Hoping to avoid a direct confrontation when he saw that Sennacherib was preparing to attack Judah, Hezekiah sent Sennacherib a substantial tribute of gold and silver, including most, if not all, of the palace and temple treasuries. He even had the gold plating taken off the temple doors and pillars. (See 2 Kgs. 18:13-16.) But Sennacherib wanted more; he demanded absolute submission, and he knew that Hezekiah was one of the leaders in the revolt against Assyrian authority. He wanted nothing less than the unconditional surrender of Jerusalem, and he wanted her king still alive, so that he could humiliate, torture, and finally slowly impale King Hezekiah upon a pointed stake, just as he had done to the rebel kings of the Philistines.

It is under these conditions that a representative from Sennacherib went to Jerusalem with a message for King Hezekiah:

36 So in the fourteenth year of King Hezekiah's reign, Sennacherib, king of Assyria, came to fight against the walled cities of Judah and conquered them. ²Then he sent his personal representative with a great army from Lachish to confer with King Hezekiah in Jerusalem. He camped near the outlet of the upper pool, along the road going past the field where cloth is bleached. (LB)

The opening scene of this chapter is very similar to that of chapter 7, in which Isaiah meets King Ahaz at the "conduit of the upper pool in the highway of the fuller's field" (KJV). In chapter 7, Isaiah warns Ahaz against any Assyrian coalition. Ahaz disregarded this counsel, however, and the Assyrians became so powerful in the area that the representative of an invading Assyrian army met King Hezekiah's delegation at the same place.

³Then Eliakim, Hilkiah's son, who was the prime minister of Israel, and Shebna, the king's scribe, and Joah (Asaph's son), the royal secretary, formed a truce team and went out of the city to meet with him. ⁴The Assyrian ambassador told them to go and say to Hezekiah, "The mighty king of Assyria says you are a fool to think that the king of Egypt will help you. ⁵What are the Pharaoh's promises worth? Mere words won't substitute for strength, yet you rely on him for help, and have rebelled against me! ⁶Egypt is a dangerous ally. She is a sharpened stick that will pierce your hand if you lean on it. That is the experience of everyone who has ever looked to her for help. ⁷But perhaps you say, 'We are trusting in the Lord our God!' Oh? Isn't he the one your king insulted, tearing down his temples and altars in the hills and making everyone in Judah worship only at the altars here in Jerusalem? ⁸,⁹My master, the king of Assyria, wants to make a little bet with you!—that you don't have 2,000 men left in your entire army!

If you do, he will give you 2,000 horses for them to ride on! With that tiny army, how can you think of proceeding against even the smallest and worst contingent of my master's troops? For you'll get no help from Egypt. ¹⁰What's more, do you think I have come here without the Lord's telling me to take this land? The Lord said to me, 'Go and destroy it!' " (LB)

The Assyrian ambassador is also known by his title, Rabshakeh. The Rabshakeh was an adept propagandist, whose mastery of Hebrew and understanding of Jewish culture were so keen that some scholars assert he must have been an apostate Jew serving as an Assyrian mercenary. He begins by referring to Hezekiah without using any title, a gross breach of diplomatic courtesy, which indicates Sennacherib's extreme hatred toward the Judean king. (Coincidentally, this hatred still persisted years later, for in the Sennacherib Prism, an Assyrian record of circa 685 B.C., in which twenty-five royal personages are named, Hezekiah is one of only two leaders who is not given any title as king.) Meanwhile, the Rabshakeh calls his own leader, Sennacherib, the "great king," and mimics a prophet-spokesman when he says, "Thus saith the great king" (v. 4, KJV). This subtle overture creates immediate feelings of inferiority and tentativeness among the Judean delegation, although their positions in the Judean government are at least equivalent to Rabshakeh's in the Assyrian government.

From the outset (and perhaps understandably in the face of their military successes) the Assyrians assume the dominant position in the negotiations. The Rabshakeh proceeds by first attacking the confidence of the Judeans in themselves, then undermining their faith in their ally, Egypt, and finally questioning their trust in God, implying that Hezekiah himself has weakened their faith, since he has abolished all the local sanctuaries in deference to the temple in Jerusalem (vs. 4-7). Taunting that the Judeans cannot muster 2,000 horsemen, and again questioning their alliance with Egypt, the Rabshakeh finally proudly claims that the Lord is with the Assyrians (vs. 8-10).

At this, the Judean officials ask the Assyrians to speak to them in Aramaic rather than Hebrew so that those on the ramparts of the city will not overhear:

¹¹Then Eliakim and Shebna and Joah said to him, "Please talk to us in Aramaic for we understand it quite well. Don't speak in Hebrew, for the people on the wall will hear." (LB)

Aramaic was the international language of diplomacy at that time, and most Jewish political leaders understood it. The Assyrian minister ignored their request:

¹²But he replied, "My master wants everyone in Jerusalem to hear this, not just you. He wants them to know that if you don't surrender, this city will be put under siege until everyone is so hungry and thirsty that he will eat his own dung and drink his own urine."

¹³Then he shouted in Hebrew to the Jews listening on the wall, "Hear the words of the great king, the king of Assyria:

¹⁴"Don't let Hezekiah fool you—nothing he can do will save you. ¹⁵Don't let him talk you into trusting in the Lord by telling you the Lord won't let you be conquered by the king of Assyria. ¹⁶Don't listen to Hezekiah, for here is the king of Assyria's offer to you: Give me a present as a token of surrender; open the gates and come out, and I will let you each have your own farm and garden and water, ¹⁷until I can arrange to take you to a country very similar to this one—a country where there are bountiful harvests of grain and grapes, a land of plenty. ¹⁸Don't let Hezekiah deprive you of all this by saying the Lord will deliver you from my armies. Have any other nation's gods ever gained victory over the armies of the king of Assyria? ¹⁹Don't you remember what I did to Hamath and Arpad? Did their gods save them? And what about Sepharvaim and Samaria? Where are their gods now? ²⁰Of all the gods of these lands, which one has ever delivered their people from my power? Name just one! And do you think this God of yours can deliver Jerusalem from me? Don't be ridiculous!" (LB)

Instead of lowering his voice or speaking in Aramaic, the Rabshakeh raises his voice to a shout. Addressing those on the wall, he says that it is to them that Sennacherib has sent him to speak. He adds the vulgar claim that they and their leaders will eat their own waste if Assyria besieges the city. He continues in his role of "propaganda minister" by seeking to undermine the popular support of King Hezekiah's government, saying that Hezekiah's call for the people to trust in the Lord is foolishness. Using a blasphemous allusion to prophecy ("hear the words of the great king of Assyria") the Rabshakeh describes Sennacherib as the advocate of the people. He promises the Jews that if they will submit, they can keep their own property until Sennacherib takes them to a good land like their own. Finally, the Rabshakeh boastfully belittles the gods of the many nations that Assyria has subjected, claiming that Jehovah can do no better at rescuing his people from Assyria.

Silent before this Assyrian arrogance, the Judean delegation returns to their leaders inside the city:

²¹But the people were silent and answered not a word, for Hezekiah had told them to say nothing in reply. ²²Then Eliakim (son of Hilkiah), the prime minister, and Shebna, the royal scribe, and Joah (son of Asaph), the royal secretary, went back to Hezekiah with clothes ripped to shreds as a sign of their despair and told him all that had happened.

37 When king Hezekiah heard the results of the meeting, he tore his robes and wound himself in coarse cloth used for making sacks, as a sign of humility and mourning, and went over to the Temple to pray. ²Meanwhile he sent Eliakim his prime minister, and Shebna his royal scribe, and the older priests—all dressed in sackcloth—to Isaiah the prophet, son of Amoz. ³They brought him this message from Hezekiah:

"This is a day of trouble and frustration and blasphemy; it is a serious time, as when a woman is in heavy labor trying to give birth, and the child does not come. ⁴But perhaps the Lord your God heard the blasphemy of the king of Assyria's representative as he scoffed at the Living God. Surely God won't let him get away with this. Surely God will rebuke him for those words. Oh, Isaiah, pray for us who are left!"

⁵So they took the king's message to Isaiah. (LB)

The Jewish leaders are so concerned about the seriousness of the situation that they rend their clothes, don sackcloth, and petition the prophet to seek divine aid. Their "day of trouble" is graphically compared to a woman's travail before birth when there is not enough strength to bring forth deliverance (v. 3; compare D&C 101:8).

In response to Sennacherib's blasphemous boasting, Isaiah sends a message of comfort to Hezekiah:

⁶Then Isaiah replied, "Tell King Hezekiah that the Lord says, Don't be disturbed by this speech from the servant of the king of Assyria, and his blasphemy. ⁷For a report from Assyria will reach the king that he is needed at home at once, and he will return to his own land, where I will have him killed." (LB)

The Lord's promised assistance calms the Jews temporarily.

Meanwhile, the Rabshakeh has returned to his leader, who is besieging the Judean cities southwest of Jerusalem. Sennacherib's attention is soon diverted from Judah, however, for he receives word that an Egyptian army is approaching from the south. Caught between the Jews on the north and the Egyptians in the south, he does not want the Jews to attack his rear or cut off his supply lines. He therefore presses for Jerusalem's immediate surrender, before Hezekiah can find out about the approaching Egyptians. He quickly sends a letter to Hezekiah:

8, 9Now the Assyrian envoy left Jerusalem and went to consult his king, who had left Lachish and was besieging Libnah. But at this point the Assyrian king received word that Tirhakah, crown prince of Ethiopia, was leading an army against him (from the south). Upon hearing this, he sent messengers back to Jerusalem to Hezekiah with this message:

10"Don't let this God you trust in fool you by promising that Jerusalem will not be captured by the king of Assyria! 11Just remember what has happened wherever the kings of Assyria have gone, for they have crushed everyone who has opposed them. Do you think you will be any different? 12Did their gods save the cities of Gozan, Haran, or Rezeph, or the people of Eden in Telassar? No, the Assyrian kings completely destroyed them! 13And don't forget what happened to the king of Hamath, to the king of Arpad, and to the kings of the cities of Sepharvaim, Hena, and Ivvah." (LB)

The substance of the letter is that no other deities have helped those who believe in them; the other rebel kings are now dead or in servitude, and Judah should not expect her fate to be any different. Judah and her God would be powerless before the Assyrians.

Most of the places mentioned in Sennacherib's letter above are listed in the Gazetteer. Many of them no longer exist except as archaeological sites, but as a point of reference they are listed below according to the modern country that controls the area of their location:

Iraq:	Gozan, Rezeph, Telassar
Syria:	Hamath, Arphad, and Sepharvaim
Turkey:	Haran
Unknown:	Hena, Ivvah

Upon receipt of the letter, Hezekiah, filled with new fear, goes to the temple to ask for the Lord's help:

14As soon as King Hezekiah had read this letter, he went over to the Temple and spread it out before the Lord, 15and prayed, saying 16, 17"O Lord of Hosts, God of Israel enthroned above the cherubim, you alone are God of all the kingdoms of the earth. You alone made heaven and earth. Listen as I plead; see me as I pray. Look at this letter from King Sennacherib, for he has mocked the Living God. 18It is true, O Lord, that the kings of Assyria have destroyed all those nations, just as the letter says, [19]and thrown their gods into the fire; for they weren't gods at all, but merely idols, carved by men from wood and stone. Of course the Assyrians could destroy them. [20]O Lord our God, save us so that all the kingdoms of the earth will know that you are God, and you alone." (LB)

In the face of extreme danger, Hezekiah still retains a true perspective about power upon this earth. His faith remains in the Lord. In spite of military threats and the idolatry surrounding him, Hezekiah keeps his trust. President Spencer W. Kimball has provided counsel concerning similar situations today:

> In spite of our delight in defining ourselves as modern, and our tendency to think we possess a sophistication that no people in the past ever had—in spite of these things, we are, on the whole, an idolatrous people—a condition most repugnant to the Lord.
>
> We are a warlike people, easily distracted from our assignment of preparing for the coming of the Lord. When enemies rise up, we commit vast resources to the fabrication of gods of stone and steel—ships, planes, missiles, fortifications—and depend on them for protection and deliverance. When threatened, we become anti-enemy instead of pro-kingdom of God.
>
> We forget that if we are righteous the Lord will either not suffer our enemies to come upon us—and this is the special promise to the inhabitants of the land of the Americas [see 2 Ne. 1:7]—or he will fight our battles for us [Ex. 14:14; D&C 98:37]." (*Ensign*, June 1976, p. 6.)

In answer to Hezekiah's prayer, Isaiah speaks for the Lord and delivers his message to Sennacherib:

[21]Then Isaiah, the son of Amoz, sent this message to King Hezekiah: "The Lord God of Israel says, This is my answer to your prayer against Sennacherib, Assyria's king. [22]"The Lord says to him: My people—the helpless virgin daughter of Zion—laughs at you and scoffs and shakes her head at you in scorn. [23]Who is it you scoffed against and mocked? Whom did you revile? At whom did you direct your violence and pride? It was against the Holy One of Israel! [24]You have sent your messengers to mock the Lord. You boast, 'I came with my mighty army against the nations of the west. I cut down the tallest cedars and choicest cypress trees. I conquered their highest mountains and destroyed their thickest forests.' [25]"You boast of wells you've dug in many a conquered land, and Egypt with all its armies is no obstacle to you! [26]But do you not yet know that it was I who decided all this long ago? That it was I who gave you all this power from ancient times? I have caused all this to happen as I planned—that you should crush walled cities into ruined heaps. [27]That's why their

people had so little power, and were such easy prey for you. They were as helpless as the grass, as tender plants you trample down beneath your feet, as grass upon the housetops, burnt yellow by the sun. [28]But I know you well—your comings and goings and all you do—and the way you have raged against me. [29]Because of your anger against the Lord—and I heard it all!—I have put a hook in your nose and a bit in your mouth and led you back to your own land by the same road you came." (LB)

With majestic poetry, the Lord reminds Sennacherib that it is only with divine sanction that he rules Assyria and has power over other nations. But, because of the Assyrian's blasphemy, the Lord's anger has now come upon Sennacherib, and he will be forced to return home humiliated.

The Lord also offers a sign to Hezekiah that the invasion will soon end and conditions will return to normal:

[30]Then God said to Hezekiah, "Here is the proof that I am the one who is delivering this city from the king of Assyria: This year he will abandon his siege. Although it is too late now to plant your crops, and you will have only volunteer grain this fall, still it will give you enough seed for a small harvest next year, and two years from now you will live in luxury again. [31]And you who are left in Judah will take root again in your own soil and flourish and multiply. [32]For a remnant shall go out from Jerusalem to repopulate the land; the power of the Lord of Hosts will cause all this to come to pass. (LB)

Soon peace will be established in the land and the people will return to their fields, resettling the devastated areas.

Isaiah concludes these two chapters by prophesying the downfall of Assyria and recording the fulfillment of his earlier prophecy (37:7):

[33]"As for the king of Assyria, his armies shall not enter Jerusalem, nor shoot their arrows there, nor march outside its gates, nor build up an earthen bank against its walls. [34]He will return to his own country by the road he came on, and will not enter this city, says the Lord. [35]For my own honor I will defend it, and in memory of my servant David." [36]That night the Angel of the Lord went out to the camp of the Assyrians and killed 185,000 soldiers; when the living wakened the next morning, all these lay dead before them.[37]Then Sennacherib, king of Assyria, returned to his own country,to Nineveh. [38]And one day while he was worshiping in the temple of Nisroch his god, his sons Adrammelech and Sharezer killed him with their swords; then they escaped into the land of Ararat, and Esar-haddon his son became king. (LB)

As prophesied, the Assyrians never attacked Jerusalem. While awaiting the surrender of Jerusalem and preparing for a conflict with the Egyptians, they were struck down by the angel of the Lord, who destroyed most of the Assyrian army in a single night.

Isaiah records very few details about the destruction of the Assyrian army. He does not say where the army was, why the men died, when they returned to Assyria, or how many, if any, Assyrian soldiers remained in the area. Fortunately, two other accounts besides the Bible contain information about this Assyrian campaign.

Sennacherib's own history of the events is very positive. One would never know from reading it that the Assyrians had suffered a major setback. Unfortunately, ancient kings and their scribes rarely recorded defeats, so it is not uncommon to read two opposite accounts of the same war, each describing what appears to be a victory for its own side. One must read between the lines to find hints of defeat. Such a hint can be found in the middle of Sennacherib's account of his Judean campaign:

> But as for Hezekiah, the Jew, who did not bow in submission to my yoke, forty-six of his strong walled towns and innumerable smaller villages in their neighbourhood I besieged and conquered . . . He himself I shut up like a caged bird within Jerusalem, his royal city. I put watchposts strictly around it and turned back to his disaster any who went out of its city gate. Moreover, I fixed upon him an increase in the amount to be given as *katre*-presents for my lordship, in addition to the former tribute, to be given annually. As for Hezekiah, the awful splendour of my lordship overwhelmed him. (From the *Taylor Prism* in the British Museum as translated by Thomas, *Documents from Old Testament Times*, p. 67.)

Sennacherib does not come right out and admit that he was unable to defeat Hezekiah or to capture Jerusalem, but he does state that Hezekiah was trapped like a "caged bird" within the city. In any case, Sennacherib's account of the conquest and the biblical record in Isaiah 36-37 and 2 Kings 18:13–19:37 are so different that they could be describing two completely different confrontations.

Another brief account of the Assyrian campaign is contained in the history of Herodotus, who wrote about 450 B.C. He records that when Sennacherib's army was close to Pelusium, a border garrison southwest of Libnah (where the Bible account first mentions their presence), mice ate the Assyrian bowstrings and caused their defeat:

> So presently came king Sanacharb [Sennacherib] against Egypt, with a great host of Arabians and Assyrians; and the warrior Egyptians would not march against him. . . . [The Egyptian King Sethos] encamped at Pelusium with such

Egyptians as would follow him, for here is the road into Egypt; and none of the warriors would go with him, but only hucksters and artificers and traders. Their enemies too came thither, and one night a multitude of fieldmice swarmed over the Assyrian camp and devoured their quivers insomuch that they fled the next day unarmed and many fell. (Herodotus, *History*, Book 2, pt. 141 as translated in the *Loeb Classical Library*, vol. 113.)

From this account, it appears that the mice played a major role in the Assyrian defeat. This sheds an interesting new light on the biblical account, for mice and rats are often carriers of plagues. And a plague might have been the means by which the angel of death struck down 185,000 soldiers in a single night.

If one combines the limited information contained in these three accounts, a composite picture emerges. Although the Assyrian record does not seem to record a defeat and the Egyptian account gives credit to the mice in turning the tide of battle, the biblical records add the important fact that the Lord was the causative force in the Assyrian defeat. The Bible may not present all the historical facts, but it does include the most essential one—the Lord defended the Jews and defeated the Assyrians.

After his defeat, Sennacherib returned to Nineveh, where he was assassinated twenty years later by his own son. It is not recorded whether or not he ever personally recognized the power of the Lord in his defeat. But it is evident from his record of the campaign that he harbored a great hatred for Hezekiah for many years after their confrontation. The manifestation of the Lord's power in defeating Assyria was apparently not so much designed to impress or convert the Assyrians as it was to witness to Judah that God was still their protector.

In conclusion, chapters 36 and 37 describe a historical event, but only in the context of demonstrating how the Lord deals with his people. Isaiah shows that the Lord's involvement with the Israelites' problems is largely dependent on their willingness to accept him. As the Lord helped and hindered Sennacherib and punished and protected Judah, it becomes clear that his actions changed only when the people changed their relationship with him. God is constant in his covenant—he blesses the faithful and punishes the wicked. These chapters of Isaiah demonstrate the extent to which the Lord must sometimes go in order to fulfill his promises.

KING HEZEKIAH AVERTS DEATH BUT ENTICES SLAVERY
ISAIAH 38-39

Chapters 38 and 39 form the second half of the historical bridge connecting the two collections of Isaiah's writings, chapters 1-35 and 40-66. (See Appendix: The Authorship of Isaiah.) Chapters 36 and 37, the first half of the bridge, conclude the prophecies to Israel during the peak of Assyrian power, while 38 and 39 introduce Isaiah's prophecies to Israel during the Babylonian and later periods. The relationship between sections can be illustrated with the following diagram:

Early Collection	*Historical Bridge*		*Later Collections*
Prophecies to Israel	Assyrian	Babylonian	Prophecies to Israel in
during Assyrian	attack	delegation	Babylonian and later
period (1-35)	(36-37)	(38-39)	periods (40-66)

This is somewhat misleading, however, since the four historical chapters are out of chronological order. The first set of chapters describe Sennacherib's attack upon Jerusalem in 701 B.C., while the second set (38-39) records Hezekiah's recovery from illness and his involvement with the Babylonians around 705-703 B.C., some few years before the Assyrian invasion.

Some evidence that the chapters are transposed is contained in the text itself. Chapters 38 and 39 both begin with phrases that can be used to introduce historical flashbacks: "In those days" and "At that time." Also, in chapter 38, Isaiah prophesies that Jerusalem will be saved from an Assyrian invasion, implying that the events of chapters 36 and 37 were, at that time, still in the future. And in chapter 39, Hezekiah proudly shows the Babylonians great treasures, which were undoubtedly given later as tribute to the victorious Assyrians. (See 2 Kgs. 18:14-15.) The correct chronology of the historical chapters in relation to the rest of Isaiah is illustrated in this diagram:

First Collection	Historical Chapters		Second Collection
Isaiah's earlier prophecies (1-35)	Hezekiah's sickness and Babylonian visitors (38-39)	Assyrian attack and defeat (36-37)	Isaiah's later prophecies (40-66)

The fact that some chapters are out of chronological order should not disturb the readers of Isaiah, since earlier collections in his book (1-12, 13-23) are organized thematically rather than chronologically. Similarly, although Isaiah's writings are roughly chronological, some other methods of arrangement were also used, possibly under the direction of Isaiah himself, though a scribe or later editor may have arranged Isaiah's writings in their present order.

Chapters 38 and 39 can be outlined as follows:

I. Hezekiah's illness and recovery (ch. 38)
   A. Hezekiah's sickness and Isaiah's prophecy (v. 1)
   B. Hezekiah prays for health (2-3)
   C. Hezekiah receives an answer to his prayer (4-8, 21-22)
      1. Fifteen more years promised to Hezekiah (5)
      2. Jerusalem will be preserved from the Assyrians (6)
      3. Isaiah heals Hezekiah (21)
      4. Hezekiah asks for and receives a sign (22, 7-8)
   D. Hezekiah's psalm of thanksgiving (9-20)

II. The Babylonian delegation (ch. 39)
   A. Merodach-baladan sends gifts and an embassy (v. 1)
   B. Hezekiah shows his treasures (2)
   C. Isaiah questions Hezekiah's actions (3-4)
   D. Isaiah prophesies of Babylonian captivity (5-7)
   E. Hezekiah responds to Isaiah's words (8)

With the exception of Hezekiah's psalm of thanksgiving, most of the material in Isaiah 38 and 39 is also recorded in 2 Kings 20. Some additional phrases are in the 2 Kings account, and a brief evaluation of Hezekiah and the Babylonian visit is also found in 2 Chronicles 32. In addition, Joseph Smith revised portions of Hezekiah's psalm in his inspired translation. In order to provide a more complete acccount of these events, the additions from the materials mentioned above will be included as the Isaianic verses are quoted.

The story of Hezekiah's illness is straightforward and easily understood. Close to death, Hezekiah reminds the Lord of his faithful life and petitions for divine aid. Isaiah, who had earlier told Hezekiah to prepare for death, is inspired by the Lord to return and pronounce a blessing upon the king. The events are recorded as follows (brackets enclose the additions from 2 Kgs. 20:4-6):

38 At this time Hezekiah fell dangerously ill and the prophet Isaiah son of Amoz came to him and said, 'This is the word of the LORD: Give your last instructions to your household, for you are a dying man and will not recover.' ²Hezekiah turned his face to the wall and offered this prayer to the LORD: ³O LORD, remember how I have lived before thee, faithful and loyal in thy service, always doing what was good in thine eyes.' And he wept bitterly. [But before Isaiah had left the citadel] ⁴Then the word of the LORD came to Isaiah: ⁵'Go and say to Hezekiah [the prince of my people]: "This is the word of the LORD the God of your father David: I have heard your prayer and seen your tears; [I will heal you and on the third day you shall go to the house of the LORD.] I will add fifteen years to your life. ⁶I will deliver you and this city from the king of Assyria and will protect this city."' (NEB)

As the material in brackets indicates, the account in 2 Kings is more complete. In particular, it contains the promise that Hezekiah will be healed within three days and then be able to visit the temple again. The account then continues with a brief description of Isaiah's healing act and Hezekiah's question about a sign that will confirm the prophet's promise. The same basic material is found in Isaiah 38, but it is placed at the end of the chapter after Hezekiah's psalm.

Here again is an example of material taken out of chronological order and placed in a thematic pattern for emphasis. The highlight of Isaiah 38 is Hezekiah's psalm of thanksgiving. This psalm is not included in the 2 Kings account, and thus its editor simply presents the story in chronological sequence. With the psalm at the center of Isaiah's account, however, the following parallelism is developed:

A. Sickness and promised health (vs. 1-6)
B. Sign given to Hezekiah (7-8)
C. Hezekiah's psalm (9-20)
A'. Symbolic act of healing (21)
B'. Hezekiah's request for a sign (22)

Hezekiah's healing and his request for a sign are presented at the end of Isaiah 38 and in verses 7 and 8 as follows (brackets enclose additions from 2 Kgs. 20:8-11):

²¹Then Isaiah told them to apply a fig-plaster; so they made one and applied it to the boil, and he recovered. ²²Then Hezekiah said, 'By what sign shall [the LORD give that] I know that I shall go up into the house of the LORD [on the third day]?' ⁷And Isaiah said, 'This shall be your sign from the LORD that he will do what he has promised. [Shall the shadow go forward ten steps or back ten steps?' Hezekiah

answered, 'It is an easy thing for the shadow to move forward ten steps; rather let it go back ten steps.' Isaiah the prophet called to the LORD, and he said,] ⁸'Watch the shadow cast by the sun on the stairway of Ahaz: I will bring backwards ten steps the shadow which has gone down on the stairway.' And the sun went back ten steps on the stairway down which it had gone. (NEB)

Although Isaiah records that he made a mixture of figs and applied it to Hezekiah's boil, or sore, he does not say what type of boil it is or why he administered a fig-plaster as a remedy. Most likely, the fig-compress had no inherent healing properties, but was used as an outward "ordinance" to concretely illustrate God's blessing upon Hezekiah. Similarly, Christ made clay packs to heal the blind (John 9:6-7), Elisha instructed the leper Naaman to dip himself seven times in the Jordan River (2 Kgs. 5), and priesthood holders anoint the sick with oil.

Hezekiah also asked for a sign to assure him that the promise would be fulfilled in time for him to visit the temple on the third day. Isaiah asked which sign he preferred—to have the shadow cast by the sun go forward or backward? The phraseology of this question requires further explanation. In Isaiah's time, the common geographic reference point was east, toward the rising sun, instead of north as today. Thus, if someone in Jerusalem said that he was going to visit the "land to the front," he would journey east, probably to Syria. (See Isa. 9:12.) On the other hand, if he said that he was going to the "sea behind," he would travel west to the Mediterranean Sea. (See Joel 2:20.) Therefore, when Isaiah asks whether Hezekiah desires the shadow to go forward or backward, he means east or west, respectively.

Now Hezekiah knew that as the day progresses, the sun's shadow naturally moves to the east, opposite to the sun's actual movement. Therefore, he requested that the shadow move backward, or west, since that would be a greater manifestation. The Lord responded and reversed the normal direction of the sun's shadow by "ten steps" or degrees (KJV).

The Hebrew word here (*ma'alot*) refers to actual steps that apparently were used as time-markers alongside a wall built by Ahaz, Hezekiah's father. The wall served as a large sundial, with steps as units measuring the movement of the sun's shadow. Although the precise dimensions and style of the wall and steps of Ahaz are not known, the following diagram illustrates the principle involved:

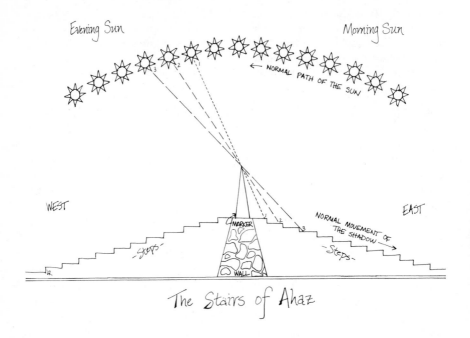

The Stairs of Ahaz

The shadow on the steps moved east as the sun moved west, and the shadow gradually moved down the steps during the afternoon. Apparently, Isaiah and Hezekiah conversed together in the afternoon, for when the Lord reversed the shadow's direction, it came "back ten steps on the stairway down which it had gone" (v. 8). The sign satisfied Hezekiah, and he composed the following psalm after his recovery (brackets enclose JST additions):

Chiastic Outline

⁹A poem of Hezekiah king of Judah after his recovery from his illness, as it was written down:

¹⁰I thought: In the prime of life I
  must pass away;
  for the rest of my years I am
    consigned to the gates of Sheol.

A. He feels that he is going to hell.

¹¹I said: I shall no longer see the
  LORD in the land of the living;
  never again, like those who live in

B. He will no longer see the Lord.

C. He will not be among the living.

the world, shall I look on a
man.
12My dwelling is taken from me,
pulled up like a shepherd's tent;
thou hast cut short my life like a
weaver
who severs the web from the
thrum [fringe].
From morning to night thou
tormentest me,
13then I am racked with pain till
the morning.
All my bones are broken, as a lion
would break them;
from morning to night thou
tormentest me.
14I twitter as if I were a swallow,
I moan like a dove.
My eyes falter as I look up to the
heights;
O Lord, pay heed, stand surety
for me.
15How can I complain, what can I
say to the LORD
when he himself has done this
[healed me]?
I wander to and fro all my life
long
[that I may not walk] in the
bitterness of my soul.
16Yet, O Lord, [thou who art the
life of my spirit,] my soul shall
live with thee,
do thou give my spirit rest.
Restore me and give me life [and
in all these things I will praise
thee].
17Bitterness had indeed been my lot
in place of prosperity;
but thou by thy love hast brought
me back from the pit of
destruction;
for thou hast cast all my sins
behind thee.

D. All ties to earth life will
be cut.

E. He experiences
physical pain.

F. He is continually
tormented.

G. He is lost and afraid.

H. He prays to the Lord

H'. The Lord heals him.

G'. He lives secure with
the Lord.

F'. He knows peace and
rest.

E'. He is freed from
spiritual anguish.

¹⁸Sheol cannot confess thee,
  Death cannot praise thee,
    nor can they who go down to
      the abyss hope for thy truth.
¹⁹The living, the living alone can
  confess thee as I do this day,
    as a father makes thy truth
      known, O God, to his sons.
²⁰The LORD is at hand to save me;
  so let us sound the music of our
    praises
  all our life long in the house of the
    LORD. (NEB)

D'. People in spirit prison
are without the gospel.

C'. The living can repent
and testify of God.

B'. The Lord is nearby.
A'. Hezekiah will sing in
the house of the Lord.

As the outline illustrates, the psalm forms a complete chiasmus, structured with many parallelisms. In the first half of the hymn, Hezekiah describes his suffering and fears; in the second half he recounts the peace and blessings he received from the Lord. Hezekiah's psalm is a special testimony to the Lord's power, which testimony is emphasized by its position in the chiastic pivot point (v. 15; see Ps. 6, 32).

Shortly after his recovery, Hezekiah receives a Babylonian delegation that brings him gifts and congratulations on the restoration of his health. Hezekiah's activities with this delegation and Isaiah's response to them are the subject of chapter 39. Also, an evaluation of Hezekiah's wealth and boastful attitude is found in a similar account in 2 Chronicles 32.

Isaiah 39

39 At this time Merodach-baladan son of Baladan king of Babylon sent envoys with a gift to Hezekiah; for he had heard that he had been ill and was well again. ²Hezekiah welcomed them and showed them all his treasury, silver and gold, spices and fragrant oil, his entire armoury and everything to be found among his treasures; there was nothing in his house and in all his realm that Hezekiah did not show them. ³Then the prophet Isaiah came to King Hezekiah and

2 Chronicles 32

²⁴About this time Hezekiah fell dangerously ill and prayed to the LORD; the LORD said, 'I will heal you', and granted him a sign. ²⁵But, being a proud man, he was not grateful for the good done to him, and Judah and Jerusalem suffered for it. ²⁶Then, proud as he was, Hezekiah submitted, and the people of Jerusalem with him, and the LORD's anger did not fall on them again in Hezekiah's time.

²⁷Hezekiah enjoyed great wealth and fame. He built for himself

asked him, 'What did these men say and where have they come from?' 'They have come from a far-off country,' Hezekiah answered, 'from Babylon.' [4]Then Isaiah asked, 'What did they see in your house?' 'They saw everything,' Hezekiah replied; 'there was nothing among my treasures that I did not show them.' [5]Then Isaiah said to Hezekiah, 'Hear the word of the LORD of Hosts: [6]The time is coming, says the LORD, when everything in your house, and all that your forefathers have amassed till the present day, will be carried away to Babylon; not a thing shall be left. [7]And some of the sons who will be born to you, sons of your own begetting, shall be taken and shall be made eunuchs in the palace of the king of Babylon.' [8]Hezekiah answered, 'The word of the LORD which you have spoken is good'; thinking to himself that peace and security would last out his lifetime. (NEB)

treasuries for silver and gold, precious stones and spices, shields and other costly things; [28]and barns for the harvests of corn, new wine, and oil; and stalls for every kind of cattle, as well as sheepfolds. [29]He amassed a great many flocks and herds; God had indeed given him vast riches. [30]It was this same Hezekiah who blocked the upper outflow of the waters of Gihon and directed them downwards and westwards to the city of David. In fact, Hezekiah was successful in everything he attempted, [31]even in the affair of the envoys sent by the King of Babylon—the envoys who came to inquire about the portent [or wonder, KJV] which had been seen in the land at the time when God left him to himself, to test him and to discover all that was in his heart. (NEB)

The chronicler is very generous in his evaluation of Hezekiah as a king: "Hezekiah . . . wrought that which was good and right and truth before the Lord his God. And in every work that he began in the service of the house of God, and in the law, and in the commandments, to seek his God, he did it with all his heart, and prospered." (2 Chr. 31:20-21.) Indeed, there is no doubt that Hezekiah did much good during his early years as king, for he was very zealous in eradicating paganism and restoring the Passover and other forms of true worship of the Lord. (See 2 Chr. 29-31.) But as 2 Chronicles 32:31 indicates, the Lord blessed Hezekiah with health and wealth not only to reward him for previous righteous behavior, but also to test the true nature of his heart.

Indeed, though the scriptures record that Hezekiah remained a righteous king over Judah and was buried in honor with his ancestors, some readers and scholars question the righteousness of Hezekiah's attitude in responding to Isaiah's prophecy of Judah's impending destruction. In 39:8, Isaiah indicates that Hezekiah is not disturbed by the warning that, in the future, his family's wealth will be lost and his descendants carried off as slaves to Babylon. He is just relieved that the disaster will not occur during his lifetime. But that is just one interpretation. It may be that Hezekiah is not as calloused as this brief account suggests. He may realize that later generations will be judged and punished for their actions, just as he has been judged and blessed for his. Still, his attitude toward the sufferings of his posterity lacks the compassion that many prophets had who foresaw similar circumstances. (For example, Enoch in Moses 7:41-42, Noah in Moses 8:25-27, Abraham in Gen. 18, and Moses in Ex. 32:12-14, 31-33.) Perhaps if Hezekiah had possessed the same concern for his posterity as he exhibited for his own health, he might have persuaded the Lord to grant a reprieve for his descendants as well as for himself.

In any case, the Lord continually tested Hezekiah, whether in sickness and invasion, or in health and prosperity. It appears that Hezekiah remained true to the Lord and was a noble ruler whose righteous leadership was a strong support to Isaiah's prophetic ministry. After Hezekiah's death, Isaiah was persecuted and, according to tradition, eventually killed by Hezekiah's son and successor, King Manasseh.

In conclusion, chapters 38 and 39 present many gospel teachings within the historical context of King Hezekiah. His story demonstrates the importance of faith and prayers in receiving a blessing from the Lord (38:1-7), as well as the necessity of a struggle for forgiveness. (Compare Isa. 38:10-14 with Alma's journey through hell in Alma 36.) Also, Hezekiah beautifully expresses the joy of being forgiven (38:15-20). His willingness to follow the prophet's counsel is evidenced by these and the preceding two chapters. Hezekiah was a good man whose righteous example stands in sharp contrast to wicked kings who preceded and followed him, and chapters 38 and 39 provide special insights into his soul.

These two chapters also give new insights into our understanding of Isaiah. The specific and immediate fulfillment of some of his prophecies are recorded along with his healing of Hezekiah and the miracle of the receding shadow. These chapters testify to Isaiah's power and authority as the Lord's prophet. Primarily historical, they witness the Lord's dealings with a prophet and king.

SCRIPTURAL NOTES AND COMMENTARY

Isaiah 39:1: Who was Merodach-Baladan?

Merodach-Baladan was the Chaldean tribal ruler of Bit-Yakin, the Sea Country, located just north of the Persian Gulf. Upon the succession of Sargon to the Assyrian throne in 721 B.C., Merodach-Baladan took advantage of the chaos that accompanied the change in leadership. With the support of the Elamites, inhabitants of southeast Mesopotamia, Merodach-Baladan was successful in making himself king of Babylon. Finally, in 710 B.C., Sargon succeeded in retaking Babylon; marching in unopposed, he made himself king. Still, he was unable to oust Merodach-Baladan from his tribal lands in Bit-Yakin. Merodach-Baladan retained his position as local ruler in his native area by submitting to Assyrian rule for the remainder of Sargon's days.

But upon Sargon's death in 705 B.C., Merodach-Baladan resumed his anti-Assyrian activites. With his confidence strengthened through a new alliance with the Arabs and by relying upon the support of the Elamites, Merodach-Baladan sent an embassy to Hezekiah (2 Kgs. 20; Isa. 39), hoping to entice the Assyrians' vassals in the west to rebellion. Unfortunately for Merodach-Baladan, Isaiah was strongly opposed to an alliance with the Babylonians and counseled Hezekiah against supporting this rebel Chaldean king.

RECEIVING THE STRENGTH
OF THE LORD
ISAIAH 40

In chapter 40, Isaiah gives a message of comfort and inspiration to countless generations, renewing hope in the advent of the Messiah (vs. 1-5) and proclaiming the immortality, power, love, knowledge, strength, creative abilities, and judgments of God (vs. 6-28). Isaiah concludes with a promise that those who wait and trust in the Lord will share in his powers and renew their strength (through the resurrection so that they will "run, and not be weary," and "walk, and not faint" [vs. 29-31]).

The dominant theme of this chapter stresses the glory of God the Father (*Elohim* in Hebrew). However, Isaiah's purpose in this discourse seems to extend beyond the extolling of God, since he concludes with a promise that those who follow Jesus Christ (*Yahweh* or *Jehovah* in Hebrew) will share God's strength. Thus Isaiah's message is twofold: (1) God is great and glorious, and (2) we can share his glory as we follow his son Jesus Christ.

God's greatness is emphasized throughout the chapter by an extensive use of synonymous parallelism that highlights a number of God's characteristics. In the following outline, the divine attributes are listed in the center column while the outside columns indicate the verses and means by which Isaiah portrays the attributes:

Example	Attribute	Example
God gives comfort and forgives his people (vs. 1-2)	Living, loving God	People build lifeless idols; give them care and attention (vs. 18-20)
Earth changed and reformed at Christ's coming (3-5)	Creative, powerful God	Earth created by Jehovah before Adam's coming (21)
Flesh is transitory; God's word is eternal (6-8)	Supreme, eternal God	People are numerous; God is incomparable (22-25)

338

Mighty God cares for his sheep and measures the earth (9-12)	Active, caring God	Mighty God calls for his children to come and be judged (26)
The Lord follows the divine plan and paths (13-14)	Mysterious, knowing God	People fear their concerns and ways are unknown to the Lord (27)
Great nations are as nothing before the Lord (15-17)	Wealthy, wise God	God and his wisdom never fade (28)

Since the synonymous parallelism will be more apparent if verses 1-17 are read as a whole, the "matching sets" of verses are printed in parallel columns below. In the first set, compare the tender love of God toward his people (vs. 1-2 on the left) with the care Judah devotes to her lifeless idols (vs. 18-20 on the right):

40 Comfort, oh comfort My people Says your God.	¹⁸To whom, then, can you liken God, What form compares to Him?
²Speak tenderly to Jerusalem, And declare to her That her term of service is over, That her iniquity is expiated; For she has received at the hand of the LORD Double for all her sins. (NJV)	¹⁹The idol? A woodworker shaped it, And a smith overlaid it with gold, Forging links of silver. ²⁰As a gift, he chooses the mulberry— A wood that does not rot— Then seeks a skillful woodworker To make a firm idol, That will not topple. (NJV)

In the first two verses, God speaks comforting words to be delivered to his people in Jerusalem. The audience he addresses is unidentified, although he apparently speaks to a number of people, since the instruction to "comfort" is a double, plural command ("you [plural] comfort, you [plural] comfort my people!"). The double imperative provides emphasis to the message and is characteristic of Isaiah's style. Some scholars assume that these verses are set in a heavenly council in which God addresses his heralds. The heralds are God's messengers to the people on earth and could include the prophets, who, like Isaiah, deliver God's words (see the discussion on vs. 3-5 following this section).

Compare God's actions with those of the people making their idols. They choose wood for the core that does not rot and design the idol so it will not easily topple over. Finally, they cover the idol with fine gold and silver and perhaps inlay it with jewels. This is their god, a god they built with their own hands, but which can do nothing for them.

On the other hand, the true and living God can speak to his messengers and provide a way in which his followers and the inhabitants of Jerusalem (who probably represent the members of his Church) can be forgiven of their sins and enjoy the finest blessings, powers, and glory that he possesses. (See Young, *The Book of Isaiah*, 3:21.)

Isaiah continues his discourse by describing the power God has to transform mountains and valleys into new formations. He also reviews the process of the creation of this earth:

³A voice rings out:
 "Clear in the desert
 A road for the LORD!
 Level in the wilderness
 A highway for our God!
⁴Let every valley be raised,
 Every hill and mount made low.
 Let the rugged ground become
  level
 And the ridges become a plain.
⁵The Presence of the LORD shall
  appear,
 And all flesh, as one, shall
  behold—
 For the mouth of the LORD has
  spoken." (NJV)

²¹Do you not know?
 Have you not heard?
 Have you not been told
 From the very first!
 Have you not discerned
 How the earth was founded?
 (NJV)

Verses 3-5 seem to deal with the role of John the Baptist in preparing the way for Jesus Christ; all four New Testament evangelists clearly indicate that the "voice of him that crieth in the wilderness (KJV)" is indeed John the Baptist. (Matt. 3:3; Mark 1:3; Luke 3:4; John 1:23.) Scriptures from the New World, both ancient and modern, also support this assertion. (See 1 Ne. 10:21; 11:27; 2 Ne. 31:4-18; D&C 13:65.)

However, John the Baptist was an "Elias" or forerunner of Christ in this dispensation as well. (See MD, pp. 221-22; Matt. 11:10.) The fact that John's mission could extend to this dispensation finds support in Luke's account of John, especially in Joseph Smith's inspired translation. (See JST Luke 3:4-11.)

Only at the second coming of Christ, however, will Jerusalem receive forgiveness and peace. John's mission was only the beginning of the fulfillment of Isaiah's prophecy. The prophecy will only be fully realized when the Lord returns to initiate his millennial reign.

Besides John the Baptist, any other "Elias" or forerunner of the Millennium is a messenger preparing the world for Christ. (See Mal. 3:1.) For example, Joseph Fielding Smith identified the Prophet Joseph Smith as a "messenger who was to come and prepare the way" before Christ as prophesied by Malachi and Isaiah. (DS 1:193-95; see also JS-H 1:36, 40.) Other leaders of this dispensation, such as Orson Hyde, were commissioned to give a voice of warning to the world. (HC 4:376.) Indeed, all ordained representatives of The Church of Jesus Christ of Latter-day Saints are called to prepare the way before Christ. (D&C 39:20.) The whole Church is responsible to make the earth ready for the time when Christ will transform the mountains and valleys. (D&C 109:74; compare Isaiah 40:4.) Finally, the "voice of one crying in the wilderness" may be the voice of any of the Lord's servants, but the voice is initially the Lord's own, carried by the Spirit to mortals here on earth and through them to the whole world. (See D&C 88:66.)

Verse 4, in which Isaiah speaks of mountains being lowered, valleys exalted, crooked paths straightened, and rough places leveled, appears to have a variety of possible interpretations. At least two literal fulfillments seem possible: (1) the events in America concurrent with Christ's death, and (2) events throughout the entire world prior to his second coming. (See 3 Ne. 8:13, 17-18; D&C 49:23, 133:21-22; compare an earlier similar occurrence during Enoch's ministry, Moses 7:13.) Figuratively, the transformation of the land may symbolize the spiritual vice and coarseness of people, which must be eliminated in order for them to receive Christ and his gospel.

The "glory of the Lord" (KJV) at his "presence" (NJV) is promised in verse 5 to all people of the earth. Elder Orson Pratt described this appearance as a time when Christ "will appear as a being whose splendor and glory will cause the sun to hide his face with shame." He also explained that those who appear with Christ will be clothed in glory, that the "brightness of their countenance will shine forth with all that refulgence and fulness of splendour that shall surround the Son of Man when he appears." (JD 8:50-52; see also D&C 133:49; TG "Jesus Christ, Glory of.")

As seen from the evaluation of verses 3-5, the message the Lord's herald delivers to the world is profound and universal. It is no wonder, then, that as Charles Jennens prepared the libretto for Handels *Messiah*, he made extensive uses of Isaiah 40:1-5. (*Messiah*, part 1, sections 2, 3, 4.) Other portions of the fortieth chapter were used in the *Messiah* and in Brahm's *Requiem*.

Isaiah continues his prophetic discourse by promising another voice that shall cry out. This herald compares the transitory nature of man with the eternity of God's word. In the companion parallel passage, Isaiah borrows the same vocabulary and highlights the power of God over the rulers of this earth:

⁶A voice rings out: "Proclaim!"
Another asks, "What shall I proclaim?"
"All flesh is grass,
All its goodness like flowers of the field:
⁷Grass withers, flowers fade
When the breath of the LORD blows on them.
Indeed, man is but grass:
⁸Grass withers, flowers fade—
But the word of our God endures forever!" (NJV)

²²It is He who is enthroned above the vault of the earth,
So that its inhabitants seem as grasshoppers;
Who spread out the skies like gauze
Stretched them out like a tent to dwell in.
²³He brings potentates to naught,
Makes rulers of the earth as nothing.
²⁴Hardly are they planted,
Hardly are they sown,
Hardly has their stem
Taken root in earth,
When He blows upon them and they dry up,
And the storm bears them off like straw.
²⁵To whom, then, can you liken Me,
To whom can I be compared?
—says the Holy One. (NJV)

Strong parallels are apparent between these two passages. In the first section (vs. 6-8), people are compared to grass that the breath of the Lord blows upon until it withers; in the second (vs. 22-25), the earth's inhabitants are like grasshoppers and their rulers like plants that the Lord blows upon until they dry up and are carried off. Isaiah employs a variety of parallelisms in these few verses, especially *emblematic* (people are like grass or grasshoppers, the Lord's power is like the wind, etc.), *antithetic* (men and their rulers are compared to God), *synthetic* (a number of questions and situations keep the reader's attention as he looks for answers and explanations), *climactic* (both sections conclude with powerful pronouncements about God's nature), and *synonymous* (the two passages each present the same basic message).

Isaiah's comparisons are found in later scriptural passages—

342

Peter used them in the New Testament (1 Pet. 1:25) and Joseph Smith included them in a revealed proclamation to the rulers of all nations. (See D&C 124:3, 5-8, especially v. 7.)

In the next verses, Isaiah contrasts the power and might of God the judge with the love and concern of God the shepherd:

⁹Ascend a lofty mountain,
O herald of joy in Zion;
Raise your voice with power,
O herald of joy to Jerusalem—
Raise it, have no fear;
Announce to the cities of Judah:
Behold your God!
¹⁰Behold, the Lord GOD comes in
  might,
And his arm wins triumph for
  Him;
See, His reward is with Him.
His recompense before Him.
¹¹Like a shepherd He pastures His
  flock:
He gathers the lambs in His arms
And carries them in His bosom;
Gently He drives the mother
  sheep.
¹²Who measured the waters with
  the hollow of his hand,
And gauged the skies with a span,
And meted earth's dust with a
  measure,
And weighed the mountains with
  a scale
And the hills with a balance?
(NJV)

²⁶Lift high your eyes and see:
Who created these?
He who sends out their host by
  count,
Who calls them each by name:
Because of His great might and
  vast power,
Not one fails to appear. (NJV)

The companion passage in verse 26, though short, continues many parallelisms from verses 9-12: "Ascend, raise, raise" (v. 9) is parallel with "lift high"; might of the Lord's arm (v. 10) is equivalent to the power of creation; a shepherd with his flock (v. 11) is like a being who can name each of his host; and an omnipotent being who can measure the universe (v. 12) is a mighty God to whom all come, at his call, for a final judgment. (See 2 Ne. 9:15-16; Alma 5:38; MD, pp. 401-4.)

The extensive creations of the Lord highlighted in verses 12 and 26 become a major theme of Isaiah in his later writings. Of the slightly more than fifty occurrences of the word *bara* (create) in the Old Testament, nearly half are in Isaiah 40-56; two are in chapter 40 alone (vs. 26, 28). *Bara* is a theological word that "does not in itself carry the meaning of creation out of nothing, but it is never used except with God as the subject" or the being who directs the creation. (North, *The Second Isaiah*, p. 88.) Isaiah's emphasis upon the creation probably reaches a peak in chapter 65, in which he speaks of the Lord creating a new heaven and a new earth. Not only does Isaiah apparently want to humble his listeners and help them fear and obey God, but he also probably wants us to appreciate what God has created and anticipate that he will yet create a new earth, first on a terrestrial level and finally on a celestial level. (See Moses 1:8-10, 35-37; D&C 45:1; 88; 93:10.)

Joseph Smith compares the divine powers and creative abilities with their value in developing man's faith as follows:

> And it is not less necessary that men should have the idea of the existence of the attribute power in the Deity; for unless God had power over all things, and was able by his power to control all things, and thereby deliver . . . [those] who put their trust in God . . . [then] men feel as though . . . he has power to save all who come to him to the very uttermost. . . . seeing he is God over all, from everlasting to everlasting, the Creator and upholder of all things, no such fear can exist in the minds of those who put their trust in him, so that in this respect their faith can be without wavering. (LOF 4:12; 3:19.)

The two parallel Isaianic sections that describe God's creations (vs. 9-12 and 26) cause man to realize he cannot match God's might. These sections also ask questions that are left unanswered: "Who can measure the earth and the skies?" (v. 12), and "Who has created the earth's inhabitants?" (v. 26). More unanswered questions about man's inability to match God's understanding comprise the next two parallel passages in which Isaiah portrays the omniscience of God:

13Who has plumbed the mind of the Lord,
What man could tell Him His plan?
14Whom did he consult, and who taught Him,
Guided Him in the way of right?
Who guided Him in knowledge
And showed Him the path of wisdom? (NJV)

27Why do you say, O Jacob,
Why declare, O Israel,
"My way is hid from the Lord,
My cause is ignored by my God"?
(NJV)

Joseph Smith records a similar comparison of man's knowledge in relation to God's wisdom: "Marvelous [are] his ways; the extent of his doings none can find out." (D&C 76:2; see Alma 26:35; Mosiah 4:9.)

Joseph Smith not only expounds upon the greatness of God's wisdom, but also promises that there is not anyone "who can stay his hand." (D&C 76:3.) Isaiah compares God's unfathomable wisdom and his divine glory with the frailty of mortals in the last set of parallel passages:

¹⁵The nations are but a drop in a bucket,
Reckoned as dust on a balance;
The very coastlands He lifts like motes.
¹⁶Lebanon is not fuel enough,
Nor its beasts enough for sacrifice.
¹⁷All nations are as naught in His sight;
He accounts them as less than nothing. (NJV)

²⁸Do you not know?
Have you not heard?
The LORD is God from of old,
Creator of the earth from end to end,
He never grows faint or weary,
His wisdom cannot be fathomed. (NJV)

In verse 15, Isaiah suggests first that the nations of this earth "are but a drop in a bucket" compared to God's dominion. Secondly, they are powerless compared to him. Verse 16 contains a few awkward phrases as it stresses that the mighty forests of Lebanon cannot nearly provide the power available to God, and its livestock cannot satisfy God's expectations for sacrifice. The pagan worshippers in Lebanon believed that as they performed burnt offerings, the smoke from the wood and offerings traveled up into the heavens, where their gods could ingest it and receive energy and health. Of course, such a source of power is not needed by the true and living God, and besides, no act of sacrifice on our part can begin to compensate him for what he has provided us. Indeed, as verse 17 says, all the nations of the earth (even those with great wealth and armies) are insignificant to him.

Much more important to God than nations, forests, and flocks are his children. Since his chosen people, Israel, fear that the Lord is unaware of them (v. 27), Isaiah stresses in verse 28 that God is the same forever, that he is their creator, and that he will never weaken in fulfilling his task to bring to pass their immortality and eternal life. (Moses 1:39.) With fine insight, Isaiah identifies Israel's expressed doubt of God's salvation as a lack of faith in God's power. To say that God will not do what he says is equivalent to saying that he cannot do it. Isaiah's first answer to this doubt is an affirmation of God's creative power. (McKenzie, *Second Isaiah*, p. 25.)

Having emphasized the everlasting dominion and strength of God in the last set of parallel passages (vs. 15-17, 28), Isaiah could conclude his message, having edified us and humbled us through his discourse on God's supreme power and glory. However, Isaiah chooses to build further upon his concept of God's glory. He suggests that its greatest value is not to serve as a measurement of God's greatness, but to be shared with his children:

[29]He gives strength to the weary, Fresh vigor to the spent.	A. Divine strength to the weary
[30]Youths may grow faint and weary, And young men stumble and fall;	B. Youths may weaken
[31]But they who trust in the LORD shall renew their strength	C. Those who trust in the Lord shall renew their strength
As eagles grow new plumes:	B'. As eagles grow new feathers
They shall run and not grow weary, They shall march and not grow faint. (NJV)	A'. People will find strength

A chiastic pattern is outlined in the right column. The two primary words in this section are antithetic to each other, "weary" and "strength." The key word is "trust." Combined in one statement, these three words declare that "weary" people who "trust" in the Lord will receive new strength."

These three terms can be evaluated through a variety of possible relationships. One scholar describes them as follows:

> What the prophet means is that Yahweh communicates some of the unfailing strength of his eternity to those who believe in him. As Yahweh always acts with full vigor, so those who trust in him find their vigor renewed to perpetual fullness. (McKenzie, *Second Isaiah*, p. 25.)

McKenzie also suggests that the sprouting of wings probably symbolizes restored strength to the feeble, for when "a person who is greatly weakened suddenly begins to run, it is as if he sprouts wings." (Ibid., p. 22.)

Another scholar compares Isaiah's imagery of an eagle growing new feathers as follows:

> They [the weary people] shall put forth fresh feathers like the moulting eagle. It has been a common and popular opinion that the eagle lives and

retains his rigour to a great age; and that beyond the common lot of other birds, he moults in his old age, and renews his feathers, and with them his youth. (*Clarke's Commentary* 14:162.)

The concept of divine strength shared with mortals is confirmed by modern revelation. The Lord promised Oliver Cowdery in the early days of this dispensation that he would give unto him "strength such as is not known among men." (D&C 24:12.) On the other hand, David Whitmer was rebuked because he did not rely upon the Lord for strength as he should. (D&C 30:1-2.) The Lord's promise of renewed bodies is given to those who magnify their priesthood callings. (D&C 84:33.)

Isaiah's metaphoric use of eagles' wings is also echoed in modern scripture where the Lord promises Lyman Wight that if he is faithful the Lord will "bear him up as on eagles' wings; and he shall beget glory and honor to himself and unto my name." (D&C 124:18.) In the same revelation, the Lord promises William Law that as he serves the Lord, he will receive great powers and blessings including the promise that "he shall mount up in the imagination of his thoughts as upon eagles' wings." (D&C 124:99.) Other phraseology from Isaiah's promise is found in the Doctrine and Covenants. For example, those who keep the Word of Wisdom are promised that they shall "run and not be weary, and shall walk and not faint." (D&C 89:20; compare Isa. 40:31, KJV.)

An apostle of this dispensation, Orson Pratt, expanded the promises of Isaiah and explained that those who renew their strength and "mount up with wings as eagles" (KJV) will be "renewed with the light of truth, and be enabled to move from place to place at accelerated velocity, even with the speed of light." (JD 3:104.)

Since God promises to share his strength (or power, glory, and dominion) with those who trust in him, Isaiah's promise compares with President Lorenzo Snow's statement: "As man now is, God once was. As now God is, so man may be." (*Improvement Era*, June 1919, p. 660.) Isaiah stresses what God now is in most of chapter 40, but concludes with a promise of what man may be as he shares God's strength.

In summary, in a new vision Isaiah receives and records God's directives for heralds to proclaim special messages to the people (vs. 1-11), and then testifies concerning God's great knowledge and powers (vs. 12-28). Isaiah does not record the means by which God has received his special qualities (vs. 14, 28), but he does promise that those who trust in the Lord will be able to receive strength and blessings from him (vs. 29-31). In short, those who follow the way of the Lord Jesus Christ in the fulfillment of God's plan will be able to share our Heavenly Father's glory and the greatest gift, eternal life. (See D&C 133:57-62.)

SCRIPTURAL NOTES AND COMMENTARY

Isa. 40:2: Why does Jerusalem have to pay "double" for her sins?

First, it was the rule under the Mosaic law that "for all manner of trespass" a man found guilty by the judges should pay double. (Ex. 22:9.) Because of the Israelites' accountability as the chosen people, the Lord required more of Judea's inhabitants when they sinned than from other nations.

As a corollary, the double punishment might refer to the physical and spiritual suffering that God's children experience after they sin. Although anyone may experience physical consequences when he transgresses laws of God, those who know that the law is one of God's commandments, and still sin against the law, receive spiritual consequences as well.

In addition, the double punishment might be a prophecy of the double scattering that the Jews experienced first at the hand of the Babylonians in the sixth century B.C. and then through the Romans in the first century A.D. Indeed, their punishment may continue into the twentieth century and the period immediately prior to the Millennium, for Elder Orson Hyde recorded in his vision of the Jews that the Lord instructed him to tell the Jews:

> The lion is come up from his thicket, and the destroyer of the Gentiles is on his way—he is gone forth from his place to make thy land [Judah] desolate, and thy cities shall be laid waste, without an inhabitant. Speak ye comfortably to Jerusalem, and cry unto her, that her warfare is accomplished—that her iniquity is pardoned, for she hath received of the Lord's hand doubly for all her sins [Isa. 40:2]. (HC 4:376.)

The main idea of verse 2 is to tell Jerusalem that she has proved herself faithful to the Lord through the trials and punishments she has experienced. She has humbled herself and come to the Lord and has more than satisfied the demands of justice. The Lord has therefore forgiven her of her trespasses so that she is ready for the Restoration and other events promised in chapter 40 and the rest of Isaiah.

TRUST IN THE LORD AND HIS SERVANT
ISAIAH 41-42

In chapters 41-42, Isaiah builds further upon the concepts developed in chapter 40; in chapter 40 Isaiah extolls the Lord's knowledge and strength and promises that those who trust in the Lord can share his strength. Chapters 41-42 present the Lord's invitation to Israel to be his servant and share his glory, but also warn Israel she will be destroyed if she rejects her opportunity.

Without a firm historical context to anchor them in any one setting, these chapters are easily applicable to any generation of God's children; indeed, Isaiah addresses his words to all nations upon the isles by the seas (which includes all land masses), indicating that people everywhere should listen to the Lord's message. At times, however, he speaks directly to Israel and challenges her to heed her special responsibility as God's servant to the world.

In order to reinforce his message, Isaiah repeats key ideas in an extensive example of synonymous parallelism (41:1-20 and 41:21-42:22). In the two parallel halves of the pronouncement, Isaiah reminds Israel of the Lord's continual efforts in her behalf and foretells how God's servant will represent him to Israel. After his "double discourse," Isaiah concludes with more insights concerning the role of the Lord's servant and a sober warning of bondage and divine wrath that will come upon those who disregard the Lord's message (42:23-25).

Isaiah begins both pronouncements by setting a scene in a courtroom. The Lord begins speaking and addresses his remarks to the nations of the earth, particularly those who worship pagan gods;

Discourse 1, Part A

41 "Be silent before me, you islands!
Let the nations renew their strength!
Let them come forward and speak;
let us meet together at the place of judgment. (NIV)

Discourse 2, Part A

21"Present your case," says the LORD.
"Set forth your arguments," says Jacob's King.
22"Bring in your idols to tell us what is going to happen.
Tell us what the former things were,
so that we may consider them and know their final outcome.
23Or declare to us the things to come,
tell us what the future holds,
so we may know that you are gods.
Do something, whether good or bad,
so that we will be dismayed and filled with fear.
24But you are less than nothing and your works are utterly worthless;
he who chooses you is detestable. (NIV)

After concluding chapter 40 with the promise that those who trust in the Lord will "renew their strength" (v. 31), Isaiah begins chapter 41 by inviting the nations to "renew their strength" if they can. Like Elijah with the priests of Baal (1 Kgs. 18), he challenges the pagans to bring forth any signs of power like those the Lord had demonstrated earlier; still their idols remain silent and powerless. (Isa. 40.) Any comparison quickly demonstrates the Lord's omnipotence in contrast to the idols' impotence.

The Lord next highlights the ministry of a prophesied leader who is divinely directed. An important sign of the Lord's power is the fact that no one else has envisioned this messenger and what he will do:

Discourse 1, Part B

2"Who has stirred up one from the east,
calling him in righteousness to his service?
He hands nations over to him and subdues kings before him.

Discourse 2, Part B

25"I have stirred up one from the north, and he comes—
one from the rising sun who calls on my name.
He treads on rulers as if they were mortar,

He turns them to dust with his
sword,
to windblown chaff with his
bow.
³He pursues them and moves on
unscathed,
by a path his feet have not
traveled before.
⁴Who has done this and carried it
through,
calling forth the generations
from the beginning?
I, the LORD—with the first of them
and with the last—I am he."
⁵The islands have seen it and fear;
the ends of the earth tremble.
⁶They approach and come forward;
each helps the other
and says to his brother, "Be
strong!"
⁷The craftsman encourages the
goldsmith,
and he who smooths with the
hammer
spurs on him who strikes the
anvil.
He says of the welding, "It is
good."
He nails down the idol so it will
not topple. (NIV)

as if he were a potter treading
the clay.
²⁶Who told of this from the
beginning, so we could
know,
or beforehand, so we could say,
'He was right'?
No one told of this, no one foretold
it,
no one heard any words from
you.
²⁷I was the first to tell Zion, 'Look,
here they are!'
I gave to Jerusalem a
messenger of good tidings.
²⁸I look but there is no one—
no one among them to give
counsel,
no one to give answer when I
ask them.
²⁹See, they are all false!
Their deeds amount to
nothing;
their images are but wind and
confusion." (NIV)

Compare the many striking parallels between the two chapter segments in these few verses:

A. An important person comes from the east (or rising sun)

B. He has power over rulers and kings

C. He turns them into dry powder or molds them as wet clay

D. His feet pursues them and treads them under

E. His coming is foretold

F. The Lord is the one who has announced it

G. People are powerless though they try to obtain counsel from each other

H. The people try to secure their idols, but they cannot ward off the ensuing wind and confusion

The powerful person who creates this havoc (vs. 2, 25) is un-named, though scholars have speculated on a number of persons who could fulfill this prophecy, from Abraham to the future Messiah. If individuals near Isaiah's time are considered, various Assyrian kings or ancient emperors, especially Cyrus, are likely candidates. But if this leader embodies as much spiritual power as he does political force, Christ is the most likely candidate—he came out of the eastern deserts after his forty-day fast to begin his mortal ministry. (Matt. 3:13–4:11.) Apparently, he will come again from the east at his political or second coming. (Isa. 63.) However, it is possible that the promised individual still belongs to the future and might be the evil king of the world (Gog of Magog) or the forces led by Michael who will oppose him. (Dan. 11:44–12:1.)

In verses 8 of chapter 41 and 1 of chapter 42, Isaiah continues his "double pronouncement" by introducing yet another entity who is identified as a servant of the Lord. In the first of these parallel sections, this servant is represented by Israel collectively, and in the corollary verses is personified by an individual messianic figure:

Discourse I, Part C

8"But you, O Israel, my servant,
    Jacob, whom I have chosen,
    you descendants of Abraham
    my friend,
9I took you from the ends of the
    earth,
    from its farthest corners I
    called you.
I said, 'You are my servant';
    I have chosen you and have not
    rejected you.
10So do not fear, for I am with you;
    do not be dismayed, for I am
    your God.
I will strengthen you and help
    you;
    I will uphold you with my
    righteous right hand."
    (NIV)

Discourse 2, Part C

42 "Here is my servant, whom
    I uphold,
    my chosen one in whom I
    delight;
I will put my Spirit on him
    and he will bring justice to the
    nations.
2He will not shout or cry out,
    or raise his voice in the streets.
A bruised reed he will not break,
    and a smoldering wick he will
    not snuff out.
3In faithfulness he will bring forth
    justice;
4   he will not falter or be
    discouraged
till he establishes justice on earth.
    In his law the islands will put
    their hope."
5This is what God the LORD says—
he who created the heavens and
    stretched them out,
    who spread out the earth and all

that comes out of it,
who gives breath to its people,
and life to those who walk on it:
6"I, the LORD, have called you in
righteousness;
I will take hold of your hand.
I will keep you and will make you
to be a covenant for the
people
and a light for the Gentiles,
7to open eyes that are blind,
to free captives from prison
and to release from the dungeon
those who sit in darkness.
8"I am the LORD; that is my name!
I will not give my glory to
another
or my praise to idols.
9See, the former things have taken
place,
and new things I declare;
before they spring into being I
announce them to you."
(NIV)

These verses contain some of Isaiah's most beautiful poetry. For example, verse 10 is paraphrased in a favorite Latter-day Saint hymn, "How Firm a Foundation": "Fear not, I am with thee, O be not dismayed, For I am thy God and will still give thee aid; I'll strengthen thee, help thee, and cause thee to stand, upheld by my righteous, . . . omnipotent hand." (*Hymns*, no. 66.)

The parallel segment to verse 10 begins chapter 42 and is identified as a hymn, psalm, or servant song of Isaiah. It expands the parallel concepts found in chapter 41 (part C, vs. 8-10). The last two verses echo the preceding B segments, both discourses (41:2-7, 25-29), promising that the Lord will bring forth some prophesied events.

Looking back, then, to the previous sets of verses in which a mysterious individual is promised to come from the east (v. 2) or the northeast (v. 25), it seems possible that the servant is not an individual, but the entire house of Israel (v. 8), which will be gathered from the corners of the earth (v. 9). Indeed, this identification can easily apply to the Jews, who have thus far had two major gatherings to their homeland, the first from the east after the Babylonian captivity (538-500 B.C.) and the second from the north (Europe) and the east (Asia) as they have returned to Palestine in the past century.

In short, the person (or people) promised to come from the east (segment B) may be the servant described in the succeeding set of verses (segment C). Although the precise identity of the person or servant has not been absolutely established, the house of Israel as a people and Jesus Christ himself seem to be the most likely possibilities.

For now, to know the exact identity of the servant is not as important as to understand his character. Reread the servant song in chapter 42 above and note the servant's qualities: spirituality and fairness (v. 2), humility and faithfulness (v. 3), perseverance and justice (v. 4), righteousness and example (v. 6), and power and light (v. 7). Until the servant can be more precisely identified, readers will find it much more valuable to emulate his characteristics than to discover his name. In fact, the servant may not represent a single individual or tribe, but may typify all those who serve the Lord. As Isaiah explains more about servants of the Lord in later chapters and servant songs, identify the traits of these servants and ponder how they can become a productive part of your own personality. In this way, the servant songs and message of Isaiah will find the greatest value and application in your own life.

Turning back to chapters 41 and 42, we see that Isaiah continues his parallel accounts by describing the Lord's protection of Israel and her song of joy to the Lord:

Discourse 1, Part D

41:11"All who rage against you
will surely be ashamed and
disgraced;
those who oppose you
will be as nothing and
perish.
12Though you search for your
enemies,
you will not find them.
Those who wage war against
you
will be as nothing at all.
13For I am the LORD, your God,
who takes hold of your right
hand

Discourse 2, Part D

42:10Sing to the LORD a new song,
his praise from the ends of
the earth,
you who go down to the sea,
and all that is in it,
you islands, and all who live
in them.
11Let the desert and its towns
raise their voices;
let the settlements where
Kedar lives rejoice.
Let the people of Sela sing for
joy;
let them shout from the
mountaintops.

and says to you, Do not fear;
I will help you.
¹⁴Do not be afraid, O worm
Jacob,
O little Israel,
for I myself will help you,"
declares the LORD,
your Redeemer, the Holy
One of Israel.
¹⁵"See, I will make you into a
threshing sledge,
new and sharp, with many
teeth.
You will thresh the mountains
and crush them,
and reduce the hills to chaff.
¹⁶You will winnow them, the
wind will pick them up,
and a gale will blow them
away.
But you will rejoice in the LORD
and glory in the Holy One of
Israel. (NIV)

¹²Let them give glory to the
LORD
and proclaim his praise in
the islands.
¹³The LORD will march out like a
mighty man,
like a warrior he will stir up
his zeal;
with a shout he will raise the
battle cry
and will triumph over his
enemies. (NIV)

Isaiah creates beautiful poetry and powerful imagery in these verses. Humble Israel (or "worm Jacob," 41:14) is counseled not to fear, for the Lord will make her into a threshing machine that will crush her enemies into dust that the wind will blow away (vs. 14-16). Righteous Israelites are destined also to inhabit the far reaches of the land, from the Mediterranean Sea to the desert boundaries of Kedar (northeast of Jerusalem in Syria) and Sela (southeast of Jerusalem in Edom; see areas D2 and C3 on Map 10). She will give glory to the Lord (41:16; 42:12) as he triumphs over his enemies (41:15; 42:13).

Isaiah's parallel accounts then describe manifestations of the Lord's power upon the geography of the land: mountains and valleys will be transformed, and water and vegetation will fill the desert. In the first account the Lord protects his followers, and in the parallel version he punishes his enemies:

Discourse 1, Part E
^{41:17}"The poor and needy search for
water,
but there is none;
their tongues are parched
with thirst.

Discourse 2, Part E
^{42:14}"For a long time I have kept
silent,
I have been quiet and held
myself back.
But now, like a woman in

355

But I the LORD will answer
   them;
   I, the God of Israel, will not
     forsake them.
¹⁸I will make rivers flow on
   barren heights,
   and springs within the
   valleys.
I will turn the desert into pools
   of water,
   and the parched ground into
   springs.
¹⁹I will put in the desert
   the cedar and the acacia, the
   myrtle and the olive.
I will set pines in the
   wasteland,
   the fir and the cypress
   together,
²⁰so that people may see and
   know,
   may consider and
   understand,
that the hand of the LORD has
   done this,
   that the Holy One of Israel
   has created it. (NIV)

childbirth,
   I cry out, I gasp and pant.
¹⁵I will lay waste the mountains
   and hills
   and dry up all their
   vegetation;
I will turn rivers into islands
   and dry up the pools.
¹⁶I will lead the blind by ways
   they have not known,
   along unfamiliar paths I will
   guide them;
I will turn the darkness into
   light before them
   and make the rough places
   smooth.
These are the things I will do:
   I will not forsake them.
¹⁷But those who trust in idols,
   who say to images, 'You are
   our gods,'
will be turned back in utter
   shame. (NIV)

Probably the most important message in these verses is the Lord's promise that he will assist those who are either physically or spiritually poor, needy, thirsty (41:17), and blind (42:16). A second major point is delivered in the concluding verses in which the Lord gives the purpose for his manifestations of power—people will see the hand of the Lord (41:20) and know the impotence of their idols (42:17).

At the conclusion of Isaiah's parallel accounts, the Lord directs a special message to the listener or reader. Isaiah continues with some earlier terminology as he talks about servants, blindness, Israel, and the Lord's manifestations upon the wicked. However, some of these verses seem full of contradictions that have baffled scholars. One apparent point of inconsistency is the representations of the Lord's servant in very derogatory imagery; he is described as completely blind and deaf. The English text was either so corrupt or confusing that Joseph Smith found it necessary to give an inspired translation of most of these concluding verses of Isaiah 42. His version, with the major changes italicized, is reproduced side-by-side with the New International Version:

42:18"Hear, you deaf;
  look, you blind, and see!
19Who is blind but my servant,
  and deaf like the messenger I send?
Who is blind like the one committed to me,
  blind like the servant of the LORD?
20You have seen many things,
  but have paid no attention;
  your ears are open, but you hear nothing."
21It pleased the LORD
  for the sake of his righteousness
  to make his law great and glorious.
22But this is a people plundered and looted,
  all of them trapped in pits or hidden away in prisons.
They have become plunder,
  with no one to rescue them;
they have been made loot,
  with no one to say, "Send them back."

23Which of you will listen to this
  or pay close attention in time to come?
24Who handed Jacob over to become loot,
  and Israel to the plunderers?
Was it not the LORD
  against whom we have sinned?
For they would not follow his ways;

18Hear, ye deaf; and look, ye blind, that ye may see.
19For I will send my servant unto you who are blind; yea, a messenger to open the eyes of the blind, and unstop the ears of the deaf;
20And they shall be made perfect notwithstanding their blindness, if they will hearken unto the messenger, the LORD's servant.
21Thou art a people, seeing many things, but thou observest not; opening the ears to hear, but thou hearest not.
22The Lord is not well pleased with such a people, but for his righteousness sake he will magnify the law and make it honorable.
23Thou art a people robbed and spoiled; thine enemies, all of them, have snared thee in holes, and they have hid thee in prison houses; they have taken thee for a prey, and none delivereth; for a spoil, and none saith, Restore.
24Who among them will give ear unto thee, or hearken and hear thee for the time to come? and who gave Jacob for a spoil, and Israel to the robbers? did not the Lord, he against whom they have sinned?
25For they would not walk in his ways, neither were they obedient unto his law; therefore he hath poured upon them the fury of his anger, and the strength of battle; and they have set them on fire round about, yet they know not, and it burned them, yet they laid it not to heart. (JST)

357

they did not obey his law.
²⁵So he poured out on them his
    burning anger,
the violence of war.
It enveloped them in flames,
    yet they did not
    understand;
    it consumed them, but they
    did not take it to heart.
    (NIV)

The major difference between the two translations is that the Joseph Smith Translation clarifies the ambiguous passages to make clear that the blindness lies with the people, not the servant. Furthermore, the Joseph Smith Translation gives the promise that the people can become perfect in spite of their blindness if they heed the Lord's servant. It also explains that Israel's enemies will be allowed to plunder her as punishment for her sins. In addition, by carefully studying the last two verses of the Joseph Smith Translation and matching the different referents to their various pronouns (thee/Israel; they, them/Israel's enemies or the Gentiles), one can see that the Gentiles will ignore the words of Israel until their sins merit divine wrath upon them.

The Joseph Smith Translation is a necessary help in understanding these important verses. With Joseph Smith's inspired revisions, Isaiah's message to Israel becomes much clearer. The relationship between God's servant (a prophet, a chosen people, or the Lord himself) and God's children is thereby more easily understood. The reader can also better appreciate why and how the Lord will bless or punish people according to their diligence in following his counsel given through his servants. Isaiah's message is valuable today, since the Lord has called many servants to deliver God's word to us in the last dispensation. The identity and role of some of these servants is discussed in the following section.

THE SERVANT SONGS OF ISAIAH

The first four verses of Isaiah 42 comprise one of the four "major songs" or major poetic passages in which Isaiah describes a servant of the Lord. (The other three are Isa. 49:1-6; 50:4-9; 52:13–53:12.) This servant is not named, so readers and scholars often disagree about the servant's identity. Generally, the Jewish scholars believe the servant is

358

either the prophet Isaiah or a representation of the people of Israel in their chosen rule as the Lord's servants to the world. Christian scholars usually believe Jesus Christ is the servant prophesied by Isaiah. Latter-day Saint readers often recognize that the covenant members of the restored gospel serve as the Lord's servants. They as a people, and the prophet of the restoration, Joseph Smith, may be identified as Isaiah's promised servant.

In order to understand how any of these identities are possible, twelve major characteristics of the servant will be listed as described by Isaiah:

1. The Lord calls the servant, attests to his authority, and foretells his coming. (See Isa. 42:1, 8-9; 42:6; compare 49:1, 3; 50:4, 10.)
2. God foreordains the servant, preserving him to come forth at a specific time and clothing him with the Spirit of God. (See Isa. 42:6; 42:1; compare 49:1, 2, 5; see also Jer. 1:5.)
3. The servant is *beloved* of God. (See Isa. 42:1.)
4. The servant is taught from on high; though uneducated after the manner of the world, he is an articulate spokesman for truth. (See JST Isa. 50:4-5, 7; 49:2).
5. The servant is refined and sanctified through suffering and adversity. Though hated and persecuted by his own people, he will prevail over all his enemies, for the result of his work will be everlasting. (See Isa. 50:5-6; 49:2, 7; 42:4, 6; compare 49:4-5; 50:7-9, 11.)
6. The servant does not use violence or coercion, but preaches peace through gentle persuasion. (See Isa. 42:2-3; 50:6.)
7. The servant is raised up at a time when Israel is scattered. He is sent to the house of Israel and leads those in spiritual darkness to light. (See Isa. 49:5; 42:6-7; 49:8; 50:10; 49:6.)
8. The servant's mission extends to the entire world. (See Isa. 42:1, 4; 49:6; 50:10-11.)
9. The servant establishes a covenant with the chosen people. (See Isa. 42:6; 49:8.)
10. The servant prompts kings and princes to righteousness through the great power given him by the Lord. (See Isa. 49:7.)
11. The servant paves the way for those in the spirit prison to hear the true gospel and be freed. (See Isa. 49:9; 42:7.)
12. The servant comes prior to the Millennium and is instrumental in the final redemption of Zion. His mission is significant, for it prepares the way for the renewal of Jerusalem and the return of Zion. (See Isa. 49:8; 9-13.)

As noted in the many references listed above, strong scriptural support can be gathered for the five possible identities of Isaiah's prophesied servant: ancient Israel, restored Israel, Isaiah, Jesus Christ, and Joseph Smith. Rather than categorically stating that Isaiah's servant songs apply only to one servant, we might be wise in recognizing that the characteristics of God's servant are best exemplified in Christ and are also demonstrated through the lives of all of God's righteous children. In short, the precise identity of the servant is not as important as studying his characteristics and seeking to develop them in our own lives.

THE LORD OF THIS EARTH
ISAIAH 43

Isaiah 43 builds upon the themes of the previous chapter and follows a pattern by opening with promise and concluding with a message of judgment. The contrast between the two chapters is sharp and clear, for Isaiah's reproach of Israel shifts abruptly to a prophecy of grace, ransom, and restoration by the Lord. (See Isa. 43, footnote 1a.) Likewise, Isaiah contrasts the glorious redemption Israel will someday enjoy (vs. 1-21) with the people's present dismal condition (vs. 22-28).

As in his earlier writings, Isaiah uses contrast and a full range of poetic techniques to express his ideas, including parallelism, repetition, word play, assonance, symbolism, and irony.

Isaiah 43 easily divides into four segments containing from 6-8 verses each:

Theme	Mood
A. Israel's future gathering (vs. 1-7)	Positive
B. A trial scene of God before Israel and the other nations (8-13)	Positive
A'. Israel's future blessings (14-21)	Positive
B'. A trial scene between God and Israel; present Israel merits condemnation (22-28)	Negative

The chapter points to an ideal relationship to come when Israel finally recognizes the Lord as the sole God of this earth; however, it also forbodes captivity and bondage as long as the people forget the Lord.

The historical context of the chapter is uncertain, although many scholars place it during the Babylonian captivity. Still, other periods of Jewish dispersion and oppression provide a likely context for Isaiah's message of a promised ransom, restoration, and divine blessing. Indeed, the context of the chapter may lie outside the political-historical realm and in the overall spiritual framework of people held captive by their own sins and desirous of a message of hope and deliverance.

Most of the chapter is written in the first person singular, with the Lord himself as the speaker, who promises the deliverance of Israel and reminds her of his power manifested in the creation and the exodus from Egypt. Surely if the Lord can create the earth, he can provide for man; if he can free Israel from Egypt, he can also free man from sin. The Lord stresses in this chapter that there is no other savior on this earth and that he alone is responsible for its inhabitants.

He uses a number of titles to emphasize his sovereign power. Any recipient of these words of the Lord through Isaiah would surely understand that Yahweh (Jehovah) is the Lord of this earth!

The Lord Promises the Gathering of Israel (vs. 1-7)

The promise of release from exile is one of Isaiah's favorite themes; it is amplified in these verses. After Israel is driven to the four corners of the earth, she will be gathered from all directions. Isaiah likens the future gathering to the earlier exodus from Egypt by associating it with similar signs and wonders:

43 But now thus says the LORD,
  he who created you,
    O Jacob,
he who formed you, O Israel:
"Fear not, for I have redeemed
    you;
I have called you by name, you
    are mine.
²When you pass through the waters
    I will be with you;
and through the rivers, they
    shall not overwhelm you;
when you walk through fire you
    shall not be burned,
    and the flame shall not consume
    you.
³For I am the LORD your God,
  the Holy One of Israel, your
    Savior.
I give Egypt as your ransom,
  Ethiopia and Seba in exchange
    for you.

⁴Because you are precious in my
    eyes,
  and honored, and I love you,
I give men in return for you,
  peoples in exchange for your
    life.
⁵Fear not, for I am with you;
  and I will bring your offspring
    from the east,
  and from the west I will gather
    you;
⁶I will say to the north, Give up,
  and to the south, Do not
    withhold;
bring my sons from afar
  and my daughters from the end
    of the earth,
⁷every one who is called by my
    name,
  whom I created for my glory,
  whom I formed and made."
(RSV)

Isaiah begins by reaffirming to exiled Israel that the Lord is the creator, the one who formed them at Sinai. The prophet uses the same words for *create* and *form* as Moses did in his creation account (Gen. 1:1, 26-27), thus emphasizing that Israel gives her survival to God, just as the earth and mankind owe their existence to him.

The Lord's discourse begins in the past tense (v. 1) and then shifts to the future (v. 2ff.), suggesting that the verbs of verse 1 do not refer to a past act. Instead, they promise a redemption yet to come. This is another example of the "prophetic perfect" tense where the fulfillment of a prophecy is so certain that it is spoken of in the perfect or past tense as though it had already happened. (See Isa. 42:9.)

Two names designate the people who will inherit God's blessings, *Jacob* and *Israel*. Isaiah uses this double designation seventeen times in chapters 40-49. Of course, the two names are synonymous because both belonged to the same person. It is the order of the two names that makes the repetition significant, for "Jacob" nearly always precedes "Israel," hinting, perhaps, that a change in Jacob's character prompted the Lord to change his name also. Jacob, the "supplanter," who worried about his relationship with his twin brother, Esau, became Israel, the "prevailer," who worked together with God to overcome wickedness. (See BD "Jacob"; "Israel.") Jacob was also at one time a deceiver and had to become as Israel, who prevailed over selfishness. Thus, Isaiah places *Jacob* before Israel in the chapter as a way of saying that the descendants of Jacob need to rise to the character of Israel; he charges them to be Israelites in deed as well as in lineage.

The name *Israel* has acquired a variety of connotations over the centuries. A brief review of the three major applications of the term *Israelite* will be helpful in understanding its different meanings in Isaiah:

1. *"Blood" Israelite.* Any descendent of the house of Israel (Jacob) now scattered throughout the earth. The most recognizable body of blood Israelites are the Jews.
2. *"Land" Israelite.* Anyone who inhabits the area known as Israel. This area has also been called Canaan, Samaria, Judea, the Holy Land, Palestine, etc. (The modern citizens of this land are identified by modern writers as "Israelis," and not "Israelites.")
3. *"Covenant" Israelite.* Anyone who accepts the God and covenants of Israel. Today this term applies specifically to members of The Church of Jesus Christ of Latter-day Saints.

So, when Isaiah addresses "Israel," he may be including any one of these categories. Usually, though, he is speaking to either blood or covenant Israelites. Given the context of Isaiah 43, it appears that the Lord is addressing covenant Israel, those whom he has called by name as his peculiar people for his own glory (vs. 1-2; see Mosiah 5:6-15; Deut. 14:2; Moses 1:39).

The Lord uses the imagery of his earlier miracles with Israel to promise future protection to the people. The "waters" and "rivers" of verse 2 allude not only to the earlier miracles at the Red Sea and the Jordan River, but, along with the fire, also represent the dangers and judgments Israel will experience. It is also possible that water and fire symbolize the twin covenants of baptism by water and the Spirit. Whether the water and fire are really physical dangers or if they represent military power (see Isa. 33:14) or covenants (Isa. 48:1; JST 55:1-3), the promise is given to righteous Israel that the Lord will accompany them through their tribulation.

Listed in verse 3 are four special names for God: The LORD (*Yahweh*), God (*Elohim*), the Holy One of Israel (*Qedosh-Yisrael*), and the Savior (*Moshiya*). Israel frequently uses the first three titles in his earlier writings, but the last term, *Savior*, first appears in this verse.[1] Many other special names for God besides the four mentioned are found in chapter 43 of Isaiah: "I am He" (v. 10); "I, I am the Lord" (v. 11); "God" (*El*, v. 12); "Redeemer" (v. 14); "your Holy One" (v. 15); "the Creator of Israel" (v. 15); and "your King" (v. 15). While some of the terms are repeated in the chapter and throughout other sections of Isaiah, the last two titles are found only in the fifteenth verse of this chapter. The variety of titles used by Isaiah in this chapter and throughout his writings demonstrates that he had a deep understanding of the Lord's involvement in the salvation of mankind. The wide range of names also suggests that Isaiah himself had a profound, personal relationship with the Lord.

After identifying himself to Israel by different titles, the Lord continues in verse 3 to promise that he will ransom Israel from the countries of Africa to the southwest. Later in this pronouncement, the Lord similarly promises a deliverance from the Babylonian invaders from the northeast (v. 14).

Verses 5 and 6 emphasize that the final gathering will be worldwide. This literal gathering has been promised by modern

---

[1] Isaiah's only earlier use of the term is in 19:20, where it may be messianic, but there the term probably applies to a political figure who will rule Egypt.

prophets, including Joseph Fielding Smith, who quoted those verses and said that "the time was to come when they [the Israelites] would be restored again." (CHMR 4:92.) Such an extensive gathering of Israel has occurred only within the past century. This gathering from the four corners of the earth has been twofold: (1) a gathering of covenant Israelites to the stakes of Zion through the missionary program, and (2) a gathering of the Jews (blood Israelites) to Palestine through the Zionist movement.

While most Latter-day Saints are familiar with much of the success of the Church's missionary program, they are less aware of the conditions surrounding the return of the Jews. In the 1880s, when the gathering of the Jews began, only a few thousand Jews lived in Palestine. Most were students of the Jewish holy books and were supported by contributions from abroad. But, as the Jewish life in Eastern Europe deterioriated because of restrictive legislation and pogroms (mass riots sanctioned by the government that resulted in the destruction of life and property), many Jews sought new homes in America or Palestine. Under the leadership of Theodor Herzl in the early 1900s, the modern Zionist movement was organized and a more systematic return of the Jews began; with restrictive immigration laws in America and the rise of Naziism in Germany, many more Jews immigrated to Palestine during the 1920s. After the catastrophe of the Holocaust, the prayers of many Jews throughout the centuries of long dispersion were finally answered May 14, 1948, when the leadership of Jewish Palestine voted to found the Jewish State of Israel. The founding of the State of Israel has not been without problems, especially in securing the rights of the Arab Palestinians, but with it came the fulfillment of many prophecies and promises to ancient Israel, of which Isaiah 43 is just one. (See Nyman, *Great Are the Words of Isaiah*, p. 159 for some references by modern prophets to this Isaiah chapter.) Today there are over three million Jews living in Israel, immigrants from over one hundred countries. Truly the gathering has been from the east, west, north, and south!

In verse 4, the Lord gives the reason for his involvement in the gathering: his love for Israel has required him to provide a ransom and to "give men in return" for them. Those sacrificed for the salvation of Israel could include the Jewish and Lamanite victims of persecution, the prophets who have sealed their testimonies with their blood, and, of course, Christ himself. After the purging judgments and sacrifices, however, Israel will be gathered in from the four corners of the earth. And since the exile symbolizes the spiritual separation between the Lord and Israel, the most important prerequisite for the full gathering of Israel is their recognition of the Lord as Savior! The invitation to gather, to be called by the Lord's name, and to take part in his glory (v. 7) is extended to all who desire to unite with covenant Israel through his church, The Church of Jesus Christ of Latter-day Saints. The relationship between covenant Israel and the Lord is highlighted in the next few verses.

Trial Scene of God before Israel and the Other Nations (vs. 8-13)

These verses are compared to a trial scene because the Lord assembles a community council, calls forth witnesses, and declares a judgment upon the people. As the Lord delivers this speech, he calls forth Israel as a special witness of his fidelity to her:

[8]Bring forth the people who are blind, yet have eyes,
who are deaf, yet have ears!
[9]Let all the nations gather together and let the peoples assemble.
Who among them can declare this,
and show us the former things?
Let them bring their witnesses to justify them,
and let them hear and say, It is true.
[10]"You are my witnesses," says the LORD,
"and my servant whom I have chosen,
that you may know and believe me

and understand that I am He.
Before me no god was formed,
nor shall there be any after me.
[11]I, I am the LORD,
and besides me there is no savior.
[12]I declared and saved and proclaimed,
when there was no strange god among you;
and you are my witnesses,"
says the LORD.
[13]"I am God, and also henceforth I am He;
there is none who can deliver from my hand;
I work and who can hinder it?"
(RSV)

The people mentioned in verse 8, the blind and deaf, are similar to those described in Isaiah 42:18-23 (JST) who ignore the prophet's message. These people are blind and deaf because they have not acknowledged God's workings on earth or listened to the Spirit declare his truths. In the time of restoration, however, their eyes and ears will be opened, and they will understand the Lord's role upon this earth. After they hear the witnesses and see the divine reality, they will all come to know the true Lord of this earth (v. 11; see Isa. 45:23).

In verse 9, the Lord summons the nations to bring forth witnesses of his divine plan, if they can. However, they are not able to testify about the former (including premortal) things the Lord has done. So, the Lord turns to Israel and calls his chosen people as witnesses; that God has fulfilled his gracious plan for the world is manifest best in the records of the house of Israel. They alone testify that the Lord has provided salvation and resurrection for the world and eternal life for those who desire to receive it. Israel is not only God's special witness, but also his servant to the world, and her inspired records are to go to all people. No other nation can give a similar witness of its gods.

Israel's message to the world is highlighted in verses 11-13. Here the pronoun *I* appears twelve times to emphasize that Jehovah alone is the savior of this earth. Verse 11 is the triumphal climax to this declaration, for three important names of God are found therein. The verse begins with "I, I am," a phrase that calls to mind the title, "I AM," the name by which God identified himself to Moses on Mount Sinai. The divine speaker of the verse then declares that he is "the Lord" (Jehovah from the Hebrew *Yahweh*). He reveals his role as redeemer by identifying himself as the only "savior" of this world. The word *savior* is the common Old Testament term used to describe the God of Israel. He is to be Israel's ultimate redeemer because he is also the "anointed one," or the *Messiah*. (Translated into Greek, the Aramaic word *Messiah* becomes Christ.) Therefore, the terms *Savior, Messiah,* and *Christ* all emphasize the importance of Jehovah's role in God's plan. The German scholar F. Delitzsch provides a helpful insight into the relationship between two of these terms:

> [Savior] and Jehovah are kindred epithets here; just as in the New Testament the name Jehovah sets, as it were, but only to rise again in the name Jesus, in which it is historically fulfilled. Jehovah's precious self-manifestation in history [as in Isa. 43:11] furnished a pledge of the coming redemption. (Keil-Delitzsch, *Commentary on the Old Testament* 2:194.)

Thus, Jehovah promises Israel that he will eventually come as the Savior of this earth.

Centuries after Isaiah composed chapter 43, Joseph Smith borrowed some of Isaiah's terminology in his praise of the Lord in the preface to the marvelous revelation on the three degrees of glory: "Hear, O ye heavens, and give ear, O earth, and rejoice ye inhabitants thereof, for the Lord is God, and beside him there is no Savior." (D&C 76:1; see Isa. 1:2; 43:11.) This verse does not say that no other Gods exist, but rather that only Jehovah (Jesus Christ) is the Savior and through him alone is salvation. (See Hel. 5:9; 2 Ne. 25:20.) The first chapter of Genesis indicates that other Gods have been involved with this earth, but the Lord, in speaking to ancient Israel, wants it clearly understood that he is to be their sole savior. (See Gen. 1:26.)

Continuing in verse 12, the Lord charges Israel to accept her role as a special witness of him. In addition to foretelling his triumph, Israel is to serve as a second witness and to announce his role as the Savior to the earth. Members of covenant Israel are now fulfilling this charge as they send missionaries into the world to testify of Jesus Christ. (Bruce R. McConkie, CR, Apr. 1977, p. 135.)

Israel's Future Blessings (vs. 14-21)

The Lord continues his discourse by telling the manner in which he will protect and bless his chosen people:

¹⁴Thus says the LORD,
 your Redeemer, the Holy One
 of Israel:
"For your sake I will send to
 Babylon
and break down all the bars,
and the shouting of the
 Chaldeans will be turned to
 lamentations.
¹⁵I am the LORD, your Holy One,
 the Creator of Israel, your
 King."
¹⁶Thus says the LORD,
 who makes a way in the sea,
 a path in the mighty waters,
¹⁷who brings forth chariot and
 horse,
 army and warrior;
they lie down, they cannot rise,
 they are extinguished,

quenched like a wick:
¹⁸"Remember not the former
 things,
 nor consider the things of old.
¹⁹Behold, I am doing a new thing;
 now it springs forth, do you
 not perceive it?
I will make a way in the
 wilderness
 and rivers in the desert.
²⁰The wild beasts will honor me,
 the jackals and the ostriches;
for I give water in the wilderness,
 rivers in the desert,
to give drink to my chosen people,
²¹ the people whom I formed for
 myself
that they might declare my
 praise." (RSV)

These verses reiterate some inspired promises given by Isaiah in chapter 35 and foreshadow the even greater promises the prophet delivers in chapters 65 and 66. The promised blessings include freedom (v. 14), miracles in the sea (v. 16), protection from every enemy army (v. 17), a restoration (v. 19), and miracles in the desert (vs. 19-20). Isaiah concludes this short discourse by stating God's reason for providing these many blessings—the Lord hopes that his chosen people will declare his praise.

A closer look at some of the verses reveals the possibility of even greater blessings in store for the Lord's righteous people. For example, in verse 14, the Lord's promise that he will break down the bars of Babylon may be twofold: he may be promising release from physical prison or, since Babylon also represents the wicked world, from spiritual captivity. The promise of miracles at sea and protection from enemies suggests a new gathering of Israel and a new exodus to their land, in which the miracles attending the exodus from Egypt are reenacted.

As the gathering Israelites forget the "things of old" (v. 18), they will forget a variety of earlier experiences: physical captivity, spiritual bondage, life and practices in a period of apostasy, lesser laws of earlier dispensations, and so forth. Hence, the new things that will come forth might include a new gospel dispensation, new prophets, new scriptures, and so forth. The miracles of the desert and the animals honoring the Lord suggest a millennial period when complete harmony will exist between God, men, animals, and the earth.

So, finally, the Lord's chosen people will not just drink from the waters of the desert, but from the living waters of the gospel as well. They will share these waters with the beasts of the desert who represent perhaps, the Gentiles. Therefore, both the Gentiles and the Israelites will enjoy the gospel waters. (See John 7:37-39.)

Some events of the new exodus and gathering seem to have occurred within the past century. The return of many Jews to their desert homeland and the Mormon missionary work among Gentiles and Lamanites fulfill some of the promises in the prophecy. However, the complete gathering, with its great miracles and millennial society, has not yet taken place. Indeed, a prophet of this dispensation, Joseph Fielding Smith, has said that this prophecy (Isa. 43) applies to the Ten Tribes, who will journey past their enemies upon miraculous highways to a desert fruitful with water. (See Ludlow, *A Companion to Your Study of the Old Testament*, pp. 44-45.) Since other important remnants of Israel, especially the Ten Tribes, have yet to be gathered, Isaiah's prophecy cannot be fulfilled until they too return to Zion.

Before moving on to the last verses of Isaiah 43, an overview of the first three sections of the chapter is appropriate. The first verses (1-7) review God's creation of the earth and the Israelites' first exodus; the next section (vs. 8-13) highlights some roles between the Lord and Israel; the third segment (vs. 14-21) promises a latter exodus in preparation for a new creation or millennial era. These sections are structured both chronologically and chiastically with the most important idea in the middle of the chapter (v. 11), where the Lord promises that he alone is to be the Savior. Christ did come to earth during the meridian of time, long after the first exodus and centuries before the second; likewise, the declaration of his special role with Israel is placed between the accounts of the two gatherings. Following is a chiastic outline of Isaiah 43:1-21:

A. The Lord called to Israel in the past (v. 1)

A'. New things to happen as the Lord blesses his chosen people (vs. 18-21)

B. Protection given through fire and water (2)

B'. Water and fire are powerless before the Lord (16-17)

C. Four titles: Lord, Thy God, Holy One. Savior (3)

C'. Four titles: Lord, Holy One, Creator, King (15)

D. Israel was ransomed from the West (Egypt) (3-4)

D'. Israel will be freed from the East (Babylon) (14)

E. Gathering of covenant Israel promised (5-7)

E'. None can stop the Lord's work (gathering) (13)

F. Let all nations produce witnesses, if they can (8-9)

F'. Everything since the beginning testifies of God's work (13)

G. Israelites are God's witnesses, "saith the Lord" (10)

G'. You (Israel) are God's witnesses, "saith the Lord" (12)

H. No other God will be for Israel (10)

H'. No strange God is among Israel (12)

I. I AM the Lord (Yahweh), there is no other Savior (Messiah) (11)

As in most chiastic parallelism, the major idea in this chapter is emphasized at the pivot point and alluded to in other verses near the middle. The idea of the "oneness" of Israel's God is stressed in items H, I, and H' of the outline.

The second most important concept in a chiasmus is usually found near the beginning and end. In A and A' of the pattern above, the relationship between the Lord and Israel is stressed.

The third most important point is often presented twice, halfway between the middle and both ends of the chiasmus. Since a chiasmus divides into two parallel sections, a concept in the middle of each section easily reinforces the major ideas found at the ends of each section. In the example above, items C and C' repeat the concept found in the chiastic pivot point and give additional titles for the Lord.

The placement of the major concepts within a chiastic pattern can be outlined as follows:

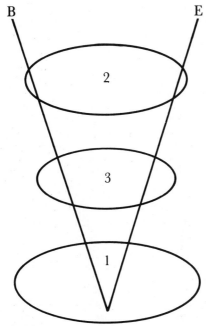

B = Beginning of chiasmus
E = End of chiasmus
1, 2, 3 = Major concepts in a chiasmus in probable order
            of importance

Trial Scene between God and Israel (vs. 22-28)

In the last section of Isaiah 43, the Lord accuses Israel of rejecting her role as servant and messenger to the world. In a court scene presided over by the Lord, Israel is found sinful and is condemned to destruction and ridicule:

22"Yet you did not call upon me, O Jacob;
  but you have been weary of me, O Israel!
23You have not brought me your sheep for burnt offerings,
  or honored me with your sacrifices.
I have not burdened you with offerings,
  or wearied you with frankincense.
24You have not bought me sweet cane with money,
  or satisfied me with the fat of your sacrifices,
But you have burdened me with your sins,
  you have wearied me with your iniquities.

25"I, I am He
  who blots out your transgressions for my own sake,
  and I will not remember your sins.
26Put me in remembrance, let us argue together;
  set forth your case, that you may be proved right.
27Your first father sinned,
  and your mediators transgressed against me.
28Therefore I profaned the princes of the sanctuary,
  I delivered Jacob to utter destruction
  and Israel to reviling." (RSV)

The Lord's accusation in these verses constitutes one of only two trial speeches in which the Lord opposes his chosen people Israel (the other is in Isa. 50:1-13). In both instances, the primary confrontation is between the Lord and the false pagan gods. The primary issue revolves around the question "Who is the true God of this earth?"

In the scene comprising 43:22-28, Israel has apparently brought a charge against the Lord asking why she has been shamed in spite of the sacrifices her people have given (vs. 22-24, 28). God challenges Israel to prove her case in the Lord's court (v. 26), but she is unable to give any evidence of divine injustice. The Lord accuses Israel of sin (v. 27) and explains why he was obliged to act toward her as he did (v. 28).

In contrast to the promise of a future restoration in the first half of chapter 43, God recounts Israel's iniquities. Still, though the Lord employs the negative *not* (*lo* in Hebrew) seven times in the first three verses, his climactic negation is an affirmation: "thy sins I will *not* remember" (v. 25). This promise stands in sharp contrast to the anticipated harsh judgment; after the Lord has described Israel's hypocrisy, one would expect him to deliver a threat. Instead, he promises forgiveness; mercy instead of punishment is extended to Israel.

Verse 25 is a profound promise for those of God's children who repent and follow him—they will benefit from his atonement since he blots out their transgressions for his sake. In other words, Christ promised to be our Savior, and in order to fulfill his own covenants and "all righteousness," it was necessary for him to provide the atoning sacrifice. Isaiah later highlights the Lord's voluntary sacrifice in chapter 53 through a song about a suffering servant. Also, a modern prophet, Spencer W. Kimball, built upon verse 25 when he exhorted modern Israelites to forgive and forget the sins of others as the Lord forgives theirs. (CR, Oct. 1949, p. 133.)

After promising that he will not remember Israel's sins, the Lord challenges Israel to remember him (v. 26). He then reminds the people that their first father and leaders had sinned against him (v. 27). It is unclear who is meant by their first father. Some commentators have suggested Adam or Abraham, but the context and the parallelism of verses 27 and 28 strongly suggest Jacob as the first father who is being discussed. The parallelism matches the *first father and mediators* who have sinned (v. 27) with the *priests* and *Jacob* who will be punished (v. 28). However, all of the ancestors or "fathers" of Israel sinned somewhat as mortal beings, and Israel's ancestors who came out of Eygpt were especially noted for their sinful behavior. (See Isa. 43, footnote 27a.) In any case, because of Israel's earlier sins and the continued wickedness of the people, the Lord promises that he will deliver them up to destruction, curses (KJV), and humiliation.

A great variety of destructions followed Israel over the centuries after Isaiah recorded this warning. During the prophet's own lifetime, the northern tribes were taken captive. Over a century later, Judah was destroyed and her people taken captive to Babylon. Similar destruction and dispersion came when the Romans warred upon the Jews shortly after the time of Christ. Centuries of harassment and persecution by Christians and Moslems followed, and, finally, the minions of Hitler destroyed one-third of the Jews. The Lamanite branch of Israel has undergone similar persecution. Israel will yet suffer before millennial peace is finally established.

Although the harshness of these last verses contrasts with the promises found in most of the chapter, the ideas parallel the same pattern outlined earlier. Verse 22 continues the theme of the Lord's relationship with Israel (items A and A' on the outline), the fire and oil of Israel's sacrifices parallel the fire and water of the Lord's protection (vs. 23-24; B and B'), the titles and role of Jehovah are given (vs. 25-26; C, C', and I), and reasons for the scattering complement promises of the gathering (vs. 27-28; D and D'). Just as these verses build upon the themes found earlier in the chapter, they also lead naturally into the first verses of chapter 44, where Israel's role with the Lord is amplified, refreshing water is promised, and the names and titles of God are highlighted. In short, although the material we now find in Isaiah 40-47 is currently divided into eight units or chapters, it actually divides into many smaller segments, all of which revolve around the Lord's relationship with his chosen people. The four segments of chapter 43 complement this section of Isaiah, since they contain many of the Lord's titles and emphasize his role with Israel—only *he* is to be their Savior!

In conclusion, at least three major principles are developed in Isaiah 43:2: first, that there is only one Lord and Savior of this earth; second, the reasons for the scattering and promises for the gathering; and third, a combination of the first two concepts, the witness relationship between Israel and the Lord—as Israel fails in this role she is scattered, and as she testifies faithfully of the Lord, she is gathered.[2] The witness relationship is very important for both parties, since Israel and the Lord will eventually testify of each other to the whole world. For now, Israel bears the responsibility of carrying God's word to the world. As she turns away from the Lord and refuses to take her message to others in peace and love, she will remain scattered among the nations in an atmosphere of war and hatred. But as she becomes the true servant of Christ, she will be blessed with a millennial society.

---

[2]Each of these three major themes is amplified by Isaiah elsewhere in his writings: the Savior's role in Isa. 53; the gathering of Israel and the watering of the desert in Isa. 32-35; the role of witnesses in Isa. 29.

JACOB, CYRUS, AND JESHUA:
SERVANTS OF GOD
ISAIAH 44-45

In chapters 44 and 45, Isaiah builds upon some themes found in chapters 40-43 (attributes and names of God, roles of his servants, and the foolishness of idolatry) and continues his pattern of alternating positive declarations with negative denouncements. A quick reading of the chapters reveals the following divisions:

+   Declaration of the Lord's redeeming role with Israel (44:1-8)
−   Denouncement of idol worshippers (44:9-20)
+   Declaration of the Lord's role with Israel and Cyrus (44:21-45:8)
−   Denouncement of unthankful, critical children (45:9-11)
+   Declaration of the Lord's creative role (45:12-15)
− + Shame and ignorance of idol worshippers contrasted with triumph and recognition of the Lord (45:16-25)

More careful study reveals further insights and what appears to be a "roller coaster" pattern of increasing polarity in chapters 40-47 of Isaiah as his promises become more profound and his warnings more pointed. This pattern can be diagrammed as follows:

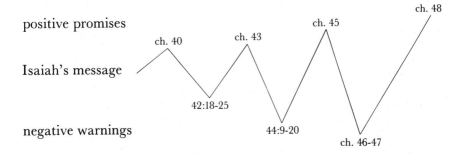

positive promises

Isaiah's message

negative warnings

ch. 40   ch. 43   ch. 45   ch. 48

42:18-25

44:9-20

ch. 46-47

Isaiah's ridicule of idolatry (44:9-20) is followed by a stronger denouncement in chapters 46 and 47. Also, his declaration that the entire earth will recognize the true Lord of this earth (45:14-25) is followed by even greater prophecies about the Lord and his people, beginning in chapter 48.

A simple A-B-C-B'-A' chiasmus develops in chapter 44:

A. The Lord will bless Israel (vs. 1-5)
B. Beside the Lord there is no other redeemer (6-8)
C. Idols are the foolish work of man (9-20)
B'. The Lord alone will redeem Israel (21-23)
A'. The Lord will protect and bless Israel (24-28)

Like its bordering chapters, 43 and 45, chapter 44 contains one of Isaiah's primary messages: the Lord alone is the god of Israel and the whole earth. However, Isaiah approaches this message negatively, for most of the verses and the pivotal point of the chiasmus center upon the futility of worshipping other gods.

Isaiah emphasizes in verse 15, the worthlessness of idols, employing strong sarcasm to effectively debase both the worshipper (idolator) and the worshipped (idol). He ridicules the man who selects wood, burning part of it for fuel and worshipping the rest. Ironically, man worships something transitory that he can control instead of the eternal Lord who controls man's destiny. Man does receive some temporary benefits from the wood used for fuel, yet nothing from the wood that forms an idol, because this image and the pagan god it represents are both lifeless. In the end, the wood, the idol, and the idolatry will all be as ashes and dust, worthless to the children of men (v. 20).

Isaiah begins chapter 44 with a short oracle of salvation. He first reminds Israel of her covenant as messenger of the Lord:

44 "But now listen, O Jacob,
    My servant;
And Israel, whom I have chosen:
²Thus says the LORD who made you
And formed you from the womb,
    who will help you,
'Do not fear, O Jacob My servant;
And you Jeshurun whom I have
    chosen.
³'For I will pour out water on the
    thirsty land

And streams on the dry ground;
I will pour out My Spirit on your
    offspring,
And My blessing on your
    descendants;
⁴And they will spring up among the
    grass
Like poplars by streams of water.'
⁵"This one will say, 'I am the
    LORD's';
And that one will call on the name

of Jacob;
And another will write on his
hand, 'Belonging to the LORD,'
And will name Israel's name with
honor." (NAS)

The oracle is introduced by a "messenger formula" consisting of three
parts: "listen," "thus says the Lord," and "do not fear" (to be God's
witness; see v. 8). Isaiah is not delivering a new charge to Israel to be
God's messenger, but is reminding her of earlier covenants with God
established by Jacob and Moses. Jacob was the father of the Israelites
both physically and spiritually. When the Lord renewed his covenant
with Abraham through Jacob, he changed Jacob's name to Israel to
signify his righteousness. (Gen. 35:9-11.) When Moses initiated a new
gospel dispensation among the Israelites, he reminded them of the
covenants made by Jacob, the "king of Jeshurun" (v. 2; see Deut.
33:5, 26; *jeshurun* is Hebrew for "upright" or "righteous"). Isaiah uses
all three names, Jacob, Israel, and Jeshurun, to remind Israel of her
covenants.

After promising physical and spiritual blessings (water and the
Holy Ghost) Isaiah repeats two of the names, Jacob and Israel, as he
continues his oracle (v. 5). He also promises that others will join with
Israel and enter into the same covenants. The promise in verse 5
obviously extends beyond the descendants of Jacob because:

> Those who adopt the names of Yahweh and Israel can scarcely be Israelites.
> Although it is not inconceivable that the prophet may represent the Israelites as
> boasting that they are the people of Yahweh, they would hardly boast of this
> after ruin and exile. The prophet surely sees foreign peoples and nations so
> impressed by this demonstration of the saving power of Yahweh that they will
> take his name and the name of his people. For the challenges uttered to the
> nations and their gods must have the effect of demonstrating that Yahweh alone
> is God, and Israel is his people. (McKenzie, *Second Isaiah*, p. 64.)

While Isaiah does not precisely identify the converts, he does describe
their growing relationship with the Lord.

The convert's first step is to say, "I am the Lord's," or, in other
words, "I want to take the Lord's name upon myself." This covenant
relationship is then established through the ordinance of baptism and
renewed through the sacrament.

The second step results from the person's desire to "call himself
by the name of Jacob" (KJV). The person probably wants to receive
the birthright blessings promised to Jacob's posterity. Also, the Holy

Ghost can literally transform a person into "the seed of Abraham." (See TPJS, p. 150.) Today, the blessings of Abraham are usually pronounced in patriarchal blessings.

Step three requires that, in addition to desiring a new name (of Jacob), the person also writes the name of Christ upon his hand. Although this might be a literal act, it is probably symbolic of using that hand to establish covenants or promises. Many scholars feel that the person does not literally write "to Yahweh" on his hand, but that he uses his hand to witness his relationship with the Lord. The witness could be that the hand writes a testimony declaring the person's covenant. (North, *The Second Isaiah*, p. 134; Young, *The Book of Isaiah* 3:169.) Or, the hand could be used in a sign, token, or witness of a person's promises and covenants with God. For example, today we still shake hands in an agreement and raise hands to sustain a Church leader.

Finally, the fourth step occurs when one is named with the name of Israel. This step is a further development of the second, in which the person desired the name of Jacob. Now he actually receives the name. The actualization of the full blessings of Abraham, Isaac, and Jacob come only to those who enter into the "new and everlasting covenant" in the temples of the Lord. Anyone who is faithful to the covenants of the endowment and sealing (or temple marriage) will receive the Lord's full approbation and become an heir to every blessing promised to Israel's righteous posterity.

In review, verse 5 can be read on one level as a simple poetic parallelism reminding the Israelites of their identity as God's chosen people. However, closer study of the verse suggests some specific ordinances that establish covenant relationships for people in each generation, for example, baptism, patriarchal blessings, sustaining of Church officers, the endowment, and temple marriage.

In the next few verses, Isaiah emphasizes Israel's covenant relationship with the Lord and the spiritual ignorance of other peoples:

6"Thus says the LORD, the King of
Israel
And his Redeemer, the LORD of
hosts:
'I am the first and I am the last,
And there is no God besides Me. A. No other god
7'And who is like Me? Let him
proclaim and declare it; B. Idols speechless

378

Yes, let him recount it to Me in order,
From the time that I established the ancient nation.
And let them declare to them the things that are coming
And the events that are going to take place.
⁸'Do not tremble and do not be afraid;
Have I not long since announced it to you and declared it?
And you are My witnesses.
Is there any God besides Me,
Or is there any *other* Rock?
I know of none.'" (NAS)

C. Mortals cannot foretell

D. Old things not foretold

E. Let them speak if they can
D'. Future things not foretold

C'. God prophesies
B'. God speaks

A'. No other gods

The chiastic pattern outlined at the right highlights the inability of other nations and their pagan gods to foretell what the Lord will do to fulfill his plan for this earth.

In verse 6, Isaiah sets forth six attributes of Jehovah. He is (1) the Lord, (2) Israel's king, (3) Israel's redeemer, (4) the leader of the heavenly hosts, (5) the Eternal, the "first" and the "last," and (6) the only true God of this earth. And the Lord then asks in verse 7, "Who is like me?" The rest of the oracle testifies that no one is like the Lord, the rock of our salvation. (See Deut. 32:15-17; Isa. 8:14.)

In contrast to the relationship between the Lord and his children, Isaiah portrays the relationship between idol worshippers and their pagan images:

⁹Those who fashion a graven image are all of them futile, and their precious things are of no profit; even their own witnesses fail to see or know, so that they will be put to shame.
¹⁰Who has fashioned a god or cast an idol to no profit?
¹¹Behold, all his companions will be put to shame, for the craftsmen themselves are mere men. Let them all assemble themselves, let them stand up, let them tremble, let them together be put to shame.
¹²The man shapes iron into a cutting tool, and does his work over the coals, fashioning it with hammers, and working it with his strong arm. He also gets hungry and his strength fails; he drinks no water and becomes weary.
¹³*Another* shapes wood, he extends a measuring line; he outlines with red chalk. He works it with

planes, and outlines it with a compass, and makes it like the form of a man, like the beauty of man, so that it may sit in a house.

[14]Surely he cuts cedars for himself and takes a cypress or an oak, and raises *it* for himself among the trees of the forest. He plants a fir, and the rain makes it grow.

[15]Then it becomes *something* for a man to burn, so he takes one of them and warms himself; he also makes a fire to bake bread. He also makes a god and worships it; he makes it a graven image, and falls down before it.

[16]Half of it burns in the fire; over *this* half he eats meat as he roasts a roast, and is satisfied. He also warms himself and says, "Aha! I am warm, I have seen the fire."

[17]But the rest of it he makes into a god, his graven image. He falls down before it and worships; he also prays to it and says, "Deliver me, for thou art my god."

[18]They do not know, nor do they understand, for He has smeared over their eyes so that they cannot see and their hearts so that they cannot comprehend.

[19]And no one recalls, nor is there knowledge or understanding to say, "I have burned half of it in the fire, and also have baked bread over its coals. I roast meat and eat *it*. Then I make the rest of it into an abomination, I fall down before a block of wood!"

[20]He feeds on ashes, a deceived heart has turned him aside. And he cannot deliver himself, nor say, "Is there not a lie in my right hand?" (NAS)

As indicated in the introduction to this chapter, Isaiah mocks the people's idolatry with sharp sarcasm in these verses. The prophet seems deliberately to reverse the process of Genesis 1:26-27: God made man in his divine image, and now man makes a god in his own frail image. The Ten Commandments strictly forbade images of God because, among other reasons, nothing material can capture the full glory of God.

However, it is also helpful to remember that the pagans of Isaiah's time did not usually believe that their gods actually lived in or were the idols themselves. The idols were merely symbolic representations of their gods. But the Lord proved the other gods lifeless, speechless, and valueless (vs. 6-8). These idolators worshipped the efforts of their craftsmanship and deprived themselves of the resources the wood, metal, and their labors could otherwise provide.

After his taunting parody of the idol worshippers, Isaiah returns to his message of salvation, calling upon Israel to repent and turn back to the Lord:

21"Remember these things, O
Jacob,
And Israel, for you are My
servant;
I have formed you, you are My
servant,
O Israel, you will not be forgotten
by Me.
22"I have wiped out your
transgressions like a thick
cloud,
And your sins like a heavy mist.
Return to Me, for I have
redeemed you."
23Shout for joy, O heavens, for the
LORD has done it!
Shout joyfully, you lower parts of
the earth;
Break forth into a shout of joy,
you mountains,
O forest, and every tree in it;
For the LORD has redeemed Jacob
And in Israel He shows forth His
glory. (NAS)

In verse 22, the Lord promises forgiveness to the repentant Israelites, speaking in the prophetic past tense. That is, God will not come to the earth and actually bring about the Atonement until centuries later, but Isaiah speaks about it in the past tense as though it had already happened. He declares that the Atonement has been made and that Israel's redemption is predicated upon her return to God. As early as the time of the councils in the premortal existence, God the Father promised and committed his son as the required sacrifice of the Atonement. Scholar E. J. Young explains:

> A command to repent is given, because God Himself has paid a price to purchase His people. It is that concept that lies at the heart of the matter. . . . The reference is not to the return from exile, for that act could not really be designated a redemption paid by God; the reference is to a ransom paid for deliverance from sin and guilt, and the price God paid for that deliverance was His own Son, in whom we have redemption through His blood, the forgiveness of sins. (*The Book of Isaiah* 3:184.)

Isaiah concludes chapter 44 with further promises to Israel, including the promise of a future political leader, Cyrus, who will serve the Lord in freeing the Jews and assist them in rebuilding their temple:

24Thus says the LORD, your
Redeemer, and the one who
formed you from the womb,
"I, the LORD, am the maker of all
things,
Stretching out the heavens by
Myself,
And spreading out the earth all
alone,
25Causing the omens of boasters to
fail,
Making fools out of diviners,
Causing wise men to draw back,
And turning their knowledge into

foolishness,
²⁶Confirming the word of His
servant,
And performing the purpose of
His messengers.
It is I who says of Jerusalem, 'She
shall be inhabited!'
And of the cities of Judah, 'They
shall be built.'
And I will raise up her ruins
again.
²⁷"It is I who says to the depth of

the sea, 'Be dried up!'
And I will make your rivers dry.
²⁸"It is I who says to Cyrus, 'He is
My shepherd!
And he will perform all My
desire.'
And he declares of Jerusalem,
'She will be built,'
And of the temple, 'Your
foundation will be laid.' "
(NAS)

As indicated on page 540, many scholars believe that these verses were written at the time of or after the death of Cyrus (c. 590-529 B.C.). There are, however, other examples in the scriptures where prophets foretell the name and mission of people centuries before they are born. For examples, see Joseph's prophecies about Moses and Joseph Smith (JST Gen. 50:24-38; 2 Ne. 3), Nephi's prophecy about Jesus (2 Ne. 25:19-20), and King Benjamin's and Alma's prophecies about Mary (Mosiah 3:8; Alma 7:10).

The mission of Cyrus was to include a number of important events, the most important being the rebuilding of Jerusalem and its temple. With new political and religious centers in Judah, the Jews could reestablish themselves as a nation that would remain in the land until a descendant of David, the Messiah, would finally be born in Bethlehem.

Isaiah prophesies further concerning Cyrus in chapter 45. In fact, Isaiah records a personal message from the Lord to Cyrus:

45 Thus says the LORD to Cyrus His anointed,
Whom I have taken by the right hand,
To subdue nations before him,
And to loose the loins of kings;
To open doors before him so that gates will not be shut:
²"I will go before you and make the rough places smooth;
I will shatter the doors of bronze, and cut through their iron bars.
³"And I will give you the treasures of darkness,

And hidden wealth of secret places,
In order that you may know that it is I,
The LORD, the God of Israel, who calls you by your name.
⁴"For the sake of Jacob My servant, And Israel My chosen one,
I have also called you by your name;
I have given you a title of honor Though you have not known Me.
⁵"I am the LORD, and there is no other;

Besides Me there is no God.
I will gird you, though you have
  not known Me;
⁶That men may know from the
  rising to the setting of the sun
That there is no one besides Me.
I am the LORD, and there is no
  other,

⁷The ONE forming light and
  creating darkness,
Causing well-being and creating
  calamity;
I am the LORD who does all these."
(NAS)

The fact that Cyrus was to be the Lord's "anointed" servant (v. 1) has confused Bible scholars. It is not recorded anywhere that one of the Lord's prophets ever anointed Cyrus in a position of political power as Samuel did Saul and David. (1 Sam. 10, 16.) However, a later Jewish historian records that Cyrus considered himself appointed by God to assist the Jews. Writing shortly after the time of Christ, Josephus recorded:

> In the first year of the reign of Cyrus [539 B.C.], which was the seventieth from the day that our people were removed out of their own land into Babylon, God commiserated the captivity and calamity of these poor people . . . for he stirred up the mind of Cyrus, and made him write this throughout all Asia:— "Thus saith Cyrus the King:—Since God Almighty hath appointed me to be king of the habitable earth, I believe that he is that God which the nation of the Israelites worship; for indeed he foretold my name by the prophets, and that I should build him a house at Jerusalem, in the country of Judea."
> This was known to Cyrus by his reading the book which Isaiah left behind him of his prophecies; for this prophet said that God had spoken thus to him in a secret vision:—"My will is, that Cyrus, whom I have appointed to be king over many and great nations, send back my people to their own land, and build my temple." This was foretold by Isaiah one hundred and forty years before the temple was demolished [c. 726 and 586 B.C.]. Accordingly, when Cyrus read this, and admired the divine power, an earnest desire and ambition seized upon him to fulfill what was so written. (Josephus, *Antiquities of the Jews*, book 11, ch. 1.)

It should be noted that other ancient documents record similar statements attributed to Cyrus, in which the Persian king claims to be the agent for other gods to help other peoples. For example, Cyrus claimed that the Babylonian god Marduk had helped him to conquer Babylon. In turn, Cyrus rebuilt a shrine to Marduk and restored him and other gods and their sanctuaries to places of prominence. (See IDB 1:755.) Although Cyrus may have felt that he was the Lord's servant in restoring the Jews in their land, he did not worship only Jehovah. He remained a polytheist throughout his life, at least as far as any available documents indicate.

The fact that Cyrus probably was not literally anointed to be the

Lord's servant and that he did not claim sole allegiance to the Lord does not discount the role he fulfilled in helping the Jews. Also, he did not require anointing here on earth in order to serve as God's servant if he had been foreordained in the pre-earth existence. President Joseph Fielding Smith stated that Cyrus did receive such a foreordination. (See AGQ 5:181.) Joseph Smith stated:

> That we may learn still further that God calls or elects particular men to perform particular works, or on whom to confer special blessings, we read, Isaiah 45:4, "For Jacob my servant's sake, and Israel mine elect, I have even called thee Cyrus by thy name," to be a deliverer to my people Israel, and help to plant them on my holy mountain, Isaiah 45:9. (HC 4:257.)

In short, although Cyrus was helpful to the Jews and very tolerant of other religions, there is no evidence that he was fully converted to the true religion of the Lord during mortality. He did, however, fulfill his foreordained mission to assist the Jews. He served well as a model or type of the Anointed One, the Messiah, who would follow him; just as Cyrus freed the Jews from political bondage and restored them to their homelands, Christ freed men from spiritual prison and prepared the way for them to return to Heavenly Father's presence.

Verse 8 provides a capstone to Isaiah's prophecy, for it promises a fruitful earth fulfilling the full measure of its creation:

8"Drip down, O heavens, from above,
And let the clouds pour down righteousness;
Let the earth open up and salvation bear fruit,
And righteousness spring up with it.
I, the LORD, have created it.
(NAS)

This verse points out that God brings forth righteousness and salvation. (See Ps. 85:11; Moses 7:62.)

The Hebrew word translated "salvation" is *jeshua*. The root of *jeshua* means (1) to open, free, or be safe, or (2) to free, rescue, or bring salvation. Isaiah uses this root thirty-eight times in his writings, seven times in chapter 45 alone.[1] *Jeshua* is a part of Isaiah's own name (*Jeshayahu*, "Jehovah has saved") and the prophet Joshua's (*Jehoshua*, "Jehovah-saved"). As the Aramaic derivation of the root *jeshua* was transmitted through the Greek New Testament into English, it became *Jesus*, the given name of Christ. A more pure Greek form of the word is *Jason*. (See BD "Jeshua," "Jesus," "Joshua.")

---

[1] This excludes the fifteen times the root shows up as a part of Isaiah's own name.

Since Isaiah uses the *jeshua* root so frequently in chapter 45, one wonders why he gives the word particular emphasis in this discourse. It shows up a number of times in verses 20-22 in passages that parallel the first part of the chapter. Many of the parallelisms are clearer in the Hebrew:

A. Way prepared (physically) for Cyrus' glory (v. 1)

A'. Way prepared (spiritually) for mankind's glory (v. 25)

B. Power of the Lord (2)

B'. Strength of the Lord (24)

C. The Lord's secret knowledge of Cyrus (3-4)

C'. People's open knowledge of the Lord (23)

D. There is no other Lord (5-6)
*a I am the Lord
 b Beside me no God
 c I have encircled you that you may come to know me
 b None beside me
 a I am the Lord

D'. There is no other God (21b-22)
*a It is I, the Lord
 c A Savior (*moshiya*, from *jeshua*) to come
 b None beside me
 c Be saved (*huyashu*, from *jeshua*)
 a I am God

E. The Lord's efforts (7-8)
**a Creation (physical)
 b Righteousness
 c Salvation (*jeshua*) will bear fruit
 b Righteousness
 a Creation (spiritual)

E'. Man's ineffectiveness (20-21a)
**a Gather together
 b Mortal ignorance
 c Success (*joshiya*, from *jeshua*) not with Gentiles
 a Counsel together
 b Divine foreknowledge

F. People questioning the Lord about his purpose (9-10)

F'. God's creation of the earth for an (eternal) habitation will be known (18-19)

G. God's handiwork demonstrated in mankind (see Moses 1:39) (11)

G'. Israel *saved* by the *Lord* with *salvation* (*jeshua, yahweh, jeshua*) (17)

H. God created man (12)

H'. Men build idols (16)

I. God has prepared a way of righteousness (13)

I'. God has preserved a Savior (*moshiya*, from *jeshua*) (15)

J. The world will finally recognize that *only among Israel is the one true God* (see outline elements D and D', vs. 5, 6, 21-22)

As illustrated by this outline, one major theme is stressed in this chapter—the way is prepared so that Israel and the world can know their Lord. Also, in order for God's plan to be fulfilled, a savior

---

*Clear chiastic patterns in the Hebrew. The concept of "there is no other God" shows up.

**Clear parallel patterns in the Hebrew.

(*jeshua*) is necessary. Since the name *jeshua* is such an important word in the discourse, one wonders if Isaiah is either using this root as a play upon his own name or perhaps upon the Savior's name, Jesus.

Since Jesus' name was revealed to Book of Mormon prophets centuries before his birth in Bethlehem (2 Ne. 25:19; Mosiah 3:8; Alma 5:44), it is possible that Isaiah also knew Jesus' name. If so, however, he probably was not allowed to divulge this information, since common knowledge of very many details of Jesus's life would have handicapped the Jews in their development of faith when Jesus finally lived among them. But even if Isaiah did not know Jesus' name, he did know and prophesy about his role as the Savior of mankind.

A prophet's knowledge about God's plan is contrasted with man's understanding in the next verses of chapter 45:

9"Woe to the one who quarrels with his Maker—
An earthenware vessel among the vessels of earth!
Will the clay say to the potter, 'What are you doing?'
Or the thing you are making say, 'He has no hands'?
10"Woe to him who says to a father, 'What are you begetting?'
Or to a woman, 'To what are you giving birth?'" (NAS)

Just as no child has the right to ask such impudent questions of his parents, Israel does not have the right to question God's purposes.

Isaiah continues by recording what God has done and planned:

11Thus says the LORD, the Holy One of Israel, and his Maker:
"Ask Me about the things to come concerning My sons,
And you shall commit to Me the work of My hands.
12"It is I who made the earth, and created man upon it.
I stretched out the heavens with My hands,
And I ordained all their host.
13"I have aroused him in righteousness,
And I will make all his ways smooth;
He will build My city, and will let My exiles go free,
Without any payment or reward," says the LORD of hosts. (NAS)

The person in verse 13 could be Cyrus or the Messiah, depending upon whether a physical or spiritual deliverance is being foretold.

The promise probably refers to both types of freedom; Israel will eventually enjoy both to such an extent that she will serve as a witness of God's blessings and protection upon the earth. Isaiah describes the humble attitude of some peoples from Africa who will finally recognize that God is with Israel:

¹⁴Thus says the LORD,
"The products of Egypt and the
merchandise of Cush
And the Sabeans, men of stature,
Will come over to you and will be
yours;
They will walk behind you,

they will come over in chains
And will bow down to you;
They will make supplication to
you:
'Surely, God is with you, and
there is none else,
No other God.' " (NAS)

As indicated earlier in the chiastic outline, this verse is the pivot point of the chiasmus and repeats the declaration that there is only one God of this earth. Indeed, there is no other *Elohim* (God) or any other Heavenly Father for this earth than the one who created our spirits and prepared the way for us to return to him.

After God initiated his plan of salvation, he left the administration of it to his Son, Jehovah. Isaiah describes the indirect involvement of God the Father in the next verses and compares his divine work with the results of idolatry:

¹⁵Truly, Thou art a God who hides
Himself,
O God of Israel, Savior!
¹⁶They will be put to shame and
even humiliated, all of them;
the manufacturers of idols will go
away together in humiliation.

¹⁷Israel has been saved by the
LORD
With an everlasting salvation;
You will not be put to shame or
humiliated
To all eternity. (NAS)

Review the outline given earlier to recall that these verses contain three references to the salvation (*jeshua*) that God will provide through Jehovah or *Yahweh* (vs. 15, 17). As Jesus fulfills and administers Heavenly Father's plan, he represents the Father's absolute authority. He speaks and acts for and in behalf of the Father through the process of divine investiture of authority. (MFP 5:31-34.)

Isaiah records one of his great testimonies in these verses and those that follow (15-25). He bears witness that the Lord Jehovah is the Savior both of Israel and the whole world. As the prophecies concerning Israel's redemption come to pass, Jehovah (Jesus) is verified as the Savior of his people and the fulfillment of God's plan (v. 17).

Isaiah reviews the Lord's creative role in an answer to the people's question in the earlier parallel verses (9-10):

¹⁸For thus says the LORD, who
created the heavens
(He is the God who formed the

earth and made it,
He established it and did not
create it a waste place,

But formed it to be inhabited),
"I am the LORD, and there is
  none else.
19"I have not spoken in secret,
In some dark land;
I did not say to the offspring of
  Jacob,

'Seek Me in a waste place';
I, the LORD, speak righteousness
Declaring things that are
  upright." (NAS)

As Isaiah stresses in these verses, God's plan was established from earliest times, so there is no need to doubt the Lord's fulfillment of this plan.

The next verses challenge the other nations to bring forth their witnesses, if they can, of God's foreordained plan. They also emphasize that there is no other means or name besides Jehovah by which man may be saved:

20"Gather yourselves and come;
Draw near together, you fugitives
  of the nations;
They have no knowledge,
Who carry about their wooden
  idol,
And pray to a god who cannot
  save.
21"Declare and set forth your case;
Indeed, let them consult together.
Who has announced this from of
  old?

Who has long since declared it?
Is it not I, the LORD?
And there is no other God besides
  Me,
A righteous God and a Savior;
There is none except Me.
22"Turn to Me, and be saved, all
  the ends of the earth;
For I am God, and there is no
  other." (NAS)

Compare the parallelisms of these verses with verses 5-7 quoted and outlined earlier to see how they reinforce Isaiah's teachings about the Lord's singular role as the God of this earth.

Isaiah understands that eventually all people will recognize Jehovah as the only true God:

23"I have sworn by Myself,
The word has gone forth from My
  mouth in righteousness
And will not turn back,
That to me every knee will bow,
  every tongue will swear
  allegiance.
24"They will say of Me, 'Only in
  the LORD are righteousness and

  strength.
Men will come to Him,
And all who were angry at Him
  shall be put to shame.
25"In the LORD all the offspring of
  Israel
Will be justified, and will glory."
(NAS)

Bowing the knee and swearing loyalty represents a total recognition of God's rule and the justice of his plan as fulfilled through Christ. (Mosiah 16:1-4; Phil. 2:10-11; D&C 88:104.) It does not mean that everyone will repent and become Christ's disciples, but that they will at least accept him as the supreme master of this earth. (DS 2:30-31.) Even the lowliest telestial beings and wicked people will be constrained to recognize Jesus Christ as the God of Israel and the author of their salvation. (D&C 76:110.)

How much better it would be if everyone on his own would receive a testimony of God's rule and Christ's role with this earth and its inhabitants. Eventually those with this faith will be justified and receive their glorious station (v. 25). Just as those who receive and maintain such a faith are comparatively rare, so those who enjoy God's eternal glory in the celestial kingdom will be all too few. Just as the way to Babylon was prepared physically for Cyrus, the spiritual path to God's Zion, where the pure in heart dwell, is available for everyone who will follow it.

THE FALL OF BABYLON
ISAIAH 46-47

Isaiah introduces no new themes in chapters 46 and 47, but does employ different poetic styles to reiterate two messages he delivered earlier: his prophecies on Babylon recorded in chapters 13 through 14 and his affirmation of the omnipotence of Jehovah in chapters 40-45. In chapters 46 and 47, Isaiah contrasts the impotence of the Babylonian gods with the supreme power of Israel's Jehovah. The Babylonian idols are carried from their defeated country into exile, while the God of Israel delivers his people from captivity and leads them to freedom.

While these prophecies are directed mainly to the Jews during the Babylonian exile, Isaiah's poetry also contains a universal warning against idol worship (46) and worldly ambition (47). "Idols" can represent any man-made object or endeavor that mortals esteem higher than God. In turn, the power of "Babylon" can symbolize the influences of wickedness that pervade the earth. Thus, these chapters are relevant today, for they warn us against the false trust we might place in earthly goods or powers.

The two chapters can be briefly outlined as follows:

I. Idolatry and Jehovah (Yahweh) compared (ch. 46)
   A. The fall of Bel (vs. 1-4)
   B. Yahweh is without equal (5-7)
   C. Yahweh is Lord of the future (8-13)
II. Lament for Babylon (ch. 47)
   A. Babylon's shame (vs. 1-5)
   B. Babylon's abuse (6-9)
   C. Babylon's sorcery (10-19)

Isaiah begins his first poem by comparing the helplessness of idols with God's constant care:

46 Bel is crouching, Nebo
cringing.
Their idols are being loaded on
animals, on beasts of burden,
carried off like bundles on weary
beasts.
²They are cringing and crouching
together,
powerless to save the ones who
carry them,
as they themselves go off into
captivity.

³'Listen to me, House of Jacob,
all you who remain of the House of
Israel,
you who have been carried since
birth,
whom I have carried since the
time you were born.

⁴'In your old age I shall be still the
same,
when your hair is gray I shall still
support you.
I have already done so, I have
carried you,
I shall still support and deliver
you.' (JB)

Bel and Nebo were the two most prominent deities in the Assyro-Babylonian pantheon. Bel was originally the god of heaven and, as such, the father and chief of the gods. He was the equivalent of the Canaanite Baal ("lord") and was also known as Bel-Marduk, the god of the city of Babylon. Nebo, the god of wisdom, divine interpretation, and writing, was the chief god of Borsippa (a neighboring city south of Babylon) and the son of Marduk. His importance is demonstrated by the many royal names formed from Nebo (or Nabu) such as Nebuchadnezzar, Nabopolassar, and so on. Nebo later became the chief god of the neo-Babylonian or Chaldean dynasty that overthrew the Assyrians a century after Isaiah's death. Bel the chief god and Nebo the god of learning were the Babylonian apostate versions of Jehovah and the Holy Ghost.

Isaiah describes how the empire represented by these gods is about to fall while the gods' images are being moved from danger and loaded on beasts of burden. Ancient man believed that each god had a certain territory in which he was to be worshiped. (Though a god could be worshiped anywhere, it was most effective to worship him in his own land.) If a person moved to another location, he would then worship and give honor to the god of that particular land. Ancient man also believed that the lives of the gods were reflected in their own lives. For example, if the people of one city were defeated by the people of another city, they believed it to be because there had been a war in heaven in which the god of the victorious nation defeated their god. Because Isaiah understood the true nature of the Gods of heaven, he describes (vs. 3-4) the ways in which Israel's God is different from the gods of the Gentile nations.

Isaiah calls upon the remnant of Israel, particularly the kingdom of Judah, to listen as he describes the ways in which the Lord has protected them since the birth of the Israelite nations. (See Isa. 43:1-2.) God's actions contrast with those of the pagan gods, who are so helpless that they have to be carried from place to place. For example, Jehovah's power contrasts with that of Bel and his son Nebo, who are carried into captivity with those who worship them. While the ancients believed that the Babylonian gods had been defeated, Isaiah proclaims that Jehovah has never been defeated and has borne his people continually.

Isaiah next speaks in the first person as if he were the Lord and challenges the Jews to compare him with the idols:

5To whom can you compare me,
   equate me,
to whom claim I am similar, or
   comparable?
6These prodigals weigh out gold
   from their purses
and silver on the scales.
They engage a goldsmith to make
   a god
then worship and prostrate

themselves before it.
7They lift it on their shoulders and
   carry it,
and put it where it is meant to
   stand.
It never moves from the spot.
You may invoke it, it never replies,
It never saves anyone in trouble.
(JB)

The utter helplessness of the pagan gods is apparent, for the people have to pay a goldsmith not only to construct their idol but to provide the materials for the statue. Upon its completion, the people must pick up and carry the god to its final resting place. What good can a god like this do for anyone? The capstone to this section is the last two lines, in which the complete uselessness of idols is summed up: "You may invoke it, it never replies, it never saves anyone in trouble." What a contrast between the God of Israel and idols!

Jewish legends, as later recorded in the Book of Jasher, include a story about Abraham's encounter with idols. This story illustrates the helplessness of idols very well. Perhaps Isaiah's prophecy recalled this story to the minds of the ancient Israelites. It seems that Terah, Abraham's father, was an idolator and had in his home a whole room full of idols, which he regularly worshiped. As Abraham grew up in the home, he wondered about these gods. One day he asked his mother about them and how he could please them. She replied that by giving them food and drink, he could gain favor in their eyes. So Abraham went out and slew a lamb and prepared a meal for the gods.

He took it in before the gods and went out. The next day he returned only to find the food still there. He thought to himself that perhaps he had not given enough and it angered the gods and therefore they did not eat. So he prepared more food and placed it before them. Again, the next day, it still was not eaten. Thinking that perhaps it was not cooked enough, he prepared yet another meal. But upon his return the third day, it still was not eaten.

Then, the account says, the Spirit of the Lord came upon Abraham, telling him that these idols were both deaf and blind, having neither life nor power because they were only wood and stone. Abraham went out, got an ax, and returned and destroyed the gods. Leaving the largest idol unharmed in the middle of the room, he placed the ax in its hand and went out. Terah, having heard all the noise, came in to see what had happened. Abraham explained that he had brought food and drink so that he might find favor in the eyes of the gods. "Upon placing the food before them," said Abraham, "the smaller gods put forth their hands to partake first before the great god could eat. This infuriated the great god who took the ax in hand and destroyed all the other gods." To this, Terah made the following reply:

41What is this tale that thou hast told? Thou speakest lies to me.

42Is there in these gods spirit, soul or power to do all thou hast told me? Are they not wood and stone, and have I not *myself* made them, and canst thou speak such lies, saying that the large god that was with them smote them? It is thou that didst place the hatchet in his hand, and then sayest he smote them all.

43And Abram answered his father and said to him: And how canst thou *then* serve these idols in whom there is no power to do anything? Can those idols in which thou trustest deliver thee? Can they hear thy prayers when thou callest upon them? Can they deliver thee from the hands of thy enemies, or will they fight thy battles for thee against thy enemies, that thou shouldest serve wood and stone which can neither speak nor hear? (BOJ 11:41-43.)

After speaking further to Terah, Abraham took the hatchet from the idol and broke the image into pieces as a demonstration of the idol's helplessness. (BOJ 11:21-49.)

Many apocryphal stories and the teachings of many prophets earlier than Isaiah continually reminded the Israelites of the helplessness of idols. Isaiah alludes to former witnesses in describing how God has been able not only to help Israel but to foretell the future and bring about the complete fulfillment of all his plans:

⁸Remember this and be dismayed,
stir your memories again, you
sinners,
⁹remember things long past.
I am God unrivaled
God who has no like.
¹⁰From the beginning I foretold the
future,
and predicted beforehand what is
to be.

I say: My purpose shall last;
I will do whatever I choose.

¹¹I call a bird of prey from the east,
my man of destiny from a far
country.
No sooner is it said than done,
no sooner planned than
performed.
¹²Listen to me, faint hearts,
who feel far from victory.
¹³I bring my victory near, already it
is close,
my salvation will not be late.
I will give salvation to Zion,
my glory shall be for Israel. (JB)

This section is a further reminder to the exiles that their God had "from ancient times" accurately predicted future events (v. 10). Leaving the immediate theme of idols, God sternly rebukes the exiles' unwillingness to believe in his promises of salvation from exile (vs. 8, 12). He appeals to the long history of miracles he performed in behalf of his people, reaffirms his uniqueness as God, and again reminds Israel that he has foretold the future from the beginning, thereby leaving no doubt that he alone is God (vs. 8-10; compare Isa. 43:8-12.) The Jews seem to have lost trust and confidence in God, and for this reason God continually reaffirms his power in these closing verses.

Verse 11 appears to be another description of Cyrus coming like "a bird of prey from the east" to serve as God's agent.[1] Continuing to give confidence to Israel, the Lord says that "no sooner is it said than done . . ." and the exiles are called upon to listen even though they "feel far from victory" (v. 12). "I bring my victory near," promises God (v. 13). Zion and Israel will finally have salvation, and the glory of the Lord will dwell with them once more.

Chapter 46, though proclaiming the helplessness of idols, has its focus in these last six verses. This chapter is one of hope, proclaiming salvation to God's people. Having earlier prophesied of Israel's salvation from the Babylonian exile through Cyrus the Great (Isa. 44-45), in chapter 46, Isaiah describes the uselessness of the Babylonian gods and the final triumph of Jehovah over them. Isaiah turns to a descrip-

---

[1]However, the deliverer coming out of the east could also be an eschatological prophecy of the Messiah coming from the direction of the rising sun as he ushers in the millennial age. (Compare Isa. 46, footnote 11a with Isa. 63:1.)

tion of the fall of Babylon itself and prophesies that she will sit on the ground, dethroned, shamed, and deserted.

Chapter 47 is a beautifully written taunt song describing the destruction of Babylon. Using poetic parallelism and descriptive imagery, Isaiah speaks both to the people of his time and of all ages in portraying Babylon's shame:

47 Down with you! Sit in the dust,
virgin, daughter of Babylon.
Sit on the ground, dethroned,
daughter of the Chaldaeans.
Never again will you be called
tender and delicate.
²Take the millstones, grind the meal.
Remove your veil,
tie up your skirt, uncover your legs.
Wade through rivers.

³Let your nakedness be seen,
and your shame exposed.
I am going to take vengeance
and no one can stop me.

⁴Our redeemer, Yahweh Sabaoth[2] his name,
the Holy One of Israel, says:
⁵Sit in silence and creep into shadows,
daughter of the Chaldaeans,
for you will no longer be called
sovereign lady of the kingdom.
(JB)

"Chaldaeans" (vs. 1, 5) is a term with double meaning, used first to describe the inhabitants of southern Babylonia and second to represent magicians, sorcerers, astrologers, and diviners of all sorts. Isaiah prophesies that the daughter of the Chaldaeans will be brought low from her high-class background to the humiliating position of a slave.

Her work is done while she sits in the dust, a sign of extreme humiliation in Babylon. (Compare Jer. 13:18.) Isaiah uses six feminine imperative verbs in verse 2 to describe her status as a slave. While sitting, she has to "take" the two millstones that formed the common hand mill and "grind" the meal, a task of the lowest menial slaves. Furthermore she has to "remove" her veil and thus subject herself to public view, an inappropriate gesture for a married woman that many Arab women still shun to this day. Then she has to "tie" or lift up her skirt and "uncover" her legs in order to be unrestricted in her work. Finally, she must "wade" through the streams and canals that must be crossed daily by a working person in Babylon. Isaiah describes the punishment of Babylon, which is similar to the way the Israelites themselves were treated earlier in Mesopotamia.

2"Lord of hosts," KJV.

Not only must a slave girl submit herself to hard labor, but she is also often sexually abused, as alluded to in verse 3. The promise that Babylon will have her nakedness revealed means that she will be seen for what she truly is. The final result will be Babylon's disgrace and her own recognition that she has fallen out of favor with men (and the Lord, v. 5).

Part of the reason for Babylon's punishment is that she has abused her power over the Israelites. Speaking for the Lord, Isaiah describes her oppression against the Lord's children and promises that she will soon be without a husband and children:

6I was angry with my people,
I profaned my heritage.
I had surrendered it into your hands,
but you showed them no mercy.
On the aged you laid
your crushing yoke.
7You said, 'for ever
I shall be sovereign lady.'
You never took these things to heart
or pondered on their outcome.

8So listen now, voluptuous woman,
lolling at ease

and saying to yourself,
'I, and none besides me.
I shall never be widowed,
never know loss of children.'
9Yet both these things shall happen to you
both suddenly and on the same day.
Loss of children, widowhood, at once
will come to you;
in spite of all your witchcraft
and the power of all your spells.
(JB)

The Lord's denouncements upon ancient Babylon for her physical abuse of the Israelites can also easily apply to spiritual Babylon's religious oppression of God's children. As promised in similar words in Revelation 18:7-8, both Babylons will meet the same fate, in spite of their magical or evil powers.

As Isaiah concludes his taunt song, he analyzes the intellectual resources at Babylon's disposal. He recognized that the connection between Babylon's absolute power and her wisdom was based upon secular learning at best and manipulative deception at worst. One scholar describes Isaiah's insights about the power of this intellectual wisdom in Babylon as follows:

This is probably the first occasion in world-history when the way of making power absolute was not conceived in material terms such as armies, armaments, and financial resources, but in terms of the intellectual substructures of power. The literature of the neo-Babylonian empire furnishes us with enough knowledge of the diversity and profusion of Mesopotamia's intellectual and religious life during the period to lead us to understand this. (Westermann, *Isaiah 40-66*, p. 192.)

Isaiah warns Babylon about the ultimate danger of her wisdom:

¹⁰You were bold in your wickedness
and said,
"There is no one to see me."
That wisdom and knowledge of
yours
led you astray.
You said to yourself,
"I, and none besides me."
¹¹A calamity shall fall on you
which you will not be able to
charm away,
a disaster shall overtake you
which you will not be able to
avert,
unforeseen ruin
will suddenly descend on you.

¹²Keep to your spells then,
and all your sorceries,
for which you have worn yourself
out since your youth.
Do you think they will help you?
Do you think they will make
anyone nervous?

¹³You have spent weary hours with
your many advisers.
Let them come forward now
and save you, these who analyze
the heavens,
who study the stars
and announce month by month
what will happen to you next.

¹⁴Oh, they will be like wisps of
straw
and the fire will burn them.
They will not save their lives
from the power of the flame.
No embers these, for baking,
no fireside to sit by.
¹⁵This is what your wizards will be
for you,
those men for whom you have
worn yourself out since your
youth.
They will all go off, each his own
way,
powerless to save you. (JB)

It appears that in Isaiah's time, as today, astrologers predicted the course of events for the people and their communities. Evidently, the people of Israel placed more credence in the words of the astrologers than in the words of the prophets.

Despite Babylon's intellectualism and craftiness, she will stand helpless like the idols of her false gods in the face of destruction. Ancient Babylon fell and became an empty desert; there will be none to save spiritual Babylon from her ultimate disgrace (v. 15, see commentary on Isaiah 13-14).

On the other hand, the Lord is constantly ready to guide, protect, and save Israel and the righteous. (Isa. 45.) His salvation will come and rest in Zion for all Israel to enjoy. (Isa. 46:13.) All who desire to share God's glory must get "out from Babylon" and gather together "in Zion" in order to maintain the purity required of God's true children. (D&C 133:4-5.)

ISRAEL, ISRAEL, ISRAEL IN THE LAST DAYS
ISAIAH 48-49

Rarely does Isaiah take a single topic and develop it extensively in a given chapter; he usually combines three or four themes by weaving segments of each in and out of his writings throughout the course of many chapters. Any given topic is customarily treated for a few verses, abandoned, then emphasized and expanded when it surfaces in later verses and chapters.

As one studies Isaiah's literary tapestry, he admires the overwhelming beauty of the entire scene created by the myriads of recurring themes so masterfully interwoven by the grand artist. In addition, he can study an individual thread of a message and contemplate its composition and setting as it is woven into the tapestry of chapters.

Chapters 48 and 49 comprise a tapestry that combines threads already spun in chapters 40-47; they intertwine them with some new themes that are emphasized further in chapters 50-58. They both review chapters 40-47 and preview chapters 50-58. Here are a few of the earlier themes repeated in chapters 48 and 49:

1. Jehovah is the Lord of this earth (48:12-13, 17; compare 41:4, 28-29; 43:11-15, 22-24; 44:6).
2. God can predict things before they occur (48:3-9, 14-16; compare 41:21-29; 45:19-21).
3. Why and how the chosen people suffer (48:1-2, 9-11, 18-19, 22; 49:14-17; compare 42:8, 14, 22-25; 43:1, 22-28).
4. How Israel is blessed (48:20-21; 49:10-13, 18-26; compare 40:9, 11; 42:10-12; 43:1, 4-8, 25).
5. Role of the Lord's righteous servant (49:1-9; compare 42:1-4; 44:1-5).

6. Role of Cyrus (48:14-15; compare 44:28; 45:1-5).

Most of the themes mentioned here are found also in chapters 50-58. However, the role of Cyrus is not mentioned or even alluded to in the later chapters. Also, God's power to know the future is alluded to only in 55:8-13. Instead of witnessing that God can predict the future, Isaiah prophesies in chapters 50-58 what the Lord will do. Most of his promises are positive, and the ways in which Israel will be blessed become the dominant message. The following list shows where four of the above themes are repeated in chapters 50-58:

1. Jehovah is the Lord (50:2; 51:5, 15; 52:6; 53:4-12; 54:5; 55:5).
2. Israel's suffering (50:1-3; 51:17-23; 57:3–58:7).
3. Israel's blessings (51:1-16; 52:1-12; 54; 55:1-7; 56; 57:1-2; 58:8-14).
4. The Lord's servant (50:4-11; 52:13–53:12).

Isaiah gradually shifts emphasis in chapters 48 and 49 by moving from the context of his own age toward the latter days, and from a voice of warning to a voice of promise. Also, his tone becomes more hopeful as he anticipates the fulfillment of the Lord's promises through the work of his servants and the gathering of Israel.

It is no wonder, then, that the Book of Mormon leaders often quoted Isaiah 48 and 49 as they taught the Nephites about their destiny. In fact, chapters 48 and 49 are the first Isaianic chapters to be quoted in their entirety in the Book of Mormon. (1 Ne. 20-21.) Also, approximately one-third of the Isaianic verses in the Book of Mormon containing major changes are located in these two chapters. Therefore, as the New Jewish Version of these chapters is quoted throughout this text, the Book of Mormon changes will be added in italics. Some of these changes help to clarify passages that have perplexed scholars over the centuries. For example, C. Westermann states that there are "serious textual difficulties" in chapter 48 and that, so far, "editors have not succeeded in finding any convincing solution." He added that editors almost unanimously agree that chapter 49 contains additions by later scribes and that "we have to take account of transpositions, and also omissions." (*Isaiah 40-66*, pp. 195, 200, 213.) Interestingly, the Book of Mormon does support the premise that a few additions and even more omissions were made to the Isaiah text of chapters 48 and 49. The changes will be highlighted later.

The format of chapter 48 is very similar to a pattern used by Moses in the Book of Deuteronomy and by ancient kings in their treaties. The classical format of a treaty between a king and his vassal or, as Moses organized it, a covenant between the Lord and his people, has the following elements:

1. Preamble ("these are the words" of the king [or of Moses]; Deut. 1:5).
2. Historical prologue (the acts of the king or the Lord with Israel are reviewed; Deut. 1:6–4:49).
3. Stipulations (the relationship between the king and vassal or between God and Israel is outlined; Deut. 5-26).
4. Witnesses (various pagan deities or the Lord's servants on earth and in heaven witness the treaty; Deut. 27:1-8; 30:19; 31:26; 32:1-43).
5. Curses and blessings (the promises for breaking and maintaining the treaty or covenant are stated; Deut. 27-33).
6. Perpetuation of the contract (the treaty or covenant states where the text is to be maintained, how often it is to be reviewed and renewed, etc.; Deut. 27-28; 31:9-13, 24-27).

Although in a slightly different order, the same six elements are present in Isaiah 48:

1. Preamble (vs. 1-2); Hearken, O Israel, to the Lord.
2. Historical prologue (3-8a); the Lord reviews his earlier actions with Israel.
3. Stipulations (8b-13a); the Lord states what he is going to do.
4. Witnesses (16); Israel is a witness of what God has done.
5. Blessings and curses (17-22); the Lord contrasts the opposites that result from their righteous and wicked acts.
6. Perpetuation (13b-15); the Lord commands Israel to assemble and review what he has done.

These will each be discussed in turn.

Preamble (vs. 1-2)

Perhaps the best introduction to chapter 48 is by Nephi:

> Hear ye the words of the prophet, ye who are a remnant of the house of Israel, a branch who have been broken off; hear ye the words of the prophet, which were written unto all the house of Israel, and liken them unto themselves, that ye may have hope as well as your brethren from whom ye have been broken off; for after this manner has the prophet written. (1 Ne. 19:24.)

Isaiah's own words of introduction are:

48 *Hearken and* listen to this,
   O House of Jacob,
Who bear the name Israel
And have issued from the waters of
   Judah,
Or out of the waters of baptism,
Who swear by the name of the
   LORD
And invoke the God of Israel—

Though *they swear* not in truth and
   sincerity—
²*Nevertheless* for you are called after
   the Holy City
And you do *not* lean on the God of
   Israel, *who is the Lord of hosts,*
Yea, whose name is LORD of Hosts.
(NJV, italicized phrases from
1 Ne.)

A number of words and phrases are added in the 1 Nephi 20 rendition of these verses. The most significant addition is the phrase identifying the "waters of Judah" as the "waters of baptism" (v. 1).

This addition fits quite well within the verse, since the people are called first by their natural name as descendants of Jacob and then by their covenant title as followers of Israel. A parallelism naturally develops if the verse is also interpreted to mean that people come first out of the "waters of Judah" (the amniotic fluids of the womb, or the "loins"; RSV, NIV, and other translations) and then out of the "waters of baptism," representing a covenant or spiritual birth. The covenant then continues through the first verses as the people also make oaths in God's name and are then called after the name of his holy city.

Interestingly, the phrase "or out of the waters of baptism" was not in the original 1830 edition of the Book of Mormon, but appeared first in the 1840 printing. Latter-Day Saint scholar Daniel H. Ludlow provides some interesting background on this phrase:

> The term "or out of the waters of baptism" did not appear in the first edition of the Book of Mormon. It first appeared in the edition of 1840 on page 53, and the sentence in which it appeared was punctuated as follows: "Hearken and hear this, O house of Jacob, who are called by the name of Israel, and are come forth out of the waters of Judah, (or out of the waters of baptism,) who swear by the name of the Lord," etc. It is not absolutely clear who was responsible for the insertion of this phrase, although the title page of this edition indicates that it was the "Third Edition, Carefully Revised by the Translator" and was published in Nauvoo, Illinois.
>
> In the "Committee Copy" of the Book of Mormon that was used by Elder James E. Talmage and his committee in making the changes for the 1920 edition, the words "or out of the waters of baptism" were not printed in the text although they had been inserted in red ink in parentheses. However, the parentheses were crossed out by red pencil. These words are printed in the current edition of the Book of Mormon without the parentheses. (CSBM, p. 120.)

It seems unlikely that the additional phrase came from the prophet Isaiah himself or was inserted by Nephi in his copy of the text. Most likely, Joseph Smith inserted it to identify or amplify the phrase "out of the waters of Judah," a phrase that may have implied baptism to the ancient Israelites but that is meaningless to modern readers. Latter-day Saint scholar Hugh Nibley feels it was Joseph Smith's prerogative as translator to insert the clarifying phrase. (*Since Cumorah*, p. 151.)

As indicated earlier in the discussion on Isaiah chapter 1, the ordinance of baptism was known to the Jewish people. (See Moses 6:64-65.) It appears that Isaiah was rebuking those in Israel who called themselves Israelites because of their lineage, but who broke the commandments and covenants that true Israelites should maintain. Their hypocrisy is emphasized in verse 2, especially in the Book of Mormon translation; they called themselves a part of God's community, but did not rely upon him for spiritual guidance. Claus Westermann explains the distinction between the lineage and covenant relationships of Israel:

> The people addressed are the 'house of Jacob'. Strictly speaking, this means Jacob's own family. This is then explained in the first two appositions—those who bear the name of the patriarch Jacob and are descended from Judah. This indicates the first basis upon which the history of Israel rests—that solidarity, initiated by the blessing, which reaches back beyond the clans (north and south) to unite the generation now alive with the patriarchs who had received the promise of a future for the chosen people. The further appositions all refer to the other bases of Israel's history—her worship. (*Isaiah 40-66*, pp. 196-97.)

The term *Israel* appears frequently in Isaiah's writings, particularly after chapter 47, and the prophet applies it in at least three ways to mean blood Israel, covenant Israel, or the land of Israel. Blood Israelites are the literal descendants of Jacob or Israel (the "house of Jacob," v. 1). Covenant Israelites are those who accept the God and covenants of Israel (and call themselves Israel, v. 1; see Isa. 44:5). Land Israelites are the inhabitants of the land that was granted to the tribes of Israel, the area called Canaan, the Holy Land, or Palestine. (In chapter 49, Isaiah promises that a "covenant people" will be restored to their ancestral land as they are gathered from afar—in other words, covenant Israelites will also become land Israelites; vs. 8, 12, 22.) In reading Isaiah's prophecies concerning the Israelites in chapters 48 and 49, one must pay careful attention in order to understand which group of Israelites the prophet is addressing.

Historical Prologue (vs. 3-8a)

As Isaiah reviews Israel's covenant relationship with the Lord, he stresses the Lord's foreknowledge (italics indicate passages added and brackets mark segments omitted in 1 Ne. 20):

3*Behold* long ago, I foretold things that happened,
From My mouth they issued, and I announced them;
Suddenly I acted [and they came to pass].
4*And I did it* because I know how stubborn you are
(Your neck is like an iron sinew
And your forehead bronze),
5Therefore I told you long beforehand,
Announced things to you ere they happened—
And I showed them that you might not say, "My idol caused them,
My carved and molten images ordained them."

6You have heard all this; look, must you not acknowledge it?
As of now, I announce to you new things,
Well-guarded secrets you did not know.
7 Only now are they created, and not of old;
Before today you had not heard them;
When they were declared unto you;
You cannot say, "I knew them already."
8You had never heard, you had never known,
Your ears were not opened of old. (NJV)

In these verses, the Lord gives some reasons why he reveals things of the future to his people. His aim is not simply to enlighten Israel about her destiny or to prepare her for future dangers or blessings. Instead, he foretells some events (about which no one else can prophesy) so that when they do finally occur, the stubborn Israelites cannot claim that their pagan idols caused the events. Eventually, all people will recognize that the Lord truly did foretell and bring about all that he promised.

As Isaiah spoke, he prophesied new things that had not been recorded earlier. In verse 7, he states that Israel had not heard of these words. Verse 8 suggests that even when the prophetic words were delivered, they did not really hear them or know what they meant. Thus, Isaiah could have been delivering new prophecies that were available but that the Israelites did not understand. In any case, Isaiah gave new, inspired insights to help his people realize that God's foreordained and prophetic work comes about through divine powers and not through idols or false gods.

Stipulations of the Covenant (vs. 8b-13a)

The Lord explains that his efforts are in fulfillment of the covenants made with Israel. He promises that in spite of Israel's rebellion, he will not completely destroy her; still, he will not let her disregard her covenant without punishment:

8bThough I know that you are treacherous,
That you were called a rebel from birth,
9*Nevertheless* for the sake of My name I control My wrath;
To My own glory, I am patient with you,
And I will not destroy you.
10See, I refine you, but not as silver;
I test you in the furnace of affliction.

11For My sake, My own sake, do I act—
Lest [My name] is dishonored!
I will not give My glory to another.

12Listen to Me, O Jacob,
Israel, whom I have called:
I am He—I am the first,
And I am the last as well.
13My own hand founded the earth,
My right hand spread out the skies. (NJV)

Verse 10 contains a discrepancy between the King James Version and the Book of Mormon. The King James Version phrase "but not with silver" is deleted from the Book of Mormon. It disrupts the flow of the verse so badly that many commentators have said that its "meaning is obscure," that it has "defeated all commentators up to the present," and that it was probably "altered by a scribe who took the meaning to be 'I have not sold thee for money.'"[1] However, by omitting the phrase "but not with silver," the verse becomes simple and clear. Perhaps this verse is an example of a "gloss," an addition made by a later scribe in order to clarify the verse as he understood it. If so, the gloss was assuredly written after 600 B.C. when the Brass Plates of Laban were taken from Jerusalem, because the phrase is not quoted in the Book of Mormon version of this verse.

In verse 13, the Lord's creation of the heavens and earth is reviewed; in a structure of synonymous parallelism, Isaiah records that the Lord's "hand founded the earth" and his "right hand spread out the skies." Identifying the Lord's hand of power as the *right* hand helps explain why the right hand is traditionally favored in secular society and in religious matters. President Joseph Fielding Smith

---

[1]Cheyne, *The Prophecies of Isaiah* 2:4; *Beacon Bible Commentary*, p. 130; Ottley, *The Book of Isaiah According to the Septuagint*, p. 329.

quoted this Isaiah passage and explained that "showing favor to the right hand or side is not something invented by man but was revealed from the heavens in the beginning. There are numerous passages in the scriptures referring to the right hand, indicating that it is a symbol of righteousness and was used in the making of covenants." (AGQ 1:156.)

Perpetuation of the Covenant (vs. 13b-15)

The Lord petitions assembled Israel to sustain his work among them:

^{13b}I call unto them, let them stand up.
¹⁴Assemble, all of you, and listen!
Who among you foretold these things *unto them*:
"He whom the LORD loves
And he will fulfill his word which he has declared by them;
And he shall work His will against Babylon,
And, with His might, against Chaldea"?
¹⁵*Also, says the Lord; I the Lord I, I predicted and I called him to declare,*
I have brought him and he shall succeed in his mission. (NJV)

To fulfill his purposes, the Lord will bring forth a servant who will foretell the future, fulfill the Lord's word, wield power over Babylon, and ultimately succeed in his foreordained mission. Although Isaiah or Cyrus could possibly fit the description of this servant, the Lord Jesus Christ best exemplifies these qualities. It seems strange that the Lord Jehovah, who is delivering this message through Isaiah, would speak of himself in the third person as "he" and "him." Yet the Lord might be a spokesman for God the Father in delivering the Father's promise about Jesus Christ. Thus Jesus could deliver a prophecy about himself and still use the third person. Identifying the servant as Jesus Christ enriches the interpretation of these verses. The Lord, Jehovah, asks assembled Israel to recognize him as Heavenly Father's servant and to believe that through him all things will be fulfilled.

Witnesses of the Covenant (v. 16)

The Lord himself testifies of his relationship to Heavenly Father as he speaks further to Israel:

¹⁶Draw near to Me [and hear this]:
From the beginning, I did not speak in secret;
From the time anything *was declared* [existed], I *have spoken* [was there].

"And now the Lord GOD has sent
me, endowed with His spirit."
(NJV)

The Book of Mormon modifies verse 16 slightly by changing one
statement about the Lord. The idea that "since the beginning, the
Lord has existed" is changed to "when anything has been declared,
the Lord has spoken it." In essence, the Book of Mormon version
describes the Lord's role as being active rather than passive.

The verse concludes with what appears to be Isaiah's own witness. He testifies through the Spirit that the Lord God ("my lord,
Jehovah") sent him. Thus, verse 16 contains the testimonies of both
divine and mortal beings, for both the Lord and Isaiah bear witness to
the people.

Blessings and Curses (vs. 17-22)

Isaiah's covenant pronouncement concludes with a listing of opposites, the good and bad that will befall Israel depending upon her
actions:

17Thus said the LORD your
Redeemer,
The Holy One of Israel:
I *have sent him*, the LORD am
your God,
Instructing you for your own
benefit.
Guiding you in the way you
should go, *has done it.*
18If only you would heed My
commands!
Then your prosperity would be
like a river,
Your triumph like the waves of
the sea.
19Your offspring would be as many
as the sand,
Their issue as many as its grains.
Their name would never be cut
off
Or obliterated from before Me.

20Go forth from Babylon,
Flee from Chaldea!
Declare this with loud shouting,
Announce this,
Bring out the word to the ends of
the earth!
Say: "The LORD has redeemed
His servant Jacob!"
21They have known no thirst
Though He led them through
parched places;
He made water flow for them
from the rock;
He cleaved the rock and water
gushed forth.
22*And notwithstanding he has done all
this, and greater also,*
There is no safety—said the
LORD—for the wicked. (NJV)

It seems the sad nature of many that, in spite of the great blessings
promised them for righteousness, they choose to rebel against the

Lord. Instead of receiving peace, joy, and great posterity, they choose confusion, misery, and isolation. These concluding verses review what the Lord has promised his people. Yet in spite of his power and all that he does, he cannot overrule the eternal laws of justice and give eternal "peace" (KJV) to the wicked (v. 22). As this chapter emphasizes, God reminds the Israelites of his covenants with them but cannot force them to receive his blessings.

COVENANT ISRAEL'S COURT SCENE

In chapter 49, Isaiah builds upon the message of chapter 48, addressing scattered Israelites throughout the ages. While chapter 48 may apply more to the ancient members of covenant Israel, chapter 49 speaks to modern Israelites who claim to be part of the covenant people. Every Latter-day Saint should carefully study this chapter to see how he or she can become a true member of the house of Israel.

President Wilford Woodruff mentioned one reason this chapter is important for Latter-day Saints:

> The revelations that are in the Bible, the predictions of the patriarchs and prophets who saw by vision and revelation the last dispensation and fulness of times plainly tell us what is to come to pass. The 49th chapter of Isaiah is having its fulfillment. (SOT, pp. 96, 112.)

Isaiah reviewed in chapter 48 Israel's covenant relationship by following a pattern developed in ancient contracts and treaties. He seems to follow a similar pattern in chapter 49 by modeling his discourse after an ancient court scene or contract lawsuit. In an ancient lawsuit, after one party broke a covenant or contract, the other party (the plaintiff) could call the accused before a judge or the elders of the community. A court would then be convened, following four steps: the summons, the plaintiff's charge, the defendant's plea, and the judge's indictment. Chapter 49 follows these four steps.

The Summons (vs. 1-6)

The Lord himself issues the summons to scattered Israel. However, since Isaiah delivers the summons, it appears that he is talking about himself as he speaks about his role with Israel:

49 *And again: hearken O house of Israel,*
All you who are broken off and are driven out,
Because of the wickedness of the pastors of my people;
Yea, all you who are broken off, who are scattered abroad,
Who are of my people, O house of Israel.
Listen, O coastlands, to me,

And give heed, O nations afar:
The LORD appointed me before I
was born,
He named me while I was in my
mother's womb.
[2]He made my mouth like a
sharpened blade,
He hid me in the shadow of His
hand,
And He made me like a polished
arrow;
He concealed me in His quiver.
[3]And He said to me, "You are My
servant,
Israel in whom I glory."
[4]I thought, "I have labored in vain,
I have spent my strength for
empty breath."
But my case rested with the LORD,
My recompense was in the hands
of my God.

[5]And now the LORD has resolved—
He who formed me in the womb to
be His servant—
To bring back Jacob to Himself,
That Israel may be restored to
Him.
And I have been honored in the
sight of the LORD,
My God has been my strength.
[6]For He has said:
"It is too little that you should be
My servant
In that I raise up the tribes of
Jacob
And restore the survivors of Israel:
I will also make you a light of
nations,
That My salvation may reach the
ends of the earth."

(NJV, italicized phrases added)

The Book of Mormon version of this chapter includes a number of phrases not found in any biblical texts. The addition specifically directs the message to the scattered remnants of Israel, while the biblical texts imply that Isaiah's message is directed to the world at large. This distinction is important because when the Lord's servant is introduced later in verse 1, the reader more clearly understands that the servant has stewardship over a specific community.

These six verses comprise one of the four recognized "servant songs" of Isaiah (along with 42:1-4; 50:4-9; and 52:13-53:12; see pp. 358-60).Various scholars offer numerous possible identities for this servant: Isaiah, the nation Israel, Jesus Christ, and even Joseph Smith.[2]

In order to appreciate how the identity of the servant might be someone besides Isaiah, who authored the servant song, a few important characteristics of the servant will be listed and then some possible reasons will be given explaining why Israel, Jesus Christ, or Joseph Smith might fit the description of the promised servant:

---

[2]Cleon Skousen, *Treasures from the Book of Mormon* 1:1172; VIP, p. 113; DNTC 2:129; Joseph F. McConkie, *His Name Shall Be Joseph*, pp. 111-20.

1. He is selected before birth (foreordained) (v. 1).
   Israel: Elder Bruce R. McConkie states that Israelites were chosen for their particular lineage based upon their worthiness in the premortal life and the foreknowledge of God. (MD, p. 216.)
   Jesus Christ: Abraham records that Jesus was called before the earth was organized. (Abr. 3:27; see Moses 4:1-4; Luke 1:31; 2:21.)
   Joseph Smith: Joseph of Egypt prophesied of Joseph Smith, and Joseph Smith testified that he was foreordained to be a prophet in this dispensation. (2 Ne. 3:15; D&C 127:2; TPJS, p. 365.)
2. He is hidden in the Lord's hand (v. 2).
   Israel: The servants of the Lord through the chosen lineage have been hid "from the world with Christ." (D&C 86:8-9.)
   Jesus Christ: For four thousand years Jehovah did his work hidden from men until he finally came to earth himself. (Isa. 52:6.)
   Joseph Smith: He was among those addressed by the Lord in the last days who was hid up. (D&C 86:9.)
3. He is like a polished shaft (v. 2).
   Israel: This people has been prepared by the Lord to receive their proper calling. (D&C 136:31; Isa. 48:12, 17.)
   Jesus Christ: He learned obedience in all things through suffering and lived a perfect life. (Heb. 5:8-9; 3 Ne. 12:48.)
   Joseph Smith: The prophet specifically quoted this characteristic in relation to himself. (TPJS, p. 304; HC 5:401.)
4. He sometimes feels that he has labored in vain (v. 4).
   Israel: Ancient Israelites were often discouraged, and modern members of Christ's kingdom sometimes believe they have failed in their opportunities. (Isa. 49:14, 21, 24; D&C 84:3-5; 124:49-50.)
   Jesus Christ: The Messiah was rejected by his own people. (John 1:11; Luke 19:14; D&C 39:3.)
   Joseph Smith: The modern prophet eloquently expressed his discouragement while imprisoned in Liberty Jail. (D&C 121:1-6; 122:1-4, see also D&C 3:4; 21:7-8; 24:7-9.)
5. He will be involved with the gathering of Israel (vs. 5-6).
   Israel: The servants of covenant Israel will assist in gathering the rest of Israel, including the Lamanites, Ten Tribes, and the Jews. (Jacob 5:61-75; D&C 133:30-32; compare Gen. 49:22-26.)
   Jesus Christ: Although Israel was not gathered during the Savior's mortal ministry, he visited the remnants of Israel after his resurrection and prophesied concerning their gathering. (Matt. 23:37; 3 Ne. 15:11-24; John 10:16; Jacob 5:50-53.)

Joseph Smith: Joseph received the keys for gathering Israel. (D&C 90:3-4; 110:11; 2 Ne. 3:13.)

In answer to the question "Who is the servant referred to in Isaiah 49:1-6?" it seems that the limited evidence suggests that the term "servant" generally applies to the house of Israel's major representatives throughout the ages:

1. Isaiah, Israel's major prophet at the end of the eighth century B.C., was the last great prophet before the scattering of Israel.
2. Jesus Christ personally fulfilled the Father's promises to Jacob.
3. Ephraim, recipient of Jacob's birthright, is responsible for Israel's spiritual welfare and especially for her restoration in the last days.
4. Joseph Smith was the head of the dispensation of the fulness of times and the first prophet with the keys of the gathering of Israel in the last days.

It appears that the servant song in chapter 49 is talking more about Ephraim than the other possibilities; however, more important than identifying the exact servant described here is understanding the servant's characteristics and desiring to incorporate his traits into our own lives so that we can become true servants of the Lord. (See Jacob 5:61-63.)

The Plaintiff's Charge (vs. 7-13)

The Lord delivers the accusation to Israel, reminding her of the actions that fulfilled his obligations in their contract or covenant:

⁷Thus said the LORD,
The Redeemer of Israel, his Holy One,
To the despised being,
To the abhorred nation,
To the slave of rulers:
Kings shall see and stand up;
Nobles, and they shall prostrate themselves—
To the honor of the LORD who is faithful,
[To the Holy One of Israel who chose you.]
⁸Thus said the LORD:
In an hour of favor I answer you,
O isles of the sea,
And on a day of salvation I help you—
I created you and appointed you
my servant for a covenant people—
Restoring the land,
Allotting anew the desolate holdings,
⁹Saying to the prisoners, "Go free,"
To those who are in darkness, "Show yourselves."
They shall pasture along the roads,
On every bare height shall be their pasture.

¹⁰They shall not hunger or thirst,
   Hot wind and sun shall not strike
      them;
   For He who loves them will lead
      them,
   He will guide them to springs of
      water.
¹¹I will make all My mountains a
      road,
   And My highways shall be built
      up.
¹²*And then, O House of Israel,*
   Look! These are coming from
      afar,
   These from the north and the
      west,
   And these from the land of Sinim.
¹³Shout, O heavens, and rejoice, O
      earth!
   For the feet of those who are in the east
      shall be established;
   Break into shouting, O hills!
   For they shall be smitten no more;
   For the LORD has comforted His
      people,
   And has taken back His afflicted
      ones in love. (NJV)

Again, the Book of Mormon version of these verses contains a number of changes.

In verse 8 the Lord not only promises Israel's return from the far continents beyond Asia (the isles of the sea) but also indicates the role covenant Israel will play in that gathering: "The picture refers primarily not to the return from the Babylonian exile, but to the reestablishment of the Davidic kingdom under the Messiah when all the true seed of Abraham will receive their promised inheritance." (Young, *The Book of Isaiah* 2:279.) All this will be done in an "acceptable time" (KJV) to the Lord, sometime in the last days. (D&C 93:51.)

The prisoners set free (v. 9) could represent these who will live when "light shall break forth among them that set in darkness, and it shall be the fulness of my gospel." (D&C 45:28.) In other words, the people will be freed from the bondage of false beliefs and traditions by the restoration of the gospel. Also, the Lord might be promising freedom from spirit prison and the bonds of sin for those who repent, as well as liberation from the grave for all of God's children. (D&C 128:22.)

The gathering promised in verse 12 will be so extensive that remnants will come from as far as the land of Sinim. There has been much debate upon the location of Sinim. Some scholars believe it to be a place near Aswan, Egypt. (See Westermann, *Isaiah 40-66*, p. 216.) Others feel that the deserts of Sinim in Egypt form no suitable contrast to the gathering from the north and the sea as promised in the earlier part of the verse, since Egypt is too close to the Holy Land. Some scholars suggest that China is the land of Sinim:

Quite possibly, therefore, the reference is to a district to the east, so far away that it stands for a quarter of the earth. China may be that reference. The Arabic *tsin* may favor this. One cannot, however, be dogmatic. What is important is that a faraway district, a quarter of the earth, is intended, for the return to God in Christ will be worldwide. (Young, *The Book of Isaiah* 2:294; see Slotki, *Isaiah*, p. 12.)

Whether Sinim is near or far from Jerusalem, the fact that Israelites gather from there seems to be an unexpected miracle.

The Defendant's Plea (vs. 14, 21, 24)

In response to the Lord's charge of a broken covenant and his claim of continual involvement with Israel, the defendant, Israel, gives three complaints: (1) the Lord has forsaken her; (2) she is left alone without any friends, childless and captive (vs. 14, 21); and (3) she fears she has been robbed of her heritage (v. 24).

The Judge's Indictment (vs. 15-20, 22-23, 25-26)

The Lord answers all three complaints in turn, promising the solutions he will bring about. As one complaint is answered, Israel responds with another:

[14]*Behold*, Zion says,
"The LORD has forsaken me,   First complaint: Israel is
My Lord has forgotten me."   forgotten
But he will show that he has not.
[15]Can a woman forget her baby,   The Lord's response
Or disown the child of her womb?
Though she might forget,
I could never forget you, *O house*
of Israel.
[16]See, I have engraved you   The Lord's promise
On the palms of My hands,
Your walls are ever before Me.
[17]Swiftly your children are coming
against
Those who ravaged *yea*, and *those*
who ruined
you shall leave you.
[18]Look up all around you and see:
They are all assembled, *they* are
come to you!
As I live

412

—declares the LORD—
You shall don them all like jewels,
Deck yourself with them *even* like
a bride.
19As for your ruins and desolate
places
And your land laid waste—
You shall soon be crowded with
settlers,
While destroyers stay far from
you.
20The children you thought you
had lost
Shall yet say in your hearing,
"The place is too crowded for me;
Make room for me to settle."
(NJV)

In verse 14, Isaiah portrays Israel's lost faith in the Lord's ability to save her. The prophet concludes by asserting that the Lord will no more forget the house of Israel than a mother will forget her child.

In verse 16, the Lord promises that his hands will bear witness of his efforts for Zion. Just as a workman's hands often indicate his type of manual labor, the Lord's hands will reveal the nature of his labors: nail prints in his hands remind Israel of his fulfillment of the Atonement covenant. (Zech. 12:10; 13:6; D&C 45:48-53.)

Walls will stand as a perpetual memorial to the successful work of the Lord (v. 16), and her numbers will grow so quickly that there will be scarcely any room for all the people (vs. 17-20).

After Israel is promised a future restoration with great numbers, she complains that she has so few friends and children as a beginning:

21And you will say to yourself,
"Who bore these for me
When I was bereaved and barren,
Exiled and disdained—
By whom, then, were these
reared?
I was left all alone—
And where have these been?"
22Thus said the Lord GOD:
I will raise My hand to nations
And lift up My ensign to peoples;
And they shall bring your sons in
their bosoms
And carry your daughters on
their backs.
23Kings shall tend your children,
Their queens shall serve you as
nurses.
They shall bow to you, face to the
ground,

Second complaint:
Israel is childless

The Lord's promise

And lick the dust of your feet.
And you shall know that I am the
LORD—
Those who trust in Me shall not
be ashamed. (NJV)

Verses 22 and 23 answer Israel's question as to how she will grow so quickly. Her growth will come from the Gentile nations who will assist both temporally and spiritually to gather Israel. (D&C 77:11; 1 Ne. 22:3.) It is a paradox that the barren and widowed woman would find herself with so many children, but the gathering of Israel will be so sudden that it will catch her by complete surprise.

This gathering of Israel through the aid of foreign nations is taking place today. Since the Church was restored in 1830, the Jewish population in the Holy Land has grown from seven thousand to over three million people. Whereas in 1830 only one out of five hundred Jews resided in Palestine, one out of five now live in the modern state of Israel. Many foreign nations have supported the movement: Britain assisted in the establishment of a Jewish homeland in Palestine after World War I; Holland and Denmark helped protect many Jews from the holocaust; the United States, Russia, and others in the United Nations voted for the creation of a Jewish free state in 1947; the United States and France assisted Israel with military equipment in the first decades of her existence after 1948; and German reparation payments and large contributions from the United States and other nations have helped Israel financially. Truly, many nations have helped provide for the Jews over the centuries, assisting in their return and reestablishment as a nation.

Isaiah was not the only prophet who recorded many prophecies about Israel in the last days. Most Old Testament prophets spoke of this time immediately preceding the Millennium. Taken collectively, they have recorded dozens, even hundreds, of prophecies about the last days. However, even when different prophets discuss the same events, they do not record them in the same order; thus, it is difficult for us to determine the exact sequence of these prophecies.

The prophets also would often mix different types of prophecies (on social conditions, political developments, miracles, signs, etc.) and then leave it to us to sort them out and to see how they might interrelate. We could select hundreds of prophecies and then compile many lists of different types of prophecies about the last days (such as weather phenomena, social disturbances, wars, growth of the Church, return and role of the Ten Tribes, building of Zion in Jackson County, return of the Jews, etc.). We would often find more than one prophet foretelling the same event (for example, the moon not giving forth light or turning "into blood"—Isa. 13:10; 60:19; Ezek. 32:7; Joel 2:10, 31; 3:15; Acts 2:20; D&C 29:14; 34:9; 45:42; 88:87). When prophets living in different times and places say the same thing, their prophecies must be important and will be fulfilled as testified by these many witnesses. (See Amos 3:7.)

Of the many possible lists of prophecies of the last days, the following list includes only a selection of scriptures about Jews in the last days. The references are from prophets living in different dispensations (including our own) and on different continents. These prophecies were not yet fulfilled in 1830 when the Church was organized, but some of them have since been fulfilled (or have begun to be fulfilled), and all of them must be fulfilled before the Millennium is over. (For further lists of Old Testament prophecies about the last days, see CSOT, pp. 23-62.)

The following chart shows some of the major prophecies about the Jews that have been fulfilled since 1830. It includes key dates and events surrounding their fulfillment.

Prophecies Pertaining to the Return of Judah That Have Been Fulfilled or at Least Partially Fulfilled

1. *Elijah the Prophet to return to the earth.* (Mal. 4:5-6; 3 Ne. 24-25; D&C 98:16-17; D&C 110:13-16; JS-H 1:36-39.) April 3, 1836, Kirtland Temple; on the same day, Moses visited Joseph Smith and restored the keys for the gathering of Israel.
2. *Descendants of Judah to gather.* (Isa. 11:12; Jer. 16:14-21; Zech. 2:11-12; 10:6-9, 12; 1 Ne. 19:13-17; 2 Ne. 10:7-8; Ether 13:11-12; D&C 110:11; JS-H 1:40; HC 4:456; 5:336-37.) In 1881, only one out of three hundred of the world's Jews were in Palestine; in 1882, Russian May Laws resulted in large-scale emigration (mostly to the United States) and the first major immigration wave to Palestine; other waves followed, until by 1980, approximately one out of five Jews were in Israel.
3. *Gold and silver from the nations to revive the land.* (Isa. 6-9, 14; Zech. 14:14; Jer. 32:41; 43-44; MS 41:244; JD 15:272.) In 1897, the first Zionist Congress was held in Basel, Switzerland. Shortly thereafter, the Jewish National Fund was organized to purchase land in Palestine as an eternal inheritance for the Jews. After 1948, large financial contributions (especially from American Jews) were necessary to keep Israel economically solvent with a large defense budget and trade balance deficiencies.
4. *The land of Jerusalem to be made productive.* (Isa. 35:1-2, 5-7, 10; Ezek. 36:34-36; Amos 9:14-15; 2 Ne. 27:28; HC 4:457.) In 1920, England assumed mandate over Palestine after the Balfour Declaration and the British conquest of Jerusalem from the Ottoman Turks; research stations were established, plagues were reduced, mil-

lions of trees were planted, Jezreel valley was drained, and citrus crops began to be exported. In 1975, Israel exported over $290 million worth of food and flowers.

5. *The descendants of Judah to be attacked and delivered.* (Isa. 54:3, 8, 17; Zech. 12:6, 9; Jer. 23:5-8; 45:28; 2 Ne. 6:8; 24:12; 3 Ne. 22:12, 17.) In 1948, Israel fought a war of independence against all her Arab neighbors. She fought Egypt in the Sinai conflict during 1956. In June 1967, she used a strong first strike and air superiority to acquire the Sinai from Egypt, East Jerusalem and the West Bank from Jordan, and the Golan Heights from Syria in the Six Day War. In October 1973, Egypt and Syria took the initiative and inflicted great losses on Israel in the Yom Kippur War before the Jews used brilliant strategy across the Suez Canal and in the Golan to gain a cease-fire. In November 1977, Anwar Sadat went to Jerusalem and encouraged peace talks. In March 1979, Egypt and Israel signed a peace treaty and exchanged ambassadors.

6. *Jerusalem will come under the control of Israel.* (Isa. 62:5-12; Zech. 2:12; 12:6 [see also Zech. 7-8]; 3 Ne. 20:29, 33-34; HC 4:457.) On June 7, 1967, with serious hand-to-hand combat, Israel used a three-pronged attack across northern Jerusalem and moved into the Old City of Jerusalem through the Lion's Gate. Israeli forces soon moved to the Wailing Wall for an emotional reunion between the Jews and their most sacred site.

7. *The Jewish people will begin to believe in Jesus Christ.* (Isa. 49:26; 66:21-23; Deut. 4:25-31; Jer. 16:21; 31:31-34; Matt. 24:14; 1 Ne. 10:14; 15:16; 3 Ne. 20:29-31, 46; Morm. 5:12-14; D&C 133:8; JD 2:200.) In October 1975, in a meeting with regional and mission representatives, President Spencer W. Kimball repeated three times, "Now is the time of the Jew." In November 1975, a special committee prepared missionary discussions and pamphlets for the Jews (which were revised four years later). In January 1977, the first "cultural representatives" of the Church entered Israel. By 1980, a few hundred missionaries were teaching Jews in the United States and some other countries with limited success.

Many other important prophecies about the Jews in the last days remain to be fulfilled:

Prophecies Pertaining to the Return of Judah That Are Largely Still in the Future

1. *A new temple will be built in Jerusalem.* (Isa. 60:13; Zech. 8:7-9; Ezek. 40:48; D&C 124:36-37; MS 52:740; HC 5:423.)
2. *A leader named David . . . will lead Israel.* (Isa. 11:1-6; 55:3-4; Ezek. 37:21-25; Jer. 23:3-8; 30:3-9; Hosea 3:4-5; Zech. 3:8-9; 6:11-13; HC 6:253; HC 4:457.)
3. *The nations . . . will gather . . . and Judah will be smitten.* (Isa. 65:11-12; Zech. 14:2; Rev. 11:1-13; D&C 45:26-27; JS-M 1:4; 12-19; WW, pp. 509-10.)
4. *Two prophets are to be raised up to the Jewish nation.* (JST Isa. 51:18-20; Rev. 11:2-3; 6:12; 2 Ne. 8:18-20; D&C 77:15; JD 16:329; IDYK, p. 197.)
5. *The Savior to appear to the descendants of Judah.* (Isa. 63:1; Zech. 12:10; 13:6; 14:9; D&C 45:51-59; JS-M 1:20-27; JD 15:277-78.)
6. *The Messiah to lead Israel to victory and rule as King of Kings.* (Isa. 63:2-6; Zech. 14:3, 9; D&C 133:41-42; WW, pp. 509-10; MS 21:583.)
7. *Two great world capitals are to be established, Zion and Jerusalem.* (Isa. 2:2-3; Heb. 12:22; Rev. 3:12; Ether 13:4-11; D&C 133:19-25, 35; *Improvement Era* 22:815-16.)

This list highlights only some major prophecies about the Jews in the last days; similar prophecies about the growth, spiritual and political strength, and gathering of the Lamanites are also finding fulfillment or preparation for their fulfillment. President Spencer W. Kimball said about the Lamanites:

> The brighter day has dawned. The scattering has been accomplished; the gathering is in process. May the Lord bless us all as we become nursing father and mothers (see Isa. 49:23 and 1 Ne. 21:23) unto our Lamanite brethren and hasten the fulfillment of the great promises made to them. (CR, Oct. 1965, p. 72.)

Prophecies concerning the Ten Tribes and their return and growth also will be fulfilled. (D&C 133:26-33; TG "Israel, Ten Lost Tribes of.") Finally, all Israel will be gathered and restored in great numbers, as promised by the Lord through Isaiah. (See TG "Israel, Gathering of.")

The gathering will be so vast that Israel issues her last complaint, or more correctly, a question about how this work could be brought forth from her powerful enemies:

²⁴Can spoil be taken from a warrior
  Or captives retrieved from a
    victor?

Third complaint: Israel is robbed

²⁵Yet thus said the LORD:

The Lord's response

  Captives shall be taken from a
    warrior
  And spoil shall be retrieved from
    a tyrant;
  For the Mighty God shall deliver his
    covenant people.

The Lord's promise

  For thus saith the Lord:
  For I will contend with your
    adversaries,
  [And I will deliver your children.]
²⁶I will make your oppressors eat
    their own flesh,
  They shall be drunk with their
    own blood as with wine.
  And all mankind shall know
  That I the LORD am your Savior,
  The Mighty One of Jacob, your
    Redeemer. (NJV)

417

The Book of Mormon changes noted above in italics are found in 2 Nephi 6:17, as quoted by Jacob. Interestingly, the same passage as quoted by Nephi in 1 Nephi 21:25 does not have these changes, but is basically the same as the King James Version. It appears that Jacob changed the order of some phrases by dropping the last phrase of verse 25, "I will save thy children" (KJV) and adding the phrase "For the Mighty God shall deliver his covenant children," which conveys the same message found earlier in the verse. The only major difference is his substitution of "covenant people" for "children," defining God's children as those who keep his covenants.

Probably the best summary of Isaiah's prophecies about the house of Israel is found in the Book of Mormon. After quoting chapters 48 and 49, Nephi gives an inspired commentary and concludes with the promise:

> Wherefore, he will bring them again out of the captivity, and they shall be gathered together to the lands of their inheritance; and they shall be brought out of obscurity and out of darkness; and they shall know that the Lord is their Savior and their Redeemer, the Mighty One of Israel. (1 Ne. 22:12; see also vs. 3, 6, 11.)

Today, we, the members of covenant Israel, have a marvelous opportunity to share the gospel with the entire house of Israel and all nations as we seek to bring all people out of spiritual darkness into a personal relationship with the Savior.

HEAR, O JERUSALEM,
THE PROPHET'S VOICE
ISAIAH 50-51

Isaiah 50 and 51 are set in the middle of the sections of chapters directed to Israel. (Isa. 48-52.) The Book of Mormon prophet Jacob expressed the value of these chapters when, after quoting Isaiah 49-52:2, he said he wanted to teach his people "concerning the covenants of the Lord that he has covenanted with all the house of Israel." (2 Ne. 9:1.) Isaiah speaks specifically to covenant Israel in chapters 50 and 51.

Isaiah begins chapter 50 with a promise of the Savior's redemption, continues with a foreshadowing of the Lord's future mission and suffering, and concludes with a terse reminder of Israel's responsibility to trust in the Lord's word. In chapter 51, Isaiah reminds Israel of her covenant heritage, promises a time when the remnants of Israel will trust in the Lord, testifies concerning the Lord's strength, and foretells the Lord's mercy toward Israel.

Chapter 50 is divided into three main sections: verses 1-3, a call to Israel to return to the Lord and make him their strength; verses 4-9, the third servant song; and verses 10-11, an injunction to all people to follow the servant, including a message of encouragement to the faithful and of warning to the unfaithful.

A Call to Israel (vs. 1-3)

Israel has gone away from the Lord and suffered much punishment, but there is no cause to fear that this separation will be permanent:

50 The Lord says,
"Do you think I sent my
people away
like a man who divorces his
wife?
Where, then, are the papers of
divorce?
Do you think I sold you into

419

captivity
like a man who sells his children
as slaves?
No, you went away captive
because of your sins;
you were sent away because of
your crimes.
2"Why did my people fail to
respond
when I went to them to save
them?
Why did they not answer when I
called?

Am I too weak to save them?
I can dry up the sea with a
command
and turn rivers into a desert,
so that the fish in them die for
lack of water.
3I can make the sky turn dark,
as if it were mourning for the
dead." (TEV; note changes in
2 Ne. 7:12)

In chapter 49, Isaiah foretells a time when scattered Israel would feel that the Lord had forsaken her, but adds, "He will show that he hath not." (Isa. 49:13-17.) This same concern and consolation is found in verse 1.

In the first verse, the Lord asks to see the bill of divorcement between him and Israel. Alluding to the law of divorce given in Deuteronomy 24:1-4, which requires a formal bill of divorcement when a man puts away his wicked wife, the Lord asks a rhetorical question because he knows he has never given such a bill to his beloved. Although they are separated, they are not divorced. (Hosea, a contemporary of Isaiah, used the same analogy in his prophecy; see Hosea 1.)

Furthermore, the Lord avers that he has not sold Israel into bondage and captivity as some fathers did in times of severe economic hardship. In the time of Isaiah, if a man was pressed by his creditors, he had the possibility of relieving his debt by selling his children as slaves. (Ex. 21:7; Neh. 1-5; Matt. 18:25.) And if he died, a creditor might take his children as payment. (2 Kgs. 4:1.) This slavery was not permanent; the person was indentured to work for a fixed number of years. In answer to the question "To whom has the Lord ever been in debt?" Isaiah answers that the Lord is indebted to no one and therefore has not been forced to sell Israel; Israel's separation and captivity is her own fault.

Indeed, verses 2 and 3 indicate that at any time, the Lord could have returned and redeemed Israel if she had just called for his help. The same invitation to call upon God and receive his strength is repeated in modern scripture:

In that day when I came unto mine own, no man among you received me, and you were driven out. When I called again there was none of you to answer; yet my arm was not shortened at all that I could not redeem, neither my power to deliver. Behold, at my rebuke I dry up the sea. I make the rivers a wilderness; their fish stink, and die for thirst. I clothe the heavens with blackness, and make sackcloth their covering. (D&C 133:66-69.)

The Lord's power is particularly manifest in the seas and the heavens, elements over which mortals have the least control. Isaiah reminds Israel that the Lord is able to save and redeem them; he recalls the miracles during the exodus from Egypt. At the Lord's command, the sea was dried and the fish shriveled up. (Ex. 7:21; 14:26-31; see Ps. 74:12-15; 107:33.) The final miracle referred to is the darkness that covered Egypt. (Ex. 10:21.) However, in describing the darkness as a covering of "sackcloth" (KJV) Isaiah presents a double picture. At the second coming of Christ, the heavens will be darkened, and the wicked will mourn in sackcloth. By closing with this symbol, Isaiah reminds Israel both of merciful redemption and the consequences of refusing his invitation.

A Servant Song (vs. 4-9)

After Isaiah and Joseph Smith (in the Doctrine and Covenants) record the Lord's ability to redeem Israel, each prophet extends an invitation to the world to heed the words of the Lord's servants. Joseph Smith records that the Lord's message was that Israel "believed not" and "received not" the Lord's servants when they were sent to her. (D&C 133:71.) Isaiah is more poetic in describing how the Lord's servant was rejected by the people:

⁴The Sovereign Lord has taught me
    what to say,
    so that I can strengthen the
    weary.
Every morning he makes me eager
    to hear what he is going to teach
    me.
⁵The Lord has given me
    understanding,
    and I have not rebelled
    or turned away from him.
⁶I bared my back to those who beat
    me.

I did not stop them when they
    insulted me,
    when they pulled out the hairs
    of my beard
    and spit in my face.
⁷But their insults cannot hurt me
    because the Sovereign Lord
    gives me help.
I brace myself to endure them.
I know that I will not be
    disgraced;
⁸   for God is near,
    and he will prove me innocent.

421

Does anyone dare bring charges
against me?
Let us go to court together!
Let him bring his accusation!
⁹The Sovereign Lord himself
defends me—

who, then, can prove me guilty?
All my accusers will disappear;
they will vanish like motheaten
cloth. (TEV; note changes in
2 Ne. 7:4, 8)

These verses, comprising the third servant song, portray the "servant" as the epitome of righteousness. As with the other servant songs, controversy surrounds the interpretation of these verses. The servant could be any number of people or peoples. Perhaps it is the prophet Isaiah himself telling how he has been insulted, or perhaps it is the nation of Israel that has suffered persecutions throughout the long centuries of their dispersal from the land of Palestine. However, as far as the Bible records, Isaiah was not persecuted during his ministry. Also, the verses do not seem to apply to Israel as a nation, since they suffered a just punishment for their disobedience, whereas the servant suffers undeservedly for others. The most acceptable identification is Christ, because these verses describe events in the life of Jesus. In reading this servant song, however, we should not limit these references to the life of Christ, but should try to apply them to many of God's chosen servants.

Verses 4 and 5 outline the ministry of the servant. The daily discharge of the servant's office is to hear and speak the word of God. God gave him an assignment, and he is not rebellious nor does he turn away from this labor.

Verse 6 is specifically messianic, describing the physical abuse endured by the servant in his service:

> The servant now presents details to show how he was not rebellious. The striking language calls to mind immediately the physical sufferings of our Lord (cf. Matt. 26:67ff.; 27:26ff.; John 19:1ff.) . . . The strikers or smiters would be those who have the public duty of beating a criminal. Beating on the back would seem also to be the custom in the punishment of evil men (cf. Prov. 10:13; 19:29; 26:3 and cf. Ps. 129:3).
>
> In addition the servant gave his cheeks to those who pluck out the hair. The reference is to those who deliberately give the most heinous and degrading of insults. The Oriental regarded the beard as a sign of freedom and respect, and to pluck out the hair of the beard (for *cheek* in effect would refer to a beard) is to show utter contempt. (Young, *The Book of Isaiah* 3:300.)

In light of his suffering and humiliation, one of Christ's commands has a fuller meaning: "But I say unto you, that ye resist not evil: but whosoever shall smite thee on thy right cheek, turn to him the other also." (Matt. 5:39.)

As he stood before the soldiers in the common hall of judgment, they spat upon him, smote him with a reed, crowned him with thorns, and bowed before him in mockery. Yet he silently endured the abuse. (Matt. 27.)

Just as Christ endured, so can we. All of us can put ourselves in the position of this servant and apply these verses to the temptations and trials we face. Just as God upheld his Son, so shall he uphold us, as promised in verses 7-9. In all that the innocent suffer, they should not be ashamed. Eventually those who condemn and contend against God's work, whether it be against Christ or one of his servants, will perish and "wax old as a garment." While the emphasis of this servant song seems to be on Christ, its universality is also apparent. Many of God's servants suffer, but as they fulfill their callings, the Lord upholds and defends them.

An Injunction to All People (vs. 10-11)

Isaiah ends this chapter with an antithetical couplet. He asks, "Who among us fears the Lord and heeds the voice of the servant?" Even though we may walk in darkness, we are admonished to trust in the Lord. We might very well understand this passage as an admonition to follow the servant of God, either Christ or his prophets:

¹⁰All of you that have reverence for the Lord and obey the words of his servant, the path you walk may be dark indeed, but trust in the Lord, rely on your God.

¹¹All of you that plot to destroy others will be destroyed by your own plots. The Lord himself will make this happen; you will suffer a miserable fate. (TEV)

In contrast to those who follow the Lord (v. 10), Isaiah speaks in verse 11 to those who "walk in the light of their own fires" (KJV). This refers to those who refuse to hear the Lord through the voice of his servants, and thus become a law unto themselves. (D&C 88:35.) This is a major problem in the world today: "They seek the Lord to establish his righteousness, but every man walketh in his own way, after the image of his own god, whose image is in the likeness of the world." (D&C 1:16.) There is no righteous reward for those who refuse to follow the Lord. They shall "suffer a miserable fate," including eternal sorrow (v. 12; see D&C 133:70-74.)

In bridging chapters 50 and 51, it is helpful to see how another ancient prophet teaches with these chapters. Jacob quotes chapters 50 and 51 in the Book of Mormon. (2 Ne. 6-8.) He says that he has read these things so that he might teach his brethren "concerning the covenants of the Lord that he has covenanted with all the house of Israel." (2 Ne. 9:1.) Using Isaiah 50:1-3 as his text, Jacob teaches his listeners that the Jews will be restored to the true church of God and reestablished in the lands of their inheritance (Palestine). (2 Ne. 9:2.) This restoration took place when the Jews returned from the Babylonian captivity between the years 538-515 B.C.

Jacob and his Nephite brethren were concerned about their fellow Jews who were in a serious state of spiritual apostasy when Lehi's family left Jerusalem. In 2 Nephi 9:3, Jacob comments that he is telling the Nephites these things so that they may rejoice. He speaks eloquently of the coming of Jesus Christ in the flesh to atone for the sins of mankind. (2 Ne. 9:4-27.) His discourse on the Atonement corresponds with Isaiah 50:4-9.

Jacob then turns his attention to the remainder of chapter 50, verses 10-11, exhorting his people not to rely upon their own wisdom ("light of your fire") but to "fear the Lord" and "listen to the voice of his servant":

> When they are learned they think they are wise, and they hearken not unto the counsel of God, for they set it aside, supposing they know of themselves, wherefore, their wisdom is foolishness and it profiteth them not. And they shall perish. (2 Ne. 9:28.)

Jacob concluded the day's teaching to his brethren by speaking extensively on the final judgment, the time when all men will stand before God to be judged. (2 Ne. 9:29-54.) This discourse parallels the end of verse 11 of Isaiah 50.

Continuing his discourse the next day, Jacob speaks more on the servant song, applying it to Christ. (2 Ne. 10:1-6.) In the rest of chapter 10 of 2 Nephi, Jacob applies Isaiah 50 to teach the full meaning of the covenants the Lord has made with the entire house of Israel: (A) he speaks of the Jews accepting Christ in the last days and returning to the lands of their inheritance (2 Ne. 10:7-9; compare Isa. 49:22-23; (B) he foresees America (Zion) being an inheritance to the righteous Gentiles (2 Ne. 10:10-18; compare 3 Ne. 23:2-4); and (C) he concludes by reminding the Nephites of their heritage and reviewing the Lord's work with the house of Israel (2 Ne. 10:18-25).

Isaiah 51, which Jacob had quoted earlier, reverses the order of Jacob's themes: (C') Isaiah begins with a reminder to Israel of her heritage and the Lord's work (51:1-8); (B') Isaiah promises that the righteous will enjoy the blessings of Zion (51:9-16); and (A') he concludes with warnings and promises to the Jews in the last days (51:17-23).

Israel's Heritage (vs. 1-3)

In order for God's covenants to be fulfilled, the Jews must remember whose children they are. It may seem peculiar that God must tell the Jews to remember their noble ancestors, Abraham and Sarah, but they need to remember God's promises with Abraham:

51 The Lord says,
"Listen to me, you that want to be saved,
you that come to me for help.
Think of the rock from which you came,
the quarry from which you were cut.
²Think of your ancestor, Abraham, and of Sarah, from whom you are descended.
When I called Abraham, he was childless,
but I blessed him and gave him children;
I made his descendants numerous.
³"I will show compassion to Jerusalem,
to all who live in her ruins.
Though her land is a desert, I will make it a garden,
like the garden I planted in Eden.
Joy and gladness will be there,
and songs of praise and thanks to me. (TEV)

New Testament scriptures tell us that Abraham was justified by his works and that his faith and belief in the Savior were counted as righteousness. (Rom. 4:33; James 2:23.) The Lord calls upon his people to do the works of Abraham, seek for the spiritual blessings that Abraham obtained, and look forward to and accept the Savior as Abraham did. (Gal. 3:6-9, 24-29; 4:28; John 8:56-58.)

Next, the Lord recounts the covenants he had made with Abraham, great posterity and lands (v. 3; see Abr. 2:8-11). As the Jews accept Abraham by doing his works and believing in Christ, Zion (Jerusalem) will be comforted and her ruins rebuilt; it will be like Eden, the garden of the Lord. (See D&C 103:17; 132:30-31.) Gladness, joy, and thanksgiving will then abide among those who follow the servant, Christ.

Of course, these ideal conditions will prevail in Palestine and over all the earth only after Christ comes and begins his millennial reign. The precise sequence of events leading to the Millennium is not given in the scriptures. Often in prophetic writings, some events are spoken of one after another in quick succession, giving the impression that the events will all take place in a very short period of time. In reality, the signs may occur over a period of years and even centuries. On the other hand, sometimes the prophet overlaps his prophecies and begins speaking of another prophecy before fully explaining the first. Because of patterns like these, prophecies of the last days are often confusing. For example, in verses 1-3 God admonishes the Jews to remember Abraham and to seek after their Lord. As they do this, they will be comforted and gathered in from their long dispersion to the lands of their inheritance, Palestine. (2 Ne. 10:6.) But this doesn't mean that they *all* will believe before they return. (The relationship between Jewish attitudes and their returning to Palestine is discussed more fully in the special topic "Return of the Jews in the Last Days" on pp. 301-3 of this book.) In a similar manner, the redemption of the land of Palestine will take time. Today we are blessed to see the beginning of the fulfillment of these covenants. In time, we will witness their complete fulfillment and sing and rejoice with the Jews and the rest of the house of Israel (v. 3).

The Lord's Work (vs. 4-8)

Continuing the theme of the Lord's deliverance, Isaiah speaks for the Lord and calls upon Israel to hearken and give ear, to listen to what the Lord says:

4"Listen to me, my people,
   listen to what I say:
I give my teaching to the nations;
   my laws will bring them light.
5I will come quickly and save them;
   the time of victory is near.
I myself will rule over the nations.
   Distant lands wait for me to
      come;
   they wait with hope for me to
      save them.
6Look up at the heavens; look at the
      earth!
The heavens will disappear like
      smoke;
   the earth will wear out like old
      clothing,

and all its people will die like
   flies.
But the deliverance I bring will
   last forever;
   my victory will be final.
7"Listen to me, you that know what
   is right,
   who have my teaching fixed in
      your hearts.
Do not be afraid when people
      taunt and insult you;
8   they will vanish like motheaten
      clothing!
But the deliverance I bring will
   last forever;
   my victory will endure for all
      time." (TEV)

The Jews are here called "my people" and "my nation" to stress the idea that they have not been forsaken by the Lord and that by accepting him they will be God's children (v. 7; Isa. 50:1-3). The Lord's way is a light to the people (v. 7; Isa. 49:6; compare D&C 93:36). Again, the idea of following one's own wisdom instead of God's is mentioned. (Isa. 50:11.) This could be because the Israelites placed more emphasis upon knowledge and study than upon giving heed to the prophets. (Jacob 4:14.)

In verse 6, the Lord speaks of his second coming and the events surrounding it. Though the telestial order of the heavens and earth may pass away, the victory and triumph of the Lord will endure forever. The passing away of heaven and earth can be interpreted in one of three ways: (1) the Lord pronounces the certainty of his word, counsel, and judgment in contrast to the transitory nature of the world (Matt. 24:35; Luke 21:33; D&C 1:38); (2) the Lord promises the righteous that their salvation or resurrection is eternal and does not depend upon the world; and (3) the Lord foretells the events immediately preceding either the Millennium or the earth's celestial transformation (Isa. 64: Rev. 21:1). In any case, the righteous will see the day when they will not be persecuted or destroyed.

Isaiah admonishes those who do accept the Lord not to fear the insults of men (v. 7). He knows that they will have opposition in following the Lord and warns them not to fear, because those who brandish such insults will pass like an old garment, like wool before a moth. But salvation will uphold those who endure and follow the servant, for God's victory endures forever (v. 8).

The Blessings of Zion (vs. 9-16)

Before Zion can be established among Israel, the Lord must exert his powers to bring it about. If Israel seeks him, he will use his strength to assist her to fulfill her destiny. (Isa. 50:2-3.) In verses 9-11, Israel finally calls upon the Lord, and the Lord responds and recounts his powers (vs. 11-16). First, Israel's petition:

9Wake up, Lord, and help us!
Use your power and save us;
use it as you did in ancient
times.
It was you that cut the sea
monster Rahab to pieces.

10It was you also who dried up the
sea
and made a path through the
water,
so that those you were saving
could cross.

427

[11]Those whom you have rescued
    will reach Jerusalem with
        gladness,
    singing and shouting for joy.
	They will be happy forever,
	    forever free from sorrow and
	        grief. (TEV)

As indicated earlier, the sea monster (Rahab) mentioned in v. 9 probably represents Satan (see commentary on Isa. 17:1), but might also represent Egypt. (See MLB text of Isa. 30:7 on p. 00 of this book.) Perhaps Isaiah is reminding the people of the Lord's victory over Satan as well as his miracles in Egypt.

The Lord will again work many miracles for Israel in her later exodus from the "world" back to her promised land. As the Israelites return from many nations, they will come with great rejoicing, for the prophecies are being fulfilled (v. 11; D&C 101:18-19; compare D&C 45:71; 66:11).

Isaiah emphasizes the source of power behind their return in the next few verses. The Lord offers assurance to those who have forgotten him:

[12]The Lord says,
    "I am the one who strengthens
        you.
    Why should you fear mortal   Question A
        man,
    who is no more enduring than
        grass?
[13]Have you forgotten the Lord who   Question B
        made you,
    who stretched out the heavens
    and laid the earth's
        foundations?
    Why should you live in constant   Question C
        fear
    of the fury of those who oppress
        you,
    of those who are ready to
        destroy you?
    Their fury can no longer touch   Answer C
        you.
[14]Those who are prisoners will soon
        be set free;
    they will live a long life
    and have all the food they need.

15"I am the Lord your God;   Answer B
   I stir up the sea
   and make its waves roar.
 My name is the Lord Almighty!
16I stretched out the heavens
   and laid the earth's
      foundations;
 I say to Jerusalem, 'You are my   Answer A
    people!
   I have given you my teaching,
   and I protect you with my
      hand.' " (TEV)

As noted in the right-hand column, the Lord asks Israel three questions: Why do you fear mortal man? Have you forgotten your creator? Why fear your oppressors? He then answers them (in reverse order): You will be freed from your oppressors. I am the great creator. You are my people; I will teach and protect you.

Although these promises seem to be extended to all types of Israelites, they apply more particularly to those who become a part of covenant Israel, members of The Church of Jesus Christ of Latter-day Saints. Joseph Smith foretells that one group of Israelites, the remnants of the Ten Tribes, will come to Ephraim at "the boundaries of the everlasting hills." (See D&C 133:32-35.)

The parallels between these three verses and Isaiah 51:9-16 are evident. They help us to understand Isaiah's words and to see their fulfillment in those who join the Church in this dispensation.

Warnings to Judah in the Last Days (vs. 17-23)

Because of wickedness, the ancient Jews were scattered and taken captive to Babylon. Later, some Jews returned to Jerusalem and rebuilt the temple. Unfortunately, this Jewish community also became wicked, and most of their descendants rejected Christ when he lived on earth. Because of their iniquities, they suffered great destruction, another scattering, and the hatred of men. (See 2 Ne. 6:10-11; 10:3-6.) But punishment, dispersion, and persecution are not to be their permanent condition. The Lord will bless, gather, and protect them as they return to the Lord, especially after they accept him as their Messiah. (2 Ne. 6:11; 10:7-9.)

Isaiah prophesies in the last verses of chapter 51 of the final effects of the Lord's judgments and the world's hatred:

17Jerusalem, wake up!
  Rouse yourself and get up!
You have drunk the cup of
    punishment
  that the Lord in his anger gave
    you to drink;
  you drank it down, and it made
    you stagger.
18There is no one to lead you,
  no one among your people
  to take you by the hand.

19A double disaster has fallen on
    you:
  your land has been devastated
    by war,
  and your people have starved.
  There is no one to show you
    sympathy.
20At the corner of every street
  your people collapse from
    weakness;

they are like deer caught in a
  hunter's net.
They have felt the force of
  God's anger.

21You suffering people of
    Jerusalem,
  you that stagger as though you
    were drunk,
22the Lord your God defends you
    and says,
  "I am taking away the cup
    that I gave you in my anger.
  You will no longer have to drink
    the wine that makes you
    stagger.
23I will give it to those who
    oppressed you,
  to those who made you lie
    down in the streets
  and trampled on you as if you
    were dirt." (TEV)

This section culminates the Lord's covenants to the house of Judah. In these verses, Isaiah speaks of the time when the covenants of the Lord are fulfilled and the Jews are brought back home again through their righteousness. Verse 17 begins this section with a command for Jerusalem (the Jews) to "rouse" and "get up," that is, to hearken to the voice of God. Isaiah describes them as those who have "drunk the cup of God's punishment." Verse 18 explains why they are suffering and lost, for it reveals the spiritual state of the Jews: they have "no one to lead," meaning that they have no prophets or inspired leaders. Since Jerusalem has no guide from among her own sons, she must look elsewhere for inspired leadership. (This probably means that she must look to the Gentiles or other remnants of Israel for this leadership.) The Book of Mormon rendition of verses 19-20 describes two sons who do come to Jerusalem and give courage and power to the Jews:

> These two sons are come unto thee, who shall be sorry for thee—why desolation and destruction, and the famine and the sword—and by whom shall I comfort thee? Thy sons have fainted save these two; they lie at the head of all the streets; as a wild bull in a net, they are full of the fury of the Lord, the rebuke of thy God. (2 Ne. 8:19-20.)

The description of these two sons calls to mind the two witnesses who will be the major factor in keeping enemy armies from totally defeating the Jews. (Rev. 11:1-6.) John the Revelator describes two great servants of God who will stand and fight for Jerusalem against the armies of the world. For three and one-half years they will have power over the heavens, earth, and their enemies. Then they will be killed. (Rev. 11:3-13; see Zech. 4:11-14.) The two sons in Isaiah's prophecy wield similar power and are depicted as a wild bull in a net; while the bull may be captive, it is still dangerous until it is worn down. In a few words, Isaiah describes the ministry of these two great sons. While they can not stop the eventual overthrow of Jerusalem, they keep away the destruction until they are finally subdued and killed.

Joseph Smith prophesied concerning these two witnesses, calling them "two prophets that are to be raised up to the Jewish nation in the last days, at the time of the restoration." (D&C 77:15.) Bruce R. McConkie suggests that these two prophets will be Latter-day Saints, most likely members of the Quorum of the Twelve Apostles or of the First Presidency. (DNTC 3:507-11.)

The Lord concludes this prophecy by again commanding the people to attend to his words. He makes a transition from predicting the persecutions of the last days to affirming that he has not forgotten his people. No longer will they have to stagger as they drink the cup of his wrath. Instead, the cup will be given to the tormentors who have trampled his people. (Lying on the ground while someone walks upon you represents captivity or conquest.) This idea of deliverance, both spiritual and temporal, is a keystone of the Savior's plan and will be realized at the time of his second coming when he fulfills all his covenants with the house of Israel.

AWAKE, O ZION, AND CALL
ISRAEL TOGETHER
ISAIAH 52

At the conclusion of Isaiah chapter 51, the Lord promises his wrath upon Israel's tormentors. As chapter 52 begins, the Lord invites Israel to wake up and put on her strength and beautiful clothing. No longer will she lie in the dust, humiliated, powerless, and dressed in rags. Now she will stand erect and alert, clothed with dignity and God's power and glory.

Isaiah 52 is an important chapter concerning the house of Israel. Many of God's greatest prophets have attested to its significance by writing about this chapter or quoting from it: Jacob, Abinadi, and Moroni in the Book of Mormon; Paul and John the Revelator in the New Testament; and Joseph Smith in the Doctrine and Covenants. No less than seventy-five verses of scripture refer directly to or expound upon this single chapter, and many other verses relate indirectly to it. However, the most important application of this chapter appears in the Book of Mormon, where the resurrected Savior himself repeats the words of Isaiah to teach the Nephites about the house of Israel in the last days. Christ's commentary on Isaiah 52 not only stresses its importance but also gives one a fuller understanding of its message.

When the resurrected Christ appeared to the Book of Mormon community, he gave many teachings found in the New Testament. After teaching the Sermon on the Mount (3 Ne. 12-14), he talked about the law of Moses and the various remnants of Israel (3 Ne. 15). In 3 Nephi 16, however, he gives teachings not recorded anywhere earlier in the Old Testament, Book of Mormon, or New Testament. In this chapter, Christ prophesies concerning the Ten Tribes (vs. 1-3), the Jews (vs. 4-5), the Gentiles and the Lamanites (vs. 6-10), the house of Israel and their relationship with the Gentiles (vs. 11-15), and the Lamanites (v. 16). The Savior continues by saying, "and then the words of the prophet Isaiah shall be fulfilled," and he then quotes verses 8-10 from Isaiah 52.

After receiving so many profound and different teachings, the Nephites were apparently unable to understand any more. Christ told them to go to their homes, ponder his words, pray about them, and prepare their minds for further instruction on the following day. (3 Ne. 17:3.) The Book of Mormon then records some of the Lord's miracles and his teachings about the sacrament, prayer, repentance, baptism, and the Holy Ghost. (3 Ne. 17-18.) After his return on the next day and further miracles, prayers, teachings, and manifestations (3 Ne. 19:1-20:9), the Lord began again to instruct the people concerning the house of Israel.

The Savior first repeated much of what he had taught earlier (as recorded in 3 Ne. 16). He may have done this to refresh the memories of his audience or to provide the same foundation for the multitudes who had not heard him on the previous day. His discourse begins in 3 Nephi 20:10 and continues through 3 Nephi 23:5. The Lord quotes some verses from Micah, most of Isaiah 52, and all of Isaiah 54. The major portion of his new teachings are given in 3 Nephi 20:10 through 3 Nephi 21:29. This portion is structured in a clear, chiastic pattern, as indicated throughout the chapter.

Christ's New World Sermon on the House of Israel

The Savior first speaks about the house of Israel and Isaiah's prophecies:

A. The Father and Son work together (3 Ne. 20:10)

B. Isaiah's words will be fulfilled (11)

C. The Father's covenant with Israel will be fulfilled (12)

These verses serve to introduce the Lord's discourse. He ties this sermon to his remarks given the day before and indicates that he instructs the people as commanded by the Father. He then stresses that at the time when Isaiah's prophecies are fulfilled, the Father's covenant with Israel will also be fulfilled.

The Savior continues his discourse on the gathering:

| D. Those scattered upon the face of the earth will be gathered (3 Ne. 20:13) | E. This land (America) an inheritance for Lamanites (14) |

In these verses, Christ promises that the remnants of Israel will be gathered and brought to a knowledge of their Lord and Redeemer. He also specifically promises America to the Nephites as their land inheritance. (These verses review the earlier teachings found in 3 Ne. 16:4-5, 11-12, 16.)

The Savior then reviews the relationship between the Gentiles and the Lamanites:

| F. If the Gentiles do not repent, Israel will tread them down and they will be cut off; the Lord's | sword of justice will hang over them. (3 Ne. 20:15-20) |

Some of this material recapitulates the earlier teachings in 3 Nephi 16:13-15 and some provides additional information. Christ quotes Isaiah's contemporary, Micah (5:8-9; 4:12-13), thus firmly placing these verses in an eschatological setting. His warning to the Gentiles is quite specific, and the power he promises the Lamanites contrasts with his earlier description of them in their relationship to the Gentiles. (See 3 Ne. 16:8-9.)

The Lord then expounds upon a variety of topics as he reviews his relationship with the house of Israel and the prophet Moses. He also reminds his listeners about their covenants, and prophesies concerning his work with the Gentiles:

G. The Lord's covenant people of Israel, Moses, and the Gentiles (3 Ne. 20:21-29)

Jesus speaks first about America as a New Jerusalem for the Lamanites (vs. 21-22), and then testifies that he is the prophet promised by Moses and the other prophets who fulfills the law of Moses (vs. 23-24; see 3 Ne. 15:2-10).

Verses 25-29 review the Father's covenants and promises to Israel. Christ tells why the gospel goes first to the house of Israel and then to the Gentiles: it goes first to Israel because of God's promises made to Abraham, and then to the Gentiles because of Israel's wickedness. Christ then warns the Gentiles that if they become wicked, they will forfeit their claim to the gospel, and then the house of Israel will be gathered to the promised land.

The Lord promises a time when the remnants of Israel will be taught the gospel and believe in him. He quotes most of Isaiah 52, but arranges the verses in a slightly different order:

³⁰And it shall come to pass that the time cometh, when the fulness of my *gospel shall be preached unto them;* ³¹And they shall believe in me, that I am Jesus Christ, the Son of God, and shall pray unto the Father in my name.	H. Great work of the Lord with Israel, his marred servant
³²Then shall their watchmen lift up their voice, and with the voice together shall they sing; for they shall see eye to eye.	Isaiah 52:8
³³Then will the Father gather them together again, and give unto them Jerusalem for the land of their inheritance.[1]	
³⁴Then shall they break forth into joy—Sing together, ye waste places of Jerusalem; for the Father hath comforted his people, he hath redeemed Jerusalem.	9
³⁵The Father hath made bare his holy arm in the eyes of all the nations; and all the ends of the earth shall see the salvation of the Father; and the Father and I are one.	10
³⁶And then shall be brought to pass that which is written: Awake, awake again, and put on thy strength, O Zion; put on thy beautiful garments, O Jerusalem, the holy city, for henceforth there shall no more come into thee the uncircumcised and the unclean.	1

---

[1]Verse 33 seems to replace the phrase "When the Lord shall bring again Zion," which has been deleted from the previous verse. (See Isa. 52:8.)

³⁷Shake thyself from the dust; arise,   2
sit down, O Jerusalem; loose thy-
self from the bands of thy neck, O
captive daughter of Zion.

³⁸For thus saith the LORD: Ye have
sold yourselves for naught, and ye
shall be redeemed without
money.

³⁹Verily, verily, I say unto you, that   6
my people shall know my name;
yea, in that day they shall know
that I am he that doth speak.

⁴⁰And then shall they say: How   7
beautiful upon the mountains are
the feet of him that bringeth good
tidings unto them, that publisheth peace; that bringeth good
tidings unto them of good, that
publisheth salvation; that saith
unto Zion: Thy God reigneth!

⁴¹And then shall a cry go forth: De-   11
part ye, depart ye, go ye out from
thence, touch not that which is
unclean; go ye out of the midst of
her; be ye clean that bear the vessels of the Lord.

⁴²For ye shall not go out with haste   12
nor go by flight; for the Lord will
go before you, and the God of
Israel shall be your rearward.

⁴³Behold, my servant shall deal   13
prudently; he shall be exalted and
extolled and be very high.

⁴⁴As many were astonished at   14
thee—his visage was so marred,
more than any man, and his form
more than the sons of men. (3 Ne.
20.)

This segment contains most of Isaiah 52, except for verses 8-10
(quoted earlier), 4 and 5 (not quoted at all), and 15 (quoted in the
following segment). It is interesting that the Lord would use these
verses in a different order when he was the one who gave the original
prophecy recorded in Isaiah. Why did he not simply give it to Isaiah

in this order originally? A close look at the segments and verses of Isaiah 52 (except verses 4 and 5) suggests that they all deal with the same general time period near the beginning of the Millennium. Perhaps the segments overlap each other so that a precise sequence is unnecessary or even undesirable.

Certainly, the Lord could reveal prophecies about the last days to his prophets in clear, precise chronological order. However, when the writings of prophets are compared, they seem to describe the same events, though their phraseology and order of description often differ. Perhaps the terminology and chronology differ so that the reader's faith and understanding will be challenged and his accountability will not be jeopardized. That is, if the Lord were to fully reveal all the prophecies of the last days in the exact order of fulfillment, and if a vision of these prophecies were recorded and passed on, we who now live in the last days would not need to search the scriptures to find what has been prophesied about our time. We would not have to develop our ability to study and understand the scriptures. And as most of the prophecies on any "list" were fulfilled, we might set our lives in order with the Lord, not because we were righteous, but because we would know that his second coming was imminent. Thus, such a complete listing of prophecies would restrict the testing of our faith and the development of our spiritual understanding.

Besides different word order, there are further minor changes in the verses of 3 Nephi 20: in verses 32 and 34 (Isa. 52:8-9), new phrases introduce the verses and one phrase is missing; in verse 35 (Isa. 52:10) the name "Father" replaces the name "Lord" at the beginning and "God" at the end of the verse, and a phrase is added: "And the Father and I are one" (these three verses quoting Isa. 52:8-10 were also quoted the previous day [3 Ne. 16:18-20]); verse 36 (Isa. 52:1) includes an introductory phrase in addition to Isaiah 52:1-3, "and then shall be brought to pass that which is written"; verse 39 (Isa. 52:6) includes another transition phrase, "verily, verily, I say unto you," and excludes the concluding phrase, "behold, it is I"; verse 40 (Isa. 52:7) adds the phrase, "and then they shall say"; verse 41 (Isa. 52:11) includes an introductory phrase, "and then shall a cry go forth."

The changes in verse order and wording do not significantly alter the major message of the chapter, but do clarify a few verses and, most importantly, firmly establish that the complete fulfillment of this prophecy will occur only in the last days.

As indicated earlier, a number of other prophets have quoted and amplified portions of Isaiah 52. The following chart lists scriptural references to this chapter outside the Bible:

Isaiah	Jacob	Abinadi	Jesus Christ	Moroni	Joseph Smith
vs. 1-2	2 Ne. 8:24-25		3 Ne. 20:36-37	Moro. 10:31	D&C 113:7-10 D&C 82:14 (see D&C 109:61-67)
3, 6			3 Ne. 20:38-39 3 Ne. 16:18-20		
7-10		Mosiah 12:20-25 Mosiah 15:13-31	3 Ne. 20:32-35, 40		D&C 19:29; 31:3; 79:1; 84:98-99; 113:10; 128:19; 133:3,
11-12			3 Ne. 20:41-42 3 Ne. 21:29		D&C 5, 14-15 (see D&C 38:42; 49:27; 84:88; 101:68)
13-15			3 Ne. 20:43-45 3 Ne. 21:8-10		D&C 101:94

A careful study of these references demonstrates why Isaiah's prophecy is so important and how it will be fulfilled in the last days.

Judging from the scriptures listed above, it seems that most of chapter 52 applies to the last days. Verses 1 and 2 foretell a time when the people of Zion and Jerusalem will be restored to power, particularly priesthood power, and will be free from oppression. Verses 3 and 6 look forward to the redeeming powers of Christ and the personal relationship he will establish with his people. Verses 4 and 5 are omitted from the Book of Mormon and Doctrine and Covenants, probably because they refer to local events of the Assyrian oppression during Isaiah's time. Verses 7-10 promise Christ's peace and power and portray the Lord's messengers (servants, prophets, missionaries, etc.) taking the gospel to the world, particularly Jerusalem. (See also Dan. 4; Matt. 28:19; D&C 1; 68:12.) Verses 11 and 12 warn the Lord's servants to be pure and prepared, and promise the Lord's presence with them. Verses 13-15 foretell a servant of the Lord.

Some readers believe that the last three verses of this chapter refer to Israel as a whole. Historically, the chosen people have been praised on the one hand (v. 13) and persecuted on the other (v. 14). They have been scattered throughout the world and have "sprinkled many na-

438

tions" (v. 15). When they finally overcome their humiliating condition in the last days, their restoration will astound many nations (v. 15).

Many people assume that the servant promised in the last three verses of Isaiah 52 is the same servant described throughout Isaiah 53. If so, these verses describe Christ, his great works, and the persecutions and suffering he endured. (See Mosiah 14; compare D&C 19:10-13.) However, in the Book of Mormon adaptations of Isaiah 52 and 53, neither Abinadi nor Christ combine Isaiah 52:13-15 with chapter 53. In fact, Christ includes this prophecy of a servant with other promises of the last days. Still, he could be foretelling his own glorious second coming and perhaps the signs of the crucifixion and anger of his judgments which will "mar" him as he appears to the world.

Unless the Savior is speaking about himself in the last days, he must have had another person in mind as the servant of the last days. Particularly as the Savior comments upon these verses later in 3 Nephi 21:7-11, it appears obvious that he is not talking about himself, but about his servant. This servant will take God's word to the Gentiles, and those who will not accept the word will be separated from God's covenant people. (3 Ne. 21:11.) Although some people will attempt to harm this servant, Jesus promises that he will heal the servant and show that Christ's power is greater than "the cunning of the devil." (3 Ne. 21:10.)

There are several reasons to consider Joseph Smith as this promised servant. This whole series of verses, as quoted by Christ in 3 Nephi, refers to the restoration of the gospel, the revelations of the Lord through his prophets, and the gathering of Israel. It would be natural to mention the servant whom the Lord would employ to carry out this great work. When Moroni visited Joseph Smith, he told him that the Lord had a great work for him to do and that Joseph's name would be known for good and ill among all nations. (JS-H 1:33.) Indeed, no one except Jesus Christ has been more important in bringing about the eternal purposes of the Lord here on earth than the Prophet Joseph Smith. (D&C 135:3.) The work of Joseph Smith demonstrates that he fulfilled that which the Lord required of him. As prophesied in Isaiah 52:13, on the one hand he has been extolled by the Saints, yet on the other hand, hardly any man has been maligned and misrepresented as much as Joseph Smith. Among other things, he has been called a money-digger, a dreamer, a liar, an imposter, and a lunatic. During his lifetime he hardly knew a period without persecution. Many have been astonished at what Joseph Smith accomplished during his lifetime, despite constant opposition by the forces of the devil. Through the work of Joseph Smith, the nations of the earth have been "sprinkled" or blessed with many missionaries and messengers of salvation. Many people, including the great ones of this earth, have heard or will hear the message of the gospel. This "new" or restored gospel is one that the people of the earth have not earlier considered, heard, nor seen. Joseph Smith was the man who made it possible for the Lord to fulfill his commitment to call, restore, and gather the house of Israel in the last days, and thus might easily be the servant promised in Isaiah 52:13-15.

Another modern prophet might be this promised servant. As Christ comments on Isaiah's words, he says that when the latter-day Lamanites begin to grow in their knowledge of the restored gospel, they will know that the Father's work is being fulfilled with the house of Israel. (3 Ne. 21:7.) When that day comes, he continues, kings will be speechless (3 Ne. 21:8; compare Isa. 52:15) at the great work declared by a man to the people (3 Ne. 21:9; compare Isa. 52:13). Christ describes his servant of the last days as one who will be marred, yet healed by the Lord. (3 Ne. 21:10; compare Isa. 52:14.)

This description can easily be applied to President Spencer W. Kimball. Evaluating President Kimball's inspired leadership, one notes a very dramatic increase in missionary work, especially among the Lamanites. He has no equal in bringing Christ's word to the Gentiles and Abraham's posterity. Indeed, the gospel *is* being "sprinkled" among many new nations as more countries open their doors and as kings and rulers see and hear things that have not been told them or considered by them earlier. (See Isa. 52:15.) President Kimball has helped "*gather* many nations" (JST v. 15, italics added), as people throughout the world are joining covenant Israel.

It is well known that President Kimball has probably suffered more physical ailments than any other latter-day seer. Yet, in spite of a larynx marred by cancer, boils and sores, and numerous heart attacks, he has always made remarkable recoveries. "Yet I will heal him," says the Lord. (3 Ne. 21:10.) God has healed President Kimball many times so that he can visit the many nations of the earth and deliver his message to hundreds of thousands.

President Kimball has made significant changes in the Church organization. He received the revelation for giving the priesthood to all worthy males. As an able administrator and inspired leader, he has "dealt prudently" in his stewardship and is "extolled" by the Lord and the Latter-day Saints for his great service. (Isa. 52:13.)

In short, the final three verses of Isaiah 52 prophesy of the Lord's servant in the last days. But one need not feel constrained to identify this servant only with Israel, Christ, Joseph Smith, or Spencer W. Kimball, since Isaiah could be describing any or all of these people. If this prophecy deals with one particular person, the servant might not yet have fulfilled his role. Some future prophet might be the servant who will perform this great work.

As Christ speaks in the Book of Mormon about this servant, he quotes the verses from Isaiah and then indicates that as these words are fulfilled, the Father's covenant with Israel will also be fulfilled. He concludes the Isaiah quotation and gives an evaluation as follows:

I. Kings shall be speechless (3 Ne. 20:45; see Isa. 52:15)

J. Covenant and work of the Father (3 Ne. 20:46)

These verses conclude 3 Nephi 20. The next chapter begins with one long sentence that spans seven verses.

In the first verse Jesus Christ indicates that he is giving the Nephites a "sign" so that they will know when the events prophesied about the establishment of Zion will take place:

K. "Sign" is when "these things" shall be made known unto the Gentiles (3 Ne. 21:1)

L. Gentiles will learn about scattered Israel (2)

These two verses contain significant promises:

1. A sign will be given for Israelites to learn when their final gathering is to take place.
2. This sign will let the Israelites know when Zion (the Lord's kingdom) will be established among them.
3. The sign will be that "these things" (Christ's words to the Nephites) will be made known unto the Gentiles.
4. The Gentiles, in turn, will know about "this people" (the Lamanites) as a remnant of Israel whom they have scattered.

The Gentiles represent the European settlers in America who received the records of the Book of Mormon and then came to know that the Indians living in America were descendants of Jacob, coming to this world centuries earlier.

Christ continues with more information about the sign and describes how the message of the Book of Mormon prophecies will go from the Gentiles to the Lamanites:

M. These things will come
from the Gentiles to the
Lamanites (3 Ne. 21:3)

M'. These works will
come from the Gentiles to
the Lamanites (5)

N. The sign (4)

The pivot point of the chiasmus, *N*, accentuates the sign that will signal to Israel that the Father's covenants will soon be fulfilled: the Book of Mormon prophecies will "come forth from them [the Gentiles] unto a remnant of your seed [the Lamanites]." Since the gospel and the Book of Mormon have been restored through the hand of the Gentiles in America, and since the record of the Book of Mormon has been given to the Lamanites, this prophesied sign has already been given in this dispensation.

The Savior delivers the same message three times in the three verses quoted above. He wanted to emphasize that the key to the fulfillment of the Father's covenants with Israel is the Gentiles' preaching of the gospel to the Lamanites. The significance of this sign is that it lets people know when the events of the last days are finally being fulfilled, since for centuries people have anticipated the coming of the Messiah in power and glory. They realized, though, that many "preparatory" prophecies had to be fulfilled before his coming. Some of these prophecies deal with phenomena of the earth, such as great earthquakes, droughts, famines, and wars. Since these types of events have occurred at various times and places, people occasionally thought they were the precursors of the Millennium. For example, many people thought World War I was the "war to end wars" that would usher in the Millennium. Obviously, however, Christ's second coming did not follow. Many people still anticipate his return, yet remain confused about the prophecies that must first be fulfilled. They wonder which earthquakes, heavenly manifestations, or other signs might possibly fulfill the prophecies. Their confusion results from the problem that there are many signs that will appear.

Christ's instruction in the Book of Mormon places the "signs of the times," or the prophecies of the last days, in a context in which they can be understood. Although earthquakes, wars, famines, and other similar signs have occurred many times, the prophecies concerning the house of Israel have not been previously fulfilled. For example, the Ten Tribes have not yet returned, and the Jews have not yet built a temple in Jerusalem. These and other prophecies concerning the house of Israel must be fulfilled before Christ returns. In 3 Nephi, Christ tells us that the sign of the house of Israel prophecies is that the gospel will go from the Gentiles to the Lamanites. After this sign is given, all the other prophecies to the house of Israel will come to pass. As they are fulfilled, all the other prophecies will also be fulfilled, and then Christ will come.

The different types of prophecies are compared in the following diagram:

1. All Prophecies

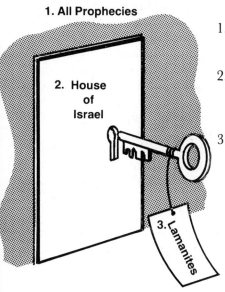

2. House of Israel

3. Lamanites

1. The prophecies of the last days are many and varied.

2. The doorway to understanding the prophecies is to see what happens to the house of Israel.

3. The key to the house of Israel prophecies is the gospel going from the Gentiles to the Lamanites.

The Lord continues his discourse on this sign of the house of Israel, repeating and reviewing the concepts he delivered earlier. He stresses why the gospel will come forth from the Gentiles to the Lamanites and why it will be a sign to the Lamanites:

L'. Some Gentiles will be remembered with the house of Israel (3 Ne. 21:6)

K'. The sign is when "these things" come to pass with the Lamanites (7)

Compare these verses with verses 1 and 2 to see how the same ideas and words are repeated.

The Savior uses further repetition in verses 7b and 8 to indicate the value of the "sign" given to the Lamanites and how this event will startle the rulers of nations:

J'. Work and covenant of the Father (3 Ne. 21:7b)	I'. Kings shall be speechless (8; see Isa. 52:15)

One reason the preaching of the gospel to the Lamanites is so important is that it indicates that the Lord's covenants with the house of Israel are already being fulfilled. The parallel verse of 3 Nephi 20:46 indicates that as the covenant is fulfilled, Jerusalem will be reinhabited. Most of the population growth in Jerusalem has occurred since 1948, long after the gospel was taken to the Lamanites. However, Jerusalem's greatest population growth has occurred since its reunification in the June 1967 war, fought two years after the first stake was organized among the Lamanites in Mexico City. Truly, the physical growth of Jerusalem parallels the spiritual growth of the Lamanites.

In a parallel segment to the long section of verses that contains most of Isaiah 52 (3 Ne. 20:30-44), Christ briefly summarizes the Father's marvelous work and his own efforts with a servant in the last days:

H'. Great work of the
Father; his marred servant
(3 Ne. 21:9-10; see Isa.
52:14)

These two verses clarify Heavenly Father's purpose in protecting the life of his servant: it will show the world that God's wisdom is "greater than the cunning of the devil." Apparently this servant will be a special witness or manifestation of the Lord's power in the last days.

Continuing his review of the earlier teachings concerning Moses and the house of Israel, Christ summarizes the two in one verse:

G'. Moses, the Gentiles,
and covenant Israel (3 Ne.
21:11)

This verse reviews the Lord's extensive teachings given in 3 Nephi 20:21-29. Earlier the Savior told of the promises made to covenant

Israel, of how he himself fulfilled the prophecies of Moses, and of the hostile relationships that would develop as the Gentiles gained power over the Lamanites. Here he warns the whole world that those who do not believe in his words will be separated from covenant Israel, as foretold in the works of Moses. (Lev. 18:29; Num. 15:30-31; see JST Gen. 50:24-33; 2 Ne. 3:5-24.)

Christ continues with an extensive description of how the Lamanites will be the Father's instruments in cutting off the spiritually unresponsive from the house of Israel:

F'. If the Gentiles do not repent, Israel will tread them down and cut them; the Lord's vengeance will come upon the unresponsive (3 Ne. 21:12-21)

Reread 3 Nephi 20:15-20 and compare it with the verses above. The Lord quotes Micah 5:8-15, and his commentary on both passages clearly places these verses of Micah in an eschatological setting. Israel will help cleanse the earth preparatory to its elevation to a higher degree of glory.

The Lord highlights the special role of America as an inheritance for the descendants of Joseph through Lehi:

E'. America an inheritance for all righteous Gentiles (3 Ne. 21:22-23)

In addition to the righteous Lamanites who will enjoy America as their inheritance, the Savior promises this land to the righteous Gentiles who join covenant Israel. This promise is a significant addition parallel to 3 Nephi 20:14. The Gentiles will help Israel build the New Jerusalem in Jackson County, the center for the Lord's kingdom.

The Gentiles will also be involved in the gathering of Israel:

D'. Gentiles help in the gathering (3 Ne. 21:24-25)

Usually, these verses are interpreted as a promise of the assistance of the Gentile nations, such as England, France, and the United States, building up modern Israel. However, the context of Christ's promises expands their meaning to include assistance in the New World and Zion as well. Thus, the Gentiles will assist both physically and spiritually in gathering Israel in both Old and New Jerusalem.

Christ concludes his marvelous sermon on the house of Israel by

445

saying that after the gospel goes to the Lamanites, it will signal the Father's work being completed among the entire house of Israel and the whole world:

C'. The Father's work with the dispersed of his people (3 Ne. 21:26-27)	Isaiah to find details about the Father's promises (28; see 3 Ne. 23:1-3)
B'. The Father's work shall commence; search	A'. The Father and Son work together (29)

Christ's concluding promise is found also in Isaiah 52:12, which highlights the relationship between God the Father and his Son. In the Hebrew, Jehovah will go before Israel, and Elohim will come behind her. The Book of Mormon stresses that both the speaker (Christ) and the Father will gather the righteous. Only the righteous who comprise covenant Israel will be worthy of the promise. Repentant and cleansed, they will have all three members of the Godhead in their company—Christ before them, the Holy Ghost with them, and God the Father behind them. Surely they will not fail in their promised destiny.

In 3 Nephi 22, Christ expresses the feelings of these righteous people by quoting Isaiah 54. He commands the people to "search these things diligently; for great are the words of Isaiah." (3 Ne. 23:1.) Although Isaiah clearly did not prophesy all things about the last days, he did touch upon "all things concerning . . . the house of Israel." (3 Ne. 23:2.) Isaiah also had much to say to the Gentiles. (3 Ne. 23:2.) The Lord himself testified of the truthfulness of Isaiah's prophecies: "All things that he spake have been and shall be, even according to the words which he spake." (3 Ne. 23:3.)

As seen in his quotation and application of Isaiah's words, the Savior took the liberty to reorder the sequence of Isaiah's verses and expound upon how they will be fulfilled. It would be helpful to us if the Lord had given similar sermons using all the chapters of Isaiah so that we could see how they either have been or will be fulfilled. However, each of us is capable of seeking divine inspiration from the Holy Ghost, so that we can understand Isaiah as clearly as if the Lord himself were to teach us.

446

SUFFERING OF THE MESSIAH
ISAIAH 53

In chapter 53, Isaiah gives the most sublime messianic prophecy in all the scriptures. Within just a few verses, he provides a preview of four major aspects of Christ's life and mission: (1) his mortal life as the "despised man" (vs. 1-3); (2) his atonement (vs. 4-6); (3) his trial and crucifixion as an "innocent lamb" (vs. 7-9); and (4) his postmortal glory as an exalted son (vs. 10-12). Elder Bruce R. McConkie has said,

> As our New Testament now stands, we find Matthew (Matt. 8:17), Philip (Acts 8:27-35), Paul (Rom. 4:25), and Peter (1 Pet. 2:24-25) all quoting, paraphrasing, enlarging upon, and applying to the Lord Jesus various of the verses in this great 53rd chapter of Isaiah. How many sermons have been preached, how many lessons have been taught, how many testimonies have been borne—both in ancient Israel and in the meridian of time—using the utterances of this chapter as the text, we can scarcely imagine. (PM, p. 235.)

Christ's Mortal Life (vs. 1-3)

Isaiah begins chapter 53 with an exclamation in the form of a rhetorical question: "Who has believed our report?" He alludes to the fact that he and other prophets have prophesied of the Messiah, yet few listeners believed. Indeed, of the Jews living during Christ's mortal ministry, only a small number believed that Jesus was their Savior.

In the first verses of the fourth servant song, which comprises all of chapter 53, Isaiah describes the Messiah growing up in arid surroundings, appearing to be like other men, and suffering silently while most of those whom he wanted to save rejected him:

53 Who has believed what we
        have heard?
And to whom has the arm of the
        Lord been revealed?

53 The people reply,
        "Who would have believed
        what we now report?
Who could have seen the Lord's

²For he grew up before him like a
    young plant
  and like a root out of dry ground;
he had no form or comeliness that
    we should look at him,
  and no beauty that we should
    desire him.
³He was despised and rejected by
    men;
  a man of sorrows, and acquainted
    with grief;
and as one from whom men hide
    their faces
  he was despised, and we esteemed
    him not. (RSV)

hand in this?
²It was the will of the Lord that his
    servant
  grow like a plant taking root in
    dry ground.
He had no dignity or beauty
  to make us take notice of him.
There was nothing attractive about
    him.
³We despised him and rejected him;
  he endured suffering and pain.
No one would even look at him—
  we ignored him as if he were
    nothing." (TEV)

(Note: To help the reader understand the content and style of this chapter, two translations are given: The RSV, a traditional, eloquent interpretation and the TEV, a contemporary, free-flowing rendition.)

Isaiah asks a second question at the beginning of verse 1: "In whom has the arm of the Lord been revealed?" He implies that the servant will be revealed by the "arm" or power of the Lord. (See Isa. 52:10; John 12:37-38; 1 Ne. 22:10-11; D&C 45:47.) Isaiah spends the rest of the chapter answering this second question.

The servant to be revealed by the Lord's power is not named, but both the prophet Abinadi and the evangelist Philip identify him as Jesus Christ. (Mosiah 15; Acts 8:26-35.) In addition, Matthew, Peter, and Paul apply various verses of Isaiah 53 to Christ. (Matt. 8:17; 1 Pet. 2:24-25; Rom. 4:25.) Modern apostles, such as James E. Talmage, Joseph Fielding Smith, and Bruce R. McConkie, have also stated that Jesus is the subject of Isaiah 53. (JTC, p. 47; DS 1:23-24; PM, pp. 234-35.)

In verse 2, Isaiah speaks of the servant as a young plant, meaning he was tenderly raised from being a newborn, helpless infant and developed like all young children. He grew up in the dry, sterile ground of apostate Judaism and achieved a natural, adult appearance like other men. Joseph Fielding Smith states that "it is expressed here by the prophet that he had no form or comeliness, that is, he was not so distinctive, so different from others that people would recognize him as the Son of God. He appeared as a mortal man." (DS 1:23; see D&C 93:11-17.)

As Isaiah describes in verse 3, Jesus was a man of sorrow and tragedy. Sensitive to the suffering of others, Jesus taught, healed, and blessed countless people during his ministry. Yet he experienced constant sorrow and rejection throughout his life. (Matt. 23:37.) Members of his own family and the people in his hometown rejected him at first. (John 7:5; Luke 4:16-30.) His own chosen people, the Jews, rejected his messianic calling. (John 1:11; 5:18.) As his mortal ministry neared completion, one of his apostles betrayed him and another temporarily denied any knowledge of him. (Luke 22:48, 54-62.) This constant persecution and rejection must have caused Christ great sorrow, for the very people he came to save first turned away from him. (See Mark 9:12; 1 Ne. 19:7-10.)

Christ's Atonement (vs. 4-6)

As much as Christ grieved over Israel's rejection of him, he sorrowed even more for their sins. Indeed, Isaiah beautifully describes how God's faithful servant suffered for the transgressions of all mankind:

4Surely he has borne our griefs
  and carried our sorrows;
yet we esteemed him stricken,
  smitten by God, and afflicted.
5But he was wounded for our
    transgressions,
  he was bruised for our iniquities,
upon him was the chastisement that
    made us whole,
  and with his stripes we are healed.
6All we like sheep have gone astray;
  we have turned every one to his
    own way;
and the Lord has laid on him
  the iniquity of us all. (RSV)

4"But he endured the suffering that
    should have been ours,
  the pain that we should have
    borne.
All the while we thought that
    his suffering
  was punishment sent by God.
5But because of our sins he was
    wounded,
  beaten because of the evil we did.
We are healed by the punishment
    he suffered,
  made whole by the blows he
    received.
6All of us were like sheep that were
    lost,
  each of us going his own way.
But the Lord made the punishment
    fall on him,
  the punishment all of us
    deserved." (TEV)

Before we can begin to appreciate Christ's atoning sacrifice, we must understand the relationship of the law of justice and the law of mercy. And these two laws are best understood when we know about the necessity of "opposition in all things" and the choices placed before Christ before he took upon himself the sins of the world.

The clearest discussion about the necessity of opposition and choice is given by Lehi in 2 Nephi 2:11-27. There are several reasons why there must be opposition before we can be free and experience joy:

1. Every law has both a punishment and a blessing attached to it.
2. Disobedience to law requires a punishment that results in misery.
3. Obedience to law provides a blessing that results in joy.
4. Without law there can be neither punishment nor blessing, neither misery nor happiness—only innocence.
5. Thus joy can exist only where the possibility of misery also exists.
6. In order to exercise agency, we must have freedom of choice; in a world without law—and thus without choice—there could be no freedom of choice and thus no exercise of agency. (See Alma 12:31-32; Alma 42:17-25.)

Lehi does not say it is necessary to choose evil in order to recognize good and evil, but he does make it clear that a choice between opposites is necessary for spiritual growth. Indeed, Christ's perfect life demonstrates that the most simple and sure way to attain eternal joy and celestial perfection is to never choose evil but to always follow the Father. (See D&C 130:20, 21; 132:5.)

The law of justice is a natural manifestation of the principles of opposition and agency. It works in relationship to the other laws of God and provides the means by which people receive their just reward. In essence, the law of justice might be explained as follows:

1. Every law has both a punishment and a blessing attached to it.
2. Whenever the law is transgressed, a punishment must be inflicted.
3. Whenever a law is obeyed, a reward must be given.

When we have a choice between good and evil, knowing the laws of God and being free agents, we can apply the law of justice in our lives and seek for whatever blessings we desire. On the other hand, as Lehi teaches, if we do not have choices, we cannot receive the full range of possible blessings and punishments. The Doctrine and Covenants references mentioned earlier indicate that blessings and punishments are predicated upon the laws of God. However, before we can live all of God's laws, we must know them and have agency. The relationship of free agency, laws, choices between good and evil, and the other elements of the law of justice are diagramed below:

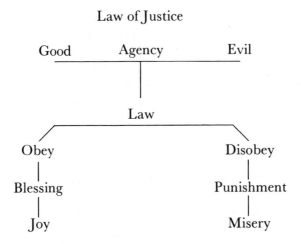

If we are free to choose between good and evil after we have obtained God's laws, then we are free to receive blessings and joy or to receive punishment and misery.

The law of justice also applies to Christ's atonement. However, as Isaiah explains in 53:4-6, Jesus did not have to suffer for any of his own sins because he lived a perfect life. God satisfied the demands of justice by allowing Christ to accept our punishment. At first thought, that Christ suffered for our sins does not seem just, since the law of justice requires that God must be a God of order and that he must be impartial. Indeed, because of the law of justice, God can inspire such statements as: "I, the Lord, am bound when ye do what I say; but when ye do not what I say, ye have no promise" (D&C 82:10), and "When we obtain any blessing from God, it is by obedience to that law upon which it is predicated" (D&C 130:20-21).

The reason that a just and loving God allowed his Son to suffer for others' sins is because of the law of mercy. The law of mercy becomes part of the law of justice, for it introduces the possibility of vicarious payment for the laws that have been broken. In essence, the law of mercy might be paraphrased as follows: whenever a law is transgressed, a payment must be made; however, the person who transgressed the law does not need to make payment *if* he will repent and *if* he can find someone else who is both *able* and *willing* to make payment. The law of mercy insists that the demands of the law of justice be fully met. As Alma stated, "Justice exerciseth all his demands, and also mercy claimeth all which is her own; and thus, none but the truly

451

penitent are saved. What, do ye suppose that mercy can rob justice? I say unto you, Nay; not one whit. If so God would cease to be God." (Alma 42:24-25.)

The law of justice made the atonement of Jesus Christ *necessary*. When Adam fell, he transgressed a law with physical and spiritual death as its punishment. Thus, the law of justice demanded payment (or atonement) for the broken law.

The law of mercy made the atonement of Jesus Christ *possible*. In order for Jesus Christ to pay fully for the law Adam transgressed, it was necessary that the Savior be both *able* and *willing* to make atonement. He was *willing* to make payment because of his great love for mankind, and he was *able* to make payment because he lived a sinless life and, as the Son of God, had the power to atone for the spiritual and physical death introduced by the Fall. Because of this atonement, he is rightfully referred to as the Savior and Redeemer of all mankind. (For further information, see MD, p. 60; DS 1:126.)

Interestingly, the word *forgive* does not appear in this chapter of Isaiah, though the Hebrew root *nasa*, from which the word *forgive* is usually translated, does appear twice, as "borne" in verse 4, and "bare" in verse 12. (See Isa. 2:9; 33:24.) Christ "bore" or carried our sins so that we do not have to carry their burden. (John 1:29; see 1 Pet. 1:18-20.) Or, as we say, "He has *forgiven* us," meaning he "gave" the price "before." Indeed, almost two thousand years before our time, he gave the necessary payment in the Garden of Gethsemane. As we take advantage of his suffering, we can find the joy God wants all men to experience as they are cleansed and worthy to live in his presence. (2 Ne. 2:25; 9:21.)

The relationship between the law of justice and the law of mercy and Christ's atonement is illustrated on the next page.

Before the law of mercy can apply in our lives, we must take advantage of Christ's atonement by repenting of our sins. As presented in the current Latter-day Saint missionary discussions, there are six steps to repentance: (1) recognition, (2) sorrow, (3) confession, (4) seeking forgiveness, (5) restitution, and (6) forsaking sin. Isaiah constantly reminded the Israelites of the necessity to repent and seek for the blessings of the Lord.

Some of the blessings promised Israel and other peoples are not conditional upon the people's repentance and righteousness.[1] For

---

[1] See the discussion on Isaiah 54:3 on pp. 459-60.

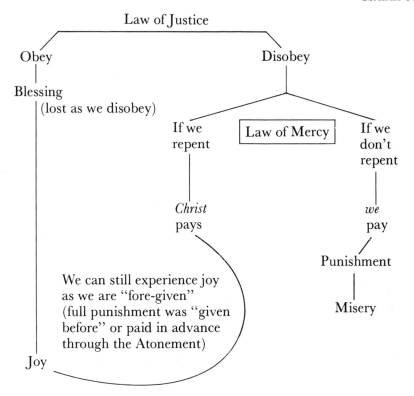

example, every person benefits *unconditionally* from one major aspect of the Atonement, the Resurrection. However, as Isaiah and other prophets indicate, there are also *conditional* aspects of the Atonement, and in order to benefit from these, we must repent of our sins. Otherwise, "mercy could have no claim" upon the person. (Mosiah 3:25-27.) (See Boyd K. Packer, "The Mediator," *Ensign*, May 1977, pp. 54-56; also published as *The Mediator* [Salt Lake City: Deseret Book Company, 1978].)

Christ's Trial and Crucifixion (vs. 7-9)

Isaiah saw beyond Christ's suffering for our sins and prophesied further abuse and suffering that Jesus endured after his atoning sacrifice in the Garden of Gethsemane. Isaiah's description of key events surrounding Christ's death clearly shows that he was a seer:

⁷He was oppressed, and he was
  afflicted,
yet he opened not his mouth;
like a lamb that is led to the
  slaughter,
and like a sheep that before
  its shearers is dumb,
so he opened not his mouth.
⁸By oppression and judgment he
  was taken away;
and as for his generation,
  who considered
that he was cut off out of
  the land of the living,
stricken for the transgression
  of my people?
⁹And they made his grave with
  the wicked
and with a rich man in his
  death,
although he had done no
  violence,
and there was no deceit in
  his mouth. (RSV)

⁷"He was treated harshly, but
  endured it humbly;
he never said a word.
Like a lamb about to be
  slaughtered,
like a sheep about to be
  sheared,
he never said a word.
⁸He was arrested and sentenced
  and led off to die,
and no one cared about his
  fate.
He was put to death for the
  sins of our people.
⁹He was placed in a grave with
  evil men,
he was buried with the rich,
even though he had never
  committed a crime
or ever told a lie." (TEV)

In each of the first three sections of chapter 53, Isaiah portrays the progressive suffering Christ had to bear: first he was despised, then he was wounded for others, and finally he was cut off from the land of the living.

In reviewing some events associated with Christ's death, Isaiah stresses the oppression that would bring about his crucifixion: Jesus was falsely accused, illegally tried, unjustly humiliated, and inhumanly executed. In spite of the evil oppression heaped upon him, Jesus remained silent, thus fulfilling Isaiah's prophecy that he would be "dumb" or quiet and submissive "as a sheep before the shearers" (v. 7; see Matt. 26:62-63; 27:12-14; John 19:9-11; Luke 23:8-10).

At his crucifixion, Jesus' weak body bore additional torture. Within the twelve sleepless hours before he was placed upon the cross, Jesus had to endure the suffering in Gethsemane, which caused him to bleed at every pore (D&C 19:18), the humiliation of the false trials before Jews and Romans, the flogging and mockery of the Romans, and the burden of the cross on the way to Golgotha. Elder James E.

Talmage wrote: "Christ's agony in the garden is unfathomable by the finite mind, both as to intensity and cause . . . he struggled and groaned under a burden such as no other being who has lived on earth might even conceive as possible." (JTC, p. 613; see D&C 19:16-18; Luke 22:44; Mosiah 3:7.) Elder Bruce R. McConkie said that the crucifixion was "the most awful moment of all":

> He was laid down upon the implement of torture. His arms were stretched along the cross-beams; and at the centre of the open palms, the point of a huge iron nail was placed, which, by the blow of a mallet, was driven home into the wood. Then through either foot separately, or possibly through both together as they were placed one over the other, another huge nail tore its way through the quivering flesh. (MM 4:211.)

Such was the means by which the Savior was cut off from the land of the living (v. 8; see Mosiah 15:10-11).

In verse 9, Isaiah adds further details about Christ's death and burial. Jesus died between two thieves and was buried in a rich man's grave. (John 19:18; Luke 22:37; 23:32-33; Matt. 27:60.) Again we see the remarkable detail with which Isaiah foretold major events of Christ's mortal mission. Verses 1-9 of chapter 53 are filled with significant details about the Savior's life, atonement, trial, death, and burial.

Christ's Postmortal Glory (vs. 10-12)

Beginning in verse 10, Isaiah signals a change in context by shifting from the past tense to the future. The earlier verbs in this fourth servant song described the grim experiences of the servant; now verbs in the future tense speak only of success and glory for the servant:

10Yet it was the will of the Lord to bruise him; he has put him to grief; when he makes himself an offering for sin, he shall see his offspring, he shall prolong his days; the will of the Lord shall prosper in his hand; 11 he shall see the fruit of the travail of his soul and be satisfied; by his knowledge shall the righteous one, my servant,	10The Lord says, "It was my will that he should suffer; his death was a sacrifice to bring forgiveness. And so he will see his descendants; he will live a long life, and through him my purpose will succeed. 11After a life of suffering, he will again have joy; he will know that he did not suffer in vain.

455

make many to be accounted
righteous;
and he shall bear their iniquities.
¹²Therefore I will divide him a
portion with the great,
and he shall divide the spoil
with the strong;
because he poured out his soul to
death,
and was numbered with the
transgressors;
yet he bore the sin of many,
and made intercession for the
transgressors. (RSV)

My devoted servant, with
whom I am pleased,
will bear the punishment of
many
and for his sake I will
forgive them.
¹²And so I will give him a place
of honor,
a place among great and
powerful men.
He willingly gave his life
and shared the fate of evil
men.
He took the place of many
sinners
and prayed that they might
be forgiven." (TEV)

Included among the promises to the suffering servant are offspring, a long (eternal) life, prosperity, satisfaction with his labors, service to others, and a royal inheritance.

These promises are applicable to everyone in the highest degree of celestial glory, but especially to Christ, because he fulfilled every desire of the Father. Obviously, God the Father was not pleased with the way people treated his Son, but he was "pleased" (KJV) or satisfied with his Son's obedience and "offering for sin" (v. 10; see 2 Ne. 9; Alma 12, 42). Christ's atonement and crucifixion met God's strictest demands of justice and thereafter guaranteed resurrection and salvation for all while making forgiveness and celestial glory possible for those who accept all God's requirements. (See Heb. 7:24-25; 9:24.) One of Isaiah's great messianic promises is that the suffering servant will see his "seed" or offspring (v. 10). Of course, all those in the highest degree of celestial glory will enjoy eternal posterity, but Christ's seed includes those who become his spiritually begotten sons and daughters, those who take his name and gospel covenants upon themselves and live accordingly. (Mosiah 5:7; 15:10-13; D&C 93:22; see 4 Ne. 1:17; Morm. 9:26; Moro. 7:19; Rom. 8.)

In verse 11, Isaiah indicates that many people will enjoy the fruits of Christ's labors. As indicated earlier, the unconditional promises of Christ's work guarantee resurrection to all God's children. In addition, his conditional promises provide the means by which God's worthy children can regain his presence and become as he is. Together, the Son and his celestial family will become joint heirs in everything the Father has: possessions, exaltation, glory, power, knowledge, truth, and godhood (v. 12; Rom. 8:17; D&C 50:26-28; 76:50-60; 88:107; 93:15-30; D&C 132:20). And why are all these marvelous eternal blessings possible? Because Christ, the suffering servant and obedient son, "willingly gave his life" (TEV) and "bore the sin of many" (RSV) that we might share eternal joy together (v. 12).

THE LORD'S EVERLASTING WAYS
WITH ISRAEL
ISAIAH 54-55

Isaiah 54 and 55 are beautiful chapters of encouragement; chapter 54 portrays the glory of Zion in the last days, and chapter 55 extends an invitation to all people to partake of the gospel. Building upon the prophecy of the Messiah (Isa. 53), these two chapters promise special blessings from the Savior's mission.

Chapters 54 and 55 also begin a short collection of Isaianic discourses addressed to the entire world. In chapter 54, the Lord promises his loyalty to Zion; in chapter 55, he testifies that his plan will be fulfilled; in chapters 56 and 57 he promises temple blessings to all righteous peoples; and in chapter 58 he testifies that righteous deeds, such as fasting, will be rewarded. This set of five chapters lays a foundation for the following eight chapters concerning the great blessings of a Zion society, a millennial reign, and a new heaven and new earth in the last days. (Isa. 59-66.)

Chapter 54 is written in beautiful poetry and provides a radiant preview of future happiness in Zion. The entire chapter is quoted by the Savior in 3 Nephi 22. But prior to his almost verbatim quotation, Christ presents some events that will precede the fulfillment of Isaiah 54: (1) the Gentiles will receive the gospel and assist in building God's kingdom and gathering Israel; (2) the gospel will be preached to the Lamanites; (3) the gosepl will be preached to all the dispersed, including the Ten Tribes; (4) Israel's remnants will gather to Zion; (5) the remnants are to return to the lands of their inheritance. (3 Ne. 20-21.) After giving these prophecies about Israel, the Savior introduces Isaiah 54 with the phrase, "Then shall that which is written come to pass. . . ." (3 Ne. 22:1.) Thus, chapter 54 ties into the prophecies of Israel in the last days, when blood Israel will join the Gentiles as a part of covenant Israel, each in their special lands of inheritances.

In this chapter Isaiah speaks of the Lord's covenants with Israel, comparing them to a marriage relationship:

54 "Sing, O barren woman,
you who never bore a
child;
burst into song, shout for joy,
you who were never in labor;
because more are the children of
the desolate woman
than of her who has a husband,"
says the Lord.
²"Enlarge the place of your tent,
stretch your tent curtains wide,
do not hold back;
lengthen your cords,
strengthen your stakes.
³For you will spread out to the right
and to the left;
your descendants will dispossess
nations
and settle in their desolate
cities." (NIV)

The barren woman of verse 1 is undoubtedly Israel, who has not yet brought forth the full fruits of her covenants with the Lord. Isaiah calls Israel barren because of her inability or unwillingness to produce spiritually strong offspring for the Lord.

The woman has been separated from her husband, the Lord, because of her wickedness. (Compare Hosea 1-2.) Thus, she has not had children. However, Isaiah tells her to break forth into song, because many children have been born to the "desolate" or forsaken woman. The desolate woman and her relationsip to the wife can be understood in two ways: (1) The desolate woman represents the Gentiles, and the wife Israel; thus the Gentiles will bring forth greater spiritual fruits than Israel has delivered; (2) the desolate woman is Israel in her scattered condition, while the wife is those people remaining in the Holy land. Thus, Israel will bring forth more children (both physically and spiritually) outside the land of her original inheritance than in it. (See Gal. 4:22-31; Rev. 12:1-6.) In either case, Isaiah, uses these images to symbolize the relationship of the Lord to Israel; those who join with covenant Israel are the children of that relationship.

In verse 2, Isaiah indicates that Israel will grow so rapidly that her habitation must be enlarged to accommodate all the new people. He compares her growth to a tent that, if one wishes to make it larger, must have its stakes moved to a further distance from the center pole. It is from Isaiah that Latter-day Saints derive the word *stake*, their basic unit of ecclesiastical organization and territorial division. Each stake of the tent (the Church or Zion) must be strong and independent enough to provide stability to the tent as it stretches to cover the whole earth. (Isa. 33:20; Moro. 10:31; D&C 45:31-32; 82:14; 109:39, 59; 115:5-6; 133:8-9; see MD, p. 764.)

Isaiah describes Israel's latter-day growth through conversion and gathering as spreading out "to the right and to the left" (v. 3) until Zion inhabits the lands of the "nations" or Gentiles (KJV). The

459

Church of Jesus Christ of Latter-day Saints fulfills this prophecy as it establishes itself in Gentile nations and spreads over all the world.

Isaiah recognizes that Israel's barren or forsaken years, though they seem long, will gradually fade from her memory after Zion is established. The prophet reminds Israel that the Lord has not forgotten her:

4"Do not be afraid; you will not suffer shame.
Do not fear disgrace; you will not be humiliated.
You will forget the shame of your youth
and remember no more the reproach of your widowhood.
5For your Maker is your husband—
the Lord Almighty is his name—
the Holy One of Israel is your Redeemer;
he is called the God of all the earth.
6The Lord will call you back
as if you were a wife deserted and distressed in spirit—
a wife who married young, only to be rejected," says your God.
7For a brief moment I abandoned you,
but with deep compassion I will bring you back.
8In a surge of anger I hid my face from you for a moment,
but with everlasting kindness I will have compassion on you,"
says the Lord your Redeemer. (NIV)

In verses 7 and 8, Isaiah stresses that Israel's period of suffering is brief when compared to her time of redemption. Likewise, our small moment of separation from God is brief when compared to the vast eternity we can live in his presence. Though Israel and we may merit divine rejection because of wickedness, we both can be welcomed back into God's company because of his "deep compassion" and "everlasting kindness."

As a reminder of the Lord's covenants with Israel, the prophet reviews an everlasting covenant God made with Noah:

9"To me this is like the days of Noah,
when I swore that the waters of Noah would never again cover the earth.
So now I have sworn not to be angry with you,
never to rebuke you again.
10Though the mountains be shaken and the hills be removed,
yet my unfailing love for you will not be shaken
nor my covenant of peace[1] be removed,"
says the LORD, who has compassion on you. (NIV)

---

[1]This word is translated as "my people" in 3 Ne. 22:10 and the JST.

After God cleansed the earth with a flood, he promised Noah that he would never again destroy the earth in that manner. (Gen. 9:13-17.) Here Isaiah impresses upon Israel that the promise God made to gather and redeem her is as valid as his promise to Noah.

As part of his promise, the Lord says that he will never again rebuke Israel (v. 9). The Lord cannot lie, and since he has sworn not to be angry with Israel nor to rebuke her, and since he has also promised that he will "chasten" or rebuke those whom he loves if they are wicked (D&C 95:1), Isaiah's prophecy means that a time will come when Israel will become righteous enough that she will need no chastisement from the Lord.

When all Israel and the earth as a whole is righteous, the Lord's millennial reign will be established. Isaiah describes Zion's beauty during such a glorious condition:

11"O afflicted city, lashed by storms and not comforted,
I will build you with stones of turquoise,
your foundations with sapphires.
12I will make your battlements of rubies,
your gates of sparkling jewels,
and all your walls of precious stones. (NIV)

The Apostle John seems to describe the same city in Revelation 21:18-21:

> The wall was made of jasper, and the city of pure gold, as pure as glass. The foundations of the city walls were decorated with every kind of precious stone. The first foundation was jasper, the second sapphire, the third chalcedony, the fourth emerald, the fifth sardonyx, the sixth carnelian, the seventh chrysolite, the eighth beryl, the ninth topaz, the tenth chrysoprase, the eleventh jacinth, and the twelfth amethyst. The twelve gates were twelve pearls, each gate made of a single pearl. The street of the city was of pure gold, like transparent glass. (NIV)

Isaiah and John are probably describing New Jerusalem. On the other hand, their description may be symbolic of the material and spiritual wealth throughout the stakes of Zion.

Isaiah concludes his description by emphasizing the peace that will prevail in Israel:

13All your sons will be taught by the Lord.
and great will be your children's peace.
14In righteousness you will be established:
Tyranny will be far from you;
you will have nothing to fear.
Terror will be far removed;
it will not come near you.
15If anyone does attack you, it will not be my doing;
whoever attacks you will surrender to you.

461

16"See, it is I who created the
 blacksmith
who fans the coals into flame
and forges a weapon fit for
 its work.
 And it is I who have created the
 destroyer to work havoc;
17 no weapon forged against you

will prevail,
 and you will refute every
 tongue that accuses you.
This is the heritage of the
 servants of the Lord,
 and this is their vindication
 from me," declares the Lord.
 (NIV)

Isaiah's promise in verse 13 that Israel's children will be taught by the Lord implies an intimate relationship between the people and Christ during the Millennium. If parents will properly teach their children here and now, then these children can enjoy the great legacy of having Christ himself as their teacher and leader. (D&C 45:58; see D&C 68:25-28.) As President Kimball said about this promise of Isaiah, "Surely every good parent would like this peace for his offspring. It comes from the simple life of the true Latter-day Saint as he makes his home and family supreme." (*Ensign*, July 1973, p. 16.)

In verses 14-15, Isaiah promises other blessings, including righteousness, freedom from oppression and fear, and protection and peace. He concludes with the Lord's promise that no power will prevail against His people. (See D&C 71:9-10; 109:25.)

In short, Isaiah 54 is a promise to Zion and her righteous members. It embodies various poetic forms to depict the relationship between the Lord and covenant Israel. The metaphor of the husband and wife is used throughout the chapter:

Husband provides wife:	Jehovah provides Israel:	Verses
Children	Great numbers	1-3
Love	Reconciliation	4-8
Commitment	Covenant relationship	9-10
Material comfort	Prosperity	11-12
Protection	Peace	13-17

The third element (a commitment and covenant relationship) becomes the pivot point for all the other promises and blessings. Because of the Lord's covenant relationship with Israel, he has an eternal commitment to bless those who want to become a part of covenant Israel. The Lord's goal in his commitment is "to bring to pass the immortality and eternal life of man." (Moses 1:38.)

Having stressed in chapter 54 the Lord's covenant with Israel, Isaiah describes in chapter 55 how the blessings of immortality and eternal life are offered to all people. He also indicates that those who do achieve eternal life in God's celestial presence become an everlasting sign that God's plan and glory is being achieved. Structured in clear chiastic parallelism, this discourse:

A. Invites all to receive the everlasting gospel (vs. 1-3).
B. Promises help (4-5).
C. Requests a turning back to the Lord (6-7).
D. States that God's plans and ways are not man's plans and ways (8).
E. Testifies that the heavens (spiritual plans) are above the earth (mortal designs) (9).
D'. States again that God's plans and ways are not like man's (9).
C'. Declares that some things have already returned back to God (10-11).
B'. Promises that we can be led back to God's presence (12).
A'. Invites us to become God's everlasting sign (13).

Through the ages, gospel truths have been taught by prophets, apostles, and other inspired teachers and servants of God. (Moses 5:12; Abr. 2:6; Deut. 4:5; Acts 5:42; Jacob 1:19; D&C 42:12-14; see TG "Teaching.") Our Heavenly Father has often extended an invitation through the prophets to his children to come and partake of his goodness. (2 Ne. 26:25; John 4:13-14; 6:47-51; Rev. 3:18; 21:6; 22:17.) In chapter 55, Isaiah extends God's invitation not only to the people of his day, but also to readers and listeners throughout the ages. This invitation to partake of the gospel establishes a positive, tender mood from the very beginning of the prophet's discourse:

55 "Come, all you who are thirsty,
come to the waters;
and you who have no money,
come, buy and eat!
Come, buy wine and milk
without money and without cost.
²Why spend money on what is not bread,
and your labor on what does not satisfy?
Listen, listen to me, and eat what is good,
and your soul will delight in the richest of fare.
³Give ear and come to me;
hear me, that your soul may live.
I will make an everlasting covenant with you,
my faithful love promised to David." (NIV)

The word "thirst" (v. 1) immediately reminds the listener of the human necessity for liquids. Isaiah mentions three common liquids: (1) water, always helpful and usually available to satisfy thirst; (2) wine, less plentiful and available only after some effort, but good for satisfying thirst and in times of rejoicing (Zech. 10:7); (3) milk, common and important for strength, growth, and nourishment. (1 Pet. 2:2.) By applying these three terms in a spiritual context, we see that Isaiah is not only inviting the people to satisfy their physical thirst, but promising them joy and strength as they spiritually drink what the Lord has to offer.

Isaiah quickly lets his audience know that his invitation is symbolic. He tells them that what he is offering can be acquired "without money and without cost" (v. !). He asks why they spend their money and effort on temporal things, which do not ultimately satisfy (v. 2). This passage was quoted by Jacob in his great sermon on the Atonement and formed the basis for his invitation that all come and partake of the blessings of redemption. (2 Ne. 9:50-51.)

Christ is clearly the "living water" and the "bread of life" (John 4:13; 6:47-51), whose gifts are free to all men. The gospel of Jesus Christ has no monetary price attached to it; one does not have to buy his Church membership or the blessing of resurrection. The invitation to come unto Christ and freely obtain these gifts does not suggest, however, that they can be obtained without effort, though one does not need worldly goods to acquire them. (See Prov. 9:4-6; Ps. 116:10; Alma 37:35 for similar promises about gaining wisdom.) The price is a pure heart and a contrite spirit.

Attracting his listener's attention with a number of imperatives (listen, eat, give ear, come, hear), Isaiah concludes his invitation by promising the Lord's everlasting covenant to the people (v. 3). Of course, the Lord has made many covenants and promises, most of which are conditional upon worthiness before they are fulfilled. For example, the covenant ordinance of baptism promises forgiveness of sins if one has faith, repents, and sins no more. The covenant promises of the sacrament, temple endowment, and temple marriage are all conditional upon righteousness. However, some promises and covenants of the Lord are unconditional; all will receive them. For example, everyone will be taught the gospel before their final judgment, either during earth life or in the spirit world. (D&C 1:2.) At the end of verse 3, Isaiah promises another unconditional blessing, the "sure mercies of David" (KJV). In Acts 13, Paul applies the phrase "sure mercies of David" to the resurrection of Christ (vs. 26-41, esp. 34). Thus, one "everlasting covenant" and "sure mercy of David" that is promised to David and all God's children is the promise of immortality with resurrected bodies. (See Ps. 89:2-4, 27-29.)

However, before God's unconditional promises can be fulfilled, Christ must come and open the gates. Isaiah alludes to Christ and others who aid in the Father's plan in the next two verses of chapter 55:

4"See, I have made him a witness to the peoples, a leader and commander of the peoples. 5Surely you will summon nations you know not, and nations that do not know you will hasten to you, because of the Lord your God, the Holy One of Israel, for he has endowed you with splendor." (NIV)

The witness, leader, and commander in verse 4 refers foremost to the Messiah, but also to David and others who represent the Messiah. (Isa. 11:1; Ezek. 34:23-24; 37:24-25; Jer. 30:9; Hosea 3:5.) Christ is the first and supreme witness of the Father and his plan. (John 18:37; Rev. 1:5.) He is also our way back to the Father's presence, and the source of all righteousness.

The strange nation of verse 5 that will help Israel probably refers to the Gentiles who restore the gospel to the house of Israel in the last days. (Eph. 2:11-12; 3 Ne. 21.) This prophecy is being fulfilled through missionary work in the Church today. (See pp. 203-10.)

Of course, before anybody can partake of the "bread and water" or saving covenants of the gospel, they must learn the truth and repent. Isaiah challenges the people to seek the Lord and repent:

6Seek the Lord while he may be found; call on him while he is near. 7Let the wicked forsake his way and the evil man his thoughts. Let him turn to the Lord, and he will have mercy on him, and to our God, for he will freely pardon. (NIV)

Isaiah's testimony that repentance will bring the Lord's forgiveness is simply but clearly stated in verse 7. His promise carries a subtle warning, however, that we have a limited period of time to draw close to the Lord and repent (v. 6). The Lord later combined this counsel with advice from the Sermon on the Mount as he spoke through Joseph Smith:

And again, verily I say unto you, my friends, I leave these sayings with you to ponder in your hearts, with this commandment which I give unto you, that ye shall call upon me while I am near—Draw near unto me and I will draw near unto you; seek me diligently and ye shall find me; ask, and ye shall receive; knock, and it shall be opened unto you. (D&C 88:62-63.)

Interestingly, the phrase "let him turn to the Lord" in verse 7 is full of meaning and is variously translated as "let him *return* unto the Lord" (KJV) or "let him *turn back* to the Lord" (NJV). The Hebrew word in the middle of the phrase is *shur*, meaning "to turn back" or "to turn away." The concept of "turning back" or returning to the Lord implies man's origin and premortal existence with God in a state of cleanliness. Now we are separated from him both physically and spiritually, but he enables us to "return" to him as we "turn away" from worldliness.

The means by which we turn away from sin and return to God is in accordance with God's foreordained plan. Isaiah next talks about this plan:

> 8"For my thoughts are not your thoughts,
> neither are your ways my ways,"
> declares the Lord.
> 9"As the heavens are higher than the earth,
> so are my ways higher than your ways
> and my thoughts than your thoughts." (NIV)

God's plans, thoughts, ways, words, and actions are not like those of men—they are higher and greater. Isaiah teaches this concept through clear, chiastic parallelism: thoughts/ways/heavens are above the earth/ways/thoughts. Simply stated, however profound men's ideas may be, the Lord's thoughts excel them. This does not mean, however, that man is forever excluded from gaining and sharing God's insights. The Book of Mormon prophet Jacob gives an important key to learning God's ways:

> Behold, great and marvelous are the works of the Lord. How unsearchable are the depths of the mysteries of him; and it is impossible that man should find out all his ways. And no man knoweth of his ways save it be revealed unto him; wherefore, brethren, despise not the revelations of God. (Jacob 4:8.)

In comparing the extreme differences between God and man, the psalmist said, "For as the heaven is high above the earth, so great is his mercy toward them that fear him." (Ps. 103:11.) However, the "fear of the Lord" is not meant to be negative, for the psalmist also said that "the fear of the Lord is the beginning of wisdom: a good understanding have all they that do his commandments." (Ps. 110:11.)

Thus, according to the psalmist, those who "fear" or respect the Lord and "do his commandments" will enjoy the "mercy" or blessings of the Lord, which are as great as "the heaven is high above the earth."

Isaiah unites the same concepts of greatness, blessings, and obedience as he concludes chapter 55. First he speaks about elements that leave God's presence, come to earth, and return to God having fulfilled their purpose:

10"As the rain and the snow
    come down from heaven,
and do not return to it
    without watering the earth
and making it bud and flourish,
    so that it yields seed for the
        sower and bread for the
        eater,

11so is my word that goes out from
    my mouth:
It will not return to me empty,
but will accomplish what I desire
    and achieve the purpose for
        which I sent it." (NIV)

Rain and snow do not descend in vain; they make the earth fertile and beautiful. (See Job 36:26-28.) Likewise God's word comes to earth for a purpose; it spiritually nourishes man and teaches him the purpose and potential of eternal life.

But God did not create this earth so that he could simply beautify it through rain, nor did he place man upon it simply to have someone to teach; his purpose is to assist his children until they are ready to return to his presence. Isaiah expressed this purpose as follows:

12"You will go out in joy
    and be led forth in peace;
the mountains and hills
    will burst into song before you,
and all the trees of the field
    will clap their hands.
13Instead of the thornbush will
    grow the pine tree,

and instead of briers the myrtle
    will grow.
This will be for the Lord's
    renown,
for an everlasting sign,
    which will not be destroyed."
(NIV)

Isaiah states that we "go out" or leave (God's presence) in joy and that we will eventually be "led home" (NJV) in peace. He did not say that leaving God was meant to be sorrowful or that we would be forced back home to God. We are here because we need the experience and because we can return to God's presence if we follow the prescribed path.

If man achieves the purpose of his creation, the earth herself and the plants and animals upon her (which were organized to provide a beautiful place for man to live) will rejoice (v. 12). Finally, the earth will blossom and reach her own destiny as she becomes the eternal dwelling place for celestial beings (v. 13). As the earth and its inhabitants achieve their full potential, they become an everlasting sign that God's word is true; his work and his glory is "to bring to pass the immortality and eternal life of man." (Moses 1:39.) Many have already reached celestial glory (D&C 132:29; 137-38); they are eternal witnesses that God's plan, which is higher than any of our plans or any designs of Satan's, does work, and they are an everlasting symbol of God's love and glory.

THE SABBATH AND TEMPLE WORSHIP
ISAIAH 56-57

Primarily a prophet and witness to the house of Israel, Isaiah also delivered important discourses to the Gentiles. In chapters 56 and 57, he specifically addresses the foreigners and others who have been excluded from the assembly of Israel. He extends to them the same promises available to the Israelites—the blessings of the Lord, especially His presence.

It seems that toward the end of Isaiah's life, he was prompted to compile his writings and edit them into a form that would inspire his readers. Some scholars wonder if Isaiah might have arranged his discourses into their present order, which is out of sequence chronologically but allows and even encourages multiple levels of meaning. When Isaiah first uttered his pronouncements, they were relevant for the Israelites of his day. But as his work achieved its final form, these same prophecies took on broader meanings by extending their message to all peoples in later ages. Christ alluded to the universal application of Isaiah's words when he said that Isaiah surely "spake as touching all things concerning my people" and "it must needs be that he must speak also to the Gentiles." (3 Ne. 23:2.)

Chapter 56 begins with God's invitation to outsiders, strangers, and the childless to come to his holy mountain and house (the temple) and take part in his eternal kingdom. These eight verses are a prelude to a later, more complete development of this idea in the closing chapters of Isaiah (65-66), in which the prophet teaches the peril of being eternally excluded from God's glory. Chapter 56 concludes and chapter 57 continues with a promise of the Gentile's unrighteous dominion over the wayward Israelites. Chapter 57 also has two short sermons: the first denounces wickedness and invites the people to trust in the Lord; the second promises blessings to the Lord's people and warns them of the consequence of wickedness. The symmetry of these two chapters provides another glimpse into Isaiah's prophetic and poetic powers. They can be divided into four sections:

1. The gathering in of the faithful outcasts (56:1-8).
2. The downfall of Israel through wickedness (56:9–57:2).
3. A rebuke of the wicked (57:3-13).
4. A promise to the righteous (57:14-21).

The Gathering In of the Faithful Outcasts (56:1-8)

The first verses of chapter 56 stress a major theme of the latter chapters of Isaiah—the return of exiles and the welcoming of Gentiles into God's fold. In a chiastic poem, Isaiah extends the Lord's invitation to all those desiring to share the blessings in Zion:

56 Be just and fair to all, the *Lord God* says. Do what's right and good, for I am *coming soon to rescue you.* ²*Blessed* is the man who refuses to work during my *Sabbath* days of rest, but honors them; and *blessed* is the man who checks himself from doing wrong.

³And my blessings are for *Gentiles*, too, when they accept the Lord; don't let them think that I will make them second-class citizens. And this is for the *eunuchs* too. They can be as much mine as anyone. ⁴For I say this to the *eunuchs* who *keep his Sabbaths* holy and *choose the things* that please him, and come to grips with *his laws*: ⁵I will give them—in my house, within my walls—a name far greater than the *honor* they would receive *from having sons and daughters.* For the name that I will give them is an everlasting one; it will never disappear.

⁶As for the *Gentiles*, the outsiders who join the people of the Lord and serve him and love his name, and are his servants and don't desecrate the *Sabbath*, and have accepted his

A. The Lord will rescue

B. The blessed people
C. Sabbath keepers

D. Blessings for Gentiles

E. Eunuchs accepted by the Lord

F. Blessings conditional upon following the Lord

E'. Blessings greater than children

D'. Invitation to Gentiles

C'. Sabbath keepers

covenant and promises, ⁷I will bring them also to my holy mountain of Jerusalem, and make them *full of joy* within my House of Prayer.

I will accept their sacrifices and offerings, for my Temple shall be called "A House of Prayer for All People"! ⁸For the *Lord God who brings back* the outcasts of Israel says, I will bring others too besides my people Israel. (LB, italics added)

B'. The joyful people

A'. The Lord will gather

The segments in italics indicate the chiastic pattern outlined in the right margin. The central idea is commitment to the Lord. Specifically, Isaiah mentions three conditions for the reception of the Lord's blessings within the temple: keeping the Sabbath holy, choosing the right, and obeying God's laws.

The next most important idea is in the opening and closing segments of the poem. Isaiah teaches that the Lord has promised that all who are righteous and obedient shall be gathered and receive salvation. Isaiah emphasizes the comprehensiveness of this deliverance and gathering, and states that these blessings are for all, Jew and Gentile. The incoming Gentiles, afraid that they will be denied some of the blessings, are assured that they will be acceptable to the Lord and brought to the "Holy Mount," that is, the temple.

Beginning in verse 1, the Lord calls upon mankind to do what is right and just. He promises that their actions will not be in vain, for his "salvation is near to come" (KJV). (The Lord's salvation came during his mortal ministry, centuries after the time of Isaiah.) Yet his "salvation" or coming to "rescue" (LB) all the righteous remains as an unfulfilled promise today. However, we know that his salvation will come soon. Thus, Isaiah's words carry relevance both for his contemporaries and for those who read them today.

Verse 2 echoes the same ideas, adding that people will be happy if they do these things. Also, the Lord admonishes the people to observe the Sabbath in order to prepare for his salvation. (This command sets the stage for verses 3-8, in which the Lord specifies certain non-Israelites, foreigners, and eunuchs who will be eligible for his salvation.) Of course, the observance of the Sabbath was traditionally practiced only by the Israelites; the Gentiles would not have observed it. But because this message is for all who will listen, both Jews and Gentiles, the Lord makes special mention of this requirement, which the incoming children are to observe in order to be prepared for his coming.

When modern Christian readers hear the term Sabbath, they think only of Sunday services, but for the ancient Israelites, the Sabbath carried far greater connotations. (Deut. 5:14-15.) More than a weekly day of worship, Sabbath observance was applied to all religious festivals, including Passover, Shavuot (Pentecost), Succot (Tabernacles), and Yom Kippur (Day of Atonement). Israel even celebrated "Sabbaths" of years (every seventh year), during which the land was not plowed, and the Sabbath year of Jubilees for release from debts and personal servitude. Thus, *Sabbaths* (v. 4) meant all the religious holidays and the remembrances these holidays invoked of the Lord's dealings with his people. These many Sabbaths reviewed many aspects of the Israelites' commitment to God and served as a sign of their covenant relationship. (Ex. 31:13, 16-17; D&C 59:9-19.) Thus, when Isaiah warns against polluting the Sabbath and admonishes Israel to keep all the Lord's Sabbaths, he means far more than simply resting from one's labors one day a week. (See BD "Sabbath," "Feasts," "Fasts.")

In verse 3, Isaiah extends the Lord's blessings to the Gentiles and the childless. These foreigners (strangers, KJV) and eunuchs were earlier restricted in their religious participation with the Israelites.

The strangers in Israel's midst were usually non-Israelites who accepted Israelite rule. (2 Sam. 1:13; Ezek. 14:7; see BD "Stranger.") Strangers were usually not full citizens, though they shared certain legal rights and responsibilities. Some were barred from entering the tabernacle and even the temple courtyards. (Deut. 23:3.) Although often ostracized and even persecuted, the strangers were under God's protection, and he commanded the Israelites to treat them kindly. (Lev. 19:33-34; Josh. 9:1–10:7; see Eph. 2:11-15, 19; Gal. 3:27-29.)

The eunuchs were particularly restricted in their social acceptance by the Israelites. Under Mosaic law, eunuchs were not allowed into full Israelite fellowship, especially in the sacrificial, tabernacle, and priesthood ordinances. (Lev. 21:17-23; Deut. 23:1-2.) This law was probably given to Israel because wholeness of body typified spiritual wholeness: those who had been emasculated were considered religiously unfit in Israel. (See BD "Eunuch.") Also, the eunuchs enjoyed no inheritance in Israel, since they could not found a family and carry on a tribal name. They were barren as a "dry tree" (v. 3, KJV).

The Lord's beautiful promise in verses 4 and 5 is that the Gentiles and eunuchs, those previously excluded from the complete Israelite covenant, will share God's full blessings if they keep his laws. The major blessing is given in verse 5 with the invitation to receive an everlasting name in the Lord's house, the temple. Particularly, the "outcasts" are promised a "name" and a "place" (KJV) or a "memorial" (NIV) or "monument" (RSV, NJV). One reason for multiple translations is that in the Hebrew the outcasts are promised a "hand and a name," and scholars vary in their interpretation of how a "hand" represents the Lord's temple promises. Of course, they assume that the "name" received is *Israel*, because these newcomers would be considered as Israelites. This is partially correct, since people willing to share Israel's religious beliefs and responsibilities are known as covenant Israelites, just as those who accept and follow Christ assume his name. (Mosiah 5:7; 3 Ne. 30:2; D&C 45:28.) However, worthy Latter-day Saints who enjoy full involvement with temple worship also recognize that names and hands play an important role in making covenants in endowment and temple sealings. These church members not only take upon themselves the name of Christ and become heirs to the blessings of Israel, but also receive a new name. (See D&C 130:11; MD, pp. 533-34.) More than receiving a hand of fellowship, they also raise their hands in the Lord's house and covenant to keep all his commandments. (See D&C 88:119-21, 130-36.) Thus, the promise of "a hand and a name" implies that the strangers and eunuchs will enjoy the full blessings and ordinances of the temple.

The "hand" of a covenant and the everlasting "name" these people receive is far more valuable than any wealth or posterity (v. 5). If one keeps his sacred covenants, he receives worlds without end and a numberless, eternal posterity. Thus, the strangers and eunuchs who were excluded from Israel and had no children can still share all of Jacob's blessings, including eternal families. And what must they do to receive these blessings? The same as any member of Israel—obey the covenant. (See DNTC 2:276.)

Apparently, the blessings received by the righteous outcasts in the Lord's house are comparable to the "mansions prepared" for the faithful "in the house of the Father" promised in Doctrine and Covenants 81:6: "And if thou art faithful unto the end thou shalt have a crown of immortality, and eternal life."

Verse 7 restates all the previously promised blessings to come upon both Jews and Gentiles. First, the promise of gathering to "my holy mountain" (KJV) is repeated. Next, the Lord promises that their sacrifices and offerings will be received upon his altars. Eventually the Lord's house will not be the exclusive privilege of blood Israel, but "a house of prayer for all people." This promise was fulfilled on June 9, 1978, when the temple blessings were made available to all worthy people, regardless of race. As the Lord promised in verse 8, he has gathered many others to him in addition to the outcasts of Israel.

The Downfall of Israel through Their Wickedness (56:9–57:2)

Isaiah turns from the righteous outcasts who would join Israel and addresses those Gentiles who will come as beasts to devour wicked Israel. He rebukes Israel's leaders who ignore the impending disaster because of their own lazy drunkenness. He also recognizes that with Israel's destruction many righteous will suffer, and he outlines their status in his discourse, which continues into chapter 57:

9Come, wild animals of the field; come, tear apart the sheep; come, wild animals of the forest, devour my people. 10For the leaders of my people—the Lord's watchmen, his shepherds—are all blind to every danger. They are featherbrained and give no warning when danger comes. They love to lie there, love to sleep, to dream. 11And they are as greedy as dogs, never satisfied; they are stupid shepherds who only look after their own interest, each trying to get as much as he can for himself from every possible source. 12"Come," they say. "We'll get some wine and have a party; let's all get drunk. This is really living; let it go on and on, and tomorrow will be better yet!"

57 The good men perish; the godly die before their time and no one seems to care or wonder why. No one seems to realize that God is taking them away from evil days ahead. 2For the godly who die shall rest in peace. (LB)

Isaiah uses pastoral imagery to describe the incompetence and ignorance of the leaders, who leave the "flock" (Israel) open to wild animals (Gentile armies). The Lord introduces this gloomy prophecy in verse 9 by calling the beasts to "come and devour." Because this pronouncement was probably written late in Isaiah's life, after the northern tribes were already taken captive, the prophet is apparently discussing the leaders of Judah in these verses. These blind, unconcerned leaders leave Judah vulnerable to the Babylonians in the sixth century B.C. and later to the Romans after the leaders' rejection of Jesus Christ in the first century A.D. Since the Babylonian captivity, the Jews were open to the false teachings of men and thereby were often led astray from the true teachings of the Lord. Long before the birth of Jesus, they lived in a state of apostasy. Christ, while teaching in Palestine, used this same imagery of wild beasts to describe apostasy and false prophets: "Beware of false prophets, which come to you in sheep's clothing, but inwardly they are ravening wolves." (Matt. 7:15.) Isaiah's imagery does not imply that the leaders themselves were the "ravening wolves," but that because of their conduct Israel was left open to those who entered and began the work of destruction.

In verses 10 and 11, Isaiah describes the conduct of the leaders themselves. He says that they are blind and compares them to dogs, dumb dogs, sleeping dogs, greedy dogs, and finally to shepherds who know not (see KJV). All of these were strong indictments against them. First, the watchmen were blind, meaning they had no vision (physically or spiritually) of the approaching danger. (See Ezek. 3:17; 34.) Not only were they unaware of the danger, but they were like "dumb dogs" who can't bark out a warning even when the danger is obvious. Even worse than their blindness or dumbness is their attitude, which prevents them from attending to their tasks. Finally, they are greedy, watching out only for themselves. Concerning the disastrous results of these "dogs," the medieval Jewish scholar Kimchi observes,

> The flock is intrusted to the care of these watchmen. The wild beasts come; these dogs bark not; and the wild beasts devour the flock. Thus they do not *profit* the flock. Yea, they *injure* it; for the owner trusts in them, that they will watch and be faithful; but they are not. These are the false teachers and careless shepherds. (Quoted in Adam Clarke, *The Holy Bible . . . with a Commentary and Critical Notes* 4:212.)

Unfortunately, Isaiah's imagery seems to describe leaders of many religions in our time. These figures seem to refer to those who possess the gospel themselves (who watch over the flock) but do not make it available to others. His words are comparable to Nephi's comments about the churches of our day (2 Ne. 28:3-9) and Moroni's prophecy about false religions in the last days (Morm. 8:31-33, 37-39.)

If the negligent watchmen were the only casualties, their loss would only serve to satisfy justice. However, along with them many innocent people suffer and are destroyed. In 57:1, Isaiah describes how good people are taken away through slavery or death because of the evil in their society. He promises, however, that the pious will still enjoy some inner peace as they "rest in their beds" (v. 2, KJV). The people resting "in their beds" or "on their couches" (NJV) could be those enjoying some peace in mortality, but this verse probably refers to the rest their bodies experience in the grave while their postmortal spirits walk in "uprightness" (v. 2, KJV) in paradise. Whether in the mortal world or in the spirit world, the righteous who suffer because of another's wickedness can still know peace and rest.

A Rebuke of the Wicked (57:3-13)

Isaiah contrasts the peace of the righteous with the acts of the wicked, which will bring the wicked into a state of eternal turmoil (57:3-13, 20-21). He vividly describes the people's wickedness:

³But you—come here, you witches' sons, you offspring of adulterers and harlots! ⁴Who is it you mock, making faces and sticking out your tongues? You children of sinners and liars! ⁵You worship your idols with great zeal beneath the shade of every tree, and slay your children as human sacrifices down in the valleys, under overhanging rocks. ⁶Your gods are the smooth stones in the valleys. You worship them and they, not I, are your inheritance. Does all this make me happy? ⁷,⁸You have committed adultery on the tops of the mountains, for you worship idols there, deserting me. Behind closed doors you set your idols up and worship someone other than me. This is adultery, for you are giving these idols your love, instead of loving me. ⁹You have taken pleasant incense and perfume to Molech as your gift. You have traveled far, even to hell itself, to find new gods to love. ¹⁰You grew weary in your search, but you never gave up. You strengthened yourself and went on. ¹¹Why were you more afraid of them than of me? How is it that you gave not even a second thought to me? Is it because I've been too gentle, that you have no fear of me?

¹²And then there is your "righteousness" and your "good works"—none of which will save you. ¹³Let's see if the whole collection of your idols can help you when you cry to them to save you! They are so weak that the wind can carry them off! A breath can puff them away. But he who trusts in me shall possess the land and inherit my Holy Mountain. (LB)

The epithets "witch," "adulterer," and "harlot" in verses 3 and 4 personify the abject wickedness of Israel; it is rare in prophetic literature that so many abusive terms are used in a single stanza. (Compare Ezek. 16; 23.) These verses seem a natural outgrowth of the preceding section, which describes the corruption of Israel's leaders. The watchmen have relaxed and evil has flooded in.

Commentators differ widely in fixing a historical background for this prophecy. It is possible that Isaiah is describing the social conditions in Judah toward the end of his life. Manasseh, who ruled Judah after his father Hezekiah, was an apostate with strong Assyrian and pagan sympathies. Manasseh's persecution of the innocent is depicted in verse 1; the sacrificing of his own son to Molech is referred to in verses 5 and 9. (See 2 Kgs. 21:6.) In another context and in keeping with the Babylonian setting for many Isaianic writings, this situation hints at the wicked condition prevailing among the Samaritans and Jews who were left behind in Palestine after Nebuchadnezzar deported many Jews in 586 B.C. The later reforms undertaken by Ezra and Nehemiah were rejected by the Samaritans, who had mixed the worship of Jehovah with idolatrous rites and beliefs similar to those described above. Either situation could have been used by Isaiah to prophesy of Judah's wickedness.

Isaiah highlights two major abuses of the people, immorality and the sacrifice of children. In verses 5, 7, and 8, he plunges into a vivid description of their wickedness. They worship with "great zeal" as they "inflame themselves" (KJV) under the terebinths (v. 5). The precise meaning of this phrase is lost to modern readers, but the Hebrew word translated as "great zeal" or "enflaming yourselves" means to arouse a person sexually. (Young, *The Book of Isaiah* 3:402.) Ancient idol worship was inseparably connected with ritual prostitution and fertility cults. Since ancient economies were founded upon agriculture, the people's dependence upon the fertility of the ground was absolute. As the pagan worship developed in ancient cultures, the belief developed that if a farmer had intercourse with a priestess at a local temple and she became pregnant, this was a sign that the fertility god would look favorably upon his crops.

Also, ancient man believed that the lives and interactions of the gods were reflected in the life of man. That is, if man acted out certain activities on earth then this would facilitate their taking place in heaven. So, if people involved themselves in fertility acts in their pagan temples, then their gods would bless the land with productivity. Thus, the pagan temples usually became centers of ritual or religious prostitution. Isaiah describes this in verse 5. As the wicked Israelites commit adultery through pagan worship, they break their covenant with God. Verses 7 and 8 give further evidence of their zeal in pursuing immorality.

The people were not only steeped in adultery through their pagan worship, but sacrificed their children. The ritual of the pagan god Molech required the worshipper to sacrifice his firstborn son. Molech was a large brass god with a hollow stomach, in which a great fire was kindled and into which the child was placed.

Both of these pagan practices are denounced in numerous scriptural references. (Deut. 12:2; 1 Kgs. 14:23; Jer. 2:20; 3:6; 13; 17:2; Hosea 4:13-14; Ezek. 6:13; Jer. 32:35; Ezek. 20:26-31.) However, in spite of God's obvious displeasure with both acts, they have found their way, metaphorically, into modern practice. No longer practiced as pagan religious rituals, the twin sins of immorality and abortion have the same evil effect in contemporary society. They strike at the root of the procreative processes and disrupt the respect people should have for life. They also indicate people's selfishness and their desire for personal gratification rather than controlling their passions, respecting marital covenants, and committing themselves to raising a family. These sins continue to take people from God and subject them to the buffetings of Satan.

In verse 9, Isaiah continues his theme: through these sexual and ritual acts the people have made covenants with the pagan gods. The oils, perfumes, and envoys are representative of tribute paid to alien cults and their prostitutes. But Isaiah exposes the true nature of this tribute and to whom it is paid. Their covenant has been with none other than Satan.

The people are so entrenched in their sins that they have lost their fear of God and his judgments (v. 12). The Lord attempts to alert them to their foolishness by asserting that their idols will profit them nothing; their idols will not hear their petitions, but will be carried away by the wind (vs. 12-13).

This brief discourse concludes with a promise that those who repent and trust in the Lord will enjoy his blessings. Indeed, the righteous will become a part of his "holy mountain," the temple and its covenants and promises.

A Promise to the Righteous (57:14-21)

In sharp contrast to the scathing denunciation and heavy style of the preceding pronouncement, Isaiah now employs flowing diction and subdued expectation as he promises the repentant sufferers the tender healing and protection of the Lord:

¹⁴I will say, Rebuild the road! Clear away the rocks and stones. Prepare a glorious highway for my people's return from captivity.

¹⁵The high and lofty one who inhabits eternity, the Holy One, says this: I live in that high and holy place where those with contrite, humble spirits dwell; and I refresh the humble and give new courage to those with repentant hearts. ¹⁶For I will not fight against you forever, nor always show my wrath; if I did, all mankind would perish—the very souls that I have made. ¹⁷I was angry and smote these greedy men. But they went right on sinning, doing everything their evil hearts desired. ¹⁸I have seen what they do, but I will heal them anyway! I will lead them and comfort them, helping them to mourn and to confess their sins. ¹⁹Peace, peace to them, both near and far, for I will heal them all. ²⁰But those who still reject me are like the restless sea, which is never still, but always churns up mire and dirt. ²¹There is no peace, says my God, for them! (LB)

The highway of salvation described in verse 14 is a common image in Isaiah (40:3; 62:10; see TG "Highway"). While the phrase "cast ye up, cast ye up, prepare the way" (KJV) generally refers to the coming of the lost Ten Tribes (D&C 133:23-28), Isaiah seems to be using it here as a figure of speech. He calls for the removal of everything that hinders spiritual growth, especially the weeds of wickedness that he denounced in the previous discourse. This spiritual way is to be the road upon which people return to spiritual health. In a latter-day context, this way could represent the restoration of the gospel through Joseph Smith. The light and knowledge restored to mankind clears the road. No longer are the people who seek God in spiritual darkness; the way of salvation is clear for them to travel back into God's presence.

God has accomplished this. He is high and lofty, his name is holy, and he dwells in holiness (v. 15). Yet his exalted position does not hinder his kindness and condescension to man. He dwells with the contrite and lowly of spirit. He heals, bringing back to life those of a lowly countenance. Indeed, verse 16 emphasizes this point as Isaiah proclaims that God, in his abundant grace, will not contend or be angry, but will give life. He retains compassion for those "souls" or premortal spirits he created. The only reason he cursed them and turned away from them is because they followed their own heart instead of his way (v. 17). Verse 18 reaffirms God's commitment to heal and comfort those who have suffered his wrath. The people of whom the Lord speaks in these verses are probably either the righteous who have suffered because of corrupt leaders (56:9–57:1-2) or those who have seen the error of their ways and have developed faith in the Lord (57:13, 15).

In closing, Isaiah makes some statements that encompass the righteous and the wicked (vs. 19-21). The righteous, wherever they may be, will be healed (v. 19), but the wicked can never rest. They are like a troubled sea that continually tosses mud and mire (v. 20). The wicked who think that they can continue in their wickedness will ultimately realize that they find no peace in their actions. (Isa. 56:12; 57:10, 21.) They will not be safe from the great judgment day when Christ comes to judge all mankind. (Moro. 10:34; see Isa. 48:22.)

President Harold B. Lee often quoted these last three verses of chapter 57 and applied them in at least three different contexts. For example, he placed them in the setting of Latter-day Saints struggling against the world (CR, Apr. 1942, p. 87); he applied them to different types of Latter-day Saints within the Church (CR, Oct. 1947, p. 67); and finally, in his last general conference, he applied them to all who seek wickedness and lack true self-love or self-respect:

> To those who fail to heed the warnings of those who are striving to teach these principles and choose to go in the opposite course, they will eventually find themselves in the pitiable state which you are witnessing so often among us. The prophet Isaiah described the tragic result most dramatically when he repeated the words of God which came to him as he sought to fortify his people against the wickedness of the world, and I quote his words: [Isa. 57:19-21.]
>
> As I have prayerfully thought of the reasons why one chooses this course which is dramatically described by the prophet Isaiah—when one who has departed from the path which would have given him peace is like the troubled sea, casting up mire and dirt—it seems to me that it all results from the failure of the individual to have self-respect. (CR, Oct. 1973, p. 4.)

Just as President Lee often returned to these verses of Isaiah and found insight and application from them, all students of the scriptures should continually reread the scriptures and seek to understand the prophets' words, which can enlighten and strengthen them.

SCRIPTURAL NOTES AND COMMENTARY

Isaiah 57: Chiastic Outline

This chapter contains a neat, clear chiasmus:

State of the Righteous and Wicked

A. The righteous enter into peace (v. 1)

A'. No peace for the wicked (v. 21)

B. Mental and spiritual rest for the righteous in paradise (2)

C. Evil seed brings forth nothing but spiritual death (3)

D. Acts of wickedness are denounced (4-12)

E. Those who continue to trust in false gods (Satan) will receive nothing; they will inherit eternal damnation (13a)

B'. Mental and spiritual anguish for the wicked in spirit prison (20)

C'. Righteousness brings forth fruits of everlasting life (19)

D'. Fruits of righteousness are promised (14-18)

E'. Those who continue to trust in the Lord will receive his blessings and inherit eternal life (13b)

LAWS AND PRINCIPLES OF THE FAST
ISAIAH 58

Chapter 58 provides a unique opportunity to study one of Isaiah's sermons to his people and to learn how the same teachings are of great value in contemporary society. Isaiah's teachings about fasting and the Sabbath are straightforward and easily understood. His poetry includes numerous parallelisms, including a chiasmus that develops throughout the whole poem, and he maintains a smooth flow of ideas from beginning to end.

The poem is essentially a dialogue between the Lord and Israel. God addresses Israel's complaints about not being rewarded for fasting by contrasting her hypocritical fasts with the true spirit of fasting. He then lists many blessings Israel can receive from fasting and concludes with some instruction about the Sabbath. The chapter naturally divides into four sections:

1. Israel vainly seeks the Lord (vs. 1-3b)
2. False and true fasts compared (3c-7)
3. Rewards for true fasting promised (8-12)
4. Counsel and promises for the Sabbath (13-14)

During Isaiah's time, just as today, the most important fixed Jewish fast was *Yom Kippur*, the Day of Atonement. (Lev. 16:29-34; Num. 29:7-11.) This fast day originated during the time of Moses as the one fast Israel was commanded to observe. Israelites could hold other public or individual fasts during times of mourning, famine, invasion, or thanksgiving, but *Yom Kippur* was to be strictly observed by the entire nation every autumn.

Yom Kippur is held on the tenth day of the seventh month of the Jewish liturgical calendar (either in September or October). During the fast, each person evaluates his life and repents of his sins in order to be at peace with God and with others. No labor is performed—the day is observed as if it were a Sabbath (whether it falls on the Sabbath or not). (Lev. 23:27-32.) *Yom Kippur* is still observed by the Jews as the most holy of all religious celebrations.

During Isaiah's day when the Israelites still had a temple, *Yom Kippur* was particularly significant because a holy convocation was held at the temple, and special sacrifices, including a particular sin offering, were made. The sin offering of an unspotted male goat represented the bringing of all Israel's sins before the Lord. The high priest took some of the blood of that sacrifice into the Holy of Holies and sprinkled it on the ground in front of the Ark of the Covenant. He also performed other sacrifices and rituals before the holy day concluded with the blowing of the *shofar*, the ram's horn. (See BD "Fasts" for more information on the Day of Atonement.)

Although every *Yom Kippur* was a special holy day, another religious commemoration was celebrated along with it twice each century—the Jubilee year. (See BD, "Jubilee, Year of."). Every fiftieth year, the blowing of trumpets on *Yom Kippur* proclaimed liberty throughout the land—all debts, slaves, and indentured servants were freed. (Lev. 25:8-17, 25-34.) When *Yom Kippur* was celebrated during the Jubilee year, Israelites had a unique opportunity to clear all their spiritual debts with the Lord and material debts with their fellow man. The celebration also provided the people an opportunity to hear a reading of the whole Mosaic law, to review their history, and to commemorate another half-century of existence and (hopefully) growth for Israel. (See BD, "Sabbatical Year.")

Note the similarities between the ritual of *Yom Kippur* (as celebrated during a Sabbatical Year, especially the Jubilee year) and the structure of Isaiah 58:

1. *Trumpet (58:1):* Isaiah's voice is raised like a trumpet; the trumpet is blown each *Yom Kippur* and proclaims the Jubilee Year. (Lev. 25:8-9.)
2. *Sins of Israel (58:1):* Isaiah is charged to remind the people of their sins; on *Yom Kippur* the High Priest sacrifices a sin offering before assembled Israel for all the sins committed during the past year. (Lev. 16:15-19.)
3. *Sabbath (58:3-4, 13):* Isaiah condemns the people for pursuing their daily business on this Sabbath fast day; the Day of Atonement and Jubilee are both special Sabbaths during which no work is to be done. (lev. 16:31; 35:1-22.)
4. *Wickedness removed (58:6, 11):* Israel is told to remove every yoke from the people, particularly wickedness and injustice; on *Yom*

Kippur the High Priest places the sins of Israel upon the scapegoat and sends it into the wilderness. (Lev. 16:20-22.)

5. *Freedom (58:6-7):* The fast that the Lord desires includes releasing burdens (debts) and freeing the oppressed; every seven years debts and slaves were to be freed, and every fifty years land was to be returned to its original tribal owners. (Lev. 25.)

6. *Mercy of the Lord (58:8):* As Israel observes a proper fast, she is promised the glory of the Lord; as the high priest sprinkles blood before the mercy seat of the Lord each *Yom Kippur*, he fulfills a ritual atonement for the people that cleanses them of their sins and enables them to be worthy of the Lord's glory. (Lev. 16:15, 30.)

Although the precise occasion of Isaiah's discourse on fasting is not recorded, it seems likely that it was on *Yom Kippur* during a Sabbatical year, and perhaps even during the Jubilee year. If so, Isaiah was addressing Israelites assembled in the Jerusalem Temple courtyards during the fall of the year. Apparently, the people were complaining about their lack of blessings, when the Lord spoke to them through his prophet:

58 "Shout it aloud, do not hold back.
Raise your voice like a trumpet.
Declare to my people their rebellion and to the house of Jacob their sins.
²For day after day they seek me out; they seem eager to know my ways,
as if they were a nation that does what is right

and has not forsaken the commands of its God.
They ask me for just decisions and seem eager for God to come near them.
³'Why have we fasted,' they say, 'and you have not seen it?
Why have we humbled ourselves, and you have not noticed?'"
(NIV)

This introduction by the Lord prefaces the entire poem. Isaiah is addressed and told to declare to Israel her sin. Isaiah's subsequent declaration answers the Israelites' complaint that the Lord is not acknowledging their fasting.

The chapter opens with a sense of urgency, which is conveyed through strong verbs ("*shout* it aloud," "*raise* your voice," "*declare* to my people") and nouns ("rebellion" and "trumpet"). In ancient Israel, the trumpet announced either an enemy attack or a special holy day. Isaiah's message needs to be delivered immediately and forcefully, not because of the people's complaints, but because of hypocrisy in their relationship with the Lord.

In verse 2, Isaiah emphasizes Israel's hypocrisy with careful word choice: "they *seem* eager, . . . *as if* they were a nation" and a righteous people, who "*seem* eager" for God's presence. In response to the people's question as to why they are not rewarded for fasting, the Lord describes their fast and reveals its true nature:

"Yet on the day of your fasting,
  you do as you please
  and exploit all your workers.
⁴Your fasting ends in quarreling
    and strife,
  and in striking each other with
    wicked fists.
You cannot fast as you do today
  and expect your voice to be
    heard on high.
⁵Is this the kind of fast I have
chosen,
  only a day for a man to humble
    himself?
Is it only for bowing one's head
    like a reed
  and for lying on sackcloth and
    ashes?
Is that what you call a fast,
  a day acceptable to the LORD?"
(NIV)

Greedily forcing their workers to labor on the fast day causes the people to argue, fight, and hold attitudes detrimental to spiritual sensitivity. Thus, although they may have sorrowful faces and may even wear sackcloth and ashes, Israel's behavior does not warrant a favorable response from the Lord.

The imagery of verse 5 portrays people who flaunt their fast with bowed heads or sad countenances (like bowed reeds or bulrushes) and with external signs of sorrow (sackcloth and ashes). Coarse sackcloth was not required when fasting, although its use seems to have been approved without question. (IDB 4:147.) Ashes, the remains of burnt offerings, were often spread upon the body and coupled with sackcloth as a sign of mourning and grief. These outward gestures and a sullen countenance do not, however, meet the true requirements of the fast. An external show of piety without inward devotion profits nothing and brings only hunger pangs, a warped soul, and the wrath of God. (See Matt. 6:16-18.)

While the Lord does not say that it is wrong to fast in sackcloth and ashes, he emphasizes proper and pure devotion over outward signs:

⁶"Is not this the kind of fasting I
    have chosen:
  to loose the chains of injustice
    and untie the cords of the yoke,
  to set the oppressed free
and break every yoke?
⁷Is it not to share your food with
    the hungry
  and to provide the poor
    wanderer with shelter—

when you see the naked, to clothe
    him,
    and not to turn away from your
      own flesh and blood?" (NIV)

Combining spiritual, social, physical, and family responsibilities, verses 6 and 7 summarize the service the people of God should render each other. These verses parallel each other both in form and theme: grammatically, they both open with a question; structurally, they follow a pattern of composite parallelism in developing similar concepts about fasting. Verse 6 stresses spiritual and social responsibilities, and verse 7 emphasizes temporal and familial opportunities for service. The climax of each verse is a phrase that includes any other service not expressly mentioned: "break every yoke" and do not "turn away from your own flesh and blood." The parallelisms are a bit more obvious in the original Hebrew, but they can still be outlined in English as follows:

Israel's spiritual responsibilities (v. 6):
  A. To loose the chains of injustice (or wickedness, KJV)
  A'. To untie the yoke bonds (of sin)
  A". and free the oppressed (from social and Satanic persecution)
  C. and break every yoke

Israel's physical responsibilities (v. 7):
  B. To feed the hungry
  B'. and provide for the homeless
  B". To cloth the naked
  C'. and fulfill duties for kin (or mankind)

To review, reread verses 6 and 7 in either the King James Version or the New International Version and note the grammatical pattern in the verses. Each begins with an interrogative and concludes with a summary phrase. Each verse follows a composite pattern of semantic parallelism in describing at least three ways in which the fast should be observed.

Careful study will reveal other forms of semantic parallelism in this set of verses: *synonymous*, since verses 6 and 7 present parallel ideas on the same theme; *synthetic*, since a question-answer format is followed; and *climactic*, since both verses build to verse 8, which describes verses 6 and 7. Studying Isaiah's poetic style should not distract from the beautiful teachings found in these verses, but should enhance them. These verses inspire the reader through style as well as content.

Another way to study these two verses about fasting is to review how they apply today. Many General Authorities have done this in general conference. (This is especially true of welfare sessions, where speakers, particularly the Church's presiding bishops, will often quote Isaiah 58. For example, see Bishop John H. Vandenberg's address, CR, Apr. 1963, pp. 28-29 and compare it with an address of Bishop Victor L. Brown, *Ensign*, Nov. 1977, p. 83.)

A third helpful approach to studying Isaiah's teachings on the fast is to review the Topical Guide entries listed in the footnotes of the Latter-day Saint edition of the Bible. Seventeen different entries are listed in Isaiah 58, ranging from common topics such as "Fasting," Hypocrisy," and "Sabbath" to other topics such as "Transgression," "Strife," and "Almsgiving." Using the Topical Guide is a particularly good way to study, since additional scriptural references will greatly enrich one's understanding of fasting as he sees what other prophets have taught on this topic.

Studying Isaiah's message in a variety of ways will help the reader understand the Lord's teachings on fasting in verses 6 and 7 and appreciate the blessings that come to those who fast. The promises are found in verses 8-12:

8Then your light will break forth
    like the dawn,
    and your healing will quickly
      appear;
then your righteousness will go
    before you,
    and the glory of the LORD will
      be your rear guard.
9Then you will call, and the LORD
    will answer;
    you will cry for help, and he
      will say: Here am I.

"If you do away with the yoke of
    oppression,
    with the pointing finger and
      malicious talk,
10and if you spend yourselves in
    behalf of the hungry
    and satisfy the needs of the
      oppressed,

then your light will rise in the
    darkness,
    and your night will become like
      the noonday.
11The LORD will guide you always;
    he will satisfy your needs in a
      sun-scorched land
    and will strengthen your frame.
You will be like a well-watered
    garden,
    like a spring whose waters will
      never fail.
12Your people will rebuild the
    ancient ruins
    and will raise up the age-old
      foundations;
you will be called Repairer of
    Broken Walls,
    Restorer of Streets with
      Dwellings." (NIV)

The introductory "then" *(az)* of verses 8 and 9 signals an important transition, for it points to the time when God's chosen people will change their ways and do those things described earlier in the chapter (see also v. 14). Then and only then will the Lord's special blessings be poured out upon them.

The promised spiritual blessings are grouped together in verse 8, the first part of verse 9, and at the end of verse 10; the temporal blessings are listed in verses 11 and 12. The spiritual blessings are, of course, the most important, and eight of them are highlighted below and matched into four sets of synonymous parallelism:

A. Light breaking forth
A'. Health springing forth
B. Righteousness before you
B'. Lord's glory after you (v.8)
C. Lord will answer your call
C'. He will respond to your cry (9)
D. Your light will rise
D'. Your night will become as the noonday (10)

"Light" is promised in blessings numbers A and D; the Lord is mentioned only twice in these verses, in blessings B' and C. This develops a chiasmus, highlighting the Lord at the pivot point with "light" at both ends receiving secondary emphasis. One can gain great insights by studying each of the eight blessings mentioned here.

President Harold B. Lee particularly loved to quote blessings C and C' as recorded in verse 9. One example is in a talk to the British Saints:

> As explained in the days of the prophet Isaiah, the children of Israel were admonished, "Is it not to deal thy bread to the hungry," meaning fasting and then paying fast offerings. If you would do that, he promised, "Then shalt thou call and the Lord shall answer; thou shalt cry, and he shall say, Here I am." (Isa. 58:7, 9.)
>
> We are saying to the Saints, How important that you keep this fundamental law to fast and to deal out your bread to the hungry through contributions so that when you call, the Lord shall answer. (England Area CR, 1971, p. 140.)

He also said in general conference:

> What a wonderful feeling of security can come in a crisis to one who has learned to pray and has cultivated listening ears so that he can "call, and the Lord shall answer;" when he can cry and the LORD shall say, "Here I am." (CR, Apr. 1972, p. 124; see also CR, Oct. 1968, p. 62.)

President Lee's remarks provide a strong witness that Isaiah's promises are just as binding today as when they were originally delivered.

The list of spiritual blessings in verses 9-10 is interrupted by some reminders about self-control, proper behavior, and charity. These ideas parallel those of verses 6 and 7, in which the people were told to help the oppressed. Just as verses 6 and 7 lead up to the promises of verses 8 and 9, verses 9 and 10 lead up to the promises of verses 10-12. Isaiah's repetition of the Israelite's responsibility toward the oppressed and needy reinforces the concept that spiritual and physical blessings are contingent upon righteousness.

An introductory phrase, "and the Lord will guide thee continually," heads the eight physical blessings that Isaiah lists again in matched sets to tell how the Lord will guide and bless Israel:

A. Quenched thirst
A'. Fed bones
B. Watered garden
B'. Running spring (v. 11)
C. Rebuilt ruins
C'. Raised buildings
D. Repaired walls
D'. Restored streets (12)

In short, the Lord will bless the whole Israelite society by renewing their bodies (A, A'), fields (B, B'), homes (C, C') and cities (D, D'). Of course, although these are physical blessings, most of them can also represent spiritual blessings: water can represent the gospel, homes and foundations the family or Church organization, and streets the path returning to God's presence.

Chapter 58 of Isaiah concludes with the promise of still more blessings for those who properly observe the Sabbath.

13"If you keep your feet from
    breaking the Sabbath
and from doing as you please
    on my holy day,
if you call the Sabbath a delight
    and the LORD's holy day
    honorable,
and if you honor it by not going
    your own way
and not doing as you please or
speaking idle words,
14then you will find your joy in the
    LORD,
and I will cause you to ride on
    the heights of the land
and to feast on the inheritance
    of your father Jacob."
The mouth of the LORD has
    spoken. (NIV)

The promises of these verses parallel those of verses 2 and 3, in which the people seek the Lord but cannot find his blessings because they neglect their Sabbath duties. Isaiah uses an "if-then" clause: the "if" being man's responsibility (v. 13), the "then" being God's obligation (v. 14). In verses 13 and 14, Isaiah promises the people that if they

489

observe the Sabbath, they will finally obtain God's greatest blessings, celestial joy as true children of Israel. (Compare D&C 59:10-24.)

Isaiah concludes his beautiful poem and profound discourse with the phrase "the mouth of the LORD has spoken." He also uses this statement in 1:20 and 40:5, and in all cases it serves as a special witness or testimony. In some ways, the phrase served the same purpose for Isaiah's listeners as does the modern phrase "In the name of Jesus Christ, amen." Isaiah's closing implies that the teachings in chapter 58 are important and that the promises are valid.

In conclusion, let me share some suggestions that I have found valuable in fasting. Fasting should not be a time of pain and sorrow, but one of joy and rejoicing. (D&C 59:14.) Based upon my experience and the testimonies of others, the following suggestions will improve the spiritual rewards of fasting:

1. Plan ahead; prepare your schedule so that you can start the fast properly on Saturday, and yourself spiritually so that you can be ready for the fast.
2. Have a particular purpose or goal in mind as you begin the fast. Perhaps you desire some answers to doctrinal questions, help in solving a problem, or inspiration in serving others. Select one primary goal on which you would like to concentrate while you fast.
3. Start the fast with a private prayer—preferably vocal—while you are alone on your knees. Remember, fasting without prayer is simply starving, and the Lord has not commanded us to starve ourselves.
4. Keep the Spirit; use Saturday evening as part of your fast period. Keep activities uplifting. Prepare yourself in all ways for the Sabbath.
5. Fast a full twenty-four hours, refraining from all food and drink, if possible. In case of health problems, fast according to your own limitations.
6. Prepare to reach your goal: study the scriptures, draft possible solutions to problems, talk with your family and home teachers, write in your journal, etc.
7. Attend all your church meetings on Sunday.
8. Pay a full fast offering as determined by what you feel you should contribute to help the poor and needy. (Remember Isaiah's counsel in 58:7, 10.)
9. Just before concluding your fast, set aside twenty or thirty min-

utes to ponder, meditate, sort out possible solutions to a problem, etc. Read Moroni 10, especially the first five verses, for helpful counsel.

10. End the fast with a private prayer and be sure to take time to listen for answers.

ARISE AND COME UP TO ZION
ISAIAH 59-60

In chapters 59 and 60, Isaiah describes a complete transformation of Israel as she moves from wickedness to righteousness through a sequence of changes: sin (58:1-8), repentance (58:9-15a), deliverance (58:15b-21), gathering (59:1-9), rebuilding (59:10-13), prosperity (59:14-18), and the presence of the Lord (59:19-22). Combining poetry and prophecy, Isaiah portrays a pattern of progression as Israel rises from the depths of spiritual death to eternal life in God's presence.

Isaiah speaks first about spiritual death, the separation of man from God. He recognizes that this death results solely from man's actions and not from any arbitrary whim of God. He tells Israel why she is not receiving answers and help from the Lord:

59 Behold, the Lord's hand is not so short
That it cannot save;
Neither is His ear so dull
That it cannot hear.
²But your iniquities have made a separation between you and your God,
And your sins have hidden His face from you, so that He does not hear.

³For your hands are defiled with blood,
And your fingers with iniquity;
Your lips have spoken falsehood,
Your tongue mutters wickedness.
⁴No one sues righteously and no one pleads honestly.
They trust in confusion, and speak lies;
they conceive mischief, and bring forth iniquity. (NAS)

There are numerous examples of synonymous parallelism in these verses. Isaiah repeats every concept so that there can be no question as to why the people are not receiving divine help—they are unworthy.

Verse 3 is particularly poetic, for Isaiah uses four body parts to portray the evil acts and words of the people. Their *hands* are defiled with blood. (Compare Isa. 1:15.) Providing further detail in a parallel expression, Isaiah states their *fingers* work iniquity. Not content with describing the instruments of their evil deeds, Isaiah rebukes their wicked speech in parallel stanzas about their *lips* and *tongue*.

Isaiah continues his description of their wickedness with imagery of snakes and spiders:

⁵They hatch adders' eggs and
  weave the spider's web;
 He who eats of their eggs dies,
 And from that which is crushed a
  snake breaks forth.
⁶Their webs will not become
  clothing,
 Nor will they cover themselves
  with their works;
 Their works are works of iniquity,
 And an act of violence is in their
  hands.
⁷Their feet run to evil,
 And they hasten to shed innocent
  blood;
 Their thoughts are thoughts of
  iniquity;
 Devastation and destruction are in
  their highways.
⁸They do not know the way of
  peace,
 And there is no justice in their
  tracks;
 They have made their paths
  crooked;
 Whoever treads on them does not
  know peace. (NAS)

The adder or cockatrice (KJV) is a very poisonous snake. Apparently, even the venom of the unhatched snakes was powerful enough to kill a person. Why would anyone want to handle these snakes or cover themselves with spiders' webs? Isaiah is really asking the people, "Why would any of you endanger your souls by entangling yourselves in sin?" The serpent represents the devil and the spider's web the bonds or chains of sin. Although the people probably would not endanger their physical lives, they gradually give themselves over to Satan's power and spiritual death as they continue their iniquities.

Verse 7 adds a fifth body part, the feet. The feet, like hands, are instruments of wickedness. The thoughts give rise to the wicked words and acts. If one's mind is continually on the path of sin, his whole body soon becomes steeped in sin. (Compare King Benjamin's admonition to guard one's thoughts, words, and deeds lest he perish; Mosiah 4:30.)

Echoing the final verses of chapter 57, Isaiah concludes his short denouncement by warning the wicked that they can find no peace in their present paths (v. 8). Having concluded his indictment, the prophet changes his role and begins to speak for the people instead of against them. Speaking in the first person, he now represents those in Israel who might recognize the error of their ways and seek deliverance from sin:

⁹Therefore, justice is far from us,
And righteousness does not
overtake us;
We hope for light, but behold,
darkness;
For brightness, but we walk in
gloom.
¹⁰We grope along the wall like blind
men,
We grope like those who have no
eyes;
We stumble at midday as in the
twilight,
Among those who are vigorous
we are like dead men.
¹¹All of us growl like bears,
And moan sadly like doves;
We hope for justice, but there is
none,
For salvation, but it is far from us.
¹²For our transgressions are
multiplied before Thee,
And our sins testify against us;
For our transgressions are with
us,
And we know our iniquities:
¹³Transgressing and denying the
Lord,
And turning away from our God,
Speaking oppression and revolt,
Conceiving in and uttering from
the heart lying words.
¹⁴And justice is turned back,
And righteousness stands far
away;
For truth has stumbled in the
street,
And uprightness cannot enter.
¹⁵Yes, truth is lacking;
And he who turns aside from evil
makes himself a prey. (NAS)

Notice again the continued use of synonymous parallelism. Isaiah's terms often have multiple meanings. For example, in verse 9, "justice," "righteousness," "light," and "brightness" are all divine attributes. Isaiah uses these for attributes to stress the people's separation from God. He repeats the separation theme twice more at the end of verse 11 after describing the stumbling actions and mournful sounds of those who are lost.

Finally the people turn from confusion and self-pity to an awareness of the primary cause for their suffering (v. 12). They admit that they have both transgressed and sinned. From the days of Moses the ancient Israelites were taught that their disobedience to God's commands could manifest itself in two forms, transgression and sin. A transgression was when a person unknowingly broke a law; a sin was willful disobedience. Thus, it is possible for a person to transgress a law without committing sin. (See 2 Ne. 2:22-23.) Under the Mosaic law, transgressors were required to bring a special sacrifice to the tabernacle or temple: if he was able to make restitution to the offended parties, he brought a trespass or guilt offering (Lev. 5:15-16; 6:2-5); if restitution was not possible, even though the person broke the law in ignorance, he was required to make the more serious sin offering (Lev.

4:1-3, 13-15, 22-24). The sin offering apparently was also the required sacrifice for those who willfully sinned but later repented and wanted to return to full fellowship with the Lord. (See BD "Sacrifices," MD, pp. 735-36, 804). In verse 12, Israel confesses to both transgression and sin. Isaiah concludes his short discourse by describing more of the consequences and dangers of wickedness (vs. 14-15a).

In the second half of verse 15, Isaiah changes to a third person narration to speak to Israel about the Lord. Through eloquent poetry, he describes the Lord's actions for His people and his judgments against His enemies:

Now the Lord saw,
And it was displeasing in His
  sight that there was no justice.
[16]And He saw that there was no
  man,
And was astonished that there
  was no one to intercede;
Then His own arm brought
  salvation to Him;
And His righteousness upheld
  Him.
[17]And He put on righteousness like
  a breastplate,
And a helmet of salvation on His
  head;
And He put on garments of
  vengeance for clothing,
And wrapped Himself with zeal
  as a mantle.

[18]According to their deeds, so He
  will repay,
Wrath to His adversaries,
  recompense to His enemies;
To the coastlands he will make
  recompense.
[19]So they will fear the name of the
  Lord from the west
And His glory from the rising of
  the sun,
For He will come like a rushing
  stream,
Which the wind of the Lord
  drives.
[20]"And a Redeemer will come to
  Zion,
And to those who turn from
  transgression in Jacob,"
declares the Lord. (NAS)

These verses obviously refer to Jesus Christ, for when he came to the earth to fulfill his foreordained role through the Atonement, there was no other man or intercessor (v. 16) who could make the requisite sacrifice.

In the first half of verse 17, Isaiah uses the imagery of a breastplate and helmet to describe the deliverance of God's people through righteousness and salvation. In the second half, he continues the imagery of clothing, but speaks of vengeance upon God's enemies. The armor mentioned is defensive, implying that powerful foes attack the Lord and seek his destruction. To withstand the evil one, people must take upon themselves the whole armor of God. (See D&C 27:15; Eph. 6:13-19.) In this verse, Isaiah depicts the Lord as the warrior of righteousness who will zealously destroy the wicked and deliver the righteous.

In verse 18, Isaiah indicates that only God brings recompense according to the offenders' deeds. In other words, the Lord is just and will not abuse his power in punishing the wicked throughout the "isles" (KJV) or continents of the earth. Verse 19 continues the theme of judgment and promises that it will come quickly to the entire earth. (See Isa. 42:13; 52:10; 63:1-6.) As the Lord brings about universal judgment, he prepares the earth for the Millennium, when he can rule with the righteous in Zion (v. 20).

In the last verse of chapter 59, Isaiah breaks out of his usual poetic mode and reiterates the Lord's personal covenant with those in Zion who have turned away from their sins:

21"And as for Me, this is My covenant with them," says the Lord: "My Spirit which is upon you, and My words which I have put in your mouth, shall not depart from your mouth, nor from the mouth of your offspring, nor from the mouth of your offspring's offspring," says the Lord, "from now and forever." (NAS)

The Lord's promise can apply either to immortal beings who live in his presence or to a religious community that never forfeits divine direction through apostasy. Only resurrected persons in the celestial kingdom fit the first category, while The Church of Jesus Christ of Latter-day Saints fits the second; they both will enjoy communion with the Lord through the eternities.

Isaiah describes in chapter 60 the inhabitants of an ideal society:

60 "Arise, shine; for your light has come, And the glory of the Lord has risen upon you. 2For behold, darkness will cover the earth, And deep darkness the peoples; But the Lord will rise upon you, And His glory will appear upon you. 3"And nations will come to your light, And kings to the brightness of your rising." (NAS)

Again, this society seems to be The Church of Jesus Christ of Latter-day Saints. Elder Orson Pratt interpreted verse 1 as a description of the Church in Zion in the latter days. (JD 16:78.) Joseph Smith applied the description in verse 2 to the world in 1837 when the Twelve Apostles were sent to the nations of the earth. (D&C 112:23.) Joseph Smith commented upon Isaiah 60:2:

Consider for a moment, brethren, the fulfillment of the words of the prophet; for we behold that darkness covers the earth, and gross darkness the minds of the inhabitants thereof—that crimes of every description are increasing among men—vices of great enormity are practiced—the rising generation growing up in the fullness of pride and arrogance. (TPJS, p. 47.)

As Zion is established in the last days, she must go through certain stages of development before she can assist the Lord in his millennial reign. The first requisite is sufficient numbers of people to establish God's kingdom. Also, these people should be geographically concentrated so that they can assist and protect one another in their work. This step requires the gathering of the remnants of Israel together with the honest in heart from among the Gentiles to establish such a nucleus. Isaiah describes this gathering in the next verses of chapter 60:

4"Lift up your eyes round about,
and see;
They all gather together, they
come to you.
Your sons will come from afar,
And your daughters will be carried
in the arms.
5"Then you will see and be radiant,
And your heart will thrill and
rejoice;
Because the abundance of the sea
will be turned to you,
The wealth of the nations will
come to you.
6"A multitude of camels will cover
you,
The young camels of Midian and
Ephah;
All those from Sheba will come;
They will bring gold and
frankincense,
And will bear good news of the
praises of the Lord.

7"All the flocks of Kedar will be
gathered together to you,
The rams of Nebaioth will
minister to you;
They will go up with acceptance
on My altar,
And I shall glorify My glorious
house.
8"Who are these who fly like a
cloud,
And like the doves to their lattices?
9"Surely the coastlands will wait
for Me;
And the ships of Tarshish will
come first,
To bring your sons from afar,
Their silver and their gold with
them,
For the name of the Lord your
God,
And for the Holy One of Israel
because He has glorified
you."(NAS)

As the people gather, the wealth of nations accumulates in Zion. Verse 6 promises riches from the areas ruled today by Jordan and Saudi Arabia, and verse 7 tells of livestock coming from the area of Syria. In

Isaiah's time, these were the prime grazing areas for camels and livestock; they also had the highest quality gold and incense. Isaiah may also be using these items and places to represent the choice people as well as goods that will become a part of Zion. Verses 8 and 9 develop this theme further and promise a return by air (doves flying) and by sea (the ships of Tarshish; see Isa. 23:1, 6, 10, 14.)

The Lord's purpose in the gathering is not the simple accumulation of people and riches, but the demonstration of his glory (v. 9). Thus, the people and their riches must be used to build a society that can attract the attention of the world. Isaiah describes how this model community will be built:

10"And foreigners will build up
    your walls,
And their kings will minister to
    you;
for in My wrath I struck you,
And in My favor I have had
    compassion on you.
11"And your gates will be open
    continually;
They will not be closed day or
    night,
So that men may bring to you the
    wealth of the nations,
With their kings led in

    procession.
12"For the nation and the kingdom
    which will not serve you will
    perish,
And the nations will be utterly
    ruined.
13"The glory of Lebanon will come
    to you,
The juniper, the box tree, and the
    cypress together,
To beautify the place of My
    sanctuary;
And I shall make the place of My
    feet glorious." (NAS)

The Gentiles and rulers of nations will help build Zion. Their labors are combined with those of Israel to produce two major symbols of the Lord's people: a city with gates continually open (meaning that it never fears attack), and a sanctuary or temple (where the Lord himself can dwell). Without fear of attack and with the presence of the Lord, this Zion people lives in peace, love, and harmony, and is thus a model of an ideal society. This model compares closely with Isaiah's earlier prophecy of the "mountain of the Lord's house" to which all nations will come. (Isa. 2:2-4; see D&C 121:29; 1 Chr. 28:2; Isa. 41:19.)

After this ideal city and its temple is built, the peoples of the earth will take notice of it. In the next three verses, Isaiah explains this and reemphasizes why the Lord will give Zion her glory:

14"And the sons of those who
    afflicted you will come bowing
    to you,

And all those who despised you
    will bow themselves at the soles
    of your feet;

And they will call you the city of
the Lord,
The Zion of the Holy one of
Israel.
15"Whereas you have been forsaken
and hated
With no one passing through,
I will make you an everlasting
pride,

A joy from generation to
generation.
16"You will also suck the milk of
nations,
And will suck the breast of kings;
Then you will know that I, the
Lord, am your Savior,
And your Redeemer, the Mighty
One of Jacob." (NAS)

The contrast of Israel's final status with her past condition is obvious: her former oppressors will humble themselves before her, and she will experience respect instead of hatred, prosperity instead of suffering, and a closeness to God instead of apostasy.

Isaiah's description of this city and the stages leading up to its final glorious state are paralleled in modern scripture where Joseph Smith records a vision of people and riches coming together in a city of refuge where the Lord's glory dwells:

> And with one heart and with one mind, gather up your riches that ye may purchase an inheritance which shall hereafter be appointed unto you. And it shall be called the New Jerusalem, a land of peace, a city of refuge, a place of safety for the saints of the Most High God; And the glory of the Lord shall be there, and the terror of the Lord also shall be there, insomuch that the wicked will not come unto it, and it shall be called Zion. (D&C 45:65-67.)

The city described by Isaiah and Joseph Smith is called Zion. Zion is patterned after Enoch's city (Moses 7) where the pure in heart dwelt (D&C 97:21). The word *Zion* is found periodically throughout the Old Testament, but commonly in Psalms (thirty-seven times) and Isaiah (forty-five times), making Isaiah the most prolific writer on the subject.

Isaiah recognized that the people establishing a Zion society needed to recognize the Lord as the Savior and love others (vs. 16, 21). Chapter 60 describes many other characteristics of Zion's capital city, Jerusalem. The following chart indicates how some of these characteristics can be applied to both the Old Jerusalem in the Holy Land and the New Jerusalem in America:

Condition to Be Fulfilled (Isa. 60)	Old Jerusalem	New Jerusalem
vs. 1-2 The Lord will appear there.	D&C 133:20-21 Zech. 13:6; 14:4, 9	D&C 84:4-5
3-5 Gentiles and kings will gather there.	Zech. 14:16	D&C 133:12
6 It will be adorned with wealth.	Zech. 14:14	D&C 124:11

Condition to Be Fulfilled (Isa. 60)	Old Jerusalem	New Jerusalem
7 Sacrifice will take place there.	Zech. 14:21	D&C 128:24
10 Gentiles and kings will help build its walls.		3 Ne. 21:23-24
11 Its gates will be continually open.		
12 Nations not subservient to it will be smitten.	Zech. 12:6, 9	D&C 97:18-22
13 A temple will be erected.	Ezek. 47:1-10	D&C 57:1-3
14 The city will be called the Zion of the Holy one of Israel.	Zech. 14:20	D&C 45:66-67
15 The city was once forsaken and hated, but will be made a joy.	Ezek. 36:34-36	D&C 45:70-71
16 It will have power over other kingdoms.	Zech. 14:1-3, 12-15	D&C 64:43
17-18 Perfect peace will prevail.	Zech. 14:11	D&C 45:66-71
19-20 The Lord will be its light.	3 Ne. 20:30-31	Rev. 22:5
21 The people will inherit its land.	2 Ne. 10:7	2 Ne. 10:10-12

As indicated above, the same general conditions will eventually develop in both Old and New Jerusalem. It appears, though, that the Zion society of the New Jerusalem will precede that which is established in Old Jerusalem. (See DS 3:67-79; AGQ 5:70-74.)

As he concludes chapter 60, the Lord promises great material and spiritual blessings to Zion:

17"Instead of bronze I will bring gold,
And instead of iron I will bring silver,
And instead of wood, bronze,
And instead of stones, iron.
And I will make peace your administrators,
And righteousness your overseers.
18"Violence will not be heard again in your land,
Nor devastation or destruction within your borders;
But you will call your walls salvation, and your gates praise.
19"No longer will you have the sun for light by day,
Nor for brightness will the moon give you light;
But you will have the Lord for an everlasting light,
And your God for your glory.
20"Your sun will set no more,
Neither will your moon wane;
For you will have the Lord for an everlasting light,
And the days of your mourning will be finished.

21"Then all your people will be
   righteous;
They will possess the land
   forever,
The branch of My planting,
The work of My hands,
That I may be glorified.

22"The smallest one will become a
   clan,
And the least one a mighty
   nation.
I, the Lord, will hasten it in its
   time." (NAS)

Verse 17 suggests an interesting multiplication and transformation of natural resources: commonplace wood and stone become bronze and iron, which in turn become gold and silver. If gold and silver were as plentiful as wood and stone, wealth would certainly abound in Zion.

The rest of verses 17 and 18 promises peace and righteousness, both of which are echoed in the names of the city gates. (See 2 Ne. 28:21.) Not only does the Lord provide safety and protection, but in verse 19 promises his glory as a source of light for the city. (See Rev. 21:23; 22:5; Ps. 27:1, D&C 88, 93.)

When the New Jerusalem is built and Jesus Christ returns to earth in glory, the need for the sun and moon to give light to Zion will disappear. The Lord himself will be "an everlasting light," as Elder Orson Pratt has explained:

> When therefore, he shall establish his throne in Zion and shall light up the habitations thereof with the glory of his presence, they will not need this light which comes from the bright luminaries that shine forth in yonder heavens, but they will be clothed upon with the glory of their God. . . . They will not need . . . lights of an artificial nature, for the Lord will be there and his glory will be upon all their assemblies. So says Isaiah the Prophet, and I believe it. Amen. (JD 14:355-56; see also D&C 133:57-58, which gives Isa. 60:22 added meaning.)

The last two verses of this chapter culminate the Lord's promises to the righteous in Zion. They will inherit the land forever, not only the Holy Land, but also Joseph's inheritance in America. In fact, the entire earth will be an eternal inheritance of all the righteous after it becomes a place of celestial glory.

In summary, in chapter 60, Isaiah portrays the Lord's glory upon Zion through superb poetry. Contrasting the conditions of wickedness described in chapter 59, Isaiah reveals the light, peace, and prosperity of a righteous people. Like the faith of a mustard seed or the great missionary success of the sons of Mosiah, the Lord's work will bloom and bring thousands to Zion. (Matt. 13:31-32; Alma 26:20.)

Eventually the least individual in Zion will become a mighty nation, because as any member of Zion establishes a righteous family that lives into the Millennium, they will become a great posterity equal to any nation on the earth (v. 22; see D&C 133:58). All these blessings will come forth in the Lord's own due time, as he has appointed it from the beginning, when enough people will have repented and sanctified themselves to be worthy of his presence. (D&C 133:60-62.)

NEW CLOTHES, NEW NAMES, AND NEW BLESSINGS
ISAIAH 61-62

Having promised in chapter 60 the future glory of Zion, Isaiah prophesies further in chapters 61 and 62 concerning the blessings of Zion. While these chapters find partial fulfillment in the return of the Jewish exiles from Babylon and the rebuilding of their temple, they are only completely fulfilled in the ministry of Christ at the meridian of time and in the fulness of times.

Isaiah begins by speaking about the earthly ministry of Christ. Jesus applied the first two verses to himself as he began his public ministry in Nazareth. He told the Jews, "This day is this scripture fulfilled in your ears." (Luke 4:21.) Isaiah prophesies at the end of verse 2 of the ministry of Christ in the fulness of times, speaking of Christ's second coming:

61 The spirit of the Lord God
is upon me,
Because the Lord has anointed me;
He has sent me as a herald of joy to the humble,
To bind up the wounded of heart,
To proclaim release to the captives,
Liberation to the imprisoned;
²To proclaim a year of the Lord's favor
And a day of vindication by our God;
To comfort all who mourn. (NJV)

Isaiah's promise of liberty to the captives can refer to both physical and spiritual bondage; the resurrection frees men from the physical bondage of death, while the Atonement frees men from sin. As Joseph Fielding Smith said, "These references to the opening of the captives evidently have reference to the dead who had been confined in darkness not knowing their fate." (AGQ 2:81.) The souls in spirit prison remained in spiritual darkness, subject to the buffetings of Satan, until the Savior initiated missionary work among them after his crucifixion. (See TG "Spirits in Prison.")

When Christ referred to these verses, he quoted only through the first phrase in verse 2. This is significant, for he said that he had come "to preach the acceptable year of the Lord" (KJV), but did not go on to say that he had come "in a day of vengeance" (KJV). His first ministry upon the earth did not complete his mission, but did accomplish the Atonement and resurrection. The "day of vengeance" will come with Christ's second coming, when the world will be judged and the wicked punished.

The compression of events centuries apart into a single verse is characteristic of Isaiah's writings. Indeed, a "compact" view of history is common among both Old and New Testament writers, who often portray the first advent of the Messiah together with his coming in glory. (See Acts 1:6-7.)

The imagery of chapter 61 is that of the year of Jubilee. A year of liberty and restoration is proclaimed (v. 1), the present tide of Judah's troubles is reversed (v. 3), and universal righteousness and hymns of praise abound (v. 11; see Lev. 25; Isa. 58). Again Isaiah applies present conditions to the future. Just as Christ provides liberty from death and sin, his followers should forgive or "free" their captives, those indebted to them. Some of the conditions in verses 1 and 2 fulfilled by Christ can likewise be fulfilled by us:

Condition	Christ's Role	Our Opportunity
Bind up the brokenhearted	Christ's atonement brings God's eternal family back together again	We can teach people the plan of salvation
Proclaim liberty to the captives	Jesus preached the gospel here and in the spirit world	We can proclaim repentance to the world
Open the prison	The Savior opened the gates to the celestial kingdom	We can do vicarious work for the dead (D&C 128:22)
Comfort the mourners	Christ's teachings and mission bring peace to those who now mourn	We can comfort those who suffer and are oppressed

There is a close relationship between the millennial condition of these first two verses of chapter 61 and the preceding chapter. Having described the future blessings of Zion in chapter 60, Isaiah here indicates *who* is to bring about Zion. Christ, first and foremost, will bring Zion to the world, but there can be no Zion society without a community of the "pure in heart." Like Isaiah's servant songs, the admonition of 61:1-2 serves as a model for all God's children who attempt to build his kingdom.

In short, Isaiah's prophecies contain a variety of possible applications. A nineteenth century scholar, Adam Clarke, distinguishes at least two levels of meaning in these first verses of Isaiah 61:

> In most of Isaiah's prophecies there is a primary and secondary sense, or a remote subject illustrated by one that is near. The deliverance of the Jews from their captivity in Babylon is constantly used to shadow forth the salvation of men by Jesus Christ. Even the prophet himself is a typical person, and is sometimes intended to represent the great Saviour. It is evident from Luke 4:18 that this is a prophecy of our blessed Lord and his preaching; and it is as evident that it primarily refers to Isaiah preaching the glad tidings of deliverance to the Jews. (*Clarke's Commentary* 4:225.)

Latter-day Saints can find at least one more level of meaning as they study Isaiah's words and apply them to the events of this dispensation.

As we become true servants of the Lord, we can help him bring about the conditions needed to establish the Zion that Isaiah describes in the next few verses of chapter 61:

3To provide for the mourners in Zion—
To give them a turban instead of ashes,
Festive ointment instead of mourning,
A garment of splendor instead of a drooping spirit.
They shall be called terebinths of victory,
Planted by the Lord for His glory.
4And they shall build the ancient ruins,
Raise up the desolations of old,
And renew the ruined cities,
The desolations of many ages.
5Strangers shall stand and pasture your flocks,
Aliens shall be your plowmen and vine-trimmers;
6While you shall be called "Priests of the Lord,"
And termed "Servants of our God."
You shall enjoy the wealth of nations
And revel in their riches.
7Because your shame was double—
Men cried, "Disgrace is their portion"—
Assuredly,
They shall have a double share in their land,
Joy shall be theirs for all time.
8For I the Lord love justice,
I hate robbery with a burnt offering.
I will pay them their wages faithfully,
And make a covenant with them for all time.
9Their offspring shall be known among the nations,
Their descendants in the midst of the peoples.
All who see them shall recognize
That they are a stock the Lord has blessed. (NJV)

In sharp contrast to the shame, destruction, and desolation promised in his earlier writings (see Isa. 1), Isaiah now prophesies prosperity—the people multiply (v. 3), cities are rebuilt (v. 4), and the land is replenished (v. 5). While others till the land and provide society's physical sustenance (v. 5), the members of covenant Israel will officiate in the Lord's priesthood and temple service (v. 6). Isaiah contrasts the wealth, reputation, joy, justice, and family security that God's chosen people will eventually enjoy with their earlier depraved condition (vs. 6-9).

Isaiah's anticipation of these events becomes so exuberant that, beginning in verse 10, he breaks forth into a song that continues to 62:9. This song is distinctly noted in the Dead Sea Scrolls in an unusual arrangement. Ordinarily, a number of Hebrew phrases that usually comprise anywhere from two to ten or more verses in our English translations are strung together from one column margin to another without any extra spacing between the phrases or verses. However, in this section of 61:10–62:9, each phrase is distinctly separated from the phrases preceding and following it by an extra wide space. For the most part, the New Jewish Version of these verses retains the separations, since each line in the English is one phrase in the Hebrew.

Isaiah sings for all of Zion in his psalm of praise:

10I greatly rejoice in the Lord,
My whole being exults in my
God.
For He has clothed me with
garments of triumph,
Wrapped me in a robe of victory,
Like a bridegroom adorned with
a turban,
Like a bride bedecked with her
finery.

11For as the earth brings forth her
growth
And a garden makes the seed
shoot up,
So the Lord God will make
Victory and renown shoot up
In the presence of all the nations.
(NJV)

In these verses, the former mourners of Zion (v. 3) are now the redeemed of the Lord and sing thanks to him for his blessings. The motifs of a wedding and the temple ceremony are a part of their rejoicing: clothed in garments, robes, and wedding attire, Israel and the Lord are ready to enter into their marriage covenant.[1] This symbolism echoes the writings of Isaiah's contemporary prophet,

---

[1]The "turban" or "ornaments" of the groom comes from the Hebrew term *pe'er*, which is used to describe the priestly mitre or cap in Ex. 39:28 and Ezek. 44.

Hosea, and calls to mind the "wedding feast" to be held at Christ's second coming. (Matt. 22; see D&C 33:17-18; 65:3; 133:10-19.)

The imagery of special clothing conveys lasting impressions to the reader. For example, Isaiah's earlier use of "armor" (59:17) brings to mind the "armor of righteousness," which all saints should wear. (2 Ne. 1:23; Eph. 6:11-12.) Armor is uncomfortable, heavy, and awkward, just as maintaining righteousness in a world of wickedness can make one feel separated from the world while living in the world. Some may feel that the armor or righteousness is too confining and shed it, thus falling to the dangers of the world. Soon they find that they have exchanged the slightly awkward armor for the absolutely confining "chains of hell." (Alma 5:7, 9-10.) On the other hand, those who faithfully wear the armor are promised a time when they will be clothed with the more comfortable "robes of righteousness." (2 Ne. 9:14.) Isaiah's repeated use of "garments," "robes," and other fine items of attire presents a picture of comfort and pleasantness (compare 59:17 with 60:3, 10).

Continuing with the symbolism of Zion, the temple, and marriage, Isaiah sings more about Jerusalem in chapter 62:

62 For the sake of Zion I will not be silent,
For the sake of Jerusalem I will not be still,
Till her victory emerge resplendent
And her triumph like a flaming torch.
²Nations shall see your victory,
And every king your majesty;
And you shall be called by a new name
Which the Lord Himself shall bestow.
³You shall be a glorious crown
In the hand of the Lord,
And a royal diadem
In the palm of your God.
⁴Nevermore shall you be called "Forsaken,"
Nor shall your land be called "Desolate";
But you shall be called "I delight in her,"
And your land "Espoused."
For the Lord takes delight in you,
And your land shall be espoused.
⁵As a youth espouses a maiden,
Your sons shall espouse you;
And as a bridegroom rejoices over his bride,
So will your God rejoice over you. (NJV)

Isaiah excels in his poetry and imagery in this majestic psalm. Undoubtedly, musical accompaniment accentuated the lyrics. Besides the many semantic parallelisms, which are obvious even in the English translations, grammatical parallelisms, rhyme, and meter give richness to the psalm. For example, the first two lines in verse 2 contain synonymous parallels in both content and form. The conceptual similarity is apparent in the English translations, while grammatical and rhyming parallels are more obvious in the original Hebrew:

ve-ra'n goy*im* tzedk*aych*
ve-kol melawch*im* kevod*aych*

Four stressed syllables in each line reinforce the poetry, which would have been sung or chanted in a pattern similar to well-known English children's songs and rounds. Just as the song "Three Blind Mice" has four beats in each line (although the lines vary in length from three to ten syllables), each line of Isaiah's poetry contains a set number of beats or stressed syllables per line (regardless of the number of syllables in each line). The first two lines of verse 2 could be translated and scanned as follows:

Nátions shall behóld your víctorý;
  kíngs all of thém your májestý.

By repeating these two lines aloud with the proper accentuation, one can begin to capture the rhythm and style of Isaiah's poetry. Because of their content, form, and beauty, Isaiah's words would have been easily remembered and passed on among the ancient Israelites.

As Isaiah develops his song in verses 1-5, he presents six themes:

A. He cannot remain *silent* (v. 1)
B. *Jerusalem* will be victorious (1-2)
C. A *new* name will be given to Zion (2)
D. She will be a *royal crown* in the Lord's hand (3)
E. She will no longer be *desolate* (4)
F. The Lord *will claim* her as his bride (5).

He repeats the same set of six themes as he concludes chapter 62:

⁶Upon your walls, O Jerusalem,
I have set watchmen,
Who shall never be silent
By day or by night.
O you, the Lord's
  remembrancers,
Take no rest
⁷And give no rest to Him.
Until He establish Jerusalem
And make her renowned on
  earth.

⁸The Lord has sworn by His right
  hand,
By His mighty arm:
Nevermore will I give your new
  grain
To your enemies for food,
Nor shall foreigners drink the new
  wine
For which you have labored.
⁹But those who harvest it shall eat
  it

And give praise to the Lord;
And those who gather it shall
    drink it
In My sacred courts.
10Pass through, pass through the
    gates!
Clear the road for the people;
Build up, build up the highway,
Remove the rocks!
Raise an ensign over the peoples!
11See, the Lord has proclaimed
To the end of the earth:
Announce to Fair Zion,
Your Deliverer is coming!
See, his reward is with Him,
His recompense before Him.
12And they shall be called, "The
    Holy People,
The Redeemed of the Lord,"
And you shall be called, "Sought
    Out,
A City Not Forsaken." (NJV)

Again, the six themes are:

A'. The watchmen (prophets) and we should never be *silent* (vs. 6-7).
B'. *Jerusalem* will be renowned (7).
C'. She will receive *new* grain and *new* wine (8).
D'. Her people will gather in the Lord's *sacred* courts (9).
E'. A highway will be *built up* (10).
F'. Zion's deliverer *will come* (11).

Verse 12 climaxes the song, promising that righteous Israel will be known as God's holy, redeemed people.

Joseph Smith provides a few insights that complement and strengthen Isaiah's psalm. The crowning of Zion (62:3) is mentioned in Doctrine and Covenants 133:32 (compare D&C 60:4). In the inspired version of Isaiah, Joseph Smith translated the merely transliterated terms of the King James Version, *Hephzi-bah* and *Beulah* (verse 4), as "delightful" and "union," an interpretation close to that of the New Jewish Version quoted earlier. Finally, in verse 5, Joseph Smith strengthened the parallelism of the first two lines in the Joseph Smith Translation by substituting the word "God" for "sons":

As a youth espouses a maiden
Your God shall espouse you [Zion].

A number of allusions to the temple ceremony are found in chapter 61 and 62. The following chart highlights some of them:

Reference	Concept	Temple Meaning
61:2	Freedom to those in spirit prison	The vicarious work for the dead (see Mal. 4:5-6; D&C 2; 138; 1 Pet. 3:18-20)
61:2	Comfort the mourners	A common practice in temple prayers is to exercise faith on behalf of the sick, afflicted, and others who mourn
61:4	Rebuilding ancient ruins	Building temples or restoring eternal family ties and keys (D&C 110)

61:8	Everlasting covenant	The new and everlasting covenant of marriage (D&C 131:1-4; 132)
61:9	Children	Promise of eternal increase to those in the highest degree of celestial glory
62:2	New name	A new name is given those who are to enter the celestial kingdom (D&C 130:11)
62:4,5	Marriage	Eternal marriages are performed in temples
62:9	Sacred courts	Only worthy people are allowed in God's house
62:10	Gates	Certain requirements are necessary to pass by Heavenly Father's servants in order to enter his presence

These examples encourage a fourth level of understanding for chapters 61 and 62 of Isaiah. As indicated earlier, these chapters might apply to (1) the Jews returning from Babylon, (2) Christ's first coming, and (3) the events surrounding his second coming. For God's faithful children in any dispensation, Isaiah's words can also refer to the temple and its ordinances and blessings.

THE MESSIAH COMES AND
DELIVERS VICTORY
ISAIAH 63-64

After describing the exaltation of Zion and her growth through the influx of Gentiles (Isa. 62), Isaiah explains in chapter 63 the destruction of Israel's enemies. In order for Zion to fill the entire earth, the enemies of righteousness must be displaced through the power of the Lord. After Isaiah prophesies concerning the Lord's power to cleanse the earth, he reminds Israel of what the Lord has already done and pleads with the Lord to bring about his promised salvation. Isaiah develops his major themes in chapter 63 and 64 as follows:

A. Dialogue with Christ about his second coming (63:1-6)
B. The Lord's former greater deed (63:7-14)
C. Isaiah's intercessory prayer for Israel (63:14–64:12)

Dialogue with Christ about His Second Coming (63:1-6)

Chapter 63 begins with a dialogue between a watchman on the walls of Jerusalem and an approaching stranger. Isaiah is the watchman, and the stranger is a mighty conqueror coming from the direction of Edom, one of Israel's worst enemies. The conversation begins with a question and the stranger's response:

> **63** Who is this coming from Edom,
> from Bozrah in garments stained with crimson,
> so richly clothed,
> marching so full of strength?
> —It is I, who speak of integrity
> and am powerful to save. (JB)

The stranger is distinguished by three characteristics: (1) he comes from Edom, (2) his fine garments are stained red, and (3) he effuses majestic strength.

The stranger's coming from Edom can be variously interpreted. First, it can mean that he is coming literally from the east, from the direction of Edom, which lies east and south of the Dead Sea. Travelers from Edom and its capital city of Bozrah usually traveled north on the King's Highway past the Dead Sea and then turned west through Jericho toward Jerusalem. (See Map 3.) Second, Edom represents the "world," or the worldly powers and nations that oppose God. (See Isa. 63, footnote 1b; D&C 1:36.) The word *Edom* in the Hebrew comes from the root meaning "earth," "dirt," or "red." Thus, Edom also means "red earth," and the stranger in red garments coming from Edom could symbolize his coming from the red hills of the earth. That is, the redness that stained his clothes may have also colored the earth. (Compare D&C 133:46.)

The stained, red clothing is the second identifying characteristic of the stranger.

The third characteristic is the stranger's dignity, heightened by his authoritative reply. Although he does not give his name, it appears that he is the Lord himself, who has come to Jerusalem with the power to save its people.

The watchman's attention, however, is attracted to the red garments or robes of the Lord. Isaiah's short question about the clothing brings forth a long response:

2—Why are your garments red,
your clothes as if you had trodden
   the winepress?

3—I have trodden the winepress
   alone.
Of the men of my people not one
   was with me.
	A

In my anger I trod them down, trampled them in my wrath.	B
Their juice spattered my garments, and all my clothes are stained.	C
4For in my heart was a day of vengeance,	D
my year of redemption had come.	E
5I looked: there was no one to help;	A'

aghast: not one could I find to
   support me.
My own arm then was my
   mainstay,	

my wrath my support.   B'
⁶I crushed the people in my fury,
trampled them in my anger,
and made the juice of them run all   C'
    over the ground. (JB)

Isaiah's question makes it apparent that Christ's clothing is unnaturally red. It looks like the clothing of servants that becomes spotted as they trample the grapes and splash the juices.

The Lord's response indicates many important qualities of his mission, as outlined in the right column above:

A. He alone could fulfill his mission
B. His anger caused him to destroy the wicked
C. Their blood (juice) stained his clothes
D. He had a day of vengeance for the wicked
E. He had a year of redemption for the righteous

Three of the ideas—A, B, C—are repeated and reinforced in verses 5 and 6. When these verses were repeated in the Doctrine and Covenants, verses 5 and 6 were not included. (See D&C 133:50-52.)

The image of Christ as a vengeful, bloodstained warrior is somewhat different from the usual Christian concept of Christ at his second coming. However, it is in line with Isaiah's earlier teachings (Isa. 59:15-20; 34:8; 61:2) and the prophecies of Joseph Smith (D&C 133:46-53; 97:22-26). The day of vengeance, however, is only upon the wicked, and the Lord's wrath is free of malice or impurity—he simply requires justice for all sinners. (D&C 133:50-51; D&C 29:17.)

The earlier verses of chapter 63 refer to the atonement of Christ. To begin with, Isaiah describes the conqueror as coming in red robes from Edom and Bozrah. As indicated earlier, the word *Edom* shares the same Hebrew root as the word *earth*. Also, the word *Bozrah* can mean "sheep fold." A figurative reading of verse 1 thus reads, "Who is this that cometh from the world (meaning Christ's earthly life), with dyed garments from the sheepfold (meaning the members of the Church)?" The sacrifices that ancient Israelites performed were symbols of the perfect sacrifice to be offered by Christ. (2 Ne. 11:4; Moses 5:6-8.) Furthermore, a part of the ancient sacrifice was to offer up a sheep or animal from among the "fold" (Lev. 1:2) that should be unblemished, the best one. Christ's life and atonement demonstrate that he was the only unblemished child of God on this earth, and therefore the only possible sacrifice for us.

Next, Isaish says that the conqueror is "mighty to save" (KJV). Assuredly, Christ was the only one mighty enough to save. But the English word *save* does not convey the full meaning of the Hebrew word *lehoshi'a*, which should be translated "cause to save." That is, Christ's atonement can "cause" salvation from sin, but his powers do not automatically save everyone; each person must repent and seek forgiveness through the proper ordinances.

The final major feature of this person is that his garments are stained red. This refers to Christ's atonement: "And being in an agony he prayed more earnestly: and his sweat was as it were great drops of blood falling down to the ground." (Luke 22:44.)

Interestingly, Isaiah notes that Christ's clothing was red "like him that treadeth in the winefat." And Christ responds, "I have trodden the winepress." The imagery of the winepress is most interesting; *geth* means "garden" and *semane* means "a press for liquids," an oil or wine press. It was in the "garden of the winepress," Gethsemane, that the Atonement took place.

Also, Christ took upon himself the sins of the world *alone* in the garden. This is emphasized in Isaiah 63:1-6.

In short, the first half dozen verses of Isaiah 63 contain strong images of Christ's atonement, which took place almost two thousand years ago. However, in their context in the book of Isaiah and in the Doctrine and Covenants, these verses have a more particular application to some time in the future when Christ comes in his "day of vengeance" upon the wicked.[1]

The Lord's Former Great Deeds (63:7-14)

Verse 4 promises a "year of redemption" that will come to the righteous. This could be the year of Jubilee, during which it was customary to free Hebrew slaves. (Lev. 25; see pp. 483-84.) However, it more likely refers to the freedom from persecution granted the righteous when the Lord's millennial reign is established.

Isaiah reinforces the hope for a future redemption by reviewing the powerful acts of the Lord in the past, particularly during the exodus from Egypt:

---

[1] Isaiah's description of the Lord's wrath in the winevat has carried over into other forms of literature. Julia Ward Howe borrowed the metaphor of the winepress in the "Battle Hymn of the Republic": "Mine eyes have seen the glory of the coming of the Lord, He is trampling out the vintage where the grapes of wrath are stored." John Steinbeck uses the same metaphor in his novel *The Grapes of Wrath*.

⁷Let me sing the praises of
Yahweh's goodness,
and of his marvelous deeds,
in return for all that he has done
for us
and for the great kindness
he has shown us in his mercy
and in his boundless goodness.

⁸He said, "Truly they are my
people,
sons and no rogues."
He proved himself their saviour
⁹in all their troubles.
It was neither messenger nor
angel
but his Presence that saved them.
In his love and pity
he redeemed them himself,
he lifted them up, carried them,
throughout the days of old.
¹⁰But they rebelled, they grieved
his holy spirit.
Then he turned enemy,
and himself waged war on them.
¹¹They remembered the days of
old,

of Moses his servant.
Where is he who brought out of
the sea
the shepherd of his flock?
Where is he who endowed him
with his holy spirit,
¹²who at the right hand of Moses
set to work with his glorious arm,
who divided the waters before
them
to win himself everlasting
renown,
¹³who made them walk through the
ocean
as easily as a horse through the
desert?
¹⁴They stumbled as little as an ox
going down to the plain.
The spirit of Yahweh led them to
rest.
This is how you guided your
people
to win yourself glorious renown.
(JB)

After an introduction in verse 7, Isaiah recounts God's kind acts toward Israel, first mentioning Israel's election as the chosen people (v. 8). Isaiah calls Israel the sons of God and adds that, as such, they should never deal falsely with God. He concludes verse 8 with the remark that God's loving kindness is best manifest in his becoming their savior.

Isaiah highlights in verse 9 the kindness and mercy of Jehovah; he reminds Israel that in all their affliction Jehovah was willing to aid them. The phrase "the angel of his presence saved them" (v. 9, KJV) echoes Moses' words. Moses indicates that this angel is the Lord himself. (Ex. 33:12-15; see D&C 133:52-53.)

In verse 10, Isaiah reminds Israel that she has rebelled against the Lord in spite of the Lord's kindness and Moses' warnings. (Compare Ex. 23:21 with Ex. 17:1-7; 32:1-14.) Instead of being faithful sons of God (v. 8), the people have dealt falsely with God, becoming his enemy. The people begin to wonder what happened to the God who has wrought such wonders for them earlier. In verses 11-14, Isaiah twists their own questions to remind them of how the Lord once guided Israel.

Isaiah's Intercessory Prayer for Israel (63:15–64:12)

Isaiah speaks for all Israel to the Lord and prays for her final redemption. Isaiah's prayer contains five elements in a loose chiastic pattern:

A. A petition to the Lord to remember Israel (63:15-18)
B. A statement on the consequences of Israel's sins (63:18-19)
C. A hope that the Lord will make his power known (64:1-5a)
B'. A statement on Israel's sinfulness (64:5b-7)
A'. A petition that the Lord will forget his anger against Israel (64:8-12)

Isaiah first addresses the Lord and then petitions him to remember and return to Israel:

15Look down from heaven, look down
from your holy and glorious dwelling.
Where is your ardour, your might,
the yearning of your inmost heart?
Do not let your compassion go unmoved,
16for you are our Father.
For Abraham does not own us
and Israel does not acknowledge us;

you, Yahweh, yourself are our Father,
Our Redeemer is your ancient name.
17Why, Yahweh, leave us to stray from your ways
and harden our hearts against fearing you?
Return, for the sake of your servants,
the tribes of your inheritance.
(JB)

Isaiah realizes that the people are so extremely wicked that neither Abraham nor Jacob would now accept the Israelites as members of their family (v. 16). Besides, these ancient patriarchs are long dead and unable to directly help the children of Israel upon the earth. However, the Lord is the father of this earth, the gospel, the Atonement, salvation, and redemption. Surely he will not forget or disclaim Israel, in spite of her wickedness.

In verse 17 it seems that Isaiah holds the Lord partially accountable for Israel's wickedness. In the King James Version, the first part of this verse reads, "O Lord, why hast thou made us to err from thy ways, and hardened our heart from thy fear?" The same is implied in the Jerusalem Bible. However, Joseph Smith clarified this verse in his translation: "O Lord, why has thou *suffered* us to err from thy ways, and *to harden* our heart from thy fear?" Instead of the Lord "making" the Israelites to sin and "hardening" their hearts, he "suffered" or allowed the Israelites to sin and harden their own hearts. The Lord does not cause anyone to stray from righteousness, but he does allow people to sin according to their own will.

As the people sinned, they brought upon themselves both physical and spiritual consequences, for new rulers gained power over them. Isaiah recognizes that the Lord has allowed these foreign leaders to control Israel because she no longer follows the Lord:

18Why have the wicked set foot in your sanctuary, why are our enemies trampling your sanctuary?

19We have long been like people you do not rule, people who do not bear your name. (JB)

Isaiah earnestly hopes for a time when the Lord will reign as sole ruler over Israel and his divine power will extend worldwide. He wishes that the Lord could come and rule immediately:

64 Oh, that you would tear the heavens open and come down
—at your Presence the mountains would melt,
2as fire sets brushwood alight, as fire causes water to boil—
to make known your name to your enemies,
and make the nations tremble at your Presence,

3working unexpected miracles
4such as no one has ever heard of before.
No ear has heard,
no eye has seen
any god but you act like this
for those who trust him.
5You guide those who act with integrity
and keep your ways in mind. (JB)

These verses are repeated in the Doctrine and Covenants in the context of the last dispensation when the gospel is preached to every nation. (See Rev. 14:6-7.) As God's servants and missionaries take the gospel to the world, they also call upon the Lord, repeating the words of Isaiah. They too request that the Lord's power be made manifest to the nations. (See D&C 133:37-45.)

When the Lord finally demonstrates his power, all the world will observe his miracles and tremble before him (v. 2; D&C 34:8). Some of these manifestations will be seen by all people, but only those who wait for him (KJV), trust in him (JB), and love him (1 Cor. 2:9) will behold all the great things that have never been previously revealed (v. 4).

Isaiah knows that his own generation is unworthy of the Lord's power and presence. He recognizes that any wicked generation does not witness the Lord's glorious powers. Instead, they give themselves over to the power of sin:

You were angry when we were sinners;
we had long been rebels against you.
⁶We were all like men unclean,
all that integrity of ours like filthy clothing.
We have all withered like leaves
and our sins blew us away like the wind.
⁷No one invoked your name
or roused himself to catch hold of you.
For you hid your face from us
and gave us up to the power of our sins. (JB)

Isaiah clearly identifies the cause of the people's separation from the Lord as their own sins. It is not that the Lord was unable to help them, but that they did not turn to him and request his aid. Therefore, the Lord hid his face from the people and turned them over to the buffetings of Satan (v. 7).

Isaiah hopes that Israel will forsake her sins and that the Lord will not have to continually chastise her. As Isaiah concludes chapter 64, he reviews the relationship between Israel and the Lord and petitions the Lord to cease his anger and punishment, to speak again to Israel and redeem her:

⁸And yet, Yahweh, you are our Father;
we the clay, you the potter,
we are all the work of your hand.
⁹Do not let your anger go too far, Yahweh,
or go on thinking of our sins for ever.
See, see, we are all your people;
¹⁰your holy cities are a wilderness,
Zion a wilderness,
Jerusalem a desolation,
¹¹our holy and glorious Temple,
in which our fathers prayed to you,
is burnt to the ground;
all that gave us pleasure lies in ruins.
¹²Yahweh, can you go unmoved by all of this,
oppressing us beyond measure by your silence? (JB)

Verse 8 contains the well-known allegory of the potter and the clay: the Lord is the potter and we are the clay. Verse 9 grows out of verse 8 and suggests that the Lord should not be too angry with us because we are all his people. Isaiah represents a humble, repentant people as he concludes the chapters and requests the Lord's action in their behalf. These repentant people are ready to be shaped by the master into vessels of eternal glory.

Isaiah continues his pattern of contrasts in these chapters. For example, in 63:4 he promises a "day of vengeance" and a "year of redemption." Due to the wickedness of his audience, most of Isaiah's discourses warn about the "day of vengeance." However, in these later chapters, Isaiah speaks more often about the "year of redemption."

The phrases "day of vengeance" and "year of redemption" show the ratio of the Lord's vengeance and redemption: he will execute vengeance for only a day, but his redemption lasts for a year. In other words, his punishments will be temporary, but his blessings permanent.

ISAIAH IN THE DOCTRINE AND COVENANTS

Except for Section 113, Isaiah is not directly quoted or mentioned in the Doctrine and Covenants, although dozens of verses from his work are quoted. A study of the Isaiah passages in the Doctrine and Covenants helps one understand both books of scripture: the Doctrine and Covenant applies Isaiah's prophecies to the last days, and the book of Isaiah expands the meaning of the Doctrine and Covenants.

Nine of the 138 sections in the Doctrine and Covenants use Isaiah's words and ideas extensively: 1, 45, 88, 101, 109, 113, 124, 128, and 133. These sections contain passages from half of the Isaiah chapters, especially Isaiah 1, 8, 11, 13, 24, 28, 35, 40, 50, 52, 60, 62-65.

Section 1

Section 1 of the Doctrine and Covenants compares with Isaiah 1 in two ways: both were written later in the ministries of the prophets who wrote them, and both serve as a preface to the books of which they are a part. Although these two chapters do not share phraseology, they share similar messages, for both denounce the broken covenants of the chosen people (D&C 1:15-16; Isa. 1:10-15), extend an invitation to repent (D&C 1:32; Isa. 1:18), and promise a future day of judgment (D&C 1:8-10; Isa. 1:25) and righteousness (D&C 1:22-28; Isa. 1:19, 26-27).

Section 45

Section 45:42 contains a prophecy very similar to Isaiah's prophecy in Isaiah 13:10 about the darkening of the sun, the moon turning to blood, and the stars falling. (See also D&C 29:14; 34:9; 88:87; 133:49.) Both chapters talk about major disturbances upon the earth (D&C 45:26; Isa. 13:13) and the Lord's destruction of the wicked (D&C 45:68-69; Isa. 13:4-13).

Section 88

Two unusual terms appear in both Isaiah and the Doctrine and Covenants. First, both works use the image of "wings" (D&C 88:45; Isa. 18:1): Isaiah gives a prophecy to a land shadowed by wings; Joseph Smith describes the earth and stars as "rolling on their wings." However, Joseph adds that the stars roll on their wings "in their glory, in the midst of the power of God." Applying this idea to Isaiah's prophecy reinforces the interpretation that the land Isaiah addresses in chapter 18 is a chosen land protected by the Lord's power.

Both scriptures use the phrase "uplifted hands" (D&C 88:132, 135; Isa. 1:15) to describe the act of prayer. Although we today do not ordinarily raise our hands while praying, it was a tradition for earlier Israelites.

Section 101

Section 101 contains strong echoes of Isaiah chapter 65, particularly verses 20-22. Phrases from Isaiah 65:20-22 are used in section 101:30 and phrases from Isaiah 65:21-22 are used in section 101:101. These verses describe the long, prosperous lives of those who live during the Millennium. Study the context of both books of scripture to appreciate how these conditions will be brought about in the last days.

Section 109

In section 109, the dedicatory prayer for the Kirtland Temple, Joseph Smith invokes the Lord's judgments upon those who spread lies about his work and servants (vs. 29-30). In chapter 28, Isaiah describes an overflowing scourge, hail, and waters that will come upon liars (vs. 15-18). Taken together, these two writings demonstrate the prophets' power to invoke judgments upon the wicked and their ability to prophesy signs of the last days. Also, these passages help explain why catastrophes come upon the earth's inhabitants.

Section 113

This is the only section in which the Isaiah passages are specifically identified, since it consists of a question-and-answer format with phrases from two Isaiah chapters as the subject matter. Terms from verses 1 and 10 of Isaiah 11 are explained in verses 1-6 of section 113, and phrases from Isaiah 52:1-2, 7-8, 10 are explained in verses 7-10 of section 113.

Section 124

One important development in the last days is that Gentiles and rulers of nations will help build Zion. This theme is stressed in verses 5-11 of section 124. Isaiah gives further details about this work in chapter 60 of his work, especially in verses 3, 10-17. A review of the earlier discussions on chapters 32-33, 48-49, and 60-61 of Isaiah highlights many Isaianic prophecies concerning the gathering of Israel and the building of Zion in the last days. The careful study of section 124 reveals many of the same prophecies. And continued study of current events in the growth of the Church throughout the world shows the fulfillment of many of these prophecies. Through further prayer and effort, all of them will be fulfilled, and the Lord's hand will be demonstrated through the Gentiles and their leaders.

Section 128

Three specific terms—*gladness, Immanuel,* and *witnesses*—found in both Isaiah and the Doctrine and Covenants can be more clearly understood as one studies their context in both works.

Glad or *gladness* shows up eight times in verses 19-23 of section 128 and only fifteen times in the rest of the Doctrine and Covenants. Similarly, the same term is found eleven times in Isaiah and only twenty-one other times in the rest of the prophetic works of the Old Testament. Therefore, section 128:19-23 and Isaiah complement each other by showing different ways God's children achieve and express "gladness." The eleven references in Isaiah are 16:10; 22:13; 25:9; 30:29; 35:1, 10; 39:2; 51:3, 11; 65:18; 66:10. (Other Isaiah passages that describe joy and gladness are: 14:7; 44:23; 48:20; 49:13; 52:7-10; see also 12:5; 26:19; 42:10; 55:9-12.)

The term *Immanuel* occurs only five times in the standard works. It appears twice in the Book of Mormon, during Nephi's quotation of Isaiah (2 Ne. 17:14; 18:8). It occurs twice in Isaiah (7:14; 8:8) and once in Doctrine and Covenants 128:22. Section 128 presents the foreordination and the redemptive role of Immanuel, while the Isaiah passages record Isaiah's original Immanuel prophecy and a declaration that this earth belongs to the Promised One.

The role of *witnesses* is very important in the Lord's plan for teaching the gospel. By comparing section 128 with Isaiah 29 and 2 Nephi 27, one quickly appreciates the role of scriptures and prophets as special witnesses in the last days. Before the Lord can bring judgment upon the people, he must give them an opportunity to hear the gospel and receive the testimonies of witnesses that the gospel is true. Then if the people reject the truth, they can be held accountable and judged according to the witnesses they have received. Further ideas about the witnesses of prophets and scriptures are discussed on pp. 268-77

Section 133

Section 133 contains more Isaiah passages than any other section of the Doctrine and Covenants. It is similar to chapters 35, 50, and 62-64 of Isaiah, as well as almost a dozen other Isaianic passages. Given originally as the appendix or conclusion to the Doctrine and Covenants, section 133 was received by Joseph Smith just two days after he received section 1. Section 133 is a proclamation to be sent to the entire world and, as such, includes promises about the return of the remnants of Israel, the Lord's glorious second coming, and the establishment of Zion. It is no wonder that it contains so many similarities to Isaiah's writings.

As Joseph Smith prophesies about the return of Israel in Doctrine and Covenants 133:27-33, he includes some of Isaiah's phraseology. (Isa. 35:7-10; see Isa. 51:9-11.) Both passages mention water in the desert, a highway for the returning remnants, and the gathering of the righteous and their songs of joy. By comparing passages and contexts, one can better understand the events surrounding the return of the Ten Tribes and other remnants of Israel in the last days.

Isaiah 50 is echoed in section 133, in which Joseph Smith speaks about the Lord's manifestation of power in the last days. Phrases and concepts from Isaiah 50:2, 3, and 11 are repeated in Doctrine and Covenants 133:66-70. These comparisons are discussed on pages 419-25.

Most of the Isaiah passages are centered in verses 40-53 of section 133, but are recorded in a different order. This shuffled order is comparable to Christ's quotations of Isaiah 52 recorded in 3 Nephi. It appears that neither section 133 nor Isaiah 62-64 is organized in a strict chronological or thematic order. The Lord probably deliberately mixes the sequence of prophecies about the last days. (See pp. 414-15, 437.) Rather than giving a complete, detailed chronological list, he reveals different items in varying sequence so that each reader can study the prophecies and search for himself to see how they are being fulfilled.

Many other cross references between the book of Isaiah and the Doctrine and Covenants can be found in the footnotes and Topical Guide entries of the Latter-day Saint edition of the King James Version of the Bible.

Before concluding this special topic on Isaiah in the Doctrine and Covenants, an important question needs to be asked and some possible answers presented: "Why is so much Isaiah phraseology found in the Doctrine and Covenants?" At least four answers are possible:

1. Joseph Smith wrote the sections of the Doctrine and Covenants under his own creative inspiration and used Isaiah's passages to give a sense of scriptural voice and authority to his work.
2. Since both Isaiah and Joseph Smith prophesied extensively about the last days, Joseph may have borrowed Isaiah's phraseology to express the impressions he received. Joseph studied the Bible carefully, and just as he used the King James phraseology in his Book of Mormon translation (see pp. 93-94), he may have simply used Isaiah's words to record his own prophecies.
3. Perhaps in a less deliberate manner, Joseph may have borrowed from the Isaiah phraseology as he transmitted his prophecies. Subtle inspirations of the Spirit coupled with his familiarity with the Bible prompted Joseph Smith to naturally record his prophecies in a style and terminology similar to Isaiah's.
4. Joseph Smith and Isaiah were both great prophets and seers who so closely communicated with the Lord that they may have received the same revelations, resulting in the close similarities of their writings.

I discount the first explanation, and doubt if the second adequately explains the similarities between the two works. I believe that either subtle inspiration (coupled with a natural use of King James phraseology) or direct revelation best explains why there is so much Isaiah phraseology in the Doctrine and Covenants.

In conclusion, the writings of Isaiah and Joseph Smith provide complementary and often overlapping accounts about many events in the last days. Studying both records together provides insights about our day that neither scripture gives by itself. These two books serve as strong witnesses for each other and testify not only that God has revealed great truths to his prophets, but also that he continues to do so. As we understand more about how God's word has been and continues to be revealed, we can better appreciate the messages of the scriptures and the personal promptings of the Spirit.

A NEW HEAVEN AND A NEW EARTH
ISAIAH 65-66

Isaiah's last two chapters comprise a set of prophecies that complement each other and serve as a bookend match to the first two chapters in Isaiah's book. Scholars generally agree that Isaiah 65 and 66 reinforce each other since they both foretell the Lord's judgment (65:1-16; 66:1-6), millennial blessings for Israel (65:17-25; 66:7-16), new heavens and a new earth (65:17; 66:22), and the Lord's presence and peace in Jerusalem (65:18-19; 66:8-12). In addition, these two chapters reiterate and complement the message of chapters 1 and 2.

In his first two chapters, Isaiah describes the Israelites' religious rebellion and lists those practices that particularly displease the Lord. He also promises redemption for Zion and the establishment of the "mountain of the Lord's house" for Israel. Similarly, in chapters 65 and 66 Isaiah warns the people and lists particularly offensive religious practices; he concludes with the promise of a glorious Zion with the presence of the Lord. These two chapters contain many parallel ideas that are also scattered through other chapters of Isaiah. Some of the more striking parallels are listed below:

The Lord almost destroys Israel (65:8-10)	The Lord barely leaves some survivors (1:9)
The Lord's sword upon the wicked (65:11-12)	The Lord's sword for the disobedient (1:19-20)
A new Jerusalem (65:17-19)	A new city in Zion (1:24-28)
Prayers answered (65:24)	Prayers rejected (1:15)
A voice from the temple (66:5-6)	The Lord's word from his house (2:3)
Jerusalem restored (66:10-14)	Jerusalem blessed (1:26; 2:3)
The Lord's anger and sword (66:15-16)	The Lord's sword and terror (1:20; 2:10, 19, 21)
Gathering of Israel from the nations (66:17-21)	Many people gather to Zion (1:26-27; 2:3-5)

It is unlikely that so many similarities would exist between the two sets of chapters without deliberate planning. Also, Isaiah 1 generally parallels chapter 65 while Isaiah 2 parallels chapter 66, indicating a highly structured composition.

In addition to comparing chapters 1 and 2 with Isaiah 65 and 66, one should also read a few selected chapters in other books of scripture that provide further parallel insights. For example, in 3 Nephi 21, Jesus Christ expands and explains Isaiah's teachings concerning a new earth and a new Jerusalem that are so well expressed in chapters 65 and 66. In Revelation 18-21, John uses the imagery of a woman quickly delivering a male son to represent the birth of Zion (compare 66:7-9 with Rev. 12:1-5) and prophesies about a new heaven and a new earth and other events described in Isaiah 65 and 66. In section 101 of the Doctrine and Covenants, Joseph Smith uses the imagery of a vineyard to represent Israel (compare Isa. 65:8 with D&C 101:45-62) and speaks about the speedy resurrection of people in the Millennium (Isa. 65:20; D&C 101:30), harmony between people and animals (Isa. 65:25; D&C 101:26), wickedness being conquered by the Lord's sword (Isa. 65:11-12; 66:15-16; D&C 101:10-11), a gathering of Israel to Zion (Isa. 66:17-21; D&C 101:67-75), and the prosperity of Zion, which the righteous will inherit (Isa. 65:21-22; D&C 101:30, 101). From the strong similarities in the writings of Nephi (as taught directly by Jesus Christ), John, and Joseph Smith it is obvious that the Lord has revealed the same glorious vision of a new heaven and a new earth to other servants besides Isaiah. (See also 2 Ne. 30:8-15; 2 Pet. 3:10-13; D&C 29.)

Isaiah's witness as a prophet, his inspiration as a seer, and his genius as a poet are all demonstrated in chapters 65 and 66.

Isaiah 65 seems to be the Lord's answer to the prophet's intercessory prayer in chapter 64. The prayer concludes with the petition, "O Lord, will you remain silent and keep punishing us?" The Lord's response is:

65 "I revealed myself to those who did not ask for me;
I was found by those who did not seek me.
To a nation that did not call on my name,
I said, 'Here am I, here am I.'

²All day long I have held out my hands
to an obstinate people,
who walk in ways not good,
pursuing their own imaginations—" (NIV)

A quick reading of these verses suggests either that the Lord is silent with Israel because he has revealed himself to a people who have not called upon him (meaning perhaps the Gentiles) or that he is ironically chastising the Israelites because he continues speaking to them though they ignore him. Joseph Smith clarifies these two verses in his inspired translation:

[1]I am *found of them who seek after me. I give unto all them that ask of me;* I am *not* found of them that sought me not, *or that inquireth not after me.* [2]I said *unto my servant,* Behold me, look upon me; *I will send you* unto a nation that is not called after my name, for I have spread out my hands all the day *to a* people *who* walketh *not* in my ways, and *their works are evil and* not good, *and they walk after* their own thoughts. (JST; italics added)

The Lord ordinarily will speak to those who seek him. However, he commissioned Isaiah to go to a nation that ignored the Lord. Most translations indicate that the Lord is rebuking a people who do not call upon and obey him. The most likely identification for this unnamed people is Israel, although the Lord could be speaking to any of Heavenly Father's children who neglect him.

Isaiah continues by describing the people's wickedness:

[3]"a people who continually provoke me
to my very face,
offering sacrifices in gardens
and burning incense on altars of brick;
[4]who sit among the graves
and spend their nights keeping secret vigil;
who eat the flesh of pigs,
and whose pots hold broth of unclean meat;
[5]who say, 'Keep away; don't come near me,
for I am too sacred for you!'
Such people are smoke in my nostrils,
a fire that keeps burning all day." (NIV)

Some of Isaiah's rebukes identify Israel as the people addressed in these verses. For example, in verse 3, he describes acts that do not readily appear to be unrighteous, such as the offering of sacrifices in gardens and the burning of incense on brick altars. However, the Israelites had been specifically instructed by Moses not to worship in groves of trees, but to destroy them. (Ex. 34:1-3; Deut. 16:21; see 2 Kgs. 23:4-6, 14.) The prophets had also instructed the people to offer sacrifices only upon altars of unhewn stone. (Ex. 20:24-25; Deut. 27:5; Josh. 8:31.) Lingering in the graveyards suggests an attempt to commune with the spirits, a practice strictly forbidden (v. 4; see Lev. 19:31; Deut. 18:10; Josh. 13:22). Also, their eating of swine and other unclean meat clearly violated God's commandments to Israel. (Lev. 11:7-8; Deut. 14:7-8.)

Earlier, the people had petitioned, "O Lord, why are you silent and angry with us?" (Isa. 64:12.) The Lord answers that the people's blatant wickedness offends him like a continual fire and smoke (v. 5). So, their cities are destroyed with fire and smoke. (Isa. 64:11.) The Lord states that he will remain silent no longer, but will let his voice be heard in retribution:

6"See, it stands written before me:
I will not keep silent but will
pay back in full;
I will pay it back into their
laps—
7both your sins and the sins of your
father,"
says the Lord.
"Because they burned sacrifices on
the mountains
and defied me on the hills,
I will measure into their laps
the full payment for their former
deeds." (NIV)

Thus, the Lord's final answer to the earlier question is that the people's sins have caused his silence and anger.

Still, the Lord desires to punish Israel, but not destroy her. As Isaiah foretold in chapter 1:9, Israel will not be utterly destroyed as was Sodom and Gomorrah; a small remnant will remain. In chapter 65, Isaiah indicates that Israel retains the potential to bring forth the sweet fruits of righteousness. He promises those of Israel who are righteous that they will possess the earth:

8This is what the Lord says:
"As when juice is still found in a
cluster of grapes
and men say, 'Don't destroy it,
there is yet some good in it,'
so will I do in behalf of my
servants;
I will not destroy them all.
9I will bring forth descendants
from Jacob,
and from Judah those who
will possess my mountains;
my chosen people will inherit
them,
and there will my servants live.
10Sharon will become a pasture for
flocks,
and the Valley of Achor a
resting place for herds,
for my people who seek me.
(NIV)

These verses begin a separate poem that continues to the end of chapter 65. The poem begins and ends with a verbal flag—"the Lord says"—that signals his listeners to witness the prophetic authority of the message. The poem is organized in a chiastic pattern with the pivot point in verse 17:

A. The Lord said not to destroy bad grapes because some good was still present (v. 8)

A'. The Lord said nothing evil or vile was to be done (everyone will be good) (v. 26)

B. Servants and animals dwell in the land (9-10)

B'. People and animals will be at peace on the earth (23-25)

C. The wicked warned (11)

C'. Chosen ones blessed (22)

D. War (12)

D'. Peace (21)

E. The righteous vs. the wicked (13)

E'. The innocent vs. sinners (JST 20)

F. Shouting, crying, and howling (14)

F'. Rejoicing, no more weeping and wailing (19)

G. Cursing (15)

G'. Blessings (18)

H. Former troubles shall be forgotten (16)

H'. Former things shall not be remembered (17)

I. The Lord is creating a new heaven and a new earth (17)

The pivot point stresses the Lord's major goal, a new heaven and earth. But before an ideal environment can be established, the earth's spiritual pollution must be removed. In verse 11, the Lord again distresses the evil polluters and prophesies their destiny:

> [11]"But as for you who forsake the Lord
> and forget my holy mountain,
> who spread a table for Fortune
> and fill bowls of mixed wine for Destiny,
> [12]I will destine you for the sword,
> and you will all bend down
> for the slaughter;
> for I called but you did not answer,
> I spoke but you did not listen.
> You did evil in my sight
> and chose what displeases me."
> (NIV)

Note the irony in Israel's imagery: the people use fortune-telling and wine to seek their *destiny*, but the Lord *destines* them to destruction by the sword; the people *bend down* as if *in* the attitude of humility or *prayer*, but they will eventually *bend down to be slaughtered*.

The Lord warns the wicked of their punishments, which are contrasted with the rewards of the righteous in the next verses:

> [13]Therefore this is what the Sovereign Lord says:
>
> "My servants will eat,
> but you will go hungry;
> my servants will drink,
> but you will go thirsty;
> my servants will rejoice,
> but you will be put to shame.
> [14]My servants will sing
> out of the joy of their hearts,
> but you will cry out
> from anguish of heart
> and wail in brokenness of spirit.

¹⁵You will leave your name
to my chosen ones as a curse;
the Sovereign Lord will put you
to death,
but to his servants he will give
another name.
¹⁶Whoever invokes a blessing in the
land

will do so by the God of truth;
he who takes an oath in the land
will swear by the God of truth.
For the past troubles will be
forgotten
and hidden from my eyes.
(NIV)

Verse 15 contains interesting implications to Christians and Latter-day Saints. Christians see the fulfillment of "another name" in Acts 11:26, where the disciples of Jesus call themselves "Christians" (v. 26). Latter-day Saints think of the "new name" mentioned in Revelation 3:12. At any rate, the Lord is preparing for something new, and the Lord's servants will share his priesthood power as they invoke blessings and make covenants in his name (v. 16).

The end of the Lord's preparations will be a new creation:

¹⁷"Behold, I will create
new heavens and a new earth.
The former things will not be

remembered,
nor will they come to mind.
(NIV)

Note the synonymous parallelism in the second half of verses 16 and 17, which highlights the pivot point of the poem:

| past troubles forgotten | former things not remembered |
| hidden from eyes (16) | gone from mind 17) |

In other words, whatever the conditions of life on earth were earlier, they will be forgotten in the bliss of the Lord's new earth. The former conditions can refer to the physical circumstances of life or the spiritual state of the people.

Some Latter-day Saint readers assume that the Lord's promise of a new heaven and earth emphasizes the earth's final state as a celestial sphere. However, President Joseph Fielding Smith repeatedly stressed that this chapter of Isaiah does not refer to a celestialized earth. Instead, the new heavens and earth prophesied by Isaiah will come at the beginning of the Millennium. (SOT, pp. 36-37; CHMR 2:217; AGQ 1:110-11; 2:20-21.)

The changes brought about at the ushering in of the Millennium will be so drastic that the earth itself will be transformed. (See MD, p. 495.) The new earth created in the Millennium will not be organized out of new materials; our present earth will come into a state of "paradisiacal glory."

The phrase "former things will not be remembered" can refer not only to the physical transformation of the earth but to changes in social order and spirituality of the people. People reared in a millennial world will have difficulty understanding what life was like when selfishness, wickedness, wars, disease, and other problems prevailed. Likewise, it is hard for us today to appreciate what millennial life will be like. (See MD, pp. 492-501.) Isaiah attempts to describe these conditions in the rest of chapter 65.

The following verses in Isaiah 65 also support a millennial setting because people will continue living and dying, missionary work will go on, and man's daily labors will continue. In contrast to the cries of the wicked as they are cleansed from the earth (vs. 14-15), the righteous will rejoice in the new millennial earth:

18But be glad and rejoice forever
  in what I will create,
for I will create Jerusalem to be a
  delight
  and its people a joy.
19I will rejoice over Jerusalem

and take delight in my people;
the sound of weeping and of
  crying
will be heard in it no more.
(NIV)

Isaiah promises long life on this new earth, but his words were apparently distorted later so that an inconsistency developed in verse 20: the verse says that all people will live at least one hundred years, but it also states that some people will die before they reach one hundred. Joseph Smith's Translation clarifies this verse:

20"Never again will there be in it
  an infant that lives but a few
    days,
  or an old man who does not live
    out his years;
he who dies at a hundred
  will be thought a mere youth;
he who fails to reach a hundred
  will be considered accursed."
(NIV)

20In those days there shall be no
more thence an infant of days, nor
an old man that hath not filled his
days; for the child shall not die,
but shall live to be an hundred
years old; but the sinner, living to
be an hundred years old, shall be
accursed. (JST)

Joseph Smith further amplifies the meaning of the verse in Doctrine and Covenants 101, in which he prophesies concering the Millennium: "In that day an infant shall not die until he is old; and his life shall be as the age of a tree." (D&C 101:30).

The Prophet Joseph also says that when people die during the Millennium their bodies will not sleep in the earth (while their spirits are in the spirit world), but that they will die and be resurrected "in the twinkling of an eye." (D&C 101:31.)

This concept of an instantaneous resurrection helps clarify verse 20, which says that sinners in the Millennium "living to be an hundred years old, shall be accursed" (JST). Ordinarily, we all have the post-earthly period in spirit prison to pay the "uttermost farthing" or every demand of justice for our sins. (Matt. 5:25-26.) As Elder Bruce R. McConkie has stated, "According to the terms and conditions of the great plan of redemption, *justice demands that a penalty be paid for every violat on of the Lord's laws.*" (MD, p. 406; italics added.) He also said that the wicked are sent to the spirit prison, where they must satisfy every demand of justice before they can be resurrected. (MD, pp. 349-51, 755, 761-62.)

However, people living during the Millennium will not be able to satisfy the demands of justice in spirit prison; they must do it completely in the flesh before their resurrection. Most people living during the Millennium will probably repent of their sins and allow Christ's atonement to satisfy justice (see pp. 449-53), but some may exercise their free agency and choose not to repent. They will then have to personally suffer for their sins here on earth before they are resurrected. (See D&C 19:17-20.) Thus, Isaiah's promise that all people living on the new earth will live to be a hundred years old can be reconciled with his words that a sinner living to be a hundred "shall be accursed." The sinner will still live a long life, but will be "accursed" or made to suffer for his own sins before his resurrection. (D&C 63:50-51; 101:29-31; see MD, pp. 495-501.)

Verse 20 shows that two characteristics of all people during the Millennium will be a long life and the retention of agency and the capacity to sin. In verse 20, Isaiah contrasts infants with old men and the righteous with sinners, just as he contrasted in verse 13 the rewards of the righteous with the punishments of the wicked. Although grossly wicked people will not live on the earth during the Millennium, people of a terrestrial order will still be here, subject to personal failings. (D&C 76:71-80; see MD, pp. 783-84.)

On the whole, however, life during the Millennium will be more glorious than under any previous society. Isaiah beautifully describes the millennial society:

21"They will build houses and
   dwell in them;
  they will plant vineyards and
         eat their fruit.
      22No longer will they build houses
        and others live in them,

or plant and others eat.
For as the days of a tree,
so will be the days of my
people;
my chosen ones will long enjoy
the works of their hands.
23They will not toil in vain
or bear children doomed to
misfortune;
for they will be a people blessed
by the Lord,
they and their descendants
with them.

24Before they call I will answer;
while they are still speaking I
will hear.
25The wolf and the lamb will feed
together,
and the lion will eat straw
like the ox,
but dust will be the serpent's
food.
They will neither harm nor
destroy
in all my holy mountain,"
says the Lord. (NIV)

Compare these verses to Isaiah's description of Israel in Isaiah 1, in which desolation visited the land, cities and vineyards were destroyed, strangers ate the fruit of the land, and the Lord cursed the Israelites. Probably the most striking promise is in verse 24, in which the Lord covenants to answer the people's prayers even before they call to him. What a pleasant contrast to Isaiah 1:15, in which Israel's prayers were rejected. (See D&C 101:27.)

Some of the promises in these verses echo earlier prophecies of Isaiah, particularly his description of millennial peace in chapter 11. In both of these chapters, Isaiah foretells harmony among all life and universal righteousness upon the Lord's "holy mountain" (the entire earth).

Isaiah repeats in chapter 66 these themes and others found in Isaiah 11 and 65. Chapter 66 contains some warnings, but primarily promises blessings. The chapter is a single long poem with nine major ideas in a chiastic pattern:

A. The Lord's work in heaven and on earth (1-2)
B. Hypocritical sacrifices and rejection of the wicked (3-4)
C. The Lord repays his enemies (5-6)
D. Zion's delivery (7-9)
E. The righteous will rejoice with Zion (10)
D'. Zion's vanquishment (11-13)
C'. The Lord's fury upon his foes (14-17)
B'. Pure sacrifices and glory of gathered Israel (18-21)
A'. The Lord's work in heaven and on earth (22-24)

The Lord's Work in Heaven and on Earth (66:1-2)

The Lord testifies concerning his handiwork, heaven and earth:

66 This is what the Lord says:
"Heaven is my throne
and the earth is my footstool.
Where is the house you will build
for me?
Where will my resting place be?
²Has not my hand made all these
things,

and so they came into being?"
declares the Lord.

"This is the one I esteem:
he who is humble and contrite in
spirit,
and trembles at my word." (NIV)

Note the transition in verse 2 from the Lord's efforts in heaven and earth to his pride in his ultimate product—a humble, obedient person. More than building the earth as a place of residence, the Lord wants the earth to be a place where a person develops righteousness. (See Moses 1:39.)

Hypocritical Sacrifices and Rejection of the Wicked (66:3-4)

With simple but powerful poetry, Isaiah portrays the people's hypocrisy and promises the Lord's punishments:

³"But whoever sacrifices a bull
is like one who kills a man,
and whoever offers a lamb,
like one who breaks a dog's neck;
whoever makes a grain offering
is like one who presents pig's
blood,
and whoever burns memorial
incense,
like one who worships an idol.
They have chosen their own ways,
and their souls delight in their

abominations;
⁴so I also will choose harsh
treatment for them
and bring upon them what they
dread.
For when I called, no one
answered,
when I spoke, no one listened.
They did evil in my sight
and chose what displeases me."
(NIV)

In verse 3, Isaiah employs four parallel phrases, each consisting of two parts, to portray opposites—a legitimate sacrifice and an act contrary to Mosaic law:

1. *Slaying an ox/killing a man.* The ox is an animal for sacrifice, but if the sacrificer lacks the spirit of faith and devotion, he has simply committed an act of murder like the killing of a man.
2. *Offering a sheep/breaking a dog's neck.* An unrighteous animal sacrifice

is unclean before the Lord, like a dog, and is to have its neck broken as an unredeemed offering. (Ex. 13:13; Deut. 21:4; compare Matt. 7:6; 2 Pet. 2:22.)

3. *Offering grain/presenting pig's blood.* In conjunction with animal sacrifice, blood was sprinkled on the altar, and in addition to animal sacrifices, grain offerings were often required. But in no case would pig's blood or grain from an unrighteous person be accepted by the Lord.

4. *Burning incense/worshipping idols.* Incense ascends from the altar toward heaven, reminding God of the offerer and bringing the two closer together. Idols deteriorate in the earth, distract the worshipper from God, and separate God from his children. (See Young, *The Book of Isaiah* 3:520 for similar comparisons.)

In essence, the Israelites took a form of Mosaic worship and turned it into a mockery. They maintained the external appearance of the ordinances, but lost the spiritual significance. Thus, the very forms of worship designed to save them became an abomination that condemned them to suffer God's wrath. By *choosing* their wicked ways, the people *chose* to have the Lord's terrible judgments come upon them (v. 4).

The Lord Repays His Enemies (66:5-6)

The Lord finally chooses to bring justice upon the oppressors of his people:

⁵Hear the word of the Lord,
  you who tremble at his word:
"Your brothers who hate you
  and exclude you because of my
    name, have said,
'Let the Lord be glorified,
  that we may see your joy!'
Yet they will be put to shame.
⁶Hear that uproar from the city,
  hear that noise from the temple!
It is the sound of the Lord
  repaying his enemies all they
    deserve." (NIV)

The wicked should be careful when they ask the Lord to demonstrate his glory, because they will be the ones to feel his wrath. (See Alma 30; 3 Ne. 1, 6, 8.)

Zion's Delivery (66:7-9)

With poetic imagery, Isaiah compares Zion to a woman who brings forth a special manchild, who represents the Millennium:

⁷"Before she goes into labor,
  she gives birth;
before the pains come upon her,
  she delivers a son.

8Who has ever heard of such a
  thing?
Who has ever seen such things?
Can a country be born in a day
  or a nation be brought forth in
  a moment?
Yet no sooner is Zion in labor
  than she gives birth to her
children.
9Do I bring to the moment of birth
  and not give delivery?" says the
  Lord.
"Do I close up the womb
  when I bring to delivery?" says
  your God. (NIV)

Ordinarily there are contractions and other physical signs preceding
the birth of a child, but Zion will give birth to an ideal millennial
society before the labor pains come upon her. In this prophecy, Isaiah
apparently promises that shortly after Zion is established in Jackson
County, great numbers of unexpected peoples, including the Ten
Tribes and other Israelite remnants, will join with Zion to prepare
the earth for the Millennium. These verses convey the feeling of
suddenness and surprise at Zion's rapid growth. (Compare Rev.
12:1-5; [vs. 1-7 in JST].)

The Righteous Will Rejoice in Zion (66:10)

Isaiah invites all people to join with Zion:

10"Rejoice with Jerusalem and be
  glad for her,
all you who love her;
rejoice greatly with her,
  all you who mourn over her."
(NIV)

Note that the people who associate with Zion will be those who love
her and mourn over her. In other words, they will be close to Zion and
sensitive to her earlier suffering, probably because they themselves
experienced it.

Zion's Nourishment (66:11-13)

Isaiah promises beautiful blessings to those who seek strength
from Zion:

11"For you will nurse and be
  satisfied
at her comforting breasts;
you will drink deeply
  and delight in her overflowing
  abundance."

12For this is what the Lord says:

"I will extend peace to her like a
  river,
and the wealth of nations like a
  flooding stream;
you will nurse and be carried on
  her arm
  and dandled on her knees.
13As a mother comforts her child,
  so will I comfort you;
and you will be comforted over
  Jerusalem." (NIV)

Isaiah's imagery of a mother and child beautifully conveys God's tender love for his children. (Compare Isa. 49:14-23; 54:1-10.)

The Lord's Fury upon His Foes (66:14-17)

Although the Lord's people will rejoice as they enjoy his millennial presence, God's kingdom will be established only after the wicked are destroyed:

14When you see this, your heart will rejoice
and you will flourish like grass;
the hand of the Lord will be made known to his servants,
but his fury will be shown to his foes.
15See, the Lord is coming with fire, and his chariots are like a whirlwind;
he will bring down his anger with fury,
and his rebuke with flames of fire.

16For with fire and with his sword
the Lord will execute judgment upon all men,
and many will be those slain by the LORD.

17"Those who consecrate and purify themselves to go into the gardens, following the one in the midst of those who eat the flesh of pigs and rats and other abominable things—they will meet their end together," declares the Lord. (NIV)

The establishment of the Millennium will be a partial judgment of the earth's inhabitants, since those worthy of a terrestrial glory will be permitted to remain on earth. All people on earth will be judged, and the wicked will be destroyed. (Matt. 25:31-46; Mal. 3:2-3; D&C 88:95-99; 101:24; 133:50-53.)

Pure Sacrifices and Glory of Gathered Israel (66:18-21)

The theme of punishment is abruptly dropped in verses 18-21, in which the Lord sends forth his servants to gather all nations to see his glory:

18"And I, because of their actions and their imaginations, am about to come and gather all nations and tongues, and they will come and see my glory.
19"I will set a sign among them, and I will send some of those who survive to the nations—to Tarshish, to the Libyans and Lydians

(famous as archers), to Tubal and Greece, and to the distant islands, that have not heard of my fame or seen my glory. They will proclaim my glory among the nations. 20And they will bring all your brothers, from all the nations, to my holy mountain in Jerusalem as an offering to the Lord—on horses, in chariots and wagons, and mules and camels," says the Lord. "They will bring them, as the Israelites bring their grain offerings, to the temple of the Lord in ceremonially clean vessels. [21]And I will select some of them also to be priests and Levites," says the Lord. (NIV)

The names in verse 19 refer to such places as modern Spain, Libya, Turkey, and Greece. (See Map 10.) These countries were considered to be the ends of the earth in Isaiah's day. Thus, he prophesies that the Lord's word will go to all the nations of the earth.

Verse 20 is amplified in Doctrine and Covenants 128. An "offering" in "clean vessels" seems symbolic of the names of the dead for whom the righteous do vicarious work in the last days. These names are brought from all over the world to the temples.

The Lord's Work in Heaven and on Earth (66:22-24)

Isaiah concludes his writings with a testimony: the heavens, the earth, and all glorified, resurrected people serve as a witness for the Lord and his righteous plan and deeds; the memorials of the wicked will be a perpetual witness of the folly of sin:

[22]"As the new heavens and the new earth that I make will endure before me," declares the Lord, "so will your name and descendants endure. [23]From one New Moon to another and from one Sabbath to another, all mankind will come and bow down before me," says the Lord. [24]"And they will go out and look upon the dead bodies of those who rebelled against me; their worm will not die, nor will their fire be quenched, and they will be loathsome to all mankind." (NIV)

It seems somewhat unusual that Isaiah concludes his prophecies with a sober tone, describing "dead bodies," "worms," and eternal "fires." However, Isaiah often mixes negative and positive messages together.

In fact, Isaiah follows a similar pattern in many chapters. He often starts in a somewhat negative tone as he rebukes the sinners and their wickedness. He quickly becomes very specific as he lists their sins, calls them to repentance, and warns them of the judgments descending upon them. However, Isaiah is not a pessimist; he usually extends a message of hope and a promise of redemption to his listeners. He then extends a prophecy of blessings and restoration for those who repent, especially in the last days. Still, Isaiah's optimism is tempered by reality. He does not usually conclude a prophecy or discourse on a high note; instead, he ends with a sober admonition. This pattern may be diagrammed as follows:

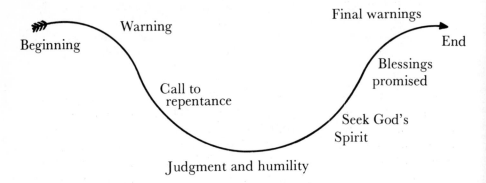

This pattern is easily identified in Isaiah 66 and is also characteristic of the entire book of Isaiah:

Warnings of wickedness (ch. 1-23)
Judgments upon the world (24-25)
Humility of Israel (36-39)
People seeking the Lord (40-47)
Blessings of the Messiah and the last days (48-64)
A final promise and warning (65-66)

In evaluating chapters 65 and 66 in the context of the whole book of Isaiah, one sees how they summarize his writings and provide a last promise and warning to Israel. As one studies these last two chapters and compares them with the first two chapters of Isaiah, he sees the opening and closing framework of the prophet's teaching. The other sixty-two chapters provide the panoramic gospel message Isaiah gives to the world.

CONCLUSION

One word can be used to describe Isaiah: *greatness*. He is a *great* prophet, seer, and poet. And, as Christ concluded, *"great* are the words of Isaiah." (3 Ne. 23:1, italics added.) Isaiah uniquely combines prophetic revelations with poetic inspiration to provide both a masterpiece of literature and a profound work of scripture.

As a great prophet, Isaiah received and bore personal witness of God the Father; the Lord, our Redeemer; and the Holy Spirit. He taught and testified about trusting in the Lord (faith), turning away from evil (repentance), washing oneself clean (baptism), seeking spiritual direction (Holy Ghost), and living true to one's commitments (enduring to the end). He warned the people against idolatry and adultery and exhorted them to seek selflessness instead of selfishness, charity instead of corruption, and integrity instead of iniquity. As a prophet, Isaiah spoke with a clear voice to ancient Israel as she began to scatter, and speaks with a strong testimony today to all God's chosen people as they gather to Zion.

As a great seer, Isaiah prophesied about the Messiah, our Savior, and he foresaw the time when everyone will recognize the Lord as the ruler of this earth and the supreme judge of the universe. He envisioned marvelous events of the last days, especially the gathering of Israel, the building of Zion, and the creation of a new millennial earth. He also revealed the role of God's servants, the prophets, priests, and kings of all ages, and particularly the Servant of all who is the Master of all.

As a great poet, Isaiah used parallelism, memory aids, repetition, and word play to stimulate his listeners and to edify their hearts.

Isaiah is also great in that he lived as he taught; he set a noble example of what a true servant of God should be. "Great are the words of Isaiah," but greater still is the revealed message his words teach and the Lord of whom they testify.

APPENDIX: THE AUTHORSHIP
OF ISAIAH

Traditionally, the book of Isaiah has been ascribed to a prophet serving Israel between 740 and 700 B.C.. However, in the past couple of centuries—with the development of schools of biblical criticism—this traditional belief has been questioned and denied. Biblical criticism essentially consists in the application of certain evaluation techniques to biblical writings. The Bible and other ancient writings are often examined in order to establish, as far as possible, the wording of the original texts, the manner and date of their composition, their sources, their authorship, and so forth. To Latter-day Saints, an examination of this kind does not usually present any immediate problems, since we believe that the Bible has not necessarily come down to us in its original form. (A of F 8.) For some Christians and Jews, however, the idea that the Bible is anything besides "the unchanged word of God" presents a major theological problem because of the orthodox belief that the Hebrew and Greek portions of the Biblical text, as we have them today, appear exactly as originally written. Recently, other Christians and Jews, especially those with more liberal religious backgrounds, have questioned the historical origins and prophetic values of the Bible.

As early as the twelfth century A.D., a Jewish commentator on the Old Testament, Ibn Ezra, challenged some biblical teachings and ideas, particularly the authorship of Isaiah, saying that the latter section of Isaiah (chs. 40-66) was not the work of Isaiah, but of some other man living a century and a half later during the Babylonian captivity. This idea remained relatively undeveloped until the late 1700s, when new critical attitudes surfaced as a product of the "Age of Reason." In about 1780, J. G. Eichhorn held that chapters 40-66 were the work of persons other than Isaiah, thus creating the idea of a "Second Isaiah" or "Deutero-Isaiah." By 1888 some scholars asserted that the last eleven chapters (56-66) were written by an individual or school of writers known as "Third Isaiah" or "Trito-Isaiah." During the past two centuries, so many scholars have questioned the Bible's validity, and particularly Isaiah's work, that now there are a wide variety of different theories regarding the date and authorship of Isaiah, with many scholars disagreeing vigorously among themselves.

As stated above, Latter-day Saint theology teaches that, in fact, the Biblical text is not absolutely correct, and therefore the work of the critics to discover the nature of the original texts has only served to demonstrate scholastically what we know by revelation—the Bible is not perfect. Unfortunately, however, this is not all that Bible critics have done. As various schools of criticism developed, many theories also developed that deny the Bible's inspired authorship. Therefore, while Latter-day Saints may find certain aspects and findings of biblical criticism valuable, they must reject others in order to maintain that the Bible, though imperfect, is still the word of God as revealed to his prophets and other inspired writers such as the psalmists, poets, and scribes.

Critical Views of Isaiah and Modern Comparisons

In order to appreciate how scholars most often evaluate Isaiah's book, a brief overview of their major arguments about the authorship of Isaiah will be helpful. Also, a brief evaluation of modern prophets and their writings will provide a helpful point of reference for comparison in relation to Isaiah and his book.

Bible critics who advocate the composite authorship theory usually mention one of four reasons for their theory: varied historical perspectives, changing theological emphasis, contrasting literary style, and shifting vocabulary and grammar patterns as supported by computer analysis. Each of these arguments for composite authorship will be discussed in turn.

Varied historical perspectives. While Isaiah 1-39 is addressed to the Israelites and other nations of the Middle East during Isaiah's time, chapters 40-66 deal with later periods. These later chapters mention specific events and people (for example, King Cyrus of Persia [Isa. 44-45]) that did not exist until centuries after Isaiah. Since the historical critics hold that no individual can foretell the future, they believe that these chapters must have been written by someone contemporary with or later than the persons and events described. For them, a prophet is always a "man of his own time" who does not speak to later generations; the pronouncements he gives can be applied only to people in his own day. The historical critics usually employ one of four methods to discount prophecy: (1) they reject the situation (time, place, etc.) recorded in the Bible and place the prophecy in a situation close enough to the time of the event that the predictive element need not exist; (2) they interpret the prophecy so that the prediction disappears or becomes so vague as to be useless; (3) they treat the prophecy as a literary device used by a contemporary or successor of the described events to speak with the authority of a prophetic voice as if from the distant past; or (4) they insist that later editors of Isaiah's works must have brought them into their present form and have in the process added the information that now appears to be prophetic. (Allis, *The Unity of Isaiah*, pp. 4, 20.)

This argument strikes at the foundation of God's relationship with people on this earth, his revelation and prophecy. God's revelations to prophets can include prophecies that no mortal power could produce. (See MD, p. 547.) As seers, prophets can reveal the truth and knowledge of things as they were, are, and will be. (D&C 93:24.) The Book of Mormon provides numerous examples of prophecies that were delivered centuries before they were fulfilled. (2 Ne. 26:6; 3 Ne. 1:4; Morm. 1:19; Ether 3:25-26; TG "Prophecy.")

When Christ appeared in America, he quoted from Isaiah and stressed Isaiah's prophetic insights. He quoted most of Isaiah 52 and all of Isaiah 54, ascribing them to Isaiah. (3 Ne. 16, 20-22.) Some critics argue that Jesus of Nazareth may have been unaware that someone else wrote the last part of Isaiah when he quoted from his writings. (See Luke 4:18-19.) But certainly the resurrected Lord, who had by this time received a fulness of knowledge, would not be deceived. (D&C 93:12-17; 3 Ne. 12:48.) He knew who wrote Isaiah 52 and 54 and called the author by name. He also realized the large scope of Isaiah's writings: "For surely he spake as touching all things concerning my people which are of the house of Israel; therefore, it must needs be that he must speak also to the Gentiles." (3 Ne. 23:2.)

It is true that in the last twenty-seven of his chapters, Isaiah does speak more on future events and persons, especially those associated with the first and second comings of Christ. It is, however, one man prophesying about the future, not later writers who recorded prophecies after the fact.

Anyone who accepts the historical critical argument that Isaiah could not have foretold future events lacks faith in a God who can reveal future events to his prophets. Just as man can now record past events and provide "instant replays" on television of earlier occurrences, so can God, with his infinitely superior system of spiritual communication, instruct a person through "forevision" of future events.

Changing theological emphasis. Since the messages of chapters 40-66 are more positive and hopeful, some Bible scholars feel that the last chapters must have been written by someone other than the eighth-century Isaiah. Instead of dreadful warnings and rebukes, this "Deutero-Isaiah" speaks of comfort, pardon, deliverance, restoration, grace, and hope. He seems to be speaking words of comfort and encouragement to a despairing people, such as to the Jews in the Babylonian captivity.

However, as already noted earlier in the evaluation of chapters 1-35, many hopeful promises are given in the first section of Isaiah. Interestingly, some scholars have removed the most positive of those chapters, especially 24-27 and 33-35, from those attributed to Isaiah ben Amoz and have credited them to Deutero-Isaiah. Careful study, though, will show that many serious warnings and punishments continue to be found in the last chapters of Isaiah, including dire pronouncements to foreign nations. (Isa. 47; 63:1-6.)

The changing theological message in the latter chapters of Isaiah need not be explained through composite authorship. Why should not Isaiah's message change when the rebellious Ten Tribes are gone, the people of Jerusalem have finally been humbled by the Assyrians, and Isaiah in his old age speaks to new and even future generations of Israelites. In addition, Isaiah's teachings could certainly be enriched if he received new insights and revelations concerning far-distant events. He might also be speaking more to future audiences than to contemporary Israelites, thus needing to change the emphasis in his message. (Compare this with the fact that many Book of Mormon writers spoke more often to future peoples than to their own contemporaries.)

Readers of Isaiah should also recognize that as an individual grows and matures, or as his Church callings change, his perspectives vary. Latter-day Saints can identify with modern prophets who have grown in wisdom and insight as they have served the Lord. For example, discourses delivered by Joseph Fielding Smith for sixty years as an apostle were generally rather stern. He usually emphasized such topics as repentance and scripture study. However, during the two years he was President of the Church, his messages were primarily of universal love and peace. The same man speaks, but since his role has changed, his message changes. Perhaps Isaiah felt a need to make similar changes in his messages, since in the latter part of his work he speaks on some new themes to an audience that is ready for more profound teachings.

Contrasting literary style. Although literary style is often difficult to evaluate, literary critics of Isaiah sense that the more positive, optimistic tone in Isaiah 40-66 is matched with a language of greater beauty and power. They also recognize that there is more use of the first person singular "I" (meaning "God") in the later chapters of Isaiah, indicating a different style of communicating God's message to the people.

However, if Isaiah were addressing new themes and a new audience in a new role, would not his style need to change somewhat? For example, any Latter-day Saint today would use completely different oratory styles, even when speaking on the same subject, if he were to address such differing audiences as a Primary class of six-year-olds, a home evening group of college students, a ward sacrament meeting, or a special meeting of the General Authorities of the Church.

Since Isaiah records very little about his method of receiving and recording his writings, it is difficult to know the answers to some questions that could explain differences in style:

1. Did Isaiah compose all the material himself?
2. Did the Lord inspire certain portions, even word for word, so that they contrast with Isaiah's own words?
3. When was the material written and by whom, and was it later edited?

I know from my own limited experiences as a missionary, father, home teacher, and bishop that when I am giving talks, prayers, or priesthood blessings I usually receive subtle impressions through the Spirit and am left to express them through my own vocabulary. However, there are times when the message is revealed so strongly that the words flow through me as I speak not in my own style but precisely as the Spirit directs me. Then I am not only delivering a message from someone else, but also more of the style of the divine being who speaks through Isaiah.

Computer analysis. Since computers allow scholars to quickly evaluate and compare vocabulary word frequencies, grammar patterns, and other writing characteristics, some early computer studies demonstrated differences between the two halves of Isaiah. However, vocabulary and speech patterns are likely to change if an author uses different approaches or delivers contrasting messages to different audiences, as Isaiah did.

More recently, other more sophisticated computer studies have not compared all or even any major vocabulary words, but have concentrated instead on items of stylometry, the subtle, minor choices of non-contextual words (prepositions, prefixes, suffixes, conjunctions, etc.). The choice of non-contextual words that form speech patterns is not greatly affected by the passage of time, change of subject matter, or differing literary forms. Computer studies that compare these "word print" patterns demonstrate that the different halves of Isaiah are much more like each other than they are like any other Old Testament book. (See L. L. Adams and A. C. Rencher, "A Computer Analysis of the Isaiah Authorship Problem," *BYU Studies*, Autumn 1974, p. 102; Wayne A. Larsen et al., "Who Wrote the Book of Mormon? An Analysis of Wordprints," *BYU Studies*, Spring 1980, pp. 225-51.) Since computers are only instruments in men's hands, they analyze as directed by their programmers, so there is a fairly large range of computer studies of Isaiah's writings. As further studies demonstrate more consistent and objective means to compare Hebrew writing styles, more precise conclusions can be made about Isaiah's work.

Additional witnesses for the single authorship of Isaiah. A variety of additional facts support Isaiah as the author of the book of Isaiah:

1. Jesus Christ named him as the author and quoted him specifically in the New Testament and the Book of Mormon. (Matt. 13:14-15; 15:8-9; Luke 4:18-19; 3 Ne. 16, 20-22.)
2. Many New Testament writers quoted from the second half of Isaiah, naming him in their quotations. (Matt. 8:17; 12:18-21; John 1:23; 12:38; Acts 8:30-33; Rom. 10:16, 20-21.)
3. The earliest Bible manuscripts, such as the Dead Sea Scrolls, have all recorded Isaiah as one book.
4. Writers and historians as early as 185 B.C. attribute authorship of Isaiah only and specifically to the eighth-century prophet and record that he prophesied concerning the future and Cyrus. (Ben Sira in *Ecclesiasticus* 49:17-25 and Josephus in *Antiquities*, XI, 1-2.)
5. The Jewish and Christian tradition from the earliest times to the last couple of centuries has supported the single authorship of

Isaiah. For example, the Septuagint and other ancient versions give no hint of multiple authorship.

6. Book of Mormon writers quoted from both halves of Isaiah (especially Isa. 48-55, in the second half) and attributed the material to Isaiah. Since Lehi left Jerusalem decades before Cyrus ruled and the "Deutero-Isaiah" lived in Babylon, many major portions of the last half of Isaiah had to have been written by 600 B.C. (Whether a prophet prophesies 60 or 160 years before the time of Cyrus, he would still have to receive revelation from God to see into the future.)

7. The critical attitudes and anti-dogmatic beliefs in the 1800s encouraged the higher criticism of the Bible beyond its natural bounds. These attitudes even called into question the authorship of Shakespeare's works and other famous writings. This "vogue" attitude of the scholars manifested itself in radical criticism, which has since moderated somewhat, especially as further evidences for the creative genius of ancient writers come forth.

8. Internal evidences in the book of Isaiah provide striking characteristics common to the whole book and support its unity. Isaiah uniquely uses some techniques and phrases uncommon in other works, such as imagery, parallelism, psalms, repetition, paronomasia, and expressions such as "the Holy One of Israel." Also, there is no record of anyone besides Isaiah writing the last half of his book. If the "Deutero-Isaiah" is one of the greatest prophets in the Old Testament, why is no mention made of him? All other prophetic writings at least mention their source, even the small, comparatively insignificant Obadiah. As one Jewish scholar records:

> If the author of the latter part [of Isaiah] were another prophet, who was contemporary and lived among the people whom he consoled, how can it possibly be believed that his name would be entirely forgotten? Isaiah ben Amoz who lived centuries before the Exile was well remembered and details of his life recorded. Furthermore it is indeed strange that Isaiah ben Amoz who denounced the people and whose message was certainly not welcome at the time should be remembered and his writings preserved but the name of this supposed Second Isaiah who preached a message of consolation whose message must have been quite welcome should be forgotten and, indeed, so completely forgotten that we do not even know his name. (Freehof, *Isaiah*, pp. 199-200.)

9. Contemporary apostles, who are prophets, seers, and revelators, have witnessed concerning Isaiah's authoring his whole book.

(James E. Talmage, CR, April 1929, pp. 45-47; Bruce R. McConkie, *Ensign*, Oct. 1973, pp. 78-83.)
10. A personal testimony about Isaiah's book and his efforts in its composition is available to everyone who seeks for a witness through the Holy Ghost.

In summary, some questions about Isaiah's reception and recording of his prophecies remain unanswered. It is also unknown how much of his writings was later changed and edited. From the evidence available, however, it appears obvious that Isaiah authored the sixty-six chapters in his book. The truth is that Isaiah received prophetic visions centuries into the future, many of his teachings and prophecies are recorded in his book, and eventually all of his prophecies will be fulfilled. (3 Ne. 23:1-3.)

In studying Isaiah's work in the light of contemporary scholarship, we should follow the Lord's admonition given in modern scripture and seek "out of the best books words of wisdom; seek learning, even by *study* and also by *faith*." (D&C 88:118, italics added.) As we combine the study of the scholars' critical evaluations with the faith of the scriptural writers, we will come to a greater understanding of Isaiah. As we build upon the best of man's knowledge about the scriptures and also follow the promptings of the Spirit, we emulate Joseph Smith, who, though endowed with the spirit of revelation, also studied Hebrew and German to better understand the Bible and Isaiah. The positive, constructive elements of biblical criticism can enrich the process of study and meditation that prepares us for the spirit of revelation, which can then tell us in our minds and hearts what we need to learn from the scriptures. (Compare D&C 8:2 and Moro. 10:3-5.)

BIBLIOGRAPHY

Abingdon Bible Commentary. New York: Abingdon-Cokesbury Press, 1929.

Adams, L. Lamar, and Rencher, Alvin C. "A Computer Analysis of the Isaiah Authorship Problem," *BYU Studies,* vol. 15, no. 1 (Autumn 1974), pp. 95-102.

Allis, O. T. *The Unity of Isaiah.* Philadelphia: Presbyterian and Reformed Publishing Co., 1950.

American Heritage Dictionary of the English Language. New York: American Heritage Publishing Co., 1969.

Amplified Bible. Grand Rapids: Zondervan, 1965.

Anderson, Mary Audentia Smith. *Ancestry and Posterity of Joseph Smith and Emma Hale.* Independence, Mo.: Herald Publishing House, 1929.

Ballard, Melvin R., ed. *Melvin J. Ballard: Crusader for Righteousness.* Salt Lake City: Bookcraft, 1966.

Barne, Albert. *Barne's Notes on Isaiah.* New York: Leavitt and Allen, 1847.

Beacon Bible Commentary. Kansas City, Mo.: Beacon Hill Press, 1964-69.

Bialik, C. N. *Selected Poems.* Edited by Israel Efros. New York: Bloch Publishing Co., 1965.

The Book of Jasher. Salt Lake City: J. H. Parry & Co., 1887.

The Book of Mormon. Salt Lake City: The Church of Jesus Christ of Latter-day Saints, 1950.

Brahms, Johannes. *Ein deutsches Requiem.* Leipzig: Ernst Eulenberg, n.d.

Calvin, John. *Calvin's Commentaries on the Prophet Isaiah,* 4 vols. Translated by Rev. William Pringle. Grand Rapids: Eerdman's Publishing Co., 1956.

Cheyne, Thomas Kelly. *The Prophecies of Isaiah.* New York: Bible House, 1892.

Church News. Salt Lake City: Deseret News Publishing Co.

Clark, James R., comp. *Messages of the First Presidency of The Church of Jesus Christ of Latter-day Saints.* 6 vols. Salt Lake City: Bookcraft, 1965-75.

Clarke, Adam. *Clarke's Commentary.* New York: Abingdon, n.d.

Conference Report. Salt Lake City: The Church of Jesus Christ of Latter-day Saints.

Conteneau, G. *Everyday Life in Babylon and Assyria.* London: E. Arnold, 1954.

Cowley, Matthias F. *Wilford Woodruff.* Salt Lake City: Bookcraft, 1964.

Bibliography

Delitzsch, Franz. *Biblical Commentary on the Prophecies of Isaiah*. New York: Funk and Wagnalls, n.d.

The Doctrine and Covenants of The Church of Jesus Christ of Latter-day Saints. Salt Lake City: The Church of Jesus Christ of Latter-day Saints, 1950.

Dummelow, J. R., ed. *A Commentary on the Whole Bible*. New York: Macmillan, 1943.

Durham, G. Homer, ed. *Discourses of Wilford Woodruff*. Salt Lake City: Bookcraft, 1969.

Encyclopedia Judaica. New York: Macmillan, 1972.

Ensign. Salt Lake City: The Church of Jesus Christ of Latter-day Saints.

Flanders, Henry Jackson. *People of the Covenant: An Introduction to the Old Testament*. New York: Ronald Press Co., 1973.

Freehof, Solomon B. *Book of Isaiah*. New York: Union of American Hebrew Congregations, 1972.

Gilbert, Martin. *Jewish History Atlas*. New York: Macmillan, 1977.

Ginsberg, Arthur. *Legends of the Jews*. Philadelphia: Jewish Publication Society of America, 1909-38.

Good News Bible. New York: American Bible Society, 1955.

Hailey, Homer. *Commentary on the Minor Prophets*. Grand Rapids: Baker Book House, 1972.

Handel, Georg Friedrich. *Messiah*. London: Scholar Press, 1974.

Hartshorn, Leon. *Joseph Smith: Prophet of the Restoration*. Salt Lake City: Deseret Book Co., 1970.

Hasel, G. *The Remnant: The History and Theology of the Remnant Idea from Genesis to Isaiah*. Berrien Springs, Mich.: Andrews University Press, 1974.

Hayes, John H. *Israelite and Judean History*. Philadelphia: Westminster Press, 1977.

Herodotus. *History*, book 2, as translated in the *Loeb Classical Library*, vol. 113, n.d.

Heschel, Abraham. *The Prophets*. New York: Jewish Publication Society of America, 1962.

The Holy Bible (King James Version). Salt Lake City: The Church of Jesus Christ of Latter-day Saints, 1980.

The Holy Scriptures. ("An Inspired Revision of the Authorized Version, by Joseph Smith, Junior.") Independence, Mo.: Herald Publishing House, 1944.

The Holy Scriptures according to the Masoretic Text. Philadelphia: The Jewish Publication Society of America, 1917.

Hymns. Rev. and enl. Salt Lake City: The Church of Jesus Christ of Latter-day Saints, 1948.

Improvement Era. Salt Lake City: The Church of Jesus Christ of Latter-day Saints.

Interpreter's Bible. New York: Abingdon-Cokesbury Press, 1951-57.

Interpreter's Dictionary of the Bible. New York: Abingdon Press, 1962.

Jerusalem Bible. Garden City, New York: Doubleday, 1966.

550

Josephus, Flavius. *Antiquities of the Jews* and *Wars of the Jews.* New York: Bigelow, Brown and Co., n.d.

Journal of Discourses. 26 vols. London: Latter-day Saints' Book Depot, 1854-56.

Journal of Rudger Clawson. Historical Department. The Church of Jesus Christ of Latter-day Saints. Salt Lake City.

Journal of Wilford Woodruff, June 15, 1878. Historical Department. The Church of Jesus Christ of Latter-day Saints. Salt Lake City.

Kaiser, Otto. *Isaiah 1-12, 13-39, 40-46.* 3 vols. Philadelphia: Westminster Press, 1972-76.

Keil, C. F., and Delitzch, F. *Biblical Commentary on the Old Testament.* 9 vols. Grand Rapids: Eerdman's Publishing Co., 1949.

Keller, Werner. *Bible as History: A Confirmation of the Book of Books.* New York: W. Morrow, 1956.

Kimball, Edward C. *Spencer W. Kimball.* Salt Lake City: Bookcraft, 1977.

Kimball, Heber C. *Life of Heber C. Kimball.* Salt Lake City: the Kimball family, 1888.

Kimball, Spencer W. "Lamanite Prophecies Fulfilled." *BYU Speeches of the Year,* 1964-1965. Provo: Brigham Young University.

Larsen, Wayne A. "Who Wrote the Book of Mormon? An Analysis of Wordprints." *BYU Studies,* vol. 20 (Spring 1980), pp. 225-51.

The Layman's Parallel Bible. [KJV, MLB, LB, RSV.] Grand Rapids: Zondervan, 1973.

The Living Bible. In *The Layman's Parallel Bible.* Grand Rapids: Zondervan, 1973.

Lowth, Robert [Bishop of London, 1710-87]. *Lectures on the Sacred Poetry of the Hebrews.* New York: Garland Pub., 1971.

Ludlow, Daniel H. *A Companion to Your Study of the Book of Mormon.* Salt Lake City: Deseret Book Co., 1976.

————. *A Companion to Your Study of the Old Testament.* Salt Lake City: Deseret Book Co., 1981.

Lytle, Elizabeth E. *The Aswan High Dam.* Monticello, Ill.: Council of Planning Librarians, 1977.

Macintosh, A. A. *Isaiah XXI.* New York: Cambridge University Press, 1980.

McConkie, Bruce R. *Doctrinal New Testament Commentary.* 3 vols. Salt Lake City: Bookcraft, 1973.

————. *Mormon Doctrine.* Salt Lake City: Bookcraft, 1966.

————. *The Mortal Messiah.* Salt Lake City: Deseret Book Co., 1981.

————. *The Promised Messiah.* Salt Lake City: Deseret Book Co., 1978.

————. "Ten Keys to Understanding Isaiah." *Ensign,* October 1973, pp. 72-81.

McConkie, Joseph F. *His Name Shall Be Joseph.* Salt Lake City: Hawkes Publishing, 1980.

McKenzie, John L., ed. *Second Isaiah.* Anchor Bible Series. Vol. 20. Garden City, New York: Anchor Press, 1968.

Messenger and Advocate. New Haven, Conn.: Research Publications, 1967.

Bibliography

Millennial Star. Official organ of the Church of Jesus Christ of Latter-day Saints in Great Britain.

Modern Language Bible. In *The Layman's Parallel Bible.* Grand Rapids: Zondervan, 1973.

New American Standard Bible. Carol Stream, Ill.: Creation House, 1973.

New English Bible. New York: Oxford University Press, 1970.

New International Version. Grand Rapids: Zondervan, 1978.

"New Jewish Version": *The Book of Isaiah: A New Translation.* Philadelphia: The Jewish Publication Society of America, 1972.

Nibley, Hugh. *An Approach to the Book of Mormon.* Salt Lake City: Deseret Book Co., 1964.

————. *Since Cumorah.* Salt Lake City: Deseret Book Co., 1967.

North, C. R. *The Second Isaiah.* Oxford: Clarendon, 1964.

Nyman, Monte. *Great Are The Words of Isaiah.* Salt Lake City: Bookcraft, 1980.

Odeberg, Hugo. *3 Enoch or The Hebrew Book of Enoch.* New York: Ktav Pub. House, 1973.

Ottley,————. *The Book of Isaiah According to the Septuagint.* Cambridge: University Press, 1906.

Packer, Boyd K. *The Mediator.* Salt Lake City, Deseret Book Co., 1978.

Patan, Lewis B. "Notes on Hosea's Marriage." *Journal of Biblical Literature,* vol. 15 (1896), p. 10.

Revised Standard Version. In *The Layman's Parallel Bible.* Grand Rapids: Zondervan, 1973.

Reynolds, Noel. "Nephi's Outline." *BYU Studies,* vol. 20 (Winter 1980), pp. 131-49.

Richards, LeGrand. *A Marvelous Work and a Wonder.* Salt Lake City: Deseret Book Co., 1958.

————. *Israel! Do You Know?* Salt Lake City: Deseret Book Co., 1954

Roberts, B. H. *New Witnesses for God.* 3 vols. Salt Lake City: Deseret News, 1909-11.

Robinson, G. L. *The Book of Isaiah,* rev. ed. Grand Rapids: Baker Book House, 1954.

Septuagint Version of the Old Testament and Apocrypha. Grand Rapids: Zondervan, 1972.

Slotki, Israel. *Isaiah.* London: Soncino Press, 1948.

Smith, George Adam. *The Book of Isaiah.* London: Hodder and Stoughton, 1900.

Smith, Joseph. *History of The Church of Jesus Christ of Latter-day Saints.* 7 vols. 2nd ed. rev. Edited by B. H. Roberts. Salt Lake City: The Church of Jesus Christ of Latter-day Saints, 1932-51.

————. *Lectures on Faith.* Compiled by N. B. Lundwall. Salt Lake City: N. B. Lundwall, n.d.

————. *The Words of Joseph Smith.* Compiled and edited by Andrew F. Ehat and Lyndon W. Cook. Provo: Religious Studies Center, Brigham Young University, 1980.

Smith, Joseph Fielding. *Answers to Gospel Questions.* 5 vols. Compiled by Joseph Fielding Smith, Jr. Salt Lake City: Deseret Book Co., 1957-66.

―――. *Church History and Modern Revelation.* Salt Lake City: Council of the Twelve Apostles of The Church of Jesus Christ of Latter-day Saints, 1953.

―――. *Doctrines of Salvation.* 3 vols. Compiled by Bruce R. McConkie. Salt Lake City: Bookcraft, 1954-56.

―――. *Signs of the Times.* Salt Lake City: Deseret News Press, 1952.

―――. *The Way to Perfection.* Salt Lake City: Genealogical Society of Utah, 1940.

Sperry, Sidney B. *Book of Mormon Compendium.* Salt Lake City: Bookcraft, 1968.

―――. *The Voice of Israel's Prophets.* Salt Lake City: Bookcraft, 1952.

Sterling, Claire. "The Trouble with Superdams." *Britannica Yearbook of Science and the Future, 1974.* Chicago: Encyclopedia Britannica, 1974.

Strong, James. *Strong's Exhaustive Concordance of the Bible.* MacLean, Va.: MacDonald Publishing Co., n.d.

Talmage, James E. *The Articles of Faith.* 12th ed. Salt Lake City: The Church of Jesus Christ of Latter-day Saints, 1924.

―――. *Jesus the Christ.* 3rd ed. Salt Lake City: The Church of Jesus Christ of Latter-day Saints, 1916.

Talmud. Jerusalem: Makor, 1972.

Thomas, D. Winston. *Documents from Old Testament Times.* New York: Harper, 1961.

Today's English Version. American Bible Society. New York: Macmillan, 1971.

Unified System For Teaching Families. Salt Lake City: The Church of Jesus Christ of Latter-day Saints.

Vine, W. E. *Isaiah.* Grand Rapids: Zondervan, 1971.

Webster's New Twentieth Century Dictionary. 2nd ed. Cleveland and New York: World Publishing Co., 1973.

Webster's Third New International Dictionary. Springfield, Mass.: G. & C. Merriam Co., 1971.

Welch, John. "Chiasmus in the Book of Mormon." *New Era,* Feb. 1972, pp. 6-11.

Westermann, Claus. *Isaiah 40-66.* Philadelphia: Westminster Press, 1969.

―――. *The Praise of God in the Psalms.* Richmond: John Knox Press, 1965.

Wright, G. Ernest. *The Book of Isaiah.* Richmond: John Knox Press, 1964.

Young, Edward J. *The Book of Isaiah.* Grand Rapids: Eerdman's Publishing Co., 1965.

―――. *Who Wrote Isaiah?* Grand Rapids: Eerdman's Publishing Co., 1958.

INDEX